MILESTONE DOCUMENTS IN AMERICAN HISTORY

Exploring the Primary Sources That Shaped America

MILESTONE DOCUMENTS
IN AMERICAN HISTORY

Exploring the Primary Sources
That Shaped America

Volume 2: 1824 – 1887

Paul Finkelman
Editor in Chief

Bruce A. Lesh
Consulting Editor

Schlager Group

Milestone Documents in American History
Copyright © 2008 by Schlager Group Inc.

All rights reserved. No part of this book may be reproduced or utilized in any form or by any means, electronic or mechanical, including photocopying, recording, or by any information storage or retrieval systems, without permission in writing from the publisher. For information, contact:

Schlager Group Inc.
2501 Oak Lawn Avenue, Suite 245
Dallas, Tex. 75219
USA

You can find Schlager Group on the World Wide Web at
http://www.schlagergroup.com
http://www.milestonedocuments.com
Text and cover design by Patricia Moritz

Printed in the United States of America

10 9 8 7 6 5 4 3 2 1

ISBN: 978-0-9797758-0-2

This book is printed on acid-free paper.

Contents

Volume 1: 1763–1823

Volume 2: 1824–1887

Volume 3: 1888–1955

Volume 4: 1956–2003

MILESTONE DOCUMENTS
IN AMERICAN HISTORY

Exploring the Primary Sources
That Shaped America

Tuesday Morning March 2ⁿᵈ 1824 —

Pursuant to adjournment the Court met this morning
at the Capitol.

Present —

The Honorable John Marshall Chief Justice

Bushrod Washington

William Johnson

The Hon'ble: Thomas Todd   associate
Gabriel Duvall   Justices
Joseph Story &
Smith Thompson

Proclamation being made the Court is opened

Thomas   Gibbons   This cause came on to be heard
29.   vs   on the Transcript of the Record
Aaron   Ogden   of the Court, For the trial of
                              Impeachments and correction

of Errors of the State of New York, and was argued by
counsel, on consideration Whereof this court is of
opinion that the several licences to the Steam Boats the
Stoudinger and the Bellona to carry on the coasting trade
Which are set up by the appellant Thomas Gibbons in
his answer to the Bill of the appellee Aaron Ogden filed
in the Court of Chancery for the State of New York, which
were granted under an act of Congress passed in pursu-

Gibbons v. Ogden (National Archives and Records Administration)

GIBBONS V. OGDEN

"Commerce, undoubtedly, is traffic, but it is something more: it is intercourse."

Overview

The U.S. Supreme Court case *Thomas Gibbons v. Aaron Ogden* (1824), often referred to as the steamboat monopoly case, is consistently ranked by historians as one of the most important landmark decisions in American jurisprudence. *Gibbons v. Ogden* represented the first Supreme Court case to tackle the thorny issue of interstate commerce and upheld the right of Congress to regulate travel between state lines. The case originated with the development of steam travel in New York. In 1798 the state chancellor Robert R. Livingston secured a legislative monopoly on steam travel in New York waters. In 1807 Livingston and his partner, the famous inventor Robert Fulton, successfully launched their prototype *North River Steam Boat* on the Hudson River.

In 1815 Fulton and the Livingston family granted the former New Jersey governor Aaron Ogden a license under the monopoly to run steamboats from Elizabethtown, New Jersey, to New York City. In 1819 Ogden sued his former partner, the Georgia businessman Thomas Gibbons, in the New York Court of Chancery for operating steamboats in New York harbor. Gibbons countered that he possessed a federal coasting license that gave him the right to conduct business in any American port, but the New York chancellor James Kent repeatedly upheld Ogden's monopoly license. Gibbons then hired the U.S. senator Daniel Webster and the U.S. attorney general William Wirt to appeal his case to the Supreme Court. Ogden secured the services of the former New York attorneys general Thomas Addis Emmet and Thomas Oakley. After extensive deliberations, on March 2, 1824, Chief Justice John Marshall ruled that Gibbons's federal coasting license invalidated Ogden's monopoly permit. The associate justice William Johnson argued in a concurring opinion that Congress's commerce powers alone defeated the New York monopoly.

The *Gibbons v. Ogden* case interested many Americans because it involved the widely popular issue of steam travel. Gibbons, Ogden, and the legal elites involved in the case believed that steam power was vital to the commercial and social development of the young nation. Working-class Americans likewise eagerly followed stories of the case in local newspapers. Although Marshall's broad decision was found favorable by the public, it ultimately failed to fully outline federal commerce powers. *Gibbons* became a legal precedent invoked by temperance supporters, labor leaders, civil rights demonstrators, and gun-control supporters.

Context

Gibbons v. Ogden occurred against a backdrop of rapid economic and social change in the young United States. Following the Revolutionary War, millions of Americans moved west across the Appalachian Mountains to settle in the newly available lands of the Midwest and Old Southwest. The American public thus became interested in newer and faster forms of transportation. Steam power had already been successfully used in Great Britain to pump water out of mines and operate looms in factories. Early American inventors like John Fitch and James Rumsey hoped to build functioning steamboats that would further aid in the westward expansion of the United States.

After the War of 1812, the United States entered a full-blown "transportation revolution," involving widespread support for steam power, canals, turnpikes, and public roads. Under the leadership of the Kentucky senator Henry Clay, Congress launched a formidable array of internal improvements, dubbed the American System, designed to link the different economic sections of the nation together into a seamless whole. At the state level, the New York governor DeWitt Clinton took the lead in promoting the Erie Canal, an ambitious attempt to connect the Hudson River to the Great Lakes and thus make New York City the leading port in the fledgling nation.

Steamboat entrepreneurs like Fitch, Rumsey, and Fulton had to secure resources, patrons, and legal protection in an ad hoc manner. Given the weakness of federal patent laws, they sought state monopolies that gave them exclusive rights to steam travel at the local level. As steamboats became more widely available, competitors emerged to challenge these monopolies. This led to a series of lawsuits in state and federal courts, which became a morass of unresolved litigation. Meanwhile, the public clamored for cheaper steamboat fares and better service. The federal

1787

■ **March 19**
The New York legislature grants John Fitch a monopoly on steam travel in state waters.

■ **August 22**
John Fitch demonstrates his steamboat *Perseverance* on the Delaware River before delegates from the Constitutional Convention.

■ **September 17**
The Founding Fathers complete the U.S. Constitution, giving Congress the power to grant patents (Article 1, Section 8, Clause 8) and regulate interstate commerce.

1790

■ **April 10**
Congress passes the first federal Patent Act.

1798

■ **March 27**
The New York legislature gives Fitch's steamboat monopoly to the state chancellor Robert R. Livingston.

1802

■ **October 10**
Livingston and Robert Fulton form a partnership to develop a working steamboat.

■ **May 2**
Livingston and James Monroe, negotiating with Napoléon Bonaparte, conclude the Louisiana Purchase.

1803

■ **August 9**
Fulton demonstrates his experimental steamboat in Paris.

1807

■ **August 17**
Fulton launches the *North River Steam Boat* on its maiden voyage from New York City to Albany.

1808

■ **April 16**
The New York legislature extends Fulton and Livingston's monopoly rights and allows them to seize unlicensed steam vessels in New York waters.

government in general and the Supreme Court in particular were reluctant to become involved in such an explosive issue, yet the persistence of Aaron Ogden and Thomas Gibbons in pursuing their legal conflict through the federal courts prompted the ultimate intervention of the Supreme Court in 1824.

About the Author

John Marshall was born near Germantown, in the "northern neck" region of western Virginia, on September 24, 1755. Marshall was the eldest of fifteen children in a family of minor frontier gentry. His mother, Mary Randolph Keith, was a cousin of Thomas Jefferson's. As a member of a landholding family, Marshall learned to function in the informal political world of the frontier. In 1775 Marshall volunteered for service in the Continental army and served with distinction in several battles before surviving a brutal winter at Valley Forge. The challenges of holding the army together and negotiating with squabbling state officials for precious resources fueled Marshall's beliefs in a strong federal union and an effective central government. In 1780 Marshall briefly studied law at the College of William and Mary before returning to the army in 1781.

In 1783, at the close of the American Revolution, Marshall married Mary Willis Ambler and pursued a career as an attorney in Richmond, Virginia. Marshall's charisma and sharp legal mind helped him secure positions in the Virginia House of Delegates and in the governor's Council of State. Marshall became a staunch Federalist and enthusiastic supporter of his former military comrades George Washington and Alexander Hamilton. In 1788 Marshall served as a delegate to the Virginia ratifying convention, where he strongly urged the adoption of the U.S. Constitution. Following the creation of the fledgling federal government, Marshall turned down offers to serve as Washington's attorney general, as ambassador to France, and as an associate justice of the U.S. Supreme Court. In 1797 President John Adams appointed Marshall, Charles Pinckney, and Elbridge Gerry to serve as delegates on a diplomatic mission to France. Rejecting demands from French officials for hefty bribes in what became known as the XYZ Affair, Marshall returned to the United States to a hero's welcome. In 1798 he successfully ran for Congress, where he became a key defender of Adams's moderate brand of federalism. Two years later Marshall began a brief stint as secretary of state. In the aftermath of Adams's defeat to Thomas Jefferson in the presidential election of 1800, the incumbent president hastily nominated Marshall to serve as chief justice of the United States.

Marshall would become the longest-serving chief justice in American history, dominating the Supreme Court until his death in 1835. With the assistance of colleagues such as Joseph Story and Bushrod Washington, Marshall handed down a series of landmark decisions that upheld federal power and established the reputation of the federal judiciary as a truly coequal branch of government. In *Fletcher v. Peck* (1810), Marshall asserted that the Georgia state legislature had to recognize the validity of land claims by out-of-state speculators, even though the sale of such land involved the wholesale bribery of state legislators. Furthermore, in *Martin v. Hunter's Lessee* (1816) Marshall recognized British land claims that had been confiscated by Virginia officials during the American Revolution. In *Trustees of Dartmouth College v. Woodward* (1819) the chief justice upheld Dartmouth's state charter as a contract that could not be changed by the New Hampshire legislature.

Although Marshall strove to deliver unanimous court opinions whenever possible, he often clashed with the associate justice William Johnson over points of law. Born in South Carolina in 1771, Johnson sprang from working-class roots. He attended Princeton, became an attorney, and served three terms as a Republican congressman, briefly serving as Speaker of the House of Representatives. In 1802 President Thomas Jefferson appointed Johnson to the Supreme Court, primarily to counterbalance the nationalist tendencies of John Marshall. Johnson, however, proved to be an independent figure, defying both Marshall and Jefferson on several occasions. For example, in *Gibbons v. Ogden*, Johnson issued a concurring opinion that argued that the commerce clause of the Constitution, the ultimate authority behind Gibbons's coasting license, invalidated the New York monopoly on its face.

Explanation and Analysis of the Document

◆ "Mr. Webster, for the Appellant"

Pages 3–33 of the record of *Gibbons v. Ogden* present the arguments given by Daniel Webster on February 4, 1824, against the New York monopoly. After noting that such a complex and controversial case deserved the right of appeal to the Supreme Court, Webster reduces his attack on the New York monopoly to two legal questions: Could the New York legislature grant a monopoly over steam travel? If so, was such a monopoly allowed by federal law and the U.S. Constitution? Webster observes, "Nothing was more complex than commerce; and in an age such as this, no words embrace a wider field than commercial regulation." As such, the framers of the Constitution had never intended for states to retain the power to grant monopolies; to allow them to do so at that time would have created tremendous legal problems. Although states retained police powers to regulate commerce for the public good, the Fulton-Livingston steamboat monopoly merely represented a legislative block to free trade. Webster states, "The people of New York have a right to be protected against this monopoly." In fact, the Act for Enrolling and Licensing Ships or Vessels to be Employed in the Coasting Trade and Fisheries, and for Regulating the Same, passed in 1793, granted Thomas Gibbons the right to trade in any American port. Furthermore, the state monopoly collided with congressional authority to collect taxes.

Time Line

1811

■ April 19
At the urging of the governor W. C. C. Claiborne, the legislature of Orleans Territory grants Fulton and Livingston a steamboat monopoly in local waters.

■ July 30
The justice Henry Brockholst Livingston dismisses the federal circuit case *Livingston v. Van Ingen*, citing lack of jurisdiction.

■ November 18
The New York chancellor John Lansing strikes down the Fulton-Livingston steamboat monopoly as unconstitutional.

1812

■ January 10
Nicholas Roosevelt successfully pilots Fulton and Livingston's steamboat *New Orleans* into its namesake city.

■ March 12
The chancellor James Kent and the New York Court for the Trial of Impeachments and the Correction of Errors uphold the New York monopoly as a valid exercise of state police powers.

1815

■ May 5
Fulton and John R. Livingston grant a monopoly license to the former New Jersey governor Aaron Ogden.

1816

■ May 20
The federal district court justice Dominic Hall declares the Louisiana steamboat monopoly unconstitutional.

■ July 16
Thomas Gibbons confronts Aaron Ogden at his home in Elizabethtown, New Jersey.

1819

■ October 6
Chancellor Kent issues an injunction against Thomas Gibbons from operating steamboats within the boundaries of New York State.

1823

■ August 7
The U.S. Supreme Court associate justice William Johnson, in a circuit court opinion for *Elkison v. Deliesseline*, strikes down a South Carolina law restricting black seamen to their ships as a violation of the commerce clause.

1824

■ March 2
Chief Justice John Marshall declares the New York steamboat monopoly unconstitutional in the Supreme Court case *Gibbons v. Ogden*.

■ June 14
The New York chancellor Nathan Sanford upholds *Gibbons v. Ogden* in *North River Steam Boat Co. v. Livingston*.

1825

■ February 28
John Savage, chief justice of the New York Court for the Trial of Impeachments and the Correction of Errors, reaffirms the *Gibbons* and *Livingston* decisions.

◆ "Mr. Oakley, for the Respondent"

Pages 33–79 chronicle Thomas Oakley's lengthy nine-hour defense of Aaron Ogden on February 4 and 5. In opposition to Webster's claims, Oakley contends that in 1787 the sovereign American states had created a limited central government of enumerated powers. As per the Tenth Amendment, state laws had to be "absolutely repugnant," not merely inconvenient, to federal authority if they were to be struck down. In any case, the steamboat monopoly did not represent a direct threat to congressional patent or commerce powers. According to Oakley, neither Livingston nor Fulton had invented the steamboat; they had, however, introduced European steam technology into the United States and deserved public compensation in the form of a state-granted monopoly for their efforts. Gibbons likewise claimed no federal patent rights, thus making the issue academic. Oakley then maintains that the state and federal governments enjoyed dual powers over commerce. States could grant monopolies for turnpikes, stagecoaches, and ferryboats as well as establish quarantine and inspection laws to promote public safety, provided such agreements did not interfere with federal powers. The term "commerce," Oakley argues, should be limited to the "transportation and sale of commodities." Since Gibbons's

steamboats transported passengers as opposed to freight, they did not fall under the terms of the Coasting Trade and Fisheries Act of 1793. The New York monopoly therefore did not directly conflict with federal law.

◆ "Mr. Emmet, on the Same Side"

Pages 79–159 present Thomas Addis Emmet's spirited reinforcement of Oakley's key arguments. Emmet begins with the observation that the burden of proof lay with Gibbons to show how the New York monopoly specifically injured him. The monopoly had been sustained numerous times by the New York legislature and courts, and it bore striking similarities to monopoly grants issued by other states ranging from Massachusetts to Georgia. Giving his own account of the creation of the U.S. Constitution, Emmet argues that the framers had given Congress broad commerce powers specifically to allow states wide latitude in governing their own commercial affairs. With respect to this case, Emmet asserts, commerce indeed consisted of "the exchange of one thing for another; the interchange of commodities; trade or traffic." To give Congress control over local trade would harm state efforts to support internal improvements. The states and federal government were therefore required to use their mutual commerce powers wisely and with due respect to one another's mutual spheres of influence. In fact, Congress had done this many times in frequently acquiescing to state taxation and inspection laws on imported goods; such comity had allowed the thirteen colonies to triumph through the American Revolution. However, in a larger, more fractious nation, the likelihood of regional antagonism would only increase. Emmet raises the specter of a future United States in which western congressman controlled foreign and interstate commerce, "without community of interest or knowledge of our local circumstances." Under such conditions, "the Union will not stand; it cannot stand; it cannot be the ordinance of God or nature, that it should stand." In any event, the New York monopoly did not prohibit steamboats in New York waters; it merely kept such vessels from using their engines while within state boundaries.

Emmet briefly touches on the issue of patent rights, echoing Oakley's observations that Gibbons claimed no patent rights and that even if he had, New York could still regulate such property under its commerce powers. Emmet finishes his defense with the observation that New York could take pride in its role supporting the development of steam power in the United States. The Empire State could thus take Aeneas's quote of despair, "What region of Earth is not full of our calamities," from Virgil's epic *Aeneid*, and turn it into an expression of triumph depicting the benefits of steam travel that would be given to the rest of the world.

◆ "The Attorney-General, for the Apellant"

Pages 159–186 of the case record trace the U.S. attorney general William Wirt's meticulous arguments on behalf of Gibbons, delivered on February 7. Wirt begins by stating that regardless of any state powers over commerce, the New York monopoly infringed upon federal law and was therefore invalid. He admits that the Founding Fathers had given the federal government vague commerce powers to accommodate state interests, but Congress still retained such authority "to be wielded by the whole Union over the whole Union, which no state could previously do." The framers had likewise given the federal government patent powers to promote scientific development in the nation. Fulton had often claimed to have invented the steamboat. To depict the New York monopoly as either an attempt to reward Fulton for merely possessing the technology in question or as a health regulation were at that time clearly shallow attempts to avoid federal patent authority. States could regulate trade as part of their police powers, but they had ceded authority over interstate trade to Congress with the ratification of the U.S. Constitution.

Wirt concludes by criticizing Emmet's earlier invocation of the *Aeneid*. He reminds the court that Aeneas's statement had been made in a moment of deepest despair, while contemplating the fall of Troy. Wirt then warns that if the federal government allowed state-granted monopolies to run unchecked, the United States might suffer the same fate as Troy.

◆ "Mr. Chief Justice Marshall Delivered the Opinion of the Court"

Pages 186–222 recount John Marshall's delivery of the unanimous decision in *Gibbons v. Ogden* against Aaron Ogden, delivered on March 2, 1824. Marshall begins by acknowledging that the monopoly had been supported "by names which have all the titles to consideration that virtue, intelligence, and office, can bestow," yet the Supreme Court still had the constitutional obligation to hear the case. He then upholds a broad view of the Constitution, stating that all power over interstate commerce had been given to Congress with the ratification of the Constitution. Out of necessity, the Constitution gave the federal government broad powers; to limit Congress to its enumerated powers "would cripple the government and render it unequal to the object for which it is declared to be instituted." In plain language, the Founders had granted Congress the power to "regulate commerce with foreign nations, and among the several States, and with the Indian tribes." They had understood that "commerce, undoubtedly, is traffic, but it is something more: it is intercourse." As such, Congress could regulate both the buying and selling of goods and the transportation of passengers and cargo across state lines. Since such commerce occurred "among" or "intermingled" with the states, congressional commerce power could "not stop at the external boundary line of each State, but may be introduced into the interior." Marshall concedes that states could pass safety or inspection laws based on their police powers. However, this did not give them concurrent powers over interstate commerce. Congress could recognize such state regulations and even give them the status of federal law as needed, but Congress still maintained ultimate control over interstate trade.

Marshall briefly considers whether the commerce clause by itself is enough to invalidate all attempts at concurrent state regulation. Nevertheless, the central point

Daniel Webster was one of the attorneys who represented Thomas Gibson during his successful appeal to the U.S. Supreme Court. (Library of Congress)

remains whether the New York monopoly impeded congressional authority. The Coasting Trade and Fisheries Act of 1793 gave registered vessels not only the status of American ships but also the right to travel between ports in different states. The act makes no mention of what such ships might be carrying in their holds or how they might be powered. Marshall concludes with a condemnation of states' rights activists who supported the monopoly, referring to them as "powerful and ingenious minds, taking as postulates that the powers expressly granted to the government of the Union are to be contracted by construction into the narrowest possible compass." Such individuals, Marshall warns, would "explain away the constitution of our country and leave it a magnificent structure, indeed, to look at, but totally unfit for use." The New York steamboat monopoly, he concludes, is unconstitutional and invalid.

◆ "Mr. Justice Johnson"

Pages 222–239 recount Justice William Johnson's concurring opinion in *Gibbons v. Ogden*. He begins with an expression of support for Marshall's decision and then stresses the need to state his own views on the matter. Johnson eschews both broad and strict interpretations of the Constitution, stating that the "simple, classical, precise, yet

"If ever a numerous and inland delegation shall wield the exclusive power of making regulations for our foreign commerce, without community of interest or knowledge of our local circumstances, the Union will not stand; it cannot stand; it cannot be the ordinance of God or nature, that it should stand."

(Thomas Addis Emmet)

"Commerce, undoubtedly, is traffic, but it is something more: it is intercourse."

(Chief Justice John Marshall)

"The mind can scarcely conceive a system for regulating commerce between nations which shall exclude all laws concerning navigation, which shall be silent on the admission of the vessels of the one nation into the ports of the other, and be confined to prescribing rules for the conduct of individuals in the actual employment of buying and selling or of barter."

(Chief Justice John Marshall)

"Powerful and ingenious minds, taking as postulates that the powers expressly granted to the government of the Union are to be contracted by construction into the narrowest possible compass and that the original powers of the States are retained if any possible construction will retain them may, by a course of well digested but refined and metaphysical reasoning founded on these premises, explain away the constitution of our country and leave it a magnificent structure indeed to look at, but totally unfit for use."

(Chief Justice John Marshall)

"The great and paramount purpose was to unite this mass of wealth and power, for the protection of the humblest individual, his rights, civil and political, his interests and prosperity, are the sole end; the rest are nothing but the means."

(Justice William Johnson)

comprehensive language in which it is couched leaves, at most, but very little latitude for construction." The Founders had created the Constitution to "unite this mass of wealth and power, for the protection of the humblest individual, his rights, civil and political, his interests and prosperity, are the sole end; the rest are nothing but the means." To overcome the economic rivalries of the era of the Articles of Confederation, the framers had given Congress extensive and complete control over interstate commerce. Such power obviously included the right to regulate navigation and commerce. This broad authority automatically swept away the New York monopoly, regardless of the Coasting Trade and Fisheries Act of 1793. In fact, Congress had created the coasting act to promote national trade, making any attempts at state regulation moot. To be certain, federal and state commerce powers intersected in some cases: "Wherever the powers of the respective governments are frankly exercised, with a distinct view to the ends of such powers, they may act upon the same object, or use the same means, and yet the powers be kept perfectly distinct." Ultimately, however, state power had to give way to federal authority. After concluding his defense of federal commerce powers, Johnson begs off a discussion on federal patent law.

◆ "Decree"

The case concludes on page 239 with John Marshall's decree of the Supreme Court. He reexamines the background of the case and his own decision, concluding that the Coasting Trade and Fisheries Act of 1793 granted Gibbons the right to trade in New York waters, state laws notwithstanding. The New York steamboat monopoly was accordingly "erroneous, and ought to be reversed, and the same is hereby reversed and annulled: and this Court doth further DIRECT, ORDER, and DECREE that the bill of the said Aaron Ogden be dismissed, and this same is hereby dismissed accordingly."

Audience

The *Gibbons v. Ogden* case was argued and adjudicated with a national audience in mind. In their invocation of the founding generation, the American Revolution, and the creation of the U.S. Constitution, attorneys like Webster and Emmet hoped to convince the American public of the righteousness of their causes. Furthermore, John Marshall recognized the importance of crafting a decision that would result in maximum public support. At that time, despite the formidable knowledge of the Supreme Court justices, the judiciary remained the weakest branch of the federal government. The concept of judicial supremacy was still a novel idea, and the Supreme Court had to inspire rather than compel the obedience of the states and the American public. Furthermore, the Marshall Court had issued several unpopular decisions in recent years, such as *McCulloch v. Maryland* (1819), *Cohens v. Virginia* (1821), and *Green v. Biddle* (1823).

Marshall accordingly handed down a broadly worded decision that appealed to many Americans. For instance, therein, he highlights the plain and common language used by the framers in the creation of the Constitution to show that they enjoyed widespread approval from the American public. He also depicts the ratification of the Constitution as an event in which the public expressed support for the new federal government and its commerce policies. Marshall also aimed part of his opinion at states' rights enthusiasts, warning them that a governmental structure that lacked the power to effectively carry out its powers was no government at all.

Impact

Public reaction to *Gibbons v. Ogden* was overwhelmingly positive. Within a month of Marshall's decision, twenty steamboats were operating in New York waters, many from other states. Middling Americans such as businessmen, merchants, artisans, and farmers quickly took advantage of the cheaper fares and better service brought by the destruction of the monopoly. Northern and western newspapers cheered the *Gibbons* decision as a victory for free trade over special interests, for social progress over provincialism. Many southerners likewise reacted favorably to the decision, although some worried that the case could prove a dangerous precedent regarding federal regulation of the interstate slave trade.

Marshall's decision in *Gibbons v. Ogden* left many issues unclear, and the particular issue of state versus federal control of commerce continued to appear before the Supreme Court. By the 1830s and 1840s, as public attention shifted from economic matters to social reform, popular perceptions of the *Gibbons* case began to change. Both social elites and ordinary citizens increasingly discussed the possibility of regulating commerce to protect public "morals" as well as public safety and property rights. Legal documents and newspaper accounts show that in the Court of Chief Justice Roger Taney, in cases such as *Mayor of New York v. Miln* (1837), *Groves v. Slaughter* (1841), the License Cases (1847), and the Passenger Cases (1849), state lawyers cited *Gibbons v. Ogden* to make the case for regulation in controversial issues as disparate as immigration, alcohol, and slavery within their states. In these and other cases, *Gibbons v. Ogden*, originally a decision designed to limit state authority, ironically helped mold society at the local level with the tacit approval of the federal court system. By the eve of the Civil War, *Gibbons v. Ogden* had thus helped to stimulate a national economy but had also been used as a model for a culture of social regulation.

Throughout the late nineteenth and early twentieth centuries, *Gibbons v. Ogden* continued to play a pivotal role in the ongoing controversy over commerce regulation. For instance, during the Gilded Age, the Supreme Court preserved a system of dual federalism by repeatedly citing *Gibbons v. Ogden* both to expand federal commerce power, such as in *Wabash, St. Louis & Pacific Railroad Co. v. Illinois* (1886), and to limit that authority, such as in *United States v. E. C. Knight Co.* (1895). In *Northern Securities Co. v. United States* (1904), the associate justice Harlan Stone took tentative steps to consider the motives behind state and federal trade regulation rather than simply the actual movement of goods and individuals. Following the Supreme Court decisions in *A. L. A. Schechter Poultry Corporation v. United States* (1935) and *United States v. Butler* (1936), President Franklin D. Roosevelt's court-packing scheme prompted the Court to retreat from the aspect of dual federalism limiting the national government. In language reminiscent of the state-based regulation movements of the nineteenth century, the Supreme Court increasingly broadened congressional commerce powers to encourage social reform.

Over the next sixty years the *Gibbons* decision became a precedent for cases involving segregation, such as *Heart of Atlanta Motel, Inc. v. United States* (1964), and labor issues, such as *Garcia v. San Antonio Metropolitan Transit Authority* (1985). The Rehnquist Court rejected a broad interpretation of *Gibbons v. Ogden* beginning with *United States v. Lopez* (1995), in which a federal commerce law banning handguns from school zones was struck down. This ruling sparked a renewed public interest in *Gibbons v. Ogden* and how the memory of that case had changed over time. Above all, *Lopez* demonstrated the continuing relevance of the steamboat monopoly case to the ongoing debate over commerce regulation as an instrument both of economic development and of social change within a federalist framework.

Related Documents

Hobson, Charles F., ed. *The Papers of John Marshall*. 12 vols. Chapel Hill: University of North Carolina Press, 1974–2006. Marshall's long tenure on the Supreme Court provided him with various opportunities to comment on important topics such as nationalism, commercial development, internal improvements, and federal-state relations. These papers reveal the evolution of Marshall's beliefs from the Revolutionary War to the 1830s.

Story, William Wetmore, ed. *Life and Letters of Joseph Story, Associate Justice of the Supreme Court of the United States, and Dane Professor of Law at Harvard University*. 2 vols. Boston: C. C. Little and J. Brown, 1851. This dated and selective collection of the letters of Joseph Story, who sat on the Court alongside Marshall for more than twenty years, nevertheless provides keen insights into his views on interstate trade and fedcralism. Particularly revealing is his correspondence with the New York chancellor James Kent.

Wiltse, Charles M., and Harold D. Moser, eds. *The Papers of Daniel Webster*. 14 vols. Hanover, N.H.: University Press of New England, 1974–1989. Daniel Webster served as Thomas Gibbons's attorney before the Supreme Court in 1824; his papers contain a wealth of information on the legal strategies used in the steamboat monopoly case.

Bibliography

■ Books

Appleby, Joyce O. *Capitalism and a New Social Order: The Republican Vision of the 1790s*. New York: New York University Press, 1984.

Baxter, Maurice G. *The Steamboat Monopoly: Gibbons v. Ogden, 1824*. New York: Knopf, 1972.

Bruchey, Stuart. *Enterprise: The Dynamic Economy of a Free People*. Cambridge, Mass.: Harvard University Press, 1990.

Currie, David P. *The Constitution in the Supreme Court: The First Hundred Years, 1789–1888*. Chicago: University of Chicago Press, 1985.

Garraty, John A., ed. *Quarrels That Have Shaped the Constitution*. New York: Perennial Library, 1987.

Gilje, Paul A., ed. *Wages of Independence: Capitalism in the Early American Republic*. Madison, Wis.: Madison House, 1997.

Hobson, Charles F. *The Great Chief Justice: John Marshall and the Rule of Law*. Lawrence: University Press of Kansas, 1996.

Horwitz, Morton J. *The Transformation of American Law, 1780–1860*. Cambridge, Mass.: Harvard University Press, 1977.

Johnson, Herbert A. *The Chief Justiceship of John Marshall, 1801–1835*. Columbia: University of South Carolina Press, 1997.

Kammen, Michael. *A Machine That Would Go of Itself: The Constitution in American Culture*. New Brunswick, N.J. : Transaction Publishers, 2006.

Newmyer, R. Kent. *Supreme Court Justice Joseph Story: Statesman of the Old Republic*. Chapel Hill: University of North Carolina Press, 1985.

Sellers, Charles. *The Market Revolution: Jacksonian America, 1815–1846*. New York: Oxford University Press, 1991.

Stokes, Melvyn, and Stephen Conway, eds. *The Market Revolution in America: Social, Political, and Religious Expressions, 1800–1880*. Charlottesville: University Press of Virginia, 1996.

White, G. Edward. *The Marshall Court and Cultural Change, 1815–1835*. New York: Oxford University Press, 1991.

■ Web Sites

"Gibbons v. Ogden." U.S. Supreme Court Media, Oyez Web site. http://www.oyez.org/cases/1792-1850/1824/1824_0/. Accessed on August 27, 2007.

"*Gibbons v. Ogden* (1824)." Landmark Supreme Court Cases Web site. http://www.landmarkcases.org/gibbons/home.html. Accessed on August 27, 2007.

"Gibbons v. Ogden (1824)." National Archives "Our Documents" Web site. http://www.ourdocuments.gov/doc.php?flash=true&doc=24. Accessed on August 27, 2007.

—By Thomas H. Cox

1. Americans first began experimenting with steam power in the 1780s, and Robert Fulton produced the first practical steamboat in 1807. Nevertheless, nearly two more decades passed before the Supreme Court addressed the issues contained in *Gibbons v. Ogden*. Given the public interest in steam travel and the lucrative profits to be made from steamboat lines, why did so much time elapse before the legal conflict over steamboats reached the nation's highest court?

2. Why did litigants, attorneys, and justices involved in *Gibbons v. Ogden* center most of their arguments on factors such as federal commerce power and state monopolies instead of the rather obvious issue of federal patent rights? What about the issue of patents made it such a controversial or irrelevant topic?

3. Why did neither John Marshall nor William Johnson issue specific guidelines for federal and state commerce regulation? Could the justices' reasons have had anything to do with the explosive issue of slavery?

4. In the 1930s, New Deal attorneys argued that *Gibbons v. Ogden* foreshadowed the rise of a strong federal government with the ability to regulate not merely economic policies but also social reform across state lines. Is this a valid interpretation of Marshall's decision?

Glossary

chancery court	court that specializes in constitutional issues and property disputes
coasting license	a license giving a vessel the right to trade in American ports
commerce	the buying and selling of goods and the transportation of passengers and goods
concurrent regulation	an area in which the jurisdictions of two governments overlap
court of errors	a court of appeals that reviews the decisions of other courts
enroll	to legally register a vessel
equity	a branch of law that specializes in fairness
injunction	a legal writ issued by a court forbidding the undertaking of a certain action
inspection laws	public safety measures designed to guarantee quality of merchandise
intercourse	communication or trade between different individuals or groups
monopoly	governmental grant giving an individual the sole right over a certain activity
police powers	the right of a sovereign government to regulate health and morals for the public good
quarantine laws	laws allowing government agents to seize and hold property for public safety
viz.	namely

GIBBONS V. OGDEN

Mr. Chief Justice MARSHALL delivered the opinion of the Court, and, after stating the case, proceeded as follows:

The appellant contends that this decree is erroneous because the laws which purport to give the exclusive privilege it sustains are repugnant to the Constitution and laws of the United States.

They are said to be repugnant:

1st. To that clause in the Constitution which authorizes Congress to regulate commerce.

2d. To that which authorizes Congress to promote the progress of science and useful arts.

The State of New York maintains the Constitutionality of these laws, and their Legislature, their Council of Revision, and their Judges, have repeatedly concurred in this opinion. It is supported by great names—by names which have all the titles to consideration that virtue, intelligence, and office can bestow. No tribunal can approach the decision of this question without feeling a just and real respect for that opinion which is sustained by such authority, but it is the province of this Court, while it respects, not to bow to it implicitly, and the Judges must exercise, in the examination of the subject, that understanding which Providence has bestowed upon them, with that independence which the people of the United States expect from this department of the government.

As preliminary to the very able discussions of the Constitution which we have heard from the bar, and as having some influence on its construction, reference has been made to the political situation of these States anterior to its formation. It has been said that they were sovereign, were completely independent, and were connected with each other only by a league. This is true. But, when these allied sovereigns converted their league into a government, when they converted their Congress of Ambassadors, deputed to deliberate on their common concerns and to recommend measures of general utility, into a

Legislature, empowered to enact laws on the most interesting subjects, the whole character in which the States appear underwent a change, the extent of which must be determined by a fair consideration of the instrument by which that change was effected.

This instrument contains an enumeration of powers expressly granted by the people to their government. It has been said that these powers ought to be construed strictly. But why ought they to be so construed? Is there one sentence in the Constitution which gives countenance to this rule? In the last of the enumerated powers, that which grants expressly the means for carrying all others into execution, Congress is authorized "to make all laws which shall be necessary and proper" for the purpose. But this limitation on the means which may be used is not extended to the powers which are conferred, nor is there one sentence in the Constitution which has been pointed out by the gentlemen of the bar or which we have been able to discern that prescribes this rule. We do not, therefore, think ourselves justified in adopting it. What do gentlemen mean by a "strict construction?" If they contend only against that enlarged construction, which would extend words beyond their natural and obvious import, we might question the application of the term, but should not controvert the principle. If they contend for that narrow construction which, in support or some theory not to be found in the Constitution, would deny to the government those powers which the words of the grant, as usually understood, import, and which are consistent with the general views and objects of the instrument; for that narrow construction which would cripple the government and render it unequal to the object for which it is declared to be instituted, and to which the powers given, as fairly understood, render it competent; then we cannot perceive the propriety of this strict construction, nor adopt it as the rule by which the Constitution is to be expounded. As men whose intentions require no concealment generally employ the words which most directly and aptly express the ideas they intend to convey, the enlightened patriots who framed our Constitution, and the people who adopted it, must be understood to have employed words in their natural sense, and to have intended what they have said. If, from the imperfection of human language, there should be serious doubts respecting the extent of any given power, it is a well settled rule that the objects for which it was given, especially when those objects are expressed in the instrument itself, should have great influence in the construction. We know of no reason for excluding this rule from the present case. The grant does not convey power which might be beneficial to the grantor if retained by himself, or which can enure solely to the benefit of the grantee, but is an investment of power for the general advantage, in the hands of agents selected for that purpose, which power can never be exercised by the people themselves, but must be placed in the hands of agents or lie dormant. We know of no rule for construing the extent of such powers other than is given by the language of the instrument which confers them, taken in connexion with the purposes for which they were conferred.

The words are, "Congress shall have power to regulate commerce with foreign nations, and among the several States, and with the Indian tribes."

The subject to be regulated is commerce, and our Constitution being, as was aptly said at the bar, one of enumeration, and not of definition, to ascertain the extent of the power, it becomes necessary to settle the meaning of the word. The counsel for the appellee would limit it to traffic, to buying and selling, or the interchange of commodities, and do not admit that it comprehends navigation. This would restrict a general term, applicable to many objects, to one of its significations. Commerce, undoubtedly, is traffic, but it is something more: it is intercourse. It describes the commercial intercourse between nations, and parts of nations, in all its branches, and is regulated by prescribing rules for carrying on that intercourse. The mind can scarcely conceive a system for regulating commerce between nations which shall exclude all laws concerning navigation, which shall be silent on the admission of the vessels of the one nation into the ports of the other, and be confined to prescribing rules for the conduct of individuals in the actual employment of buying and selling or of barter.

If commerce does not include navigation, the government of the Union has no direct power over that subject, and can make no law prescribing what shall constitute American vessels or requiring that they shall be navigated by American seamen. Yet this power has been exercised from the commencement of the government, has been exercised with the consent of all, and has been understood by all to be a commercial regulation. All America understands, and has uniformly understood, the word "commerce" to comprehend navigation. It was so understood, and must have been so understood, when the Constitution was framed. The power over commerce, including navigation, was one of the primary objects for which the people of America adopted their government, and must have been contemplated in forming it. The convention must have used the word in that sense, because all have understood it in that sense, and the attempt to restrict it comes too late.

If the opinion that "commerce," as the word is used in the Constitution, comprehends navigation also, requires any additional confirmation, that additional confirmation is, we think, furnished by the words of the instrument itself.

It is a rule of construction acknowledged by all that the exceptions from a power mark its extent, for it would be absurd, as well as useless, to except from a granted power that which was not granted—that which the words of the grant could not comprehend. If, then, there are in the Constitution plain exceptions from the power over navigation, plain inhibitions to the exercise of that power in a particular way, it is a proof that those who made these exceptions, and prescribed these inhibitions, understood the power to which they applied as being granted.

The 9th section of the 1st article declares that "no preference shall be given, by any regulation of commerce or revenue, to the ports of one State over those of another." This clause cannot be understood as applicable to those laws only which are passed for the purposes of revenue, because it is expressly applied to commercial regulations, and the most obvious preference which can be given to one port over another in regulating commerce relates to navigation. But the subsequent part of the sentence is still more explicit. It is, "nor shall vessels bound to or from one State be obliged to enter, clear, or pay duties, in another." These words have a direct reference to navigation.

The universally acknowledged power of the government to impose embargoes must also be considered as showing that all America is united in that construction which comprehends navigation in the word commerce. Gentlemen have said in argument that this is a branch of the war-making power, and that an embargo is an instrument of war, not a regulation of trade.

That it may be, and often is, used as an instrument of war cannot be denied. An embargo may be imposed for the purpose of facilitating the equipment or manning of a fleet, or for the purpose of concealing the progress of an expedition preparing to sail from a particular port. In these, and in similar cases, it is a military instrument, and partakes of the nature of war. But all embargoes are not of this description. They are sometimes resorted to without a view to war, and with a single view to commerce. In such case, an embargo is no more a war measure than a merchantman is a ship of war because both are vessels which navigate the ocean with sails and seamen.

When Congress imposed that embargo which, for a time, engaged the attention of every man in the United States, the avowed object of the law was the protection of commerce, and the avoiding of war. By its friends and its enemies, it was treated as a commercial, not as a war, measure. The persevering earnestness and zeal with which it was opposed in a part of our country which supposed its interests to be vitally affected by the act, cannot be forgotten. A want of acuteness in discovering objections to a measure to which they felt the most deep-rooted hostility will not be imputed to those who were arrayed in opposition to this. Yet they never suspected that navigation was no branch of trade, and was therefore not comprehended in the power to regulate commerce. They did, indeed, contest the constitutionality of the act, but, on a principle which admits the construction for which the appellant contends. They denied that the particular law in question was made in pursuance of the Constitution not because the power could not act directly on vessels, but because a perpetual embargo was the annihilation, and not the regulation, of commerce. In terms, they admitted the applicability of the words used in the Constitution to vessels, and that in a case which produced a degree and an extent of excitement calculated to draw forth every principle on which legitimate resistance could be sustained. No example could more strongly illustrate the universal understanding of the American people on this subject.

The word used in the Constitution, then, comprehends, and has been always understood to comprehend, navigation within its meaning, and a power to regulate navigation is as expressly granted as if that term had been added to the word "commerce."

To what commerce does this power extend? The Constitution informs us, to commerce "with foreign nations, and among the several States, and with the Indian tribes."

It has, we believe, been universally admitted that these words comprehend every species of commercial intercourse between the United States and foreign nations. No sort of trade can be carried on between this country and any other to which this power does not extend. It has been truly said that "commerce," as the word is used in the Constitution, is a unit every part of which is indicated by the term.

If this be the admitted meaning of the word in its application to foreign nations, it must carry the same meaning throughout the sentence, and remain a unit, unless there be some plain intelligible cause which alters it.

The subject to which the power is next applied is to commerce "among the several States." The word "among" means intermingled with. A thing which is among others is intermingled with them. Commerce among the States cannot stop at the external boundary line of each State, but may be introduced into the interior.

It is not intended to say that these words comprehend that commerce which is completely internal, which is carried on between man and man in a State, or between different parts of the same State, and which does not extend to or affect other States. Such a power would be inconvenient, and is certainly unnecessary.

Comprehensive as the word "among" is, it may very properly be restricted to that commerce which concerns more States than one. The phrase is not one which would probably have been selected to indicate the completely interior traffic of a State, because it is not an apt phrase for that purpose, and the enumeration of the particular classes of commerce to which the power was to be extended would not have been made had the intention been to extend the power to every description. The enumeration presupposes something not enumerated, and that something, if we regard the language or the subject of the sentence, must be the exclusively internal commerce of a State. The genius and character of the whole government seem to be that its action is to be applied to all the external concerns of the nation, and to those internal concerns which affect the States generally, but not to those which are completely within a particular State, which do not affect other States, and with which it is not necessary to interfere for the purpose of executing some of the general powers of the government. The completely internal commerce of a State, then, may be considered as reserved for the State itself.

But, in regulating commerce with foreign nations, the power of Congress does not stop at the jurisdictional lines of the several States. It would be a very useless power if it could not pass those lines. The commerce of the United States with foreign nations is that of the whole United States. Every district has a right to participate in it. The deep streams which penetrate our country in every direction pass through the interior of almost every State in the Union, and furnish the means of exercising this right. If Congress has the power to regulate it, that power must be exercised whenever the subject exists. If it exists within the States, if a foreign voyage may commence or terminate at a port within a State, then the power of Congress may be exercised within a State.

This principle is, if possible, still more clear, when applied to commerce "among the several States." They either join each other, in which case they are separated by a mathematical line, or they are remote from each other, in which case other States lie between them. What is commerce "among" them, and how is it to be conducted? Can a trading expedition between two adjoining States, commence and terminate outside of each? And if the trading intercourse be between two States remote from each other, must it not commence in one, terminate in the other, and probably pass through a third? Commerce among the States must, of necessity, be commerce with the States. In the regulation of trade with the Indian tribes, the action of the law, especially when the Constitution was made, was chiefly within a State. The power of Congress, then, whatever it may be, must be exercised within the territorial jurisdiction of the several States. The sense of the nation on this subject is unequivocally manifested by the provisions made in the laws for transporting goods by land between Baltimore and Providence, between New York and Philadelphia, and between Philadelphia and Baltimore.

We are now arrived at the inquiry—What is this power?

It is the power to regulate, that is, to prescribe the rule by which commerce is to be governed. This power, like all others vested in Congress, is complete in itself, may be exercised to its utmost extent, and acknowledges no limitations other than are prescribed in the Constitution. These are expressed in plain terms, and do not affect the questions which arise in this case, or which have been discussed at the bar. If, as has always been understood, the sovereignty of Congress, though limited to specified objects, is plenary as to those objects, the power over commerce with foreign nations, and among the several States, is vested in Congress as absolutely as it would be in a single government, having in its Constitution the same restrictions on the exercise of the power as are found in the Constitution of the United States. The wisdom and the discretion of Congress, their identity with the people, and the influence which their constituents possess at elections are, in this, as in many other instances, as that, for example, of declaring war, the sole restraints on which they have relied, to secure them from its abuse. They are the restraints on which the people must often they solely, in all representative governments.

The power of Congress, then, comprehends navigation, within the limits of every State in the Union, so far as that navigation may be in any manner connected with "commerce with foreign nations, or among the several States, or with the Indian tribes." It may, of consequence, pass the jurisdictional line of New York and act upon the very waters to which the prohibition now under consideration applies.

But it has been urged with great earnestness that, although the power of Congress to regulate commerce with foreign nations and among the several States be coextensive with the subject itself, and have no other limits than are prescribed in the Constitution, yet the States may severally exercise the same power, within their respective jurisdictions. In support of this argument, it is said that they possessed it as an inseparable attribute of sovereignty, before the formation of the Constitution, and still retain it except so far as they have surrendered it by that instrument; that this principle results from the nature of the government, and is secured by the tenth amendment; that an affirmative grant of power is not exclusive unless in its own nature it be such that the continued exercise of it by the former possessor is inconsistent with the grant, and that this is not of that description.

The appellant, conceding these postulates except the last, contends that full power to regulate a particular subject implies the whole power, and leaves no residuum; that a grant of the whole is incompatible with the existence of a right in another to any part of it.

Both parties have appealed to the Constitution, to legislative acts, and judicial decisions, and have drawn arguments from all these sources to support and illustrate the propositions they respectively maintain.

The grant of the power to lay and collect taxes is, like the power to regulate commerce, made in general terms, and has never been understood to interfere with the exercise of the same power by the State, and hence has been drawn an argument which has been applied to the question under consideration. But the two grants are not, it is conceived, similar in their terms or their nature. Although many of the powers formerly exercised by the States are transferred to the government of the Union, yet the State governments remain, and constitute a most important part of our system. The power of taxation is indispensable to their existence, and is a power which, in its own nature, is capable of residing in, and being exercised by, different authorities at the same time. We are accustomed to see it placed, for different purposes, in different hands. Taxation is the simple operation of taking small portions from a perpetually accumulating mass, susceptible of almost infinite division, and a power in one to take what is necessary for certain purposes is not, in its nature, incompatible with a power in another to take what is necessary for other purposes. Congress is authorized to lay and collect taxes, &c. to pay the debts and provide for the common defence and general welfare of the United States. This does not interfere with the power of the States to tax for the support of their own governments, nor is the exercise of that power by the States an exercise of any portion of the power that is granted to the United States. In imposing taxes for State purposes, they are not doing what Congress is empowered to do. Congress is not empowered to tax for those purposes which are within the exclusive province of the States. When, then, each government exercises the power of taxation, neither is exercising the power of the other. But, when a State proceeds to regulate commerce with foreign nations, or among the several States, it is exercising the very power that is granted to Congress, and is doing the very thing which Congress is authorized to do. There is no analogy, then, between the power of taxation and the power of regulating commerce.

In discussing the question whether this power is still in the States, in the case under consideration, we may dismiss from it the inquiry whether it is surrendered by the mere grant to Congress, or is retained until Congress shall exercise the power. We may dismiss that inquiry because it has been exercised, and the regulations which Congress deemed it proper to make are now in full operation. The sole question is can a State regulate commerce with foreign nations and among the States while Congress is regulating it?

The counsel for the respondent answer this question in the affirmative, and rely very much on the restrictions in the 10th section as supporting their opinion. They say very truly that limitations of a power furnish a strong argument in favour of the existence of that power, and that the section which prohibits the States from laying duties on imports or exports proves that this power might have been exercised had it not been expressly forbidden, and consequently that any other commercial regulation, not expressly forbidden, to which the original power of the State was competent may still be made.

That this restriction shows the opinion of the Convention that a State might impose duties on exports and imports, if not expressly forbidden, will be conceded, but that it follows as a consequence from this concession that a State may regulate commerce with foreign nations and among the States cannot be admitted.

We must first determine whether the act of laying "duties or imposts on imports or exports" is considered in the Constitution as a branch of the taxing power, or of the power to regulate commerce. We think it very clear that it is considered as a branch of the taxing power. It is so treated in the first clause of the 8th section: "Congress shall have power to lay and collect taxes, duties, imposts, and excises;" and, before commerce is mentioned, the rule by which the exercise of this power must be governed is declared. It is that all duties, imposts, and excises shall be uniform. In a separate clause of the enumeration, the power to regulate commerce is given, as being entirely distinct from the right to levy taxes and imposts and as being a new power, not before conferred. The Constitution, then, considers these powers as substantive, and distinct from each other, and so places them in the enumeration it contains. The power of imposing duties on imports is classed with the power to levy taxes, and that seems to be its natural place. But the power to levy taxes could never be considered as abridging the right of the States on that subject, and they might, consequently, have exercised it by levying duties on imports or exports, had the Constitution contained no prohibition on this subject. This prohibition, then, is an exception from the acknowledged power of the States to levy taxes, not from the questionable power to regulate commerce.

"A duty of tonnage" is as much a tax as a duty on imports or exports, and the reason which induced the prohibition of those taxes extends to this also. This tax may be imposed by a State, with the consent of Congress, and it may be admitted that Congress cannot give a right to a State in virtue of its own powers. But a duty of tonnage being part of the power of imposing taxes, its prohibition may certainly be made to depend on Congress, without affording any implication respecting a power to regulate commerce. It is true that duties may often be, and in fact often are, imposed on tonnage with a view to the regulation of commerce, but they may be also imposed with a view to revenue, and it was therefore a prudent precaution to prohibit the States from exercising this power. The idea that the same measure might, according to circumstances, be arranged with different classes of power was no novelty to the framers of our Constitution. Those illustrious statesmen and patriots had been, many of them, deeply engaged in the discussions which preceded the war of our revolution, and all of them were well read in those discussions. The right to regulate commerce, even by the imposition of duties, was not controverted, but the right to impose a duty for the purpose of revenue produced a war as important, perhaps, in its consequences to the human race as any the world has ever witnessed.

These restrictions, then, are on the taxing power, not on that to regulate commerce, and presuppose the existence of that which they restrain, not of that which they do not purport to restrain.

But the inspection laws are said to be regulations of commerce, and are certainly recognised in the Constitution as being passed in the exercise of a power remaining with the States.

That inspection laws may have a remote and considerable influence on commerce will not be denied, but that a power to regulate commerce is the source from which the right to pass them is derived cannot be admitted. The object of inspection laws is to improve the quality of articles produced by the labour of a country, to fit them for exportation, or, it may be, for domestic use. They act upon the subject before it becomes an article of foreign commerce or of commerce among the States, and prepare it for that purpose. They form a portion of that immense mass of legislation which embraces everything within the territory of a State not surrendered to the General Government; all which can be most advantageously exercised by the States themselves. Inspection laws, quarantine laws, health laws of every description, as well as laws for regulating the internal commerce of a State, and those which respect turnpike roads, ferries, &c., are component parts of this mass.

No direct general power over these objects is granted to Congress, and, consequently, they remain subject to State legislation. If the legislative power of the Union can reach them, it must be for national purposes, it must be where the power is expressly given for a special purpose or is clearly incidental to some power which is expressly given. It is obvious that the government of the Union, in the exercise of its express powers—that, for example, of regulating commerce with foreign nations and among the States—may use means that may also be employed by a State in the exercise of its acknowledged powers—that, for example, of regulating commerce within the State. If Congress license vessels to sail from one port to another in the same State, the act is supposed to be necessarily incidental to the power expressly granted to Congress, and implies no claim of a direct power to regulate the purely internal commerce of a State or to act directly on its system of police. So, if a State, in passing laws on subjects acknowledged to be within its control, and with a view to those subjects, shall adopt a measure of the same character with one which Congress may adopt, it does not derive its authority from the particular power which has been granted, but from some other, which remains with the State and may be executed by the same means. All experience shows that the same measures, or measures scarcely distinguishable from each other, may flow from distinct powers, but this does not prove that the powers themselves are identical. Although the means used in their execution may sometimes approach each other so nearly as to be confounded, there are other situations in which they are sufficiently distinct to establish their individuality.

In our complex system, presenting the rare and difficult scheme of one General Government whose action extends over the whole but which possesses only certain enumerated powers, and of numerous State governments which retain and exercise all powers not delegated to the Union, contests respecting power must arise. Were it even otherwise, the measures taken by the respective governments to execute their acknowledged powers would often be of the same description, and might sometimes interfere. This, however, does not prove that the one is exercising, or has a right to exercise, the powers of the other.

The acts of Congress passed in 1796 and 1799, 2 U.S.L. 345, 3 U.S.L. 126, empowering and directing the officers of the General Government to conform to and assist in the execution of the quarantine and health laws of a State proceed, it is said, upon the idea that these laws are constitutional. It is undoubtedly true that they do proceed upon that idea, and the constitutionality of such laws has never, so far as we are informed, been denied. But they do not imply an acknowledgment that a State may rightfully regulate commerce with foreign nations or among the States, for they do not imply that such laws are an exercise of that power, or enacted with a view to it. On the contrary, they are treated as quarantine and health laws, are so denominated in the acts of Congress, and are considered as flowing from the acknowledged power of a State to provide for the health of its citizens. But as it was apparent that some of the provisions made for this purpose and in virtue of this power might interfere with and be affected by the laws of the United States made for the regulation of commerce, Congress, in that spirit of harmony and conciliation which ought always to characterize the conduct of governments standing in the relation which that of the Union and those of the States bear to each other, has directed its officers to aid in the execution of these laws, and has, in some measure, adapted its own legislation to this object by making provisions in aid of those of the States. But, in making these provisions, the opinion is unequivocally manifested that Congress may control the State laws so far as it may be necessary to control them for the regulation of commerce. The act passed in 1803, 3 U.S.L. 529, prohibiting the importation of slaves into any State which shall itself prohibit their importation, implies, it is said, an admission that the States possessed the power to exclude or admit them, from which it is inferred that they possess the same power with respect to other articles.

If this inference were correct, if this power was exercised not under any particular clause in the Constitution, but in virtue of a general right over the subject of commerce, to exist as long as the Constitution itself, it might now be exercised. Any State might now import African slaves into its own territory. But it is obvious that the power of the States over this subject, previous to the year 1808, constitutes an exception to the power of Congress to regulate commerce, and the exception is expressed in such words, as to manifest clearly the intention to continue the preexisting right of the States to admit or exclude, for a limited period. The words are

> the migration or importation of such persons as any of the States, now existing, shall think proper to admit shall not be prohibited by the Congress prior to the year 1808.

The whole object of the exception is to preserve the power to those States which might be disposed to exercise it, and its language seems to the Court to convey this idea unequivocally. The possession of this particular power, then, during the time limited in the Constitution, cannot be admitted to prove the possession of any other similar power.

It has been said that the act of August 7, 1789, acknowledges a concurrent power in the States to regulate the conduct of pilots, and hence is inferred an admission of their concurrent right with Congress to regulate commerce with foreign nations and amongst the States. But this inference is not, we think, justified by the fact.

Although Congress cannot enable a State to legislate, Congress may adopt the provisions of a State on any subject. When the government of the Union was brought into existence, it found a system for the regulation of its pilots in full force in every State. The act which has been mentioned adopts this system, and gives it the same validity as if its provisions had been specially made by Congress. But the act, it may be said, is prospective also, and the adoption of laws to be made in future presupposes the right in the maker to legislate on the subject.

The act unquestionably manifests an intention to leave this subject entirely to the States until Congress should think proper to interpose, but the very enactment of such a law indicates an opinion that it was necessary, that the existing system would not be applicable to the new state of things unless expressly applied to it by Congress. But this section is confined to pilots within the "bays, inlets, rivers, harbours, and ports of the United States," which are, of course, in whole or in part, also within the limits of some particular state. The acknowledged power of a State to regulate its police, its domestic trade, and to govern its own citizens may enable it to legislate on this subject to a considerable extent, and the adoption of its system by Congress, and the application of it to the whole subject of commerce, does not seem to the Court to imply a right in the States so to apply it of their own authority. But the adoption of the State system being temporary, being only "until further legislative provision shall be made by Congress," shows conclusively an opinion that Congress could control the whole subject, and might adopt the system of the States or provide one of its own.

A State, it is said, or even a private citizen, may construct light houses. But gentlemen must be aware that if this proves a power in a State to regulate commerce, it proves that the same power is in the citizen. States or individuals who own lands may, if not forbidden by law, erect on those lands what buildings they please, but this power is entirely distinct from that of regulating commerce, and may, we presume, be restrained if exercised so as to produce a public mischief.

These acts were cited at the bar for the purpose of showing an opinion in Congress that the States possess, concurrently with the Legislature of the Union, the power to regulate commerce with foreign nations and among the States. Upon reviewing them, we think they do not establish the proposition they were intended to prove. They show the opinion that the States retain powers enabling them to pass the laws to which allusion has been made, not that those laws proceed from the particular power which has been delegated to Congress.

It has been contended by the counsel for the appellant that, as the word "to regulate" implies in its nature full power over the thing to be regulated, it excludes necessarily the action of all others that would perform the same operation on the same thing. That regulation is designed for the entire result, applying to those parts which remain as they were, as well as to those which are altered. It produces a uniform whole which is as much disturbed and deranged by changing what the regulating power designs to leave untouched as that on which it has operated.

There is great force in this argument, and the Court is not satisfied that it has been refuted.

Since, however, in exercising the power of regulating their own purely internal affairs, whether of trading or police, the States may sometimes enact laws the validity of which depends on their interfering with, and being contrary to, an act of Congress passed in pursuance of the Constitution, the Court will enter upon the inquiry whether the laws of New York, as expounded by the highest tribunal of that State, have, in their application to this case, come into collision with an act of Congress and deprived a citizen of a right to which that act entitles him. Should this collision exist, it will be immaterial whether those laws were passed in virtue of a concurrent power "to regulate commerce with foreign nations and among the several States" or in virtue of a power to regulate their domestic trade and police. In one case and the other, the acts of New York must yield to the law of Congress, and the decision sustaining the privilege they confer against a right given by a law of the Union must be erroneous.

This opinion has been frequently expressed in this Court, and is founded as well on the nature of the government as on the words of the Constitution. In argument, however, it has been contended that, if a law passed by a State, in the exercise of its acknowledged sovereignty, comes into conflict with a law passed by Congress in pursuance of the Constitution, they affect the subject and each other like equal opposing powers.

But the framers of our Constitution foresaw this state of things, and provided for it by declaring the supremacy not only of itself, but of the laws made in pursuance of it. The nullity of any act inconsistent with the Constitution is produced by the declaration that the Constitution is the supreme law. The appropriate application of that part of the clause which confers the same supremacy on laws and treaties is to such acts of the State Legislatures as do not transcend their powers, but, though enacted in the execution of acknowledged State powers, interfere with, or are contrary to, the laws of Congress made in pursuance of the Constitution or some treaty made under the authority of the United States. In every such case, the act of Congress or the treaty is supreme, and the law of the State, though enacted in the exercise of powers not controverted, must yield to it.

In pursuing this inquiry at the bar, it has been said that the Constitution does not confer the right of intercourse between State and State. That right derives its source from those laws whose authority is acknowledged by civilized man throughout the world. This is true. The Constitution found it an existing right, and gave to Congress the power to regulate it. In the exercise of this power, Congress has passed "an act for enrolling or licensing ships or vessels to be employed in the coasting trade and fisheries, and for regulating the same." The counsel for the respondent contend that this act does not give the right to sail from port to port, but confines itself to regulating a preexisting right so far only as to confer certain privileges on enrolled and licensed vessels in its exercise.

It will at once occur that, when a Legislature attaches certain privileges and exemptions to the exercise of a right over which its control is absolute, the law must imply a power to exercise the right. The privileges are gone if the right itself be annihilated. It would be contrary to all reason, and to the course of human affairs, to say that a State is unable to strip a vessel of the particular privileges attendant on the exercise of a right, and yet may annul the right itself; that the State of New York cannot prevent an enrolled and licensed vessel, proceeding from Elizabethtown, in New Jersey, to New York, from enjoying, in her course, and on her entrance into port, all the privileges conferred by the act of Congress, but can shut her up in her own port, and prohibit altogether her entering the waters and ports of another State. To the Court, it seems very clear that the whole act on the subject of the coasting trade, according to those principles which govern the construction of statutes, implies unequivocally an authority to licensed vessels to carry on the coasting trade.

But we will proceed briefly to notice those sections which bear more directly on the subject.

The first section declares that vessels enrolled by virtue of a previous law, and certain other vessels enrolled as described in that act, and having a license in force, as is by the act required,

> and no others, shall be deemed ships or vessels of the United States, entitled to the privileges of ships or vessels employed in the coasting trade.

This section seems to the Court to contain a positive enactment that the vessels it describes shall be entitled to the privileges of ships or vessels employed in the coasting trade. These privileges cannot be separated from the trade and cannot be enjoyed unless the trade may be prosecuted. The grant of the privilege is an idle, empty form, conveying nothing, unless it convey the right to which the privilege is attached and in the exercise of which its whole value consists. To construe these words otherwise than as entitling the ships or vessels described to carry on the coasting trade would be, we think, to disregard the apparent intent of the act.

The fourth section directs the proper officer to grant to a vessel qualified to receive it, "a license for carrying on the coasting trade," and prescribes its form. After reciting the compliance of the applicant with the previous requisites of the law, the operative words of the instrument are,

> license is hereby granted for the said steamboat *Bellona* to be employed in carrying on the coasting trade for one year from the date hereof, and no longer.

These are not the words of the officer, they are the words of the legislature, and convey as explicitly the authority the act intended to give, and operate as effectually, as if they had been inserted in any other part of the act, than in the license itself.

The word "license" means permission or authority, and a license to do any particular thing is a permission or authority to do that thing, and if granted by a person having power to grant it, transfers to the grantee the right to do whatever it purports to authorize. It certainly transfers to him all the right

which the grantor can transfer, to do what is within the terms of the license.

Would the validity or effect of such an instrument be questioned by the respondent, if executed by persons claiming regularly under the laws of New York?

The license must be understood to be what it purports to be, a legislative authority to the steamboat *Bellona* "to be employed in carrying on the coasting trade, for one year from this date."

It has been denied that these words authorize a voyage from New Jersey to New York. It is true that no ports are specified, but it is equally true that the words used are perfectly intelligible, and do confer such authority as unquestionably as if the ports had been mentioned. The coasting trade is a term well understood. The law has defined it, and all know its meaning perfectly. The act describes with great minuteness the various operations of a vessel engaged in it, and it cannot, we think, be doubted that a voyage from New Jersey to New York is one of those operations.

Notwithstanding the decided language of the license, it has also been maintained that it gives no right to trade, and that its sole purpose is to confer the American character.

The answer given to this argument that the American character is conferred by the enrollment, and not by the license, is, we think, founded too clearly in the words of the law to require the support of any additional observations. The enrollment of vessels designed for the coasting trade corresponds precisely with the registration of vessels designed for the foreign trade, and requires every circumstance which can constitute the American character. The license can be granted only to vessels already enrolled, if they be of the burthen of twenty tons and upwards, and requires no circumstance essential to the American character. The object of the license, then, cannot be to ascertain the character of the vessel, but to do what it professes to do—that is, to give permission to a vessel already proved by her enrollment to be American, to carry on the coasting trade.

But if the license be a permit to carry on the coasting trade, the respondent denies that these boats were engaged in that trade, or that the decree under consideration has restrained them from prosecuting it. The boats of the appellant were, we are told, employed in the transportation of passengers, and this is no part of that commerce which Congress may regulate.

If, as our whole course of legislation on this subject shows, the power of Congress has been universally understood in America to comprehend navigation, it is a very persuasive, if not a conclusive, argument to prove that the construction is correct, and if it be correct, no clear distinction is perceived between the power to regulate vessels employed in transporting men for hire and property for hire. The subject is transferred to Congress, and no exception to the grant can be admitted which is not proved by the words or the nature of the thing. A coasting vessel employed in the transportation of passengers is as much a portion of the American marine as one employed in the transportation of a cargo, and no reason is perceived why such vessel should be withdrawn from the regulating power of that government which has been thought best fitted for the purpose generally. The provisions of the law respecting native seamen and respecting ownership are as applicable to vessels carrying men as to vessels carrying manufactures, and no reason is perceived why the power over the subject should not be placed in the same hands. The argument urged at the bar rests on the foundation that the power of Congress does not extend to navigation as a branch of commerce, and can only be applied to that subject incidentally and occasionally. But if that foundation be removed, we must show some plain, intelligible distinction, supported by the Constitution or by reason, for discriminating between the power of Congress over vessels employed in navigating the same seas. We can perceive no such distinction.

If we refer to the Constitution, the inference to be drawn from it is rather against the distinction. The section which restrains Congress from prohibiting the migration or importation of such persons as any of the States may think proper to admit until the year 1808 has always been considered as an exception from the power to regulate commerce, and certainly seems to class migration with importation. Migration applies as appropriately to voluntary as importation does to involuntary arrivals, and, so far as an exception from a power proves its existence, this section proves that the power to regulate commerce applies equally to the regulation of vessels employed in transporting men, who pass from place to place voluntarily, and to those who pass involuntarily.

If the power reside in Congress, as a portion of the general grant to regulate commerce, then acts applying that power to vessels generally must be construed as comprehending all vessels. If none appear to be excluded by the language of the act, none can be excluded by construction. Vessels have always been employed to a greater or less extent in the transportation of passengers, and have never been supposed to be, on that account, withdrawn from the control or protection of Congress. Packets which ply along the coast, as well as those which make voyages between Europe and America, consider the transportation of passengers as an important part of their business. Yet it has never been suspected that the general laws of navigation did not apply to them.

The duty act, sections 23 and 46, contains provisions respecting passengers, and shows that vessels which transport them have the same rights, and must perform the same duties, with other vessels. They are governed by the general laws of navigation.

In the progress of things, this seems to have grown into a particular employment, and to have attracted the particular attention of government. Congress was no longer satisfied with comprehending vessels engaged specially in this business, within those provisions which were intended for vessels generally, and, on the 2d of March, 1819, passed "an act regulating passenger ships and vessels." This wise and humane law provides for the safety and comfort of passengers, and for the communication of everything concerning them which may interest the government, to the Department of State, but makes no provision concerning the entry of the vessel or her conduct in the waters of the United States. This, we think, shows conclusively the sense of Congress (if, indeed, any evidence to that point could be required) that the preexisting regulations comprehended passenger ships among others, and, in prescribing the same duties, the Legislature must have considered them as possessing the same rights.

If, then, it were even true that the *Bellona* and the *Stoudinger* were employed exclusively in the conveyance of passengers between New York and New Jersey, it would not follow that this occupation did not constitute a part of the coasting trade of the United States, and was not protected by the license annexed to the answer. But we cannot perceive how the occupation of these vessels can be drawn into question in the case before the Court. The laws of New York, which grant the exclusive privilege set up by the respondent, take no notice of the employment of vessels, and relate only to the principle by which they are propelled. Those laws do not inquire whether vessels are engaged in transporting men or merchandise, but whether they are moved by steam or wind. If by the former, the waters of New York are closed against them, though their cargoes be dutiable goods, which the laws of the United States permit them to enter and deliver in New York. If by the latter, those waters are free to them though they should carry passengers only. In conformity with the law is the bill of the plaintiff in the State Court. The bill does not complain that the *Bellona* and the *Stoudinger* carry passengers, but that they are moved by steam. This is the injury of which he complains, and is the sole injury against the continuance of which he asks relief. The bill does not even allege specially that those vessels were employed in the transportation of passengers, but says generally that they were employed "in the transportation of passengers, or otherwise." The answer avers only that they were employed in the coasting trade, and insists on the right to carry on any trade authorized by the license. No testimony is taken, and the writ of injunction and decree restrain these licensed vessels not from carrying passengers, but from being moved through the waters of New York by steam for any purpose whatever.

The questions, then, whether the conveyance of passengers be a part of the coasting trade and whether a vessel can be protected in that occupation by a coasting license are not, and cannot be, raised in this case. The real and sole question seems to be whether a steam machine in actual use deprives a vessel of the privileges conferred by a license.

In considering this question, the first idea which presents itself is that the laws of Congress for the regulation of commerce do not look to the principle by which vessels are moved. That subject is left entirely to individual discretion, and, in that vast and complex system of legislative enactment concerning it, which embraces everything that the Legislature thought it necessary to notice, there is not, we believe, one word respecting the peculiar principle by which vessels are propelled through the water, except what may be found in a single act granting a particular privilege to steamboats. With this exception, every act, either prescribing duties or granting privileges, applies to every vessel, whether navigated by the instrumentality of wind or fire, of sails or machinery. The whole weight of proof, then, is thrown upon him who would introduce a distinction to which the words of the law give no countenance.

If a real difference could be admitted to exist between vessels carrying passengers and others, it has already been observed that there is no fact in this case which can bring up that question. And, if the occupation of steamboats be a matter of such general notoriety that the Court may be presumed to know it, although not specially informed by the record, then we deny that the transportation of passengers is their exclusive occupation. It is a matter of general history that, in our western waters, their principal employment is the transportation of merchandise, and all know that, in the waters of the Atlantic, they are frequently so employed.

But all inquiry into this subject seems to the Court to be put completely at rest by the act already mentioned, entitled, "An act for the enrolling and licensing of steamboats."

This act authorizes a steamboat employed, or intended to be employed, only in a river or bay of the United States, owned wholly or in part by an alien, resident within the United States, to be enrolled and licensed as if the same belonged to a citizen of the United States.

This act demonstrates the opinion of Congress that steamboats may be enrolled and licensed, in common with vessels using sails. They are, of course, entitled to the same privileges, and can no more be restrained from navigating waters and entering ports which are free to such vessels than if they were wafted on their voyage by the winds, instead of being propelled by the agency of fire. The one element may be as legitimately used as the other for every commercial purpose authorized by the laws of the Union, and the act of a State inhibiting the use of either to any vessel having a license under the act of Congress comes, we think, in direct collision with that act.

As this decides the cause, it is unnecessary to enter in an examination of that part of the Constitution which empowers Congress to promote the progress of science and the useful arts.

The Court is aware that, in stating the train of reasoning by which we have been conducted to this result, much time has been consumed in the attempt to demonstrate propositions which may have been thought axioms. It is felt that the tediousness inseparable from the endeavour to prove that which is already clear is imputable to a considerable part of this opinion. But it was unavoidable. The conclusion to which we have come depends on a chain of principles which it was necessary to preserve unbroken, and although some of them were thought nearly self-evident, the magnitude of the question, the weight of character belonging to those from whose judgment we dissent, and the argument at the bar demanded that we should assume nothing.

Powerful and ingenious minds, taking as postulates that the powers expressly granted to the government of the Union are to be contracted by construction into the narrowest possible compass and that the original powers of the States are retained if any possible construction will retain them may, by a course of well digested but refined and metaphysical reasoning founded on these premises, explain away the Constitution of our country and leave it a magnificent structure indeed to look at, but totally unfit for use. They may so entangle and perplex the understanding as to obscure principles which were before thought quite plain, and induce doubts where, if the mind were to pursue its own course, none would be perceived. In such a case, it is peculiarly necessary to recur to safe and fundamental principles to sustain those principles, and when sustained, to make them the tests of the arguments to be examined.

Mr. Justice JOHNSON

The judgment entered by the Court in this cause, has my entire approbation, but, having adopted my conclusions on views of the subject materially different from those of my brethren, I feel it incumbent on me to exhibit those views. I have also another inducement: in questions of great importance and great delicacy, I feel my duty to the public best discharged by an effort to maintain my opinions in my own way.

In attempts to construe the Constitution, I have never found much benefit resulting from the inquiry whether the whole or any part of it is to be construed strictly or literally. The simple, classical, precise, yet comprehensive language in which it is couched leaves, at most, but very little latitude for construction, and when its intent and meaning is discovered, nothing remains but to execute the will of those who made it in the best manner to effect the purposes intended. The great and paramount purpose was to unite this mass of wealth and power, for the protection of the humblest individual, his rights, civil and political, his interests and prosperity, are the sole end; the rest are nothing but the means. But the principal of those means, one so essential as to approach nearer the characteristics of an end, was the independence and harmony of the States that they may the better subserve the purposes of cherishing and protecting the respective families of this great republic.

The strong sympathies, rather than the feeble government, which bound the States together during a common war dissolved on the return of peace, and the very principles which gave rise to the war of the revolution began to threaten the Confederacy with anarchy and ruin. The States had resisted a tax imposed by the parent State, and now reluctantly submitted to, or altogether rejected, the moderate demands of the Confederation. Everyone recollects the painful and threatening discussions which arose on the subject of the five percent. duty. Some States rejected it altogether; others insisted on collecting it themselves; scarcely any acquiesced without reservations, which deprived it altogether of the character of a national measure; and at length, some repealed the laws by which they had signified their acquiescence.

For a century, the States had submitted, with murmurs, to the commercial restrictions imposed by the parent State; and now, finding themselves in the unlimited possession of those powers over their own commerce which they had so long been deprived of and so earnestly coveted, that selfish principle which, well controlled, is so salutary, and which, unrestricted, is so unjust and tyrannical, guided by inexperience and jealousy, began to show itself in iniquitous laws and impolitic measures from which grew up a conflict of commercial regulations destructive to the harmony of the States and fatal to their commercial interests abroad.

This was the immediate cause that led to the forming of a convention.

As early as 1778, the subject had been pressed upon the attention of Congress by a memorial from the State of New Jersey, and in 1781, we find a resolution presented to that body by one of the most enlightened men of his day, Dr. Witherspoon, affirming that

> it is indispensably necessary that the United States, in Congress assembled, should be vested with a right of superintending the commercial regulations of every State that none may take place that shall be partial or contrary to the common interests.

The resolution of Virginia, January 21, 1781, appointing her commissioners to meet commissioners from other States, expresses their purpose to be

> to take into consideration the trade of the United States, to consider how far an uniform system in their commercial regulations may be necessary to their common interests and their permanent harmony.

And Mr. Madison's resolution, which led to that measure, is introduced by a preamble entirely explicit to this point:

> Whereas, the relative situation of the United States has been found, on trial, to require uni-

formity in their commercial regulations as the only effectual policy for obtaining, in the ports of foreign nations, a stipulation of privileges reciprocal to those enjoyed by the subjects of such nations in the ports of the United States, for preventing animosities, which cannot fail to arise among the several States, from the interference of partial and separate regulations,

&c. "therefore, resolved," &c.

The history of the times will therefore sustain the opinion that the grant of power over commerce, if intended to be commensurate with the evils existing and the purpose of remedying those evils, could be only commensurate with the power of the States over the subject. And this opinion is supported by a very remarkable evidence of the general understanding of the whole American people when the grant was made.

There was not a State in the Union in which there did not at that time exist a variety of commercial regulations; concerning which it is too much to suppose that the whole ground covered by those regulations was immediately assumed by actual legislation under the authority of the Union. But where was the existing statute on this subject that a State attempted to execute? or by what State was it ever thought necessary to repeal those statutes? By common consent, those laws dropped lifeless from their statute books for want of the sustaining power that had been relinquished to Congress.

And the plain and direct import of the words of the grant is consistent with this general understanding.

The words of the Constitution are, "Congress shall have power to regulate commerce with foreign nations, and among the several States, and with the Indian tribes."

It is not material, in my view of the subject, to inquire whether the article a or the should be prefixed to the word "power." Either or neither will produce the same result: if either, it is clear that the article "the" would be the proper one, since the next preceding grant of power is certainly exclusive, to-wit: "to borrow money on the credit of the United States." But mere verbal criticism I reject.

My opinion is founded on the application of the words of the grant to the subject of it.

The "power to regulate commerce" here meant to be granted was that power to regulate commerce which previously existed in the States. But what was that power? The States were unquestionably supreme, and each possessed that power over commerce which is acknowledged to reside in every sovereign State. The definition and limits of that power are to be sought among the features of international law, and, as it was not only admitted but insisted on by both parties in argument that, "unaffected by a state of war, by treaties, or by municipal regulations, all commerce among independent States was legitimate," there is no necessity to appeal to the oracles of the *jus commune* for the correctness of that doctrine. The law of nations, regarding man as a social animal, pronounces all commerce legitimate in a state of peace until prohibited by positive law. The power of a sovereign state over commerce therefore amounts to nothing more than a power to limit and restrain it at pleasure. And since the power to prescribe the limits to its freedom necessarily implies the power to determine what shall remain unrestrained, it follows that the power must be exclusive; it can reside but in one potentate, and hence the grant of this power carries with it the whole subject, leaving nothing for the State to act upon.

And such has been the practical construction of the act. Were every law on the subject of commerce repealed tomorrow, all commerce would be lawful, and, in practice, merchants never inquire what is permitted, but what is forbidden commerce. Of all the endless variety of branches of foreign commerce now carried on to every quarter of the world, I know of no one that is permitted by act of Congress any otherwise than by not being forbidden. No statute of the United States that I know of was ever passed to permit a commerce unless in consequence of its having been prohibited by some previous statute.

I speak not here of the treaty-making power, for that is not exercised under the grant now under consideration. I confine my observation to laws properly so called. And even where freedom of commercial intercourse is made a subject of stipulation in a treaty, it is generally with a view to the removal of some previous restriction, or the introduction of some new privilege, most frequently, is identified with the return to a state of peace. But another view of the subject leads directly to the same conclusion. Power to regulate foreign commerce is given in the same words, and in the same breath, as it were, with that over the commerce of the States and with the Indian tribes. But the power to regulate foreign commerce is necessarily exclusive. The States are unknown to foreign nations, their sovereignty exists only with relation to each other and the General Government. Whatever regulations foreign commerce should be subjected to in the ports of the Union, the General Government would be held responsible for them, and all other regulations but those which Congress had imposed would be regarded by foreign nations as trespasses and violations of national faith and comity.

But the language which grants the power as to one description of commerce grants it as to all, and, in fact, if ever the exercise of a right or acquiescence in a construction could be inferred from contemporaneous and continued assent, it is that of the exclusive effect of this grant.

A right over the subject has never been pretended to in any instance except as incidental to the exercise of some other unquestionable power.

The present is an instance of the assertion of that kind, as incidental to a municipal power; that of superintending the internal concerns of a State, and particularly of extending protection and patronage, in the shape of a monopoly, to genius and enterprise.

The grant to Livingston and Fulton interferes with the freedom of intercourse, and on this principle, its constitutionality is contested.

When speaking of the power of Congress over navigation, I do not regard it as a power incidental to that of regulating commerce; I consider it as the thing itself, inseparable from it as vital motion is from vital existence.

Commerce, in its simplest signification, means an exchange of goods, but in the advancement of society, labour, transportation, intelligence, care, and various mediums of exchange become commodities, and enter into commerce, the subject, the vehicle, the agent, and their various operations become the objects of commercial regulation. Shipbuilding, the carrying trade, and propagation of seamen are such vital agents of commercial prosperity that the nation which could not legislate over these subjects would not possess power to regulate commerce.

That such was the understanding of the framers of the Constitution is conspicuous from provisions contained in that instrument.

The first clause of the 9th section not only considers the right of controlling personal ingress or migration, as implied in the powers previously vested in Congress over commerce, but acknowledges it as a legitimate subject of revenue. And, although the leading object of this section undoubtedly was the importation of slaves, yet the words are obviously calculated to comprise persons of all descriptions, and to recognise in Congress a power to prohibit where the States permit, although they cannot permit when the States prohibit. The treaty-making power undoubtedly goes further. So the fifth clause of the same section

furnishes an exposition of the sense of the Convention as to the power of Congress over navigation: "nor shall vessels bound to or from one State be obliged to enter, clear, or pay duties in another."

But it is almost labouring to prove a self-evident proposition, since the sense of mankind, the practice of the world, the contemporaneous assumption and continued exercise of the power, and universal acquiescence, have so clearly established the right of Congress over navigation, and the transportation of both men and their goods, as not only incidental to, but actually of the essence of, the power to regulate commerce. As to the transportation of passengers, and passengers in a steamboat, I consider it as having been solemnly recognised by the State of New York as a subject both of commercial regulation and of revenue. She has imposed a transit duty upon steamboat passengers arriving at Albany, and unless this be done in the exercise of her control over personal intercourse, as incident to internal commerce, I know not on what principle the individual has been subjected to this tax. The subsequent imposition upon the steamboat itself appears to be but a commutation, and operates as an indirect, instead of a direct, tax upon the same subject. The passenger pays it at last.

It is impossible, with the views which I entertain of the principle on which the commercial privileges of the people of the United States among themselves rests, to concur in the view which this Court takes of the effect of the coasting license in this cause. I do not regard it as the foundation of the right set up in behalf of the appellant. If there was any one object riding over every other in the adoption of the Constitution, it was to keep the commercial intercourse among the States free from all invidious and partial restraints. And I cannot overcome the conviction that, if the licensing act was repealed tomorrow, the rights of the appellant to a reversal of the decision complained of would be as strong as it is under this license. One half the doubts in life arise from the defects of language, and if this instrument had been called an exemption instead of a license, it would have given a better idea of its character. Licensing acts, in fact, in legislation, are universally restraining acts, as, for example, acts licensing gaming houses, retailers of spiritous liquors, &c. The act in this instance is distinctly of that character, and forms part of an extensive system the object of which is to encourage American shipping and place them on an equal footing with the shipping of other nations. Almost every commercial nation reserves to its own subjects a monopoly of its coasting trade, and a countervailing privilege in favour of American shipping is contemplated in the whole legislation of the United States on this subject. It is not to give the vessel an American character that the license is granted; that effect has been correctly attributed to the act of her enrollment. But it is to confer on her American privileges, as contradistinguished from foreign, and to preserve the government from fraud by foreigners in surreptitiously intruding themselves into the American commercial marine, as well as frauds upon the revenue in the trade coastwise, that this whole system is projected. Many duties and formalities are necessarily imposed upon the American foreign commerce which would be burdensome in the active coasting trade of the States, and can be dispensed with. A higher rate of tonnage also is imposed, and this license entitles the vessels that take it to those exemptions, but to nothing more. A common register equally entitles vessels to carry on the coasting trade, although it does not exempt them from the forms of foreign commerce or from compliance with the 16th and 17th sections of the enrolling act. And even a foreign vessel may be employed coastwise upon complying with the requisitions of the 24th section. I consider the license therefore as nothing more than what it purports to be, according to the first section of this act, conferring on the licensed vessel certain privileges in that trade not conferred on other vessels; but the abstract right of commercial intercourse, stripped of those privileges, is common to all.

Yet there is one view in which the license may be allowed considerable influence in sustaining the decision of this Court.

It has been contended that the grants of power to the United States over any subject do not necessarily paralyze the arm of the States or deprive them of the capacity to act on the same subject. The this can be the effect only of prohibitory provisions in their own Constitutions, or in that of the General Government. The *vis vitae* of power is still existing in the States, if not extinguished by the Constitution of the United States. That, although as to all those grants of power which may be called aboriginal, with relation to the Government, brought into existence by the Constitution, they, of course, are out of the reach of State power, yet, as to all concessions of powers which previously existed in the States, it was otherwise. The practice of our Government certainly has been, on many subjects, to occupy so much only of the field opened to them as they think the public interests require. Witness the jurisdiction of the Cir-

cuit Courts, limited both as to cases and as to amount, and various other instances that might to cited. But the license furnishes a full answer to this objection, for, although one grant of power over commerce, should not be deemed a total relinquishment of power over the subject, but amounting only to a power to assume, still the power of the States must be at an end, so far as the United States have, by their legislative act, taken the subject under their immediate superintendence. So far as relates to the commerce coastwise, the act under which this license is granted contains a full expression of Congress on this subject. Vessels, from five tons upwards, carrying on the coasting trade are made the subject of regulation by that act. And this license proves that this vessel has complied with that act, and been regularly ingrafted into one class of the commercial marine of the country.

It remains, to consider the objections to this opinion, as presented by the counsel for the appellee. On those which had relation to the particular character of this boat, whether as a steamboat or a ferry boat, I have only to remark that, in both those characters, she is expressly recognised as an object of the provisions which relate to licenses.

The 12th section of the Act of 1793 has these words: "That when the master of any ship or vessel, ferry boats excepted, shall be changed," &c. And the act which exempts licensed steamboats from the provisions against alien interests shows such boats to be both objects of the licensing act and objects of that act when employed exclusively within our bays and rivers.

But the principal objections to these opinions arise,

1st. From the unavoidable action of some of the municipal powers of the States upon commercial subjects.

2d. From passages in the Constitution which are supposed to imply a concurrent power in the States in regulating commerce.

It is no objection to the existence of distinct, substantive powers that, in their application, they bear upon the same subject. The same bale of goods, the same cask of provisions, or the same ship that may be the subject of commercial regulation may also be the vehicle of disease. And the health laws that require them to be stopped and ventilated are no more intended as regulations on commerce than the laws which permit their importation are intended to innoculate the community with disease. Their different purposes mark the distinction between the powers brought into action, and while frankly exercised, they can produce no serious collision. As to laws affecting ferries, turnpike roads, and other subjects of the same class, so far from meriting the epithet of commercial regulations, they are, in fact, commercial facilities for which, by the consent of mankind, a compensation is paid upon the same principle that the whole commercial world submit to pay light money to the Danes. Inspection laws are of a more equivocal nature, and it is obvious that the Constitution has viewed that subject with much solicitude. But so far from sustaining an inference in favour of the power of the States over commerce, I cannot but think that the guarded provisions of the 10th section on this subject furnish a strong argument against that inference. It was obvious that inspection laws must combine municipal with commercial regulations, and, while the power over the subject is yielded to the States, for obvious reasons, an absolute control is given over State legislation on the subject, as far as that legislation may be exercised, so as to affect the commerce of the country. The inferences to be correctly drawn from this whole article appear to me to be altogether in favour of the exclusive grants to Congress of power over commerce, and the reverse of that which the appellee contends for.

This section contains the positive restrictions imposed by the Constitution upon State power. The first clause of it specifies those powers which the States are precluded from exercising, even though the Congress were to permit them. The second, those which the States may exercise with the consent of Congress. And here the sedulous attention to the subject of State exclusion from commercial power is strongly marked. Not satisfied with the express grant to the United States of the power over commerce, this clause negatives the exercise of that power to the States as to the only two objects which could ever tempt them to assume the exercise of that power, to-wit, the collection of a revenue from imposts and duties on imports and exports, or from a tonnage duty. As to imposts on imports or exports, such a revenue might have been aimed at directly, by express legislation, or indirectly, in the form of inspection laws, and it became necessary to guard against both. Hence, first, the consent of Congress to such imposts or duties is made necessary, and, as to inspection laws, it is limited to the minimum of expenses. Then the money so raised shall be paid into the Treasury of the United States, or may be sued for, since it is declared to be for their use. And lastly, all such laws may be modified or repealed by an act of Congress. It is impossible for a right to be more guarded. As to a

tonnage duty that could be recovered in but one way, and a sum so raised, being obviously necessary for the execution of health laws and other unavoidable port expenses, it was intended that it should go into the State treasuries, and nothing more was required therefore than the consent of Congress. But this whole clause, as to these two subjects, appears to have been introduced *ex abundanti cautela*, to remove every temptation to an attempt to interfere with the powers of Congress over commerce, and to show how far Congress might consent to permit the States to exercise that power. Beyond those limits, even by the consent of Congress, they could not exercise it. And thus we have the whole effect of the clause. The inference which counsel would deduce from it is neither necessary nor consistent with the general purpose of the clause.

But instances have been insisted on with much confidence in argument in which, by municipal laws, particular regulations respecting their cargoes have been imposed upon shipping in the ports of the United States, and one in which forfeiture was made the penalty of disobedience.

Until such laws have been tested by exceptions to their constitutionality, the argument certainly wants much of the force attributed to it; but, admitting their constitutionality, they present only the familiar case of punishment inflicted by both governments upon the same individual. He who robs the mail may also steal the horse that carries it, and would unquestionably be subject to punishment at the same time under the laws of the State in which the crime is committed and under those of the United States. And these punishments may interfere, and one render it impossible to inflict the other, and yet the two governments would be acting under powers that have no claim to identity.

It would be in vain to deny the possibility of a clashing and collision between the measures of the two governments. The line cannot be drawn with sufficient distinctness between the municipal powers of the one and the commercial powers of the other. In some points, they meet and blend so as scarcely to admit of separation. Hitherto, the only remedy has been applied which the case admits of—that of a frank and candid cooperation for the general good. Witness the laws of Congress requiring its officers to respect the inspection laws of the States and to aid in enforcing their health laws, that which surrenders to the States the superintendence of pilotage, and the many laws passed to permit a tonnage duty to be levied for the use of their ports. Other instances could be cited abundantly to prove that collision must be sought to be produced, and when it does arise, the question must be decided how far the powers of Congress are adequate to put it down. Wherever the powers of the respective governments are frankly exercised, with a distinct view to the ends of such powers, they may act upon the same object, or use the same means, and yet the powers be kept perfectly distinct. A resort to the same means therefore is no argument to prove the identity of their respective powers.

I have not touched upon the right of the States to grant patents for inventions or improvements generally, because it does not necessarily arise in this cause. It is enough for all the purposes of this decision if they cannot exercise it so as to restrain a free intercourse among the States.

DECREE. This cause came on to be heard on the transcript of the record of the Court for the Trial of Impeachments and Correction of Errors of the State of New York, and was argued by counsel. On consideration whereof, this Court is of opinion that the several licenses to the steamboats the *Stoudinger* and the *Bellona* to carry on the coasting trade, which are set up by the appellant Thomas Gibbons in his answer to the bill of the respondent, Aaron Ogden, filed in the Court of Chancery for the State of New York, which were granted under an act of Congress, passed in pursuance of the Constitution of the United States, gave full authority to those vessels to navigate the waters of the United States, by steam or otherwise, for the purpose of carrying on the coasting trade, any law of the State of New York to the contrary notwithstanding, and that so much of the several laws of the State of New York as prohibits vessels, licensed according to the laws of the United States, from navigating the waters of the State of New York by means of fire or steam is repugnant to the said Constitution, and void. This Court is therefore of opinion that the decree of the Court of New York for the Trial of Impeachments and the Correction of Errors affirming the decree of the Chancellor of that State, which perpetually enjoins the said Thomas Gibbons, the appellant, from navigating the waters of the State of New York with the steamboats the *Stoudinger* and the *Bellona* by steam or fire, is erroneous, and ought to be reversed, and the same is hereby reversed and annulled, and this Court doth further DIRECT, ORDER, and DECREE that the bill of the said Aaron Ogden be dismissed, and the same is hereby dismissed accordingly.

uncommitted to any other course than the strict line of constitutional duty; and that the securities for this independence may be rendered as strong as the nature of power and the weakness of its possessor will admit, — I cannot too earnestly invite your attention to the propriety of promoting such an amendment of the constitution as will render him ineligible after one term of service.

It gives me pleasure to announce to Congress that the benevolent policy of the Government, steadily pursued for nearly thirty years in relation to the removal

Andrew Jackson: On Indian Removal (National Archives and Records Administration)

ANDREW JACKSON: ON INDIAN REMOVAL

"Rightly considered, the policy of the General Government toward the red man is not only liberal, but generous."

Overview

In the spring of 1830 Congress passed the Indian Removal Act, and on May 28 of that year President Andrew Jackson signed the bill into law. The act gave the president the authority to negotiate "removal" treaties with all of the Indian tribes east of the Mississippi River. Under these agreements, each tribe would surrender its homeland in the East and relocate within a stated period of time to a territory west of that great waterway.

On December 6, 1830, in his annual message to the nation—now commonly referred to as the president's State of the Union address—Jackson praised Congress for putting into law an Indian removal policy that he had recommended for over a decade. In addition, in this speech he attempted to provide Congress and the public with justifications for why Native Americans in the East needed to be removed beyond the reach of American settlement.

Context

During the early years of its existence, the U.S. government struggled to establish peace and order with the many Indian tribes that resided within and adjacent to the country's borders. American policy makers, including George Washington and his secretary of war, Henry Knox, intended for the United States to expand westward. At the same time, they realized that the Indian peoples possessed rights to lands under the law of nations, and they expressed the intent to treat these nations in an honorable fashion. By the late 1780s policy makers had developed a strategy to acquire Indian territory—a strategy that they believed would respect the autonomy and territorial rights of the tribal nations and, at the same time, prepare Native peoples for their eventual social and political assimilation.

Pursuant to Washington's instructions, the United States followed British colonial precedent and acquired tribal lands through diplomatic treaties, an indication that the American government respected the sovereign rights of the Indian nations. Washington and Knox also maintained that the U.S.

government should encourage Native Americans to abandon their traditional ways of life and learn how to live, subsist, and worship in the manner of white Americans. Those two American leaders believed that when Indians abandoned their customary ways of hunting, gathering, and horticulture and adopted Anglo-American-style farming, tribes would no longer need much of their territory. At that time, Washington and Knox theorized, the United States would purchase the excess lands, and the Indian peoples would assimilate with the white Americans who moved in around them. In 1790 Congress passed the first in a series of "trade and intercourse" acts, which included provisions for this "civilization plan," and federal agents began including inducements for Indians to acculturate in U.S.-Indian treaties.

The federal government's "civilization" plan indeed transformed the lives and cultures of most Native societies. Many individuals converted to Christianity, learned to read and write in English, and integrated themselves into the American market economy. Some tribes, the Cherokee Nation being the earliest example, transformed their political and legal institutions by adopting legal codes, court systems, and republican governments. Some tribal leaders believed that if their people embraced the civilization program, the United States would respect their efforts and allow them to retain their land and their political independence. At the same time, many Native American people resisted the pressure to acculturate, and divisions developed among several tribes over how their people should live in the future.

The civilization and expansion program did not eliminate diplomatic and cultural tensions, as Washington and Knox had hoped it would. As the population of the United States began to grow, many Americans migrated west in search of fertile land and economic opportunity. Some of these migrants settled illegally on Indian Territory, and the trespasses often provoked violence between Indians and Americans. To make matters worse, although many Indians attempted to acculturate to Anglo-American ways, most white people in the southern and western states refused to accept them as their social equals. Instead, they called for political representatives to seize lands belonging to the Native Americans and remove the peoples themselves beyond the reach of white settlement.

Time Line

1767

■ **March 15**
Andrew Jackson is born in Waxhaw settlement, along the border between North and South Carolina.

1776

■ **August 13**
Thomas Jefferson raises the idea of a general removal of the Indian tribes in a letter to the Virginia politician Edmund Pendleton.

1802

■ **April 24**
The United States promises to remove the Creeks and Cherokees from Georgia in the Compact of 1802.

1803

■ **April 30**
Thomas Jefferson's administration concludes the Louisiana Purchase; Jefferson believed that he had secured the United States space for the relocation of Indian tribes.

1809–1810

■ At Jefferson's insistence, a large group of Cherokees migrate to the Arkansas River valley.

1814

■ **March 27**
Jackson's militia troops defeat the Red Stick faction of Creeks at the battle of Horseshoe Bend.

1815

■ **January 8**
Jackson leads American forces to victory over the British army at the battle of New Orleans.

1820–1830

■ Georgia lobbies the national government to remove the Creeks and Cherokees from the state.

1827–1832

■ The states of Georgia, Alabama, Mississippi, and Tennessee extend their jurisdiction over the Indian tribes within their borders.

These calls for removal were not without important support or precedent. Since at least 1776 Thomas Jefferson had considered the possibility of relocating the eastern tribes beyond the Mississippi River. He believed that the United States could allow the tribes to continue living there as they wanted, free from the trespasses of American settlers. In the West they would have plenty of time to become "civilized." In 1803 Jefferson, now president, oversaw the Louisiana Purchase from France. He believed that he had secured a destination for the general removal of tribes, and in 1808 he persuaded a large group of Cherokees to relocate to the Arkansas River valley. Most Native peoples in the East, however, deflected Jefferson's removal overtures; they preferred to remain exactly where they were.

The history of violence between whites and Indians, as well as the prejudice of white southerners and westerners toward Indians, compelled many Americans to demand the expulsion of the tribes. Economic factors also prompted calls for removal. The profitability of cotton made the arable land in the Black Belt of the South and Southwest—named so for its rich soil—extremely valuable. Many speculators and entrepreneurial sorts wanted to acquire this land, much of which was inhabited and claimed as national territory by the Cherokee, Creek, Choctaw, and Chickasaw nations.

After the War of 1812, Andrew Jackson, now an American hero due largely to his victory at the battle of New Orleans, called for the United States to end what he called the "absurdity" of negotiating with the tribes as sovereign nations. Political representatives of the southern class of speculators and ambitious farmers, such as Jackson himself and John C. Calhoun, of South Carolina, revived Jefferson's "removal" plan. They proposed that the United States induce the tribes to exchange their lands for a portion of the unsettled territory west of the Mississippi River. Perhaps the most powerful impetus for removal came from Georgia, where political leaders were pressuring the national government to fulfill the Compact of 1802; in that agreement, Jefferson's administration had promised that the United States would at some point in the future extinguish the land rights of the Cherokees and Creeks in Georgia and remove them from the state. In exchange for that assurance, the state had surrendered its claim to lands west of the Chattahoochee River. By 1820 the state was bringing heavy pressure to bear on Congress and President James Monroe to remove the two tribal nations.

The Native peoples in the East, however, did not want to leave their homes and abandon their property. Native leaders pointed out that removal plans did not take into account the fact that other Indian peoples were already residing on lands across the Mississippi. Leaders of the major southeastern tribes said as much to Monroe, president from 1817 to 1825, and to his successor, John Quincy Adams, who served one term, and those executives decided not to force relocation on the tribes.

During the 1820s political leaders in Georgia continued to increase pressure on the federal government to remove the Creeks and Cherokees. The Creeks finally relented and ceded their remaining lands in the state in 1826. The Cherokees, on the other hand, continued to resist, and in 1827 their nation adopted and ratified a republican constitution. This declaration of independence on the part of the Cherokees infuriated removal proponents in Georgia; in response, the state declared that it was extending its jurisdiction over Cherokee territory. In December 1827 the Georgia legislature began passing laws designed to force the Cherokees out of the state. The assembly resolved that Cherokee laws were null and void within Georgia's borders, and it also declared that the lands of the Cherokee people would be seized, divided into small parcels, and distributed to white Georgians in a lottery. The discovery of gold on Cherokee territory in 1828 and the consequent gold rush only accelerated Georgia's fever to expel the Cherokees. The governments of Mississippi, Alabama, and Tennessee, following Georgia's lead, also adopted laws extending state jurisdiction over the Indian tribes within their borders. By the end of the 1820s, congressmen from the South formed a formidable pro-removal caucus.

When Andrew Jackson arrived in Washington to assume the presidency in the spring of 1829, he was well known as an advocate of the policy of removal, and the southerners who had voted for him fully expected him to implement such a policy in gratitude for their support. Not long after his inauguration, Jackson and his Democratic Party were able to push the Indian Removal Act through Congress by very slim margins; the Senate passed the bill by a vote of 28 to 19, the House of Representatives by a vote of 102 to 97. Jackson then moved quickly to bring about a general removal of all of the eastern tribes, in the North and South alike.

About the Author

When he delivered his second annual message to Congress, Andrew Jackson was sixty-three years old and in the middle of the second year of his first term as the seventh president of the United States. (He served two terms, from 1829 to 1837.) Jackson was born in the Waxhaw settlement, along the border of North and South Carolina, on March 15, 1767. He received little formal education and left home at the age of thirteen to join the Continental army during the American Revolution. He served as a courier and was held briefly as a prisoner of war by the British. After the war, he tried teaching school for a short time. He then read law for two years in Salisbury, North Carolina, and in 1787 he was admitted to the North Carolina bar. He moved to Jonesboro to begin a law practice, and in 1788 he was appointed solicitor for the western district of North Carolina, which would later be part of Tennessee; in 1796 Tennessee joined the Union as the sixteenth state. Jackson was a delegate at the new state's constitutional convention and was elected as its first congressman. In 1797 the Tennessee legislature sent Jackson to the U.S. Senate, but Jackson did not enjoy his service there and returned home after one session. He then moved to the bench, serving for six years on the Tennessee Superior Court (now known as the Supreme Court). After that, Jackson devoted most of his time to his planting and mercantile businesses.

	Time Line
1829	■ **March 4** Jackson is inaugurated as the seventh president of the United States.
1830— 1851	■ The United States ratifies removal treaties with many of the tribes in New York and the Old Northwest.
1830	■ **April 24** The Senate passes the Indian Removal Act by a 28–19 vote. ■ **May 26** The House of Representatives passes the Indian Removal Act by a 102–97 vote. ■ **May 27** Jackson vetoes the Maysville Road bill. ■ **May 28** Jackson signs the Indian Removal Act. ■ **September 27** The Choctaws agree to remove in the Treaty of Dancing Rabbit Creek. ■ **December 6** Jackson's second annual message to Congress, in which he discusses Indian removal.
1831— 1833	■ The Choctaws relocate to Indian Territory.
1831	■ **March 18** Supreme Court declares that the Cherokee Nation is not a "foreign state" but a "domestic, dependent nation" in *Cherokee Nation v. Georgia*.
1832	■ **March 3** In *Worcester v. Georgia*, the Supreme Court declares that the Cherokee Nation is a sovereign nation holding legal title to its territory; Jackson and Georgia refuse to recognize the decision. ■ **March 24** The Treaty of Cusseta calls for the allotment of Creek lands and for the removal of those Creeks who sell their allotments.

Time Line

1832

■ **July 10**
Jackson vetoes a bill to recharter the Second Bank of the United States.

■ **October 20**
The Chickasaws agree to remove in the Treaty of Pontotoc.

■ **November 2**
Jackson is reelected president.

1835–1842

■ Second Seminole War; most Seminoles are rounded up and relocated to Indian Territory.

1835

■ **December 29**
A small faction commits the entire Cherokee Nation to removal in the Treaty of New Echota.

1837

■ **1837**
The Chickasaws remove to Indian Territory.

1838–1839

■ The Trail of Tears; the Cherokees are rounded up, placed in internment camps, and forced to relocate to Indian Territory, with at least one-quarter of the nation dying as a consequence of the removal.

Jackson was elected as major general of the Tennessee militia in 1802 and served in that capacity until 1813–1814, when he led a force that put down an uprising by the Red Sticks, a faction of Creek Indians that wanted to eliminate the American presence and influence from their society. As a reward for his triumph, Jackson received a commission as a major general in the U.S. Army. He achieved national renown at the end of the War of 1812 when his forces soundly defeated a British invasion force at New Orleans.

In 1818, during the First Seminole War, Jackson led an expedition into Florida to put down resistance by the Seminoles and a group of fugitive slaves. He served as governor of the Florida Territory in 1821, and he returned to the U.S. Senate on behalf of Tennessee from 1823 to 1825. In 1824 he was defeated in his first candidacy for president of the United States. Although Jackson received a plurality of the popular vote, no candidate achieved a majority in the Electoral College. The House of Representatives then

selected John Quincy Adams to be the sixth president of the United States; Jackson, in turn, declared that Adams and Henry Clay, a senator from Kentucky, had concocted a plan to put Adams in the White House and make Clay his favored successor. From that point on, Jackson and his supporters worked toward defeating Adams in the next election. In 1828 Jackson indeed won the presidency, with strong support from the South, the West, and New York State; Jackson was reelected in 1832.

As a candidate and as president, Jackson represented himself as a self-made individualist and representative of the common man. He became a standard-bearer of egalitarian government, and a coalition that he founded evolved into the Democratic Party. He became so connoted with the idea of democratic politics that historians came to describe the period of the 1830s and 1840s, when property requirements for voting and serving in office were eliminated in most states, as the Age of Jackson and as the era of Jacksonian democracy. Subsequent studies have shown that Jackson was perhaps not as committed to the common man as early scholars and political allies maintained; most of Jackson's presidential appointments were, in fact, landed lawyers.

Historians have identified several of Jackson's acts as especially noteworthy in the history of the United States. First, he forestalled the American System, a plan put forth by his opponents (who came to be known as the Whig Party) entailing protective tariffs and financial support for internal improvements, by vetoing a bill to construct a federal road to connect Lexington and Maysville, Kentucky. Second, although he has been characterized as a president who favored state's rights, Jackson solidified the Union when he forced South Carolina by 1833 to discontinue its attempts to nullify the Tariff of 1828. Third, in 1832 he vetoed legislation that would have extended the charter for the Second Bank of the United States, which he believed to be an institution that favored people of privilege, and transferred the federal government's deposits to a number of "pet" state banks. Fourth, Jackson pushed the Indian Removal Act through Congress. Finally, he expanded the executive power of the president by firing entrenched officeholders who disagreed with his politics and replacing them with his allies. This "spoils system" became a common practice for Jackson's successors in the Oval Office.

In 1837, having ensured that his protégé, Martin Van Buren, would succeed him as president, Jackson retired from public life to the Hermitage, his plantation outside Nashville. From there he often pressured Van Buren to conclude the removal of the eastern tribes to the West. Andrew Jackson died on June 8, 1845.

Explanation and Analysis of the Document

President Andrew Jackson's discussion of Indian removal is an excerpt from a much longer address: Jackson's annual message to Congress of December 6, 1830. Today, this report is generally known as the president's

State of the Union address. Although the message was directed toward Congress, the president was well aware that his words would be published in newspapers throughout the country.

In the speech, Jackson reports on the progress the government has made in relocating the eastern tribes since Congress passed the Indian Removal Act several months earlier. He notes that several tribes, including the Choctaws, have signed or are considering removal proposals. The president further suggests that he hopes that the act and the Choctaw treaty will create momentum for a general removal of all of the eastern tribes. Jackson's comments on the removal policy contain three major themes: The relocation was in the national interest of the United States, it was in the best interests of American Indians, and it would be implemented in a fair and generous manner.

◆ National Interests

At the beginning of the speech, Jackson argues that the removal of the Indian tribes promotes the general well-being of the United States. In particular, the broader removal would eliminate a source of antagonism that had developed between southern states and the national government at a time when South Carolina was claiming the power to nullify a national law, the Tariff of 1828. During the 1820s the state of Georgia had complained bitterly about the federal government's failure to complete the Compact of 1802 and remove the Cherokees from its borders. One governor of the state, George Troup, had threatened to invade the nation of the Cherokees and force them out of the state if the federal government did not remove them. Being aware of this history, Jackson points out that a general removal would end the animosity that Indian relations had created between Georgia and the federal government.

Jackson then suggests that the removal will enhance the national security of the United States. His familiarity with the history of the region had led him to long argue that the southwestern flank of the nation was in danger of an attack from an alliance of a southern tribe and a European power such as Great Britain or Spain. Jackson could recall that the Cherokees had allied with Great Britain at the beginning of the American Revolution and that the Choctaws had maintained trade and diplomatic relations with Spain. By removing the tribes beyond the Mississippi River and opening more of the South to settlement by white Americans, Jackson hoped to develop an American population capable of providing a militia force to defend the region and eliminate the threat of European attack. In describing the security that a broader removal would bring to the nation, he also admits that the acquisition of Indian territory would benefit the economies of the southern states and, thereby, of the nation.

◆ Paternalism

The speech reeks of paternalism, with the federal government, in its assumed guise as the Great Father (a euphemism that U.S. officials often used to describe its relationship to the Indian tribes, and vice versa), determin-

Andrew Jackson (Library of Congress)

ing what is best for its Indian children. Jackson's comment that removal will "retard the progress of decay, which is lessening their numbers," was not unusual for these times. Most Americans who claimed to know something about Native peoples during this era believed that Indians were a "vanishing race." According to Jackson, removal would protect Indians in the East from the danger of extinction.

Jackson's speech is representative of the arguments that removal proponents presented to Native leaders and to opponents of the policy. He attempts to put the displacement of the Indian tribes in the best of lights. For instance, in the first paragraph, Jackson describes the policy as "benevolent." In the second, he declares that removal would free the southern tribes from encroachments, trespasses, and intimidation by the states and allow them to "pursue happiness in their own way." He also maintains that removal would provide time for Native Americans to "gradually" abandon their traditional culture and become acclimated to American society. Once this happened, removal proponents claimed, Indians could be assimilated by the American people.

Jackson's particular paternalism is revealed in his tendency to speak disparagingly of Native American culture. In the second paragraph he states that the removal would allow Indians to maintain their "rude institutions" and that over time they would be able to "cast off their savage habits." In the third paragraph, he declares that any rational person would prefer an "extensive Republic, studded with cities, towns, and prosperous farms" over "a country covered with forests and ranged by a few thousand savages." This ethnocentrism, which held that people of non-European descent should strive toward becoming "an interesting, civilized, and Christian community," was quite common through the antebellum era. Even those white Americans who opposed the removal of the Indians generally believed that Native culture was inferior to that of Americans of European descent.

In the speech, Jackson maintains that the Indian Removal Act was the culmination of an effort that the United States had "steadily pursued for nearly thirty years." Jackson is most likely referring to the fact that Thomas Jefferson, the third president, had proposed the idea of moving the eastern tribes across the Mississippi after his conclusion of the Louisiana Purchase in 1803.

◆ A "Fair Exchange"

Jackson tries to convince his listeners that the removal will be imminently "fair," "liberal," and "generous." He declares that the United States is going to provide the removing Indian with "a new and extensive territory, to pay the expense of his removal, and support him a year in his new abode." Although Jackson promises that the government will pay fair value for the lands of the tribal nations and that they will not be removed without their consent, American agents in fact subsequently hectored tribal leaders into signing removal treaties. When the Cherokee government refused to sign such a treaty, the United States avoided dealing with the official Cherokee leaders by sending an agent to secure a treaty with a dissident minority of the tribe. When the Seminoles refused to remove, Jackson ordered American troops into Florida to subdue and deport them. As far as paying for the costs of removal, the United States purchased removal supplies from low bidders and political cronies; the Native American emigrants were forced to consume spoiled and rancid food on their migration west. As a consequence, hundreds died from malnutrition, intestinal disease, and exposure.

Jackson also contends that removal is "milder" than the government's previous efforts to acquire Indian land, and he compares the expected effects of the removal policy with the fates of the tribes that had resided along the coast of North America when European settlers arrived. Those peoples were decimated by disease and pushed off their lands with little, if any, compensation. This argument was commonly put forth by southern proponents of removal when missionary societies and politicians from New England accused them of pressing for an immoral policy; only after they had eliminated the Indian peoples from their region, southern removers argued, did New Englanders deign to consider the rights and interests of Native Americans.

Native American leaders such as John Ross (also known as Cooweescoowe), the principal chief of the Cherokees, often lamented that removal would require their people to leave their homelands and the burial grounds of their ancestors. Jackson attempts to diminish the harshness of removal by juxtaposing the plan with the historical migrations of Europeans to the New World and with the westward movements of Americans across the Appalachians. He makes light of this point of opposition by noting that many Americans and their ancestors had left their homes on the Atlantic Coast and back in Europe in order to better their lives and improve prospects for themselves and their children. The ancestors of white Americans, Jackson maintains, would have been overjoyed to receive the deal that was being offered to the Indians. Of course, most of those immigrants left of their own behest; with removal, the U.S. government was forcing Native Americans to abandon their homes and the graves of their loved ones.

Instead of looking back to the past, Jackson argues, Americans should consider a future where "our young population may range unconstrained in body or in mind, developing the power and facilities of man in their highest perfection." This language reveals that the Age of Jackson was overlapped by another movement, most prominent in the North, in which people believed that individuals and societies could improve toward the goal of perfection. The use of the idea of perfection was common in this reform era, which was marked by the emergence of organizations that supported the abolition of slavery, the equality of women, humane criminal punishment, and the development of schools for the deaf and blind. As far as Jackson was concerned, however, Native Americans would not be allowed to participate in the American march toward perfection until they became "civilized." In reality, very few white Americans were willing to accept Native Americans on an equal social plane at this time, even if they were fully acculturated.

Audience

Historians have assumed that Jackson's speech was well received by his admirers. The president had been elected with overwhelming support in the southern and western states. Voting citizens in these regions, who wanted Native Americans out of their vicinity, cared little for the interests of those peoples and did not need rationalizations for the policy. They already agreed with Jackson's objective of pushing the Indians west.

The speech had very little influence on Jackson's political opponents, who believed that the president was an "Indian hater" who simply wanted to dispossess Native Americans of their land. Jackson's opponents included men who were affiliated with the Whig Party. While some found removal morally offensive, others simply opposed the policy to contradict Jackson. One could also assume that the speech had little effect on voters who lived in New England, some of whom were members of religious societies and other groups that defended the rights of Native Americans.

As was politically appropriate, Jackson's speech was aimed at a group of Americans in the middle—people who were troubled by the idea of taking the land of others but who were willing to accept the policy if they could be con-

"[Removal] will separate the Indians from immediate contact with settlements of whites; free them from the power of the States; enable them to pursue happiness in their own way and under their own rude institutions; will retard the progress of decay, which is lessening their numbers, and perhaps cause them gradually, under the protection of the Government and through the influence of good counsels, to cast off their savage habits and become an interesting, civilized, and Christian community."

(Paragraph 2)

"What good man would prefer a country covered with forests and ranged by a few thousand savages to our extensive Republic, studded with cities, towns, and prosperous farms embellished with all the improvements which art can devise or industry execute, occupied by more than 12,000,000 happy people, and filled with all the blessings of liberty, civilization and religion?"

(Paragraph 3)

"The present policy of the Government is but a continuation of the same progressive change by a milder process."

(Paragraph 4)

"Doubtless it will be painful to leave the graves of their fathers; but what do they more than our ancestors did or than our children are now doing?"

(Paragraph 4)

"Rightly considered, the policy of the General Government toward the red man is not only liberal, but generous. He is unwilling to submit to the laws of the States and mingle with their population. To save him from this alternative, or perhaps utter annihilation, the General Government kindly offers him a new home, and proposes to pay the whole expense of his removal and settlement."

(Paragraph 5)

vinced that it was in the best interests of the Indians and the United States. This address provided Americans who had reservations about Indian removal with reasons to believe that the policy was both moral and necessary.

Impact

Jackson's annual message of 1830 was a symbolic beginning of the end of a long history of Indian residency in the eastern United States. After the speech, Jackson's administration worked expeditiously to conclude removal treaties with the tribes in the Southeast. The Choctaws had already signed a removal treaty earlier that year, and the Creeks and the Chickasaws signed removal treaties not long thereafter, both in 1832. In 1834 Congress carved an area west of Arkansas out of the Louisiana Territory—the state of Oklahoma is now located in generally the same area—and designated it Indian Territory, the destination for the removed southern tribes. The Jackson administration quickly moved to expel every tribe in the East. The tribes residing in the northern states and territories were relocated to new homes across the Mississippi River and north of Indian Territory.

The removal treaties typically called for the Indian nations to exchange their national lands for new territory west of the Mississippi. The federal government promised to pay for the value of buildings and improvements left behind, for the costs of relocation, and for one year's provisions thereafter. The United States also declared that it would guarantee each tribe's title to its new territory and protect its people from trespass. Further, the government stated that it would respect the political autonomy of tribes when they arrived in the West and continue to provide assistance to prepare peoples for their eventual assimilation.

The Cherokees and Seminoles were unconvinced by these promises, and their governments refused to sign removal agreements. Their resistance was undone by federal duplicity and military force. With Congress and the president pursuing removal, the Cherokee Nation asked the U.S. Supreme Court to protect it from Georgia's trespasses. In *Cherokee Nation v. Georgia* (1831), John Marshall, the chief justice of the United States, wrote that the Cherokees were a "domestic dependent nation" that lived under the protection and guidance of the United States. The Court, however, did not relieve the Cherokees from Georgia's assault on its sovereignty. The following year, in *Worcester v. Georgia*, the Court declared that the Cherokee people constituted a sovereign nation and that Georgia had violated the national rights of the Cherokees and unlawfully interfered in U.S.-Cherokee relations. Jackson refused to enforce the decision, however, and continued to pressure the Cherokees to leave the Southeast. In 1835 the United States sent an agent, John F. Schermerhorn, to secure a removal treaty from a small group of dissidents at the Cherokee national capital of New Echota. In the summer of 1838 the U.S. Army and local volunteers rounded up approximately 15,000 Cherokees, and during the brutal winter of 1838–1839 the nation moved to Indian Territory along the tragic Trail of Tears.

The Seminoles suffered an even more egregious fate. Although some of their tribe were duped into signing a removal treaty at Fort Gibson, they refused to remove. In response, the United States sent its army into Florida to round up the Seminoles and relocate them to Indian Territory. They resisted for almost eight years before surrendering and agreeing to remove. Many Seminoles and Cherokees escaped removal and formed the core of reemergent Native nations in the Southeast.

By 1843, when most of the Seminoles had been removed, the United States had relocated almost every major tribe in the East. According to the U.S. Army, about 90,000 Native Americans, roughly three-quarters of the Indian population in the East, were removed from their homelands. The Indian nations of the South had moved to Indian Territory in a series of catastrophic "long walks." Scholars estimate that between one-quarter and one-half of the Cherokees, Creeks, and Seminoles died as a direct consequence of their roundup and removal. Although most of the removal controversy centered around the Cherokees and the other Indian tribes in the South, the Indian Removal Act also resulted in the relocation of almost all of the tribes in the North, including the Cayugas, Delawares, Kaskaskias, Kickapoos, Menominees, Miamis, Ojibwas, Oneidas, Ottawas, Peorias, Piankashaws, Potawatomis, Senecas, Shawnees, Tuscaroras, and Winnebagos.

Related Documents

American State Papers: Indian Affairs. 2 vols. Washington, D.C.: Gales and Seaton, 1832–1834. *New American State Papers: Indian Affairs.* 13 vols. Wilmington, Del.: Scholarly Resources, 1972. These are bound collections of government documents pertaining to removal and other Indian issues, available on the Web at http://memory.loc.gov/ammem/am law/lwsp.html.

Bassett, John S., ed. *Correspondence of Andrew Jackson.* 7 vols. Washington, D.C.: Carnegie Institution, 1926–1935. While Jackson's papers continue to be located and edited, this is a useful early collection.

Cobbett, William. *Life of Andrew Jackson.* New York: R. J. Richards, 1834. This is a biography written by an English radical during Jackson's presidency.

Eaton, John Henry. *The Life of Andrew Jackson, Major-General in the Service of the United States: Comprising a History of the War in the South, from the Commencement of the Creek Campaign, to the Termination of Hostilities before New Orleans.* Philadelphia: M. Carey, 1817. One of the earliest biographies of Jackson was authored by his loyal protégé; Eaton served briefly as Jackson's secretary of war before resigning during the infamous "Petticoat Affair."

Richardson, James D., ed. *A Compilation of the Messages and Papers of the Presidents.* Washington, D.C.: U.S. Government Printing Office, 1897–1914. These bound collections of important presidential papers contain many that pertain to the development of U.S.-

Indian policy. Included are remarks on removal by Thomas Jefferson, James Madison, John Quincy Adams, and Andrew Jackson.

www.milestonedocuments.com

Bibliography

■ Books

Anderson, William L., ed. *Cherokee Removal: Before and After*. Athens: University of Georgia Press, 1991.

Brands, H. W. *Andrew Jackson: His Life and Times*. New York: Doubleday, 2005.

Burstein, Andrew. *The Passions of Andrew Jackson*. New York: Knopf, 2003.

De Rosier, Arthur H., Jr. *The Removal of the Choctaw Indians*. Knoxville: University of Tennessee Press, 1970.

Foreman, Grant. *Indian Removal: The Emigration of the Five Civilized Tribes of Indians*. Norman: University of Oklahoma Press, 1953.

Garrison, Tim Alan. *The Legal Ideology of Removal: The Southern Judiciary and the Sovereignty of Native American Nations*. Athens: University of Georgia Press, 2002.

Ingersoll, Thomas N. *To Intermix with Our White Brothers: Indian Mixed Bloods in the United States from Earliest Times to the Indian Removals*. Albuquerque: University of New Mexico Press, 2005.

Norgren, Jill. *The Cherokee Cases: The Confrontation of Law and Politics*. New York: McGraw-Hill, 1996.

Perdue, Theda, and Michael D. Green. *The Cherokee Nation and the Trail of Tears*. New York: Viking, 2007.

Prucha, Francis Paul. *The Great Father: The United States Government and the American Indians*. 2 vols. Lincoln: University of Nebraska Press, 1984.

————. *American Indian Treaties: The History of a Political Anomaly*. Berkeley: University of California Press, 1994.

Remini, Robert V. *Andrew Jackson and the Course of American Freedom, 1822–1832*. New York: Harper & Row, 1981.

————. *Andrew Jackson and His Indian Wars*. New York: Viking, 2001.

Rogin, Michael Paul. *Fathers and Children: Andrew Jackson and the Subjugation of the American Indian*. New York: Knopf, 1975.

Satz, Ronald N. *American Indian Policy in the Jacksonian Era*. Lincoln: University of Nebraska Press, 1975.

Wallace, Anthony F. C. *The Long, Bitter Trail: Andrew Jackson and the Indians*. New York: Hill and Wang, 1993.

■ Web Sites

"Indian Removal Act." Library of Congress Web site. http://www.loc.gov/rr/program/bib/ourdocs/Indian.html. Accessed on September 14, 2007.

"The Hermitage: Home of President Andrew Jackson." The Hermitage Web site. http://www.thehermitage.com. Accessed on September 14, 2007.

"Trail of Tears Association: Supporting the Trail of Tears National Historic Trail." Trail of Tears Association Web site. http://www.nationaltota.org. Accessed on September 14, 2007.

—By Tim Alan Garrison

Questions for Further Study

1. Why did so many white Americans want their Indian neighbors removed from their vicinity?

2. Compare and contrast Jackson's justification for removal with apologias for slavery from the same era.

3. To what extent did the removal plan enacted by the United States contrast with previous policies toward Native Americans? What precedents did it set for the way Indian peoples in the West would be treated by the United States?

4. Were Jackson's justifications for removal genuine? In other words, did Jackson have motivations for removal that were not expressed in this document? What do the public and private evidence together reveal—that Jackson hated Indian people and wanted them eliminated or that he, as stated in this speech, had their best interests at heart?

a new and extensive territory	Indian Territory, in what is now Oklahoma
afflicting	causing pain
animate	living
benevolent	well meaning or kindly
consummation	completion or conclusion
embellish	to make more attractive or to add details
facilities	abilities
General Government	the federal government of the United States
inanimate	dead
Indian occupancy	the right of Native Americans to live on their lands
liberal	generous
pecuniary	related to money
progressive	advancing or improving
red men	Native Americans
removal	relocation or exile
render	provide or give
retard	slow the progress of
12,000,000 happy people	the population of the United States in 1830

ANDREW JACKSON: ON INDIAN REMOVAL

It gives me pleasure to announce to Congress that the benevolent policy of the Government, steadily pursued for nearly thirty years, in relation to the removal of the Indians beyond the white settlements is approaching to a happy consummation. Two important tribes have accepted the provision made for their removal at the last session of Congress, and it is believed that their example will induce the remaining tribes also to seek the same obvious advantages.

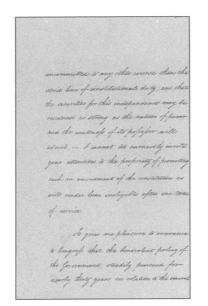

The consequences of a speedy removal will be important to the United States, to individual States, and to the Indians themselves. The pecuniary advantages which it promises to the Government are the least of its recommendations. It puts an end to all possible danger of collision between the authorities of the General and State Governments on account of the Indians. It will place a dense and civilized population in large tracts of country now occupied by a few savage hunters. By opening the whole territory between Tennessee on the north and Louisiana on the south to the settlement of the whites it will incalculably strengthen the southwestern frontier and render the adjacent States strong enough to repel future invasions without remote aid. It will relieve the whole State of Mississippi and the western part of Alabama of Indian occupancy, and enable those States to advance rapidly in population, wealth, and power. It will separate the Indians from immediate contact with settlements of whites; free them from the power of the States; enable them to pursue happiness in their own way and under their own rude institutions; will retard the progress of decay, which is lessening their numbers, and perhaps cause them gradually, under the protection of the Government and through the influence of good counsels, to cast off their savage habits and become an interesting, civilized, and Christian community.

What good man would prefer a country covered with forests and ranged by a few thousand savages to our extensive Republic, studded with cities, towns, and prosperous farms embellished with all the improvements which art can devise or industry execute, occupied by more than 12,000,000 happy people, and filled with all the blessings of liberty, civilization and religion?

The present policy of the Government is but a continuation of the same progressive change by a milder process. The tribes which occupied the countries now constituting the Eastern States were annihilated or have melted away to make room for the whites. The waves of population and civilization are rolling to the westward, and we now propose to acquire the countries occupied by the red men of the South and West by a fair exchange, and, at the expense of the United States, to send them to land where their existence may be prolonged and perhaps made perpetual. Doubtless it will be painful to leave the graves of their fathers; but what do they more than our ancestors did or than our children are now doing? To better their condition in an unknown land our forefathers left all that was dear in earthly objects. Our children by thousands yearly leave the land of their birth to seek new homes in distant regions. Does Humanity weep at these painful separations from everything, animate and inanimate, with which the young heart has become entwined? Far from it. It is rather a source of joy that our country affords scope where our young population may range unconstrained in body or in mind, developing the power and facilities of man in their highest perfection. These remove hundreds and almost thousands of miles at their own expense, purchase the lands they occupy, and support themselves at their new homes from the moment of their arrival. Can it be cruel in this Government when, by events which it can not control, the Indian is made discontented in his ancient home to purchase his lands, to give him a new and extensive territory, to pay the expense of his removal, and support him a year in his new abode? How many thousands of our own people would gladly embrace the opportunity of removing to the West on such conditions! If the offers made to the Indians were extended to them, they would be hailed with gratitude and joy.

And is it supposed that the wandering savage has a stronger attachment to his home than the settled, civilized Christian? Is it more afflicting to him to leave the graves of his fathers than it is to our brothers and children? Rightly considered, the policy of the General Government toward the red man is not only liberal, but generous. He is unwilling to submit to the laws of the States and mingle with their population. To save him from this alternative, or perhaps utter annihilation, the General Government kindly offers him a new home, and proposes to pay the whole expense of his removal and settlement.

William Lloyd Garrison (Library of Congress)

WILLIAM LLOYD GARRISON'S FIRST *LIBERATOR* EDITORIAL

"Let all the enemies of the persecuted blacks tremble."

Overview

On January 1, 1831, a twenty-five-year-old editor named William Lloyd Garrison leaped to prominence as an advocate of immediate slave emancipation with the first publication of the *Liberator*. Garrison's new weekly journal was only four pages in size and boasted few initial subscribers, but it sent shock waves through the nation by virtue of its relentless attacks upon slavery and its unwillingness to make peace with more moderate slavery opponents. The *Liberator*'s inaugural editorial spelled out Garrison's essential beliefs, ones he adhered to during the thirty-five years of his publication's existence. Provocative, accusatory, and steeped in religious fervor, the editorial's words served as the opening shot in a campaign of ideas that would cease only with the emancipation of America's slaves.

Slavery did not rank high among the controversies that troubled America's political life during the 1830s. A desire to keep peace within the Union, a preoccupation with such issues as the tariff and westward expansion, and a pervasive racism in both the North and South kept slavery largely out of the public debate. Until the publication of the *Liberator*, the antislavery sentiment that existed was largely channeled into supporting the colonization of freed slaves overseas, with only a few dedicated souls actively working to free the millions of African Americans in bondage.

Context

In 1776 the newly approved Declaration of Independence asserted "that all men are created equal, that they are endowed by their Creator with certain unalienable rights." By the time the U.S. Constitution was officially declared in effect in 1789, however, it was clear that this statement of equality did not include the millions of slaves held in both the northern and southern states. Thomas Jefferson, Patrick Henry, and other Revolutionary leaders of southern birth considered slavery a moral evil and wished—in theory—to see it eradicated. While antislavery sentiment existed in Virginia and other southern states in

the early nineteenth century, the growing profitability of the slave-based plantation system helped keep the South wedded to the institution. The northern states gradually freed their own slaves, but they showed no real inclination to interfere with slavery south of the Mason-Dixon Line. Few organized bodies of private citizens cared to oppose slavery publicly. Among the established religious denominations, only the Quakers sought to convince others that slavery was wrong. The nation's unease over the idea of human servitude was reflected in the federal suppression of the African slave trade in 1808 (with a supplementary act in 1819) and in the controversy over slavery extension leading up to the Missouri Compromise of 1820. For the most part, though, the subject was not a matter of wide concern among America's free white citizens. Abolitionists—those dedicated to abolishing slavery—were looked upon as impractical dreamers or dangerous fanatics.

Still, there were signs of a slowly growing antislavery sentiment scattered around the country. The mildest form was represented by the American Colonization Society, an organization established in 1816 to encourage the resettlement of freed slaves in overseas colonies. Those who favored more vigorous efforts to end slavery took encouragement from the work of Benjamin Lundy, a Quaker abolitionist who began publishing his newspaper the *Genius of Universal Emancipation* in 1821. Although he advocated gradual rather than immediate emancipation, Lundy won a small band of converts for his courage in attacking slavery at all. This group included a young William Lloyd Garrison, who became the coeditor of the *Genius* in 1829. That same year, David Walker, a free black man living in Boston, asserted the right of slaves to rebel against their masters in his pamphlet *Walker's Appeal ... to the Colored Citizens of the World*. This angry document—which even Garrison condemned—marked the early stirrings of a new militancy among antislavery forces.

By 1830 a number of social, political, and religious trends in America increased sympathy for antislavery views. Such evangelical Protestant preachers as Charles G. Finney advocated the doctrine of perfectionism, which stressed personal responsibility for one's own salvation and encouraged involvement in humanitarian causes. Finney's teachings were widely embraced in the North during the 1820s

Time Line

1775	**■ April 14** The first U.S. antislavery society formed in Philadelphia, with Benjamin Franklin as the president.
1808	**■ January 1** Importation of slaves into the United States is prohibited.
1816	**■ December** First meeting of American Colonization Society is held.
1820	**■ March 3** Missouri Compromise is passed by Congress, banning slavery west of the Mississippi River north of the 36°30' latitude line.
1829	**■ July 4** William Lloyd Garrison delivers an important antislavery address at Park Street Church in Boston.
1831	**■ January 1** First issue of the *Liberator* is published. **■ November 11** Nat Turner is hanged for leading a slave rebellion in Virginia.
1833	**■ December 4** American Anti-Slavery Society is organized in Philadelphia.
1835	**■ October 21** Garrison is attacked by mob at Female Anti-Slavery Society meeting in Boston.
1848	**■ March 10** U.S. Senate ratifies the Guadalupe Hidalgo Treaty, ending the Mexican-American War and potentially opening new territories to slavery.
1854	**■ May 30** President Franklin Pierce signs the Kansas-Nebraska Act, reigniting the slavery controversy.

and helped spread abolitionist beliefs to newly founded communities in the Midwest. In New England, writers like Ralph Waldo Emerson and Margaret Fuller spearheaded an emerging transcendentalist movement during the mid-1830s that stressed the natural rights and individual worth of every man and woman—ideas with obvious antislavery implications. These stirrings began to affect American politics as well. The right of citizens to have antislavery petitions received by the U.S. Congress was vigorously debated in 1835, which in turn led to a larger debate over the rights of free speech, press, and assembly for abolitionists. The launching of Garrison's *Liberator* in January 1831 both benefitted from these trends and helped advance them further.

About the Author

William Lloyd Garrison was born on December 10, 1805, in Newburyport, Massachusetts. His early years were disrupted when his father, the sailor Abijah Garrison, deserted his wife, Fanny, and their three children and disappeared into Canada. Childhood poverty shaped Garrison's youth and contributed to his later resentment of New England's ruling elite. His deeply religious mother instilled in her son an intense Christian faith, one that guided his life and work as an adult. After an unsuccessful apprenticeship to a Baltimore shoemaker, Garrison came home to Newburyport in 1818 and learned to set type at a local newspaper office. He quickly advanced to writing for and occasionally editing the publication. He went on to edit a series of periodicals before establishing the *Journal of the Times* in Bennington, Vermont, in 1828. He made his deepening antislavery views known in the *Journal* and began to lecture on the topic as well. His talk on slavery at Boston's Park Street Church on July 4, 1829, was particularly well received. His eloquence attracted the notice of the abolitionist Benjamin Lundy, who later that year asked Garrison to relocate to Baltimore and edit his *Genius of Universal Emancipation*, a small but influential antislavery paper.

As the editor of the *Genius*, Garrison grew increasingly hostile both toward slave owners and toward those who aided them. His condemnation of a Newburyport ship owner who carried slaves to the South led to a libel suit, resulting in Garrison's serving a forty-nine-day jail sentence. Lundy felt that Garrison's legal troubles had harmed his paper, and the two parted ways in July 1830. Garrison returned to Massachusetts in 1830 and began to attract followers through a series of antislavery lectures in Boston. By that time, he had become an advocate of immediate emancipation, rejecting Lundy's gradualist views. His tone of uncompromising righteousness (as well as his humble beginnings) earned him the opposition of many upper-class Bostonians, who considered his provocation of the South dangerous both to the Union and to their own financial interests. After considering a move to Washington, D.C., Garrison remained in Boston and, together with his business partner, Isaac Knapp, launched a new publication on January 1, 1831. Far more ambitious and militant than the

Genius, the *Liberator* set out to attack slavery within the broader context of universal human rights. The publication's masthead declared, "Our Country Is the World—Our Countrymen Are Mankind." This motto—so much at variance with the pervasive American nationalism of the time—served notice that the *Liberator*'s scope would be as wide as it would be controversial.

From the start, Garrison risked legal action and physical harm by publishing the *Liberator.* Rather than hide behind his editor's chair, he traveled and spoke widely during the 1830s to promote his causes. After meeting with antislavery leaders in England during the summer of 1833, he was determined to help found an effective abolitionist group in America. In December 1833, he played a key role in organizing the American Anti-Slavery Society at its first convention in Philadelphia. By the end of the decade, though, Garrison was embroiled in a series of controversies with fellow abolitionists over a range of issues. His advocacy of full equality for blacks and women and his attacks upon organized Christianity for its tolerance of slavery made him enemies within the antislavery movement. At an 1838 peace conference, he helped write a statement rejecting allegiance to all governments and calling for the abolition of all military forces—views that added to his reputation as an extremist. He also disagreed with those who sought to organize an abolitionist political party, believing that it was impossible to deal with a moral issue through electoral politics. To his detractors, Garrison was unrealistic, arrogant, and domineering; to his supporters, he was selfless, inspired, and heroic. The latter image was reinforced by his near escape from a violent Boston mob after an antislavery meeting in October 1835.

By most accounts, Garrison was personally warm and mild mannered. His marriage to Helen Benson in 1834 and the birth of his seven children allowed him to take refuge in a peaceful and satisfying family life. As an advocate for what he believed in, however, he only grew more confrontational as he aged. At a meeting of the Massachusetts Anti-Slavery Society in the spring of 1843, he offered a resolution advocating separation between the North and South, declaring the U.S. Constitution "a covenant with death and an agreement with Hell" (Nye, p. 143). His refusal to take part directly in political events of his era placed him on the sidelines as Americans debated the annexation of Texas, the Compromise of 1850, and the Kansas-Nebraska Act. As tempers rose in the North and South, he reiterated his disunionist stance, going so far as to publicly burn a copy of the Constitution in 1854.

Reactions to the U.S. Supreme Court's 1857 decision in the *Dred Scott* case and John Brown's 1859 raid on Harpers Ferry drove the North and South further apart and made Garrison's views seem less extreme. When the Civil War broke out in 1861, he gave qualified support to the Union cause as the best hope of abolishing slavery. When President Lincoln issued his preliminary Emancipation Proclamation in September 1862, Garrison offered guarded approval of this limited measure. By the close of the war, however, he took satisfaction in seeing slavery abolished at last. The final

Time Line

1854	■ **July 4** Garrison publicly burns the U.S. Constitution at a Framingham, Massachusetts, antislavery protest.
1859	■ **October 16** The radical abolitionist John Brown seizes the federal armory at Harpers Ferry, Virginia.
1861	■ **April 12** Civil War begins with Confederate attack on Fort Sumter in Charleston, South Carolina.
1863	■ **January 1** President Abraham Lincoln issues the Emancipation Proclamation.
1865	■ **December 18** Thirteenth Amendment to U.S. Constitution becomes law, abolishing slavery. ■ **December 29** Final issue of the *Liberator* is published.

issue of the *Liberator* was published on December 29, 1865, shortly after the ratification of the Thirteenth Amendment ended slavery. Believing that his work was largely done, Garrison resigned the presidency of the Massachusetts Anti-Slavery Society in January 1866. He continued to write and travel into the 1870s; financial gifts by admirers helped ensure a comfortable old age. Garrison died on May 24, 1879, in New York and is buried in Boston. At the funeral, his fellow antislavery crusader Wendell Phillips addressed Garrison: "Your heart, as it ceased to beat, felt certain, *certain,* that whether one flag or two shall rule this continent in time to come, one thing is settled—it never henceforth can be trodden by a slave!" (Mayer, p. 629).

Explanation and Analysis of the Document

Garrison opens his editorial by noting that his initial attempt to launch the *Liberator* in Washington, D.C., was thwarted by "public indifference." In August 1830 he had circulated a proposal for a periodical to be called the *Public Liberator, and Journal of the Times,* to be published in the nation's capital. Although he raised modest funds, the American Colonization Society blocked him by buying out the printing establishment Garrison had hoped to purchase. This action—as well as the relocation of the *Genius of Universal Emancipation* to Washington—helped motivate him to try Boston as a base of operations.

However, Garrison found New England far from hospitable to his views. In the second paragraph, he states that opposition to the antislavery cause is greater in the North than in the South. This statement seems based upon his recent experience of denouncing (and being successfully sued by) a New Englander who profited from the interstate slave trade as well as the efforts of conservative civic leaders to stop him from speaking in Boston and Newburyport. Despite the "detraction" and "apathy" he faces, he intends to preach his message in the shadow of Bunker Hill, the birthplace of America's struggle for freedom. (His statement was literally true; the famous battlefield was within sight of his office.) In the paragraph's final two sentences, Garrison adopts the tone that readers of the *Liberator* came to know well: militant, righteous, unyielding. He uses the language of a crusader, stating emphatically that his fight will continue until slavery is ended. It is indicative of Garrison's unshakable moral certainty that he—a poor and obscure advocate of an unpopular cause—demands that his foes "tremble" before him.

In paragraph 3, Garrison reaffirms the goals mentioned in his August 1830 proposal, which include "the abolition of slavery" and the "elevation of our colored population" (Mayer, p. 100). To these he adds his intention to avoid partisan politics. This stance eventually placed him in opposition to other abolitionists, particularly the founders of the Liberty Party, who nominated James G. Birney for president on an antislavery platform in 1840 and 1844. From Garrison's perspective, participation in the political system established under the U.S. Constitution (a document which, in his view, upheld the legality of slavery) compromised an abolitionist's moral authority. Supporting a candidate with personal ambitions would degrade the integrity of the antislavery cause. Instead, Garrison takes an expansive view and seeks to influence individuals no matter what their religious or political affiliations might be.

In contrast to the fatally flawed Constitution, the Declaration of Independence offered confirmation that Garrison's antislavery position aligned with American ideals. In paragraph 4, Garrison quotes the declaration's preamble to bolster his advocacy of the immediate enfranchisement (a stronger word than mere *emancipation*) of slaves. In homing in on this theme, he makes it clear that his abolitionist views have changed over the past two years. He specifically renounces the position he advocated in his landmark address on July 4, 1829, at Park Street Church in Boston. While his remarks that day vigorously condemned slavery and the hypocrisy of supposedly Christian Americans in tolerating it, Garrison stopped short of advocating immediate emancipation. Further reading and consideration convinced him that gradual methods only represented a compromise with evil. By the time he had moved to Baltimore in August 1829, he had come to consider his earlier position one of "timidity, injustice and absurdity." By publically

asking forgiveness from God, his country, and "my brethren the poor slaves," he makes it plain that his dedication to the abolitionist cause is both a personal spiritual commitment and a larger humanitarian obligation.

The fifth paragraph contains the most frequently quoted lines of the editorial. Garrison acknowledges that his way of speaking is severe, but he immediately goes on to say that the times call for nothing less. With the fervor of a biblical prophet, he pledges to embody the principles of Truth and Justice. The direct, forceful words that follow have the cadence and visual impact of poetry. They pointedly ridicule the idea of attacking the evil of slavery with "moderation," drawing upon intensely emotional images (a burning house, a rape victim, a threatened child) to make his case. The tone of the language here is reminiscent of the Old Testament's book of Jeremiah in its denunciations of sin and moral blindness. As Garrison builds to a crescendo and declares, "I WILL BE HEARD," the defiance in his editorial voice is palpable. The reason for his wrathful tone is the public indifference toward evil; the apathy around him is wicked enough to hasten Judgment Day upon the world.

Garrison dismisses the idea that his intemperate language and uncompromising stance will do the abolitionist cause more harm than good. In paragraph 6, he asserts that his efforts will yield positive results in the short term and will be judged favorably by history in the long term. He quotes Proverbs 29:25 from the Old Testament in reaffirming his refusal to cower before public opinion. Finally, he closes his editorial with the poem "To Oppression," from the 1828 collection *Ephemerides; or, Occasional Poems* by Thomas Pringle. Well known in abolitionist circles, Pringle had championed the rights of native Africans as a British colonist in South Africa before serving as the secretary for the Anti-Slavery Society in London.

Audience

Garrison had no illusions about the willingness of the American people to consider the possibility of abolishing slavery in 1831. He considered the vast majority of his countrymen—especially his fellow New Englanders—to be selfish materialists who practiced a smug, lazy form of Christianity. In earlier years, his antislavery efforts had been condemned by respectable clergymen and hampered by government authorities. Even antislavery groups like the American Colonization Society had proved timid and hypocritical. It was not to institutions that Garrison spoke. Instead, the first editorial of the *Liberator* was aimed most broadly at the consciences of individuals wherever he could find them. By utilizing language explicitly and implicitly drawn from the Bible, he reached across class and racial lines to stir the most basic shared values of decency and justice. Fundamentally, Garrison desired to touch the common chord of humanity that would link the slaveholder and the slave.

More narrowly, Garrison spoke to the relatively small numbers of Americans who supported emancipation. His work with Lundy had already earned him a measure of

"*Let Southern oppressors tremble—let their secret abettors tremble—let their Northern apologists tremble—let all the enemies of the persecuted blacks tremble.*"

(Paragraph 2)

"*I shall not array myself as the political partisan of any man. In defending the great cause of human rights, I wish to derive the assistance of all religions and of all parties.*"

(Paragraph 3)

"*I will be as harsh as truth, and as uncompromising as justice.*"

(Paragraph 5)

"*I am in earnest—I will not equivocate—I will not excuse—I will not retreat a single inch—AND I WILL BE HEARD.*"

(Paragraph 5)

"*I desire to thank God, that he enables me to disregard 'the fear of man which bringeth a snare,' and to speak his truth in its simplicity and power.*"

(Paragraph 6)

notice among reform-minded northern citizens. Despite his complaints of "public indifference" in the editorial, he had already developed a reputation as an energetic (if controversial) opponent of slavery. Garrison knew that his heated advocacy of immediate emancipation would lead to divisions among abolitionists. He also knew that he would receive a sympathetic hearing from free African Americans in Boston, Philadelphia, and other northern cities. They would take heart from his words, even if white Americans turned away.

In a real sense, Garrison's target audience also included God and Garrison himself. His editorial was an act of individual confession and spiritual affirmation as well as a message to the public. The idea of personal responsibility was an essential part of his religious faith; to place himself in the forefront of the antislavery battle without fear of the consequences was vital to his own salvation. Much of the editorial (particularly paragraphs 4–6) is a statement of personal belief as much as an attempt to persuade others.

In writing and publishing its words, Garrison was pledging before God to stand firm.

Impact

According to Garrison, the first issue of the *Liberator* was met with "suspicion and apathy" (Nye, p. 48). The exception was the free African American community of the Northeast, which gave the publication significant support. Garrison visited Philadelphia, New Haven, Hartford, and other cities to drum up interest; by the end of 1831, he counted more than five hundred free blacks among his subscribers. Although the *Liberator*'s paid circulation remained small for some years, its impact was far greater than the number of copies sold indicated. Its attacks upon the American Colonization Society stirred up debate within abolitionist circles across the North. Newspaper editors across the South reprinted its editorials as examples of northern antislavery extremism, increasing Garrison's influence and importance in the process. (Garrison in turn happily reprinted the denunciations of his fellow editors.) Even though it had no subscribers in the South, the *Liberator* was accused of inciting violence among slaves, especially after Nat Turner's slave rebellion in August 1831. A number of southern states and towns took steps to prosecute anyone caught circulating the paper. Garrison received death threats and was targeted for arrest (with a five-thousand-dollar reward offered) by the Georgia state legislature.

As time went on, the *Liberator* helped Garrison build a small but intensely loyal following among antislavery activists. Such notable figures as Wendell Phillips, Samuel J. May, Parker Pillsbury, Lydia Maria Child, and Maria Weston Chapman were among those he inspired to fight for immediate emancipation. He desired to attract allies who were as fervent and unyielding as he was. It has often been said that Garrison's editorials repelled far more than they persuaded. He was well aware of this effect and even reveled in the fact. "My language," he told May, "is exactly such as suits me; it will displease many, I know—to displease them is my intention" (Nye, p. 50).

While Garrison's militancy was straightforward, its effect had roundabout consequences that ultimately aided his cause. In 1836 four southern state legislatures sent formal requests to ten northern states asking them to make the publication and distribution of inflammatory antislavery material a penal offense—a move clearly aimed at publications like the *Liberator*. In the North, these actions raised freedom of speech issues and aroused a measure of sympathy for Garrison. The refusal to suppress the *Liberator* increased the level of mistrust and resentment between North and South, a situation exacerbated by the acquisition of potential slave territory following the Mexican-American War (1846–1848) and the enforcement of the Compromise of 1850's Fugitive Slave Act provision. The *Liberator* never spoke for the more moderate (and more numerous) elements within the abolitionist community during the controversies of the 1840s and 1850s. Its advocacy of racial equality, women's rights, pacifism, and other causes—as well as its bitter attacks upon organized Christianity and the U.S. Constitution—likewise found little favor. However, it did manage to put many northerners in the position of defending its freedom to publish in the face of southern opposition, which in turn increased doubts among northern public opinion about the South's commitment to basic political and human rights.

The *Liberator* could never claim more than twenty-five hundred subscribers at any point in its thirty-five-year history. Garrison often had to appeal to his followers for financial support to keep his publication going. Yet its impact was pervasive in direct and indirect ways. Its use of highly charged moral language paved the way for such respectable politicians as William H. Seward, a senator from New York, to speak of a higher law than the U.S. Constitution in considering the evils of slavery. Garrison quoted the biblical admonition "A house divided against itself cannot stand" (Matthew 12:25) in his editorials decades before Abraham

Lincoln began using the phrase. While the future president did not agree with most of Garrison's views, it is worth noting that Lincoln's law partner, William H. Herndon, was a *Liberator* reader who traveled to Boston to meet its editor in 1858. The Civil War and the Emancipation Proclamation were seen by many as vindications of the publication's views. While visiting Petersburg, Virginia, on April 6, 1865, Lincoln remarked that he was not chiefly responsible for freeing the slaves. "I have been only the instrument," he said. "The logic and moral power of Garrison, and the Anti-slavery people of the country, and the army have done all" (Barzun p. 120).

Related Documents

Cain, William E., ed. *William Lloyd Garrison and the Fight against Slavery: Selections from "The Liberator"*. Boston: Bedford Books of St. Martin's Press, 1995. Many of Garrison's most powerful and influential editorials can be found in this useful collection.

Garrison, Wendell Phillips, and Francis Jackson. *William Lloyd Garrison, 1805–1879: The Story of His Life, Told by His Children*. 4 vols. 1885. Reprint. New York: Negro Universities Press, 1969. This massive work gathers together most of Garrison's letters and speeches, along with many of his writings for publications. These volumes remain the best primary resource for Garrison scholars.

Merrill, Walter M., ed. *The Letters of William Lloyd Garrison*. 6 vols. Cambridge: Belknap Press of Harvard University Press, 1971–1981. These collected letters offer a window into Garrison's family life as well as his thoughts on the major social and political events of his time.

Bibliography

■ Books

Barnes, Gilbert H. *The Antislavery Impulse, 1830–1844*. New York: American Historical Association.,1933.

Barzun, Jacques, ed. *The Selected Writings of John Jay Chapman*. New York: Farrar, Straus, and Cudahy, 1957.

Duberman, Martin, ed. *The Antislavery Vanguard: New Essays on the Abolitionists*. Princeton, N.J.: Princeton University Press, 1965.

Jacoby, Susan. *Freethinkers: A History of American Secularism*. New York: Metropolitan Books, 2004.

Korngold, Ralph. *Two Friends of Man: The Story of William Lloyd Garrison and Wendell Phillips and Their Relationship with Abraham Lincoln*. Boston: Little, Brown, 1950.

Mayer, Henry. *All on Fire: William Lloyd Garrison and the Abolition of Slavery*. New York: St. Martin's Press, 1998.

Merrill, Walter M. *Against Wind and Tide: A Biography of William Lloyd Garrison*. Cambridge: Harvard University Press, 1963.

Nye, Russel B. *William Lloyd Garrison and the Humanitarian Reformers*. Boston: Little, Brown, 1955.

Smith, Goldwin. *The Moral Crusader, William Lloyd Garrison: A Biographical Essay*. New York: Funk and Wagnalls, 1892.

Stewart, James B. *William Lloyd Garrison and the Challenge of Emancipation*. Arlington Heights, Ill.: H. Davidson, 1992.

Thomas, John L. *The Liberator, William Lloyd Garrison, a Biography*. Boston: Little, Brown, 1963.

■ **Web Sites**

Garrison, William Lloyd. "On the Constitution and the Union." Fair Use Repository Web site.
  http://fair-use.org/the-liberator/1832/12/29/on-the-constitution-and-the-union. Accessed on November 14, 2007.

"The Liberator Files." Boston African American National Historic Site Web site.
  http://www.theliberatorfiles.com/. Accessed on November 14, 2007.

"William Lloyd Garrison, 1805–1879." Public Broadcasting System "Africans in America" Web site.
  http://www.pbs.org/wgbh/aia/part4/4p1561.html. Accessed on November 14, 2007.

"William Lloyd Garrison." NNDB Web site.
  http://www.nndb.com/people/966/000049819/. Accessed on November 14, 2007.

—By Barry Alfonso

1. The angry, aggressive thrust of the *Liberator*'s inaugural editorial is unmistakable, yet Garrison always claimed he favored nonviolent approaches to ending slavery. Critics charged that despite his public commitment to pacifism, his writings at least indirectly encouraged slaves to revolt. By denouncing moderation in the face of absolute evil, Garrison could be seen as inspiring such militant abolitionists as John Brown to take direct action. How responsible was Garrison for increasing the likelihood of violence over the slavery issue? Were his stated pacifist beliefs in conflict with the content and tone of the first editorial in the *Liberator*?

2. Many southerners (and some northerners) called for the suppression of the *Liberator*. Attempts to stop Garrison from publishing won him defenders, even among those who disagreed with his views. Did the *Liberator* in fact threaten the peace and safety of southern society? If so, were southerners justified in attempting to suppress it? Are there issues involving freedom of the press and speech from Garrison's era that are relevant to America today?

3. Garrison favored ending slavery by appealing to the Christian morality of individuals, rather than by direct political or military action. As it happened, the Civil War ultimately brought about emancipation. Is there any historical evidence that Garrison's nonviolent, conscience-oriented approach could have been successful? In discussing this, contrast America's struggles over ending slavery with those in other countries (including Great Britain and Brazil).

4. As his first *Liberator* editorial makes clear, Garrison was unwilling to compromise over the issue of immediate emancipation. This inflexible stance earned him much criticism, particularly from other abolitionists. Was Garrison ultimately right in rejecting the gradual emancipation of slaves and denouncing those who disagreed with him? Could he have done more good—and possibly helped avert the Civil War—by being more moderate?

5. From its start, the *Liberator* drew heavily from both the Old and New Testaments to define its moral position and fashion its literary style. Garrison's form of Christianity—which led him into opposition with most established churches—stressed individual responsibility and advocated defiance of man-made law when it conflicted with biblical teachings. Southern supporters of slavery also drew upon the Bible to support their positions. What does the debate over slavery say about the role of religion in American politics? How have the religious implications of the antislavery debate been echoed in recent debates over abortion, gay rights, preemptive war, and other issues?

6. Compare the public careers of William Lloyd Garrison and Abraham Lincoln with respect to the slavery issue. Both considered slavery wrong, yet they radically diverged over how to bring about its end. Contrast their words and actions dealing with the subject, particularly during the 1850s as the country headed toward civil war. In retrospect, did Garrison or Lincoln uphold a higher moral standard? Which one had the most rational approach to abolishing slavery?

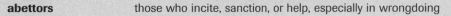

abettors	those who incite, sanction, or help, especially in wrongdoing
abhorrence	a feeling of aversion or loathing
discourses	communications, especially lectures or writings
hirelings	persons whose loyalty or services are for hire
imperious	urgent, imperative
inculcated	impressed upon the mind by frequent repetition or strong urging
palsied	afflicted with paralysis of any voluntary muscle
pernicious	causing great injury, destruction, or ruin
prospectus	a document outlining the main features of a new enterprise or project
recantation	an act of withdrawal or renunciation, especially in a public setting

WILLIAM LLOYD GARRISON'S FIRST *LIBERATOR* EDITORIAL

TO THE PUBLIC.

In the month of August, I issued proposals for publishing "The Liberator" in Washington City; but the enterprise, though hailed in different sections of the country, was palsied by public indifference. Since that time, the removal of the *Genius of Universal Emancipation* to the Seat of Government has rendered less imperious the establishment of a similar periodical in that quarter.

During my recent tour for the purpose of exciting the minds of the people by a series of discourses on the subject of slavery, every place that I visited gave fresh evidence of the fact, that a greater revolution in public sentiment was to be effected in the free States—*and particularly in New-England*—than at the South. I found contempt more bitter, opposition more active, detraction more relentless, prejudice more stubborn, and apathy more frozen, than among slave-owners themselves. Of course, there were individual exceptions to the contrary. This state of things afflicted, but did not dishearten me. I determined, at every hazard, to lift up the standard of emancipation in the eyes of the nation, *within sight of Bunker Hill and in the birthplace of liberty*. That standard is now unfurled; and long may it float, unhurt by the spoliations of time or the missiles of a desperate foe—yea, till every chain be broken, and every bondman set free! Let Southern oppressors tremble—let their secret abettors tremble—let their Northern apologists tremble—let all the enemies of the persecuted blacks tremble.

I deem the publication of my original Prospectus unnecessary, as it has obtained a wide circulation. The principles therein inculcated will be steadily pursued in this paper, excepting that I shall not array myself as the political partisan of any man. In defending the great cause of human rights, I wish to derive the assistance of all religions and of all parties.

Assenting to the "self-evident truth" maintained in the American Declaration of Independence, "that

all men are created equal, and endowed by their Creator with certain inalienable rights—among which are life, liberty and the pursuit of happiness," I shall strenuously contend for the immediate enfranchisement of our slave population. In Park-Street Church, on the Fourth of July, 1829, I unreflectingly assented to the popular but pernicious doctrine of *gradual* abolition. I seize this moment to make a full and unequivocal recantation, and thus publicly to ask pardon of my God, of my country, and of my brethren the poor slaves, for having uttered a sentiment so full of timidity, injustice, and absurdity. A similar recantation, from my pen, was published in the *Genius of Universal Emancipation* at Baltimore, in September, 1829. My conscience is now satisfied.

I am aware that many object to the severity of my language; but is there not cause for severity? I *will be* as harsh as truth, and as uncompromising as justice. On this subject, I do not wish to think, or to speak, or write, with moderation. No! no! Tell a man whose house is on fire to give a moderate alarm; tell him to moderately rescue his wife from the hands of the ravisher; tell the mother to gradually extricate her babe from the fire into which it has fallen;—but urge me not to use moderation in a cause like the present. I am in earnest—I will not equivocate—I will not excuse—I will not retreat a single inch—AND I WILL BE HEARD. The apathy of the people is enough to make every statue leap from its pedestal, and to hasten the resurrection of the dead.

It is pretended, that I am retarding the cause of emancipation by the coarseness of my invective and the precipitancy of my measures. *The charge is not true.* On this question of my influence,—humble as it is,—is felt at this moment to a considerable extent, and shall be felt in coming years—not perniciously, but beneficially—not as a curse, but as a blessing; and posterity will bear testimony that I was right. I desire to thank God, that he enables me to disregard "the fear of man which bringeth a snare," and to speak his truth in its simplicity and power. And here I close with this fresh dedication:

> Oppression! I have seen thee, face to face,
> And met thy cruel eye and cloudy brow,
> But thy soul-withering glance I fear not now—
> For dread to prouder feelings doth give place
> Of deep abhorrence! Scorning the disgrace
> Of slavish knees that at thy footstool bow,
> I also kneel—but with far other vow
> Do hail thee and thy herd of hirelings base:—
> I swear, while life-blood warms my throbbing veins,
> Still to oppose and thwart, with heart and hand,
> Thy brutalising sway—till Afric's chains
> Are burst, and Freedom rules the rescued land,—
> Trampling Oppression and his iron rod:
> *Such is the vow I take*—SO HELP ME GOD!
> [by the Scottish poet Thomas Pringle (1789–1834)]

William Lloyd Garrison.
Boston, January, 1831.

This cartoon from 1836 depicts Andrew Jackson's battle to destroy the Second Bank of the United States. The snake's heads represent the states. (Library of Congress)

"The opinion of the judges has no more authority over Congress than the opinion of Congress has over the judges, and on that point the President is independent of both."

Overview

Andrew Jackson's refusal to recharter the Second Bank of the United States was accomplished through one of the most important presidential vetoes ever issued. Of the few vetoes employed by earlier presidents, only a tiny number had dealt with important matters, and all had rested on the single argument that the legislation in question violated the U.S. Constitution. In his veto of the Second Bank recharter, Jackson cites unconstitutionality but also states that a president could kill a bill for any reason if he thought that it injured the nation. This radical view essentially gave the chief executive a more substantial role in the legislative process. In the veto, Jackson also emphasizes a philosophy of minimal centralized government and his belief that the judiciary did not have sole responsibility for interpreting the Constitution. Although it is seriously flawed in its logic and economic reasoning, the veto is a masterpiece of propaganda, virtually a call to class warfare and xenophobia.

Practically speaking, the veto meant that the Second Bank of the United States could not operate as a federal bank once its initial twenty-year charter expired in 1836. This left the young nation without a central bank until the Federal Reserve System came into being in 1913. The consequence of this absence was a series of financial upheavals, starting with the Panic of 1837. In fact, Jackson did not wait for the charter to expire before removing federal deposits from the bank, leading to another first in American history: In 1834 the Senate voted to censure the president for violating the terms of the original bank charter. Owing to the vigorous efforts of the Missouri senator Thomas Hart Benton, however, Senate Democrats successfully expunged the censure resolution in early 1837.

Context

The First Bank of the United States was chartered by Congress in 1791 under the influence of Alexander Hamilton, then the secretary of the treasury. It was modeled upon the Bank of England and was conceived to help pay off debts arising from the American Revolution and to stabilize the monetary system. Its demise resulted from animosity toward its power, sparked in part by Jeffersonian influence and in part by antagonism toward its leader, Albert Gallatin.

After the First Bank's charter expired, the nation again bore arms against Great Britain, in the War of 1812. The lack of a central bank made raising revenue and paying bills difficult, and the country suffered inflation and financial chaos. President James Madison approved the charter of the Second Bank of the United States in 1816, appointing five directors and allowing for twenty additional elected directors. A total of 80 percent of the bank's $35 million in capital was privately funded and paid in specie (in gold and silver); the rest was funded by federal government bonds. This was a very large bank—the entire nation held less than $50 million in specie at the time of the charter.

The Second Bank, like the First Bank, enjoyed a special position in U.S. finance. The landmark Supreme Court ruling in *McCulloch v. Maryland* (1819) denied states the ability to tax notes issued by the Second Bank. The Second Bank also served as a repository for the federal government, receiving funds collected from customs and land-office administrators, mostly in the form of notes issued by state banks. The bank president Nicholas Biddle extended the Second Bank's influence considerably, using its power to request specie, or money in the form of coins, in exchange for these notes. This effectively curtailed the ability of state banks to issue paper currency at will. Because the Second Bank held a large proportion of the nation's specie and specie served as international money, the bank played an important role in international trade and finance as well.

By most accounts, the United States enjoyed a period of financial stability during the Second Bank's existence, although agrarians in the West and South thought that the bank unfairly restricted credit to agriculture. Meanwhile, Wall Street enthusiasts—including the New Yorker Martin Van Buren, a crony of Andrew Jackson's—resented the power held in the bank's Philadelphia headquarters.

Biddle himself was regarded as a financial wizard by some and an evil megalomaniac by others, including Andrew Jackson. Leery of the Second Bank's size, wealth, and power, Jackson also mistrusted any form of money other than "hard money"—gold and silver. Jackson's allies

1811
- The charter of the First Bank of the United States expires.

1812–1815
- The War of 1812 and its aftermath create financial chaos, inflation, governmental difficulty in paying bills and raising revenue, and the suspension of specie payments in exchange for paper currency.

1816
- President James Madison approves the charter of the Second Bank, which is designed to provide a national paper currency and to manage federal finances. Of the $35 million raised to capitalize the bank, 20 percent is owned by the federal government.

1819
- In *McCulloch v. Maryland* the Supreme Court affirms the constitutionality of the Second Bank and denies states the ability to tax bank notes issued by the bank.

1823
- The Philadelphian Nicholas Biddle becomes president of the Second Bank.

1828
- **November**
Andrew Jackson is elected to his first term as president of the United States.

1832
- **July 3**
Congress approves the recharter of the Second Bank four years before the initial charter expires.

- **July 10**
Jackson vetoes the Second Bank recharter.

- **July 11**
The senators Daniel Webster and Henry Clay respond to Jackson's veto, with Webster calling the president a despot.

- **November**
Jackson is reelected.

included an odd mix: other hard-money zealots (many belonging to a group of radical Democrats known as Locofocos) and jealous state-chartered banks that resented the restrictions imposed by the Second Bank and wanted a chance at the profits associated with lending out federal deposits. Both Locofocos and state banks essentially hated the Second Bank and wanted to replace it with very different monetary systems.

Jackson announced his intent to torpedo the Second Bank early in his first term of office. The bank president Biddle brought matters to a head shortly before Jackson stood for reelection by having congressional allies pass a recharter bill four years early. Jackson, ill in bed at the time, famously stated to the soon-to-be vice president Martin Van Buren that although the bank was trying to kill him, he instead would kill it. Jackson's mood did not improve when his first vice president, John C. Calhoun, nixed Van Buren's appointment as minister to England just before Congress voted on the recharter bill. In an eerie foreshadowing of Jackson's veto, Nicholas Biddle's brother, a director of the Second Bank's St. Louis branch, lost his life in a September 1831 duel over the recharter.

About the Author

Andrew Jackson was born on March 15, 1767, in Waxhaw, a community straddling the border of North and South Carolina. He served in the Revolutionary War as a boy, though he was wounded and captured by the British. Later, Jackson earned his license as an attorney and practiced law first in North Carolina and then in Tennessee, where he settled for the remainder of his life. He married Rachel Donelson Robards in August 1791; the two held a second ceremony on January 17, 1794, after allegations surfaced that Rachel was still married to her first husband in 1791. Rumors of bigamy and adultery dogged Jackson and his wife for years, particularly during election season.

Jackson won fame—and a nickname—during the War of 1812: His soldiers considered him as "tough as old hickory," especially after his victorious stand at the battle of New Orleans on January 8, 1815. Old Hickory served as territorial governor of Florida and as a senator from Tennessee before winning the popular vote for president in 1824— only to lose the election to John Quincy Adams in the House of Representatives, in part due to the influence of his nemesis Henry Clay. Andrew Jackson proceeded to become and remain president by defeating John Quincy Adams in 1828 and Clay in 1832. Among his most-known exploits as president was his bitter fight against the Second Bank of the United States. Jackson also refused to allow South Carolina to nullify the federal Tariff of 1828, calling nullification the equivalent of treason. In addition, he signed the Indian Removal Act in 1830 and enforced the expulsion of the Cherokee Nation from Georgia in 1838, driving the tribe along the Trail of Tears to Indian Territory. Jackson died on June 8, 1845, and is buried next to his wife at the Hermitage, his estate outside Nashville.

Andrew Jackson was the most dominant president between Thomas Jefferson and Abraham Lincoln, and he was a founder of the Democratic Party. When Jackson's opponents portrayed him as a jackass, he laughingly adopted the symbol, which later served as inspiration for the Democrats' donkey mascot. Jackson was an avowed champion of individual and states' rights, and he was a foe of concentrated power and wealth and of paper currency. He strengthened the role of the executive office and originated the "spoils system," placing his cronies in strategic positions of power. As a young man in Tennessee, Jackson suffered a major financial loss when he accepted from a Philadelphia merchant a large amount in bank notes that later turned out to be worthless. Thereafter, he advocated hard money and viewed central banks with great suspicion. Ironically, his visage now appears on the most commonly used U.S. note: the $20 bill.

Explanation and Analysis of the Document

Andrew Jackson's veto of the recharter of the Second Bank of the United States, issued on July 10, 1832, begins with a bang: In paragraph 1, he states bluntly that the bill designed to allow the bank to continue operation after the expiration of its initial twenty-year charter "ought not become a law." Although he opens the second paragraph by saying that a central bank is "convenient for the Government and useful to the people," he never elaborates, instead spending the remainder of the long document excoriating the bank and its supporters. Jackson states in paragraph 2 that the recharter contains no modifications to make the bank compatible with justice or sound policy, despite his earlier warnings to Congress. In fact, Jackson did briefly mention the Second Bank in his first annual message to Congress, delivered on December 8, 1829, but devoted far more time in that speech to the questions of Indian removal, public debt, and the direct election of the president. His inability to perceive appropriate modifications to the bank charter may therefore have stemmed from the fact that he never clarified what these modifications should have been. In this message, in paragraphs 10 and 40, Jackson merely criticizes the suggestions offered in the recharter bill.

◆ Monopoly Power and the Corporate Status of the Bank

Jackson's first objection, expressed in paragraphs 3–7, is to the monopoly aspect of a central bank. Of course, all central banks are monopolies to some degree; here, Jackson is referring to certain special privileges enjoyed by the Second Bank. For example, the bank was the sole recipient of federal government funds, which it could then lend out at a profit. It was also permitted to open branches in different states, something state-chartered banks could not do. Further, at a time when most people paid customs duties and bought federal land using notes issued by the various state banks (at least until Jackson required specie for fed-

Time Line

1833–1834

■ September 23, 1833
After dismissing his secretary of the treasury, Jackson appoints Roger Taney to the position; Taney agrees to move government deposits to certain state-chartered banks, largely run by allies of Jackson (the so-called pet banks).

■ August 1833–June 1834
Biddle calls in numerous loans, contracting the supply of money and credit.

■ March 28, 1834
Congress censures Jackson for violating the terms of the Second Bank charter of 1816 by depositing federal money in other banks.

■ April 15, 1834
Jackson issues a protest of the censure and states that he is the direct representative of the American people and is responsible to them, not to Congress.

1836

■ February
When the federal charter of the Second Bank of the United States expires, Pennsylvania issues the bank a state charter.

■ June
The Deposit Act of 1836 (sometimes referred to as the Distribution Act) authorizes the disbursement of federal surpluses to the states in proportion to their populations.

■ July 11
The specie circular of 1836 requires that purchasers of federal land use specie instead of paper currency for payment.

1837

■ January 16
The Senate expunges the resolution of Jackson's censure.

■ May 10
The Panic of 1837 begins when New York banks suspend redemption of bank notes for gold and silver.

Time Line

1839

■ October 9
A second wave of bank
suspensions begins, and a
multiyear financial crisis
ensues.

1841

■ The Pennsylvania-
chartered Second Bank fails.

eral land purchases), the Second Bank could request specie from the relevant state banks in exchange for these notes at any time. As a result, the Second Bank held a large proportion of the nation's specie, which served both as international currency and as backing for banknotes.

The Second Bank's privileges gave it power, but they also offered benefits that Jackson fails to mention in his veto message. Because the Second Bank could compel state banks to exchange specie for notes, state banks could not print paper currency whenever they wanted. A recharter simply removing monopoly power from the Second Bank would have also destroyed its capacity to regulate the financial system.

The Second Bank's corporate status also annoyed Jackson, despite the commonplace nature of such a business organization. Like most banks and many other enterprises at the time, the Second Bank was a corporation and was therefore owned by its stockholders. Anyone could buy stock in the Second Bank, and a robust secondary market existed; in other words, bank stock freely changed hands throughout its existence, although Jackson never mentions this salient fact. Instead, he implies that only the rich and the foreign owned stock in the Second Bank. Likewise, Jackson fails to acknowledge that the federal government owned the largest share—20 percent—of the bank.

As Jackson notes in paragraphs 4 and 5, those who own stock in a monopoly might well expect to earn monopoly profits. This is a perfectly reasonable statement. Yet he then contradicts himself by claiming that no one could have foreseen such a situation at the time of the original Second Bank charter. To muddle things further, immediately after this claim Jackson estimates to the dollar what additional profits could have been enjoyed by extending the charter. He cannot have it both ways: either people (including investors and Jackson himself) foresee earning monopoly profits from a monopoly, or they do not.

◆ Foreign Stockholders

Jackson seems particularly incensed that some stockholders of the Second Bank lived in other countries, and he uses charged language (in paragraphs 4, 8, 14–18, and 29–30) to insinuate that foreigners—along with rich Americans—were therefore enjoying gifts and gratuities at the expense of small-time American taxpayers. Interestingly, Jackson and his followers did not discourage foreign borrowing as a matter of general principle; the sections concerning foreigners largely seem a sop to nativist-minded, ill-educated voters.

With regard to this issue, what Jackson left out of his message is telling. He does not bring up the fact that foreigners owned stock in many American enterprises, including state banks. Nor does he initially concede that while foreigners could own stock in the Second Bank, they could not vote for bank directors, like domestic shareholders could. Furthermore, Jackson fails to note that the inflow of capital from abroad can have large benefits for the typical American—a point Daniel Webster makes in his response to the veto.

Later in the document, in paragraph 16, Jackson admits to the voting restriction on foreigners only to use it as ammunition against wealthy Americans. He notes that if more Second Bank stock were to be purchased by foreigners, less would remain in the hands of wealthy citizens. Jackson then claims that if foreigners were to begin to own more and more of the bank, eventually only a few rich Americans would own bank stock and would thus enjoy unsupervised financial power over the nation. This point ignores reality: Second Bank stock was widely held and traded by people who had varying amounts of wealth (although some were certainly rich).

Jackson declares in paragraph 19 that Americans could have easily held the full amount of stock if he had been in charge of operations. (Presumably, he could have also ensured that poor Americans could and would have afforded substantial numbers of shares.) Here, he disregards the sheer size of the Second Bank; the domestic purchase of all of the bank's stock, particularly if Jackson had required that specie be used in transactions, simply would have been impossible.

◆ Fractional Reserve Banking

In paragraph 9, Jackson sneers at the argument that closing the Second Bank would cause loans to contract. Here, he reveals his lack of understanding of the essential nature of fractional reserve banking. Now as then, banks hold only a portion of their deposits in reserve, lending out the rest at a profit. Financial stability ensues—as does lubrication of the economy via credit—only if banks keep sufficient amounts in reserve.

By removing federal deposits from the Second Bank, Jackson gave it no choice: The bank had to call in loans as its reserves contracted. Some scholars speculate that Biddle, the Second Bank president, called in loans more abruptly and in higher quantities than needed so as to cause problems for the economy and thus for President Jackson. Because Biddle refused to allow examiners to look at the bank's books, his contemporaries could not determine whom to hold accountable for the financial woes of the mid-1830s; many chose to blame Biddle rather than Jackson.

Initially, the bank's contraction of loans caused upheaval for businesses, which had to scramble to repay borrowings sooner than expected. In the longer run, the demise of the Second Bank gave rise to a plethora of state banks and wildcat banks—that is, financially unreliable ones—not all of which maintained sufficient reserves. As a consequence, people began to generally mistrust the integrity of banks, increase their personal holdings of specie, and reduce the amount of credit available to the economy. Jackson anticipates none of these fairly foreseeable events in his veto message.

◆ The Clearinghouse Role for Banks

Jackson's next objection, offered in paragraph 11, shows his ignorance of the bank's role as an institutional clearinghouse. He protests the policy that a state bank could pay a debt to the Second Bank with notes from a different bank but ordinary citizens could not. Jackson avers that this practice united the interests of the Second Bank and state banks against those of the common man.

Jackson fails to demonstrate an understanding of the interweaving of institutions that gave rise to this policy. In fact, this policy has features in common with the modern-day practice that allows a person to deposit a check issued by one bank in an account at another but does not permit the deposit of an IOU from a neighbor. Because the Second Bank had ongoing official relations with state banks, it could engage in certain sorts of transactions with them that it could not with persons on the street. Likewise, a modern bank has reason to trust that another bank has funds available to pay its debt, whereas it cannot be sure that a person's neighbor does.

Incidentally, Jackson's apparent fear that the Second Bank would join forces in some way with state banks was unfounded and probably deliberately misleading. State banks disliked the regulatory power and privileges enjoyed by the Second Bank, and most were quite happy to see it close.

◆ *McCulloch v. Maryland* and the Value of Precedent

When Jackson rails against the inability of states to tax the operations of the Second Bank, in paragraphs 13–14 and 36–39, he is effectively opposing the judgment in *McCulloch v. Maryland*, which approved the constitutionality of the Second Bank and forbade states to tax notes issued by the bank. This is a huge statement by a chief executive. In effect, as in paragraphs 20–24, he is questioning the authority of the Supreme Court to declare whether state legislation accords with the U.S. Constitution.

In fact, Jackson not only states that the Supreme Court does not have the final say in any matter but also claims that one Congress is not bound by the actions of a previous Congress, nor is a president bound by his predecessors (paragraphs 20–21, 26–28, 31–35, and 40). His veto, then, suggests both that the Supreme Court was wrong in the *McCulloch* case and that President James Madison was even more wrong in allowing the original Second Bank charter. Certainly, presidents before Jackson had disagreed with their earlier counterparts, yet Jackson's comments are far bolder. They are bald statements designed to demonstrate the president's affinity for and protection of ordinary individuals when larger forces—including other branches of the government—appeared to align against them.

◆ Federalism, States' Rights, and Individual Rights

Jackson's objection to *McCulloch v. Maryland* raises fundamental questions about federalism and states' rights. He elaborates on his view near the end of the veto message, stating in paragraph 45 that the "true strength" of the federal government consists in leaving individuals and states alone. In Jackson's opinion, the potential evil of federal government is that it might concentrate power, particularly among the wealthy (paragraph 46).

In his attacks on the Second Bank's ability to restrict state banks from issuing excessive amounts of paper notes, Jackson never acknowledges that this regulatory power might have benefits. Instead, he suggests that the bank offends state sovereignty and acts solely as an oppressor. Behind this nefarious behavior are the bank's directors, supporters, and wealthy owners, as Jackson asserts in paragraphs 42–44 and 46. He uses the veto to portray the Second Bank as an institution that favors the rich and the foreign and to cast the president as the savior of the little man, protecting him from the powerful legislative and judicial branches. In doing so, Jackson forever changed the role of the executive branch.

Jackson's support of states in opposition to the federal government sowed the seeds of regional conflict as well. Notwithstanding his position against South Carolina in the nullification crisis, Jackson shows his true colors in paragraphs 45–47: he considers individuals and the states they live in—not the national government—to be the font of power.

Audience

Andrew Jackson hoped to reach the entire U.S. population with the messages contained in his veto. Certainly, he aims particular barbs at the administrators and supporters of the Second Bank as well as at his enemies in Congress—yet Jackson's broad statements about his responsibility to individuals, disdain for the moneyed class, distaste for foreigners, and aversion to corporations all reveal his desire to let common citizens know he was on their side. Jackson makes clear his belief that the president looks out for the nation and its people and, if necessary, will protect them against the follies of the other branches of government.

Regrettably, Jackson never understood either the benefits of fractional reserve banking and central banks or the desire of ordinary people to obtain credit from trustworthy sources. In his vitriol against stock owners, Jackson neglects the important fact that a stable financial system can benefit labor as well as capital, debtors as well as creditors, and the poor as well as the rich. Remarkably, however, the veto message seems to speak to all sorts of people, including some who suffered mightily from the demise of the Second Bank.

Amos Kendall, a Kentucky newspaperman, probably contributed to the first draft of the veto, with help from Roger Taney. Kendall's experience gave him vocabulary and phrasing that would appeal to a wide array of citizens.

The Second Bank of the United States, Philadelphia, Pennsylvania. (AP Photo/Jacqueline Larma)

Impact

The Massachusetts senator Daniel Webster, who had argued for the winning side in *McCulloch v. Maryland*, offered a blistering response to the veto one day after Jackson made it public. He noted that every bank must have stockholders, that people own stock because they think they will make money, and that this behavior is not necessarily at odds with the public interest. Webster reminded Jackson that foreign ownership of stocks was common—state banks had foreign stockholders, after all—and that noncitizens had no voice in Second Bank policy anyway. Most important, by arguing that the original Second Bank charter was unconstitutional, even though Congress had passed it, President Madison had approved it, and the Supreme Court had sanctioned it, Jackson revealed himself to be a despot who considered himself unbound by established authority.

Although Webster had his supporters, including Henry Clay, Jackson convinced many contemporaries that the Second Bank was evil and that its destruction was a momentous victory for majoritarian rule. Nicholas Biddle did little to dispel these sentiments, refusing to open the Second Bank's books or correspondence to a congressional investigatory committee.

The Second Bank recharter veto, in conjunction with Jackson's placement of federal deposits into "pet banks," the Deposit Act, and the 1836 specie circular, opened the way for a spectacular explosion in the number of state commercial banks. States initiated ambitious new canal and rail construction projects, working closely with their respective state banks to finance these operations. Indeed, the death of the Second Bank gave birth to a freewheeling free-banking era, which allowed anyone with enough capital the capability of setting up a bank—and which generated more than 9,000 types of banknotes by 1860. Ironically, Jackson's success at ridding the nation of the hated Second Bank also brought about the decreased use of hard money.

Not surprisingly, these radical changes led to major financial upheavals. In early May 1837, New York banks suspended the redemption of bank notes for gold; nearly every other bank in the nation quickly followed. The Panic of 1837 subsided within a few months, only to be followed by a second wave of suspensions starting in Philadelphia on October 9, 1839. Although this wave was less widespread, the crisis lasted much longer and had more profound effects, including numerous bank failures, unfinished state transportation projects, plummeting stock prices, and stagnation in land markets. Recovery took most of a decade.

The classical explanation for the financial crises of the late 1830s rests blame squarely on Andrew Jackson's shoulders. Set against this traditional school of thought are some revisionist economic historians who argue that the United States easily fell victim to international shifts in specie demand and supply. More recently, empirical studies of specie flows and bank records have shifted the accountability back to Jackson. Some scholars even argue that the cycles of monetary panic unleashed by Jackson's veto led inexorably to the establishment of the U.S. Federal Reserve System, a development that would have appalled Jackson nearly as much as his face being on the $20 bill.

President Andrew Jackson's veto of the Second Bank recharter not only altered the course of American economic and financial history but also made fundamental changes to the American political process. Foremost, the veto greatly expanded the role of the chief executive: By threatening legislation on virtually any ground the president might think appropriate, it forced Congress to consider more seriously the reaction of the executive branch before proposing new laws. The veto also cast the executive as an instrument of the people rather than of Congress, and it articulated concepts of state and individual rights that would resonate with the southern states three decades later. What is more, it helped lead to the first censure of a U.S. president.

As a last note regarding the document's impact, one of Jackson's chief henchmen in gutting the Second Bank was Roger Taney. Angry congressmen later refused to approve Taney's appointment as secretary of the treasury; as a consequence, Jackson ultimately rewarded Taney with the position of chief justice of the United States. Taney is perhaps best known for his opinion in the 1857 Supreme Court case *Dred Scott v. Sandford*.

Related Documents

An Act to Incorporate the Subscribers to the Bank of the United States, Statutes at Large of the United States of America, 1789–1873 3 (1816): 266–277. This act is the original charter incorporating the Second Bank of the United States, of April 10, 1816, available on the Web at http://memory.loc.gov/cgi-bin/ampage?collId=llsl&fileName=003/llsl003.db&recNum=0307.

Clay, Henry. *The Works of Henry Clay*. Vol. 7. New York: G. P. Putnam's Sons, 1904. This volume of Henry Clay's writings includes

"I sincerely regret that in the act before me I can perceive none of those modifications of the bank charter which are necessary, in my opinion, to make it compatible with justice, with sound policy, or with the Constitution of our country."

(Paragraph 2)

"It is maintained by the advocates of the bank that its constitutionality in all its features ought to be considered as settled by precedent and by the decision of the Supreme Court. To this conclusion I can not assent. Mere precedent is a dangerous source of authority, and should not be regarded as deciding questions of constitutional power except where the acquiescence of the people and the States can be considered as well settled."

(Paragraph 20)

"The Congress, the Executive, and the Court must each for itself be guided by its own opinion of the Constitution. Each public officer who takes an oath to support the Constitution swears that he will support it as he understands it, and not as it is understood by others. ... The opinion of the judges has no more authority over Congress than the opinion of Congress has over the judges, and on that point the President is independent of both."

(Paragraph 21)

"Distinctions in society will always exist under every just government. Equality of talents, of education, or of wealth can not be produced by human institutions. ... But when the laws undertake to add to these natural and just advantages artificial distinctions, to grant titles, gratuities, and exclusive privileges, to make the rich richer and the potent more powerful, the humble members of society—the farmers, mechanics, and labors—who have neither the time nor the means of securing like favors to themselves, have a right to complain of the injustice of their Government."

(Paragraph 44)

"Nor is our Government to be maintained or our Union preserved by invasions of the rights and powers of the several States. In thus attempting to make our General Government strong we make it weak."

(Paragraph 45)

his response to Jackson's veto, which in particular is available on the Web at http://alpha.furman.edu/~benson/docs/clay.htm.

"Expunged Senate Censure Motion against President Andrew Jackson." National Archives and Records Administration, Records of the U.S. Senate, January 16, 1837. The original senatorial document shows the black lines and "strong letters" that were used to expunge Jackson's censure, viewable on the Web at http://www.archives.gov/exhibits/treasures_of_congress/Images/page_9/29a.html.

Hamilton, Alexander. "Opinion as to the Constitutionality of the Bank of the United States, 1791." This document provides Hamilton's argument, presented when he was secretary of the treasury, against the First Bank of the United States, available on the Web at http://www.constitution.org/mon/ah-bank.htm.

Jackson, Andrew. "Message of Protest to the Senate," April 15, 1834. "Message to the Senate Clarifying the Protest Message," April 21, 1834. These documents record Andrew Jackson's protest of his censure and clarify certain points raised in the protest, available on the Web at http://www.yale.edu/lawweb/avalon/presiden/jackpap.htm.

Jefferson, Thomas. "Opinion on the Constitutionality of a National Bank, 1791." This document provides Jefferson's argument in favor of the First Bank of the United States, available on the Web at http://www.constitution.org/mon/tj-bank.htm.

McCulloch v. Maryland, 17 U.S. 316 (1819). The Supreme Court decided in this case that the establishment of the Second Bank of the United States did not violate the terms of the U.S. Constitution and that states did not have the power to tax the notes issued by this federally chartered bank.

U.S. Congress. *Congressional Debates*, 22nd Cong., 1st sess., 1221–1240. This record contains Daniel Webster's speech on the floor of the U.S. Senate of July 11, 1832, in which he strongly argues against Andrew Jackson's veto of the recharter of the Second Bank of the United States. It is available on the Web at http://memory.loc.gov/cgi-bin/ampage?collId=llrd&fileName=011/llrd011.db&recNum=614.

Bibliography

■ Articles

Engerman, Stanley L. "A Note on the Economic Consequences of the Second Bank of the United States." *Journal of Political Economy* 78, no. 4 (1970): 725–728.

Fraas, Arthur. "The Second Bank of the United States: An Instrument for an Interregional Monetary Union." *Journal of Economic History* 34, no. 2 (1974): 447–467.

Green, Edward. "Economic Perspective on the Political History of the Second Bank of the United States." *Economic Perspectives* 27 (2003): 59–67.

Hammond, Bray. "Jackson, Biddle, and the Bank of the United States." *Journal of Economic History* 7, no. 1 (1947): 1–23.

Macesich, George. "Sources of Monetary Disturbances in the U.S., 1834–1845." *Journal of Economic History* 20 (1960): 407–434.

Rousseau, Peter. "Jacksonian Monetary Policy, Specie Flows, and the Panic of 1837." *Journal of Economic History* 62, no. 2 (2002): 457–488.

Sushka, Marie E. "The Antebellum Money Market and the Economic Impact of the Bank War." *Journal of Economic History* 36, no. 4 (1976): 809–835.

Sylla, Richard. "American Banking and Growth in the 19th Century: A Partial View of the Terrain." *Explorations in Economic History* 9 (1971–1972): 197–227.

Temin, Peter. "The Economic Consequences of the Bank War." *Journal of Political Economy* 76, no. 2 (1968): 257–274.

Timberlake, Richard, Jr.. "The Specie Circular and the Distribution of the Surplus." *Journal of Political Economy* 68, no. 2 (1960): 109–117.

Wallis, John. "What Caused the Crisis of 1839?" National Bureau of Economic Research Historical Working Paper 133, Cambridge, Mass., 2001.

■ Books

Catterall, Ralph C. H. *The Second Bank of the United States.* Chicago: University of Chicago Press, 1903.

Hammond, Bray. *Banks and Politics in America, from the Revolution to the Civil War.* Princeton, N.J.: Princeton University Press, 1957.

Kaplan, Edward S. *The Bank of the United States and the American Economy.* Westport, Conn.: Greenwood Press, 1999.

McGrane, Reginald C. *The Panic of 1837: Some Financial Problems of the Jacksonian Era.* Chicago: University of Chicago Press, 1924.

Macesich, George. *Money and Monetary Regimes: Struggle for Monetary Supremacy.* Westport, Conn.: Praeger, 2002.

Redlich, Fritz. *The Molding of American Banking: Men and Ideas.* 2 vols. New York: Johnson Reprint, 1968.

Remini, Robert V. *Andrew Jackson and the Bank War: A Study in the Growth of Presidential Power.* New York: Norton, 1967.

———. *The Life of Andrew Jackson.* New York: Harper & Row, 1988.

Rockoff, Hugh. "Money, Prices and Banks in the Jacksonian Era." In *The Reinterpretation of American Economic History*, eds. Robert Fogel and Stanley Engerman. New York: Harper & Row, 1971.

Schlesinger, Arthur, Jr. *The Age of Jackson.* Boston: Little, Brown, 1945.

Taylor, George, ed. *Jackson versus Biddle: The Struggle over the Second Bank of the United States.* Boston: Heath, 1949.

Temin, Peter. *The Jacksonian Economy.* New York: Norton, 1969.

Timberlake, Richard, Jr. *The Origins of Central Banking in the United States.* Cambridge, Mass.: Harvard University Press, 1978.

Wahl, Jenny. "He Broke the Bank, but Did Andrew Jackson Also Father the Fed?" In *Congress and the Emergence of Sectionalism: From the Missouri Compromise to the Age of Jackson,* eds. Paul Finkelman and Donald Kennon. Athens, Ohio: Ohio University Press, 2008.

Wilburn, Jean. *Biddle's Bank: The Crucial Years.* New York: Columbia University Press, 1967.

■ **Web Sites**

"Andrew Jackson: Biography." The Papers of Andrew Jackson, University of Tennessee Web site.

http://thepapersofandrewjackson.utk.edu/biography.htm. Accessed on September 19, 2007.

"Andrew Jackson: A Life in Brief." Miller Center of Public Affairs, University of Virginia Web site.
   http://www.millercenter.virginia.edu/academic/americanpresident/jackson/essays/biography/1. Accessed on September 19, 2007.

Gordon, John Steele. "Andrew Jackson Knocks Out the Bank—and the Nation Takes a Full Century to Recover." AmericanHeritage Web site.
   http://www.americanheritage.com/articles/web/20070710-andrew-jackson-nicholas-biddle-henry-clay-bank-of-the-united-states-federal-reserve.shtml. Accessed on September 19, 2007.

"The Papers of Andrew Jackson." The Avalon Project at Yale Law School Web site.
   http://www.yale.edu/lawweb/avalon/presiden/jackpap.htm. Accessed on September 19, 2007.

—By Jenny Bourne Wahl

Questions for Further Study

1. Compare the arguments raised in the Second Bank recharter veto—about centralization of power, foreign influence, and fractional reserve banking, for instance—to those made in the twentieth century when the nation decided to establish the Federal Reserve System, during the savings-and-loan crisis of the 1980s, and upon the near failure of the Long-Term Capital Management hedge fund during the ruble crisis of 1998.

2. Evaluate the document's arguments about inequality and the role of government. What does President Andrew Jackson say the government should and should not do? Would modern-day politicians agree? What specific policies might a government implement that would address Jackson's concerns?

3. President Jackson objected to the monopoly power enjoyed by the Second Bank. What was the source of this power? What are the costs and benefits associated with central banking, particularly with regard to the ordinary citizen?

4. Compare and contrast Jackson's arguments in the veto of the Second Bank recharter to those made by Alexander Hamilton and Thomas Jefferson regarding the First Bank and by the various parties in the case of *McCulloch v. Maryland.*

5. Foreign involvement in the American economy is frequently a hot-button political issue, such as with the virulent opposition to the North American Free Trade Agreement spearheaded by the presidential candidate Ross Perot, campaigns to "Buy America First," and the like. How do Andrew Jackson's sentiments about foreign ownership of U.S. stock compare with positions taken by modern-day Americans? Evaluate the merit of Jackson's claims.

Glossary

capital	assets, usually in the form of money or property, owned by a person or business and used to produce additional assets
charter	a document that incorporates an institution and specifies its functions
dividend	a share of a company's profits paid to holders of its stock
gratuity	a gift, usually in the form of money, given in return for a service
monopoly	the exclusive control by a single entity, usually over the production or sale of a commodity or service
par value	the face price of a share of stock; the amount the company would pay a stockholder to redeem the share
specie	a commodity metal, usually gold or silver, used as coin or as backing for paper currency
stock	a portion of ownership in a corporation; also known as equity or share

President Jackson's Veto Message Regarding the Second Bank of the United States

WASHINGTON, July 10, 1832.
To the Senate.

The bill "to modify and continue" the act entitled "An act to incorporate the subscribers to the Bank of the United States" was presented to me on the 4th July instant. Having considered it with that solemn regard to the principles of the Constitution which the day was calculated to inspire, and come to the conclusion that it ought not to become a law, I herewith return it to the Senate, in which it originated, with my objections.

A bank of the United States is in many respects convenient for the Government and useful to the people. Entertaining this opinion, and deeply impressed with the belief that some of the powers and privileges possessed by the existing bank are unauthorized by the Constitution, subversive of the rights of the States, and dangerous to the liberties of the people, I felt it my duty at an early period of my Administration to call the attention of Congress to the practicability of organizing an institution combining all its advantages and obviating these objections. I sincerely regret that in the act before me I can perceive none of those modifications of the bank charter which are necessary, in my opinion, to make it compatible with justice, with sound policy, or with the Constitution of our country.

The present corporate body, denominated the president, directors, and company of the Bank of the United States, will have existed at the time this act is intended to take effect twenty years. It enjoys an exclusive privilege of banking under the authority of the General Government, a monopoly of its favor and support, and, as a necessary consequence, almost a monopoly of the foreign and domestic exchange. The powers, privileges, and favors bestowed upon it in the original charter, by increasing the value of the stock far above its par value, operated as a gratuity of many millions to the stockholders.

An apology may be found for the failure to guard against this result in the consideration that the effect of the original act of incorporation could not be certainly foreseen at the time of its passage. The act before me proposes another gratuity to the holders of the same stock, and in many cases to the same men, of at least seven millions more. This donation finds no apology in any uncertainty as to the effect of the act. On all hands it is conceded that its passage will increase at least so or 30 per cent more the market price of the stock, subject to the payment of the annuity of $200,000 per year secured by the act, thus adding in a moment one-fourth to its par value. It is not our own citizens only who are to receive the bounty of our Government. More than eight millions of the stock of this bank are held by foreigners. By this act the American Republic proposes virtually to make them a present of some millions of dollars. For these gratuities to foreigners and to some of our own opulent citizens the act secures no equivalent whatever. They are the certain gains of the present stockholders under the operation of this act, after making full allowance for the payment of the bonus.

Every monopoly and all exclusive privileges are granted at the expense of the public, which ought to receive a fair equivalent. The many millions which this act proposes to bestow on the stockholders of the existing bank must come directly or indirectly out of the earnings of the American people. It is due to them, therefore, if their Government sell monopolies and exclusive privileges, that they should at least exact for them as much as they are worth in open market. The value of the monopoly in this case may be correctly ascertained. The twenty-eight millions of stock would probably be at an advance of 50 per cent, and command in market at least $42,000,000, subject to the payment of the present bonus. The present value of the monopoly, therefore, is $17,000,000, and this the act proposes to sell for three millions, payable in fifteen annual installments of $200,000 each.

It is not conceivable how the present stockholders can have any claim to the special favor of the Government. The present corporation has enjoyed its monopoly during the period stipulated in the original contract. If we must have such a corporation, why should not the Government sell out the whole stock and thus secure to the people the full market value of the privileges granted? Why should not Congress create and sell twenty-eight millions of stock, incorporating the purchasers with all the powers and privileges secured in this act and putting the premium upon the sales into the Treasury?

But this act does not permit competition in the purchase of this monopoly. It seems to be predicated on the erroneous idea that the present stockholders have a prescriptive right not only to the favor but to the bounty of Government. It appears that more than a fourth part of the stock is held by foreigners and the residue is held by a few hundred of our own citizens, chiefly of the richest class. For their benefit does this act exclude the whole American people from competition in the purchase of this monopoly and dispose of it for many millions less than it is worth. This seems the less excusable because some of our citizens not now stockholders petitioned that the door of competition might be opened, and offered to take a charter on terms much more favorable to the Government and country.

But this proposition, although made by men whose aggregate wealth is believed to be equal to all the private stock in the existing bank, has been set aside, and the bounty of our Government is proposed to be again bestowed on the few who have been fortunate enough to secure the stock and at this moment wield the power of the existing institution. I can not perceive the justice or policy of this course. If our Government must sell monopolies, it would seem to be its duty to take nothing less than their full value, and if gratuities must be made once in fifteen or twenty years let them not be bestowed on the subjects of a foreign government nor upon a designated and favored class of men in our own country. It is but justice and good policy, as far as the nature of the case will admit, to confine our favors to our own fellow-citizens, and let each in his turn enjoy an opportunity to profit by our bounty. In the bearings of the act before me upon these points I find ample reasons why it should not become a law.

It has been urged as an argument in favor of rechartering the present bank that the calling in its loans will produce great embarrassment and distress. The time allowed to close its concerns is ample, and

if it has been well managed its pressure will be light, and heavy only in case its management has been bad. If, therefore, it shall produce distress, the fault will be its own, and it would furnish a reason against renewing a power which has been so obviously abused. But will there ever be a time when this reason will be less powerful? To acknowledge its force is to admit that the bank ought to be perpetual, and as a consequence the present stockholders and those inheriting their rights as successors be established a privileged order, clothed both with great political power and enjoying immense pecuniary advantages from their connection with the Government.

The modifications of the existing charter proposed by this act are not such, in my view, as make it consistent with the rights of the States or the liberties of the people. The qualification of the right of the bank to hold real estate, the limitation of its power to establish branches, and the power reserved to Congress to forbid the circulation of small notes are restrictions comparatively of little value or importance. All the objectionable principles of the existing corporation, and most of its odious features, are retained without alleviation.

The fourth section provides "that the notes or bills of the said corporation, although the same be, on the faces thereof, respectively made payable at one place only, shall nevertheless be received by the said corporation at the bank or at any of the offices of discount and deposit thereof if tendered in liquidation or payment of any balance or balances due to said corporation or to such office of discount and deposit from any other incorporated bank." This provision secures to the State banks a legal privilege in the Bank of the United States which is withheld from all private citizens. If a State bank in Philadelphia owe the Bank of the United States and have notes issued by the St. Louis branch, it can pay the debt with those notes, but if a merchant, mechanic, or other private citizen be in like circumstances he can not by law pay his debt with those notes, but must sell them at a discount or send them to St. Louis to be cashed. This boon conceded to the State banks, though not unjust in itself, is most odious because it does not measure out equal justice to the high and the low, the rich and the poor. To the extent of its practical effect it is a bond of union among the banking establishments of the nation, erecting them into an interest separate from that of the people, and its necessary tendency is to unite the Bank of the United States and the State banks in any measure which may be thought conducive to their common interest.

The ninth section of the act recognizes principles of worse tendency than any provision of the present charter.

It enacts that "the cashier of the bank shall annually report to the Secretary of the Treasury the names of all stockholders who are not resident citizens of the United States, and on the application of the treasurer of any State shall make out and transmit to such treasurer a list of stockholders residing in or citizens of such State, with the amount of stock owned by each." Although this provision, taken in connection with a decision of the Supreme Court, surrenders, by its silence, the right of the States to tax the banking institutions created by this corporation under the name of branches throughout the Union, it is evidently intended to be construed as a concession of their right to tax that portion of the stock which may be held by their own citizens and residents. In this light, if the act becomes a law, it will be understood by the States, who will probably proceed to levy a tax equal to that paid upon the stock of banks incorporated by themselves. In some States that tax is now 1 per cent, either on the capital or on the shares, and that may be assumed as the amount which all citizen or resident stockholders would be taxed under the operation of this act. As it is only the stock held in the States and not that employed within them which would be subject to taxation, and as the names of foreign stockholders are not to be reported to the treasurers of the States, it is obvious that the stock held by them will be exempt from this burden. Their annual profits will therefore be 1 per cent more than the citizen stockholders, and as the annual dividends of the bank may be safely estimated at 7 per cent, the stock will be worth 10 or 15 per cent more to foreigners than to citizens of the United States. To appreciate the effects which this state of things will produce, we must take a brief review of the operations and present condition of the Bank of the United States.

By documents submitted to Congress at the present session it appears that on the 1st of January, 1832, of the twenty-eight millions of private stock in the corporation, $8,405,500 were held by foreigners, mostly of Great Britain. The amount of stock held in the nine Western and Southwestern States is $140,200, and in the four Southern States is $5,623,100, and in the Middle and Eastern States is about $13,522,000. The profits of the bank in 1831, as shown in a statement to Congress, were about $3,455,598; of this there accrued in the nine western States about $1,640,048; in the four Southern

States about $352,507, and in the Middle and Eastern States about $1,463,041. As little stock is held in the West, it is obvious that the debt of the people in that section to the bank is principally a debt to the Eastern and foreign stockholders; that the interest they pay upon it is carried into the Eastern States and into Europe, and that it is a burden upon their industry and a drain of their currency, which no country can bear without inconvenience and occasional distress. To meet this burden and equalize the exchange operations of the bank, the amount of specie drawn from those States through its branches within the last two years, as shown by its official reports, was about $6,000,000. More than half a million of this amount does not stop in the Eastern States, but passes on to Europe to pay the dividends of the foreign stockholders. In the principle of taxation recognized by this act the Western States find no adequate compensation for this perpetual burden on their industry and drain of their currency. The branch bank at Mobile made last year $95,140, yet under the provisions of this act the State of Alabama can raise no revenue from these profitable operations, because not a share of the stock is held by any of her citizens. Mississippi and Missouri are in the same condition in relation to the branches at Natchez and St. Louis, and such, in a greater or less degree, is the condition of every Western State. The tendency of the plan of taxation which this act proposes will be to place the whole United States in the same relation to foreign countries which the Western States now bear to the Eastern. When by a tax on resident stockholders the stock of this bank is made worth 10 or 15 per cent more to foreigners than to residents, most of it will inevitably leave the country.

Thus will this provision in its practical effect deprive the Eastern as well as the Southern and Western States of the means of raising a revenue from the extension of business and great profits of this institution. It will make the American people debtors to aliens in nearly the whole amount due to this bank, and send across the Atlantic from two to five millions of specie every year to pay the bank dividends.

In another of its bearings this provision is fraught with danger. Of the twenty-five directors of this bank five are chosen by the Government and twenty by the citizen stockholders. From all voice in these elections the foreign stockholders are excluded by the charter. In proportion, therefore, as the stock is transferred to foreign holders the extent of suffrage in the choice of directors is curtailed. Already is almost a third of the stock in foreign hands and not represented in elections. It is constantly passing out of the country, and this act will accelerate its departure. The entire control of the institution would necessarily fall into the hands of a few citizen stockholders, and the ease with which the object would be accomplished would be a temptation to designing men to secure that control in their own hands by monopolizing the remaining stock. There is danger that a president and directors would then be able to elect themselves from year to year, and without responsibility or control manage the whole concerns of the bank during the existence of its charter. It is easy to conceive that great evils to our country and its institutions millet flow from such a concentration of power in the hands of a few men irresponsible to the people.

Is there no danger to our liberty and independence in a bank that in its nature has so little to bind it to our country? The president of the bank has told us that most of the State banks exist by its forbearance. Should its influence become concentered, as it may under the operation of such an act as this, in the hands of a self-elected directory whose interests are identified with those of the foreign stockholders, will there not be cause to tremble for the purity of our elections in peace and for the independence of our country in war? Their power would be great whenever they might choose to exert it; but if this monopoly were regularly renewed every fifteen or twenty years on terms proposed by themselves, they might seldom in peace put forth their strength to influence elections or control the affairs of the nation. But if any private citizen or public functionary should interpose to curtail its powers or prevent a renewal of its privileges, it can not be doubted that he would be made to feel its influence.

Should the stock of the bank principally pass into the hands of the subjects of a foreign country, and we should unfortunately become involved in a war with that country, what would be our condition? Of the course which would be pursued by a bank almost wholly owned by the subjects of a foreign power, and managed by those whose interests, if not affections, would run in the same direction there can be no doubt. All its operations within would be in aid of the hostile fleets and armies without. Controlling our currency, receiving our public moneys, and holding thousands of our citizens in dependence, it would be more formidable and dangerous than the naval and military power of the enemy.

If we must have a bank with private stockholders, every consideration of sound policy and every impulse of American feeling admonishes that it should be *purely American*. Its stockholders should be composed exclusively of our own citizens, who at least ought to be friendly to our Government and willing to support it in times of difficulty and danger. So abundant is domestic capital that competition in subscribing for the stock of local banks has recently led almost to riots. To a bank exclusively of American stockholders, possessing the powers and privileges granted by this act, subscriptions for $200,000,000 could be readily obtained. Instead of sending abroad the stock of the bank in which the Government must deposit its funds and on which it must rely to sustain its credit in times of emergency, it would rather seem to be expedient to prohibit its sale to aliens under penalty of absolute forfeiture.

It is maintained by the advocates of the bank that its constitutionality in all its features ought to be considered as settled by precedent and by the decision of the Supreme Court. To this conclusion I can not assent. Mere precedent is a dangerous source of authority, and should not be regarded as deciding questions of constitutional power except where the acquiescence of the people and the States can be considered as well settled. So far from this being the case on this subject, an argument against the bank might be based on precedent. One Congress, in 1791, decided in favor of a bank; another, in 1811, decided against it. One Congress, in 1815, decided against a bank; another, in 1816, decided in its favor. Prior to the present Congress, therefore, the precedents drawn from that source were equal. If we resort to the States, the expressions of legislative, judicial, and executive opinions against the bank have been probably to those in its favor as 4 to 1. There is nothing in precedent, therefore, which, if its authority were admitted, ought to weigh in favor of the act before me.

If the opinion of the Supreme Court covered the whole ground of this act, it ought not to control the coordinate authorities of this Government. The Congress, the Executive, and the Court must each for itself be guided by its own opinion of the Constitution. Each public officer who takes an oath to support the Constitution swears that he will support it as he understands it, and not as it is understood by others. It is as much the duty of the House of Representatives, of the Senate, and of the President to decide upon the constitutionality of any bill or resolution which may be presented to them for passage or approval as it is of the supreme judges when it may be brought before them for judicial decision. The opinion of the judges has no more authority over Congress than the opinion of Congress has over the judges, and on that point the President is independent of both. The authority of the Supreme Court must not, therefore, be permitted to control the Congress or the Executive when acting in their legislative capacities, but to have only such influence as the force of their reasoning may deserve.

But in the case relied upon the Supreme Court have not decided that all the features of this corporation are compatible with the Constitution. It is true that the court have said that the law incorporating the bank is a constitutional exercise of power by Congress; but taking into view the whole opinion of the court and the reasoning by which they have come to that conclusion, I understand them to have decided that inasmuch as a bank is an appropriate means for carrying into effect the enumerated powers of the General Government, therefore the law incorporating it is in accordance with that provision of the Constitution which declares that Congress shall have power "to make all laws which shall be necessary and proper for carrying those powers into execution." Having satisfied themselves that the word *"necessary"* in the Constitution means *"needful," "requisite," "essential," "conducive to,"* and that *"a bank"* is a convenient, a useful, and essential instrument in the prosecution of the Government's "fiscal operations," they conclude that to "use one must be within the discretion of Congress" and that "the act to incorporate the Bank of the United States is a law made in pursuance of the Constitution;" "but," say they, *"where the law is not prohibited and is really calculated to effect any of the objects intrusted to the Government, to undertake here to inquire into the degree of its necessity would be to pass the line which circumscribes the judicial department and to tread on legislative ground."*

The principle here affirmed is that the "degree of its necessity," involving all the details of a banking institution, is a question exclusively for legislative consideration. A bank is constitutional, but it is the province of the Legislature to determine whether this or that particular power, privilege, or exemption is "necessary and proper" to enable the bank to discharge its duties to the Government, and from their decision there is no appeal to the courts of justice. Under the decision of the Supreme Court, therefore, it is the exclusive province of Congress and the President to decide whether the particular features of this act are *necessary* and *proper* in order to enable the bank to perform conveniently and efficiently the public duties assigned to it as a fiscal agent, and therefore constitutional, or *unnecessary* and *improper*, and therefore unconstitutional.

Without commenting on the general principle affirmed by the Supreme Court, let us examine the details of this act in accordance with the rule of legislative action which they have laid down. It will be found that many of the powers and privileges conferred on it can not be supposed necessary for the purpose for which it is proposed to be created, and are not, therefore, means necessary to attain the end in view, and consequently not justified by the Constitution.

The original act of incorporation, section 21, enacts "that no other bank shall be established by any future law of the United States during the continuance of the corporation hereby created, for which the faith of the United States is hereby pledged: *Provided*, Congress may renew existing charters for banks within the District of Columbia not increasing the capital thereof, and may also establish any other bank or banks in said District with capitals not exceeding in the whole $6,000,000 if they shall deem it expedient." This provision is continued in force by the act before me fifteen years from the ad of March, 1836.

If Congress possessed the power to establish one bank, they had power to establish more than one if in their opinion two or more banks had been "necessary" to facilitate the execution of the powers delegated to them in the Constitution. If they possessed the power to establish a second bank, it was a power derived from the Constitution to be exercised from time to time, and at any time when the interests of the country or the emergencies of the Government might make it expedient. It was possessed by one Congress as well as another, and by all Congresses alike, and alike at every session. But the Congress of 1816 have taken it away from their successors for twenty years, and the Congress of 1832 proposes to abolish it for fifteen years more. It can not be *"necessary"* or *"proper"* for Congress to barter away or divest themselves of any of the powers vested in them by the Constitution to be exercised for the public good. It is not "necessary" to the efficiency of the bank, nor is it *"proper"* in relation to themselves and their successors. They may *properly* use the discretion vested in them, but they may not limit the discretion of their successors. This restriction on themselves and grant of a monopoly to the bank is therefore unconstitutional.

In another point of view this provision is a palpable attempt to amend the Constitution by an act of legislation. The Constitution declares that "the Congress shall have power to exercise exclusive legislation in all cases whatsoever" over the District of Columbia. Its constitutional power, therefore, to establish banks in the District of Columbia and increase their capital at will is unlimited and uncontrollable by any other power than that which gave authority to the Constitution. Yet this act declares that Congress shall not increase the capital of existing banks, nor create other banks with capitals exceeding in the whole $6,000,000. The Constitution declares that Congress *shall* have power to exercise exclusive legislation over this District *"in all cases whatsoever,"* and this act declares they shall not. Which is the supreme law of the land? This provision can not be *"necessary"* or *"proper"* or *constitutional* unless the absurdity be admitted that whenever it be "necessary and proper" in the opinion of Congress they have a right to barter away one portion of the powers vested in them by the Constitution as a means of executing the rest.

On two subjects only does the Constitution recognize in Congress the power to grant exclusive privileges or monopolies. It declares that "Congress shall have power to promote the progress of science and useful arts by securing for limited times to authors and inventors the exclusive right to their respective writings and discoveries." Out of this express delegation of power have grown our laws of patents and copyrights. As the Constitution expressly delegates to Congress the power to grant exclusive privileges in these cases as the means of executing the substantive power "to promote the progress of science and useful arts," it is consistent with the fair rules of construction to conclude that such a power was not intended to be granted as a means of accomplishing any other end. On every other subject which comes within the scope of Congressional power there is an ever-living discretion in the use of proper means, which can not be restricted or abolished without an amendment of the Constitution. Every act of Congress, therefore, which attempts by grants of monopolies or sale of exclusive privileges for a limited time, or a time without limit, to restrict or extinguish its own discretion in the choice of means to execute its delegated powers is equivalent to a legislative amendment of the Constitution, and palpably unconstitutional.

This act authorizes and encourages transfers of its stock to foreigners and grants them an exemption from all State and national taxation. So far from being *"necessary and proper"* that the bank should possess this power to make it a safe and efficient agent of the Government in its fiscal operations, it is calculated to convert the Bank of the United States

into a foreign bank, to impoverish our people in time of peace, to disseminate a foreign influence through every section of the Republic, and in war to endanger our independence.

The several States reserved the power at the formation of the Constitution to regulate and control titles and transfers of real property, and most, if not all, of them have laws disqualifying aliens from acquiring or holding lands within their limits. But this act, in disregard of the undoubted right of the States to prescribe such disqualifications, gives to aliens stockholders in this bank an interest and title, as members of the corporation, to all the real property it may acquire within any of the States of this Union. This privilege granted to aliens is not *"necessary"* to enable the bank to perform its public duties, nor in any sense *"proper,"* because it is vitally subversive of the rights of the States.

The Government of the United States have no constitutional power to purchase lands within the States except "for the erection of forts, magazines, arsenals, dockyards, and other needful buildings," and even for these objects only "by the consent of the legislature of the State in which the same shall be." By making themselves stockholders in the bank and granting to the corporation the power to purchase lands for other purposes they assume a power not granted in the Constitution and grant to others what they do not themselves possess. It is not *necessary* to the receiving, safe-keeping, or transmission of the funds of the Government that the bank should possess this power, and it is not *proper* that Congress should thus enlarge the powers delegated to them in the Constitution.

The old Bank of the United States possessed a capital of only $11,000,000, which was found fully sufficient to enable it with dispatch and safety to perform all the functions required of it by the Government. The capital of the present bank is $35,000,000—at least twenty-four more than experience has proved to be *necessary* to enable a bank to perform its public functions. The public debt which existed during the period of the old bank and on the establishment of the new has been nearly paid off, and our revenue will soon be reduced. This increase of capital is therefore not for public but for private purposes.

The Government is the only *"proper"* judge where its agents should reside and keep their offices, because it best knows where their presence will be "necessary." It can not, therefore, be *"necessary"* or *"proper"* to authorize the bank to locate branches where it pleases to perform the public service, without consulting the Government, and contrary to its will. The principle laid down by the Supreme Court concedes that Congress can not establish a bank for purposes of private speculation and gain, but only as a means of executing the delegated powers of the General Government. By the same principle a branch bank can not constitutionally be established for other than public purposes. The power which this act gives to establish two branches in any State, without the injunction or request of the Government and for other than public purposes, is not *"necessary"* to the due *execution* of the powers delegated to Congress.

The bonus which is exacted from the bank is a confession upon the face of the act that the powers granted by it are greater than are *"necessary"* to its character of a fiscal agent. The Government does not tax its officers and agents for the privilege of serving it. The bonus of a million and a half required by the original charter and that of three millions proposed by this act are not exacted for the privilege of giving "the necessary facilities for transferring the public funds from place to place within the United States or the Territories thereof, and for distributing the same in payment of the public creditors without charging commission or claiming allowance on account of the difference of exchange," as required by the act of incorporation, but for something more beneficial to the stockholders. The original act declares that it (the bonus) is granted "in consideration of the exclusive privileges and benefits conferred by this act upon the said bank," and the act before me declares it to be "in consideration of the exclusive benefits and privileges continued by this act to the said corporation for fifteen years, as aforesaid." It is therefore for "exclusive privileges and benefits" conferred for their own use and emolument, and not for the advantage of the Government, that a bonus is exacted. These surplus powers for which the bank is required to pay can not surely be *"necessary"* to make it the fiscal agent of the Treasury. If they were, the exaction of a bonus for them would not be *"proper."*

It is maintained by some that the bank is a means of executing the constitutional power "to coin money and regulate the value thereof." Congress have established a mint to coin money and passed laws to regulate the value thereof. The money so coined, with its value so regulated, and such foreign coins as Congress may adopt are the only currency known to the Constitution. But if they have other power to regulate the currency, it was conferred to be exercised by themselves, and not to be transferred to a corporation. If the bank be established for that purpose, with a char-

ter unalterable without its consent, Congress have parted with their power for a term of years, during which the Constitution is a dead letter. It is neither necessary nor proper to transfer its legislative power to such a bank, and therefore unconstitutional.

By its silence, considered in connection with the decision of the Supreme Court in the case of McCulloch against the State of Maryland, this act takes from the States the power to tax a portion of the banking business carried on within their limits, in subversion of one of the strongest barriers which secured them against Federal encroachments. Banking, like farming, manufacturing, or any other occupation or profession, is a *business*, the right to follow which is not originally derived from the laws. Every citizen and every company of citizens in all of our States possessed the right until the State legislatures deemed it good policy to prohibit private banking by law. If the prohibitory State laws were now repealed, every citizen would again possess the right. The State banks are a qualified restoration of the right which has been taken away by the laws against banking, guarded by such provisions and limitations as in the opinion of the State legislatures the public interest requires. These corporations, unless there be an exemption in their charter, are, like private bankers and banking companies, subject to State taxation. The manner in which these taxes shall be laid depends wholly on legislative discretion. It may be upon the bank, upon the stock, upon the profits, or in any other mode which the sovereign power shall will.

Upon the formation of the Constitution the States guarded their taxing power with peculiar jealousy. They surrendered it only as it regards imports and exports. In relation to every other object within their jurisdiction, whether persons, property, business, or professions, it was secured in as ample a manner as it was before possessed. All persons, though United States officers, are liable to a poll tax by the States within which they reside. The lands of the United States are liable to the usual land tax, except in the new States, from whom agreements that they will not tax unsold lands are exacted when they are admitted into the Union. Horses, wagons, any beasts or vehicles, tools, or property belonging to private citizens, though employed in the service of the United States, are subject to State taxation. Every private business, whether carried on by an officer of the General Government or not, whether it be mixed with public concerns or not, even if it be carried on by the Government of the United States itself, separately or in partnership, falls within the scope of the taxing power of the State. Nothing comes more fully within it than banks and the business of banking, by whomsoever instituted and carried on. Over this whole subject-matter it is just as absolute, unlimited, and uncontrollable as if the Constitution had never been adopted, because in the formation of that instrument it was reserved without qualification.

The principle is conceded that the States can not rightfully tax the operations of the General Government. They can not tax the money of the Government deposited in the State banks, nor the agency of those banks in remitting it; but will any man maintain that their mere selection to perform this public service for the General Government would exempt the State banks and their ordinary business from State taxation? Had the United States, instead of establishing a bank at Philadelphia, employed a private banker to keep and transmit their funds, would it have deprived Pennsylvania of the right to tax his bank and his usual banking operations? It will not be pretended. Upon what principal, then, are the banking establishments of the Bank of the United States and their usual banking operations to be exempted from taxation? It is not their public agency or the deposits of the Government which the States claim a right to tax, but their banks and their banking powers, instituted and exercised within State jurisdiction for their private emolument—those powers and privileges for which they pay a bonus, and which the States tax in their own banks. The exercise of these powers within a State, no matter by whom or under what authority, whether by private citizens in their original right, by corporate bodies created by the States, by foreigners or the agents of foreign governments located within their limits, forms a legitimate object of State taxation. From this and like sources, from the persons, property, and business that are found residing, located, or carried on under their jurisdiction, must the States, since the surrender of their right to raise a revenue from imports and exports, draw all the money necessary for the support of their governments and the maintenance of their independence. There is no more appropriate subject of taxation than banks, banking, and bank stocks, and none to which the States ought more pertinaciously to cling.

It can not be *necessary* to the character of the bank as a fiscal agent of the Government that its private business should be exempted from that taxation to which all the State banks are liable, nor can I conceive it *"proper"* that the substantive and most essential powers reserved by the States shall be thus attacked and annihilated as a means of executing the powers delegated to the General Government. It may be safely assumed that none of those sages who had an agency in forming or adopting our Constitution ever imagined that any portion of the taxing power of the States not prohibited to them nor delegated to Congress was to be swept away and annihilated as a means of executing certain powers delegated to Congress.

If our power over means is so absolute that the Supreme Court will not call in question the constitutionality of an act of Congress the subject of which "is not prohibited, and is really calculated to effect any of the objects intrusted to the Government," although, as in the case before me, it takes away powers expressly granted to Congress and rights scrupulously reserved to the States, it becomes us to proceed in our legislation with the utmost caution. Though not directly, our own powers and the rights of the States may be indirectly legislated away in the use of means to execute substantive powers. We may not enact that Congress shall not have the power of exclusive legislation over the District of Columbia, but we may pledge the faith of the United States that as a means of executing other powers it shall not be exercised for twenty years or forever. We may not pass an act prohibiting the States to tax the banking business carried on within their limits, but we may, as a means of executing our powers over other objects, place that business in the hands of our agents and then declare it exempt from State taxation in their hands. Thus may our own powers and the rights of the States, which we can not directly curtail or invade, be frittered away and extinguished in the use of means employed by us to execute other powers. That a bank of the United States, competent to all the duties which may be required by the Government, might be so organized as not to infringe on our own delegated powers or the reserved rights of the States I do not entertain a doubt. Had the Executive been called upon to furnish the project of such an institution, the duty would have been cheerfully performed. In the absence of such a call it was obviously proper that he should confine himself to pointing out those prominent features in the act presented which in his opinion make it incompatible with the Constitution and sound policy. A general discussion will now take place, eliciting new light and settling important principles; and a new Congress, elected in the midst of such discussion, and furnishing an equal representation of the people according to the last census, will bear to the Capitol the verdict of public opinion, and, I doubt not, bring this important question to a satisfactory result.

Under such circumstances the bank comes forward and asks a renewal of its charter for a term of fifteen years upon conditions which not only operate as a gratuity to the stockholders of many millions of dollars, but will sanction any abuses and legalize any encroachments.

Suspicions are entertained and charges are made of gross abuse and violation of its charter. An investigation unwillingly conceded and so restricted in time as necessarily to make it incomplete and unsatisfactory discloses enough to excite suspicion and alarm. In the practices of the principal bank partially unveiled, in the absence of important witnesses, and in numerous charges confidently made and as yet wholly uninvestigated there was enough to induce a majority of the committee of investigation—a committee which was selected from the most able and honorable members of the House of Representatives—to recommend a suspension of further action upon the bill and a prosecution of the inquiry. As the charter had yet four years to run, and as a renewal now was not necessary to the successful prosecution of its business, it was to have been expected that the bank itself, conscious of its purity and proud of its character, would have withdrawn its application for the present, and demanded the severest scrutiny into all its transactions. In their declining to do so there seems to be an additional reason why the functionaries of the Government should proceed with less haste and more caution in the renewal of their monopoly.

The bank is professedly established as an agent of the executive branch of the Government, and its constitutionality is maintained on that ground. Neither upon the propriety of present action nor upon the provisions of this act was the Executive consulted. It has had no opportunity to say that it neither needs nor wants an agent clothed with such powers and favored by such exemptions. There is nothing in its legitimate functions which makes it necessary or proper. Whatever interest or influence, whether public or private, has given birth to this act, it can not be found either in the wishes or necessities of the executive department, by which present action is deemed premature, and the powers conferred upon its agent not only unnecessary, but dangerous to the Government and country.

It is to be regretted that the rich and powerful too often bend the acts of government to their selfish purposes. Distinctions in society will always exist under every just government. Equality of talents, of education, or of wealth can not be produced by

human institutions. In the full enjoyment of the gifts of Heaven and the fruits of superior industry, economy, and virtue, every man is equally entitled to protection by law; but when the laws undertake to add to these natural and just advantages artificial distinctions, to grant titles, gratuities, and exclusive privileges, to make the rich richer and the potent more powerful, the humble members of society—the farmers, mechanics, and laborers—who have neither the time nor the means of securing like favors to themselves, have a right to complain of the injustice of their Government. There are no necessary evils in government. Its evils exist only in its abuses. If it would confine itself to equal protection, and, as Heaven does its rains, shower its favors alike on the high and the low, the rich and the poor, it would be an unqualified blessing. In the act before me there seems to be a wide and unnecessary departure from these just principles.

Nor is our Government to be maintained or our Union preserved by invasions of the rights and powers of the several States. In thus attempting to make our General Government strong we make it weak. Its true strength consists in leaving individuals and States as much as possible to themselves—in making itself felt, not in its power, but in its beneficence; not in its control, but in its protection; not in binding the States more closely to the center, but leaving each to move unobstructed in its proper orbit.

Experience should teach us wisdom. Most of the difficulties our Government now encounters and most of the dangers which impend over our Union have sprung from an abandonment of the legitimate objects of Government by our national legislation, and the adoption of such principles as are embodied in this act. Many of our rich men have not been content with equal protection and equal benefits, but have besought us to make them richer by act of Congress. By attempting to gratify their desires we have in the results of our legislation arrayed section against section, interest against interest, and man against man, in a fearful commotion which threatens to shake the foundations of our Union. It is time to pause in our career to review our principles, and if possible revive that devoted patriotism and spirit of compromise which distinguished the sages of the Revolution and the fathers of our Union. If we can not at once, in justice to interests vested under improvident legislation, make our Government what it ought to be, we can at least take a stand against all new grants of monopolies and exclusive privileges, against any prostitution of our Government to the advancement of the few at the expense of the many, and in favor of compromise and gradual reform in our code of laws and system of political economy.

I have now done my duty to my country. If sustained by my fellow citizens, I shall be grateful and happy; if not, I shall find in the motives which impel me ample grounds for contentment and peace. In the difficulties which surround us and the dangers which threaten our institutions there is cause for neither dismay nor alarm. For relief and deliverance let us firmly rely on that kind Providence which I am sure watches with peculiar care over the destinies of our Republic, and on the intelligence and wisdom of our countrymen. Through His abundant goodness and heir patriotic devotion our liberty and Union will be preserved.

—ANDREW JACKSON.

would be poverty and utter desolation; her citizens, in despair, would emigrate to more fortunate regions, and the whole frame and constitution of her civil polity be impaired and deranged, if not dissolved entirely.

Deeply impressed with these considerations, the representatives of the good people of this commonwealth, anxiously desiring to live in peace with their fellow-citizens, and to do all that in them lies to preserve and perpetuate the union of the states, and liberties of which it is the surest pledge, but feeling it to be their bounden duty to expose and resist all encroachments upon the true spirit of the Constitution, lest an apparent acquiescence in the system of protecting duties should be drawn into pre- cedent — do, in the name of the commonwealth of South Carolina, claim to enter upon the Journal of the Senate their *protest* against it as uncon- stitutional, oppressive, and unjust.

PRESIDENT JACKSON'S PROCLAMATION,

OF THE 10TH DECEMBER, 1833,

CONCERNING

THE ORDINANCE OF SOUTH CAROLINA. ON THE SUBJECT OF THE TARIFF,

ON THE 24TH NOVEMBER, 1832.

WHEREAS a convention assembled in the state of South Carolina have passed an ordinance, by which they declare " that the several acts, and parts of acts, of the Congress of the United States, purporting to be laws for the imposing duties and imposts on the importation of foreign com- modities, and now having actual operation and effect within the United States," and more especially, two acts for the same purposes, passed on the 29th of May, 1828, and on the 14th of July, 1832, " are unauthorized by the Constitution of the United States, and violate the true meaning and intent thereof, and are null and void, and no law," not binding on the citizens of that state or its officers; and by the said ordinance it is further declared to be unlawful for any of the constituted authorities of the state, or of the United States, to enforce the payment of the duties imposed by the said acts within the same state, and that it is the duty of the legis- lature to pass such laws as may be necessary to give full effect to the said ordinance:

Andrew Jackson's Proclamation to the People of South Carolina (Library of Congress)

SOUTH CAROLINA ORDINANCE OF NULLIFICATION AND ANDREW JACKSON'S PROCLAMATION REGARDING NULLIFICATION

"We will not submit to the application of force on the part of the federal government, to reduce this State to obedience."

Overview

The issue of tariffs had been the subject of controversy since 1819, when Congress began to consider tariffs a form of protection for manufacturing rather than purely a revenue-raising measure. When Congress passed the Tariff of 1832, South Carolinians, who had long opposed the tariff, organized a campaign to reject the legislation. Nullifiers rode the issue to victory in the state elections in October, defeating unionists and gaining a two-thirds control of the legislature. In a special session, legislators called for a convention, which convened November 19. A committee drafted an Ordinance of Nullification, authored by William Harper, as well as addresses explaining the ordinance. Convention delegates passed on November 24 the Ordinance of Nullification, which declared the tariffs of 1828 and 1832 null in the state as of February 1, 1833. It pledged that any effort by the federal government to enforce the tariff would be met by secession.

In his annual message to Congress, Andrew Jackson called for reduction in the tariff on December 4, in accordance with states' rights principles; just days later, however, he issued the Proclamation regarding Nullification. This proclamation rejected the nullifiers' claims that the states retain sovereignty and the right of secession under the Constitution. Jackson maintained that such action was treason against the federal government. By rejecting the idea that the federal nation was formed by a compact of states, Jackson undercut his credibility as a states' rights champion. It was his determination to put down what he viewed as treason with the force of the federal military, however, that caused dissention in Jackson's own party, the Democratic Party, and strengthened his political opposition.

Context

The South Carolina Ordinance of Nullification emerged from a climate of economic and political strain that characterized the state following the War of 1812. Economically, cotton growers in the state suffered from a decline in

cotton prices. While state politicians like John C. Calhoun approved of the tariffs passed in 1816, their nationalism was conditional, linked to issues of national defense. With an economy dependent on the export of rice and cotton, South Carolinians generally favored free trade. With the passage of the Tariff of 1824 and the collapse in cotton prices in 1825, public support for nationalism declined in the state, while political leaders criticized a tariff policy that benefited northeastern and western manufacturing and threatened South Carolina's export trade with the prospect of foreign retaliation. During the same period, many whites in the Carolina Low Country were anxious about the stability of slavery. In a state where African American slaves had long been in the majority, white residents were terrified to learn of a planned uprising led by Denmark Vesey, a free black from Charleston. The alleged conspirators were hanged, but elites organized to enforce laws against black residents, including the imprisonment of all black seamen arriving in state ports. When the law was successfully challenged in the federal circuit court, the state legislature defied the ruling.

Congressional debates over increased woolen duties and colonization kept the tariff and slavery at the forefront of politics in the state. Both issues were important in convincing South Carolina politicians that the state was threatened by the tyranny of the majority. When Congress passed a tariff increase in 1828, to many in South Carolina it seemed that the state was being taxed to benefit northeastern and western interests. Tariff opponents declared the legislation unconstitutional because it destroyed rather than regulated commerce and it illegally promoted industry rather than raising revenue. Calhoun expounded on these theories in an anonymously written pamphlet, arguing that states had the authority to determine the constitutionality of legislation because each state was sovereign before the individual states ratified the Constitution. The Union, therefore, was a compact of individual states.

Knowledge of Calhoun's authorship quickly spread, contributing to the vice president's growing breech with Jackson. Jackson, facing reelection in 1832, had come out in favor of the Tariff of 1832. At the same time, nullifiers in South Carolina had gained control of the state legislature and called for a convention on the tariff issue. The Ordi-

1822

- The Denmark Vesey conspiracy contributes to Low Country planters' anxiety over slavery.

1823

- **July 24**
The South Carolina Association is formed in Charleston by Low Country elites to enforce laws against black residents, including the imprisonment of black seamen arriving in South Carolina ports.

- **August 7**
In *Elkinson v. Deliesseline* before the U.S. Circuit Court in South Carolina, Judge William Johnson rules that federal treaties are the supreme law of the land and trump state laws, including the Negro Seamen Act of 1823.

1825

- **December 9**
The South Carolina legislature considers resolutions, which are passed by both houses, declaring tariff and internal improvements unconstitutional.

1827

- **July 2**
Thomas Cooper, president of South Carolina College, addresses an antitariff meeting at Columbia and questions the wisdom of South Carolina's position within the Union.

- **October 22**
Robert J. Turnbull collects previously published essays with new essays in *The Crisis; or, Essays on the Usurpations of the Federal Government*, in which he opposes an increase in the duty on woolens and federal aid to colonization, which are issues being debated in the U.S. Congress.

1828

- The so-called Tariff of Abominations (Tariff of 1828) is passed.

- **Fall**
John Calhoun anonymously writes *South Carolina Exposition and Protest* at the request of the state legislature.

nance of Nullification was passed on November 24. In Jackson's message to Congress weeks later, he seemed to reverse his course on the tariff, calling for its reduction to revenue levels. In the same address, he advocated policies that were staunchly states' rights. Just days later, however, he addressed the Ordinance of Nullification in his Proclamation regarding Nullification. The document, authored by his secretary of state, Edward Livingston, embodied Jackson's commitment to the idea of perpetual union and the rejection of the idea of undivided state sovereignty. Jackson suggested instead that the Constitution was formed by the people, rather than the states. He also threatened to use force to uphold federal policies in South Carolina, giving the nullifiers their needed ammunition. When Jackson sent what has been called his "Force Bill" message to Congress, he sought the means to collect the tariff and requested expedient measures for calling on the state militia and federal military to enforce the laws. Public opinion throughout the southern states, and in many northern states, focused on the threat of military force and what seemed like a dangerous expansion of executive power. Nullifiers used this issue to their advantage, shifting debate from the constitutionality of nullification to Jackson's threat of force, thereby gaining support for their political position.

About the Author

Governor James Hamilton presided over the South Carolina Nullification Convention. The delegates included nullifiers Robert Hayne, Robert J. Turnbull, Robert Barnwell, and William Harper. Harper, former speaker of the South Carolina House of Representatives and judge on the court of appeals, wrote the Ordinance of Nullification. Secretary of State Edward Livingston, in consultation with Jackson, wrote Jackson's Proclamation of Nullification. Livingston was a native of New York and a former senator from Louisiana who had drafted the state's legal code.

Explanation and Analysis of the Document

♦ South Carolina Ordinance of Nullification

The Ordinance of Nullification states that Congress has acted unconstitutionally in passing tariff laws that seek to protect certain industries and individuals at the expense of others. The Constitution gives Congress the power to pass tariffs to raise revenue, but not for any other purpose, including the protection of domestic manufacturing of particular individuals involved in such industries. The ordinance proceeds to declare that the tariffs passed on May 19, 1828, and on July 14, 1832, are null and void. It further states that South Carolina and its people are neither bound by these laws nor required to pay the tariffs. Having declared the laws null, the ordinance turns to the specific actions the state will take if the legislation is not repealed by February 1, 1833. In this case, the legislature of South Carolina will pass all necessary legislation to prevent the federal government from collecting tariffs. Any efforts to appeal state court decisions relating to the nullification to the United States Supreme Court will be considered in contempt of state courts. The ordinance mandates that all officeholders in the state and jurors, with the exception of the legislators, take an oath to uphold the ordinance or lose their positions. Further, if a court case or a piece of legislation related to the ordinance is under consideration, individuals will have to take an oath to uphold "the true intent and meaning" of the ordinance.

The ordinance closes with a pledge that the people of South Carolina will not submit to the federal government's force. If Congress passes legislation authorizing the federal government to use the army or navy against the state, to close its ports, to interfere with trading vessels, or to enforce the tariff, South Carolina will withdraw from the Union and organize a separate government under their rights as a sovereign state.

◆ **Jackson's Proclamation Regarding Nullification**

President Jackson's Proclamation regarding Nullification begins by stating that the South Carolina convention advocates a course of action contrary to South Carolinians responsibilities as citizens, which violates the Constitution. Appealing to Revolutionary heritage, the patriotism of South Carolinians, and the idea that the Union has been sanctioned by God, the proclamation outlines Jackson's reasons for nullification. Deeming nullification "strange," the proclamation argues that a state cannot be a part of the Union and reject federal laws. The proclamation defines the relationship between the people and the federal government as a "social compact," one that dates from colonial times, and it maintains the supremacy of federal laws and treaties over state and local interests. It also rejects the argument that South Carolina is uniquely and unfairly burdened by the tariff, noting that states have at times shared unequally in the burden of sustaining the federal government. It also suggests the improbability that the nullifiers have found a new and legitimate right within the Constitution.

The Proclamation regarding Nullification focuses on a significant weakness in the Ordinance of Nullification, the argument that the tariff legislation is intended to benefit manufacturing interests and is therefore unconstitutional. It suggests that it is impossible to divine intent and that it is "an absurd and dangerous doctrine" to believe so. Further, if the Constitution has within it the power to both make and disobey laws, then it is "self-destroying." The proclamation, again appealing to Revolutionary memory, states that the Founders could not draft a document with such a flaw. The document notes that the Constitution gives Congress the right to pass revenue legislation and suggests that, even if it does not and people have a choice between allowing the states or Congress to determine revenue policy, the rights of the people would be protected by their representation in Congress. It also charges the nullifiers with disregarding the constitutional provisions for the judiciary as well as with nullifying the judiciary act by prohibiting an appeal to federal courts.

Time Line

1830

■ **January 19**
Senator Robert Hayne, South Carolina, begins a debate with Senator Daniel Webster over the disposition of federal lands, which evolves into a debate over state sovereignty and the power of the federal government.

1832

■ **October 8–9**
The state legislative elections result in victory for nullifiers and defeat for unionists.

■ **November 19–24**
The Nullification Convention convenes in South Carolina and adopts the Ordinance of Nullification by a vote of 136 to 26.

■ **November 27**
The South Carolina legislature convenes.

■ **December 4**
In his annual message to Congress, Jackson recommends a tariff reduction.

■ **December 10**
A unionist convention at Columbia is unable to agree on how to oppose the Ordinance of Nullification.

■ **December 10**
Jackson issues the Proclamation regarding Nullification.

■ **December 20**
South Carolina's governor, Robert Hayne, issues a proclamation focusing on Jackson's threat to states' rights, not on the tariff itself.

1833

■ **January 16**
Jackson sends the "Force Bill" message to Congress.

■ **January 21**
The Senate Judiciary Committee recommends legislation to support Jackson.

■ **January 21**
A meeting in Charleston extends the date for voluntary compliance until the end of the March congressional session.

Time Line

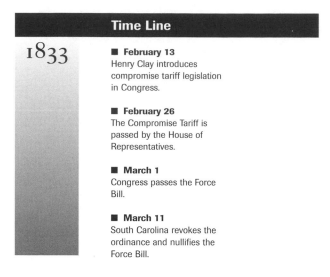

1833

- **February 13**
  Henry Clay introduces compromise tariff legislation in Congress.

- **February 26**
  The Compromise Tariff is passed by the House of Representatives.

- **March 1**
  Congress passes the Force Bill.

- **March 11**
  South Carolina revokes the ordinance and nullifies the Force Bill.

The proclamation refutes the nullifiers' theory of government, arguing that the Constitution has produced a nation, not a league of sovereign states. It agrees that the government is formed by a compact, as the nullifiers maintain, but argues that a compact is a "binding obligation" that the parties to it cannot depart from it and that the federal government possesses the means to execute its laws. The proclamation tries to affirm Jackson's respect for states' rights, while supporting the power of the federal government. It takes up two propositions: the argument that states retain sovereignty when entering into the Constitution and the right of state secession. Repeating the argument that the people created a union that was made more perfect only by the Constitution, the proclamation rejects claims of state sovereignty and the right of a state to remove itself from its responsibilities under the Constitution. It denies the right of secession because a government formed for the benefit of all cannot permit a single state to involve others "in these and countless other evils." The proclamation blames nullification on a small majority of its citizens who demand citizens either repeal the tariff or accede to secession without exhausting constitutional means to redress grievances through a convention of the states. Finally, observing that the governor suggests raising an army to effect secession, the proclamation warns the people of the state not to obey the "illegal and disorganizing ordinance of the convention."

The final sections adopt Jackson's personal voice, identifying South Carolina as the president's native state. Jackson's role as president is akin to a father trying to prevent his children from approaching danger. The proclamation acknowledges that the tariff economically hurts South Carolina but maintains that the claims are exaggerated and charges nullifiers with using passion, pride, courage, and injury to manipulate public opinion and erroneously link nullification with the Revolutionary right to oppose unconstitutional laws. The people of South Carolina neither are the heirs of Revolutionaries' efforts to defend liberty nor are they oppressed by something akin to colonial vassalage, but instead they are "free members of a flourishing and happy

Union." Noting that the nation is attempting to reduce the tariff, the proclamation catalogues the benefits of the Union, including promoting commerce, protecting the frontier, and advancing arts and education. The proclamation contrasts these images with those of an independent South Carolina, warring with its neighbors, divided in opinion, and fearful of insurrections. Appealing to the Revolutionary heritage of South Carolinians, it calls upon its people to reset their course and tell their leaders that they will not tolerate disunion and will not take up arms in its cause.

In its conclusion, the document addresses not the people of South Carolina but the citizens of the United States, framing the nullification controversy as a threat to national prosperity, the country's political existence, and the cause of free governments throughout the world. It promises that Jackson will use "moderate but firm measures" to preserve the Union but that if force is necessary, it will not be the fault of the federal government. In return, it appeals to the citizens of the United States for their support and to the "Great Ruler of nations" for his continued blessings and to show the nullifiers the error of their ways so that the divinely sanctioned Union will be preserved.

Audience

The audience of both documents was broad. The ordinance sought both to solidify support among South Carolinians and other southern states and to shape legislative policy. Jackson's Proclamation regarding Nullification was directed to the people of South Carolina but to a national audience as well, including politicians who flirted with the doctrine in the other southern states, unionists in the South to whom Jackson wanted to assure of federal support, and protectionists who supported the tariff.

Impact

Jackson's Proclamation regarding Nullification alienated some Democrats, especially in the South, who viewed it as a repudiation of states' rights and, as such, as undercutting issues central to the party, such as opposition to federal aid to internal improvements and federal banking. In addition, many southern state legislatures rejected the validity of nullification. National Republicans, including many of Jackson's political opponents, heartily approved of the proclamation. The political landscape shifted, however, with Jackson's attempt to gain congressional authority for using the military against the nullifiers. The Force Bill politically isolated Jackson, split the Democratic Party, and strengthened the nullifiers' position by uniting those who disagreed with nullification but who feared the expansion of executive power at the expense of states' rights. Nullifiers in South Carolina had not repudiated the doctrine and had achieved tariff reduction, which they used to gain political control over the state. In Congress, the nullification crisis precipitated an alliance between national Republicans and nullifiers, including Clay and Calhoun, resulting in

> *"And we, the people of South Carolina, to the end that it may be fully understood by the government of the United States, and the people of the co-States, that we are determined to maintain this our ordinance and declaration, at every hazard, do further declare that we will not submit to the application of force on the part of the federal government, to reduce this State to obedience ... and that the people of this State will henceforth hold themselves absolved from all further obligation to maintain or preserve their political connection with the people of the other States; and will forthwith proceed to organize a separate government, and do all other acts and things which sovereign and independent States may of right do."*

(Ordinance of Nullification)

> *"I consider, then, the power to annul a law of the United States, assumed by one State,* incompatible with the existence of the Union, contradicted expressly by the letter of the Constitution, unauthorized by its spirit, inconsistent with every principle on which It was founded, and destructive of the great object for which it was formed."

(Proclamation regarding Nullification)

a compromise tariff that reduced the tariff incrementally over nine years and bound the federal government to using the tariff for revenue only from 1842 on. It also contributed to the formation of the Whig Party by uniting Jackson's opponents. The crisis did not legitimize nullification but instead strengthened support for states' rights interpretations of the Constitution, the right of secession, and calls to protect the rights of minority, specifically those who had an interest in the institution of slavery, from the majority.

Related Documents

"Force Bill of 1833." TeachingAmericanHistory.org Web site. http://www.teachingamericanhistory.com/library/index.asp?document=844. Accessed on January 10, 2008. Passed by Congress on March 2, 1833, after Jackson's message to Congress, the Force Bill allowed for the establishment of floating customhouses, the collection of customs duties in cash, and the trial of tariff violations in federal courts. It also gave Jackson the power to use the federal military and to call out the state militia to put down insurrection, a power Jackson already had. In responding to the bill's passage, Jackson denied a state's right to secede.

"The Kentucky Resolutions of 1798." The Constitution Society Web site. http://www.constitution.org/cons/kent1798.htm. Accessed on November 22, 2007. Passed by the Kentucky state legislature in November 1798 in reaction to the Alien and Sedition Acts, they were actually written by Thomas Jefferson. The resolutions were an early expression of states' rights theory in that they rejected Federalists' broad interpretation of the Constitution and argued that the Constitution provided for a compact of states.

"The Old Senate Chamber: Hayne Webster Debate, 1830." United States Senate Web site. http://www.senate.gov/vtour/webhayn.htm. Accessed on November 22, 2007. The Hayne-Webster debate occurred in the Senate in January 1830 when Robert Hayne of South Carolina and Daniel Webster of Massachusetts debated the constitutional nature of the Union. Originating from a debate over public lands, it evolved into Hayne's position that the Union consisted of a compact of sovereign states and Webster's declaration that the Union was indivisible.

"South Carolina Exposition and Protest." In *The Papers of John C. Calhoun*, Vol. 10: *1825–1829*, eds. Clyde N. Wilson and W. Edwin Hemphill. Columbia: University of South Carolina Press, 1977, pp. 442–539. The Exposition and Protest consists of two documents written during the South Carolina legislature's 1828 session that considered the tariff. The Exposition, or essay, was written by John C. Calhoun at the request of the special legislative committee and finished in November 1828, although his authorship was not publicly known. In it he criticizes the tariff and articulates the theory of nullification. The Protest consists of the resolutions passed by both branches of the South Carolina legislature.

"Virginia Resolution of 1798." The Constitution Society Web site. http://www.constitution.org/cons/virg1798.htm. Accessed on November 22, 2007. This resolution was written by James Madison and passed by the Virginia state legislature in December 1798. Like the Kentucky Resolutions, the Virginia Resolution protested the Alien and Sedition Acts and argued for a compact theory of government. The Virginia Resolution was more vague, however, seeing collective state action as producing the Union and stopping short of endorsing separate state nullification.

Bibliography

■ Articles

Bolt, William K. "Founding Father and Rebellious Son: James Madison, John C. Calhoun, and the Use of Precedents." *American Nineteenth Century History* 53, no. 3 (Fall 2004): 1–27.

Ericson, David F. "The Nullification Crisis, American Republicanism, and the Force Bill Debate." *Journal of Southern History* 61, no. 2 (1995): 249–270.

Maier, Pauline. "The Road Not Taken: Nullification, John C. Calhoun, and the Revolutionary Tradition in South Carolina." *South Carolina Historical Magazine* 82, no. 1 (1981): 1–19.

Pease, Jane H., and William H. Pease. "The Economics and Politics of Charleston's Nullification Crisis." *Journal of Southern History* 47, no. 3 (August 1981): 335–362.

Ratcliffe, Donald J. "The Nullification Crisis, Southern Discontents, and the American Political Process." *American Nineteenth Century History* 1, no. 2 (Summer 2000): 1.

Stampp, Kenneth M. "The Concept of a Perpetual Union." *Journal of American History* 65, no. 1 (June 1978): 5–33.

Stewart, James Brewer. "'A Great Talking and Eating Machine': Patriarchy, Mobilization and the Dynamics of Nullification in South Carolina." *Civil War History* 27, no. 3 (September 1981): 197–220.

Wood, W. Kirk. "In Defense of the Republic: John C. Calhoun and State Interposition in South Carolina, 1776–1833." *Southern Studies* 10, nos. 1–2 (2003): 9–48.

■ Books

Ellis, Richard E. *The Union at Risk: Jacksonian Democracy, States' Rights and the Nullification Crisis.* New York: Oxford University Press, 1987.

Ericson, David F. *The Shaping of American Liberalism: The Debates over Ratification, Nullification, and Slavery.* Chicago: University of Chicago Press, 1993.

Freehling, William W. *Prelude to Civil War: The Nullification Controversy in South Carolina, 1818–1836.* New York: Harper and Row, 1965.

Niven, John. *John C. Calhoun and the Price of Union.* Baton Rouge: Louisiana State University Press, 1988.

Peterson, Merrill D. *Olive Branch and Sword: The Compromise of 1833.* Baton Rouge: Louisiana State University Press, 1982.

Remini, Robert V. *Andrew Jackson: The Course of American Democracy, 1833–1845.* Baltimore: Johns Hopkins University Press, 1998.

■ Web Sites

"1816-1860: The Second American Party System and the Tariff." Tax History Museum Web site.
    http://www.tax.org/Museum/1816-1860.htm. Accessed on November 21, 2007.

"Jacksonian Democracy:Nullification." Digital History Web site.
    http://www.digitalhistory.uh.edu/database/article_display.cfm? HHID=639. Accessed on November 21, 2007.

"Nullification Proclamation." Library of Congress "Primary Documents in American History" Web site.
    http://www.loc.gov/rr/program/bib/ourdocs/Nullification.html. Accessed on November 21, 2007.

—By Christine Dee

Questions for Further Study

1. What are the differences between how the ordinance and the proclamation interpret the formation of the Constitution and the nature of federal government?

2. How is the memory of the American Revolution used in both documents?

3. Did nullification enjoy public support among South Carolinians and among other southerners? How do we know?

4. Does nullification strengthen or weaken states' rights ideology?

5. What questions remain unanswered or unaddressed in these documents?

Glossary

affirmance	affirmation; support
coeval	being in existence for the same period of time
egress	exit; the act of leaving
fallacious	based on incorrect information or belief
imposts	taxes or other forms of imposed payments
ingress	the act of entering
profanation	the act of treating with disdain or disregard
redress	to correct or amend a wrong
refutation	demonstration of wrongness or error
remonstrances	protestations or objections
sanguinary	involving bloodshed
tariffs	duties on imports

SOUTH CAROLINA ORDINANCE OF NULLIFICATION

November 24, 1832

An ordinance to nullify certain acts of the Congress of the United States, purporting to be laws laying duties and imposts on the importation of foreign commodities.

Whereas the Congress of the United States by various acts, purporting to be acts laying duties and imposts on foreign imports, but in reality intended for the protection of domestic manufactures and the giving of bounties to classes and individuals engaged in particular employments, at the expense and to the injury and oppression of other classes and individuals, and by wholly exempting from taxation certain foreign commodities, such as are not produced or manufactured in the United States, to afford a pretext for imposing higher and excessive duties on articles similar to those intended to be protected, hath exceeded its just powers under the constitution, which confers on it no authority to afford such protection, and hath violated the true meaning and intent of the constitution, which provides for equality in imposing the burdens of taxation upon the several States and portions of the confederacy: And whereas the said Congress, exceeding its just power to impose taxes and collect revenue for the purpose of effecting and accomplishing the specific objects and purposes which the constitution of the United States authorizes it to effect and accomplish, hath raised and collected unnecessary revenue for objects unauthorized by the constitution.

We, therefore, the people of the State of South Carolina, in convention assembled, do declare and ordain and it is hereby declared and ordained, that the several acts and parts of acts of the Congress of the United States, purporting to be laws for the imposing of duties and imposts on the importation of foreign commodities, and now having actual operation and effect within the United States, and, more especially, an act entitled "An act in alteration of the several acts imposing duties on imports," approved on the nineteenth day of May, one thousand eight hundred and twenty-eight and also an act entitled "An act to alter and amend the several acts imposing duties on imports," approved on the fourteenth day of July, one thousand eight hundred and thirty-two, are unauthorized by the constitution of the United States, and violate the true meaning and intent thereof and are null, void, and no law, nor binding upon this State, its officers or citizens; and all promises, contracts, and obligations, made or entered into, or to be made or entered into, with purpose to secure the duties imposed by said acts, and all judicial proceedings which shall be hereafter had in affirmance thereof, are and shall be held utterly null and void.

And it is further ordained, that it shall not be lawful for any of the constituted authorities, whether of this State or of the United States, to enforce the payment of duties imposed by the said acts within the limits of this State; but it shall be the duty of the legislature to adopt such measures and pass such acts as may be necessary to give full effect to this ordinance, and to prevent the enforcement and arrest the operation of the said acts and parts of acts of the Congress of the United States within the limits of this State, from and after the first day of February next, and the duties of all other constituted authorities, and of all persons residing or being within the limits of this State, and they are hereby required and enjoined to obey and give effect to this ordinance, and such acts and measures of the legislature as may be passed or adopted in obedience thereto.

And it is further ordained, that in no case of law or equity, decided in the courts of this State, wherein shall be drawn in question the authority of this ordinance, or the validity of such act or acts of the legislature as may be passed for the purpose of giving effect thereto, or the validity of the aforesaid acts of Congress, imposing duties, shall any appeal be taken or allowed to the Supreme Court of the United States, nor shall any copy of the record be permitted or allowed for that purpose; and if any such appeal shall be attempted to be taken, the courts of this State shall proceed to execute and enforce their judgments according to the laws and usages of the State, without reference to such attempted appeal, and the person or persons attempting to take such appeal may be dealt with as for a contempt of the court.

And it is further ordained, that all persons now holding any office of honor, profit, or trust, civil or military, under this State (members of the legislature excepted), shall, within such time, and in such manner as the legislature shall prescribe, take an oath well and truly to obey, execute, and enforce this ordinance, and such act or acts of the legislature as may be passed in pursuance thereof, according to the true intent and meaning of the same, and on the neglect or omission of any such person or persons so to do, his or their office or offices shall be forthwith vacated, and shall be filled up as if such person or persons were dead or had resigned; and no person hereafter elected to any office of honor, profit, or trust, civil or military (members of the legislature excepted), shall, until the legislature shall otherwise provide and direct, enter on the execution of his office, or be he any respect competent to discharge the duties thereof until he shall, in like manner, have taken a similar oath; and no juror shall be impaneled in any of the courts of this State, in any cause in which shall be in question this ordinance, or any act of the legislature passed in pursuance thereof, unless he shall first, in addition to the usual oath, have taken an oath that he will well and truly obey, execute, and enforce this ordinance, and such act or acts of the legislature as may be passed to carry the same into operation and effect, according to the true intent and meaning thereof.

And we, the people of South Carolina, to the end that it may be fully understood by the government of the United States, and the people of the co-States, that we are determined to maintain this our ordinance and declaration, at every hazard, do further declare that we will not submit to the application of force on the part of the federal government, to reduce this State to obedience, but that we will consider the passage, by Congress, of any act authorizing the employment of a military or naval force against the State of South Carolina, her constitutional authorities or citizens; or any act abolishing or closing the ports of this State, or any of them, or otherwise obstructing the free ingress and egress of vessels to and from the said ports, or any other act on the part of the federal government, to coerce the State, shut up her ports, destroy or harass her commerce or to enforce the acts hereby declared to be null and void, otherwise than through the civil tribunals of the country, as inconsistent with the longer continuance of South Carolina in the Union; and that the people of this State will henceforth hold themselves absolved from all further obligation to maintain or preserve their political connection with the people of the other States; and will forthwith proceed to organize a separate government, and do all other acts and things which sovereign and independent States may of right do.

Done in convention at Columbia, the twenty-fourth day of November, in the year of our Lord one thousand eight hundred and thirty-two, and in the fifty-seventh year of the Declaration of the Independence of the United States of America.

Andrew Jackson's Proclamation regarding Nullification

December 10, 1832

Whereas a convention, assembled in the State of South Carolina, have passed an ordinance, by which they declare that the several acts and parts of acts of the Congress of the United States, purporting to be laws for the imposing of duties and imposts on the importation of foreign commodities, and now having actual operation and effect within the United States, and more especially "two acts for the same purposes, passed on the 29th of May, 1828, and on the 14th of July, 1832, are unauthorized by the Constitution of the United States, and violate the true meaning and intent thereof, and are null and void, and no law," nor binding on the citizens of that State or its officers, and by the said ordinance it is further declared to he unlawful for any of the constituted authorities of the State, or of the United States, to enforce the payment of the duties imposed by the said acts within the same State, and that it is the duty of the legislature to pass such laws as may be necessary to give full effect to the said ordinances:

And whereas, by the said ordinance it is further ordained, that, in no case of law or equity, decided in the courts of said State, wherein shall be drawn in question the validity of the said ordinance, or of the acts of the legislature that may be passed to give it effect, or of the said laws of the United States, no appeal shall be allowed to the Supreme Court of the United States, nor shall any copy of the record be permitted or allowed for that purpose; and that any person attempting to take such appeal, shall be punished as for a contempt of court:

And, finally, the said ordinance declares that the people of South Carolina will maintain the said ordinance at every hazard, and that they will consider the passage of any act by Congress abolishing or closing the ports of the said State, or otherwise obstructing the free ingress or egress of vessels to and from the said ports, or any other act of the Federal Government to coerce the State, shut up her ports, destroy or harass her commerce, or to enforce the said acts otherwise than through the civil tribunals of the country, as inconsistent with the longer continuance of South Carolina in the Union; and that the people of the said State will thenceforth hold themselves absolved from all further obligation to maintain or preserve their political connection with the people of the other States, and will forthwith proceed to organize a separate government, and do all other acts and things which sovereign and independent States may of right do.

And whereas the said ordinance prescribes to the people of South Carolina a course of conduct in direct violation of their duty as citizens of the United States, contrary to the laws of their country, subversive of its Constitution, and having for its object the instruction of the Union—that Union, which, coeval with our political existence, led our fathers, without any other ties to unite them than those of patriotism and common cause, through the sanguinary struggle to a glorious independence—that sacred Union, hitherto inviolate, which, perfected by our happy Constitution, has brought us, by the favor of Heaven, to a state of prosperity at home, and high consideration abroad, rarely, if ever, equaled in the history of nations; to preserve this bond of our political existence from destruction, to maintain inviolate this state of national honor and prosperity, and to justify the confidence my fellow-citizens have reposed in me, I, Andrew Jackson, President of the United States, have thought proper to issue this my PROCLAMATION, stating my views of the Constitution and laws applicable to the measures adopted by the Convention of South Carolina, and to the reasons they have put forth to sustain them, declaring the course which duty will require me to pursue, and, appealing to the understanding and patriotism of the people, warn them of the consequences that must inevitably result from an observance of the dictates of the Convention.

Strict duty would require of me nothing more than the exercise of those powers with which I am now, or may hereafter be, invested, for preserving the Union, and for the execution of the laws. But the imposing aspect which opposition has assumed in this case, by clothing itself with State authority, and the deep interest which the people of the United States must all feel in preventing a resort to stronger measures, while there is a hope that anything will be yielded to reasoning and remonstrances, perhaps demand, and will certainly justify, a full exposition to South Carolina and the nation of the views I entertain of this important question, as well as a distinct enunciation of the course which my sense of duty will require me to pursue.

The ordinance is founded, not on the indefeasible right of resisting acts which are plainly unconstitutional, and too oppressive to be endured, but on the strange position that any one State may not only declare an act of Congress void, but prohibit its execution—that they may do this consistently with the Constitution—that the true construction of that instrument permits a State to retain its place in the Union, and yet be bound by no other of its laws than those it may choose to consider as constitutional. It is true they add, that to justify this abrogation of a law, it must be palpably contrary to the Constitution, but it is evident, that to give the right of resisting laws of that description, coupled with the uncontrolled right to decide what laws deserve that character, is to give the power of resisting all laws. For, as by the theory, there is no appeal, the reasons alleged by the State, good or bad, must prevail. If it should be said that public opinion is a sufficient check against the abuse of this power, it may be asked why it is not deemed a sufficient guard against the passage of an unconstitutional act by Congress. There is, however, a restraint in this last case, which makes the assumed power of a State more indefensible, and which does not exist in the other. There are two appeals from an unconstitutional act passed by Congress—one to the judiciary, the other to the people and the States. There is no appeal from the State decision in theory; and the practical illustration shows that the courts are closed against an application to review it, both judges and jurors being sworn to decide in its favor. But reasoning on this subject is superfluous, when our social compact in express terms declares, that the laws of the United States, its Constitution, and treaties made under it, are the supreme law of the land; and for greater caution adds, "that the judges in every State shall be bound thereby, anything in the Constitution or laws of any State to the contrary notwithstanding." And it may be asserted, without fear of refutation, that no federative government could exist without a similar provision. Look, for a moment, to the consequence. If South Carolina considers the revenue laws unconstitutional, and has a right to prevent their execution in the port of Charleston, there would be a clear constitutional objection to their collection in every other port, and no revenue could be collected anywhere; for all imposts must be equal. It is no answer to repeat that an unconstitutional law is no law, so long as the question of its legality is to be decided by the State itself, for every law operating injuriously upon any local interest will be perhaps thought, and certainly represented, as unconstitutional, and, as has been shown, there is no appeal.

If this doctrine had been established at an earlier day, the Union would have been dissolved in its infancy. The excise law in Pennsylvania, the embargo and non-intercourse law in the Eastern States, the carriage tax in Virginia, were all deemed unconstitutional, and were more unequal in their operation than any of the laws now complained of; but, fortunately, none of those States discovered that they had the right now claimed by South Carolina. The war into which we were forced, to support the dignity of the nation and the rights of our citizens, might have ended in defeat and disgrace instead of victory and honor, if the States, who supposed it a ruinous and unconstitutional measure, had thought they possessed the right of nullifying the act by which it was declared, and denying supplies for its prosecution. Hardly and unequally as those measures bore upon several members of the Union, to the legislatures of none did this efficient and peaceable remedy, as it is called, suggest itself. The discovery of this important feature in our Constitution was reserved to the present day. To the statesmen of South Carolina belongs the invention, and upon the citizens of that State will, unfortunately, fall the evils of reducing it to practice.

If the doctrine of a State veto upon the laws of the Union carries with it internal evidence of its impracticable absurdity, our constitutional history will also afford abundant proof that it would have been repudiated with indignation had it been proposed to form a feature in our Government.

In our colonial state, although dependent on another power, we very early considered ourselves as connected by common interest with each other. Leagues were formed for common defense, and before the Declaration of Independence, we were known in our aggregate character as the United Colonies of America. That decisive and important step was taken jointly. We declared ourselves a nation by a joint, not by several acts; and when the terms of our confederation were reduced to form, it was in that of a solemn league of several States, by which they agreed that they would, collectively, form one nation, for the purpose of conducting some certain domestic concerns, and all foreign relations. In the instrument forming that Union, is found an article which declares that "every State shall abide by the determinations of Congress on all questions which by that Confederation should be submitted to them."

Under the Confederation, then, no State could legally annul a decision of the Congress, or refuse to submit to its execution, but no provision was made to enforce these decisions. Congress made requisitions, but they were not complied with. The Government could not operate on individuals. They had no judiciary, no means of collecting revenue.

But the defects of the Confederation need not be detailed. Under its operation we could scarcely be called a nation. We had neither prosperity at home nor consideration abroad. This state of things could not be endured, and our present happy Constitution was formed, but formed in vain, if this fatal doctrine prevails. It was formed for important objects that are announced in the preamble made in the name and by the authority of the people of the United States, whose delegates framed, and whose conventions approved it.

The most important among these objects, that which is placed first in rank, on which all the others rest, is *"to form a more perfect Union."* Now, is it possible that, even if there were no express provision giving supremacy to the Constitution and laws of the United States over those of the States, it can be conceived that an Instrument made for the purpose of *"forming; a more perfect Union"* than that of the confederation, could be so constructed by the assembled wisdom of our country as to substitute for that confederation a form of government, dependent for its existence on the local interest, the party spirit of a State, or of a prevailing faction in a State? Every man, of plain, unsophisticated understanding, who hears the question, will give such an answer as will preserve the Union. Metaphysical subtlety, in pursuit of an impracticable theory, could alone have devised one that is calculated to destroy it.

I consider, then, the power to annul a law of the United States, assumed by one State, *incompatible with the existence of the Union, contradicted expressly by the letter of the Constitution, unauthorized by its spirit, inconsistent with every principle on which It was founded, and destructive of the great object for which it was formed.*

After this general view of the leading principle, we must examine the particular application of it which is made in the ordinance.

The preamble rests its justification on these grounds: It assumes as a fact, that the obnoxious laws, although they purport to be laws for raising revenue, were in reality intended for the protection of manufactures, which purpose it asserts to be unconstitutional; that the operation of these laws is unequal, that the amount raised by them is greater than is required by the wants of the Government; and, finally, that the proceeds are to be applied to objects unauthorized by the Constitution. These are the only causes alleged to justify an open opposition to the laws of the country, and a threat of seceding from the Union, if any attempt should be made to enforce them. The first virtually acknowledges that the law in question was passed under a power expressly given by the Constitution, to lay and collect imposts, but its constitutionality is drawn in question from the motives of those who passed it. However apparent this purpose may be in the present case, nothing can be more dangerous than to admit the position that an unconstitutional purpose, entertained by the members who assent to a law enacted under a constitutional power, shall make that law void; for how is that purpose to be ascertained? Who is to make the scrutiny? How often may bad purposes be falsely imputed? In how many cases are they concealed by false professions? In how many is no declaration of motive made? Admit this doctrine and you give to the States an uncontrolled right to decide, and every law may be annulled under this pretext. If, therefore, the absurd and dangerous doctrine should be admitted, that a State may annul an unconstitutional law, or one that it deems such, it will not apply to the present case.

The next objection is, that the laws in question operate unequally. This objection may be made with truth to every law that has been or can be passed. The wisdom of man never yet contrived a system of taxation that would operate with perfect equality. If the unequal operation of a law makes it unconstitutional and if all laws of that description may be abrogated by any State for that cause, then, indeed, is the federal Constitution unworthy of the slightest effort for its preservation. We have hitherto relied on it as the perpetual bond of our Union. We have received it as the work of the assembled wisdom of the nation. We have trusted to it as to the sheet-anchor of our safety, in the stormy times of conflict with a foreign or domestic foe. We have looked to it with sacred awe as the palladium of our liberties, and with all the solemnities of religion have pledged to each other our lives and fortunes here, and our hopes of happiness hereafter, in its defense and support. Were we mistaken, my countrymen, in attaching this importance to the Constitution of our country? Was our devotion paid to the wretched, inefficient, clumsy contrivance, which this new doctrine would make it? Did we pledge ourselves to the support of an airy nothing—a bubble that must be blown away by the first breath of disaffection? Was this self-destroying, visionary theory the work of the profound statesmen, the exalted patriots, to whom the task of constitutional reform was intrusted? Did the name of Washington sanction, did the States deliberately ratify, such an anomaly in the history of fundamental legislation? No. We were not mistaken. The letter of this great instrument is free from this radical fault; its language directly contradicts the imputation, its spirit, its evident intent, contradicts it. No, we did not err. Our Constitution does not contain the absurdity of giving power to make laws, and another power to resist them. The sages, whose memory will always be reverenced, have given us a practical, and, as they hoped, a permanent constitutional compact. The Father of his Country did not affix his revered name to so palpable an absurdity. Nor did the States, when they severally ratified it, do so under the impression that a veto on the laws of the United States was reserved to them, or that they could exercise it by application. Search the debates in all their conventions—examine the speeches of the most zealous opposers of federal authority—look at the amendments that were proposed. They are all silent—not a syllable uttered, not a vote given, not a motion made, to correct the explicit supremacy given to the laws of the Union over those of the States, or to show that implication, as is now contended, could defeat it. No, we have not erred! The Constitution is still the object of our reverence, the bond of our Union, our defense in danger, the source of our prosperity in peace. It shall descend, as we have received it, uncorrupted by sophistical construction to our posterity; and the sacrifices of local interest, of State prejudices, of personal animosities, that were made to bring it into existence, will again be patriotically offered for its support.

The two remaining objections made by the ordinance to these laws are, that the sums intended to be raised by them are greater than are required, and that the proceeds will be unconstitutionally employed. The Constitution has given expressly to Congress the right of raising revenue, and of determining the sum the public exigencies will require. The States have no control over the exercise of this right other than that which results from the power of changing the representatives who abuse it, and thus procure redress. Congress may undoubtedly abuse this discretionary power, but the same may be said of others with which they are vested. Yet the discretion must exist somewhere. The Constitution has given it to the representatives of all the people, checked by the representatives of the States, and by the executive power. The South Carolina construction gives it to the legislature, or the convention of a single State, where neither the people of the different States, nor the States in their separate capacity, nor the chief magistrate elected by the people, have any representation. Which is the most discreet disposition of the power? I do not ask you, fellow-citizens, which is the constitutional disposition—that instrument speaks a language not to be misunderstood. But if you were assembled in general convention, which would you think the safest depository of this discretionary power in the last resort? Would you add a clause giving it to each of the States, or would you sanction the wise provisions already made by your Constitution? If this should be the result of your deliberations when providing for the future, are you—can you—be ready to risk all that we hold dear, to establish, for a temporary and a local purpose, that which you must acknowledge to be destructive, and even absurd, as a general provision? Carry out the consequences of this right vested in the different States, and you must perceive that the crisis your conduct presents at this day would recur whenever any law of the United States displeased any of the States, and that we should soon cease to be a nation.

The ordinance with the same knowledge of the future that characterizes a former objection, tells you that the proceeds of the tax will be unconstitutionally applied. If this could be ascertained with certainty, the objection would, with more propriety, be reserved for the law so applying the proceeds, but surely cannot be urged against the laws levying the duty.

These are the allegations contained in the ordinance. Examine them seriously, my fellow-citizens—judge for yourselves. I appeal to you to determine whether they are so clear, so convincing, as to leave no doubt of their correctness, and even if you should come to this conclusion, how far they justify the reckless, destructive course which you are directed to pursue. Review these objections and the conclusions drawn from them once more. What are they! Every law, then, for raising revenue, according to the South Carolina ordinance, may be rightfully annulled, unless it be so framed as no law ever will or can be framed. Congress have a right to pass laws for raising revenue, and each State has a right to oppose their execution—two rights directly opposed to each other; and yet is this absurdity supposed to be contained in an instrument drawn for the express purpose of avoiding collisions between the States and the general government, by an assembly of the most enlightened statesmen and purest patriots ever embodied for a similar purpose.

In vain have these sages declared that Congress shall have power to lay and collect taxes, duties, imposts, and excises—in vain have they provided that they shall have power to pass laws which shall be necessary and proper to carry those powers into execution, that those laws and that Constitution shall be the "supreme law of the land; that the judges in every State shall be bound thereby, anything in the constitution or laws of any State to the contrary notwithstanding." In vain have the people of the several States solemnly sanctioned these provisions, made them their paramount law, and individually sworn to support them whenever they were called on to execute any office.

Vain provisions! Ineffectual restrictions! Vile profanation of oaths! Miserable mockery of legislation! If a bare majority of the voters in any one State may, on a real or supposed knowledge of the intent with which a law has been passed, declare themselves free from its operation—say here it gives too little, there too much, and operates unequally—here it suffers articles to be free that ought to be taxed, there it taxes those that ought to be free—in this case the proceeds are intended to be applied to purposes which we do not approve, in that the amount raised is more than is wanted. Congress, it is true, are invested by the Constitution with the right of deciding these questions according to their sound discretion. Congress is composed of the representatives of all the States, and of all the people of all the states; but WE, part of the people of one State, to whom the Constitution has given no power on the subject from whom it has expressly taken it away—we, who have solemnly agreed that this Constitution shall be our law—we, most of whom have sworn to support it—we now abrogate this law, and swear, and force others to swear, that it shall not be obeyed—and we do this, not because Congress have no right to pass such laws; this we do not allege; but because they have passed them with improper views. They are unconstitutional from the motives of those who passed them, which we can never with certainty know, from their unequal operation; although it is impossible from the nature of things that they should be equal—and from the disposition which we presume may be made of their proceeds, although that disposition has not been declared. This is the plain meaning of the ordinance in relation to laws which it abrogates for alleged unconstitutionality. But it does not stop here. It repeals, in express terms, an important part of the Constitution itself, and of laws passed to give it effect, which have never been alleged to be unconstitutional. The Constitution declares that the judicial powers of the United States extend to cases arising under the laws of the United States, and that such laws, the Constitution and treaties, shall be paramount to the State constitutions and laws. The judiciary act prescribes the mode by which the case may be brought before a court of the United States, by appeal, when a State tribunal shall decide against this provision of the Constitution. The ordinance declares there shall be no appeal; makes the State law paramount to the Constitution and laws of the United States; forces judges and jurors to swear that they will disregard their provisions; and even makes it penal in a suitor to attempt relief by appeal. It further declares that it shall not be lawful for the authorities of the United States, or of that State, to enforce the payment of duties imposed by the revenue laws within its limits.

Here is a law of the United States, not even pretended to be unconstitutional, repealed by the authority of a small majority of the voters of a single State. Here is a provision of the Constitution which is solemnly abrogated by the same authority.

On such expositions and reasonings, the ordinance grounds not only an assertion of the right to annul the laws of which it complains, but to enforce it by a threat of seceding from the Union if any attempt is made to execute them.

This right to secede is deduced from the nature of the Constitution, which they say is a compact between sovereign States who have preserved their whole sovereignty, and therefore are subject to no superior; that because they made the compact, they can break it when in their opinion it has been departed from by the other States. Fallacious as this course of reasoning is, it enlists State pride, and finds advocates in the honest prejudices of those who have not studied the nature of our government sufficiently to see the radical error on which it rests.

The people of the United States formed the Constitution, acting through the State legislatures, in making the compact, to meet and discuss its provisions, and acting in separate conventions when they ratified those provisions; but the terms used in its construction show it to be a government in which the people of all the States collectively are represented. We are ONE PEOPLE in the choice of the President and Vice President. Here the States have no other agency than to direct the mode in which the vote shall be given. The candidates having the majority of all the votes are chosen. The electors of a majority of States may have given their votes for one candidate, and yet another may be chosen. The people, then, and not the States, are represented in the executive branch.

In the House of Representatives there is this difference, that the people of one State do not, as in the case of President and Vice President, all vote for all the members, each State electing only its own representatives. But this creates no material distinction. When chosen, they are all representatives of the United States, not representatives of the particular State from which they come. They are paid by the United States, not by the State; nor are they accountable to it for any act done in performance of their legislative functions; and however they may in practice, as it is their duty to do, consult and prefer the interests of their particular constituents when they come in conflict with any other partial or local interest, yet it is their first and highest duty, as representatives of the United States, to promote the general good.

The Constitution of the United States, then, forms a government, not a league, and whether it be formed by compact between the States, or in any other manner, its character is the same. It is a government in which ale the people are represented, which operates directly on the people individually, not upon the States; they retained all the power they did not grant. But each State having expressly parted with so many powers as to constitute jointly with the other States a single nation, cannot from that period possess any right to secede, because such secession does not break a league, but destroys the unity of a nation, and any injury to that unity is not only a breach which would result from the contravention of a compact, but it is an offense against the whole Union. To say that any State may at pleasure secede from the Union, is to say that the United States are not a nation because it would be a solecism to contend that any part of a nation might dissolve its connection with the other parts, to their injury or ruin, without committing any offense. Secession, like any other revolutionary act, may be morally justified by the extremity of oppression; but to call it a constitutional right, is confounding the meaning of terms, and can only be done through gross error, or to deceive those who are willing to assert a right, but would pause before they made a revolution, or incur the penalties consequent upon a failure.

Because the Union was formed by compact, it is said the parties to that compact may, when they feel themselves aggrieved, depart from it; but it is precisely because it is a compact that they cannot. A compact is an agreement or binding obligation. It may by its terms have a sanction or penalty for its breach, or it may not. If it contains no sanction, it may be broken with no other consequence than moral guilt; if it have a sanction, then the breach incurs the designated or implied penalty. A league between independent nations, generally, has no sanction other than a moral one; or if it should contain a penalty, as there is no common superior, it cannot be enforced. A government, on the contrary, always has a sanction, express or implied; and, in our case, it is both necessarily implied and expressly given. An attempt by force of arms to destroy a government is an offense, by whatever means the constitutional compact may have been formed; and such government has the right, by the law of self-defense, to pass acts for punishing the offender, unless that right is modified, restrained, or resumed by the constitutional act. In our system, although it is modified in the case of treason, yet authority is expressly given to pass all laws necessary to carry its powers into effect, and under this grant provision has been made for punishing acts which obstruct the due administration of the laws.

It would seem superfluous to add anything to show the nature of that union which connects us; but as erroneous opinions on this subject are the foundation of doctrines the most destructive to our peace, I must give some further development to my views on this subject. No one, fellow-citizens, has a higher reverence for the reserved rights of the States than the magistrate who now addresses you. No one would make greater personal sacrifices, or official exertions, to defend them from violation; but equal care must be taken to prevent, on their part, an improper interference with, or resumption of, the rights they have vested in the nation.

The line has not been so distinctly drawn as to avoid doubts in some cases of the exercise of power. Men of the best intentions and soundest views may differ in their construction of some parts of the Constitution, but there are others on which dispassionate reflection can leave no doubt. Of this nature appears to be the assumed right of secession. It rests, as we have seen, on the alleged undivided sovereignty of the States, and on their having formed in this sovereign capacity a compact which is called the Constitution, from which, because they made it, they have the right to secede. Both of these positions are erroneous, and some of the arguments to prove them so have been anticipated.

The States severally have not retained their entire sovereignty. It has been shown that in becoming parts of a nation, not members of a league, they surrendered many of their essential parts of sovereignty. The right to make treaties, declare war, levy taxes, exercise exclusive judicial and legislative powers, were all functions of sovereign power. The States, then, for all these important purposes, were no longer sovereign. The allegiance of their citizens was transferred in the first instance to the government of the United States; they became American citizens, and owed obedience to the Constitution of the United States, and to laws made in conformity with the powers vested in Congress. This last position has not been, and cannot be, denied. How then, can that State be said to be sovereign and independent whose citizens owe obedience to laws not made by it, and whose magistrates are sworn to disregard those laws, when they come in conflict with those passed by another? What shows conclusively that the States cannot be said to have reserved an undivided sovereignty, is that they expressly ceded the right to punish treason—not treason against their separate power, but treason against the United States. Treason is an offense against sovereignty, and sovereignty must reside with the power to punish it. But the reserved rights of the States are not less sacred because they have for their common interest made the general government the depository of these powers. The unity of our political character (as has been shown for another purpose) commenced with its very existence. Under the royal government we had no separate character; our opposition to its oppression began as UNITED COLONIES. We were the UNITED STATES under the Confederation, and the name was perpetuated and the Union rendered more perfect by the federal Constitution. In none of these stages did we consider ourselves in any other light than as forming one nation. Treaties and alliances were made in the name of all. Troops were raised for the joint defense. How, then, with all these proofs, that under all changes of our position we had, for designated purposes and with defined powers, created national governments—how is it that the most perfect of these several modes of union should now be considered as a mere league that may be dissolved at pleasure? It is from an abuse of terms. Compact is used as synonymous with league, although the true term is not employed, because it would at once show the fallacy of the reasoning. It would not do to say that our Constitution was only a league, but it is labored to prove it a compact (which, in one sense, it is), and then to argue that as a league is a compact, every compact between nations must, of course, be a league, and that from such an engagement every sovereign power has a right to recede. But it has been shown that in this sense the States are not sovereign, and that even if they were, and the national Constitution had been formed by compact, there would be no right in any one State to exonerate itself from the obligation.

So obvious are the reasons which forbid this secession, that it is necessary only to allude to them. The Union was formed for the benefit of all. It was produced by mutual sacrifice of interest and opinions. Can those sacrifices be recalled? Can the States, who magnanimously surrendered their title to the territories of the West, recall the grant? Will the inhabitants of the inland States agree to pay the duties that may be imposed without their assent by those on the Atlantic or the Gulf, for their own benefit? Shall there be a free port in one State, and enormous duties in another? No one believes that any right exists in a single State to involve all the others in these and countless other evils, contrary to engagements solemnly made. Everyone must see that the other States, in self-defense, must oppose it at all hazards.

These are the alternatives that are presented by the convention: A repeal of all the acts for raising revenue, leaving the government without the means of support; or an acquiescence in the dissolution of our Union by the secession of one of its members. When the first was proposed, it was known that it could not be listened to for a moment. It was known if force was applied to oppose the execution of the laws, that it must be repelled by force—that Congress could not, without involving itself in disgrace and the country in ruin, accede to the proposition; and yet if this is not done in a given day, or if any attempt is made to execute the laws, the State is, by the ordinance, declared to be out of the Union. The majority of a convention assembled for the purpose have dictated these terms, or rather this rejection of all terms, in the name of the people of South Carolina. It is true that the governor of the State speaks of the submission of their grievances to a convention of all the States; which, he says, they "'sincerely and anxiously seek and desire." Yet this obvious and constitutional mode of obtaining the sense of the other States on the construction of the federal compact, and amending it, if necessary, has never been attempted by those who have urged the State on to this destructive measure. The State might have proposed a call for a general convention to the other States, and Congress, if a sufficient number of them concurred, must have called it. But the first magistrate of South Carolina, when he expressed a hope that "on a review by Congress and the functionaries of the general government of the merits of the controversy," such a convention will be accorded to them, must have known that neither Congress, nor any functionary in the general government, has authority to call such a convention, unless it be demanded by two-thirds of the States. This suggestion, then, is another instance of the reckless inattention to the provisions of the Constitution with which this crisis has been madly hurried on; or of the attempt to persuade the people that a constitutional remedy has been sought and refused. If the legislature of South Carolina "anxiously desire" a general convention to consider their complaints, why have they not made application for it in the way the Constitution points out? The assertion that they "earnestly seek" is completely negatived by the omission.

This, then, is the position in which we stand. A small majority of the citizens of one State in the Union have elected delegates to a State convention; that convention has ordained that all the revenue laws of the United States must be repealed, or that they are no longer a member of the Union. The governor of that State has recommended to the legislature the raising of an army to carry the secession into effect, and that he may be empowered to give clearances to vessels in the name of the State. No act of violent opposition to the laws has yet been committed, but such a state of things is hourly apprehended, and it is the intent of this instrument to PROCLAIM, not only that the duty imposed on me by the Constitution, "to take care that the laws be faithfully executed," shall be performed to the extent of the powers already vested in me by law or of such others as the wisdom of Congress shall devise and Entrust to me for that purpose; but to warn the citizens of South Carolina, who have been deluded into an opposition to the laws, of the danger they will incur by obedience to the illegal and disorganizing ordinance of the convention—to exhort those who have refused to support it to persevere in their determination to uphold the Constitution and laws of their country, and to point out to all the perilous situation into which the good people of that State have been led, and that the course they are urged to pursue is one of ruin and disgrace to the very State whose rights they affect to support.

Fellow-citizens of my native State! let me not only admonish you, as the first magistrate of our common country, not to incur the penalty of its laws, but use the influence that a father would over his children whom he saw rushing to a certain ruin. In that paternal language, with that paternal feeling, let me tell you, my countrymen, that you are deluded by men who are either deceived themselves or wish to deceive you. Mark under what pretenses you have been led on to the brink of insurrection and treason on which you stand! First a diminution of the value of our staple commodity, lowered by over-production in other quarters and the consequent diminution in the value of your lands, were the sole effect of the tariff laws. The effect of those laws was confessedly injurious, but the evil was greatly exaggerated by the unfounded theory you were taught to believe, that its burdens were in proportion to your exports, not to your consumption of imported articles. Your pride was aroused by the assertions that a submission to these laws was a state of vassalage, and that resistance to them was equal, in patriotic merit, to the opposition our fathers offered to the oppressive laws of Great Britain. You were told that this opposition might be peaceably—might be constitutionally made—that you might enjoy all the advantages of the Union and bear none of its burdens. Eloquent appeals to your passions, to your State pride, to your native courage, to your sense of real injury, were used to prepare you for the period when the mask which concealed the hideous features of DISUNION should be taken off. It fell, and you were made to look with complacency on objects which not long since you would have regarded with horror. Look back to the arts which have brought you to this state—look forward to the consequences to which it must inevitably lead! Look back to what was first told you as an inducement to enter into this dangerous course. The great political truth was repeated to you that you had the revolutionary right of resisting all laws that were palpably unconstitutional and intolerably oppressive—it was added that the right to nullify a law rested on the same principle, but that it was a peaceable remedy! This character which was given to it, made you receive with too much confidence the assertions that were made of the unconstitutionality of the law and its oppressive effects. Mark, my fellow-citizens, that by the admission of your leaders the unconstitutionality must be *palpable*, or it will not justify either resistance or nullification! What is the meaning of the word *palpable* in the sense in which it is here used? that which is apparent to everyone, that which no man of ordinary intellect will fail to perceive. Is the unconstitutionality of these laws of that description? Let those among your leaders who once approved and advocated the principles of protective duties, answer the question; and let them choose whether they will be considered as incapable, then, of perceiving that which must have been apparent to every man of common understanding, or as imposing upon your confidence and endeavoring to mislead you now. In either case, they are unsafe guides in the perilous path they urge you to tread. Ponder well on this circumstance, and you will know how to appreciate the exaggerated language they address to you. They are not champions of liberty emulating the fame of our Revolutionary fathers, nor are you an oppressed people, contending, as they repeat to you, against worse than colonial vassalage. You are free members of a flourishing and happy Union. There is no settled design to oppress you. You have, indeed, felt the unequal operation of laws which may have been unwisely, not unconstitutionally passed; but that inequality must necessarily be removed. At the very moment when you were madly urged on to the unfortunate course you have begun, a change in public opinion has commenced. The nearly approaching payment of the public debt, and the consequent necessity of a diminution of duties, had already caused a considerable reduction, and that, too, on some articles of general consumption in your State. The importance of this change was underrated, and you were authoritatively told that no further alleviation of your burdens was to be expected, at the very time when the condition of the country imperiously demanded such a modification of the duties as should reduce them to a just and equitable scale. But as apprehensive of the effect of this change in allaying your discontents, you were precipitated into the fearful state in which you now find yourselves.

I have urged you to look back to the means that were used to burly you on to the position you have now assumed, and forward to the consequences they will produce. Something more is necessary. Contemplate the condition of that country of which you still form an important part; consider its government uniting in one bond of common interest and general protection so many different States—giving to all their inhabitants the proud title of AMERICAN CITIZEN—protecting their commerce—securing their literature and arts—facilitating their intercommunication—defending their frontiers—and making their name respected in the remotest parts of the earth! Consider the extent of its territory its increasing and happy population, its advance in arts, which render life agreeable, and the sciences which elevate the mind! See education spreading the lights of religion, morality, and general information into every cottage in this wide extent of our Territories and States! Behold it as the asylum where the wretched and the oppressed find a refuge and support! Look on this picture of happiness and honor, and say, WE TOO, ARE CITIZENS OF AMERICA—Carolina is one of these proud States her arms have defended—her best blood has cemented this happy Union! And then add, if you can, without horror and remorse this happy Union we will dissolve—this picture of peace and prosperity we will deface—this free intercourse we will interrupt—these fertile fields we will deluge with blood—the protection of that glorious flag we renounce—the very name of Americans we discard. And for what, mistaken men! For what do you throw away these inestimable blessings—for what would you exchange your share in the advantages and honor of the Union? For the dream of a separate independence—a dream interrupted by bloody conflicts with your neighbors, and a vile dependence on a foreign power. If your leaders could succeed in establishing a separation, what would be your situation? Are you united at home—are you free from the apprehension of civil discord, with all its fearful consequences? Do our neighboring republics, every day suffering some new revolution or contending with some new insurrection—do they excite your envy? But the dictates of a high duty oblige me solemnly to announce that you cannot succeed. The laws of the United States must be executed. I have no discretionary power on the subject—my duty is emphatically pronounced in the Constitution. Those who told you that you might peaceably prevent their execution, deceived you—they could not have been deceived themselves. They know that a forcible opposition could alone prevent the execution of the laws, and they know that such opposition must be repelled. Their object is disunion, hut be not deceived by names; disunion, by armed force, is TREASON. Are you really ready to incur its guilt? If you are, on the head of the instigators of the act be

the dreadful consequences—on their heads be the dishonor, but on yours may fall the punishment—on your unhappy State will inevitably fall all the evils of the conflict you force upon the government of your country. It cannot accede to the mad project of disunion, of which you would be the first victims—its first magistrate cannot, if he would, avoid the performance of his duty—the consequence must be fearful for you, distressing to your fellow-citizens here, and to the friends of good government throughout the world. Its enemies have beheld our prosperity with a vexation they could not conceal—it was a standing refutation of their slavish doctrines, and they will point to our discord with the triumph of malignant joy. It is yet in your power to disappoint them. There is yet time to show that the descendants of the Pinckneys, the Sumpters, the Rutledges, and of the thousand other names which adorn the pages of your Revolutionary history, will not abandon that Union to support which so many of them fought and bled and died. I adjure you, as you honor their memory—as you love the cause of freedom, to which they dedicated their lives—as you prize the peace of your country, the lives of its best citizens, and your own fair fame, to retrace your steps. Snatch from the archives of your State the disorganizing edict of its convention—hid its members to re-assemble and promulgate the decided expressions of your will to remain in the path which alone can conduct you to safety, prosperity, and honor—tell them that compared to disunion, all other evils are light, because that brings with it an accumulation of all—declare that you will never take the field unless the star-spangled banner of your country shall float over you—that you will not be stigmatized when dead, and dishonored and scorned while you live, as the authors of the first attack on the Constitution of your country!—its destroyers you cannot be. You may disturb its peace—you may interrupt the course of its prosperity—you may cloud its reputation for stability— but its tranquillity will be restored, its prosperity will return, and the stain upon its national character will be transferred and remain an eternal blot on the memory of those who caused the disorder.

Fellow-citizens of the United States! the threat of unhallowed disunion—the names of those, once respected, by whom it is uttered—the array of military force to support it—denote the approach of a crisis in our affairs on which the continuance of our unexampled prosperity, our political existence, and perhaps that of all free governments, may depend.

The conjuncture demanded a free, a full, and explicit enunciation, not only of my intentions, but of my principles of action, and as the claim was asserted of a right by a State to annul the laws of the Union, and even to secede from it at pleasure, a frank exposition of my opinions in relation to the origin and form of our government, and the construction I give to the instrument by which it was created, seemed to be proper. Having the fullest confidence in the justness of the legal and constitutional opinion of my duties which has been expressed, I rely with equal confidence on your undivided support in my determination to execute the laws—to preserve the Union by all constitutional means—to arrest, if possible, by moderate but firm measures, the necessity of a recourse to force; and, if it be the will of Heaven that the recurrence of its primeval curse on man for the shedding of a brother's blood should fall upon our land, that it be not called down by any offensive act on the part of the United States.

Fellow-citizens! the momentous case is before you. On your undivided support of your government depends the decision of the great question it involves, whether your sacred Union will be preserved, and the blessing it secures to us as one people shall be perpetuated. No one can doubt that the unanimity with which that decision will be expressed, will he such as to inspire new confidence in republican institutions, and that the prudence, the wisdom, and the courage which it will bring to their defense, will transmit them unimpaired and invigorated to our children.

May the Great Ruler of nations grant that the signal blessings with which he has favored ours may not, by the madness of party or personal ambition, be disregarded and lost, and may His wise providence bring those who have produced this crisis to see the folly, before they feel the misery, of civil strife, and inspire a returning veneration for that Union which, if we may dare to penetrate his designs, he has chosen, as the only means of attaining the high destinies to which we may reasonably aspire.

In testimony whereof, I have caused the seal of the United States to be hereunto affixed, having signed the same with my hand.

Done at the City of Washington, this 10th day of December, in the year of our Lord one thousand eight hundred and thirty-two, and of the independence of the United States the fifty-seventh.

ANDREW JACKSON.

By the President

EDW. LIVINGSTON, Secretary of State.

John Tyler

President John Tyler supported the Texas Annexation in 1844. (Library of Congress)

"The territory properly included within, and rightfully belonging to the Republic of Texas, may be erected into a new state, to be called the state of Texas."

Overview

On March 1, 1845, John Tyler, the outgoing U.S. president, signed into law a joint resolution that authorized the admission of the Republic of Texas to the United States as a state. On December 29, 1845, the new president, James Polk, signed into law the act of Congress accepting the constitution of the State of Texas and bringing Texas into the Union. Polk's signature completed a process begun nine years earlier, when Texas won its independence from Mexico at the battle of San Jacinto and offered itself to be annexed to the United States.

The annexation of Texas involved far more than the addition of another state to the rapidly growing United States. It unleashed forces that radically transformed the United States: the country's acquisition of additional territory, its emergence as the continental power, and increasing clashes over slavery that culminated in the early 1860s with secession and civil war. Texas's annexation also was the defining event that colored relations between the United States and Mexico throughout the nineteenth and twentieth centuries. Most immediately, it provoked a war between the United States and Mexico that brought vast territories of the Southwest into the country and ignited the debate over slavery in these territories. By 1854 the United States had reached its modern-day contiguous continental limits with the Gadsden Purchase of additional land from Mexico. The debate over the expansion of slavery led directly to the Civil War and the abolition of slavery.

Context

At the beginning of the nineteenth century, Texas was a sparsely settled, largely undeveloped outpost of Spain's large North American territory. In 1809 there were only about 4,100 inhabitants of Spanish Texas, and about a thousand of them were soldiers. With the establishment of Stephen Austin's colony in 1821, which encouraged immigration from the United States, Texas was transformed into a predominately Anglo-American frontier province of the newly independent Republic of Mexico. In 1836 the Anglo settlers rebelled against Mexican rule and, after suffering defeats at the Alamo and Goliad, defeated the Mexican army at the battle of San Jacinto. The citizens of the new Republic of Texas voted overwhelmingly in a referendum on September 5, 1836, to instruct their government to seek Texas's immediate annexation to the United States.

Texas's first president, Samuel Houston, submitted a formal request asking the United States to approve Texas's annexation, starting down a path to statehood that took almost ten years. In the fall of 1836, Andrew Jackson delayed action on annexation because he did not want to inject the issue into that year's presidential election. Following the election, President Jackson did recognize Texas's independence and established diplomatic relations with the new republic, but he took no action on annexation. His successor, Martin Van Buren, was cool to the idea of annexation, and in 1838 Texas withdrew its request to join the United States.

The United States hesitated to annex Texas for a number of reasons. First, Mexico had renounced the Treaty of Velasco, which recognized Texas's independence, insisting that Texas remained a part of Mexico and that any U.S. interference in the issue would be viewed as an act of war. A number of prominent American politicians, most notably Henry Clay, refused to support the annexation of Texas in the face of Mexican opposition. U.S. expansion also was complicated by the issue of slavery. For some, this was a question of political power: Would the federal government be controlled by those states committed to a plantation-based agricultural economy or those states that pursued an industrial economy? Others—the increasingly vocal abolitionists and related groups—attacked slavery and its expansion on moral terms. The economy of Texas was based on slavery. Early settlers had brought slaves with them to clear the land. At the time of independence, there were about five thousand slaves in Texas; in 1847 there were more than thirty-eight thousand. Opponents of slavery opposed the annexation of Texas.

In 1843 President Tyler reopened the issue of Texas annexation. A southerner and a supporter of territorial expansion, Tyler saw Texas as a way to build his political future. He instructed his secretary of state, Abel Upshur, to open negotiations with the Texas ambassador to the Unit-

1836

■ **March 2**
Texas declares its independence from Mexico.

■ **May 14**
The Mexican general Antonio López de Santa Anna, who is captured following the battle of San Jacinto on April 21, 1836, signs the Treaty of Velasco, recognizing Texas's independence and ordering Mexican troops to leave the territory and move south of the Rio Grande. One year later, back in Mexico, Santa Anna renounces the treaty.

1837

■ **August 4**
The Texas ambassador to the United States presents a formal offer from the Republic of Texas to annex itself to the United States.

1838

■ **October 12**
Following the failure of the U.S. Congress to act on Texas annexation, Texas withdraws the offer to be annexed.

1844

■ **April 12**
The Treaty of Annexation between the United States and Texas is signed by negotiators from both nations.

■ **June 8**
The U.S. Senate rejects the Texas Treaty of Annexation by a vote of thirty-five to sixteen.

1845

■ **February 28**
U.S. Congress approves the joint resolution annexing Texas and admitting it as a state. President Tyler signs the resolution on March 1 and transmits it to Texas two days later.

■ **July 4**
A convention meets in Texas to consider both the Cuevas-Smith Treaty between Mexico and Texas and the U.S. annexation resolution. The convention votes fifty-five to one to accept the offer of annexation.

ed States, Isaac Van Zandt. Meanwhile, Texas was negotiating with the British, who were very interested in keeping the state independent and were willing to pressure Mexico to accept an independent Texas, if it also remained separate from the United States. James Pinckney Henderson joined Van Zandt to negotiate for Texas, while John C. Calhoun took over the negotiations for the United States following Upshur's death. On April 12, 1844, the negotiators signed the treaty and submitted it to their governments for ratification. The United States was in the midst of another presidential election campaign, with widespread opposition to the treaty from both political leaders and antislavery forces. Prospects for the treaty's passage were dim, and on June 8, 1844, the Senate rejected the treaty.

The election of James Polk as the U.S. president in November 1844 revived efforts to annex Texas. Polk, a southerner, built his campaign around supporting the annexation of Texas and U.S. expansion into Oregon and other areas. Tyler considered Polk's victory a mandate for annexation. Increased British efforts to broker peace between Mexico and Texas raised the specter of a British-dominated Texas, free of slavery, challenging the South's dominance in cotton production. To avoid another treaty vote in the Senate, Tyler and his allies in Congress introduced a joint resolution admitting Texas as a state, under terms more acceptable to Texas and the United States. In Texas, public opinion overwhelmingly favored annexation. Anson Jones, the republic's president, submitted the joint resolution to the Texas congress along with the Cuevas-Smith Treaty, which the British had negotiated with Mexico. Texans had a choice: independence guaranteed by Mexico and Great Britain or admission to the United States. The Texas congress voted to accept annexation and to reject the treaty on June 23, 1845; a state convention endorsed annexation on July 4, 1845; and the people of Texas voted for annexation 7,664 to 430 in a referendum on October 13, 1845. The U.S. Congress formally admitted Texas to the United States on December 29, 1845.

About the Author

The joint resolution was authored by the Congress of the United States and signed by the presiding officer of the House and the Senate and by President Tyler. However, several congressmen played major roles in crafting the final bill. In January 1845 Milton Brown, a congressman from Tennessee, introduced a resolution to admit Texas as a state, which contained much of the language that appears in the joint resolution. It was Brown who responded to critics concerned about the Texas debt by requiring Texas to pay its own debts and to retain control of its public lands to do so. He also added the provision allowing Texas to divide into additional new states if needed, which could maintain a balance between free and slave states and address Texas's potentially overwhelming political power based on its size. He also inserted the language dealing with slavery in the additional states. Brown's bill was approved by the House on January 25, 1845. The Senate was more difficult to convince. Thomas Hart Benton, a senator from Missouri, introduced a bill that contained the contents of the third paragraph of the final resolution. Robert J. Walker of Mississippi suggested amending Brown's House resolution by adding Benton's bill to it. This compromise broke the Senate deadlock on February 27. The House passed the amended bill the following day.

Explanation and Analysis of the Document

On Friday, March 1, 1845, three days before Polk's inauguration, Congress enacted a joint resolution for the annexation of the Republic of Texas to the United States and sent the measure to President Tyler for his approval and implementation. The Twenty-eighth Congress had struggled with the issue of annexation for the better part of a year. The brief resolution (only three paragraphs) reflects the completion of this process and the effort to resolve many of the issues that arose during the debates. To understand exactly what Congress decided in this resolution, it is important to keep in mind the terms of the failed effort to annex Texas by treaty in the late spring of 1844.

The resolution begins with three lines, which identify the session of Congress that passed the bill and the bill's title. In this case, the Joint Resolution for the Annexation of Texas to the United States is passed by the Twenty-eighth Congress in its second session. Under the terms of the U.S. Constitution (prior to the Twentieth Amendment of 1933), Congress was required to meet at least once every year, and this meeting was to commence on the first Monday in December. The Twenty-eighth Congress held its first session from December 4, 1843, until June 17, 1844; this was the session that defeated the 1844 Treaty of Annexation between the United States and Texas. The same Congress assembled for its second session on December 2, 1844, and met until March 3, 1845. An oddity of this initial calendar was that the second, or short, session of any Congress began after the November elections. Thus, the second session of the Twenty-eighth Congress convened after the election of Polk as the president and of the Twenty-ninth Congress. The joint resolution was a last-minute deal, rushed through just two days before Congress adjourned and three days before the new president took office.

◆ Paragraph 1

The three paragraphs that follow provide the act's content. Each is in the form of a resolution; together these three resolutions provide for the annexation of Texas and define the terms under which Texas will enter the Union. The first paragraph addresses the question of annexation; it is significant to note what this resolution does and does not do. It does not admit Texas as a state of the United States, but it does begin the process for this to happen. Congress gives its consent that the territory belonging to the Republic of Texas may be "erected into a new state." That is, the people of Texas may prepare a state constitution; if this is done, Texas

Time Line

1845

■ **December 29**
President Polk signs the joint resolution. Texas officially enters the union as the twenty-eighth state.

1846

■ **May 13**
U.S. Congress declares war on Mexico.

■ **August 8**
David Wilmot introduces the Wilmot Proviso, which proposes to ban slavery from any territory acquired during the Mexican War. This proposal launches a prolonged debate over slavery in the territories.

1848

■ **February 2**
Treaty of Guadalupe Hidalgo is signed, ending the Mexican War and transferring Arizona, California, New Mexico, and parts of Colorado, Nevada, and Utah to the United States.

1850

■ **September 9**
Congress enacts the Compromise of 1850 in an unsuccessful effort to resolve the issue of slavery in the territories acquired from Mexico. The compromise does settle the Texas–New Mexico border dispute.

1861

■ **February 2**
Texas secedes from the Union.

may be admitted to the Union. However, when the process is complete, Texas will enter the Union as a state, not as a territory. Texas is unique as the only land added to the United States that did not go through the territorial process.

Two other issues are raised in this first paragraph. The first is the assurance that the annexation of Texas will be carried out with the consent and participation of its people and its current government. The state government and its constitution will be "adopted by the people" of Texas with the "consent of the existing government." The second is the question of the rightful territory of the Republic of Texas (and the future state of Texas). While the resolution does not attempt to define the territory of Texas, it recognizes the boundary problem by saying "the territory properly included within, and rightfully belonging to." This problem of the proper and rightful territory of Texas precipitated the Mexican War and created a conflict between the state of

Texas and the U.S. government that was resolved by Congress in the Compromise of 1850.

Finally, there is a fundamental difference between the process by which Texas is to join the Union under the terms of the joint resolution and the process proposed in the 1844 Treaty of Annexation. In the joint resolution, Texas enters the Union directly as a state; in the treaty, it enters the Union as a territory, subject to the same constitutional provisions as the other territories. Statehood will come later, although the implication is that this will happen quickly, as soon as the territory "complied with the principles of the federal constitution" (Article 2). Of course, the treaty was not ratified. Politically the joint resolution was easier to enact, since its approval required only a simple majority of both houses of Congress, while the treaty required a two-thirds vote from the Senate.

◆ **Paragraph 2**

The second paragraph of the joint resolution provides additional detail related to the implementation of annexation and the resolution of issues affecting Texas's relationship with the United States. The paragraph opens with the words "And be it further resolved" and then cites specific "conditions" and "guarantees" included in three areas of the resolution. The first of these addresses the formation of the state of Texas and the completion of the process of bringing the new state into the Union. The terms of this process are straightforward: Texas must provide "proper evidence" that the state constitution has been approved by its people, and this constitution must be presented to Congress for final approval no later than January 1, 1846. Less straightforward is the statement addressing Texas's boundaries; it simply notes that the United States will address and, if necessary, adjust all "questions of boundary that may arise with other governments."

The second set of conditions and guarantees addresses the connected issues of public lands and Texas's debts. The terms are clear but unusual. Upon entering the Union, Texas will transfer to the United States all of its buildings, developed property, and military installations and equipment; however, it will keep possession of all of its public lands—all territory that has not been sold or assigned to its citizens. Texas then becomes the only state, other than the original thirteen, to retain possession of its public lands. Balancing this, Texas also remains responsible for its own considerable debts. The disposition of public lands and debts in the joint resolution contrasts with the terms of the 1844 Treaty of Annexation. Had it been approved, the treaty would have required Texas to cede its public lands to the United States and the United States to assume responsibility for Texas's debts. This change satisfied some critics who did not want U.S. responsibility for Texas's debts.

The third set of conditions is the most interesting. These conditions address the number of states that can be created out of the territory of Texas and the status of slavery in the territory. The provision that Texas can create up to four additional states out of its territory is a right that was not granted to any other state. There are several explanations

for why this was done. First, Texas was considerably larger than any other state. Including all the land claimed by Texas in 1844, it was almost four times the size of Michigan, then the second-largest state. Thus, dividing Texas into four or five states "of convenient size" would not be unreasonable and would prevent a fully populated, oversized Texas from exercising too much influence in Congress. There was another consideration: In the highly politicized atmosphere of the mid-1840s, admitting one slave state was controversial; admitting four or five new slave states was unthinkable to most northern politicians. At the time the joint resolution was passed, there were twenty-six states, divided equally between slave and free states. A number of congressmen were reluctant to see slavery expand west to the Rio Grande; others were equally determined that slavery must expand.

To defuse this situation the joint resolution includes language on slavery. If Texas remains intact as one state, it will be a slave state. However, if it divides itself into additional states, the status of slavery in each will be determined by its location. In any new states whose territory extends north of the Missouri Compromise line, slavery will be prohibited; in states that lay south of that line, slavery will be allowed or prohibited according to the desire of "the people of each state asking admission." Since any new states carved out of the territory of Texas will have to seek admission "under the provisions of the federal constitution," Congress ultimately will approve or disapprove of their admission.

Of course Texas did not divide itself into additional states. Under the terms of the Compromise of 1850, it also ceded to the United States almost 97,000 square miles of land it claimed in the modern states of New Mexico, Kansas, Oklahoma, Colorado, and Wyoming. During the debate over the Compromise of 1850, the issue of dividing Texas came up, but no action was taken. The issue arose again following the Civil War, when the Texas constitutional convention of 1868 to 1869 sent Congress a proposal to divide Texas into three states. Congress did not act on the proposal.

◆ **Paragraph 3**

The third paragraph of the joint resolution completes the process by giving the U.S. president two options: to proceed with the implementation of the measures contained in the first two paragraphs and admit Texas as a state or to reopen negotiations with Texas on the terms of its annexation. If the president chooses the latter option, the state formed out of the territory of Texas shall be admitted to the Union under the terms of the first paragraph of the joint resolution; any additional land claimed by Texas, but not included in this state, will be ceded to the United States on terms worked out by the Texas and U.S. governments. This alternative process can take the form of a treaty or another joint resolution, and it requires approval by Congress or, in the case of a treaty, by the Senate. Furthermore, the new state of Texas will be awarded two seats in the House of Representatives until the next census and subsequent reapportionment determines its actual representation in Congress. Finally, this paragraph appropriates funds to cover the costs of any new negotiations. Since President Tyler and Presi-

> *"The territory properly included within, and rightfully belonging to the Republic of Texas, may be erected into a new state, to be called the state of Texas, with a republican form of government, to be adopted by the people of said republic, by deputies in Convention assembled, with the consent of the existing government, in order that the same may be admitted as one of the states of this Union."*
>
> (Paragraph 1)

> *"Said state ... shall retain all the public funds, debts, taxes, and dues of every kind which may belong to or be due and owing said republic; and shall also retain all the vacant and unappropriated lands lying within its limits, to be applied to the payment of the debts and liabilities of said republic of Texas."*
>
> (Paragraph 2)

> *"New states, of convenient size, not exceeding four in number, in addition to said state of Texas, and having sufficient population, may hereafter, by the consent of said state, be formed out of the territory thereof, which shall be entitled to admission under the provisions of the federal constitution."*
>
> (Paragraph 2)

> *"Such states as may be formed out of that portion of said territory lying south of ... the Missouri compromise line, shall be admitted into the Union with or without slavery, as the people of each state asking admission may desire. And in such state or states as shall be formed out of said territory north of said Missouri compromise line, slavery, or involuntary servitude, (except for crime,) shall be prohibited."*
>
> (Paragraph 2)

dent Polk carried out the annexation of Texas under the terms of the first two paragraphs, the renegotiations authorized by the third paragraph were never implemented.

Audience

The members of Congress were the joint resolution's initial audience. The resolution was first introduced in the House of Representatives and approved on January 25, 1845. A month later, on February 27, the Senate approved an amended version of the House resolution by a one-vote margin (27 to 25); the House approved the amended resolution on February 28 by a vote of 132 to 76. On March 1, President Tyler signed the bill and two days later had it dispatched by courier to Anson Jones, the president of the Republic of Texas. On March 4, the incoming U.S. president, James Polk, communicated his full support for the annexation of Texas in his inaugural address.

The joint resolution's audience also included the people and government of Texas. Sam Houston and Anson Jones were not enthusiastic supporters of annexation in early 1845. Both Texas leaders seemed to feel that the independence guaranteed by both Mexico and Great Britain was Texas's best option. President Jones waited to call the Texas legislature into session until the British completed their treaty efforts. When the congress convened, he presented two options: guaranteed independence or annexation and statehood. Both the congress and the people of Texas embraced annexation. With little dissent, the Texas legislature approved the offer of annexation, as did the convention called under the terms of the joint resolution. On October 13, 1845, almost 95 percent of the voters approved annexation.

The third audience included the European powers, especially England and France, and Mexico. Initially the Mexican government took a belligerent stance against the United States. In the summer of 1844, while Congress debated the Texas treaty, Mexico broke off diplomatic relations with the United States, began to make military preparations, and transmitted a declaration of war to Texas. Meanwhile, the British and French intensified their efforts to keep Texas independent. They pressured Mexico to accept a treaty with Texas that would preserve Texas's independence.

Impact

The most obvious impact of the annexation of Texas was that it precipitated a series of events that led to the Mexican War, the crisis over slavery in the territories, and the U.S. Civil War. More significantly, the joint resolution represented a major turning point in the history of North America. Potentially, Texas could have remained independent with British and French backing and become a significant barrier to the United States and its ultimate hegemony in North America. Texas's political leaders saw this potential as a real possibility, and American political leaders viewed it as a serious threat to the United States.

Initially, the resolution's actual impact was more benign, but it, too, led to serious problems. The joint resolution of 1845 started the process that brought Texas into the United States. Then the Texas convention convened on July 4, quickly approved the joint resolution, and drafted a state constitution. In the referendum of October 13, the voters of Texas endorsed annexation and approved the new state constitution. On December 29 the president signed the resolution and Texas was admitted to the Union. Almost as quickly, war broke out between the United States and Mexico. Even before the annexation process had been completed, Polk moved troops into Texas to protect it against a feared invasion and opened negotiations with Mexico. These negotiations broke down, and, following a border clash between U.S. and Mexican forces, Polk sought and received a declaration of war against Mexico on May 13, 1846.

The war was a total American victory. The Treaty of Guadalupe Hidalgo, which was signed on February 2, 1848, ended the war. Mexico accepted the Rio Grande as the boundary between Texas and Mexico and sold about one-third of its territory to the United States. The war also intensified the crisis over slavery. Early in the war, David Wilmot, a Democratic congressman from Pennsylvania, attached an amendment to a war appropriations bill that would exclude slavery from any territory acquired from Mexico as a result of the war. The bill did not pass, but it launched a debate over the expansion of slavery that threatened to split the country apart before it was temporarily resolved by the Compromise of 1850.

The Mexican War and the acquisition of new southwestern territories also created a crisis between Texas and the federal government over the boundary between Texas and New Mexico. Texas, which claimed the Rio Grande as its western boundary, was incensed when New Mexico, with support from President Taylor and the U.S. military commander in New Mexico, ignored Texas's territorial claims as they organized the New Mexico territory. As the crisis intensified, some Texans threatened military action to support their claims and suggested that they should separate from the United States. The Compromise of 1850 resolved the issue. The Texas boundary was redrawn, and the state transferred its western territory to the United States in exchange for $10 million, much of which was used to pay Texas's debts.

The Compromise of 1850 was less successful in resolving the slavery issue. The Kansas-Nebraska Act of 1854 reopened the crisis over slavery in the territories. The admission of California as a free state in 1850, followed by Oregon and Minnesota in the late 1850s, upset the longstanding balance between slave and free states. The election of Abraham Lincoln as the president in 1860 triggered the secession of South Carolina and five other states of the Deep South in December 1860 and January 1861. On February 1, 1861, Texas seceded from the Union as well.

Related Documents

"Joint Resolution of the Congress of the United States, December 29, 1845." The Avalon Project at Yale Law School Web site. http://www.yale.edu/lawweb/avalon/texan04.htm. Accessed on November 12, 2007. This resolution acknowledges that Texas has complied with the process of admission contained in the joint resolution of March 1, 1845, and admits Texas to the United States as a state.

"Ordinance of the Convention of Texas, July 4, 1845." The Avalon Project at Yale Law School Web site. http://www.yale.edu/lawweb/avalon/texan03.htm. Accessed on November 12, 2007. This ordinance was approved by a convention of delegates in Texas called to consider the admission of Texas to the United States under the terms of the joint resolution of March 1, 1845.

"The Treaty of Annexation, April 12, 1844." The Avalon Project at Yale Law School Web site. http://www.yale.edu/lawweb/avalon/texan05.htm. Accessed on November 12, 2007. This treaty was negotiated by representatives of Texas and the United States, but the Senate refused to ratify the treaty in the politically charged atmosphere of the summer of 1844.

Bibliography

■ Articles

Narrett, David E. "A Choice of Destiny: Immigration Policy, Slavery, and the Annexation of Texas." *Southwestern Historical Quarterly* 100 (January 1997): 271–302.

Schroeder, John H. "Annexation or Independence: The Texas Issue in American Politics, 1836–1845." *Southwestern Historical Quarterly* 89 (October 1985): 137–164.

Vasquez, Josefina Zoraida. "The Texas Question in Mexican Politics, 1836–1845." *Southwestern Historical Quarterly* 89 (January 1986): 309–344.

■ Books

Madis, Franklin. *The Taking of Texas: A Documentary History.* Austin, Tex.: Eakin Press, 2002.

Merk, Frederick. *Slavery and the Annexation of Texas.* New York: Knopf, 1972.

Pletcher, David M. *The Diplomacy of Annexation: Texas, Oregon, and the Mexican War.* Columbia: University of Missouri Press, 1973.

Silbey, Joel H. *Storm over Texas: The Annexation Controversy and the Road to Civil War.* New York: Oxford University Press, 2005.

Stegmaier, Mark J. *Texas, New Mexico, and the Compromise of 1850: Boundary Dispute and Sectional Crisis.* Kent, Ohio: Kent State University Press, 1996.

■ Web Sites

"The Handbook of Texas Online." Texas State Historical Association Web site.
   http://www.tsha.utexas.edu/handbook/online/. Accessed on November 10, 2007.

"Hard Road to Texas: Texas Annexation, 1836–1845." Texas State Library and Archives Commission Web site.
   http://www.tsl.state.tx.us/exhibits/annexation/index.html. Accessed on November 12, 2007.

"Texas—From Independence to Annexation." The Avalon Project at Yale Law School Web site.
   http://www.yale.edu/lawweb/avalon/texmenu.htm. Accessed on November 12, 2007.

—By Cary D. Wintz

Questions for Further Study

1. Why did the U.S. presidents Andrew Jackson and Martin Van Buren refuse to annex Texas in 1836 and 1837? Were their reasons the same?

2. What factors changed between June 1844, when the Treaty of Annexation was defeated, and February 1845, when the joint resolution was passed by Congress? How did these changes affect the debate over annexation?

3. Compare and contrast the terms of the failed 1844 Treaty of Annexation with the terms of the joint resolution of 1845. Explain which document gave Texas better terms for joining the United States.

4. Assess the validity of the idea that the annexation of Texas in 1845 was the first step in a series of events that led to the outbreak of the Civil War in 1861.

Glossary

apportionment   official distribution of seats in the U.S. House of Representatives following each decennial census

ceding   transferring, usually of land, from one country to another, usually by virtue of a treaty

deem   consider or think

defray   pay or cover the cost of

deputies   elected representatives in a legislative body or convention

edifices   large or imposing buildings

involuntary servitude   forced labor or service without compensation or pay; slavery

magazines   places for the storage of military equipment, especially ammunition

Missouri compromise line   a line located at 36°30' north latitude, extending west from the southwestern corner of Missouri, which divided the remaining unorganized territory of the Louisiana Purchase between free territory and slave territory

overture   formal or informal initiative toward an agreement, an action, or the establishment of a relationship

said   aforementioned

unappropriated lands   lands held in common, usually by a government, that have not passed into private ownership

JOINT RESOLUTION OF CONGRESS FOR THE ANNEXATION OF TEXAS

March 1, 1845

28th Congress Second Session

Begun and held at the city of Washington, in the District of Columbia, on Monday the second day of December, eighteen hundred and forty-four.

Joint Resolution for annexing Texas to the United States.

Resolved by the Senate and House of Representatives of the United States of America in Congress assembled, That Congress doth consent that the territory properly included within, and rightfully belonging to the Repub-

John Tyler

lic of Texas, may be erected into a new state, to be called the state of Texas, with a republican form of government, to be adopted by the people of said republic, by deputies in Convention assembled, with the consent of the existing government, in order that the same may be admitted as one of the states of this Union.

2. And be it further resolved, That the foregoing consent of Congress is given upon the following conditions, and with the following guarantees, to wit: First—said state to be formed, subject to the adjustment by this government of all questions of boundary that may arise with other governments; and the constitution thereof, with the proper evidence of its adoption by the people of said republic of Texas, shall be transmitted to the President of the United States, to be laid before Congress for its final action, on or before the first day of January, one thousand eight hundred and forty-six. Second—said state, when admitted into the Union, after ceding to the United States all public edifices, fortifications, barracks, ports and harbors, navy and navy-yards, docks, magazines, arms, armaments, and all other property and means pertaining to the public defence belonging to said republic of Texas, shall retain all the public funds, debts, taxes, and dues of every kind which may belong to or be due and owing said republic; and shall also retain all the vacant and unappropriated lands lying within its limits, to be applied to the payment of the debts and liabilities of said republic of

Texas; and the residue of said lands, after discharging said debts and liabilities, to be disposed of as said state may direct; but in no event are said debts and liabilities to become a charge upon the government of the United States. Third—New states, of convenient size, not exceeding four in number, in addition to said state of Texas, and having sufficient population, may hereafter, by the consent of said state, be formed out of the territory thereof, which shall be entitled to admission under the provisions of the federal constitution. And such states as may be formed out of that portion of said territory lying south of thirty-six degrees thirty minutes north latitude, commonly known as the Missouri compromise line, shall be admitted into the Union with or without slavery, as the people of each state asking admission may desire. And in such state or states as shall be formed out of said territory north of said Missouri compromise line, slavery, or involuntary servitude, (except for crime,) shall be prohibited.

3. And be it further resolved, That if the President of the United States shall in his judgment and discretion deem it most advisable, instead of proceeding to submit the foregoing resolution to the Republic of Texas, as an overture on the part of the United States for admission, to negotiate with that Republic; then, Be it resolved, that a state, to be formed out of the present Republic of Texas, with suitable extent and boundaries, and with two representatives in Congress, until the next apportionment of representation, shall be admitted into the Union, by virtue of this act, on an equal footing with the existing states, as soon as the terms and conditions of such admission, and the cession of the remaining Texan territory to the United States shall be agreed upon by the governments of Texas and the United States: And that the sum of one hundred thousand dollars be, and the same is hereby, appropriated to defray the expenses of missions and negotiations, to agree upon the terms of said admission and cession, either by

treaty to be submitted to the Senate, or by articles to be submitted to the two Houses of Congress, as the President may direct.

J W JONES, Speaker of the House of Representatives.

WILLIE P. MANGUM, President, pro tempore, of the Senate.

Approv'd March 1. 1845
JOHN TYLER

DECLARATION OF SENTIMENTS.

When, in the course of human events, it becomes necessary for one portion of the family of man to assume among the people of the earth a position different from that which they have hitherto occupied, but one to which the laws of nature and of nature's God entitle them, a decent respect to the opinions of mankind requires that they should declare the causes that impel them to such a course.

We hold these truths to be self-evident: that all men and women are created equal; that they are endowed by their Creator with certain inalienable rights, that among these are life, liberty, and the pursuit of happiness; that to secure these rights governments are instituted, deriving their just powers from the consent of the governed. Whenever any form of government becomes destructive of these ends, it is the right of those who suffer from it to refuse allegiance to it, and to insist upon the institution of a new government, laying its foundation on such principles, and organizing its powers in such form as to them shall seem most likely to effect their safety and happiness. Prudence, indeed, will dictate that governments long established should not be changed for light and transient causes; and accordingly, all experience hath shown that mankind are more disposed to suffer, while evils are sufferable, than to right themselves by abolishing the forms to which they were accustomed. But when a long train of abuses and usurpations, pursuing invariably the same object evinces a design to reduce them under absolute despotism, it is their duty to throw off such government, and to provide new guards for their future security. Such has been the patient sufferance of the women under this government, and such is now the necessity which constrains them to demand the equal station to which they are entitled.

The history of mankind is a history of repeated injuries and usurpations on the part of man toward woman, having in direct object the establishment of an absolute tyranny over her. To prove this, let facts be submitted to a candid world.

The Seneca Falls Declaration of Sentiments (Library of Congress)

SENECA FALLS CONVENTION DECLARATION OF SENTIMENTS

"The history of mankind is a history of repeated injuries and usurpations on the part of man toward woman."

Overview

The Declaration of Sentiments was written by Elizabeth Cady Stanton and was presented to the participants at a convention in Seneca Falls, New York, on July 19–20, 1848. Modeling her work on the Declaration of Independence, the author sought to address the wrongs perpetrated against womankind and called for redress of those wrongs. The Seneca Falls meeting was the first convention specifically devoted to the issue of women's rights. Organized by Stanton, Lucretia Coffin Mott, Mary Ann McClintock, Martha Wright, and Jane Hunt, the convention's goal was to address "the social, civil and religious rights of women," according to the *Seneca County Courier* of July 14, 1848 ("Rights for Women," http://www.nwhm.org/Rightsfor Women/SenecaFalls.html). The Declaration of Sentiments summed up the current state of women's rights in the United States and served notice that women would no longer stand for being treated inequitably.

While antebellum reformers, many of whom were abolitionists, connected the situation of women with that of slaves, in that neither could vote, hold office, sit on juries, or have property rights, the Seneca Falls Convention marked the first time that men and women publicly discussed the issue of women's rights. The people who gathered at Seneca Falls realized that they were taking an unprecedented—not to mention controversial—step in calling for full citizenship for American women. The Declaration of Sentiments was considered radical for its time, especially in the clause calling for suffrage of women. In the context of antebellum America, this document is indeed a radical one. While it took seventy-two years for women to get the vote and even longer to abolish other forms of discrimination, the Declaration of Sentiments marked the first step in the long struggle for women's rights.

Context

The United States in the 1840s seethed with a variety of reform movements, inspired by the religious upheaval known as the Second Great Awakening as well as the rise of transcendentalism. (Transcendentalism was a new way of looking at life, spirituality, and religion that emerged in the mid-nineteenth century. Transcendentalists, among them Ralph Waldo Emerson, generally believed that they could gain knowledge of spiritual reality through the use of intuition rather than through established religion.) The men and women reformers thought they could improve American society by changing some of the ills they perceived as plagues upon the nation. Some of the reformers' causes included better treatment of the mentally ill, opposition to capital punishment and war, temperance, and most notably, abolitionism. The first publication of William Lloyd Garrison's antislavery newspaper the *Liberator* on January 1, 1831, traditionally marks the beginning of the American abolitionist movement. Garrison's newspaper proclaimed on its masthead that there should "no union with slaveholders" and demanded the end of slavery immediately. This call for immediate abolition set the abolitionists apart from antislavery advocates who were more moderate and willing to accept the gradual dismantling of the slave system. The formation of the American Anti-Slavery Society in 1833 created an organization committed to the immediate abolition of slavery. Throughout the North activists formed antislavery organizations loosely affiliated with the American Anti-Slavery Society.

Men of conscience, however, were not the only ones who wanted to free the enslaved. Organized antislavery encouraged women to participate in the movement, although the more conservative preferred that women form auxiliary organizations rather than joining with the men in the same group. Others, like Garrison and his friend Stephen S. Foster, believed that women should participate in the same organizations alongside the men. The role of women in the American Anti-Slavery Society became one of several issues that finally split the organization in 1840. Those who supported full participation of women stayed in the American Anti-Slavery Society, while the dissenters formed the American and Foreign Anti-Slavery Society. Those who stayed in the American Anti-Slavery Society also viewed the U.S. Constitution as a proslavery document and eschewed involvement with political parties.

Time Line

1831

■ **January 1**
First issue is published of William Lloyd Garrison's *Liberator*, which traditionally marks the rise of the abolitionist movement, demanding an immediate end to slavery.

1833

■ **December 4**
Formation of the American Anti-Slavery Society, marking the beginnings of organized abolitionism focused on immediate abolition.

1840

■ Conservative abolitionists bolt the American Anti-Slavery Society and form the American and Foreign Anti-Slavery Society, placing the discussion of the role of women in organized abolition on the national stage.

■ **June 12**
Beginning of the World Anti-Slavery Convention in London, England, where female delegates are refused seats and Stanton and Mott meet for the first time.

1848

■ **July 19**
The first women's rights convention, in Seneca Falls, New York, opens. The Declaration of Sentiments is presented to the convention; on July 20 members of the convention sign the document.

1850

■ Amelia Jenks Bloomer launches her dress reform crusade with the appearance of the women's outfit bearing her name.

■ **April 19**
First women's rights convention west of the Alleghenies opens in Salem, Ohio. It is the only women's rights convention where men were not permitted to participate.

■ **October 23**
First national women's rights convention opens in Worcester, Massachusetts.

Female abolitionists played a number of roles in the fight to end slavery, circulating petitions to Congress, holding antislavery fairs, contributing articles to antislavery publications, and organizing antislavery societies. Some even took the daring step of speaking out publicly against slavery. The sisters Sarah and Angelina Grimké were among the first women who gave public orations to mixed-gender audiences on the issue of abolition. This was considered so outrageous that they were often on the receiving end of abuse, both verbal and physical. The Grimkés paved the way for other women orators such as Abby Kelley Foster. The abolitionist movement, as well as other contemporary reform movements such as temperance and anti-capital punishment, was fertile ground for inspiring women's activity beyond the home. Their work in reform motivated many women to question their role in society and begin to work to improve their own lot. It was in this atmosphere that Elizabeth Cady Stanton, Lucretia Coffin Mott, Jane Hunt, Mary Ann McClintock, and Martha Wright called for a convention to discuss the issue of women's rights.

The seed for what became the Seneca Falls Convention in 1848 was actually planted several years earlier at the 1840 World Anti-Slavery Convention in London. Mott and Stanton met for the first time at the London convention. Stanton was accompanying her husband, Henry, who was a delegate to the convention. Mott was actually a delegate herself but, because of her gender, was denied a seat at the convention. This blatant discrimination forced the women to rethink their treatment in American society and call for their rights as free citizens of the United States.

The immediate impetus for the Seneca Falls Convention was the impending passage of a married women's property law in New York State. Traditionally women had no legal rights to property; once married, everything from the clothes on their backs to their children belonged to the husband. The New York legislature was considering legislation to give married women some property rights. The convention's organizers hoped that by meeting they would bring awareness to the inequitable treatment of women and gain support for passage of the law. Mott's husband, James, chaired the convention; the participants feared that having a woman preside would only increase hostility toward their cause. Seneca Falls was the last time that a male presided over a women's rights convention. The Declaration of Sentiments was one of two documents produced at the convention. The other was a preamble followed by a series of eleven resolutions making various demands for women's rights. Resolution number nine was the most radical—it called for the right of women to vote. All eleven resolutions passed, ten of them unanimously. Only the demand for the vote was not passed unanimously. Indeed, even Lucretia Mott felt that asking for votes for women would harm their cause.

About the Author

Elizabeth Cady Stanton was born on November 12, 1815, in Johnstown, New York, the daughter of Margaret

Livingstone and Daniel Cady. Stanton's father was a distinguished lawyer and jurist who ultimately served on the state's highest court. Stanton was one of eleven of children, many of whom did not survive to adulthood. Young Elizabeth received tutoring in Greek and mathematics; she also became an accomplished equestrian. Judge Cady allowed her free run of his library, giving her access to any book she wished to read, including law books. Cady alternated praising his daughter's accomplishments with telling her he wished she had been born male, creating in her a determination to succeed at academic as well as domestic activities. By reading her father's law books, she also learned that women were accorded a second-class status in the legal realm, planting the seed that eventually matured into her campaign for women's rights.

Stanton furthered her education at Emma Willard's Troy Female Seminary in Troy, New York. Willard's school provided the best female education available for its time. Stanton studied the classics, algebra, geometry, philosophy, and history as well as proper female deportment and etiquette. After her graduation in 1833, Stanton lived with a cousin, the abolitionist Gerrit Smith, in whose circle she was exposed to reformist sentiment. It was at Smith's residence that she met a fellow abolitionist, Henry Stanton, whom she married in 1840. Stanton accompanied her husband to London in that year, where he was a delegate to the World Anti-Slavery Convention. She met another American delegate, Lucretia Coffin Mott, who, because of her gender, could not take her seat at the convention. All the female delegates were allowed only to observe the proceedings in silence. Mott and Stanton commiserated about the injustice dealt the women and vowed to do something about it. This fateful meeting eventually culminated in the Seneca Falls Convention.

Upon their return from Europe, the Stantons settled with her family so that Henry could study to law. They moved to Boston in 1842, where Henry practiced law. The couple also began their family in 1842; their last of six children was born in 1856. Elizabeth became an avid participant in Boston's intellectual life, where she met luminaries such as Frederick Douglass, Louisa May Alcott, and Ralph Waldo Emerson. Henry actively participated in antislavery activities, although he was more closely allied with the conservative wing of abolitionism, rather than the Garrisonian wing. He and Elizabeth disagreed on a number of issues, particularly that of women's rights. Indeed, throughout her life she refused to refer to herself as "Mrs. Henry Stanton"; instead she used "Elizabeth Cady Stanton" or "E. C. Stanton." In 1847 the Stantons left Boston for Seneca Falls, in Upstate New York, because of Henry's health.

Seneca Falls was a small community in the Finger Lakes region. While children and her household occupied some of Stanton's time, she missed the intellectual stimulation of city life. As she became involved in her new home, Stanton made the acquaintance of women who agreed that something needed to be done to improve the rights of women. Stanton, Lucretia Mott, Jane Hunt, Martha Wright, and Mary Ann McClintock organized a convention to discuss

www.milestonedocuments.com

Time Line

1866

■ Elizabeth Cady Stanton and Susan B. Anthony form the Equal Rights Association with the goal of universal suffrage.

1868

■ **July 9**
Fourteenth Amendment to the U.S. Constitution is passed; this is the first time that voters are equated with male citizens only.

1869

■ The organized women's rights movement splits into two organizations over the Fourteenth Amendment and pending Fifteenth Amendment (which gives black men the right to vote); Stanton and Anthony form the National Woman Suffrage Association; Lucy Stone, Henry Blackwell, and Julia Ward Howe form the more conservative American Woman Suffrage Association.

■ **December 10**
Wyoming Territory gives women right to vote.

1870

■ **February 3**
Fifteenth Amendment to the U.S. Constitution is ratified.

1872

■ **November 21**
Susan B. Anthony is arrested after voting in the presidential election of 1872, casting her ballot for Ulysses S. Grant. Anthony also convinces her three sisters and ten other women to vote; all of them are arrested as well. Anthony claims women are enfranchised by the Fourteenth and Fifteenth Amendments.

1878

■ Woman suffrage amendment is introduced into Congress for the first time.

1890

■ National Woman Suffrage Association and American Woman Suffrage Association is reunited as the National American Woman Suffrage Association under the leadership of Stanton. It is this organization that leads the way to the federal woman suffrage amendment.

1890

■ March 27
Wyoming enters the Union
with woman suffrage provision
intact.

1920

■ August 18
The Nineteenth Amendment
to the U.S. Constitution,
enfranchising women, is
ratified.

the rights of women. The Seneca Falls Convention, where Stanton presented her Declaration of Sentiments, gave birth to other women's rights conventions around the country, including the first national convention, in Worcester, Massachusetts, in 1850. The conventions continued until the outbreak of the Civil War.

In 1851 Amelia Bloomer introduced Stanton to the woman who would become her lifelong friend, Susan B. Anthony. The two women had complementary gifts; Stanton was the better writer and Anthony the superior organizer. The unmarried Anthony was free to travel and speak out on women's rights, while Stanton stayed home and saw to her family but wrote Anthony's speeches. Together Stanton and Anthony provided decades of leadership for the nascent feminist movement. Following the Civil War, Stanton and Anthony formed the Equal Rights Association supporting universal suffrage and tried to get women included in the Fourteenth Amendment, which defined citizens as exclusively male for the first time in the Constitution. Stanton took a hard-line stance that neither the Fourteenth nor the Fifteenth Amendment (which gave black men the right to vote) should be passed unless woman suffrage was included. The women were told that it was "the Negro's hour" ("Suffrage Activity in the Nineteenth Century," http://www.nwhm.org/exhibits/tour_02-02d.html), and both amendments passed without provisions for woman suffrage, but some of the feminists embarked on their own crusade to gain the vote for women.

Stanton and Anthony split from the more conservative feminists like Lucy Stone and Julia Ward Howe, differing on passage of the Fourteenth and Fifteenth Amendments as well as the approach to organizing the suffrage movement. Stanton and Anthony organized the National Woman Suffrage Association (NWSA) and Stone and Howe the American Woman Suffrage Association (AWSA), both in 1869. The NWSA believed that the goal should be an amendment to the U.S. Constitution, with the Fifteenth Amendment as the model. The organization also propounded a broader agenda of women's rights in general, not just the vote. The AWSA, on the other hand, supported the Fourteenth and Fifteenth Amendments and worked on gaining votes for women state by state. The NWSA counted among its supporters Sojourner Truth and Matilda Joslyn Gage, who became a leader in the suffrage move-

ment and, in an interesting aside, was the mother-in-law of L. Frank Baum, author of *The Wizard of Oz*.

Stanton put her writing skills to good use on behalf of the feminist movement. Together with Anthony and the feminist Parker Pillsbury, she wrote and edited a feminist periodical called *Revolution* in 1868. She also published a number of works including her autobiography, *Eighty Years and More* (1898). With Anthony and Gage she wrote volumes 1 through 3 of *The History of Woman Suffrage* (published in six volumes 1881–1922, with the later volumes completed by Anthony, Gage, and Ida Husted Harper). Stanton's *Woman's Bible* (1895) is an intriguing publication, offering a feminist interpretation of scripture.

As Stanton's children matured, she was able to more actively pursue the cause of women's rights. She made speeches and worked to pass suffrage laws in several states, including New York, Michigan, and Kansas. Senator Aaron A. Sargent of California introduced the woman suffrage amendment to the U.S. Senate for the first time in 1878 at the behest of Stanton and Anthony. It contained the exact wording that would finally become law in 1920.

The suffrage movement gained strength when the NWSA and AWSA merged in 1890 to form the National American Woman Suffrage Association and elected Stanton its first president. Stanton served the organization until her death on October 26, 1902. Throughout her long life, Stanton worked tirelessly for women's rights. Her ideas were often considered too radical for the mainstream, and eventually it was Anthony who received most of the adulation from young suffragists, whose primary goal was the vote. In a great disservice to Stanton, the Nineteenth Amendment is also referred to as the "Susan B. Anthony amendment." With the revitalization of the feminist movement in the 1960s, Stanton has been restored to her proper place of importance as a founding mother of modern feminism.

Explanation and Analysis of the Document

The Declaration of Sentiments echoes the language and structure of the Declaration of Independence's preamble. Its opening justifies the actions of those who support women's rights and prepares the reader for the litany of the wrongs perpetrated against womankind. Stanton uses the religious language of the Declaration of Independence when she refers to "nature's God" and points out that the rights women are demanding come not from government but from "nature" as well as the Supreme Being.

Stanton goes on to state, "We hold these truths to be self-evident: that all men and women are created equal." This ringing proclamation comes directly from the Declaration of Independence, with only the words "and women" added. Women, like men, are entitled to "life, liberty, and the pursuit of happiness," and the government was instituted to make sure that all people are guaranteed these rights. Stanton states that people who have been denied their rights have the right to "refuse allegiance" to their government and "insist upon the institution of a new govern-

Bronze statues at the Women's Rights National Historical Park depict Elizabeth Cady Stanton, Frederick Douglass, Lucretia Mott and other attendees to the 1848 convention held in Seneca Falls, New York. (AP Photo/Michael Okoniewski)

ment." In fact, those who are abused in this way have a responsibility and duty "to throw off such government." These are the words Thomas Jefferson used to justify the American people's break from Great Britain and formation of a new government. Stanton added, however, language stating that women have suffered patiently under the current government, which has denied them their full rights, and "such is now the necessity which constrains them to demand the equal station to which they are entitled."

A statement that the "history of mankind is a history of repeated injustices and usurpations on the part of man toward woman" introduces the lengthy portion of the document that lists the wrongs visited upon womankind. The first five focus on women's political rights—or lack thereof. The list begins with the fact that women are denied the vote. Logically, from lacking the vote, women are subject to laws that they had no say in making. The next item argues that women have been denied simple rights possessed by even the "most ignorant and degraded" men, not only native-born but even foreign. This statement was an appeal to the nativist element that was emerging in the late nineteenth century. The next statement again makes mention of the denial of "the elective franchise" in the context of denying women "representation in the halls of the legislation."

The next set of wrongs deals with marriage and property rights. Stanton observes that the institution of marriage

has been particularly destructive to women, given that married women are defined outright as "civilly dead" in the eyes of the law. Because of that, married women have no rights to property, even their own wages. The next clause states that because of the usurpation of these rights, the law has essentially rendered woman "an irresponsible being" who can commit any crime without fear of punishment, as long as it is done "in the presence of her husband." Stanton further notes that women must obey their husbands unquestioningly and that the law gives him the power "to deprive her of her liberty" and physically and emotionally abuse her without recourse. Divorce is the next topic, and here women are denied the guardianship of their children, no matter what the cause for ending the marriage. Single women are mentioned in the next clause, which points out that if a single woman is a property owner, then she is subject to taxes; thus the government "recognizes her only when her property can be made profitable to it."

Clauses on employment, education, and religion make up the next set. Stanton states that men have "monopolized nearly all the profitable employments." Not only that, but in the professions women could enter, they were not equitably paid. At the time the Declaration of Sentiments was written, the only acceptable profession for "respectable" women was teaching—and even that was restricted to edu-

> "We hold these truths to be self-evident: that all men and women are created equal."
>
> (Paragraph 2)

> "The history of mankind is a history of repeated injuries and usurpations on the part of man toward woman, having in direct object the establishment of an absolute tyranny over her."
>
> (Paragraph 3)

> "He has never permitted her to exercise her inalienable right to the elective franchise."
>
> (Paragraph 4)

> "He has withheld from her rights which are given to the most ignorant and degraded men—both natives and foreigners."
>
> (Paragraph 6)

> "Having deprived her of this first right of a citizen, the elective franchise, thereby leaving her without representation in the halls of legislation, he has oppressed her on all sides."
>
> (Paragraph 7)

cating young children. Stanton believed that women should have access to any profession they wished. The next clause focuses on education, noting that all colleges are "closed against her." Stanton actually slightly exaggerates in this clause, as Oberlin College did admit women equally with men by 1848, but that was the exception rather than the rule. Organized religion comes under attack next, for it keeps women "in a subordinate position," barring them from the ministry and generally from any "public participation in the affairs of the church." Not only are women discriminated against by "the church," but also in the realm of morals they are subjected to a double standard; as the clause puts it, there is "a different code of morals for men and women." The penultimate clause makes reference to God and states that man has "usurped" the Lord's "prerogative" by assigning woman a sphere of action "when that belongs to her conscience and to her God." Finally, the last clause states that man has decreed women should be sub-

missive and dependent, destroying "her confidence in her own powers" and lessening "her self-respect."

The last paragraph sums up the entire document. Stanton states that in light of the aforementioned grievances, including "the disenfranchisement of one-half the people of this country," American women "insist that they have immediate admission to all the rights and privileges which belong to them as citizens of the United States."

Audience

The Declaration of Sentiments was written for several audiences. The first audience was the men and women who participated in the Seneca Falls Convention. Following the form and adapting many of the key concepts of the Declaration of Independence, the Declaration of Sentiments sought to set forth the wrongs done to women and offer a redress of those wrongs. Thus, another audience was the men who served as the lawmakers of the United States, both in the federal government and in each state and territory. These people made the laws and needed to be aware that women were treated as second-class citizens and were not granted all the rights of other American citizens. The last audience was the people of the United States. The document was intended to raise the awareness of all Americans regarding the treatment of women in the nation that proclaimed that "all men are created equal." Stanton and the other women's rights advocates understood that in order to improve women's legal and social standing, they would need to win the support of those in power as well as influencing popular opinion.

Impact

Following its adoption at the Seneca Falls Convention, the Declaration of Sentiments became a flash point for criticism and ridicule of the nascent women's rights movement. The newspapers that reported on the convention derided the document and its signers. The press generally expressed fears that by demanding equal rights, women were stepping out of the role ordained for them not only by society but also by God and nature. The only newspaper that actually applauded the Declaration of Sentiments was Frederick Douglass's *North Star*, which called it the "grand basis for attaining the civil, social, political, and religious rights of women" (July 28, 1848). A second women's rights convention met a few weeks later, on August 2, 1848, in Rochester, New York. This convention was the first to have a female president, Abigail Bush. The participants adopted the Declaration of Sentiments from Seneca Falls. The Rochester convention was also subject to ridicule and derision by the general public. By the time that the first women's rights convention was held west of the Alleghenies, at Salem, Ohio, in 1850, supporters of feminism no longer considered the suffrage clause radical. Indeed, the vote was now seen as an essential element in women's rights reform and eventually became the centerpiece of the movement.

From its introduction in 1848 through the present, the Declaration of Sentiments has been a central part of feminist thought. While the women's movement focused solely on the vote following the Civil War, there were still many feminists who had a broader vision of women's rights. Alice Paul and the National Woman's Party, which was founded in 1914 as the Congressional Union, saw beyond the vote to full equality for women, not only in the United States but indeed worldwide. The revitalized feminist movement in the 1960s was more in the spirit of the Declaration of Sentiments, demanding full participation in society. In 1998, at the 150th anniversary of the Seneca Falls Convention, the National Organization for Women issued its own Declaration of Sentiments modeled on the Seneca Falls document. The demands expressed generations ago still have relevance for men and women seeking justice for all in the contemporary world.

Elizabeth Cady Stanton (Library of Congress)

Related Documents

Anthony, Susan B., et al. *The History of Woman Suffrage*. 6 vols. 1886–1922. Reprint. New York: Arno Press, 1969. The coauthors of this documentary collection—along with Anthony, Elizabeth Cady Stanton and Matilda Joslyn Gage in volumes 1–3 and Gage and Ida Husted Harper in volumes 4–6—not only included their own reminiscences but also collected the stories of other suffrage activists. This is an indispensable source for studying the first American feminist movement. Volume 1 includes the text of the Declaration of Sentiments.

DuBois, Ellen Carol, ed. *The Elizabeth Cady Stanton–Susan B. Anthony Reader: Correspondence, Writings, Speeches*. Revised edition. Boston: Northeastern University Press, 1992. Gerda Lerner, one of the premier historians of women's history, contributed a foreword to this volume of primary documents by Stanton and Anthony.

Sherr, Lynn. *Failure Is Impossible: Susan B. Anthony in Her Own Words* Pittsburgh, Pa.: Three Rivers Press, 1996. This is a collection of Anthony's speeches and correspondence.

Stanton, Elizabeth Cady. *The Woman's Bible*. Boston: Northeastern University Press, 1993. This is Stanton's critique of the Bible from a feminist perspective.

———. *The Solitude of Self*. Ashfield, Mass.: Paris Press, 2001. This is the text of a speech by Stanton, which she considered the most important she ever gave.

———. *Eighty Years and More: Reminiscences, 1815–1897.* Unabridged edition. Amherst, N.Y.: Humanity Books, 2002. Stanton's autobiography.

Bibliography

■ Articles

"The Rights of Women." *The North Star*, July 28, 1848.

■ Books

Baker, Jean H., ed. *Votes for Women: The Struggle for Suffrage Revisited.* New York: Oxford University Press, 2002.

DuBois, Ellen Carol. *Feminism and Suffrage: The Emergence of an Independent Women's Movement in the United States, 1848–1869.* Revised edition. Ithaca, N.Y.: Cornell University Press, 1999.

Flexner, Eleanor, and Ellen Fitzpatrick. *Century of Struggle: The Woman's Rights Movement in the United States.* Enlarged edition. Cambridge, Mass.: Belknap Press of Harvard University Press, 1996.

Ginzberg, Lori. *Untidy Origins: A Story of Woman's Rights in Antebellum New York.* Chapel Hill: University of North Carolina Press, 2005.

Griffith, Elisabeth. *In Her Own Right: The Life of Elizabeth Cady Stanton.* New York: Oxford University Press, 1985.

Isenberg, Nancy. *Sex and Citizenship in Antebellum America.* Chapel Hill: University of North Carolina Press, 1998.

Kraditor, Aileen. *The Ideas of the Woman Suffrage Movement, 1890–1920.* Reprint, New York: W. W. Norton, 1981.

McMillen, Sally. *Seneca Falls and the Origins of the Women's Rights Movement.* New York: Oxford University Press, 2008.

Ward, Geoffrey C. [based on a documentary film by Ken Burns and Paul Barnes]. *Not for Ourselves Alone: The Story of Elizabeth Cady Stanton and Susan B. Anthony: An Illustrated History.* New York. Alfred A. Knopf, 1999.

Wellman, Judith. *The Road to Seneca Falls: Elizabeth Cady Stanton and the First Woman's Rights Convention.* Urbana: University of Illinois Press, 2004.

■ Web Sites

"Not for Ourselves Alone: The Story of Elizabeth Cady Stanton and Susan B. Anthony." Public Broadcasting Service Web site.
    http://www.pbs.org/stantonanthony/. Accessed on November 26, 2007.

"Rights for Women: The Suffrage Movement and Its Leaders." National Women's History Museum Web site.
    http://www.nwhm.org/RightsforWomen/SenecaFalls.html. Accessed on January 10, 2008.

"Seneca Falls Convention." American Treasures of the Library of Congress Web site.
    http://www.loc.gov/exhibits/treasures/trr040.html. Accessed on November 26, 2007.

"Suffrage Activity in the Nineteenth Century." National Women's History Museum Web site.
    http://www.nwhm.org/exhibits/tour_02-02d.html. Accessed on January 10, 2008.

Susan B. Anthony House Web site.
    http://www.susanbanthonyhouse.org/. Accessed on November 26, 2007.

"Women's Rights." National Park Service U.S. Department of the Interior Web site.
    http://www.nps.gov/wori. Accessed on November 26, 2007.

—By Donna M. DeBlasio

Questions for Further Study

1. Compare and contrast the Declaration of Sentiments with the Declaration of Independence. How do these documents differ, and how are they alike? In your response, consider the time they were written, the audience, and the reaction.

2. Why was the demand for the vote so radical when first proposed at Seneca Falls?

3. It is July 1848. You are a reporter for a local newspaper. Write an article on the Seneca Falls Convention, which you have just attended. You can either support or attack the convention and the Declaration of Sentiments. In either case, you must defend your position.

candid	impartial
chastisement	discipline, especially physical punishment
constrains	forces; compels
covenant	formal agreement of legal validity
disfranchisement	denial of a right, especially the right to vote
franchise	the right to vote
hitherto	up to this time; until now
impunity	immunity from punishment
inalienable	incapable of being repudiated or transferred to another
Jehovah	a name for God in the Old Testament
prerogative	exclusive entitlement
prudence	caution regarding practical matters
remuneration	payment or consideration received for services or employment
sufferance	capacity to endure hardship
supposition	an assumption
usurped	used without authority or right; employed wrongfully

SENECA FALLS CONVENTION SENTIMENTS

The Declaration of Sentiments

When, in the course of human events, it becomes necessary for one portion of the family of man to assume among the people of the earth a position different from that which they have hitherto occupied, but one to which the laws of nature and of nature's God entitle them, a decent respect to the opinions of mankind requires that they should declare the causes that impel them to such a course.

We hold these truths to be self-evident: that all men and women are created equal; that they are endowed by their Creator with certain inalienable rights; that among these are life, liberty, and the pursuit of happiness; that to secure these rights governments are instituted, deriving their just powers from the consent of the governed. Whenever any form of government becomes destructive of these ends, it is the right of those who suffer from it to refuse allegiance to it, and to insist upon the institution of a new government, laying its foundation on such principles, and organizing its powers in such form, as to them shall seem most likely to effect their safety and happiness. Prudence, indeed, will dictate that governments long established should not be changed for light and transient causes; and accordingly all experience hath shown that mankind are more disposed to suffer, while evils are sufferable, than to right themselves by abolishing the forms to which they are accustomed. But when a long train of abuses and usurpations, pursuing invariably the same object, evinces a design to reduce them under absolute despotism, it is their duty to throw off such government, and to provide new guards for their future security. Such has been the patient sufferance of the women under this government, and such is now the necessity which constrains them to demand the equal station to which they are entitled. The history of mankind is a history of repeated injuries and usurpations on the part of man toward woman, having in

direct object the establishment of an absolute tyranny over her. To prove this, let facts be submitted to a candid world.

The history of mankind is a history of repeated injuries and usurpations on the part of man toward woman, having in direct object the establishment of an absolute tyranny over her. To prove this, let facts be submitted to a candid world.

He has never permitted her to exercise her inalienable right to the elective franchise.

He has compelled her to submit to laws, in the formation of which she had no voice.

He has withheld from her rights which are given to the most ignorant and degraded men—both natives and foreigners.

Having deprived her of this first right of a citizen, the elective franchise, thereby leaving her without representation in the halls of legislation, he has oppressed her on all sides.

He has made her, if married, in the eye of the law, civilly dead.

He has taken from her all right in property, even to the wages she earns.

He has made her, morally, an irresponsible being, as she can commit many crimes with impunity, provided they be done in the presence of her husband. In the covenant of marriage, she is compelled to promise obedience to her husband, he becoming, to all intents and purposes, her master—the law giving him power to deprive her of her liberty, and to administer chastisement.

He has so framed the laws of divorce, as to what shall be the proper causes, and in case of separation, to whom the guardianship of the children shall be given, as to be wholly regardless of the happiness of women—the law, in all cases, going upon a false supposition of the supremacy of man, and giving all power into his hands.

After depriving her of all rights as a married woman, if single, and the owner of property, he has taxed her to support a government which recognizes her only when her property can be made profitable to it.

He has monopolized nearly all the profitable employments, and from those she is permitted to follow, she receives but a scanty remuneration. He closes against her all the avenues to wealth and distinction which he considers most honorable to himself. As a teacher of theology, medicine, or law, she is not known.

He has denied her the facilities for obtaining a thorough education, all colleges being closed against her.

He allows her in church, as well as state, but a subordinate position, claiming apostolic authority for her exclusion from the ministry, and, with some exceptions, from any public participation in the affairs of the church.

He has created a false public sentiment by giving to the world a different code of morals for men and women, by which moral delinquencies which exclude women from society, are not only tolerated, but deemed of little account in man.

He has usurped the prerogative of Jehovah himself, claiming it as his right to assign for her a sphere of action, when that belongs to her conscience and to her God.

He has endeavored, in every way that he could, to destroy her confidence in her own powers, to lessen her self-respect, and to make her willing to lead a dependent and abject life.

Now, in view of this entire disfranchisement of one-half the people of this country, their social and religious degradation—in view of the unjust laws above mentioned, and because women do feel themselves aggrieved, oppressed, and fraudulently deprived of their most sacred rights, we insist that they have immediate admission to all the rights and privileges which belong to them as citizens of the United States.

It being desirable, for the peace, concord and harmony of t[he]
[Uni]on of these States, to settle and adjust amicably all questions
existing
controversy ~~between them~~ between them, arising out of the
[insti]tution of Slavery, upon a fair equitable and just basis: Therefor[e]
1st Resolved that California, with suitable boundaries, oug[ht]
her application
be admitted as one of the States of this Union, without the im[posi-]
tion by Congress of any restriction in respect to the exclus[ion]
[or] introduction of Slavery within those boundaries.

[2.] Resolved that as Slavery does not exist by law, and is not l[ikely]
[to] be introduced into any of the Territory acquired by the Unite[d]
[Stat]es from the Republic of Mexico, it is inexpedient for Cong[ress]
[to] provide by law either for its introduction into or exclusion
[fr]om any part of the said Territory; and that appropriate Terri[tor-]
[i]al Governments ought to be established by Congress in all of [sai]d territory, not assigned as the boundaries of the proposed State [of] California, without the adoption of any restriction or conditi[on on] the subject of Slavery.

3. Resolved that the Western boundary of the State of Texas oug[ht]
[to] be fixed on the Rio del Norte, commencing one Marine league
[from] its mouth, and running up that river to the Southern line of
New Mexico, thence with that line Eastwardly, and so continuing in the s[ame]
between the U.S. and Spain;
[direc]tion to the line as established, excluding any portion of New Mexico, whe[ther]
lying

The Compromise of 1850 (National Archives and Records Administration)

COMPROMISE OF 1850

"It being desirable ... to settle and adjust amicably all existing questions of controversy ... arising out of the institution of slavery."

Overview

After years of simmering tension, disagreements between the northern and southern states erupted as a result of the Mexican-American War (1846–1848). The acquisition of thousands of miles of western territory from Mexico raised questions about the expansion of slavery. The controversy grew especially intense in the U.S. Congress, where antislavery and proslavery factions used increasingly hostile language and threatened to break up the Union. Undertaking the difficult challenge of calming the situation was Senator Henry Clay, a veteran Kentucky legislator and three-time presidential nominee. Then in the twilight of his career, Clay used his legendary political skills to persuade both northern and southern states to make concessions in order to avoid civil war.

Clay embodied his compromise proposals in a series of resolutions dealing with the statehood of California; the organization of the New Mexico and Utah territories; the adjustment of the Texas–New Mexico border; the slave trade in Washington, D.C.; and the supplementation and increased enforcement of the Fugitive Slave Act of 1793. The resolutions were vigorously debated in Congress for seven months. The Massachusetts senator Daniel Webster came out in favor of the compromise, angering antislavery forces in the North by supporting a strengthened fugitive slave law. South Carolina's John C. Calhoun opposed the compromise because it failed to protect slavery in the territories. New York's senator William H. Seward, in turn, claimed that the compromise conceded too much to proslavery forces and also asserted that a "higher law" (Potter, p. 102) than the Constitution should guide national policy on slavery.

Clay's legislative package—nicknamed the Omnibus Bill—was defeated. Nevertheless, the Illinois senator Stephen A. Douglas quickly revived the proposals as separate bills and secured their collective passage. As time would tell, however, these acts, collectively known as the Compromise of 1850, represented more of a truce between hostile forces than a long-lasting agreement.

Context

Slavery had been a point of division between the northern and southern states at least since the Constitutional Convention of 1787. In fact, citizens in both the North and South at that time widely believed that slavery was slowly headed toward extinction. However, after the 1793 invention of the cotton gin made the plantation system more profitable, the South became increasingly attached to slavery and more firmly resistant to its abolition. Moreover, the arguments regarding slavery became part of a broader economic rivalry between the regions. An unstable harmony was maintained through the balanced admission of new free states and slave states during the first two decades of the nineteenth century.

In 1819 a proposal to admit Missouri as a free state immediately raised objections from southern leaders, sparking a crisis that the former president Thomas Jefferson called "the most portentous one that has yet threatened our Union" (Ellis, p. 264).

Talk of disunion and civil war began to be heard. Finally, a compromise was reached: Missouri would be admitted without restrictions on slavery, but slavery would be prohibited in all other parts of the Louisiana Purchase north of latitude 36°30' north. While the Missouri Compromise was not rooted in any constitutional principle, most political leaders accepted it as a permanent arrangement.

The 1830s saw the rise of antislavery sentiment in the North and the increasingly militant defense of the institution in the South. The hope of maintaining peace between the sections fell victim to the desire of Americans in the North and in the South to acquire more national territory. The annexation of Texas in 1845 led to war with Mexico, which eventually resulted in the transfer of more than 500,000 square miles of Mexican territory to the United States. In August 1846 the Pennsylvania representative David Wilmot offered an amendment prohibiting slavery in territory acquired from Mexico. The Wilmot Proviso failed to pass the Senate but was continually debated for the next several years. Southerners openly talked about accomplishing disunion if the proviso became law. Other proposals were floated in Congress, such as to extend the Missouri Compromise line to the Pacific and to allow territorial gov-

1820

■ **March 6**
In the Missouri Compromise, President James Madison signs an act banning slavery north of latitude 36°30' north, excluding within the boundaries of the newly forming state of Missouri.

1846

■ **May 11**
President James K. Polk asks Congress to declare war on Mexico.

■ **August 8**
In the House of Representatives, David Wilmot introduces the Wilmot Proviso, which would exclude slavery from all new territory acquired by the United States from Mexico.

1848

■ **March 10**
Senate approves peace treaty with Mexico, by which the United States gains California, New Mexico, and other western territories.

1850

■ **January 29**
Henry Clay introduces his compromise proposals in the Senate.

■ **March 7**
Daniel Webster endorses the compromise in an influential Senate speech.

■ **July 9**
President Zachary Taylor, an opponent of the compromise, dies; Millard Fillmore, a compromise supporter, succeeds him.

■ **July 31**
The compromise legislative package is defeated in the Senate.

■ **September 9**
As part of the Compromise of 1850, an act settling the Texas boundary and organizing New Mexico Territory, an act granting statehood to California, and an act organizing Utah Territory all pass the Senate.

ernments to settle the slavery question themselves. None of these ideas mustered enough support to pass. Meanwhile, the territories of California and New Mexico lacked organized governments. President Zachary Taylor, though he himself was a slaveholder, took a hard line against southern secessionist threats. The situation in Congress was becoming dangerously heated when Senator Henry Clay presented his set of compromise proposals in January 1850.

About the Author

Henry Clay was born in Hanover County, Virginia, in 1777. After earning a law license in 1797, he relocated to Lexington, Kentucky. He gained a reputation as an adept trial lawyer before entering local politics. Elected to the state legislature in 1803, he interrupted his service to act as a defense counsel for the former vice president Aaron Burr in the latter's trial for treason. After serving as speaker of the Kentucky House of Representatives and filling out two unexpired terms in the U.S. Senate, he was elected to the U.S. House of Representatives and became its speaker in 1811. Clay's charismatic personality and dramatic oratorical style made him a natural leader. As the guiding force behind the so-called War Hawks in Congress, Clay helped spur the United States into the War of 1812, against Great Britain. He went on to serve as a peace commissioner in 1814, helping to negotiate the Treaty of Ghent.

During his years in Congress, Clay promoted his American System, which entailed protective tariffs for manufacturers and federally supported internal improvements (including construction and the maintenance of roads, rivers, and canals). His vision was national, rather than sectional—though he was a slaveholder, he championed the interests of the United States as a whole rather than those of his native South alone. His role in shaping the Missouri Compromise in 1820 strengthened his stature as a conciliator between the free and slave states.

In 1824 Clay ran for the presidency, coming in last in a four-way election that was ultimately decided in the House of Representatives. When Clay swung his crucial support to John Quincy Adams, charges that a "corrupt bargain" had been struck were raised by supporters of Andrew Jackson, who had received the most popular votes. Criticism only intensified after Adams selected Clay as his secretary of state. Adams's presidency never recovered from these charges, which damaged Clay's career as well. Clay's second bid for the White House, against Jackson, failed in 1832. His next move was to help found the Whig Party, in opposition to Jackson's Democratic Party. He ran as the Whig candidate for president in 1844, losing narrowly to the Democrat James K. Polk.

Denied another Whig nomination in 1848, Clay announced his retirement from politics. He changed his mind, however, and returned to the Senate a year later. Even though he was in declining health, he decided to use his still-considerable influence to attempt to end the crisis over slavery. Speaking for hours before a packed Senate gallery on February 5, 1850, the seventy-two-year-old Clay predicted a long and bloody civil war if his compromise measures failed to pass. Clay lived to see his proposals become law in modified form. He died in Washington, D.C., on June 29, 1852.

Explanation and Analysis of Document

◆ Henry Clay's Resolutions of January 29, 1850

In the eight resolutions that he presented to the Senate, Henry Clay stresses the need for unity and good feeling between the North and South. Implicit in his opening statement is a call for both sections to give up something—either materially or in principle—in order to maintain national unity.

The resolutions broadly sketch out proposals regarding the statehood of California, the organization of the remaining territories acquired from Mexico, the settlement of the Texas boundary controversy, the status of slavery in the District of Columbia, the enactment of a strengthened fugitive slave law, and the protection of the interstate slave trade. The eight resolutions are not organized around a defined constitutional principle or any other legal tenet. The moral implications of slavery are avoided. Revealing his attention to issues of practicality, Clay speaks of "inexpedient" and "expedient" aspects of slavery's abolition or protection in the second, fifth, and sixth resolutions. He also claims in the second resolution that slavery "is not likely to be introduced" into the newly acquired Mexican territories, an assertion based upon the region's climate and geography. Taken as a whole, Clay's resolutions base their appeal for all-inclusive compromise legislation upon an overriding desire to protect the Union rather than upon any detailed or closely reasoned arguments.

◆ Act to Establish Texas's Borders and a Territorial Government for New Mexico

This act—like the four other legislative measures of the Compromise of 1850—was taken from the package proposed by a select Senate committee on May 8, 1850, nicknamed the Omnibus Bill. After the Omnibus Bill was defeated, Senator Stephen A. Douglas reintroduced its sections in somewhat rewritten form as separate bills. This act, the act granting statehood to California, and the act organizing Utah Territory all passed on September 9, 1850.

In Section 1 of this act, Congress offers a proposal to settle an ongoing dispute with the state of Texas over its borders with the still-unorganized territory of New Mexico. The first and second articles propose specific boundary lines, corresponding to the present-day Texas–New Mexico border. This was a compromise between two vastly different land claims. The Texas state government had asserted that the Rio Grande formed its western border and had claimed additional territory north to the forty-second parallel as well; this covered the eastern half of New Mexico, including Santa Fe and Albuquerque. At the other extreme, Henry Clay had proposed extending New Mexico's southern border

Time Line

1850

■ **September 18**
Also as part of the Compromise of 1850, President Fillmore signs the controversial Fugitive Slave Act of 1850.

■ **September 20**
As the final legislative piece of the Compromise of 1850, an act prohibiting the slave trade in the District of Columbia is signed into law.

1854

■ **May 30**
President Franklin Pierce signs the Kansas-Nebraska Act, effectively repealing the Missouri Compromise and reigniting the slavery controversy.

from the city of El Paso east to the Sabine River—which forms part of the present Texas-Louisiana border—adding the northern half of Texas to the new territory.

The third through fifth articles of Section 1 work out the details of a financial settlement between the federal and Texas governments in compensation for Texas's dropping its claims to New Mexican territory. Under these terms, Texas would forgo any compensation for turning over public property—such as military posts, ships, and customhouses—to the United States. The United States would in turn assume Texas's state debt, an amount of $10 million.

The closing sentence of the fifth article of Section 1 refers back to the congressional resolution annexing Texas to the Union in 1845. Specifically, it reaffirms the right of Texas to divide into one or more additional states. This was important, considering the fierce debate over maintaining a balance of free and slave states in the Union. Several proposals to carve new slave states out of Texas were made during the 1850 compromise debates, though none was acted upon.

Section 2 of the act sets the western boundaries of New Mexico Territory and reserves the possibility of dividing it into new territories in the future. (Parts of the territories of Arizona and Colorado were later carved out of New Mexican land.) The last sentence of this section implicitly rejects the Wilmot Proviso by specifying that New Mexico could apply for statehood in the future regardless of whether its constitution allowed slavery or not.

Sections 3–12 are devoted to largely uncontroversial details regarding the establishment of the New Mexico territorial government, calling for a federally appointed governor and locally elected state legislature. As was typical at the time, the voting franchise was restricted to free white males over age twenty-one. The most significant detail is found toward the end of Section 10, where the right to take writs of error and appeal from the territory to the federal Supreme Court is discussed. Specifically, the right to take cases involving titles to slaves and "any writ of habeas corpus involving the question of personal freedom" to the Supreme Court is affirmed. This was an attempt to shift the responsibility for regulating slavery to the Court, dodging the question of whether Congress or a territory's citizens had the right to do so.

The remaining sections of the act are devoted to territorial organization and follow the model of the recently created Oregon Territory. Sections 11–13 deal with the creation of law enforcement and judicial offices and the establishment of a state capitol. Section 14 grants the territory the right to send a nonvoting delegate to the U.S. House of Representatives. Section 15 calls for reserving land for schools. Section 16 gives the territorial governor the right to draw judicial district boundaries. The slavery question arises again (at least indirectly) in Section 19, which was added as a last-minute amendment. The amendment was originally offered by the Georgia representative Robert Toombs to prevent slaveholders from being deprived of "life, liberty, or property" in the territory—the "property" in question being slaves. However, in its final form, the amendment appeared to have the opposite effect. By stipulating that property could be regulated by "the laws of the land" within the territory, the section seems to refer back to the laws of Mexico, which prohibited slavery.

The Texas–New Mexico bill—known as "the little omnibus"—passed the Senate by a 31–20 vote. The negative votes came from antislavery northerners and extreme southern partisans. The bill went on to pass the House by a vote of 108 to 97.

◆ Act for the Admission of the State of California into the Union

Thanks to the discovery of gold in 1848, California experienced fast population growth and had an immediate need for government. Its application for admission as a free state became stalled at the start of 1850. Southern congressmen contended that admitting California would upset the balance between slave and free states, and they sought to obtain some sort of compensation, such as the guaranteed protection of slavery in New Mexico. Northern antislavery congressmen objected to linking California's statehood to any other measure. In the end, California was indeed admitted as part of the Compromise of 1850.

The act granting statehood to California begins by accepting its request for admission into the Union "on an equal footing with the original States in all respects whatever." Section 2 grants the new state two representatives to the U.S. Congress, a number that could change following an official census. In Section 3 the ability to tax or interfere with the disposal of federal lands within California is prohibited, as is any restriction of the use of the state's waterways.

The act for the admission of California passed the Senate by a vote of 34 to 18 and the House by a vote of 150 to 56. The negative votes came entirely from southern legislators.

◆ Act to Establish a Territorial Government for Utah

When Clay's Omnibus Bill came up for a vote in the Senate on July 31, 1850, the measure was so riddled with amendments that only the provision for the organization of the territory of Utah survived. This passed on a 32–18 vote.

In nearly all respects, the Utah act resembles the one establishing the territory of New Mexico. Section 1 sets the boundaries of the territory, declares that slavery will not be a barrier to the territory's later admission as a state, and leaves open the possibility of dividing the territory in the future. The language of Sections 2–17 is largely identical to comparable sections in the Texas–New Mexico act. Exceptions are found in Sections 12 and 14, where funds are appropriated to construct public buildings and purchase a library. In Section 9 the right to take writs of error and appeal involving titles to slaves from the territory to the federal Supreme Court is affirmed. As in the case of New Mexico, this blocks the application of the Wilmot Proviso to the territory.

On September 7, 1850, the House voted 97–85 to establish the Utah Territory. The measure subsequently passed the Senate on September 9, 1850.

◆ Fugitive Slave Act of 1850

The legislation popularly known as the Fugitive Slave Act of 1850 was intended to strengthen Article IV, Section 2, Clause 3, of the U.S. Constitution, which states, "No person held in service or labor in one State, under the laws thereof, escaping into another, shall, in consequence of any law or regulation therein, be discharged from such service or labor, but shall be delivered up on claim of the party to whom such service or labor may be due." Clay's proposal to aid in the enforcement of this clause recognized the fact that several northern states had passed personal liberty laws protecting the rights of persons claimed as fugitive slaves. Indeed, the states had done so in reaction to the Fugitive Slave Act of 1793, which provided that a slave (or "servant") could be captured by a slaveholder or his agent and brought before a federal or local judge. If the judge ruled that the charges against the fugitive were true, he or she would be returned to slavery. The act was challenged in the free states as a violation of the right to trial by jury.

The increase of antislavery activity in the North and the growth of the Underground Railroad caused southern proslavery forces to demand a new fugitive slave law. Pro-compromise leaders from both the North and the South aligned themselves with this position. In his famous speech of March 7, 1850, the Massachusetts senator Daniel Webster stated that the South's only legitimate grievance against the North was "the want of a proper regard to the injunctions of the Constitution for the delivery of fugitive slaves." (Tefft, p. 527). Many in the North disagreed with him, making the Fugitive Slave Act the most controversial part of the Compromise of 1850. President Millard Fillmore signed the act into law on September 18, 1850.

Section 1 of the act authorizes the U.S. circuit courts to appoint commissioners to act as law enforcement officers in runaway slave cases. Their authority was similar to that granted to justices of the peace under Section 33 of the

Judiciary Act of 1789. They were given the power to arrest and imprison fugitive slaves. Section 2 includes organized U.S. territories within the same system. Section 3 allows for the possibility of enlarging the number of commissioners in the future.

Section 4 gives the commissioners in question the power to "grant certificates to such claimants, upon satisfactory proof being made, with authority to take and remove such fugitives from service or labor ... to the State or Territory from which such persons may have escaped or fled." The fact that this section denied an alleged fugitive slave any right to a jury trial raised intense northern opposition. Some argued that the legal presumption of innocence prevented the return of an alleged slave to a claimant without a trial. This view was rejected by supporters of the Fugitive Slave Act of 1850. Implicit here is the principle that a slave is not a person but "property." Moreover, a presumption made in this act is that anyone claimed as a slave was of African descent. After the act became law, this led to cases of free blacks being mistakenly arrested in the North and sent into slavery in the South. Behind the Fugitive Slave Act of 1850 stood the belief that African Americans were not recognized under the Constitution as citizens—a belief later made explicit by the U.S. Supreme Court in its 1857 *Dred Scott* decision.

Section 5 states that local marshals and their deputies would be required to aid commissioners in the capture of fugitive slaves. Failure to comply would result in a $1,000 fine. If an alleged slave was to escape from a local law officer's custody, the officer was to be liable for the full value of the slave. This section also empowered commissioners to appoint their own deputies for assistance in slave catching—and even to compel ordinary citizens to perform such functions. In addition, the act states, "All good citizens are hereby commanded to aid and assist in the prompt and efficient execution of this law." This provision, in particular, was widely disliked in the free states. While many northerners considered slavery wrong, they were content to leave the South to manage its own affairs; even those northerners who did not favor the abolition of slavery objected to being involved in the process of recapturing slaves.

In Section 6, the owner of a slave is given the right to pursue and reclaim his property in any state or territory, either by procuring a warrant or seizing and arresting the slave personally. The captured slave was then to be brought before a judge or magistrate and, "upon satisfactory proof being made," the slave was to be handed over to the claimant. The affidavit of the claimant would be the primary evidence in the case; the testimony of the alleged fugitive slave would be inadmissible. Once a judicial officer had determined the claim to be valid, a certificate was to be issued authorizing the claimant or his or her agent "to use such reasonable force and restraint as may be necessary" to return the fugitive slave to bondage. No court or law officer would be legally permitted to interfere once the certificate had been issued.

Section 7 prohibits anyone from interfering with the arrest of a fugitive slave. Harboring or concealing a slave is

Stephen A. Douglas helped shepherd the series of laws known as the Compromise of 1850 through the Senate. (Library of Congress)

likewise deemed a crime. Anyone accused of these offenses was to be tried before a U.S. district court in the district where the alleged offenses took place. A maximum fine of $1,000 and a maximum six-month prison term would be the penalties in the case of conviction. In addition, a $1,000 fine for civil damages was to be payable to the claimant for each fugitive slave involved.

Section 8 specifies that marshals, deputies, and clerks of the district and territorial courts would receive fees for their services in fugitive slave cases comparable to those for similar services in other cases. A commissioner issuing a certificate to a claimant allowing for the arrest of a fugitive slave was to be paid $10; a commissioner declining to issue a certificate would be paid $5. (Critics charged that the commissioners were in effect given $5 bribes for issuing certificates.) Those authorized to arrest fugitive slaves were to be paid $5, along with compensation for expenses incurred in keeping the slaves in custody.

Section 9 requires the local arresting officer to physically return the fugitive slave to the claimant or his agent or attorney. The officer would receive compensation for expenses, including the hiring of assistants to help confine and transport the slave.

"*It being desirable, for the peace, concord, and harmony of the Union of these States, to settle and adjust amicably all existing questions of controversy between them arising out of the institution of slavery upon a fair, equitable and just basis.*"

(Henry Clay's Resolutions, Preamble)

"*Secession! Peaceable secession! Sir, your eyes and mine are never destined to see the miracle. The dismemberment of this vast country without convulsion! The breaking up of the fountains of the great deep without ruffling the surface! Who is so foolish—I beg everybody's pardon—as to expect to see any such thing?*"

(Daniel Webster, in Senate speech of March 7, 1850; Tefft, p. 530)

"*The Constitution regulates our stewardship; the Constitution devotes the domain to union, to justice, to defense, to welfare, and to liberty. But there is a higher law than the Constitution, which regulates our authority over the domain, and devotes it to the same noble purposes.*"

(William H. Seward, in Senate speech of March 11, 1850; Seward, p. 126)

"*Let us go to the fountains of unadulterated patriotism, and, performing a solemn lustration, return divested of all selfish, sinister, and sordid impurities, and think alone of our God, our country, our conscience, and our glorious Union.*"

(Henry Clay, in Senate speech of July 22, 1850; Schurz, p. 356)

"*In no trial or hearing under this act shall the testimony of such alleged fugitive be admitted as evidence.*"

(Fugitive Slave Act of 1850, Section 6)

◆ **Act to Suppress the Slave Trade in the District of Columbia**

This bill ended the practice of selling slaves in Washington, D.C. For many years, a desire—even among southerners—to close the slave markets in the nation's capital had been building. The controversial aspect of this was the acknowledgment of the right of Congress, versus the rights of individual states, to restrict slavery. If Congress could

regulate slavery in the District of Columbia, some argued, it could do likewise in other areas under congressional jurisdiction, such as the New Mexico and Utah territories. Most southern leaders opposed the bill for this reason.

Section 1 of the bill makes the slave trade illegal in the District of Columbia as of January 1, 1851. Thenceforth, any slave brought into the district for the purpose of being sold would be declared free. Section 2 gives local governments the power to close down slave markets. The prohibition of the slave trade in the District of Columbia passed the Senate by a 33–19 vote and the House by a 124–59 vote, becoming law on September 20, 1850.

Audience

The legislation making up the Compromise of 1850 was written to gain the support of a sufficient number of members of Congress. The ideas that these bills contained, however, were aimed at a much wider public. In proposing the original compromise resolutions, Henry Clay reached out to Union-loving citizens in the North and South, calling for "an equal amount of concession and forbearance on both sides" (Milton, p. 54). Americans who considered peace and stability more important than the moral arguments surrounding slavery were receptive to Clay's appeal. They responded to the suggestion that since slavery could not prosper in the new western territories, it was not worth fighting about. By distinguishing between "expedient" and "inexpedient" ways of dealing with slavery, Clay appealed to the practicality of the American people. Many citizens in both the North and the South could not be persuaded to support the compromise, but an even larger group—including many influential businessmen, clergymen, and educators—proved open to the approach.

Impact

The historians David Potter and William Freehling call the Compromise of 1850 an "armistice" rather than a true compromise (Freehling, p. 487). No central point of agreement was established, aside from the broader aims of avoiding disunion and war. The five separate bills that made up the Compromise of 1850 were each passed by different combinations of northern and southern votes; only four senators ended up voting for all of the individual bills. The fact that none of the compromise legislation declared whether Congress could regulate slavery in the territories proved to be both a strength and a weakness. The vague language in the New Mexico and Utah territorial bills enabled their passage but did not provide any guiding principles to help the nation avoid future battles over slavery. As a result, the Compromise of 1850 proved a temporary cure rather than the long-lasting solution it was intended to be.

The voting patterns in Congress for the compromise bills fell along regional rather than party lines. The divisions split the Whig Party the most deeply. In the 1852 presidential election, both the Democratic nominee, Franklin Pierce, and his Whig opponent, Winfield Scott, endorsed the Compromise of 1850. However, the Democrats were more nationally unified in their support of the legislation, while many northern Whigs disliked the compromise and distrusted those in their party who approved of it. Pierce was overwhelmingly elected, and the Whig Party dissolved over the next several years.

The Compromise of 1850 proved too fragile to survive. In particular, northern opposition to the Fugitive Slave Act grew in intensity, which enraged the South and increased support for disunion. In 1854 the Kansas-Nebraska Act repealed the Missouri Compromise, opening the territories to the expansion of slavery. This, in turn, led to the rise of the antislavery Republican Party, which achieved the election of Abraham Lincoln to the presidency in 1860 with only northern support. The outbreak of the Civil War in 1861 was the final evidence that, however good its intentions, the Compromise of 1850 had only delayed the final conflict over slavery.

Overall, the Compromise of 1850 probably aided the preservation of the Union in delaying the Civil War by a decade. During that time the North expanded its population and industrial bases, enabling it to ultimately defeat the Confederacy.

Related Documents

Cheek, H. Lee, Jr., ed. *John C. Calhoun: Selected Writings and Speeches.* Washington, D.C.: Regnery Publishing, 2003. Calhoun was considered the most brilliant American political theorist of his time, even by his opponents. His defense of southern rights influenced generations.

Hopkins, James F., ed. *The Papers of Henry Clay, 1797–1852.* 11 vols. Lexington: University of Kentucky Press, 1959–1992. Clay's writings display both his strong nationalism and his flair for language. Through all his political maneuverings and personal feuds, his commitment to keeping the Union intact remained ever present.

Seward, William H. *William H. Seward: An Autobiography from 1801 to 1834.* 3 vols. New York: Derby and Miller, 1891. These volumes contain many extracts from Seward's journals and speeches, revealing how he tempered his desire to directly oppose slavery with a shrewd feel for practical politics.

Wiltse, Charles M., ed. *The Papers of Daniel Webster.* 14 vols. Hanover, N.H.: University Press of New England, 1974–1989. This massive collection of Webster's writings gives a sense of his gifts as a legal scholar and his broad vision as a national leader.

Bibliography

■ Books

Coit, Margaret L. *John C. Calhoun: American Portrait.* Boston: Houghton Mifflin, 1950.

Ellis, Joseph J. *American Sphinx: The Character of Thomas Jefferson.* New York: Alfred A. Knopf, 1997.

Freehling, William W. *The Road to Disunion.* 2 vols. New York: Oxford University Press, 1990–2007.

Hamilton, Holman. *Zachary Taylor.* 2 vols. Indianapolis: Bobbs-Merrill, 1941–1951.

Holt, Michael F. *The Rise and Fall of the American Whig Party: Jacksonian Politics and the Onset of the Civil War*. New York: Oxford University Press, 1999.

McLaughlin, Andrew C. *A Constitutional History of the United States*. New York: D. Appleton-Century, 1935.

McPherson, James M. *Battle Cry of Freedom: The Civil War Era*. New York: Oxford University Press, 1988.

Milton, George F. *The Eve of Conflict: Stephen A. Douglas and the Needless War*. Boston: Houghton Mifflin, 1934.

Nevins, Allan. *Ordeal of the Union*. 2 vols. New York: Scribner, 1947.

Potter, David M. *The Impending Crisis, 1848–1861*. Completed and edited by Don E. Fehrenbacher. New York: Harper & Row, 1976.

Remini, Robert V. *Henry Clay: Statesman for the Union*. New York: W. W. Norton, 1991.

Schurz, Carl. *Henry Clay*. 2 vols. Boston: Houghton, Mifflin, 1887.

Tefft, B. F. *Speeches of Daniel Webster and his Master-Pieces*. Philadelphia: Henry T. Coates, 1854.

■ **Web Sites**

Calhoun, John C. "The Clay Compromise Measures." National Center for Public Policy Research Web site.
　http://www.nationalcenter.org/CalhounClayCompromise.html. Accessed on September 1, 2007.

"On the Compromise of 1850." History Channel Web site.
　http://www.thehistorychannel.co.uk/site/encyclopedia/article_show/Compromise_of_1850/l0000493.html?&searchtermold=m0022791&searchtermold=m0022791. Accessed on September 1, 2007.

"The Seventh of March Speech." Daniel Webster: Dartmouth's Favorite Son, Dartmouth College Web site.
　http://www.dartmouth.edu/~dwebster/speeches/seventh-march.html. Accessed on September 1, 2007.

"The Territorial Question: Speech of Mr. Douglas." Furman University Web site.
　http://facweb.furman.edu/~benson/docs/Douglas50.htm. Accessed on September 1, 2007.

—By Barry Alfonso

Questions for Further Study

1. In supporting the Compromise of 1850, leaders like Henry Clay and Daniel Webster made the preservation of the Union their highest priority. Was this the best position to take at the time? Analyze this topic from both the northern and southern perspectives.

2. Write a critique of the compromise measures from any of these points of view: (a) a citizen who opposes slavery, (b) a slaveholder, (c) a unionist without strong opinions about slavery, (d) a slave.

3. At the time of the passage of the Compromise of 1850, many Americans thought that the legislation could hold the nation together indefinitely. If the citizens of the North had obeyed the Fugitive Slave Act more consistently, would the bloodshed of the Civil War have been avoided? Specifically consider if the war *should* have been avoided, given the stakes involved.

4. Have any political compromises been made to avert wars or other crises in recent times? Are such compromises still possible, or are political choices—both in the United States and elsewhere—more black and white today? If so, is the world consequently a more dangerous place?

5. As discussed earlier, the Fugitive Slave Act of 1850 disallowed any alleged runaway slave from testifying on his own behalf. Describe how such a rule could affect an ordinary person in a modern-day legal situation.

6. Extremists in both the proslavery and antislavery camps opposed the Compromise of 1850. Is extremism ever productive in politics? Consider what forms of extremism—in the debates over abortion, the environment, and gay rights, for instance—might be justifiable today.

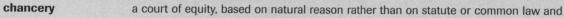

Glossary

chancery	a court of equity, based on natural reason rather than on statute or common law and involving nonmonetary settlements
concord	friendly and peaceful relations
deem	to think, believe, or judge
effectual	able to produce the desired effect
emoluments	gains from employment or a position
habeas corpus	in law, a writ or order requiring a person to attend a court hearing
impost	tax
precepts	in law, writs or warrants
vested	not contingent upon anything; fixed

COMPROMISE OF 1850

Henry Clay's Resolutions of January 29, 1850

It being desirable, for the peace, concord, and harmony of the Union of these States, to settle and adjust amicably all existing questions of controversy between them arising out of the institution of slavery upon a fair, equitable and just basis: therefore,

1. Resolved, That California, with suitable boundaries, ought, upon her application to be admitted as one of the States of this Union, without the imposition by Congress of any restriction in respect to the exclusion or introduction of slavery within those boundaries.

2. Resolved, That as slavery does not exist by law, and is not likely to be introduced into any of the territory acquired by the United States from the republic of Mexico, it is inexpedient for Congress to provide by law either for its introduction into, or exclusion from, any part of the said territory; and that appropriate territorial governments ought to be established by Congress in all of the said territory, not assigned as the boundaries of the proposed State of California, without the adoption of any restriction or condition on the subject of slavery.

3. Resolved, That the western boundary of the State of Texas ought to be fixed on the Rio del Norte, commencing one marine league from its mouth, and running up that river to the southern line of New Mexico; thence with that line eastwardly, and so continuing in the same direction to the line as established between the United States and Spain, excluding any portion of New Mexico, whether lying on the east or west of that river.

4. Resolved, That it be proposed to the State of Texas, that the United States will provide for the payment of all that portion of the legitimate and bona fide public debt of that State contracted prior to its annexation to the United States, and for which the duties on foreign imports were pledged by the said State to its creditors, not exceeding the sum of dollars, in consideration of the said duties so pledged having been no longer applicable to that object after the said annexation, but having thenceforward become payable to the United States; and upon the condition, also, that the said State of Texas shall, by some solemn and authentic act of her legislature or of a convention, relinquish to the United States any claim which it has to any part of New Mexico.

5. Resolved, That it is inexpedient to abolish slavery in the District of Columbia whilst that institution continues to exist in the State of Maryland, without the consent of that State, without the consent of the people of the District, and without just compensation to the owners of slaves within the District.

6. But, resolved, That it is expedient to prohibit, within the District, the slave trade in slaves brought into it from States or places beyond the limits of the District, either to be sold therein as merchandise, or to be transported to other markets without the District of Columbia.

7. Resolved, That more effectual provision ought to be made by law, according to the requirement of the constitution, for the restitution and delivery of persons bound to service or labor in any State, who may escape into any other State or Territory in the Union. And,

8. Resolved, That Congress has no power to promote or obstruct the trade in slaves between the slaveholding States; but that the admission or exclusion of slaves brought from one into another of them, depends exclusively upon their own particular laws.

An Act proposing to the State of Texas the Establishment of her Northern and Western Boundaries, the Relinquishment by the said State of all Territory claimed by her exterior to said boundaries, and of all her Claims upon the United States, and to establish a territorial Government for New Mexico

Be it enacted by the Senate and House of Representatives of the United States of America in Congress assembled, That the following propositions shall be, and the same hereby are, offered to the State of Texas, which, when agreed to by the said State, in an act passed by the general assembly, shall be binding and obligatory upon the United States, and upon the said State of Texas: Provided, The said agreement by the said general assembly shall be given on or before the first day of December, eighteen hundred and fifty:

FIRST. The State of Texas will agree that her boundary on the north shall commence at the point at which the meridian of one hundred degrees west from Greenwich is intersected by the parallel of thirty-six degrees thirty minutes north latitude, and shall run from said point due west to the meridian of one hundred and three degrees west from Greenwich; thence her boundary shall run due south to the thirty-second degree of north latitude; thence on the said parallel of thirty-two degrees of north latitude to the Rio Bravo del Norte, and thence with the channel of said river to the Gulf of Mexico.

SECOND. The State of Texas cedes to the United States all her claim to territory exterior to the limits and boundaries which she agrees to establish by the first article of this agreement.

THIRD. The State of Texas relinquishes all claim upon the United States for liability of the debts of Texas, and for compensation or indemnity for the surrender to the United States of her ships, forts, arsenals, custom-houses, custom-house revenue, arms and munitions of war, and public buildings with their sites, which became the property of the United States at the time of the annexation.

FOURTH. The United States, in consideration of said establishment of boundaries, cession of claim—to territory, and relinquishment of claims, will pay to the State of Texas the sum of ten millions of dollars in a stock bearing five per cent. interest, and redeemable at the end of fourteen years, the interest payable half-yearly at the treasury of the United States.

FIFTH. Immediately after the President of the United States shall have been furnished with an authentic copy of the act of the general assembly of Texas accepting these propositions, he shall cause the stock to be issued in favor of the State of Texas, as provided for in the fourth article of this agreement: Provided, also, That no more than five millions of said stock shall be issued until the creditors of the State holding bonds and other certificates of stock of Texas for which duties on imports were specially pledged, shall first file at the treasury of the United States releases of all claim against the United States for or on account of said bonds or certificates in such form as shall be prescribed by the Secretary of the Treasury and approved by the president of the United States: Provided, That nothing herein contained. shall be construed to impair or qualify any thing contained in the third article of the second section of the "joint resolution for annexing Texas to the United States," approved March first, eighteen hundred and forty-five; either as regards the number of States that may hereafter be formed out of the State of Texas, or otherwise.

◆ **SEC. 2.**

And be it further enacted, That all that portion of the Territory of the United States bounded as follows: Beginning at a point in the Colorado River where the boundary line with the republic of Mexico crosses the same; thence eastwardly with the said boundary line to the Rio Grande; thence following the main channel of said river the parallel of the thirty-second degree of north latitude; thence east with said degree to its intersection with the one hundred and third degree of longitude west of Greenwich; thence north with said degree of longitude to the parallel of thirty-eighth degree of north latitude; thence west with said parallel to the summit of the Sierra Madre; thence south with the crest of said mountains to the thirty-seventh parallel of north latitude; thence west with said parallel to its intersection with the boundary line of the State of California; thence with said boundary line to the place of beginning be, and the same is hereby, erected into a temporary government, by the name of the Territory of New Mexico: Provided, That nothing in this act contained shall be construed to inhibit the government of the United States from dividing said Territory into two or more Territories, in such manner and at such times as Congress shall deem convenient and proper, or from attaching any portion thereof to any other Territory or State: And provided, further, That, when admitted as a State, the said Territory, or any portion of the same, shall be received into the Union, with or without slavery, as their constitution may prescribe at the time of their admission.

◆ **SEC. 3.**

And be it further enacted, That the executive power and authority in and over said Territory of New Mexico shall be vested in, a governor, who shall hold his office for four years, and until his successor shall be appointed and qualified, unless sooner removed by the President of the United States. The governor shall reside within said Territory, shall be commander-in-chief of the militia thereof, shall perform the duties and receive the emoluments of superintendent of Indian affairs, and shall approve all laws passed by the legislative assembly before they shall take effect; he may grant pardons for offences against the laws of said Territory, and reprieves for offences against the laws of the United States, until the decision of the President can be made known thereon. he shall commission all officers who shall be appointed to office under the laws of the said Territory, and shall take care that the laws be faithfully executed.

◆ SEC. 4.

And be it further enacted, That there shall be a secretary of said Territory, who shall reside therein, and hold his office for four years, unless sooner removed by the President of the United States; he shall record and preserve all the laws and proceedings of the legislative assembly hereinafter constituted and all the acts and proceedings of the governor in his executive department; he shall transmit one copy of the laws and one copy of the executive proceedings, on or before the first day of December in each year, to the President of the United States, and, at the same time, two copies of the laws to the Speaker of the House of Representatives and the President of the Senate, for the use of Congress. And, in case of the death, removal, resignation, or other necessary absence of the governor from the Territory, the secretary shall have, and he is hereby authorized and required to execute and perform all the powers and duties of the governor during such vacancy or necessary absence, or until another governor shall be duly appointed to fill such vacancy.

◆ SEC. 5.

And be it further enacted, That the legislative power and authority of said Territory shall be vested in the governor and a legislative assembly. The legislative assembly shall consist of a Council and House of Representatives. The Council shall consist of thirteen members, having the qualifications of voters as hereinafter prescribed, whose term of service shall continue two years. The House of Representatives shall consist of twenty-six members, possessing the same qualifications as prescribed for members of the Council, and whose term of service shall continue one year. An apportionment shall be made, as nearly equal as practicable, among the several counties or districts, for the election of the Council and House of Representatives, giving to each section of the Territory representation in the ratio of its population, (Indians excepted,) as nearly as may be. And the members of the Council and of the House of Representatives shall reside in, and be inhabitants of, the district for which they may be elected respectively. Previous to the first election, the governor shall cause a census or enumeration of the inhabitants of the several counties and districts of the Territory to be taken, and the first election shall be held at such time and places, and be conducted in such manner, as the governor shall appoint and direct; and he shall, at the same time, declare the number of the members of the Council and House of Representatives to which each of the counties or districts shall be entitled under this act. The number of persons authorized to be elected having the highest number of votes in each of said Council districts, for members of the Council, shall be declared by the governor to be duly elected to the Council; and the person or persons authorized to be elected having the greatest number of votes for the House of Representatives, equal to the number to which each county or district shall be entitled, shall be declared by the governor to be duly elected members of the House of Representatives: Provided, That in case of a tie between two or more persons voted for, the governor shall order a new election to supply the vacancy made by such tie. And the persons thus elected to the legislative assembly shall meet at such place and on such day as the governor shall appoint; but thereafter, the time, place, and manner of holding and conducting all elections by the people, and the apportioning the representation in the several counties or districts to the Council and House of Representatives according to the population, shall be prescribed by law, as well as the day of the commencement of the regular sessions of the legislative assembly: Provided, That no one session shall exceed the term of forty days.

◆ SEC. 6.

And be it further enacted, That every free white male inhabitant, above the age of twenty-one years, who shall have been a resident of said Territory at the time of the passage of this act, shall be entitled to vote at the first election, and shall be eligible to any office within the said Territory; but the qualifications of voters and of holding office, at all subsequent elections, shall be such as shall be prescribed by the legislative assembly: Provided, That the right of suffrage, and of holding office, shall be exercised only by citizens of the United States, including those recognized as citizens by the treaty with the republic of

Mexico, concluded February second, eighteen hundred and forty-eight.

◆ SEC. 7.

And be it further enacted, That the legislative power of the Territory shall extend to all rightful subjects of legislation, consistent with the Constitution of the United States and the provisions of this act; but no law shall be passed interfering with the primary disposal of the soil; no tax shall be imposed upon the property of the United States; nor shall the lands or other property of non-residents be taxed higher than the lands or other property of residents. All the laws passed by the legislative assembly and governor shall be submitted to the Congress of the United States, and, if disapproved, shall be null and of no effect.

◆ SEC. 8.

And be it further enacted, That all township, district, and county officers. not herein otherwise provided for, shall be appointed or elected, as the case may be, in such manner as shall be provided by the governor and legislative assembly of the Territory of New Mexico. The governor shall nominate, and, by and with the advice and consent of the legislative Council, appoint, an officers not herein otherwise provided for; and in the first instance the governor alone may appoint all said officers, who shall hold their offices until the end of the first session of the legislative assembly, and shall lay off the necessary districts for members of the Council and House of Representatives, and all other officers.

◆ SEC. 9.

And be it further enacted, That no member of the legislative assembly shall hold, or be appointed to, any office which shall have been created, or the salary or emoluments of which shall have been increased while he was a member, during the term for which he was elected, and for one year after the expiration of such term; and no person holding a commission or appointment under the United

States, except postmasters, shall be a member of the legislative assembly, or shall hold any office under the government of said Territory.

◆ SEC. 10.

And be it further enacted, That the judicial power of said Territory shall be vested in a Supreme Court, District Courts, Probate Courts, and in justices of the peace. The Supreme Court shall consist of a chief justice and two associate justices, any two of whom shall constitute a quorum, and who shall hold a term at the seat of government of said Territory annually, and they shall hold their offices during the period of four years. The said Territory shall be divided into three judicial districts, and a District Court shall be held in each of said districts by one of the justices of the Supreme Court, at such time and place as may be prescribed by law; and the said judges shall, after their appointments, respectively, reside in the districts which shall be assigned them. The jurisdiction of the several courts herein provided for, both appellate and original, and that of the Probate Courts and of justices of the peace, shall be as limited by law: Provided, That justices of the peace shall not have jurisdiction of any matter in controversy when the title or boundaries of land may be in dispute, or where the debt or sum claimed shall exceed one hundred dollars; and the said Supreme and District Courts, respectively, shall possess chancery as well as common law jurisdiction. Each District Court, or the judge thereof, shall appoint its clerk, who shall also be the register in chancery, and shall keep his office at the place where the court may be held. Writs of error, bills of exception, and appeals, shall be allowed in all cases from the final decisions of said District Courts to the Supreme Court, under such regulations as may be prescribed by law, but in no case removed to the Supreme Court shall trial by jury be allowed in said court. The Supreme Court, or the justices thereof, shall appoint its own clerk, and every clerk shall hold his office at the pleasure of the court for which he shall have been appointed. Writs of error and appeals from the final decisions of said Supreme Court shall be allowed, and may be taken to the Supreme Court of the United States, in the same manner and under the same regulations as from the Circuit Courts of the United States, where the value of the property or the amount in controversy, to be ascertained by the oath or affirmation of either party, or other competent witness, shall exceed one thousand dollars; except only that in all cases involving title to slaves, the said writs of error or appeals shall be allowed and decided by the said Supreme Court without regard to the value of the matter, property, or title in controversy; and except also that a writ of error or appeal shall also be allowed to the Supreme Court of the United States from the decision of the said Supreme Court created by this act, or of any judge thereof, or of the District Courts created by this act, or of any judge thereof, upon any writ of habeas corpus involving the question of personal freedom; and each of the said District Courts shall have and exercise the same jurisdiction in all cases arising under the Constitution and laws of the United States as is vested in the Circuit and District Courts of the United States; and the said Supreme and District Courts of the said Territory, and the respective judges thereof, shall and may grant writs of habeas corpus in all cases in which the same are grantable by the judges of the United States in the District of Columbia; and the first six days of every term of said courts, or so much thereof as shall be necessary, shall be appropriated to the trial of causes arising under the said Constitution and laws; and writs of error and appeals in all such cases shall be made to the Supreme Court of said Territory, the same as in other cases. The said clerk shall receive in all such cases the same fees which the clerks of the District Courts of Oregon Territory now receive for similar services.

◆ SEC. 11.

And be it further enacted, That there shall be appointed an attorney for said Territory, who shall continue in office for four years, unless sooner removed by the President, and who shall receive the same fees and salary as the attorney of the United States for the present Territory of Oregon. There shall also be a marshal for the Territory appointed, who shall hold his office for four years, unless sooner removed by the president, and who shall execute all processes issuing from the said courts when exercising their jurisdiction as Circuit and District Courts of the United States: he shall perform the duties, be subject to the same regulation and penalties, and be entitled to the same fees as the marshal of the District Court of the United States for the present Territory of Oregon, and shall, in addition, be paid two hundred [dollars] annually as a compensation for extra services.

◆ SEC. 12.

And be it further enacted, That the governor secretary, chief justice and associate justices, attorney and marshal shall be nominated, and, by and with the advice and consent of the Senate, appointed by the President of the United States. The governor and secretary, to be appointed as aforesaid, shall, before they act as such, respectively take an oath or affirmation, before the district judge, or some justice of the peace in the limits of said Territory, duly authorized to administer oaths and affirmations by the laws now in force therein, or before the chief justice or some associate justice of the Supreme Court of the United States, to support the Constitution of the United States, and faithfully to discharge the duties of their respective offices; which said oaths, when so taken, shall be certified by the person by whom the same shall have been taken, and such certificates shall be received and recorded by the said secretary among the executive proceedings; and the chief justice and associate justices, and all other civil officers in said Territory, before they act as such, shall take a like oath or affirmation, before the said governor or secretary, or some judge or justice of the peace of the Territory, who may be duly commissioned and qualified, which said oath or affirmation shall be certified and transmitted, by the person taking the same, to the secretary, to be by him recorded as aforesaid; and afterwards, the like oath or affirmation shall be taken, certified, and recorded, in such manner and form as may be prescribed by law. The governor shall receive an annual salary of fifteen hundred dollars as governor, and one thousand dollars as superintendent of Indian affairs. The chief justice and associate justices shall each receive an annual salary of eighteen hundred dollars. The secretary shall receive an annual salary of eighteen hundred dollars. The said salaries shall be paid quarter-yearly, at the treasury of the United States. The members of the legislative assembly shall be entitled to receive three dollars each per day during their attendance at the sessions thereof, and three dollars each for every twenty miles' travel in going to and returning from the said sessions, estimated according to the nearest usually travelled route. There shall be appropriated annually the sum of one thousand dollars, to be expended by the governor, to defray the contingent expenses of the Territory; there shall also be appropriated annually a sufficient sum to be expended by the secretary of the Territory, and upon an estimate to be made by the Secretary of the Treasury of the United States, to defray the expenses of the legislative assembly, the printing of the laws, and other incidental expenses; and the secretary of the Territory shall annually account to the Secretary of the Treasury of the United States for the manner in which the aforesaid sum shall have been expended.

◆ SEC. 13.

And be it further enacted, That the legislative assembly of the Territory of New Mexico shall hold its first session at such time and place in said Territory as the Governor thereof shall appoint and direct; and at said first session, or as soon thereafter as they shall deem expedient, the governor and legislative assembly shall proceed to locate and establish the seat of government for said Territory at such place as they may deem eligible; which place, however, shall thereafter be subject to be changed by the said governor and legislative assembly.

◆ **SEC. 14.**

And be it further enacted, That a delegate to the House of Representatives of the United States, to serve during each Congress of the United States, may be elected by the voters qualified to elect members of the legislative assembly, who shall be entitled to the same rights and privileges as are exercised and enjoyed by the delegates from the several other Territories of the United States to the said House of Representatives. The first election shall be held at such time and places, and be conducted in such manner, as the governor shall appoint and direct; and at all subsequent elections, the times, places, and manner of holding the elections shall be prescribed by law. The person having the greatest number of votes shall be declared by the governor to be duly elected, and a certificate thereof shall be given accordingly: Provided, That such delegate shall receive no higher sum for mileage than is allowed by law to the delegate from Oregon.

◆ **SEC. 15.**

And be it further enacted, That when the lands in said Territory shall be surveyed under the direction of the government of the United States, preparatory to bringing the same into market, sections numbered sixteen and thirty-six in each township in said Territory shall be, and the same are hereby, reserved for the purpose of being applied to schools in said Territory, and in the States and Territories hereafter to be erected out of the same.

◆ **SEC. 16.**

And be it further enacted, That temporarily and until otherwise provided by law, the governor of said Territory may define the judicial districts of said Territory, and assign the judges who may be appointed for said Territory to the several districts, and also appoint the times and places for holding courts in the several counties or subdivisions in each of said judicial districts, by proclamation to be issued by him; but the legislative assembly, at their first or any subsequent session, may organize, alter, or modify such judicial districts, and assign the judges, and alter the times and places of holding the courts, as to them shall seem proper and convenient.

◆ **SEC. 17.**

And be it further enacted, That the Constitution, and all laws of the United States which are not local-ly inapplicable, shall have the same force and effect within the said Territory of New Mexico as elsewhere within the United States.

◆ **SEC. 18.**

And be it further enacted, That the provisions of this act be, and they are hereby, suspended until the boundary between the United States and the State of Texas shall be adjusted; and when such adjustment shall have been effected, the President of the United States shall issue his proclamation, declaring this act to be in full force and operation, and shall proceed to appoint the officers herein provided to be appointed in and for said Territory.

◆ **SEC. 19.**

And be it further enacted, That no citizen of the United States shall be deprived of his life, liberty, or property, in said Territory, except by the judgment of his peers and the laws of the land.

APPROVED, September 9, 1850.

An Act for the admission of the State of California into the Union

Whereas the people of California have presented a constitution and asked admission into the Union, which constitution was submitted to Congress by the President of the United States, by message dated February thirteenth, eighteen hundred and fifty, and which, on due examination, is found to be republican in its form of government:

Be it enacted by the Senate and House of Representatives of the United States of America in Congress assembled, That the State of California shall be one, and is hereby declared to be one, of the United States of America, and admitted into the Union on an equal footing with the original States in all respects whatever.

◆ **SEC. 2.**

And be it further enacted, That, until the representatives in Congress shall be apportioned according to an actual enumeration of the inhabitants of the United States, the State of California shall be entitled to two representatives in Congress.

◆ **SEC. 3.**

And be it further enacted, That the said State of California is admitted into the Union upon the express condition that the people of said State, through their legislature or otherwise, shall never

interfere with the primary disposal of the public lands within its limits, and shall pass no law and do no act whereby the title of the United States to, and right to dispose of, the same shall be impaired or questioned; and that they shall never lay any tax or assessment of any description whatsoever upon the public domain of the United States, and in no case shall non-resident proprietors, who are citizens of the United States, be taxed higher than residents; and that all the navigable waters within the said State shall be common highways, and forever free, as well to the inhabitants of said State as to the citizens of the United States, without any tax, impost, or duty therefor: Provided, That nothing herein contained shall be construed as recognizing or rejecting the propositions tendered by the people of California as articles of compact in the ordinance adopted by the convention which formed the constitution of that State.

APPROVED, September 9, 1850.

An Act to establish a Territorial Government for Utah

Be it enacted by the Senate and House of Representatives of the United States of America in Congress assembled, That all that part of the territory of the United States included within the following limits, to wit: bounded on the west by the State of California, on the north by the Territory of Oregon, and on the east by the summit of the Rocky Mountains, and on the south by the thirty-seventh parallel of north latitude, be, and the same is hereby, created into a temporary government, by the name of the Territory of Utah; and, when admitted as a State, the said Territory, or any portion of the same, shall be received into the Union, with or without slavery, as their constitution may prescribe at the time of their admission: Provided, That nothing in this act contained shall be construed to inhibit the government of the United States from dividing said Territory into two or more Territories, in such manner and at such times as Congress shall deem convenient and proper, or from attaching any portion of said Territory to any other State or Territory of the United States.

◆ SEC. 2.

And be it further enacted, That the executive power and authority in and over said Territory of Utah shall be vested in a governor, who shall hold his office for four years, and until his successor shall be appointed and qualified, unless sooner removed by the President of the United States. The governor shall reside within said Territory, shall be commander-in-chief of the militia thereof, shall perform the duties and receive the emoluments of superintendent of Indian affairs, and shall approve all laws passed by the legislative assembly before they shall take effect: he may grant pardons for offences against the laws of said Territory, and reprieves for offences against the laws of the United States, until the decision of the President can be made known thereon; he shall commission all officers who shall be appointed to office under the laws of the said Territory, and shall take care that the laws be faithfully executed.

◆ SEC. 3.

And be it further enacted, That there shall be a secretary of said Territory, who shall reside therein, and hold his office for four years, unless sooner removed by the President of the United States: he shall record and preserve all the laws and proceedings of the legislative assembly hereinafter constituted, and all the acts and proceedings of the governor in his executive department; he shall transmit one copy of the laws and one copy of the executive proceedings, on or before the first day of December in each year, to the President of the United States, and, at the same time, two copies of the laws to the Speaker of the House of Representatives, and the President of the Senate, for the use of Congress. And in the case of the death, removal, resignation, or other necessary absence of the governor from the Territory, the secretary shall have, and he is hereby authorized and required to execute and perform, all the powers and duties of the governor during such vacancy or necessary absence, or until another governor shall be duly appointed to fill such vacancy.

◆ SEC. 4.

And be it further enacted, That the legislative power and authority of said Territory shall be vested in the governor and a legislative assembly. The legislative assembly shall consist of a Council and House of Representatives. The Council shall consist of thirteen members, having the qualifications of voters as hereinafter prescribed, whose term of service shall continue two years. The House of Representatives shall consist of twenty-six members, possessing the same qualifications as prescribed for members of the Council, and, whose term of service shall continue one year. An apportionment shall be made, as nearly equal as practicable, among the several counties or districts, for the election of the Council and House of Representatives, giving to each section of the Territory representation in the ratio of its population, Indians excepted, as nearly as may be. And the members of the Council and of the House of Representatives shall reside in, and be inhabitants of, the district for which they may be elected respectively. Previous to the first election, the governor shall cause a census or enumeration of the inhabitants of the several counties and districts of the Territory to be taken, and the first election shall be held at such time and places, and be conducted in such manner, as the governor shall appoint and direct; and he shall, at the same time, declare the number of members of the Council and House of Representatives to which each of the counties or districts shall be entitled under this act. The number of persons authorized to be elected having the highest number of votes in each of said Council districts for members of the Council, shall be declared by the governor to be duly elected to the Council; and the person or persons authorized to be elected having the highest number of votes for the House of Representatives, equal to the number to which each county or district shall be entitled, shall be declared by the governor to be duly elected members or the House of Representatives: Provided, That in case of a tie between two or more persons voted for, the governor shall order a new election to supply the vacancy made by such a tie. And the persons thus elected to the legislative assembly shall meet at such place, and on such day, as the governor shall appoint; but thereafter, the time, place, and manner of holding and conducting all elections by the people, and the apportioning the representation in the several counties or districts to the Council and House of Representatives, according to population, shall be prescribed by law, as well as the day of the commencement of the regular sessions of the legislative assembly: Provided That no one session shall exceed the term of forty days.

◆ SEC. 5.

And be it further enacted, That every free white male inhabitant above the age of twenty-one years, who shall have been a resident or said Territory at the time of the passage of this act, shall he entitled to vote at the first election, and shall be eligible to any office within the said Territory; but the qualifications of voters and of holding office, at all subsequent elections, shall be such as shall be prescribed by the legislative assembly: Provided, That the right of suffrage and of holding office shall be exercised only by

citizens of the United States, including those recognized as citizens by the treaty with the republic of Mexico, concluded February second, eighteen hundred and forty-eight.

◆ SEC. 6.

And be it further enacted, That the legislative power of said Territory shall extend to all rightful subjects of legislation, consistent with the Constitution of the United States and the provisions of this act; but no law shall be passed interfering with the primary disposal of the soil; no tax shall be imposed upon the property of the United States; nor shall the lands or other property of non-residents be taxed higher than the lands or other property of residents. All the laws passed by the legislative assembly and governor shall be submitted to the Congress of the United States, and, if disapproved, shall be null and of no effect.

◆ SEC. 7.

And be it further enacted, That all township, district, and county officers, not herein otherwise provided for, shall be appointed or elected, as the case may be, in such manner as shall be provided by the governor and legislative assembly of the territory of Utah. The governor shall nominate, and, by and with the advice and consent of the legislative Council, appoint all officers not herein otherwise provided for; and in the first instance the governor alone may appoint all said officers, who shall hold their offices until the end of the first session of the legislative assembly, and shall layoff the necessary districts for members of the Council and House of Representatives, and all other offices.

◆ SEC. 8.

And be it further enacted, That no member of the legislative assembly shall hold or be appointed to any office which shall have been created, or the salary or emoluments of which shall have been increased while he was a member, during the term for which he was elected, and for one year after the expiration of such term; and no person holding a commission or appointment under the United States, except postmasters, shall be a member of the legislative assembly, or shall hold any office under the government of said Territory.

◆ SEC. 9.

And be it further enacted, That the judicial power of said Territory shall be vested in a Supreme Court,

District Courts, Probate Courts, and in justices of the peace. The Supreme Court shall consist of a chief justice and two associate justices, any two of whom shall constitute a quorum, and who shall hold a term at the Beat of government of said Territory annually, and they shall hold their offices during the period of four years. The said Territory shall be divided into three judicial districts, and a District Court shall be held in each of said districts by one of the justices of the Supreme Court, at such time and place as may be prescribed by law; and the said judges shall, after their appointments, respectively, reside in the districts which shall be assigned them. The jurisdiction of the several courts herein provided for, both appellate and original, and that of the Probate Courts and of justices of the peace, shall be as limited by law: Provided, That justices of the peace shall not have jurisdiction of any matter in controversy when the title or boundaries of land may be in dispute, or where the debt or sum claimed shall exceed one hundred dollars; and the said Supreme and District Courts, respectively, shall possess chancery as well as common law jurisdiction. Each District Court, or the judge thereof, shall appoint its clerk, who shall also be the register in chancery, and shall keep his office at the place where the court may be held. Writs of error, bills of exception, and appeals shall be allowed in all cases from the final decisions of said District Courts to the Supreme Court, under such regulations as may be prescribed by law; but in no case removed to the Supreme Court shall trial by jury be allowed in said court. The Supreme Court, or the justices thereof, shall appoint its own clerk, and every clerk shall hold his office at the pleasure of the court for which he shall have been appointed. Writs of error, and appeals from the final decisions of said Supreme Court, shall be allowed, and may be taken to the Supreme Court of the United States, in the same manner and under the same regulations as from the Circuit Courts of the United States, where the value of the property or the amount in controversy, to be ascertained by the oath or affirmation of either party, or other competent witness, shall exceed one thousand dollars, except only that, in all cases involving title to slaves, the said writs of error or appeals shall be allowed and decided by the said Supreme Court, without regard to the value of the matter, property, or title in controversy; and except also, that a writ of error or appeal shall also be allowed to the Supreme Court of the United States, from the decisions of the said Supreme Court created by this act or of any judge thereof or of the District Courts created by this act or of any judge thereof, upon any writ of habeas corpus involving the question of personal freedom; and each of the said District Courts shall have and exercise the same jurisdiction in all cases arising under the Constitution and laws of the United States as is vested in the Circuit and District Courts of the United States; and the said Supreme and District Courts of the said Territory, and the respective judges thereof shall and may grant writs of habeas corpus in all cases in which the same are granted by the judges of the United States in the District of Columbia; and the first six days of every term of said courts, or so much thereof as shall be necessary. shall be appropriated to the trial of causes arising under the said Constitution and laws; and writs of error and appeal, in all such cases, shall be made to the Supreme Court of said Territory, the same as in other cases. The said clerk shall receive in all such cases the same fees which the clerks of the District Courts of Oregon Territory now receive for similar services.

◆ **SEC. 10.**

And be it further enacted, That there shall be appointed an attorney for said Territory, who shall continue in office for four years, unless sooner removed by the President, and who shall receive the same fees and salary as the attorney of the United States for the present Territory of Oregon. There shall also be a marshal for the Territory appointed, who shall hold his office for four years, unless sooner removed by the President, and who shall execute all processes issuing from the said courts, when exercising their jurisdiction as Circuit and District Courts of the United States: he shall perform the duties, be subject to the same regulation and penalties, and be entitled to the same fees as the marshal of the District Court of the United States for the present Territory of Oregon; and shall, in addition, be paid two hundred dollars annually as a compensation for extra services.

◆ **SEC. 11.**

And be it further enacted, That the governor, secretary, chief justice and associate justices, attorney and marshal, shall be nominated, and, by and with the advice and consent of the Senate, appointed by the President of the United States. The governor and secretary to be appointed as aforesaid shall, before they act as such. respectively, take an oath or affirmation, before the district judge, or some justice of the peace in the limits of said Territory, duly authorized to administer oaths and affirmations by the laws now in force therein or before the chief justice or some associate justice of the Supreme Court of the United States, to support the Constitution of the United States, and faithfully to discharge the duties of their respective offices; which said oaths, when so taken, shall be certified by the person by whom the same shall have been taken, and such certificates shall be received and recorded by the said secretary among the executive proceedings; and the chief justice and associate justices, and all other civil officers in said Territory, before they act as such, shall take a like oath or affirmation, before the said governor or secretary, or some judge or justice of the peace of the Territory who may be duly commissioned and qualified, which said oath or affirmation shall be certified and transmitted, by the person taking the same, to the secretary, to be by him recorded as aforesaid; and afterwards, the like oath or affirmation shall be taken, certified, and recorded, in such manner and form as may he prescribed by law. The governor shall receive an annual salary of fifteen hundred dollars as governor, and one thousand dollars as superintendent of Indian affairs. The chief justice and associate justices shall each receive an annual salary of eighteen hundred dollars. The secretary shall receive an annual salary of eighteen hundred dollars. The said salaries shall be paid quarter yearly, at the treasury of the United States. The members of the legislative assembly shall be entitled to receive three dollars each per day during their attendance at the sessions thereof, and three dollars each for twenty miles' travel, in going to and returning from the said sessions, estimated according to the nearest usually travelled route. There shall be appropriated annually the sum of one thousand dollars, to be expended by the governor, to defray the contingent expenses of the Territory. There shall also be appropriated, annually, a sufficient sum, to be expended by the secretary of the Territory, and upon an estimate to be made by the Secretary of the Treasury of the United States, to defray the expenses of the legislative assembly, the printing of the laws, and other incidental expenses; and the secretary of the Territory shall annually account to the Secretary of the Treasury of the United States for the manner in which the aforesaid sum shall have been expended.

◆ SEC. 12.

And be it further enacted, That the legislative assembly of the Territory of Utah shall hold its first session at such time and place in said Territory as the governor thereof shall appoint and direct; and at said first session, or as soon thereafter as they shall deem expedient, the governor and legislative assembly shall proceed to locate and establish the seat of government for said Territory at such place as they may deem eligible; which place, however, shall thereafter be, subject to be changed by the said governor and legislative assembly. And the sum of twenty thousand dollars, out of any money in the treasury not otherwise appropriated, is hereby appropriated and granted to said Territory of Utah to be applied by the governor and legislative assembly to the erection of suitable public buildings at the seat of government.

◆ SEC. 13.

And be it further enacted, That a delegate to the House of Representatives of the United States, to serve during each Congress of the United States, may be elected by the voters qualified to elect members of the legislative assembly, who shall be entitled to the same rights and privileges as are exercised and enjoyed by the delegates from the several other Territories of the United States to the said House of Representatives. The first election shall be held at such time and places, and be conducted in such manner, as the governor shall appoint and direct; and at all subsequent elections, the times, places, and manner of holding the elections shall be prescribed by law. The person having the greatest number of votes shall be declared by the governor to be duly elected, and a certificate thereof shall be given accordingly: Provided, That said delegate shall receive no higher sum for mileage than is allowed by law to the delegate from Oregon.

◆ SEC. 14.

And be it further enacted, That the sum of five thousand dollars be, and the same is hereby, appropriated out of any moneys in the treasury not otherwise appropriated, to be expended by and under the direction of the said governor of the territory of Utah, in the purchase of a library, to be kept at the seat of government for the use of the governor, legislative assembly, judges of the Supreme Court, secretary, marshal, and attorney of said Territory, and such other persons, and under such regulations, as shall be prescribed by law.

◆ SEC. 15.

And be it further enacted, That when the lands in the said Territory shall be surveyed under the direction of the government of the United States preparatory to bringing the same into market, sections numbered sixteen and thirty-six in each township in said Territory shall be, and the same are hereby, reserved for the purpose of being applied to schools in said Territory, and in the States and Territories hereafter to be erected out of the same.

◆ **SEC. 16.**

And be it further enacted, That temporarily, and until otherwise provided by law, the governor of said Territory may define the judicial districts of said Territory, and assign the judges who maybe appointed for said Territory to the several districts, and also appoint the times and places for holding courts in the several counties or subdivisions in each of said judicial districts, by proclamation to be issued by him; but the legislative assembly, at their first or any subsequent session, may organize, alter, or modify such judicial districts, and assign the judges, and alter the times and places of holding the courts, as to them shall seem proper and convenient.

◆ **SEC. 17.**

And be it further enacted, That the Constitution and laws of the United States are hereby extended over and declared to be in force in said Territory of Utah, so far as the same, or any provision thereof, may be applicable.

APPROVED, September 9, 1850.

An Act to amend, and supplementary to, the Act entitled "An Act respecting Fugitives from Justice, and Persons escaping from the Service of their Masters," approved February twelfth, one thousand seven hundred and ninety-three

Be it enacted by the Senate and House of Representatives of the United States of America in congress assembled, That the persons who have been, or may hereafter be, appointed commissioners, in virtue of any act of Congress, by the Circuit Courts of the United States and who, in consequence of such appointment, are authorized to exercise the powers that any justice of the peace, or other magistrate of any of the United States, may exercise in respect to offenders for any crime or offence against the United States, by arresting, imprisoning, or bailing the same under and by virtue of the thirty-third section of the act of the twenty-fourth of September seventeen hundred and eighty-nine, entitled "An Act to establish the Judicial courts of the United States,"

shall be, and are hereby, authorized and required to exercise and discharge all the powers and duties conferred by this act.

◆ **SEC. 2.**

And be it further enacted, That the Superior Court of each organized Territory of the United States shall have the same power to appoint commissioners to take acknowledgements of bail and affidavits and to take depositions of witnesses in civil causes, which is now possessed by the Circuit Court of the United States; and all commissioners who shall hereafter be appointed for such purposes by the Superior Court of any organized Territory of the United States, shall possess all the powers, and exercise all the duties, conferred by law upon the commissioners appointed by the Circuit Courts of the United States for similar purposes, and shall moreover exercise and discharge all the powers and duties conferred by this act.

◆ **SEC. 3.**

And be it further enacted, That the Circuit Courts of the United States, and the Superior Courts of each organized Territory of the United States, shall from time to time enlarge the number of commissioners, with a view to afford reasonable facilities to reclaim fugitives from labor, and to the prompt discharge of the duties imposed by this act.

◆ **SEC. 4.**

And be it further enacted, That the commissioners above named shall have concurrent jurisdiction with the judges of the Circuit and District Courts of the United States, in their respective circuits and districts within the several States, and the judges of the Superior Courts of the Territories, severally and collectively, in term time and vacation; and shall grant certificates to such claimants, upon satisfactory proof being made, with authority to take and remove such fugitives from service or labor, under the restrictions herein contained, to the State or Territory from which such persons may have escaped or fled.

◆ **SEC. 5.**

And be it further enacted, That it shall be the duty of all marshals and deputy marshals to obey and execute all warrants and precepts issued under the provisions of this act, when to them directed; and should any marshal or deputy marshal refuse to receive such warrant, or other process, when tendered, or to use all proper means diligently to execute the same, he shall, on conviction thereof, be fined in the sum of one thousand dollars, to the use of such claimant, on the motion of such claimant, by the Circuit or District Court for the district of such marshal; and after arrest of such fugitive, by such marshal or his deputy, or whilst at any time in his custody under the provisions of this act, should such fugitive escape, whether with or without the assent of such marshal or his deputy, such marshal shall be liable, on his official bond, to be prosecuted for the benefit of such claimant, for the full value of the service or labor of said fugitive in the State, Territory, or District whence he escaped: and the better to enable the said commissioners, when thus appointed, to execute their duties faithfully and efficiently, in conformity with the requirements of the Constitution of the United States and of this act, they are hereby authorized and empowered, within their counties respectively, to appoint, in writing under their hands, anyone or more suitable persons, from time to time, to execute all such warrants and other process as may be issued by them in the lawful performance of their respective duties; with authority to such commissioners, or the persons to be appointed by them, to execute process as aforesaid, to summon and call to their aid the bystanders, or posse comitatus of the proper county, when necessary to ensure a faithful observance of the clause of the Constitution referred to, in conformity with the provisions of this act; and all good citizens are hereby commanded to aid and assist in the prompt and efficient execution of this law, whenever their services may be required, as aforesaid, for that purpose; and said warrants shall run, and be executed by said officers, any where in the State within which they are issued.

◆ SEC. 6.

And be it further enacted, That when a person held to service or labor in any State or Territory of the United States, has heretofore or shall hereafter escape into another State or Territory of the United States, the person or persons to whom such service or labor may be due, or his, her, or their agent or attorney, duly authorized, by power of attorney, in writing, acknowledged and certified under the seal of some legal officer or court of the State or Territory in which the same may be executed, may pursue and reclaim such fugitive person, either by procuring a warrant from some one of the courts, judges, or commissioners aforesaid, of the proper circuit, district, or county, for the apprehension of such fugitive from service or labor, or by seizing and arresting such fugitive, where the same can be done without process, and by taking, or causing such person to be taken, forthwith before such court, judge, or commissioner, whose duty it shall be to hear and determine the case of such claimant in a summary manner; and upon satisfactory proof being made, by deposition or affidavit, in writing, to be taken and certified by such court, judge, or commissioner, or by other satisfactory testimony, duly taken and certified by some court, magistrate, justice of the peace, or other legal officer authorized to administer an oath and take depositions under the laws of the State or Territory from which such person owing service or labor may have escaped, with a certificate of such magistracy or other authority, as aforesaid, with the seal of the proper court or officer thereto attached, which seal shall be sufficient to establish the competency of the proof, and with proof, also by affidavit, of the identity of the person whose service or labor is claimed to be due as aforesaid, that the person so arrested does in fact owe service or labor to the person or persons claiming him or her, in the State or Territory from which such fugitive may have escaped as aforesaid, and that said person escaped, to make out and deliver to such claimant, his or her agent or attorney, a certificate setting forth the substantial facts as to the service or labor due from such fugitive to the claimant, and of his or her escape from the State or Territory in which such service or labor was due, to the State or Territory in which he or she was arrested, with authority to such claimant, or his or her agent or attorney, to use such reasonable force and restraint as may be necessary, under the circumstances of the case, to take and remove such fugitive person back to the State or Territory whence he or she may have escaped as aforesaid. In no trial or hearing under this act shall the testimony of such alleged fugitive be admitted in evidence; and the certificates in this and the first [fourth] section mentioned, shall be conclusive of the right of the person or persons in whose favor granted, to remove such fugitive to the State or Territory from which he escaped, and shall prevent all molestation of such person or persons by any process issued by any court judge, magistrate, or other person whomsoever.

◆ SEC. 7.

And be it further enacted, That any person who shall knowingly and willingly obstruct, hinder, or prevent such claimant, his agent or attorney, or any person or persons lawfully assisting him, her, or them, from arresting such a fugitive from service or labor, either with or without process as aforesaid, or shall rescue, or attempt to rescue such fugitive from service or labor, from the custody of such claimant, his or her agent or attorney, or other person or persons lawfully assisting as aforesaid, when so arrested, pursuant to the authority herein given and declared; or shall aid, abet, or assist such person so owing service or labor as aforesaid, directly or indirectly, to escape from such claimant, his agent or attorney, or other person or persons legally authorized as aforesaid; or shall harbor or conceal such fugitive, so as to prevent the discovery and arrest of such person, after notice or knowledge of the fact that such person was a fugitive from service or labor as aforesaid, shall, for either of said offences, be subject to a fine not exceeding one thousand dollars, and imprisonment not exceeding six months, by indictment and conviction before the District Court of the United States for the district in which such offence may have been committed, or before the proper court of criminal jurisdiction, if committed within anyone of the organized Territories of the United States; and shall moreover forfeit and pay, by way of civil damages to the party injured by such illegal conduct, the sum of one thousand dollars, for each fugitive so lost as aforesaid, to be recovered by action of debt, in any of the District or Territorial Courts aforesaid, within whose jurisdiction the said offence may have been committed.

♦ **SEC. 8.**

And be it further enacted, That the marshals, their deputies, and the clerks of the said District and Territorial Courts, shall be paid, for their services, the like fees as may be allowed to them for similar services in other cases; and where such services are rendered exclusively in the arrest, custody, and delivery of the fugitive to the claimant, his or her agent or attorney, or where such supposed fugitive may be discharged out of custody for the want of sufficient proof as aforesaid, then such fees are to be paid in the whole by such claimant, his agent or attorney; and in all cases where the proceedings are before a commissioner, he shall be entitled to a fee of ten dollars in full for his services in each case, upon the delivery of the said certificate to the claimant, his or her agent or attorney; or a fee of five dollars in cases where the proof shall not, in the opinion of such commissioner, warrant such certificate and delivery, inclusive of all services incident to such arrest and examination, to be paid, in either case, by the claimant, his or her agent or attorney The person or persons authorized to execute the process to be

issued by such commissioners for the arrest and detention of fugitives from service or labor as aforesaid, shall also be entitled to a fee of five dollars each for each person he or they may arrest and take before any such commissioner as aforesaid, at the instance and request of such claimant, with such other fees as may be deemed reasonable by such commissioner for such other additional services as may be necessarily performed by him or them; such as attending at the examination, keeping the fugitive in custody, and providing him with food and lodging during his detention, and until the final determination of such commissioner; and, in general, for performing such other duties as may be required by such claimant, his or her attorney or agent, or commissioner in the premises, such fees to be made up in conformity with the fees usually charged by the officers of the courts of justice within the proper district or county, as near as may be practicable, and paid by such claimants, their agents or attorneys, whether such supposed fugitives from service or labor be ordered to be delivered to such claimants by the final determination of such commissioners or not.

♦ **SEC. 9.**

And be it further enacted, That, upon affidavit made by the claimant of such fugitive, his agent or attorney, after such certificate has been issued, that he has reason to apprehend that such fugitive will be rescued by force from his or their possession before he can be taken beyond the limits of the State in which the arrest is made, it shall be the duty of the officer making the arrest to retain such fugitive in his custody, and to remove him to the State whence he fled, and there to deliver him to said claimant, his agent, or attorney. And to this end, the officer aforesaid is hereby authorized and required to employ so many persons as he may deem necessary to overcome such force, and to retain them in his service so long as circumstances may require. The said officer and his assistants, while so employed, to receive the same compensation, and to be allowed the same expenses, as are now allowed by law for transportation of criminals, to be certified by the judge of the district within which the arrest is made, and paid out of the treasury of the United States.

♦ **SEC. 10.**

And be it further enacted, That when any person held to service or labor in any State or Territory, or in the District of Columbia, shall escape therefrom, the party to whom such service or labor shall be due, his,

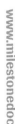

her, or their agent or attorney, may apply to any court of record therein, or judge thereof in vacation, and make satisfactory proof to such court, or judge in vacation, of the escape aforesaid, and that the person escaping owed service or labor to such party. Whereupon the court shall cause a record to be made of the matters so proved, and also a general description of the person so escaping, with such convenient certainty as may be; and a transcript of such record, authenticated by the attestation of the clerk and of the seal of the said court, being produced in any other State, Territory, or district in which the person so escaping may be found, and being exhibited to any judge, commissioner, or other officer authorized by the law of the United States to cause persons escaping from service or labor to be delivered up, shall be held and taken to be full and conclusive evidence of the fact of escape, and that the service or labor of the person escaping is due to the party in such record mentioned. And upon the production by the said party of other and further evidence if necessary, either oral or by affidavit, in addition to what is contained in the said record of the identity of the person escaping, he or she shall be delivered up to the claimant. And the said court, commissioner, judge, or other person authorized by this act to grant certificates to claimants of fugitives, shall, upon the production of the record and other evidences aforesaid, grant to such claimant a certificate of his right to take any such person identified and proved to be owing service or labor as aforesaid, which certificate shall authorize such claimant to seize or arrest and transport such person to the State or Territory from which he escaped: Provided, That nothing herein contained shall be construed as requiring the production of a transcript of such record as evidence as aforesaid. But in its absence the claim shall be heard and determined upon other satisfactory proofs, competent in law.

APPROVED, September 18, 1850.

An Act to suppress the Slave Trade in the District of Columbia

Be it enacted by the Senate and House of Representatives of the United States of America in Congress assembled, That from and after the first day of January, eighteen hundred and fifty-one, it shall not be lawful to bring into the District of Columbia any slave whatever, for the purpose of being sold, or for the purpose of being placed in depot, to be subsequently transferred to any other State or place to be sold as merchandize. And if any slave shall be brought into the said District by its owner, or by the authority or consent of its owner, contrary to the provisions of this act, such slave shall thereupon become liberated and free.

◆ SEC. 2.

And be it further enacted, That it shall and may be lawful for each of the corporations of the cities of Washington and Georgetown, from time to time, and as often as may be necessary, to abate, break up, and abolish any depot or place of confinement of slaves brought into the said District as merchandize, contrary to the provisions of this act, by such appropriate means as may appear to either of the said corporations expedient and proper. And the same power is hereby vested in the Levy Court of Washington county, if any attempt shall be made, within its jurisdictional limits, to establish a depot or place of confinement for slaves brought into the said District as merchandize for sale contrary to this act.

APPROVED, September 20, 1850.

Frederick Douglass (Library of Congress)

Frederick Douglass's "Fourth of July" Speech

1852

"What, to the American slave, is your 4th of July? I answer: a day that reveals to him ... the gross injustice and cruelty to which he is the constant victim."

Overview

Frederick Douglass's "Fourth of July" Speech is the most famous speech delivered by the abolitionist and civil rights advocate Frederick Douglass. In the nineteenth century, many American communities and cities celebrated Independence Day with a ceremonial reading of the Declaration of Independence, which was usually followed by an oral address or speech dedicated to the celebration of independence and the heritage of the American Revolution and the Founding Fathers. On July 5, 1852, the Ladies' Anti-Slavery Society of Rochester, New York, invited Douglass to be the keynote speaker for their Independence Day celebration.

The "Fourth of July" Speech, scheduled for Rochester's Corinthian Hall, attracted a crowd of between five hundred and six hundred, each of whom paid twelve and a half cents admission. The meeting opened with a prayer offered by the Reverend S. Ottman of Rush, New York, followed by a reading of the Declaration of Independence by the Reverend Robert R. Raymond of Syracuse, New York. Douglass then delivered his address, which the local press reported to be eloquent and admirable and which drew much applause. Upon conclusion of the address, the crowd thanked Douglass and called for the speech to be published in pamphlet form. Douglass complied, publishing a widely distributed pamphlet of the address. He also reprinted a text of the speech in his newspaper *Frederick Douglass' Paper* on July 9, 1852.

Context

The 1850s were a time of rising sectional tensions as slavery became the single most divisive issue in the United States. The United States' war with Mexico (1846–1848) resulted in the acquisition of a continental United States that stretched from the Atlantic to Pacific oceans. Even before the war concluded, Americans began debating whether slavery should be allowed in California and the New Mexico territories. The matter was settled with the Compromise of 1850, which admitted California as a free state but left the matter of slavery open in the territory that would become the states of Utah, New Mexico, and Arizona. In exchange for agreeing to the compromise, southerners in Congress demanded more protection for slavery where it existed, which resulted in the Fugitive Slave Act of 1850. The new law, passed in September 1850, superseded the Fugitive Slave Act of 1793 and required northerners to assist in returning escaped slaves. It also provided an unfair fee structure for fugitive slave commissioners, failed to provide jury trials, and did not permit an alleged fugitive to testify in his or her own defense. The Fugitive Slave Act led a number of northern states to pass personal liberty laws that aimed to skirt the act by routing fugitive slave cases through state courts.

The Fugitive Slave Act of 1850 also led many formerly pacifistic antislavery activists to take a more militant stance against slavery. On numerous occasions in the 1850s, abolitionists planned and executed the escape of fugitive slaves held in custody or liable for capture. In September 1851 antislavery activists killed the Maryland slaveholder Edward Gorsuch near Christiana, Pennsylvania, as he attempted to capture some fugitives. The following month abolitionists in Syracuse, New York, successfully rescued a slave by the name of Jerry Henry from fugitive slave commissioners in that city. Although Douglass did not participate in that rescue, many of his closest friends did, and he often spoke at annual "Jerry Rescue" celebrations.

If the Fugitive Slave Act served to heighten awareness and prompt physical action against slavery among abolitionists, the March 1852 publication of Harriet Beecher Stowe's *Uncle Tom's Cabin* succeeded in bringing the evils of slavery to the citizens of the northern states. This novel, which provided a vivid depiction of the lives of slaves, sold an amazing three hundred thousand copies in 1852, but many in Douglass's audience had already read the novel, as it had been published in forty installments beginning in June 1851 in the abolitionist weekly newspaper the *National Era*. Arriving on the heels of the highly publicized injustices of the Fugitive Slave Act, the novel had a profound effect on American attitudes toward slavery.

Douglass's "Fourth of July" Speech came in the early years of the turbulent 1850s, which began with the Fugitive Slave Act of 1850. Advocates and opponents of slavery

1845

■ The *Narrative of the Life of Frederick Douglass* is published in Boston.

1846–1848

■ The United States' war with Mexico results in the acquisition of California and New Mexico territories and escalates the debate over the extension of slavery into the new territories.

1850

■ The Compromise of 1850 is negotiated, including the Fugitive Slave Act of 1850, which requires northerners to assist in the return of escaped slaves.

1852

■ Harriet Beecher Stowe's antislavery novel *Uncle Tom's Cabin* is published and widely read.

■ **July 5**
Frederick Douglass delivers his "Fourth of July" Speech at Corinthian Hall in Rochester, New York.

1854

■ **May 30**
The Kansas-Nebraska Act is passed, allowing new territories to enter as slave or free states on the basis of popular sovereignty.

1857

■ **March 6**
The Supreme Court rules in *Dred Scott v. Sandford* that African Americans have "no rights whites are bound to obey" (60 U.S. 393; 1857).

1859

■ **October 16–18**
John Brown, an abolitionist, leads a failed raid on the federal arsenal at Harpers Ferry, Virginia, in an attempt to overthrow slavery; he is convicted of treason and hanged on December 2.

1860

■ **November 6**
Abraham Lincoln is elected as the president of the United States; the southern states begin to secede from the Union.

clashed again in 1854 when the Kansas-Nebraska Act opened up those territories to slavery if the residents so desired. In 1857 the U.S. Supreme Court stepped into the debate with Chief Justice Roger Taney's ruling in *Dred Scott v. Sandford*, which proclaimed that African Americans, enslaved or not, were not citizens of the United States and that Congress had no authority to prohibit slavery in the territories. Two years later, in October 1859, the abolitionist John Brown led a failed slave uprising and raid on the federal arsenal at Harpers Ferry, Virginia. Brown, a friend of Douglass's, was hanged for treason in December 1859. The 1850s ended with a nation more divided than ever before on the issue of slavery and teetering on the edge of civil war.

About the Author

Frederick Douglass, abolitionist and civil rights activist, was born into slavery on a Maryland plantation in February 1818—the exact date of his birth cannot be determined. He was known in his youth as Frederick Washington Augustus Bailey, and he spent twenty years in bondage— first on Wye Plantation near St. Michaels in Talbot County, Maryland, and then in the shipbuilding city of Baltimore. His mother, Harriet Bailey, was a fieldworker, and his father was most likely his first owner, Aaron Anthony.

During his enslavement, Douglass gained literacy, learning the basics of reading from his mistress, Sophia Auld, and improving his reading and writing on his own after Auld's husband chastised her for illegally teaching a slave to read. While living and working in Baltimore, Douglass obtained a copy of *The Columbian Orator*, a collection of famous speeches published in a single, portable volume by the bookseller Caleb Bingham. Douglass poured over the speeches, improving his reading skills and beginning to develop the oratory style for which he would become famous. In September 1838 Douglass borrowed the free papers of a friend and boarded a train for the North. This rather uneventful escape from the bonds of slavery marked the beginning of his life as a crusader against the evils of slavery and in favor of civil rights for African Americans and women.

By 1841 Douglass had been hired as a field lecturer for the Massachusetts Anti-Slavery Society, and he was well on his way to becoming one of the most powerful orators of the nineteenth century. In 1845 the publication of his first autobiography, *Narrative of the Life of Frederick Douglass*, afforded him an international reputation as America's most famous fugitive slave. In 1847 he moved his family to Rochester, New York, where he began publishing an antislavery newspaper called the *North Star*, later renamed *Frederick Douglass' Paper*. In 1852 the Rochester Ladies' Anti-Slavery Society invited Douglass to offer the annual Fourth of July address at their July 5 event.

During and after the Civil War, Douglass was a strong advocate for civil rights. During the war, he recruited African American troops and advised President Abraham Lincoln on the best plan to incorporate blacks into the

Union war effort. In 1872 Douglass moved his family to Washington, D.C., where he accepted a post as president of the Freedman's Savings Bank in 1874. In 1877 President Rutherford B. Hayes appointed him U.S. marshal for the District of Columbia, and in 1881 he became recorder of deeds for the District of Columbia. His highest federal post came as U.S. resident minister and consul general (ambassador) to Haiti. He died at Cedar Hill, his home in Washington, D.C., on February 20, 1895.

Explanation and Analysis of the Document

In the opening three paragraphs of the introductory section of his "Fourth of July" Speech, Douglass establishes a tone of humility, expressing his gratitude to the event's organizers for deeming him worthy of addressing American independence. Here he juxtaposes himself as a former slave with those in the audience who he deems the true beneficiaries of the Declaration of Independence. He notes the considerable distance between "this platform and the slave plantation, from which I escaped." He further reveals humility by discounting the amount of preparation put into the address. In reality, the oration is carefully crafted to offer the utmost contrast between the celebration of Independence Day and the continuance of racial slavery in the United States. Douglass would write to his friend and fellow abolitionist Gerrit Smith on July 7, 1852, that writing the oration took "much of my extra time for the last two or three weeks" (Blassingame, p. 359).

Although traditional Fourth of July addresses tended to emphasize the achievements of the American Revolution and its legacy, Douglass's address intends to bring focus to the present. To this end, in the introductory section he carefully distances himself from the historical events of the Revolution, preparing the way to contrast the rights white Americans enjoy and the oppression of slavery. He describes the day as one celebrating "your National Independence" and "your political freedom."

Once he establishes that he is not a beneficiary of the freedom and benefits of the Revolution, Douglass compares the abolitionist reformers of the 1850s with the independence-seekers of the founding generation. Douglass tells the assembled crowd that "your fathers" spoke out and acted in opposition to the unjust government of the British Crown. They petitioned, complained, and eventually declared their independence from tyranny and slavery. Although it seemed that achieving the goal of independence was insurmountable owing to a lack of organization, a widely scattered population, insufficient resources, and other factors, the founding generation prevailed, and independence was achieved.

The paragraphs near the end of this section provide a transition into the heart of the address. Douglass heaps praise on the Revolutionary generation and assures the audience that "I am not wanting in respect for the fathers of this republic." He clearly states that he is transitioning into matters affecting the present state of the nation, not-

Time Line

1861

- ■ **April 14**
  Shots are fired at Fort Sumter in the harbor at Charleston, South Carolina, which hails the beginning of the Civil War.

1863

- ■ **January 1**
  The Emancipation Proclamation, which abolishes slavery in the states under rebellion, takes effect.

1865

- ■ The states ratify the Thirteenth Amendment, which abolishes slavery in the United States.

ing that he intends to leave "the great deeds of your fathers to other gentlemen," most notably to those who were not born into slavery as he was.

◆ The Present

Douglass's tone changes to a critical assessment of the way that Americans reap the benefits of the founding generation's achievements in this section as he turns toward the influence of those achievements in the present. He quotes a stanza from Henry Wadsworth Longfellow's poem "A Psalm of Life" at the start of the section, which emphasizes the importance of acting in the present instead of dwelling on the future or past. The problem of the present that most concerns Douglass is the existence of slavery in the United States and the inherent contradiction between celebrating American independence while many suffer under the bonds of slavery. His allusion to Sydney Smith (1771–1845) refers to an Anglican minister who wrote satirically in criticism of the British Crown and who was a strong activist for Catholic emancipation in that country. Douglass also alludes to the biblical passage Luke 3:8: "Bring forth therefore fruits worthy of repentance, and begin not to say within yourselves, We have Abraham to *our* father: for I say unto you, That God is able of these stones to raise up children to Abraham." He points out that George Washington, the most revered of the Founders, freed his slaves in his will. Douglass argues that many of those celebrating American independence and the legacy of the Revolutionary generation are hypocrites who hold slaves and engage in slave trafficking. The quote that follows, noting that men's evil deeds often follow them to the grave, originates from William Shakespeare's *Julius Caesar* (act 3, scene 2).

After outlining a series of rhetorical questions about the application of the principles of freedom and justice to all, Douglass powerfully asks the crowd if it was their intention to mock him by inviting him to speak on the Fourth of July. He notes in the seventh paragraph, "The rich inheritance of justice, liberty, prosperity, and independence, bequeathed by your fathers, is shared by you, not by me." Douglass quotes Psalms 135:1 to 135:6 in the eighth paragraph of this section, comparing the experiences of American slaves to the unjust biblical enslavement of the Jews. In the following passages, Douglass transitions from the celebration of the Fourth of July to a more familiar topic, American slavery. Many in the audience were abolitionist-minded, and most would have anticipated the shift in topic. He argues that the character and conduct of the nation "never looked blacker." Following the passage of the federal Fugitive Slave Act of 1850, northern states were required to take a more active role in returning fugitive slaves to the South, greatly angering abolitionists and others who viewed the new law as a demonstration of the federal government's support for slavery. Douglass condemns the use of religion and the U.S. Constitution to support slavery and vows to actively oppose slavery in every way he can, taking the quote "I will not equivocate; I will not excuse" from the first issue of William Lloyd Garrison's antislavery newspaper, the *Liberator*, which appeared January 1, 1831.

Douglass next examines a series of issues commonly found in abolitionists' denunciations of slavery, including the humanity of the enslaved, their entitlement to liberty, and biblical justifications for the institution. The tone of these passages is full of irony, as Douglass argues that each of these issues has already been settled and really requires no additional comment. He turns first to the question of the humanity of slaves. An early justification for slavery argued that men and women of African descent were descended from a different species than whites. Their full humanity was sometimes considered questionable. Douglass argues persuasively in the tenth and eleventh paragraphs that the question of the humanity of slaves has been put to rest and that even in the South, the slave is considered a man. He cites a series of seventy-two crimes for which a black man might be given the death penalty in Virginia as partial evidence that southerners recognize the humanity of slaves. Douglass likely pulls this information from the writings of the abolitionist Theodore Dwight Weld, whose 1839 book *American Slavery As It Is* included a careful exploration of slave laws and punishments. At the close of this section, Douglass turns to the argument that slaves as men are entitled to liberty. He proclaims that this issue is also widely settled; in fact, he remarks, "There is not a man beneath the canopy of heaven, that does not know that slavery is wrong *for him*." Likewise, he touches on the fact that slavery is neither divinely sanctioned nor created by God. Such common arguments, Douglass contends, have run their course, and now a new course of action must be undertaken. He announces to the crowd, "We need the storm, the whirlwind, and the earthquake." The speech changes course again as Douglass begins a scathing condemnation of the country with the famous title line "What, to the American slave, is your 4th of July?"

Douglass argues that, for enslaved Americans, the Fourth of July is the one day of the year that most represents the "gross injustice and cruelty to which he is the constant victim." He finds that the celebration of liberty and equality is hypocritical while slavery continues to exist in the United States. In the final paragraph of the section, he claims that the hypocrisy of the United States is deeper than the abuses of European and other world monarchies and that even the cruelties of South American slavery do not match the cruelty brought about by the contradiction between slavery and freedom in America. This is an especially harsh criticism, because it is widely known that South American slavery was particularly callous.

◆ **The Internal Slave Trade**

In the next section of the speech, Douglass's critical eye turns to the slave trade within the United States. Although the importation of slaves from Africa or the Caribbean was outlawed after 1808, the boom in cotton production after the War of 1812 increased the need for labor in the developing, southwestern cotton states. The labor gap was filled by moving large numbers of enslaved men and women from the Upper South states, such as Virginia and Maryland, to the Lower South. It is estimated that between 1820 and 1860 about 900,000 slaves were sold or moved into the developing cotton fields in such states as Alabama, Mississippi, Louisiana, and Texas. The practice often separated family members and is considered one of the cruelest elements of U.S. slavery. Douglass references the former senator Thomas Hart Benton (1782–1858), who served as a U.S. senator from Missouri from 1821 to 1851 and as one of that state's congressmen from 1853 to 1855.

In the first paragraph of this section, Douglass points out that some important ministers have spoken out against the slave trade and slavery but that many of them support a movement to colonize free blacks in Africa. This movement began in earnest with the creation of the American Colonization Society in 1816, which established the colony of Liberia on the west coast of Africa. Although a number of freed blacks did emigrate to Liberia and other places, the movement was largely unsuccessful. Douglass adamantly opposes colonization and other expatriation schemes.

Douglass follows this with a condemnation of the internal slave trade. These passages offer some details about the ways that the slave trade functioned and of how it affected and dehumanized those who were subjected to sale and movement. Douglass describes men, women, and children being bound in chains, screams, whippings, and the separation of mothers and children. In the second paragraph he asks his audience to tell him "WHERE, under the sun, you can witness a spectacle more fiendish and shocking." The following passages detail Douglass's own experiences as he recalls the Baltimore slave market controlled by a man he remembers as Austin Woldfolk. This notorious man's name was actually Austin Woolfolk of Augusta, Georgia. He came to Baltimore around 1819 and was the most prominent slave trader in the area during the 1820s and 1830s, exporting between 230 and 460 slaves to New Orleans each year. This discussion concludes with a slight alteration of the first four lines of the poem "Stanzas for the Times" by the abolitionist poet John Greenleaf Whittier.

In the final two paragraphs of this section, Douglass heartily condemns the Fugitive Slave Act, which was passed as a part of the Compromise of 1850 and was negotiated to settle matters of territorial and slavery expansion following the United States' war with Mexico (1846–1848). The Fugitive Slave Act angered abolitionists and led many who had previously been neutral on the issue of slavery to speak out against the measure. The law required northern states to aid in returning fugitive slaves. It established commissioners and special hearings to handle the cases of alleged fugitives. As Douglass describes in the seventh paragraph, the commissioner received a fee of $10 if an individual was determined to be a fugitive but only $5 if he or she was determined to be free. Although the law did not specify the number of witnesses needed to establish one as a fugitive, it did specify that evidence or testimony from the alleged fugitive was inadmissible. The injustice inherent in this law led many formerly pacifistic abolitionists to take more active roles in helping fugitives to escape, sometimes physically rescuing them from jails and courthouses across the North.

◆ **Religious Liberty**

In a section comprising two paragraphs, Douglass places blame on the established churches and denominations of the United States for their failure to condemn the Fugitive Slave Act as "one of the grossest infringements of Christian Liberty." He makes his case for the churches' culpability in this section. Douglass argues that if the matter involved financial benefit or harm to the church, clergy would call for the law's repeal. The following passage refers to the struggle against Mary Stuart's (Mary, Queen of Scots) attempt to halt the Protestant Reformation and bring Scotland back under the fold of the Roman Catholic Church. John Knox was the most outspoken minister fighting to push the Protestant Reformation forward in Scotland. Douglass believes that American ministers should fight to repeal the Fugitive Slave Act in the same way that Knox fought against Catholicism. The other person mentioned in this brief section is President Millard Fillmore, who presided over the Senate as vice president during the negotiation of the Compromise of 1850. He became president in July 1850, following the death of President John Tyler. The "mint, anise, and cumin" allusion at the end of the section is drawn from Matthew 23:23: "Woe unto you, scribes and Pharisees, hypocrites! For ye pay tithe of mint, anise and cumin, and have omitted the weightier matters of the law, judgment, mercy and faith; these ought ye to have done, and not to leave the other undone."

◆ **The Church Responsible**

In this section of the address, Douglass condemns the established churches in the United States, claiming that they have taken the side of slaveholders in the debate over slavery. He refers to three famous supporters of Deism from the eighteenth and nineteenth centuries: Thomas Paine (1737–1809), an American Revolutionary and author of *Common Sense*; François-Marie Arouet de Voltaire (1694–1778), a French playwright and author; and Henry St. John, Viscount Bolingbroke, an English statesmen and author. In the second paragraph of the section, Douglass quotes biblical passages from James 1:27, "Pure religion and undefiled … is this," and James 3:17, "But the wisdom that is from above is first pure, then peaceable, gentle, and easy to be intreated, full of mercy and good fruits, without partiality and without hypocrisy." The second series of quotes originates from Isaiah 1.13 to 1:17. The fourth paragraph refers to the radical New Light Presbyterian minister Albert Barnes (1798–1870), who opposed slavery and made a similar condemnation of the complicity of the American church in maintaining slavery. In the sixth paragraph of this section, he names several well-known American ministers as individuals particularly supportive of slaveholding and teaching "that we ought to obey man's laws before the law of God," including John Chase Lord, Gardiner Spring, Leonard Elijah Lathrop, Samuel Hanson Cox, Ichabod Smith Spencer, Ezra Stiles Gannett, Daniel Sharp, and Orville Dewey. Douglass concludes this section by reminding the audience that although his words apply to the majority of American ministers, notable exceptions include the Reverend Robert R. Raymond, who also spoke at the Corinthian Hall event.

◆ **Religion in England and Religion in America**

To draw a clear contrast between the antislavery activism of the British and those in the United States, Douglass includes this segment juxtaposing prominent antislavery British activists including Granville Sharp, Thomas Clarkson, William Wilberforce, Thomas Fowell Buxton, Thomas Burchell, and William Knibb. Douglass had traveled for a year and a half in Great Britain and Ireland in 1845 to 1847, during which time he met and worked with a number of British reformers. Unlike the U.S. antislavery movement, when Great Britain ended slavery under the Slavery Abolition Act of 1833, the established Anglican Church supported the abolition of slavery in the British West Indies. In the second paragraph of the section, Douglass contrasts the failure of American clergy to oppose slavery with their sympathy for such foreign causes as the movement of Hungarians to shake off an invasion by Russian and Austrian troops in 1849. Near the end of this lengthy paragraph, Douglass paraphrases Acts 17:26, "And [God] hath made of one blood all the nations of men for to dwell upon the earth," and quotes the Declaration of Independence. Douglass attributes the quote to a letter written on June 26, 1786 by Thomas Jefferson to the French author and politician Jean-Nicolas Démeunier.

◆ **The Constitution**

The final section of the speech turns to the constitutionality of slavery. Although Douglass once held the view that the U.S. Constitution was a proslavery document, by 1852 he was committed to using political means to end slavery. In the opening paragraph he paraphrases Shakespeare's *Macbeth* to emphasize the fallacy of those who believe that the Constitution sanctions slavery. He men-

"This Fourth [of] July is yours, not mine. You may rejoice, I must mourn."

("The Present," paragraph 7)

"What, to the American slave, is your 4th of July? I answer: a day that reveals to him, more than all other days in the year, the gross injustice and cruelty to which he is the constant victim."

("The Present," paragraph 16)

tions several prominent northerners committed to antislavery politics, each of whom had published works arguing that the Constitution does not support slavery. Beginning with the third paragraph, Douglass outlines the evidence for his argument, pointing especially to the fact that the words *slave* and *slavery* do not appear anywhere in the document. Although some historians argue that slavery was implicitly protected in several articles of the Constitution, Douglass does not see a single proslavery clause. In support of his position, he points to prominent politicians outside the antislavery circle, including George Mifflin Dallas, who served as vice president under James Polk; the Georgia senator John MacPherson Berrien; the Illinois Democrat Sidney Breese; and Lewis Cass, Michigan senator and Democratic candidate for president in 1848.

Douglass turns more hopeful for the speech's conclusion. He believes that slavery will one day be abolished, paraphrasing Isaiah 59:1 in the sixth paragraph of the section: "Behold, the Lord's hand is not shortened, that it cannot save, neither His ear heavy, that it cannot hear." He takes inspiration that the Declaration of Independence will one day apply to all. In the final paragraph, he proclaims that slavery will end when the light of freedom reaches the United States, alluding to Psalms 68:31: "Princes shall come out of Egypt; Ethiopia shall soon stretch out her hands unto God." The essay concludes with the poem "The Triumph of Freedom" authored by the famous abolitionist William Lloyd Garrison.

Audience

Douglass's speech was delivered before a crowd of reform-minded citizens of Rochester, New York. Many in the audience probably shared his belief that slavery was a moral sin and should be immediately ended. With publication of the speech in pamphlet form, Douglass was able to increase the number of Americans who heard his words. At least seven hundred copies of the speech were printed and distributed for a nominal fee that covered printing. Douglass aimed

his message at the American public and hoped his words might persuade many to join in the antislavery cause.

Impact

Douglass's "Fourth of July" Speech made an immediate impact on the northern American reading public. It was published in pamphlet form in the weeks following the address and read by hundreds who had not attended the Rochester event. The speech endures as one of the most articulate expressions of what it means to be excluded from the republican experiment that resulted in the democracy of the United States. Yet beyond a condemnation of slavery, the speech endures because Douglass adopted a hopeful tone, believing that the United States would be more complete once slavery ended. Today scholars and students of American history still widely read Douglass's "Fourth of July" Speech.

Related Documents

"Declaration of Independence." National Archives "Our Documents" Web site. http://www.ourdocuments.gov/doc.php?flash= true&doc=2. Accessed on January 3, 2008. This document, framed by a committee of the Second Continental Congress and largely authored by Thomas Jefferson, is the core document of the United States. In July 1776 it announced the original thirteen colonies' freedom from Great Britain. In Frederick Douglass's era, Fourth of July celebrations often included a reading of the Declaration, as did the one at Rochester, New York, where Douglass delivered his address in 1852.

Douglass, Frederick. *Narrative of the Life of Frederick Douglass, An American Slave.* Boston, 1845. *Narrative,* the first of three autobiographies authored by Douglass, provides a detailed account of his life as a slave in Maryland and concludes with his escape from slavery in 1838. The book has been in continuous print since its publication in 1845, and it is one of the best documented, first-person records of slave life in antebellum America.

Bibliography

■ Books

Blassingame, John W., et al., eds. *The Frederick Douglass Papers*, Series One: *Speeches, Debates, and Interviews*, Vol. 2: 1847–54. New Haven, Conn.: Yale University Press, 1982.

Colaiaco, James A. *Frederick Douglass and the Fourth of July*. New York: Palgrave Macmillan, 2006.

Douglass, Frederick. *Oration, Delivered in Corinthian Hall, Rochester, July 5, 1852*. Rochester, New York, 1852.

—By L. Diane Barnes

Questions for Further Study

1. How does Douglass align himself with the audience while still expressing a point of view that differs from theirs?

2. Douglass was a renowned orator who drew large audiences to hear him speak on many topics. What rhetorical and persuasive devices does he employ in this address?

3. For Douglass, freedom is clearly tied to the idea of the progress of the American empire. What portions of the speech best reflect this assertion?

Glossary

despotisms	absolute rules
ecclesiastics	priests and ministers
euphonious	agreeable sound or spoken words
exordium	introduction, especially in a classic or rhetorical text
fettered	shackled or chained together
mammon	riches
perambulate	walk around

FREDERICK DOUGLASS'S "FOURTH OF JULY" SPEECH

Mr. President, Friends and Fellow Citizens:

He who could address this audience without a quailing sensation, has stronger nerves than I have. I do not remember ever to have appeared as a speaker before any assembly more shrinkingly, nor with greater distrust of my ability, than I do this day. A feeling has crept over me, quite unfavorable to the exercise of my limited powers of speech. The task before me is one which requires much previous thought and study for its proper performance. I know that apologies of this sort are generally considered flat and unmeaning. I trust, however, that mine will not be so considered. Should I seem at ease, my appearance would much misrepresent me. The little experience I have had in addressing public meetings, in country school houses, avails me nothing on the present occasion.

The papers and placards say, that I am to deliver a 4th July oration. This certainly, sounds large, and out of the common way, for me. It is true that I have often had the privilege to speak in this beautiful Hall, and to address many who now honor me with their presence. But neither their familiar faces, nor the perfect gage I think I have of Corinthian Hall, seems to free me from embarrassment.

The fact is, ladies and gentlemen, the distance between this platform and the slave plantation, from which I escaped, is considerable—and the difficulties to be overcome in getting from the latter to the former, are by no means slight. That I am here today, is, to me, a matter of astonishment as well as of gratitude. You will not, therefore, be surprised, if in what I have to say, I evince no elaborate preparation, nor grace my speech with any high sounding exordium. With little experience and with less learning, I have been able to throw my thoughts hastily and imperfectly together; and trusting to your patient and generous indulgence, I will proceed to lay them before you.

This, for the purpose of this celebration, is the 4th of July. It is the birthday of your National Independence, and of your political freedom. This, to you, is what the Passover was to the emancipated people of God. It carries your minds back to the clay, and to the act of your great deliverance; and to the signs, and to the wonders, associated with that act that day. This celebration also marks the beginning of another year of your national life; and reminds you that the Republic of America is now 76 years old. I am glad, fellow-citizens, that your nation is so young. Seventy-six years, though a good old age for a man, is but a mere speck in the life of a nation. Three score years and ten is the allotted time for individual men; but nations number their years by thousands. According to this fact, you are, even now only in the beginning of you national career, still lingering in the period of childhood. I repeat, I am glad this is so. There is hope in the thought, and hope is much needed, under the dark clouds which lower above the horizon. The eye of the reformer is met with angry flashes, portending disastrous times; but his heart may well beat lighter at the thought that America is young, and that she is still in the impressible stage of her existence. May he not hope that high lessons of wisdom, of justice and of truth, will yet give direction to her destiny? Were the nation older, the patriot's heart might be sadder, and the reformer's brow heavier. Its future might be shrouded in gloom, and the hope of its prophets go out in sorrow. There is consolation in the thought, that America is young. Great streams are not easily turned from channels, worn deep in the course of ages. They may sometimes rise in quiet and stately majesty, and inundate the land, refreshing and fertilizing the earth with their mysterious properties. They may also rise in wrath and fury, and bear away, on their angry waves, the accumulated wealth of years of toil and hardship. They, however, gradually flow back to the same old channel, and flow on as serenely as ever. But, while the river may not be turned aside, it may dry up, and leave nothing behind but the withered branch, and the unsightly rock, to howl in the abyss-sweeping wind, the sad tale of departed glory. As with rivers so with nations.

Fellow-citizens, I shall not presume to dwell at length on the associations that cluster about this day. The simple story of it is, that, 76 years ago, the people of this country were British subjects. The style and title of your "sovereign people" (in which you now glory) was not then born. You were under the British Crown. Your fathers esteemed the English Government as the home government and England as the fatherland. This home government, you know, although a considerable distance from your home, did, in the exercise of its parental prerogatives, impose upon its colonial children, such restraints, burdens and limitations, as, in its mature judgment, it deemed wise, right and proper.

But, your fathers, who had not adopted the fashionable idea of this day, of the infallibility of government, and the absolute character of its acts, presumed to differ from the home government in respect to the wisdom and the justice of some of those burdens and restraints. They went so far in their excitement as to pronounce the measures of government unjust, unreasonable, and oppressive, and altogether such as ought not to be quietly submitted to. I scarcely need say, fellow-citizens, that my opinion of those measures fully accords with that of your fathers. Such a declaration of agreement on my part, would not be worth much to anybody. It would, certainly, prove nothing, as to what part I might have taken, had I lived during the great controversy of 1776. To say now that America was right, and England wrong, is exceedingly easy. Everybody can say it; the dastard, not less than the noble brave, can flippantly discant on the tyranny of England towards the American Colonies. It is fashionable to do so; but there was a time when, to pronounce against England, and in favor of the cause of the colonies, tried men's souls. They who did so were accounted in their day, plotters of mischief, agitators and rebels, dangerous men. To side with the right, against the wrong, with the weak against the strong, and with the oppressed against the oppressor! here lies the merit, and the one which, of all others, seems unfashionable in our day. The cause of liberty may be stabbed by the men who glory in the deeds of your fathers. But, to proceed.

Feeling themselves harshly and unjustly treated, by the home government, your fathers, like men of honesty, and men of spirit, earnestly sought redress. They petitioned and remonstrated; they did so in a decorous, respectful, and loyal manner. Their conduct was wholly unexceptionable. This, however, did not answer the purpose. They saw themselves treated with sovereign indifference, coldness and scorn. Yet they persevered. They were not the men to look back.

As the sheet anchor takes a firmer hold, when the ship is tossed by the storm, so did the cause of your fathers grow stronger, as it breasted the chilling blasts of kingly displeasure. The greatest and best of British statesmen admitted its justice, and the loftiest eloquence of the British Senate came to its support. But, with that blindness which seems to be the unvarying characteristic of tyrants, since Pharaoh and his hosts were drowned in the Red sea, the British Government persisted in the exactions complained of.

The madness of this course, we believe, is admitted now, even by England; but, we fear the lesson is wholly lost on our present rulers.

Oppression makes a wise man mad. Your fathers were wise men, and if they did not go mad, they became restive under this treatment. They felt themselves the victims of grievous wrongs, wholly incurable in their colonial capacity. With brave men there is always a remedy for oppression. Just here, the idea of a total separation of the colonies from the crown was born! It was a startling idea, much more so, than we, at this distance of time, regard it. The timid and the prudent (as has been intimated) of that day, were, of course, shocked and alarmed by it.

Such people lived then, had lived before, and will, probably, ever have a place on this planet; and their course, in respect to any great change, (no matter how great the good to be attained, or the wrong to be redressed by it,) may be calculated with as much precision as can be the course of the stars. They hate all changes, but silver, gold and copper change! Of this sort of change they are always strongly in favor.

These people were called tories in the days of your fathers; and the appellation, probably, conveyed the same idea that is meant by a more modern, though a somewhat less euphonious term, which we often find in our papers, applied to some of our old politicians.

Their opposition to the then dangerous thought was earnest and powerful; but, amid all their terror and affrighted vociferations against it, the alarming and revolutionary idea moved on, and the country with it.

On the 2d of July, 1776, the old Continental Congress, to the dismay of the lovers of ease, and the worshippers of property, clothed that dreadful idea with all the authority of national sanction. They did so in the form of a resolution; and as we seldom hit upon resolutions, drawn up in our day, whose transparency is at all equal to this, it may refresh your minds and help my story if I read it.

Resolved, That these united colonies are, and of right, ought to be free and Independent States; that they are absolved from all allegiance to the British Crown; and that all political connection between them and the State of Great Britain is, and ought to be, dissolved.

Citizens, your fathers Made good that resolution. They succeeded; and today you reap the fruits of their success. The freedom gained is yours; and you, therefore, may properly celebrate this anniversary. The 4th of July is the first great fact in your nation's history—the very ring-bolt in the chain of your yet undeveloped destiny.

Pride and patriotism, not less than gratitude, prompt you to celebrate and to hold it in perpetual remembrance. I have said that the Declaration of Independence is the RINGBOLT to the chain of your nation's destiny; so, indeed, I regard it. The principles contained in that instrument are saving principles. Stand by those principles, be true to them on all occasions, in all places, against all foes, and at whatever cost.

From the round top of your ship of state, dark and threatening clouds may be seen. Heavy billows, like mountains in the distance, disclose to the leeward huge forms of flinty rocks! That bolt drawn, that chain, broken, and all is lost. Cling to this day—cling to it, and to its principles, with the grasp of a storm-tossed mariner to a spar at midnight.

The coining into being of a nation, in any circumstances, is an interesting event. But, besides general considerations, there were peculiar circumstances which make the advent of this republic an event of special attractiveness.

The whole scene, as I look back to it, was simple, dignified and sublime.

The population of the country, at the time, stood at the insignificant number of three millions. The country was poor in the munitions of war. The population was weak and scattered, and the country a wilderness unsubdued. There were then no means of concert and combination, such as exist now. Neither steam nor lightning had then been reduced to order and discipline. From the Potomac to the Delaware was a journey of many days. Under these, and innumerable other disadvantages, your fathers declared for liberty and independence and triumphed.

Fellow Citizens, I am not wanting in respect for the fathers of this republic. The signers of the Declaration of Independence were brave men. They were great men too—great enough to give fame to a great age. It does not often happen to a nation to raise, at one time, such a number of truly great men. The point from which I am compelled to view them is not, certainly the most favorable; and yet I cannot contemplate their great deeds with less than admiration. They were statesmen, patriots and heroes, and for the good they did, and the principles they contended for, I will unite with you to honor their memory.

They loved their country better than their own private interests; and, though this is not the highest form of human excellence, all will concede that it is a rare virtue, and that when it is exhibited, it ought to command respect. He who will, intelligently, lay down his life for his country, is a man whom it is not in human nature to despise. Your fathers staked their lives, their fortunes, and their sacred honor, on the cause of their country. In their admiration of liberty, they lost sight of all other interests.

They were peace men; but they preferred revolution to peaceful submission to bondage. They were quiet men; but they did not shrink from agitating against oppression. They showed forbearance; but that they knew its limits. They believed in order; but not in the order of tyranny. With them, nothing was "settled" that was not right. With them, justice, liberty and humanity were "final;" not slavery and oppression. You may well cherish the memory of such men. They were great in their day and generation. Their solid manhood stands out the more as we contrast it with these degenerate times.

How circumspect, exact and proportionate were all their movements! How unlike the politicians of an hour! Their statesmanship looked beyond the passing moment, and stretched away in strength into the distant future. They seized upon eternal principles, and set a glorious example in their defence. Mark them!

Fully appreciating the hardships to be encountered, firmly believing in the right of their cause, honorably inviting the scrutiny of an on-looking world, reverently appealing to heaven to attest their sincerity, soundly comprehending the solemn responsibility they were about to assume, wisely measuring the terrible odds against them, your fathers, the fathers of this republic, did, most deliberately, under the inspiration of a glorious patriotism, and with a sublime faith in the great principles of justice and freedom, lay deep, the corner-stone of the national super-structure, which has risen and still rises in grandeur around you.

Of this fundamental work, this day is the anniversary. Our eyes are met with demonstrations of joyous enthusiasm. Banners and penants wave exultingly on the breeze. The din of business, too, is hushed. Even mammon seems to have quitted his grasp on this day. The ear-piercing fife and the stirring drum unite their accents with the ascending peal of a thousand church bells. Prayers are made, hymns are sung, and sermons are preached in honor of this day; while the quick martial tramp of a great and multitudinous nation, echoed back by all the hills, valleys and mountains of a vast continent, bespeak the occasion one of thrilling and universal interest—a nation's jubilee.

Friends and citizens, I need not enter further into the causes which led to this anniversary. Many of you understand them better than I do. You could instruct me in regard to them. That is a branch of knowledge in which you feel, perhaps, a much deeper interest than your speaker. The causes which led to the separation of the colonies from the British crown have never lacked for a tongue. They have all been taught in your common schools, narrated at your firesides, unfolded from your pulpits, and thundered from your legislative halls, and are as familiar to you as household words. They form the staple of your national poetry and eloquence.

I remember, also, that, as a people, Americans are remarkably familiar with all facts which make in in their own favor. This is esteemed by some as a national trait—perhaps a national weakness. It is a fact, that whatever makes for the wealth or for the reputation of Americans, and can be had cheap! will be found by Americans. I shall not be charged with slandering Americans, if I say I think the Americans can side of any question may be safely left in American hands.

I leave, therefore, the great deeds of your fathers to other gentlemen whose claim to have been regularly descended will be less likely to be disputed than mine!

◆ The Present

My business, if I have any here today, is with the present. The accepted time with God and his cause is the ever-living now.

"Trust no future, however pleasant, Let the dead past bury its dead; Act, act in the living present, Heart within, and God overhead."

We have to do with the past only as we can make it useful to the present and to the future. To all inspiring motives, to noble deeds which can be gained from the past, we are welcome. But now is the time, the important time. Your fathers have lived, died, and have done their work, and have done much of it well. You live and must die, and you must do your work. You have no right to enjoy a child's share in the labor of your fathers, unless your children are to be blest by your labors. You have no right to wear out and waste the hard-earned fame of your fathers to cover your indolence. Sydney Smith tells us that men seldom eulogize the wisdom and virtues of their fathers, but to excuse some folly or wickedness of their own. This truth is not a doubtful one. There are illustrations of it near and remote, ancient and modern. It was fashionable, hundreds of years ago, for the children of Jacob to boast, we have "Abraham to our father," when they had long lost Abraham's faith and spirit. That people contented themselves under the shadow of Abraham's great name, while they repudiated the deeds which made his name great. Need I remind you that a similar thing is being done all over this country today? Need I tell you that the Jews are not the only people who built the tombs of the prophets, and garnished the sepulchres of the righteous? Washington could not die till he had broken the chains of his slaves. Yet his monument is built up by the price of human blood, and the traders in the bodies and souls of men, shout, "We have Washington to 'our father.' Alas! that it should be so; yet so it is.

"The evil that men do, lives after them, The good is oft interred with their bones."

Fellow-citizens, pardon me, allow me to ask, why am I called upon to speak here today? What have I, or those I represent, to do with your national independence? Are the great principles of political freedom and of natural justice, embodied in that Declaration of Independence, extended to us? and am I, therefore, called upon to bring our humble offering to the national altar, and to confess the benefits and express devout gratitude for the blessings resulting from your independence to us?

Would to God, both for your sakes and ours, that an affirmative answer could be truthfully returned to these questions! Then would my task be light, and my burden easy and delightful. For who is there so cold, that a nation's sympathy could not warm him? Who so obdurate and dead to the claims of gratitude, that would not thankfully acknowledge such priceless benefits? Who so stolid and selfish, that would not give his voice to swell the hallelujahs of a nation's jubilee, when the chains of servitude had been torn from his limbs? I am not that man. In a case like that, the dumb might eloquently speak, and the "lame man leap as an hart."

But, such is not the state of the case. I say it with a sad sense of the disparity between us. I am not included within the pale of this glorious anniversary! Your high independence only reveals the immeasurable distance between us. The blessings in which you, this day, rejoice, are not enjoyed in common. The rich inheritance of justice, liberty, prosperity and independence, bequeathed by your fathers, is shared by you, not by me. The sunlight that brought life and healing to you, has brought stripes and death to me. This Fourth July is yours, not mine. You may rejoice, I must mourn. To drag a man in fetters into the grand illuminated temple of liberty, and call upon him to join you in joyous anthems, were inhuman mockery and sacrilegious irony. Do you mean, citizens, to mock me, by asking me to speak today? If so, there is a parallel to your conduct. And let me warn you that it is dangerous to copy the example of a nation whose crimes, towering up to heaven, were thrown down by the breath of the Almighty, burying that nation in irrecoverable ruin! I can today take up the plaintive lament of a peeled and woe-smitten people!

"By the rivers of Babylon, there we sat down. Yea! we wept when we remembered Zion. We hanged our harps upon the willows in the midst thereof. For there, they that carried us away captive, required of us a song; and they who wasted us required of us mirth, saying, Sing us one of the songs of Zion. How can we sing the Lord's song in a strange land? If I forget thee, O Jerusalem, let my right hand forget her cunning. If I do not remember thee, let my tongue cleave to the roof of my mouth."

Fellow citizens; above your national, tumultuous joy, I hear the mournful wail of millions! whose chains, heavy and grievous yesterday, are, today, rendered more intolerable by the jubilee shouts that reach them. If I do forget, if I do not faithfully remember those bleeding children of sorrow this day, "may my right hand forget her cunning, and may my tongue cleave to the roof of my mouth!" To forget them, to pass lightly over their wrongs, and to chime in with the popular theme, would be treason most scandalous and shocking, and would make me a reproach before God and the world. My subject, then, fellow-citizens, is AMERICAN SLAVERY. I shall see, this day, and its popular characteristics, from the slave's point of view. Standing, there, identified with the American bondman, making his wrongs mine, I do not hesitate to declare, with all my soul, that the character and conduct of this nation never looked blacker to me than on this 4th of July! Whether we turn to the declarations of the past, or

to the professions of the present, the conduct of the nation seems equally hideous and revolting. America is false to the past, false to the present, and solemnly binds herself to be false to the future. Standing with God and the crushed and bleeding slave on this occasion, I will, in the name of humanity which is outraged, in the name of liberty which is fettered, in the name of the constitution and the Bible, which are disregarded and trampled upon, dare to call in question and to denounce, with all the emphasis I can command, everything that serves to perpetuate slavery—the great sin and shame of America! "I will not equivocate; I will not excuse;" I will use the severest language I can command; and yet not one word shall escape me that any man, whose judgment is not blinded by prejudice, or who is not at heart a slaveholder, shall not confess to be right and just.

But I fancy I hear some one of my audience say, it is just in this circumstance that you and your brother abolitionists fail to make a favorable impression on the public mind. Would you argue more, and denounce less, would you persuade more, and rebuke less, your cause would be much more likely to succeed. But, I submit, where all is plain there is nothing to be argued. What point in the anti-slavery creed would you have me argue? On what branch of the subject do the people of this country need light? Must I undertake to prove that the slave is a man? That point is conceded already. Nobody doubts it. The slave-holders themselves acknowledge it in the enactment of laws for their government. They acknowledge it when they punish disobedience on the part of the slave. There are seventy-two crimes in the State of Virginia, which, if committed by a black man (no matter how ignorant he be), subject him to the punishment of death; while only two of the same crimes will subject a white man to the like punishment. What is this but the acknowledgement that the slave is a moral, intellectual and responsible being. The manhood of the slave is conceded. It is admitted in the fact that Southern statute books are covered with enactments forbidding, under severe fines and penalties, the teaching of the slave to read or to write. When you can point to any such laws, in reference to the beasts of the field, then I may consent to argue the manhood of the slave. When the dogs in your streets, when the fowls of the air, when the cattle on your hills, when the fish of the sea, and the reptiles that crawl, shall be unable to distinguish the slave from a brute, then will I argue with you that the slave is a man.

For the present, it is enough to affirm the equal manhood of the negro race. Is it not astonishing that, while we are ploughing, planting and reaping, using all kinds of mechanical tools, erecting houses, constructing bridges, building ships, working in metals of brass, iron, copper, silver and gold; that, while we are reading, writing and cyphering, acting as clerks, merchants and secretaries, having among us lawyers, doctors, ministers, poets, authors, editors, orators and teachers; that, while we are engaged in all manner of enterprises common to other men, digging gold in California, capturing the whale in the Pacific, feeding sheep and cattle on the hillside, living, moving, acting, thinking, planning, living in families as husbands, wives and children, and, above all, confessing and worshipping the Christian's God, and looking hopefully for life and immortality beyond the grave, we are called upon to prove that we are men!

Would you have me argue that man is entitled to liberty? that he is the rightful owner of his own body? You have already declared it. Must I argue the wrongfulness of slavery? Is that a question for Republicans? Is it to be settled by the rules of logic and argumentation, as a matter beset with great difficulty, involving a doubtful application of the principle of justice, hard to be understood? How should I look today, in the presence of Americans, dividing, and subdividing a discourse, to show that men have a natural right to freedom? speaking of it relatively, and positively, negatively, and affirmatively. To do so, would be to make myself ridiculous, and to offer an insult to your understanding. There is not a man beneath the canopy of heaven, that does not know that slavery is wrong for him.

What, am I to argue that it is wrong to make men brutes, to rob them of their liberty, to work them without wages, to keep them ignorant of their relations to their fellow men, to beat them with sticks, to flay their flesh with the lash, to load their limbs with irons, to hunt them with dogs, to sell them at auction, to sunder their families, to knock out their teeth, to burn their flesh, to starve them into obedience and submission to their masters? Must I argue that a system thus marked with blood, and stained with pollution, is wrong? No I will not. I have better employment for my time and strength, than such arguments would imply.

What, then, remains to be argued? Is it that slavery is not divine; that God did not establish it; that our doctors of divinity are mistaken? There is blasphemy in the thought. That which is inhuman, cannot be divine! Who can reason on such a proposition? They that can, may; I cannot. The time for such argument is past.

At a time like this, scorching irony, not convincing argument, is needed. O! had I the ability, and could I reach the nation's ear, I would, to day, pour out a fiery stream of biting ridicule, blasting reproach, withering sarcasm, and stern rebuke. For it is not light that is needed, but fire; it is not the gentle shower, but thunder. We need the storm, the whirlwind, and the earthquake. The feeling of the nation must be quickened; the conscience of the nation must be roused; the propriety of the nation must be startled; the hypocrisy of the nation must be exposed; and its crimes against God and man must be proclaimed and denounced.

What, to the American slave, is your 4th of July? I answer: a day that reveals to him, more than all other days in the year, the gross injustice and cruelty to which he is the constant victim. To him, your celebration is a sham; your boasted liberty, an unholy license; your national greatness, swelling vanity; your sounds of rejoicing are empty and heartless; your denunciations of tyrants, brass fronted impudence; your shouts of liberty and equality, hollow mockery; your prayers and hymns, your sermons and thanksgivings, with all your religious parade, and solemnity, are, to him, mere bombast, fraud, deception, impiety, and hypocrisy—a thin veil to cover up crimes which would disgrace a nation of savages. There is not a nation on the earth guilty of practices, more shocking and bloody, than are the people of these United States, at this very hour.

Go where you may, search where you will, roam through all the monarchies and despotisms of the old world, travel through South America, search out every abuse, and when you have found the last, lay your facts by the side of the every day practices of this nation, and you will say with me, that, for revolting barbarity and shameless hypocrisy, America reigns without a rival.

◆ **The Internal Slave Trade**

Take the American slave-trade, which we are told by the papers, is especially prosperous just now. Ex-Senator Benton tells us that the price of men was never higher than now. He mentions the fact to show that slavery is in no danger. This trade is one of the peculiarities of American institutions. It is carried on in all the large towns and cities in one half of this confederacy; and millions are pocketed every year, by dealers in this horrid traffic. In several states, this trade is a chief source of wealth. It is called (in contradistinction to the foreign slave-trade) "the internal slave-trade." It is, probably, called so, too, in order to divert from it the horror with which the foreign slave-trade is contemplated. That trade has long since been denounced by this government, as piracy. It has been denounced with burning words, from the high places of the nation, as an execrable traffic. To arrest it, to put an end to it, this nation keeps a squadron, at immense cost, on the coast of Africa. Every-where, in this country, it is safe to speak of this foreign slave-trade, as a most inhuman traffic, opposed alike to the laws of God and of man. The duty to extirpate and destroy it, is admitted even by our DOCTORS OF DIVINITY. In order to put an end to it, some of these last have consented that their colored brethren (nominally free) should leave this country, and establish themselves on the western coast of Africa! It is, however, a notable fact, that, while so much execration is poured out by Americans, upon those engaged in the foreign slave-trade, the men engaged in the slave-trade between the states pass without condemnation, and their business is deemed honorable.

Behold the practical operation of this internal slave-trade, the American slave-trade, sustained by American politics and American religion. Here you will see men and women, reared like swine, for the market. You know what is a swine-drover? I will show you a man-drover. They inhabit all our Southern States. They perambulate the country, and crowd the highways of the nation, with droves of human stock. You will see one of these human flesh jobbers, armed with pistol, whip and bowie-knife, driving a company of a hundred men, women, and children, from the Potomac to the slave market at New Orleans. These wretched people are to be sold singly, or in lots, to suit purchasers. They are food for the cotton-field, and the deadly sugar-mill. Mark the sad procession, as it moves wearily along, and the inhuman wretch who drives them. Hear his savage yells and his blood-chilling oaths, as he hurries on his affrighted captives! There, see the old man, with locks thinned and gray. Cast one glance, if you please, upon that young mother, whose shoulders are bare to the scorching sun, her briny tears falling on the brow of the babe in her arms. See, too, that girl of thirteen, weeping, yes! weeping, as she thinks of the mother from whom she has been torn! The drove moves tardily. Heat and sorrow have nearly consumed their strength; suddenly you hear a quick snap, like the discharge of a rifle; the fetters clank, and the chain rattles simultaneously; your ears are saluted with a scream, that seems to have torn its way to the centre of your soul! The crack you heard, was the sound of the slave-whip;

the scream you heard, was from the woman you saw with the babe. Her speed had faltered under the weight of her child and her chains! that gash on her shoulder tells her to move on. Follow this drove to New Orleans. Attend the auction; see men examined like horses; see the forms of women rudely and brutally exposed to the shocking gaze of American slave-buyers. See this drove sold and separated for ever; and never forget the deep, sad sobs that arose from that scattered multitude. Tell me citizens, WHERE, under the sun, you can witness a spectacle more fiendish and shocking. Yet this is but a glance at the American slave-trade, as it exists, at this moment, in the ruling part of the United States.

I was born amid such sights and scenes. To me the American slave-trade is a terrible reality. When a child, my soul was often pierced with a sense of its horrors. I lived on Philpot Street, Fell's Point, Baltimore, and have watched from the wharves, the slave ships in the Basin, anchored from the shore, with their cargoes of human flesh, waiting for favorable winds to waft them down the Chesapeake. There was, at that time, a grand slave mart kept at the head of Pratt Street, by Austin Woldfolk. His agents were sent into every town and county in Maryland, announcing their arrival, through the papers, and on flaming "hand-bills," headed CASH FOR NEGROES. These men were generally well dressed men, and very captivating in their manners. Ever ready to drink, to treat, and to gamble. The fate of many a slave has depended upon the turn of a single card; and many a child has been snatched from the arms of its mother, by bargains arranged in a state of brutal drunkenness.

The flesh-mongers gather up their victims by dozens, and drive them, chained, to the general depot at Baltimore. When a sufficient number have been collected here, a ship is chartered, for the purpose of conveying the forlorn crew to Mobile, or to New Or-leans. From the slave prison to the ship, they are usually driven in the darkness of night; for since the anti-slavery agitation, a certain caution is observed.

In the deep still darkness of midnight, I have been often aroused by the dead heavy footsteps, and the piteous cries of the chained gangs that passed our door. The anguish of my boyish heart was intense; and I was often consoled, when speaking to my mistress in the morning, to hear her say that the custom was very wicked; that she hated to hear the rattle of the chains, and the heart-rending cries. I was glad to find one who sympathized with me in my horror.

Fellow-citizens, this murderous traffic is, to-day, in active operation in this boasted republic. In the solitude of my spirit, I see clouds of dust raised on the highways of the South; I see the bleeding footsteps; I hear the doleful wail of fettered humanity, on the way to the slave-markets, where the victims are to be sold like horses, sheep, and swine, knocked off to the highest bidder. There I see the tenderest ties ruthlessly broken, to gratify the lust, caprice and rapacity of the buyers and sellers of men. My soul sickens at the sight.

"Is this the land your Fathers loved, The freedom which they toiled to win? Is this the earth whereon they moved? Are these the graves they slumber in?"

But a still more inhuman, disgraceful, and scandalous state of things remains to be presented.

By an act of the American Congress, not yet two years old, slavery has been nationalized in its most horrible and revolting form. By that act, Mason & Dixon's line has been obliterated; New York has become as Virginia; and the power to hold, hunt, and sell men, women and children, as slaves, remains no longer a mere state institution, but is now an institution of the whole United States. The power is co-extensive with the star-spangled banner, and American Christianity. Where these go, may also go the merciless slave-hunter. Where these are, man is not sacred. He is a bird for the sportsman's gun. By that most foul and fiendish of all human decrees, the liberty and person of every man are put in peril. Your broad republican domain is hunting ground for men. Not for thieves and robbers, enemies of society, merely, but for men guilty of no crime. Your law-makers have commanded all good citizens to engage in this hellish sport. Your President, your Secretary of State, your lords, nobles, and ecclesiastics, enforce, as a duty you owe to your free and glorious country, and to your God, that you do this accursed thing. Not fewer than forty Americans, have, within the past two years, been hunted down, and, without a moment's warning, hurried away in chains, and consigned to slavery, and excruciating torture. Some of these have had wives and children, dependent on them for bread; but of this, no account was made. The right of the hunter to his prey, stands superior to the right of marriage, and to all rights in this republic, the rights of God included! For black men there are neither law, justice, humanity, nor religion.

The Fugitive Slave Law makes MERCY TO THEM, A CRIME; and bribes the judge who tries them. An American JUDGE GETS TEN DOLLARS FOR EVERY VICTIM HE CONSIGNS to slavery, and five, when he fails to do so. The oath of any two villains is sufficient, under this hell-black enactment, to send the most pious and exemplary black man into the remorseless jaws of slavery! His own testimony is nothing. He can bring no witnesses for himself. The minister of American justice is bound, by the law to hear but one side; and that side, is the side of the oppressor. Let this damning fact be perpetually told. Let it be thundered around the world, that, in tyrant-killing, king-hating, people-loving, democratic, Christian America, the seats of justice are filled with judges, who hold their offices under an open and palpable bribes, and are bound, in deciding in the case of a man's liberty, to hear only his accusers!

In glaring violation of justice, in shameless disregard of the forms of administering law, in cunning arrangement to entrap the defenceless, and in diabolical intent, this Fugitive Slave Law stands alone in the annals of tyrannical legislation. I doubt if there be another nation on the globe, having the brass and the baseness to put such a law on the statute-book. If any man in this assembly thinks differently from me in this matter, and feels able to disprove my statements, I will gladly confront him at any suitable time and place he may select.

◆ Religious Liberty

I take this law to be one of the grossest infringements of Christian Liberty, and, if the churches and ministers of our country were not stupidly blind, or most wickedly indifferent, they, too, would so regard it.

At the very moment that they are thanking God for the enjoyment of civil and religious liberty, and for the right to worship God according to the dictates of their own consciences, they are utterly silent in respect to a law which robs religion of its chief significance, and makes it utterly worthless to a world lying in wickedness. Did this law concern the "mint, anise and cummin,"—abridge the right to sing psalms, to partake of the sacrament, or to engage in any of the ceremonies of religion, it would be smitten by the thunder of a thousand pulpits. A general shout would go up from the church, demanding repeal, repeal, instant repeal! And it would go hard with that politician who presumed to solicit the votes of the people without inscribing this motto on his banner. Further, if this demand were not complied with, another Scotland would be added to the history of religious liberty, and the stern old covenanters would be thrown into the shade. A John Knox would be seen at every church door, and heard from every pulpit, and Fillmore would have no more quarter than was shown by

Knox, to the beautiful, but treacherous Queen Mary of Scotland. The fact that the church of our country, (with fractional exceptions,) does not esteem "the Fugitive Slave Law" as a declaration of war against religious liberty, implies that that church regards religion simply as a form of worship, an empty ceremony, and not a vital principle, requiring active benevolence, justice, love and good will towards man. It esteems sacrifice above mercy; psalm-singing above right doing; solemn meetings above practical righteousness. A worship that can be conducted by persons who refuse to give shelter to the houseless, to give bread to the hungry, clothing to the naked, and who enjoin obedience to a law forbidding these acts of mercy, is a curse, not a blessing to mankind. The Bible addresses all such persons as "scribes, pharisees, hypocrites, who pay tithe of mint, anise, and cumin, and have omitted the weightier matters of the law, judgment, mercy and faith."

◆ **The Church Responsible**

But the church of this country is not only indifferent to the wrongs of the slave, it actually takes sides with the oppressors. It has made itself the bulwark of American slavery, and the shield of American slave-hunters. Many of its most eloquent Divines, who stand as the very lights of the church, have shamelessly given the sanction of religion, and the bible, to the whole slave system. They have taught that man may, properly, be a slave; that the relation of master and slave is ordained of God; that to send back an escaped bondman to his master is clearly the duty of all the followers of the Lord Jesus Christ; and this horrible blasphemy is palmed off upon the world for Christianity.

For my part, I would say, welcome infidelity! welcome atheism! welcome anything! in preference to the gospel, as preached by those Divines! They convert the very name of religion into an engine of tyranny, and barbarous cruelty, and serve to confirm more infidels, in this age, than all the infidel writings of Thomas Paine, Voltaire, and Bolingbroke, put together, have done? These ministers make religion a cold and flinty-hearted thing, having neither principles of right action, nor bowels of compassion. They strip the love of God of its beauty, and leave the throne of religion a huge, horrible, repulsive form. It is a religion for oppressors, tyrants, man-stealers, and thugs. It is not that "pure and undefiled religion" which is from above, and which is "first pure, then peaceable, easy to be entreated, full of mercy and good fruits, without partiality, and without hypocrisy." But a religion which favors the rich against the poor; which exalts the proud above the humble; which divides mankind into two classes, tyrants and slaves; which says to the man in chains, stay there; and to the oppressor, oppress on; it is a religion which may be professed and enjoyed by all the robbers and enslavers of mankind; it makes God a respecter of persons, denies his fatherhood of the race, and tramples in the dust the great truth of the brotherhood of man. All this we affirm to be true of the popular church, and the popular worship of our land and nation—a religion, a church and a worship which, on the authority of inspired wisdom, we pronounce to be an abomination in the sight of God. In the language of Isaiah, the American church might be well addressed, "Bring no more vain oblations; incense is an abomination unto me: the new moons and Sabbaths, the calling of assemblies, I cannot away with it is iniquity, even the solemn meeting. Your new moons, and your appointed feasts my soul hatest. They are a trouble to me; I am weary to bear them; and when ye spread forth your hands I will hide mine eyes from you. Yea! when ye make many prayers, I will not hear. YOUR HANDS ARE FULL OF BLOOD; cease to do evil, learn to do well; seek judgment; relieve the oppressed; judge for the fatherless; plead for the widow."

The American church is guilty, when viewed in connection with what it is doing to uphold slavery; but it is superlatively guilty when viewed in connection with its ability to abolish slavery.

The sin of which it is guilty is one of omission as well as of commission. Albert Barnes but uttered what the common sense of every man at all observant of the actual state of the case will receive as truth, when he declared that "There is no power out of the church that could sustain slavery an hour, if it were not sustained in it."

Let the religious press, the pulpit, the Sunday school, the conference meeting, the great ecclesiastical, missionary, bible and tract associations of the land array their immense powers against slavery, and slave-holding; and the whole system of crime and blood would be scattered to the winds, and that they do not do this involves them in the most awful responsibility of which the mind can conceive.

In prosecuting the anti-slavery enterprise, we have been asked to spare the church, to spare the ministry; but how, we ask, could such a thing be done? We are met on the threshold of our efforts for the redemption of the slave, by the church. and ministry of the country, in battle arrayed against us; and we are compelled to fight or flee. From what quarter,

I beg to know, has proceeded a fire so deadly upon our ranks, during the last two years, as from the Northern pulpit? As the champions of oppressors, the chosen men of American theology have appeared—men, honored for their so called piety, and their real learning. The LORDS of Buffalo, the SPRINGS of New York, the LATHROPS of Auburn, the COXES and SPENCERS of Brooklyn, the GANNETS and SHARPS of Boston, the DEWEYS of Washington, and other great religious lights of the land, have, in utter denial of the authority of Him, by whom they professed to be called to the ministry, deliberately taught us, against the example of the Hebrews, and against the remonstrance of the Apostles, they teach that we ought to obey man's law before the law of God.

My spirit wearies of such blasphemy; and how such men can be supported, as the "standing types and representatives of Jesus Christ," is a mystery which I leave others to penetrate. In speaking of the American church, however, let it be distinctly understood that I mean the great mass of the religious organizations of our land. There are exceptions, and I thank God that there are. Noble men may be found, scattered all over these Northern States, of whom Henry Ward Beecher, of Brooklyn, Samuel J. May, of Syracuse, and my esteemed friend on the platform, are shining examples; and let me say further, that, upon these men lies the duty to inspire our ranks with high religious faith and zeal, and to cheer us on in the great mission of the slave's redemption from his chains.

◆ Religion in England and Religion in America

One is struck with the difference between the attitude of the American church towards the anti-slavery movement, and that occupied by the churches in England towards a similar movement in that country. There, the church, true to its mission of ameliorating, elevating, and improving the condition of mankind, came forward promptly, bound up the wounds of the West Indian slave, and restored him to his liberty. There, the question of emancipation was a high religious question. It was demanded, in the name of humanity, and according to the law of the living God. The Sharps, the Clarksons, the Wilberforces, the Buxtons, the Burchells and the Knibbs, were alike famous for their piety, and for their philanthropy. The anti-slavery movement there, was not an anti-church movement, for the reason that the church took its full share in prosecuting that movement: and the anti-slavery movement in this country will cease to be an anti-church movement, when the church of this country shall assume a favorable, instead of a hostile position towards that movement.

Americans! your republican politics, not less than your republican religion, are flagrantly inconsistent. You boast of your love of liberty, your superior civilization, and your pure Christianity, while the whole political power of the nation, (as embodied in the two great political parties, is solemnly pledged to support and perpetuate the enslavement of three millions of your countrymen. You hurl your anathemas at the crowned headed tyrants of Russia and Austria, and pride yourselves on your Democratic institutions, while you yourselves consent to be the mere tools and body-guards of the tyrants of Virginia and Carolina. You invite to your shores fugitives of oppression from abroad, honor them with banquets, greet them with ovations, cheer them, toast them, salute them, protect them, and pour out your money to them like water; but the fugitives from your own land, you advertise, hunt, arrest, shoot and kill. You glory in your refinement, and your universal education; yet you maintain a system as barbarous and dreadful, as ever stained the character of a nation—a system begun in avarice, supported in pride, and perpetuated in cruelty. You shed tears over fallen Hungary, and make the sad story of her wrongs the theme of your poets, statesmen and orators, till your gallant sons are ready to fly to arms to vindicate her cause against her oppressors; but, in regard to the ten thousand wrongs of the American slave, you would enforce the strictest silence, and would hail him as an enemy of the nation who dares to make those wrongs the subject of public discourse! You are all on fire at the mention of liberty for France or for Ireland; but are as cold as an iceberg at the thought of liberty for the enslaved of America. You discourse eloquently on the dignity of labor; yet, you sustain a system which, in its very essence, casts a stigma upon labor. You can bare your bosom to the storm of British artillery, to throw off a three-penny tax on tea; and yet wring the last hard earned farthing from the grasp of the black laborers of your country. You profess to believe "that, of one blood, God made all nations of men to dwell on the face of all the earth," and hath commanded all men, everywhere to love one another; yet you notoriously hate, (and glory in your hatred,) all men whose skins are not colored like your own. You declare, before the world, and are understood by the world to declare, that you "hold these truths to be self evident, that all men are created equal; and are endowed by their Creator with certain, inalienable rights; and that, among these are, life, liberty, and the pursuit of happiness"; and yet, you hold securely, in a bondage, which according to your own Thomas Jefferson, "is worse than ages of that which your fathers rose in rebellion to oppose," a seventh part of the inhabitants of your country.

Fellow-citizens! I will not enlarge further on your national inconsistencies. The existence of slavery in this country brands your republicanism as a sham, your humanity as a base pretence, and your Christianity as a lie. It destroys your moral power abroad it corrupts your politicians at home. It saps the foundation of religion; it makes your name a hissing, and a bye-word to a mocking earth. It is the antagonistic force in your government, the only thing that seriously disturbs and endangers your Union. It fetters your progress; it is the enemy of improvement, the deadly foe of education; it fosters pride; it breeds insolence; it promotes vice; it shelters crime; it is a curse to the earth that supports it; and yet, you cling to it, as if it were the sheet anchor of all your hopes. Oh! be warned! be warned! a horrible reptile is coiled up in your nation's bosom; the venomous creature is nursing at the tender breast of your youthful republic; for the love of God, tear away, and fling from you the hideous monster, and let the weight of twenty millions, crush and destroy it forever!

◆ The Constitution

But it is answered in reply to all this, that precisely what I have now denounced is, in fact, guaranteed and sanctioned by the Constitution of the United States; that, the right to hold, and to hunt slaves is a part of that Constitution framed by the illustrious Fathers of this Republic. Then, I dare to affirm, notwithstanding all I have said before, your fathers stooped, basely stooped. "To palter with us in a double sense: And keep the word of promise to the ear, But break it to the heart."

And instead of being the honest men I have before declared them to be, they were the veriest imposters that ever practiced on mankind. This is the inevitable conclusion, and from it there is no escape; but I differ from those who charge this baseness on the framers of the Constitution of the United States. It is a slander upon their memory, at least, so I believe. There is not time now to argue the constitutional question at length; nor have I the ability to discuss it as it ought to be discussed. The subject has been handled with masterly power by Lysander Spooner, Esq., by William Goodell, by Samuel E. Sewall, Esq., and last, though not least, by Gerritt

Smith, Esq. These gentlemen have, as I think, fully and clearly vindicated the Constitution from any design to support slavery for an hour.

Fellow-citizens! there is no matter in respect to which, the people of the North have allowed themselves to be so ruinously imposed upon, as that of the pro-slavery character of the Constitution. In that instrument I hold there is neither warrant, license, nor sanction of the hateful thing; but interpreted, as it ought to be interpreted, the Constitution is a GLORIOUS LIBERTY DOCUMENT. Read its preamble, consider its purposes. Is slavery among them? Is it at the gateway? or is it in the temple? it is neither. While I do not intend to argue this question on the present occasion, let me ask, if it be not somewhat singular that, if the Constitution were intended to be, by its framers and adopters, a slave-holding instrument, why neither slavery, slaveholding, nor slave can anywhere be found in it. What would be thought of an instrument, drawn up, legally drawn up, for the purpose of entitling the city of Rochester to a track of land, in which no mention of land was made? Now, there are certain rules of interpretation, for the proper understanding of all legal instruments. These rules are well established. They are plain, common-sense rules, such as you and I, and all of us, can understand and apply, without having passed years in the study of law. I scout the idea that the question of the constitutionality, or unconstitutionality of slavery, is not a question for the people. I hold that every American citizen has a right to form an opinion of the constitution, and to propagate that opinion, and to use all honorable means to make his opinion the prevailing one. With out this right, the liberty of an American citizen would be as insecure as that of a Frenchman. Ex-Vice-President Dallas tells us that the constitution is an object to which no American mind can be too attentive, and no American heart too devoted. He further says, the constitution, in its words, is plain and intelligible, and is meant for the home-bred, unsophisticated understandings of our fellow-citizens. Senator Berrien tells us that the Constitution is the fundamental law, that which controls all others. The charter of our liberties, which every citizen has a personal interest in understanding thoroughly. The testimony of Senator Breese, Lewis Cass, and many others that might be named, who are everywhere esteemed as sound lawyers, so regard the constitution. I take it, therefore, that it is not presumption in a private citizen to form an opinion of that instrument.

Now, take the constitution according to its plain reading, and I defy the presentation of a single proslavery clause in it. On the other hand it will be found to contain principles and purposes, entirely hostile to the existence of slavery.

I have detained my audience entirely too long already. At some future period I will gladly avail myself of an opportunity to give this subject a full and fair discussion.

Allow me to say, in conclusion, notwithstanding the dark picture I have this day presented, of the state of the nation, I do not despair of this country. There are forces in operation, which must inevitably, work the downfall of slavery. "The arm of the Lord is not shortened," and the doom of slavery is certain.

I, therefore, leave off where I began, with hope. While drawing encouragement from "the Declaration of Independence," the great principles it contains, and the genius of American Institutions, my spirit is also cheered by the obvious tendencies of the age. Nations do not now stand in the same relation to each other that they did ages ago. No nation can now shut itself up, from the surrounding world, and trot round in the same old path of its fathers without interference. The time was when such could be done. Long established customs of hurtful character could formerly fence themselves in, and do their evil work with social impunity. Knowledge was then confined and enjoyed by the privileged few, and the multitude walked on in mental darkness. But a change has now come over the affairs of mankind. Walled cities and empires have become unfashionable. The arm of commerce has borne away the gates of the strong city. Intelligence is penetrating the darkest corners of the globe. It makes its pathway over and under the sea, as well as on the earth. Wind, steam, and lightning are its chartered agents. Oceans no longer divide, but link nations together. From Boston to London is now a holiday excursion. Space is comparatively annihilated. Thoughts expressed on one side of the Atlantic, are distinctly heard on the other.

The far off and almost fabulous Pacific rolls in grandeur at our feet. The Celestial Empire, the mystery of ages, is being solved. The fiat of the Almighty, "Let there be Light," has not yet spent its force. No abuse, no outrage whether in taste, sport or avarice, can now hide itself from the all-pervading light. The iron shoe, and crippled foot of China must be seen, in contrast with nature. Africa must rise and put on her yet unwoven garment. "Ethiopia shall stretch out her hand unto God." In the fervent aspirations of William Lloyd Garrison, I say, and let every heart join in saying it:

God speed the year of jubilee
The wide world o'er!
When from their galling chains set free, Th' oppress'd shall vilely bend the knee, And wear the yoke of tyranny
Like brutes no more.
That year will come, and freedom's reign, To man his plundered rights again Restore.
God speed the day when human blood
Shall cease to flow!
In every clime be understood,
The claims of human brotherhood,
And each return for evil, good, Not blow for blow;
That day will come all feuds to end,
And change into a faithful friend
Each foe.
God speed the hour, the glorious hour, When none on earth
Shall exercise a lordly power,
Nor in a tyrant's presence cower; But all to manhood's stature tower, By equal birth!
THAT HOUR WILL COME, to each, to all,
And from his prison-house, the thrall Go forth.
Until that year, day, hour, arrive,
With head, and heart, and hand I'll strive, To break the rod, and rend the gyve, The spoiler of his prey deprive
So witness Heaven!
And never from my chosen post,
Whate'er the peril or the cost,
Be driven.

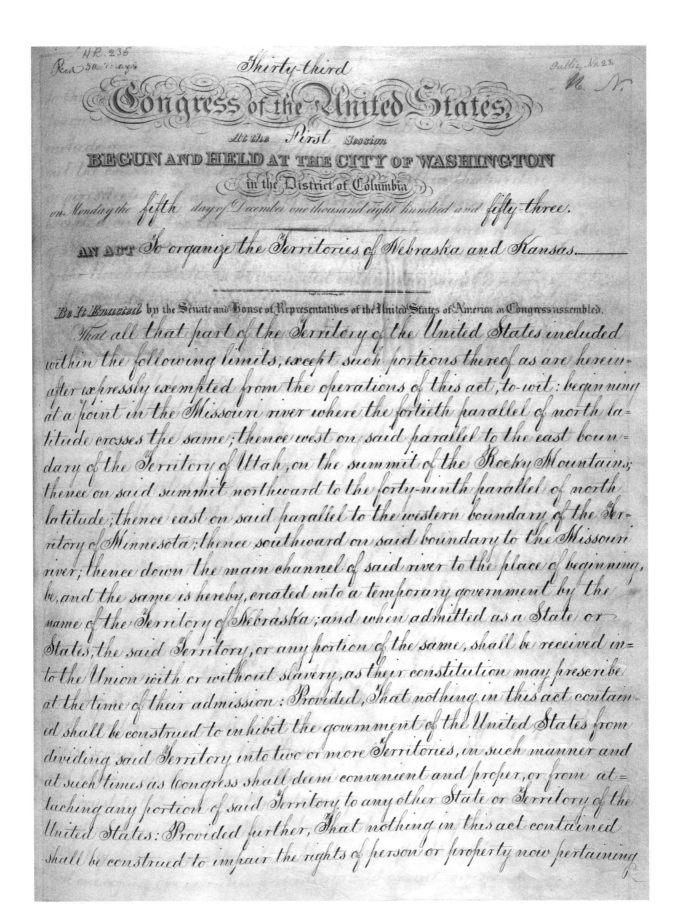

Thirty-third

Congress of the United States,

At the *First Session*

BEGUN AND HELD AT THE CITY OF WASHINGTON

in the District of Columbia

on Monday the *fifth* day of December one thousand eight hundred and *fifty-three.*

AN ACT *To organize the Territories of Nebraska and Kansas.*

Be it Enacted by the Senate and House of Representatives of the United States of America in Congress assembled, That all that part of the Territory of the United States included within the following limits, except such portions thereof as are herein-after expressly exempted from the operations of this act, to-wit: beginning at a point in the Missouri river where the fortieth parallel of north latitude crosses the same; thence west on said parallel to the east boundary of the Territory of Utah, on the summit of the Rocky Mountains; thence on said summit northward to the forty-ninth parallel of north latitude; thence east on said parallel to the western boundary of the Territory of Minnesota; thence southward on said boundary to the Missouri river; thence down the main channel of said river to the place of beginning, be, and the same is hereby, created into a temporary government by the name of the Territory of Nebraska; and when admitted as a State or States, the said Territory, or any portion of the same, shall be received into the Union with or without slavery, as their constitution may prescribe at the time of their admission: Provided, That nothing in this act contained shall be construed to inhibit the government of the United States from dividing said Territory into two or more Territories, in such manner and at such times as Congress shall deem convenient and proper, or from attaching any portion of said Territory to any other State or Territory of the United States: Provided further, That nothing in this act contained shall be construed to impair the rights of person or property now pertaining

The Kansas-Nebraska Act (National Archives and Records Administration)

"Said Territory or any portion of the same, shall be received into the Union with or without slavery, as their constitution may prescribe at the time of admission."

Overview

In the early months of 1854 the contentious issue of slavery spreading into America's western territories once again reared its head after a brief respite following the Compromise of 1850 and the so-called finality campaign of 1852 (between Democrat Franklin Pierce and Whig Winfield Scott). For decades American politicians, working through a very competitive national political party system, had worked tirelessly to avoid the divisive issue altogether or to craft a workable compromise position that would successfully put the matter to rest. In the span of a few short months, however, their collective efforts were negated by the passage of the Kansas-Nebraska Act of 1854.

The bill, first reported to Congress on January 4 by the Illinois senator Stephen Douglas, the Democratic chair of the Senate Committee on Territories and the architect of the measure, underwent major revisions before its final passage on May 26 and approval by President Franklin Pierce four days later. The act, which explicitly repealed the Missouri Compromise of 1820—with its prohibition against slavery in the region—initiated a storm of protest and indignation throughout the northern states, spawning a new political party, the Republicans, and setting in motion a dramatic increase in sectional tensions, which shortly thereafter plunged the nation into four years of bloody civil war.

Context

The invention of the cotton gin in 1793 paved the way for the rapid expansion of the institution of slavery into the American Southwest (it was precluded by law, and many assumed climate, from the Northwest Territory) in the early decades of the nineteenth century. Nationally, little was said about this trend until 1819, when Missouri, the first territory to be created within the confines of the Louisiana Purchase, applied for admission as a slave state. The ensuing debate thrust the issue of slavery into the national consciousness and exposed a growing sectional rift over the question of slavery's expansion. The following year

Henry Clay's Missouri Compromise eased tensions: admitting Missouri into the Union as a slave state paired with the admission of Maine as a free state and establishing a boundary line between slave and free territory at parallel 36°30' north through the remainder of the Louisiana Purchase, including the area that would later be designated as Kansas and Nebraska.

Debate over the issue flared once again with the annexation of Texas and its proslavery state constitution into the United States in December 1845 and the subsequent war with Mexico that resulted in the appropriation of nearly half of Mexico's territory between 1846 and 1848. Viewing the conflict as a war to promote slavery and intent upon preserving the newly acquired Mexican Cession for "free" white settlers, a number of northern politicians supported a proviso attached to a wartime appropriations bill by Pennsylvania congressman David Wilmot calling for a prohibition of slavery from all territories obtained from Mexico. Wilmot's controversial proviso, pitting northern and southern interests against one another, brought Congress to a standstill. Hoping to end the impasse, Senator Lewis Cass, a Democrat from Michigan and a presidential hopeful in 1848, proposed allowing the people residing within the territories to decide the fate of slavery's expansion themselves, a policy that became known as "popular sovereignty." Although Cass was defeated in his quest for the presidency by the Whig candidate Zachary Taylor, his policy emerged as the Democratic Party's position on slavery's expansion from that point through the commencement of hostilities between North and South in April 1861.

The gold rush of 1849 triggered explosive and chaotic growth in the newly obtained California region and, once again, propelled the controversy over slavery's extension into the political forefront. Eager to establish order in California and to avoid the touchy issue of the extent of congressional authority over slavery in the federal territories, President Taylor proposed that California be admitted directly into the Union as a free state, forgoing the usual territorial stage. The resulting opposition threatened a state of perpetual gridlock in Congress. Once again Senator Clay stepped forward to craft a far-reaching compromise (which included a controversial new fugitive slave law) bill to prevent the issue from doing further damage. After the omnibus bill's defeat,

1820

■ **March 6**
President James Monroe signs the Missouri Compromise, which establishes future Kansas-Nebraska territories as free areas and temporarily diffuses controversy over slavery's extension.

1845

■ **December 29**
Texas is admitted into the Union, which paves the way for war with Mexico and helps to reignite national debate over slavery's expansion.

1846

■ **August 8**
Wilmot Proviso is introduced into Congress and deepens sectional tension.

1847

■ **December 24**
Lewis Cass outlines the principle of popular sovereignty in a letter to A. O. P. Nicholson, which becomes a critical position for Democratic politicians, especially Stephen Douglas, up through the Civil War.

1850

■ **September 17**
The final bills constituting the Compromise of 1850 are signed into law by President Millard Fillmore; the measure temporarily blunts sectional hostility.

1851

■ **June 5**
The first segment of Harriet Beecher Stowe's *Uncle Tom's Cabin* appears in print in the *Washington National Era.*

1854

■ **January 4**
The Kansas-Nebraska bill is first reported to Congress; the initial bill's adherence to slavery's ban in the region initiates a sectional conflict in Senate.

■ **January 16**
Douglas amends the Kansas-Nebraska bill, repealing the Missouri Compromise; a revised bill is created to reflect the Democratic Party's commitment to the new principle of popular sovereignty.

Senator Douglas of Illinois assumed responsibility for the measure, breaking the bill into its component parts and successfully guiding the so-called Compromise of 1850 through Congress by forging a series of sectional and cross-party alliances in support of the now separate measures. Taylor's untimely death removed the final obstacle to the compromise, and it became law in September 1850.

Although they were punctuated by moments of heightened sectional tension such as the publication of Harriet Beecher Stowe's *Uncle Tom's Cabin* in 1852, the years immediately following the Compromise of 1850 were relatively free of strife over slavery. Weakened by the previous sectional conflict and by a growing consensus on other critical political issues, the nation's two main parties, the Democrats and Whigs, looked to take advantage of the relative calm to promote new programs and to rebuild party strength. Among the political issues garnering attention was the proposal to construct a transcontinental railroad to link the new state of California to the rest of the federal Union. Faced with a well-organized, determined lobbying effort by southern congressmen wedded to a southern route to California, Senator Douglas, hoping to promote the interests of his home state of Illinois, moved quickly to organize the territory immediately to the west of Illinois and Iowa to facilitate the construction of a northerly route to California. Douglas's initial proposal left the Missouri Compromise's prohibition of slavery in the region intact, but southern opposition (as well as Douglas's own belief that the area in question was inhospitable to slave-based plantation agriculture) quickly prompted Douglas to revise his bill and to organize the new territory according to the principle of popular sovereignty.

About the Author

Stephen Arnold Douglas was born on April 23, 1813, in Brandon, Vermont. After his father's untimely death and his mother's remarriage, young Douglas was taken to Canandaigua, New York. There he obtained his only formal education. Upon completion of his studies, Douglas headed west to the Illinois frontier, where he assumed a post as a teacher. Eager to make a name for himself, the five-foot, four-inch Douglas taught himself law and became active in local Democratic politics. His efforts bore immediate fruit, and within one year of his arrival, the young man became a state's attorney and, soon thereafter, a member of the Illinois state legislature and a justice on the Illinois Supreme Court.

In 1843 Douglas was elected to the U.S. House of Representatives. Four years later he assumed a seat in the Senate. Douglas, dubbed the "Little Giant" for his oratory skills and legislative acumen, led the battle for the Compromise of 1850 after poor health sidelined its author, Henry Clay. In 1854 Douglas drafted the Kansas-Nebraska bill in order to promote the construction of a northern-based transcontinental railroad. The bill's substitution of popular sovereignty for the Missouri Compromise's ban on slavery in the area initiated intense sectional tensions and doomed Douglas's presidential aspirations. After losing the Democratic

Party's nomination in 1856, Douglas returned to Illinois in 1858 to campaign against the Republican Abraham Lincoln for his Senate seat. A series of highly publicized debates between the two men highlighted the divisive nature of the slavery question. While Douglas won the election, his critique of the recent *Dred Scott* ruling undermined his presidential standing among southern voters. Nonetheless, Douglas succeeded in winning the nomination of the northern wing of a hopelessly divided Democratic Party in 1860 only to lose the general election to his Republican competitor (and Illinois political rival) Abraham Lincoln. As the nation slid into civil war, Douglas actively sided with the northern cause. Unfortunately, however, the Union lost his powerful voice on June 3, 1861, when he died of typhoid fever.

Explanation and Analysis of the Document

◆ Section 1

In Section 1 of "An Act to Organize the Territories of Nebraska and Kansas," Douglas defines the geographic boundaries for the first of the two new territories to be established—Nebraska. Importantly, Douglas also includes a provision, in direct contradiction to the Missouri Compromise's prohibition of slavery in this specific region, establishing the principle of popular sovereignty for the territory, noting "said Territory or any portion of the same, shall be received into the Union with or without slavery, as their constitution may prescribe at the time of admission." The section also contains a provision guaranteeing the rights and privileges of the native peoples living in the area "so long as such rights shall remain unextinguished by treaty between the United States and such Indians."

◆ Section 2

Section 2, following the historical precedent of the Northwest Ordinance of 1787, establishes the executive power and authority in the Nebraska Territory within the office of an appointed territorial governor. The section further describes the term for the governor and outlines the basic powers and responsibilities assigned to the office of governor.

◆ Section 3

Section 3, again following the pattern established by the Northwest Ordinance, outlines the responsibilities of the federally appointed territorial secretary for Nebraska—to "record and preserve all the laws and proceedings of the Legislative Assembly hereinafter constituted, and all the acts and proceedings of the Governor in his executive department." It further designates the secretary as the alternate to administer the territory in cases where the governor is absent, dies, is removed, or resigns.

◆ Section 4

This section defines the legislative power (exercised by the governor and the Legislative Assembly) for the Nebras-

Time Line

1854

■ **March 4**
The U.S. Senate passes the Kansas-Nebraska bill.

■ **May 22**
The U.S. House of Representatives passes the Kansas-Nebraska bill.

■ **May 30**
President Franklin Pierce signs the Kansas-Nebraska Act into law; this initiates an immediate negative response from northerners.

■ **July 6**
The Republican Party is organized in Jackson, Michigan; this marks the end of the old Jacksonian party system and the beginning of the new, sectionally oriented party system.

1856

■ **May 19**
Senator Charles Sumner of Massachusetts delivers his "Crime against Kansas" speech in response to pro- and antislavery violence in the Kansas Territory.

■ **May 21**
Proslavery partisans sack Lawrence, Kansas.

■ **May 22**
South Carolina representative Preston Brooks canes Charles Sumner in the Senate chamber; the caning is delivered in retaliation for Sumner's May 19 speech.

■ **May 24**
The Pottawatomie Creek massacre, the murder of proslavery settlers in Kansas by the abolitionist John Brown and a handful of supporters, occurs.

1857

■ **March 6**
U.S. Supreme Court hands down its ruling in *Dred Scott v. Sandford*; the decision challenges the validity of the Democratic policy of popular sovereignty as well as the Republican policy of halting slavery's expansion into federal territories.

ka Territory. The section divides the territorial legislature into two houses—a Council comprising thirteen members serving two-year terms and a House of Representatives comprising twenty-six individuals elected annually. Apportionment between the two houses is to occur according to the recommendation of the governor, with the total number of assembly members limited to thirty-nine. The section concludes by outlining residency requirements for council members and the general parameters to be followed for legislative elections.

◆ **Section 5**

Section 5 establishes voting rights and qualifications for office holding within the Nebraska Territory, relegating these rights to "every free white male inhabitant above the age of twenty-one years who shall be an actual resident of said Territory" and to those who are either citizens of the United States or who "shall have taken an oath to support the Constitution of the United States and the provisions of this act." The section closes by excluding military personal stationed in the territory from voting and holding office.

◆ **Section 6**

This section limits the power of the Nebraska territorial legislature to measures that are consistent with the U.S. Constitution and with the various provisions of the act itself. This section describes the process by which a bill becomes law in the territory, the governor's veto prerogative, the override process, and the deadlines for gubernatorial signatures on proposed legislation.

◆ **Section 7**

Section 7 stipulates that local governmental officials, "not herein otherwise provided for," will be appointed or elected in a manner determined by the Nebraska territorial governor and Legislative Assembly. Initial appointments to such positions are made by the governor with the consent of the Council, with the terms running to the end of the first session of the Legislative Assembly.

◆ **Section 8**

This provision makes it impossible for members of the Legislative Assembly (with the exception of the members of the first assembly) to hold or accept any appointment or salary to any post created during (or within the first year after) their service in the assembly. It further excludes those with federal appointments, with the exception of postmasters, from serving in the Legislative Assembly.

◆ **Section 9**

Section 9 outlines the structure of the Nebraska Territory's judicial branch, the terms of judicial service, and the jurisdictions and powers of the various territorial judicial entities.

◆ **Section 10**

This section extends the provisions of the federal fugitive slave laws of 1793 and 1850 to the Nebraska Territory.

◆ **Section 11**

Section 11 requires the federal appointment of an attorney and federal marshal for the Nebraska Territory (each to serve a four-year term) to ensure the enforcement of federal laws in the territory. The section also dictates that they be paid a salary commensurate with their peers in the newly organized Utah Territory.

◆ **Section 12**

Section 12 explains how the territorial governor, secretary, chief justice, associate justices, attorney, and marshal are to be appointed by the president of the United States and confirmed by the Senate. The section goes on to describe the oath to be taken by the appointees as well as the annual salaries to be paid to these officials. Additionally, the provision calls for an annual meeting of the territorial legislature and stipulates that funds will also be distributed to the governor and secretary to defray the costs of the territorial legislature and the "contingent expenses of the territory."

◆ **Section 13**

This section authorizes the governor of the Nebraska Territory to call for the first session of the territorial legislature at a time and place of his choosing. The measure goes on to require the legislature to "locate and establish the seat of government for said Territory at such place as they may deem eligible; which place, however, shall thereafter be subject to be changed by the said Governor and Legislative Assembly."

◆ **Section 14**

This segment of the act provides for the election of a nonvoting delegate to the U.S. House of Representatives to represent the Nebraska Territory. The section also outlines the method of electing the delegate. Most importantly, Section 14 has the controversial provision stating that the Constitution and all laws of the United States are in full effect in Nebraska

except the eighth section of the act preparatory to the admission of Missouri into the Union approved March sixth, eighteen hundred and twenty, which, being inconsistent with the principle of non-intervention by Congress with slaves in the States and Territories, as recognized by the legislation of eighteen hundred and fifty, commonly called the Compromise Measures, is hereby declared inoperative and void; it being the true intent and meaning of this act not to legislate slavery into any Territory or State, nor exclude it therefrom, but to leave the people thereof perfectly free to form and regulate their domestic institutions in their own way, subject only to the Constitution of the United States.

This clause renders the Missouri Compromise's exclusion of slavery from the region null and void and thus paves the way for the renewal of intense sectional division.

Section 15

Section 15 provides for federal funds to be expended under the direction of Nebraska's territorial governor for the construction of public buildings at the seat of government and for the creation of a library for use by territorial officials.

Section 16

Section 16 is patterned after provisions that originally appeared in the Northwest Ordinance. It stipulates that the proceeds of land sales in sections 16 and 36 in each township surveyed are to be reserved to finance public schools in Nebraska during both its territorial and state phases.

Section 17

This section empowers the governor of the Nebraska Territory to define the judicial districts within the territory, to assign justices to those districts, and to determine when and where court sessions will be held within the individual districts. These boundaries, assignments, times, and locations can be revised or altered by the territorial legislature as deemed appropriate.

Section 18

This section requires that all federally appointed territorial officials who have responsibility for dispersing federal funds post security as directed by the secretary of the treasury.

Section 19

In Section 19, Douglas defines the geographic boundaries for the second of the two new territories to be established—Kansas. Importantly, Douglas also includes a provision, in direct contradiction to the Missouri Compromise's prohibition of slavery in this specific region, establishing the principle of popular sovereignty for the territory. This provision notes that "said Territory, or any portion of the same, shall be received into the Union with or without slavery, as their constitution may prescribe at the time of admission." It has been suggested that Douglas created a second territory in the belief that he would be able to establish one new free state and one new slave state so as to placate both the North and the South. The section also contains a provision guaranteeing the rights and privileges of the native peoples living in the area "so long as such rights shall remain unextinguished by treaty between the United States and such Indians."

Section 20

Section 20 establishes the executive power and authority in the Kansas Territory within the office of an appointed territorial governor. The section further describes the term for the governor and outlines the basic powers and responsibilities assigned to the office of governor.

Section 21

Section 21 outlines the responsibilities of the federally appointed territorial secretary for Kansas—to "record and preserve all the laws and proceedings of the Legislative Assembly hereinafter constituted, and all the acts and proceedings of the Governor in his Executive Department." It further designates the secretary as the alternate to administer the territory in cases where the governor is absent, dies, is removed, or resigns.

Section 22

This section defines the legislative power (exercised by the governor and a legislature) for the Kansas Territory. The section divides the territorial legislature into two houses—a Council comprising thirteen members serving two-year terms and a House of Representatives comprising twenty-six individuals elected annually. Apportionment between the two houses is to occur according to the recommendation of the governor, with the total number of assembly members limited to thirty-nine. The section concludes by outlining residency requirements for council members and the general parameters to be followed for legislative elections.

Section 23

Section 23 establishes voting rights and qualifications for office-holding within the Kansas Territory, relegating these rights to "every free white male inhabitant above the age of twenty-one years, who shall be an actual resident of said Territory" and to those who are either citizens of the United States or who "shall have taken an oath to support the Constitution of the United States and the provisions of this act." The section closes by excluding military personal stationed in the territory from voting and holding office.

Section 24

This section of the act limits the power of the Kansas territorial legislature to measures consistent with the U.S. Constitution and with the various provisions of the act itself. This section describes the process by which a bill becomes law in the territory, the governor's veto prerogative, the override process, and the deadlines for gubernatorial signatures on proposed legislation.

Section 25

Section 25 stipulates that local governmental officials, "not herein otherwise provided for," will be appointed or elected in a manner determined by the Kansas territorial governor and Legislative Assembly. Initial appointments to such positions are to be made by the governor with the consent of the Council, with the terms running to the end of the first session of the Legislative Assembly.

Section 26

This provision makes it impossible for members of the Kansas Legislative Assembly (with the exception of the members of the first assembly) to hold or accept any appointment or salary to any post created during (or within the first year after) their service in the assembly. It further excludes those with federal appointments, with the exception of postmasters, from serving in the Legislative Assembly.

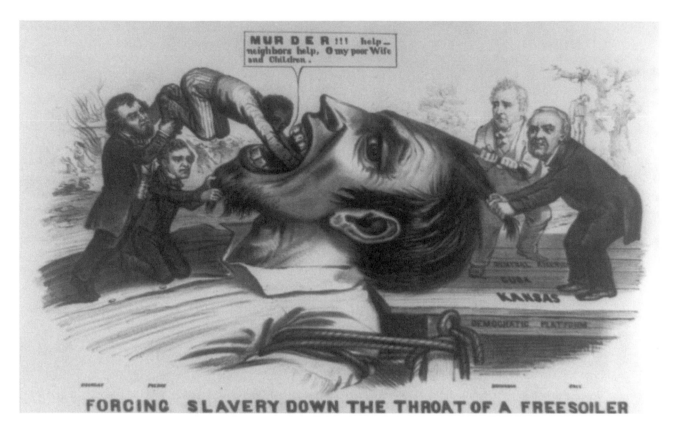

FORCING SLAVERY DOWN THE THROAT OF A FREESOILER

This 1856 cartoon by John L. Magee depicts the violence that followed the passage of the Kansas-Nebraska Act.
(Library of Congress)

◆ **Section 27**

Section 27 outlines the structure of the Kansas Territory's judicial branch, the terms of judicial service, and the jurisdictions and powers of the various territorial judicial entities.

◆ **Section 28**

This section extends the provisions of the federal Fugitive Slave Laws of 1793 and 1850 to the Kansas Territory.

◆ **Section 29**

Section 29 requires the federal appointment of an attorney and federal marshal for the Kansas Territory (each to serve a four-year term) to ensure the enforcement of federal laws in the territory. The section also dictates that they be paid a salary commensurate with their peers in the newly organized Utah Territory.

◆ **Section 30**

Section 30 explains how the territorial governor, secretary, chief justice, associate justices, attorney, and marshal are to be appointed by the president of the United States and confirmed by the Senate. The section goes on to describe the oath to be taken by the appointees as well as the annual salaries to be paid to these officials. Additionally, the provision calls for an annual meeting of the territorial legislature and stipulates that funds will also be distributed to the gov-

ernor and secretary to defray the costs of the territorial legislature and the "contingent expenses of the Territory."

◆ **Section 31**

This section establishes Fort Leavenworth as the temporary seat of government for the Kansas Territory and authorizes the governor and territorial legislature of the Kansas Territory to make use of any unused public buildings within the fort.

◆ **Section 32**

This segment of the act provides for the election of a nonvoting delegate to the U.S. House of Representatives to represent the Kansas Territory. The section also outlines the method of electing the delegate. Section 32 also mirrors Section 14 in rendering the Missouri Compromise's exclusion of slavery from the region null and void and thus paving the way for the renewal of intense sectional division.

◆ **Section 33**

Section 33 provides for federal funds to be expended under the direction of Kansas's territorial governor for the construction of public buildings at the seat of government and for the creation of a library for use by territorial officials.

◆ **Section 34**

Section 34 is patterned after provisions that originally appeared in the Northwest Ordinance. It stipulates that the

> "*Said Territory or any portion of the same, shall be received into the Union with or without slavery, as their constitution may prescribe at the time of admission.*"
>
> (Sections 1 and 19)

> "*That the Constitution, and all Laws of the United States which are not locally inapplicable, shall have the same force and effect within the said Territory of Nebraska as elsewhere within the United States, except the eighth section of the act preparatory to the admission of Missouri into the Union approved March sixth, eighteen hundred and twenty, which, being inconsistent with the principle of non-intervention by Congress with slaves in the States and Territories, as recognized by the legislation of eighteen hundred and fifty, commonly called the Compromise Measures, is hereby declared inoperative and void; it being the true intent and meaning of this act not to legislate slavery into any Territory or State, nor exclude it therefrom, but to leave the people thereof perfectly free to form and regulate their domestic institutions in their own way, subject only to the Constitution of the United States.*"
>
> (Section 14)

proceeds of land sales in sections 16 and 36 in each township surveyed are to be reserved to finance public schools in Kansas during both its territorial and state phases.

◆ Section 35

This section empowers the governor of the Kansas Territory to define the judicial districts within the territory, to assign justices to those districts, and to determine when and where court sessions will be held within the individual districts. These boundaries, assignments, times, and locations can be revised or altered by the territorial legislature as deemed appropriate.

◆ Section 36

Section 36 requires that all federally appointed territorial officials who have responsibility for dispersing federal funds post security as directed by the secretary of the treasury.

◆ Section 37

This final section specifies that "all treaties, laws, and other engagements made by the government of the United States with the Indian tribes inhabiting the territories embraced within this act, shall be faithfully and rigidly observed."

Audience

The Kansas-Nebraska Act was written for a national audience. Douglas, aware of the harmful effect that the slavery debate could have upon both his beloved Democratic Party and the nation at large, played an active role in trying to suppress the controversy. He guided the Compromise of 1850, including its provisions establishing the doctrine of popular sovereignty in the newly formed far-western territories, through Congress and into law. Douglas believed that this doctrine, with its democratic foundation, along with the geography of the West, would ensure that slavery did not spread beyond its current geographic boundaries.

Firm in his dedication to the theoretical principle of self-rule (though recognizing a growing northern majority) and believing that the Kansas-Nebraska area was not climatically hospitable to slavery, Douglas did not hesitate to revise his bill by substituting the principle of popular sovereignty for the Missouri Compromise's explicit omission of slavery. Even though he claimed not to care one way or the other, Douglas believed that the net result would most likely be the same—new western territories and states that were free of slavery. Thus, through his Kansas-Nebraska bill, Douglas hoped to show the American people (whom he also intended to court in a quest for the presidency) that the controversy over slavery spreading to the West was a nonissue and that sectionalism could be peacefully and permanently muzzled.

Impact

The Kansas-Nebraska Act had a profound and immediate impact upon the American people and the nation's subsequent history. Southerners generally embraced the act, viewing it as validation of their way of life and their interpretation of the intentions of the Founding Fathers to establish a slave-based republic. Many northerners, however, increasingly predisposed to suspicion of their southern peers as a result of years of heightened sectional tensions, were mortified by the act, lamenting the potential loss to slavery of territory long reserved for free settlers. Accordingly, scores of protest meetings condemning Douglas and his controversial legislation and calling for coordinated political opposition to the act were staged throughout the North. The uproar over the Kansas-Nebraska Act upended an already fragile political system and doomed a reeling Whig Party.

Shortly after the Kansas-Nebraska Act became law, political activists in the North, committed to an agenda of preserving the western territories for free settlers, began to pull together elements from the fractured Democratic and Whig Parties into new political coalitions designed to advocate for an end to slavery's expansion and to the seeming control of slavery's supporters over Washington. In short order, these coalitions began to coordinate their activities, banding together under such names as "Anti-Nebraska," "Fusion," and, most famously, the "Republican Party." In spite of the intense hostility to the Kansas-Nebraska Act, throughout late 1854 and into 1855 and 1856, the Republican agenda was merely one of many competing for northern electoral support. Events in Kansas, however, soon gave the Republicans a leg up on their opponents.

In the immediate aftermath of the passage of the Kansas-Nebraska Act, settlers from the contiguous slave state of Missouri rapidly organized to ensure victory for their particular way of life in the new Kansas Territory, migrating to the territory and occupying land along the Missouri River. Antislavery activists quickly followed suit, establishing settlements at Topeka and Lawrence. Rapid settlement in the region spurred territorial governor Andrew Reeder to call for a legislative election in the spring of 1855. Marred by voter fraud and intimidation, the balloting resulted in the election of a stridently proslavery territorial legislature. Free-state settlers responded by rejecting the proslavery laws created by the new legislature and by creating an antislavery shadow government in Topeka. By late 1855 the two sides had begun to take up arms, and

stories about "Bleeding Kansas" permeated the nation's newspapers. The violence escalated in 1856, culminating with the sack of Lawrence, Kansas, the beating of Senator Charles Sumner by South Carolina's Preston Brooks in retaliation for a speech decrying the civil war in Kansas, and the murder of proslavery settlers on Pottawatomie Creek by the abolitionist John Brown.

The bloody events of 1856 seemingly lent credence to the Republican Party's condemnation of the Kansas-Nebraska Act and its claim of a slave power conspiracy determined to force slavery into the western territories and to undermine the intentions of the nation's Founders. As a result, the party quickly rose to prominence throughout the North and, by the fall of 1856, stood as the primary opposition to Democratic Party. Although the party was unsuccessful in the presidential election of 1856, its rise to prominence, along with the Democratic Party's increasingly prosouthern stance, sectionalized American politics and thus made compromise and moderation virtually impossible.

For their part, Democrats, despite the obvious problems in Kansas, clung tenaciously to the principle of popular sovereignty. Debate over Kansas's attempt to join the Union as a slave state under the Lecompton Constitution and the Supreme Court's decision in the case of *Dred Scott v. Sandford*, however, dramatically undermined the appeal of their platform and further bolstered their Republican opponents. The subsequent election of Republican Abraham Lincoln in the 1860 presidential race sounded the death knell for popular sovereignty. Thrust into the White House because of northern votes alone, Lincoln embodied a commitment to antislavery extension and thus, from a southern point of view, a commitment to the destruction of their liberty. Convinced that secession was their only viable option, the states of the Deep South withdrew from the Union beginning in December 1860, and the United States rapidly slid into civil war.

Related Documents

Dred Scott v. John F. A. Sandford, 60 U.S. 393 (1857). One of the most influential court cases in American history; the decision rendered in this case negated the Democratic Party's policy of popular sovereignty and triggered intense sectional debate.

"Lewis Cass to Alfred Nicholson, December 24, 1847." Printed in the *Washington Daily Union*, December 30, 1847. Cass's letter represents the first major expression of the doctrine that came to be known as popular sovereignty.

Stowe, Harriet Beecher. *Uncle Tom's Cabin; Or, Life among the Lowly*. Boston: John P. Jewett and Company, 1852. Written in response to the Fugitive Slave Act of 1850, this seminal work galvanized North and South alike and served as the backdrop for the debate over the Kansas-Nebraska Act.

Sumner, Charles. "On the Crime against Kansas." United States Senate, May 19–20, 1856. http://www.iath.virginia.edu/seminar/

unit4/sumner.html. Accessed on January 31, 2008. Delivered in response to the escalating violence in Kansas between pro- and antislavery partisans, Sumner's speech articulated a growing fear among northerners, especially after the beating of Sumner by South Carolina congressman Preston Brooks.

U.S. Congress. Senate. *Conference Committee Report on the Missouri Compromise.* 16th Cong., 1st sess., 1820. The Missouri Compromise of 1820, with its exclusion of slavery from the territory north of 36°30' north (which included the area later set aside as Kansas and Nebraska), was at the center of the national debate over slavery's extension into the West and was explicitly repealed by the Kansas-Nebraska Act.

U.S. Congress. Senate. *Resolution Introduced by Senator Clay in Relation to the Adjustment of All Existing Questions of Controversy between the States Arising Out of the Institution of Slavery.* 31st Cong., 1st sess., 1850. This legislation, which became the Compromise of 1850, stood as a concerted effort to span the sectional debate over slavery's encroachment into the West and gave rise to the Fugitive Slave Act of 1850.

Wilmot Proviso, *Congressional Globe*, August 12, 1846. http://memory.loc.gov/cgi-bin/ampage?collId=llcg&fileName=016/llcg016.db&recNum=1264. Accessed on January 31, 2008. Attached to a Mexican War appropriations bill, David Wilmot's proviso became the foundation for northern antislavery parties (such as the Free-Soil and Republican parties) and served as a foil to the Democrats' policy of popular sovereignty.

Bibliography

■ Articles
Russel, Robert R. "The Issues in the Congressional Struggle over the Kansas-Nebraska Bill, 1854." *Journal of Southern History* 29, no. 2 (May 1963): 187–210.

■ Books
Basler, Roy Prentice, ed. *The Collected Works of Abraham Lincoln.* 4 vols. New Brunswick, N.J.: Rutgers University Press, 1953–1955.

Foner, Eric. *Free Soil, Free Labor, Free Men: The Ideology of the Republican Party before the Civil War.* Reprint edition. New York: Oxford University Press, 1995.

Gienapp, William E. *The Origins of the Republican Party, 1852–1856.* New York: Oxford University Press, 1987.

Holt, Michael F. *The Fate of Their Country: Politicians, Slavery Extension, and the Coming of the Civil War.* New York: Hill and Wang, 2004.

Johannsen, Robert W. *Stephen A. Douglas.* Urbana: University of Illinois Press, 1997.

Levine, Bruce. *Half Slave and Half Free: The Roots of Civil War.* Revised edition. New York: Hill and Wang, 2005.

Potter, David Morris. *The Impending Crisis, 1848–1861.* New York: Harper and Row, 1976.

Sewell, Richard H. *A House Divided: Sectionalism and Civil War, 1848–1861.* Baltimore: Johns Hopkins University Press, 1988.

■ Web Sites
"Kansas-Nebraska Act (1854)." National Archives "Our Documents" Web site.
    http://www.ourdocuments.gov/doc.php?flash=true&doc=28/. Accessed on July 10, 2007.

Monroe, R. D. "The Kansas-Nebraska Act and the Rise of the Republican Party, 1854–1856." Lincoln/Net Web site.
    http://lincoln.lib.niu.edu/biography6text.html. Accessed on July 10, 2007.

—By Martin J. Hershock

1. Was Douglas justified in believing that the principle of popular sovereignty would diffuse the sectional crisis in the United States?

2. In 1850 many Americans believed that the compromise measures crafted by Congress had produced a final resolution of the slavery controversy in the United States. Only eleven years later the nation found itself enmeshed in a bloody civil war. What role, if any, did the Kansas-Nebraska Act play in precipitating that war?

3. In a speech about the Kansas-Nebraska Act delivered in the fall of 1850, Abraham Lincoln argued,

> Whether slavery shall go into Nebraska, or other new territories, is not a matter of exclusive concern to the people who may go there. The whole nation is interested that the best use shall be made of these territories. We want them for the homes of free white people. This they cannot be, to any considerable extent, if slavery shall be planted within them. Slave States are places for poor white people to remove FROM; not to remove TO. New free States are the places for poor people to go to and better their condition. For this use, the nation needs these territories. (Lincoln, vol. 2, p. 268).

How might Douglas have responded to this critique of his bill?

Glossary

appellate	having the power to review the judgment of another tribunal
chancery	having to do with providing equity without making rulings on issues of law
common law	referring to a body of law developed primarily from judicial decisions based on custom and precedent and forming the basis of U.S. law
emoluments	compensation deriving from holding an office
habeas corpus	a common law writ obtained to bring someone before a court or judge
prescribed	ordained
respites	delays
suffrage	the vote
to wit	that is to say
vested	conferred as a power
writ	a formal legal document

KANSAS-NEBRASKA ACT

An Act to Organize the Territories of Nebraska and Kansas

Be it enacted by the Senate and House of Representatives of the United States of America in Congress assembled, That all that part of the territory of the United States included within the following limits, except such portions thereof as are hereinafter expressly exempted from the operations of this act, to wit: beginning at a point in the Missouri River where the fortieth parallel of north latitude crosses the same; then west on said parallel to the east boundary of the Territory of Utah, the summit of the Rocky Mountains; thence on said summit northwest to the forty-ninth parallel of north latitude; thence east on said parallel to the western boundary of the territory of Minnesota; thence southward on said boundary to the Missouri River; thence down the main channel of said river to the place of beginning, be, and the same is hereby, created into a temporary government by the name of the Territory Nebraska; and when admitted as a State or States, the said Territory or any portion of the same, shall be received into the Union with without slavery, as their constitution may prescribe at the time of the admission: Provided, That nothing in this act contained shall be construed to inhibit the government of the United States from dividing said Territory into two or more Territories, in such manner and at such tin as Congress shall deem convenient and proper, or from attaching a portion of said Territory to any other State or Territory of the United States: *Provided further*, That nothing in this act contained shall construed to impair the rights of person or property now pertaining the Indians in said Territory so long as such rights shall remain unextinguished by treaty between the United States and such Indians, or include any territory which, by treaty with any Indian tribe, is not, without the consent of said tribe, to be included within the territorial line or jurisdiction of any State or Territory; but all such territory shall excepted out of the boundaries, and constitute no part of the Territory of Nebraska, until said tribe shall signify their assent to the President of the United States to be included within the said Territory of Nebraska. or to affect the authority of the government of the United States make any regulations respecting such Indians, their lands, property, or other rights, by treaty, law, or otherwise, which it would have been competent to the government to make if this act had never passed.

SEC. 2. *And be it further enacted*, That the executive power and authority in and over said Territory of Nebraska shall be vested in a Governor who shall hold his office for four years, and until his successor shall be appointed and qualified, unless sooner removed by the President of the United States. The Governor shall reside within said Territory, and shall be commander-in-chief of the militia thereof. He may grant pardons and respites for offences against the laws of said Territory, and reprieves for offences against the laws of the United States, until the decision of the President can be made known thereon; he shall commission all officers who shall be appointed to office under the laws of the aid Territory, and shall take care that the laws be faithfully executed.

SEC. 3. *And be it further enacted*, That there shall be a Secretary of said Territory, who shall reside therein, and hold his office for five years, unless sooner removed by the President of the United States; he shall record and preserve all the laws and proceedings of the Legislative Assembly hereinafter constituted, and all the acts and proceedings of the Governor in his executive department; he shall transmit one copy of the laws and journals of the Legislative Assembly within thirty days after the end of each session, and one copy of the executive proceedings and official correspondence semi-annually, on the first days of January and July in each year to the President of the United States, and two copies of the laws to the President of the Senate and to the Speaker of the House of Representatives, to be deposited in the libraries of Congress, and in or case of the death, removal, resignation, or absence of the Governor from the Territory, the Secretary shall be, and he is hereby, authorized and required to execute and perform all the powers and duties of the Governor during such vacancy or absence, or until another Governor shall be duly appointed and qualified to fill such vacancy.

SEC 4. *And be it further enacted,* That the legislative power and authority of said Territory shall be vested in the Governor and a Legislative Assembly. The Legislative Assembly shall consist of a Council and House of Representatives. The Council shall consist of thirteen members, having the qualifications of voters, as hereinafter prescribed, whose term of service shall continue two years. The House of Representatives shall, at its first session, consist of twenty-six members, possessing the same qualifications as prescribed for members of the Council, and whose term of service shall continue one year. The number of representatives may be increased by the Legislative Assembly, from time to time, in proportion to the increase of qualified voters: *Provided,* That the whole number shall never exceed thirty-nine. An apportionment shall be made, as nearly equal as practicable, among the several counties or districts, for the election of the council and representatives, giving to each section of the Territory representation in the ratio of its qualified voters as nearly as may be. And the members of the Council and of the House of Representatives shall reside in, and be inhabitants of, the district or county, or counties for which they may be elected, respectively. Previous to the first election, the Governor shall cause a census, or enumeration of the inhabitants and qualified voters of the several counties and districts of the Territory, to be taken by such persons and in such mode as the Governor shall designate and appoint; and the persons so appointed shall receive a reasonable compensation therefor. And the first election shall be held at such time and places, and be conducted in such manner, both as to the persons who shall superintend such election and the returns thereof, as the Governor shall appoint and direct; and he shall at the same time declare the number of members of the Council and House of Representatives to which each of the counties or districts shall be entitled under this act. The persons having the highest number of legal votes in each of said council districts for members of the Council, shall be declared by the Governor to be duly elected to the Council; and the per-

sons having the highest number of legal votes for the House of Representatives, shall be declared by the Governor to be duly elected members of said house: *Provided,* That in case two or more persons voted for shall have an equal number of votes, and in case a vacancy shall otherwise occur in either branch of the Legislative Assembly, the Governor shall order a new election; and the persons thus elected to the Legislative Assembly shall meet at such place and on such day as the Governor shall appoint; but thereafter, the time, place, and manner of holding and conducting all elections by the people, and the apportioning the representation in the several counties or districts to the Council and House of Representatives, according to the number of qualified voters, shall be prescribed by law, as well as the day of the commencement of the regular sessions of the Legislative Assembly: *Provided, That no session in any one year shall exceed the term of forty days, except the first session, which may continue sixty days.*

SEC. 5. *And be it further enacted,* That every free white male inhabitant above the age of twenty-one years who shall be an actual resident of said Territory, and shall possess the qualifications hereinafter prescribed, shall be entitled to vote at the first election, and shall be eligible to any office within the said Territory; but the qualifications of voters, and of holding office, at all subsequent elections, shall be such as shall be prescribed by the Legislative Assembly: *Provided,* That the right of suffrage and of holding office shall be exercised only by citizens of the United States and those who shall have declared on oath their intention to become such, and shall have taken an oath to support the Constitution of the United States and the provisions of this act: And provided further, That no officer, soldier, seaman, or marine, or other person in the army or navy of the United States, or attached to troops in the service of the United States, shall be allowed to vote or hold office in said Territory, by reason of being on service therein.

SEC. 6. *And be it further enacted,* That the legislative power of the Territory shall extend to all rightful subjects of legislation consistent with the Constitution of the United States and the provisions of this act; but no law shall be passed interfering with the primary disposal of the soil; no tax shall be imposed upon the property of the United States; nor shall the lands or other property of non-residents be taxed higher than the lands or other property of residents. Every bill which shall have passed the Council and House of Representatives of the said Territory shall, before it become a law, be presented to the

Governor of the Territory; if he approve, he shall sign it; but if not, he shall return it with his objections to the house in which it originated, who shall enter the objections at large on their journal, and proceed to reconsider it. If, after such reconsideration two thirds of that house shall agree to pass the bill, it shall be sent, together with the objections, to the other house, by which it shall likewise be reconsidered, and if approved by two thirds of that house, it shall become a law. But in all such cases the votes of both houses shall be determined by yeas and nays, to be entered on the journal of each house respectively. If any bill shall not be returned by the Governor within three days (Sundays excepted) after it shall have been presented to him, the same shall be a law in like manner as if he had signed it, unless the Assembly, by adjournment, prevents its return, in which case it shall not be a law.

SEC. 7. *And be it further enacted*, That all township, district, and county officers, not herein otherwise provided for, shall be appointed or elected, as the case may be, in such manner as shall be provided by the Governor and Legislative Assembly of the Territory of Nebraska. The Governor shall nominate, and, by and with the advice and consent of the Legislative Council, appoint all officers not herein otherwise provided for; and in the first instance the Governor alone may appoint all said officers, who shall hold their offices until the end of the first session of the Legislative Assembly; and shall lay off the necessary districts for members of the Council and House of Representatives, and all other officers.

SEC. 8. *And be it further enacted*, That no member of the Legislative Assembly shall hold, or be appointed to, any office which shall have been created, or the salary or emoluments of which shall have been increased, while he was a member, during the term for which he was elected, and for one year after the expiration of such term; but this restriction shall not be applicable to members of the first Legislative Assembly; and no person holding a commission or appointment under the United States, except Postmasters, shall be a member of the Legislative Assembly, or hold any office under the government of said Territory.

SEC. 9. *And be it further enacted*, That the judicial power of said Territory shall be vested in a Supreme Court, District Courts, Probate Courts, and in Justices of the Peace. The Supreme Court shall consist of a chief justice and two associate justices, any two of whom shall constitute a quorum, and who shall hold a term at the seat of government of said Territory annually, and they shall hold their offices during the period of four years, and until their successor shall be appointed and qualified. The said Territory shall be divided into three judicial districts, and a district court shall be held in each of said districts by one of the justices of the Supreme Court, at such times and places as may be prescribed by of law; and the said judges shall, after their appointments, respectively, reside in the districts which shall be assigned them. The jurisdiction of the several courts herein provided for, both appellate and original, and that of the probate courts and of justices of the peace, shall be as limited by law: *Provided*, That justices of the peace shall not have jurisdiction of any matter in controversy when the title or boundaries of land may be in dispute, or where the debt or sum claimed shall exceed one hundred dollars; and the said supreme and districts courts, respectively, shall possess chancery as well as common law jurisdiction. Each District Court, or the judge thereof, shall appoint its clerk, who shall also be the register in chancery, and shall keep his office at the place where the court may, be held. Writs of error, bills of exception, and appeals, shall be allowed in all cases from the final decisions of said district courts to the Supreme Court, under such regulations as may be prescribed by law; but in no case removed to the Supreme Court shall trial by jury be allowed in said court. The Supreme Court, or the justices thereof, shall appoint its own clerk, and every clerk shall hold his office at the pleasure of the court for which he shall have been appointed. Writs of error, and appeals from the final decisions of said Supreme Court, shall be allowed, and may be taken to the Supreme Court of the United States, in the same manner and under the same regulations as from the circuit courts of the United States, where the value of the property, or the amount in controversy, to be ascertained by the oath or affirmation of either party, or other competent witness, shall exceed one thousand dollars; except only that in all cases involving title to slaves, the said writs of error, or appeals shall be allowed and decided by the said Supreme Court, without regard to the value of the matter, property, or title in controversy; and except also that a writ of error or appeal shall also be allowed to the Supreme Court of the United States, from the decision of the said Supreme Court created by this act, or of any judge thereof, or of the district courts created by this act, or of any judge thereof, upon any writ of habeas corpus, involving the question of personal freedom: *Provided*, that nothing herein contained shall be construed to apply to or affect the provisions to the "act respecting fugitives from justice, and persons escaping from the service of their masters," approved February twelfth, seventeen hundred and ninety-three, and the "act to amend and supplementary to the aforesaid act," approved September eighteen, eighteen hundred and fifty; and each of the said district courts shall have and exercise the same jurisdiction in all cases arising under the Constitution and Laws of the United States as is vested in the Circuit and District Courts of the United States; and the said Supreme and District Courts of the said Territory, and the respective judges thereof, shall and may grant writs of habeas corpus in all cases in which the same are granted by the judges of the United States in the District of Columbia; and the first six days of every term of said courts, or so much thereof as shall be necessary, shall be appropriated to the trial of causes arising under the said constitution and laws, and writs of error and appeal in all such cases shall be made to the Supreme Court of said Territory, the same as in other cases. The said clerk shall receive in all such cases the same fees which the clerks of the district courts of Utah Territory now receive for similar services.

SEC. 10. *And be it further enacted*, That the provisions of an act entitled "An act respecting fugitives from justice, and persons escaping from the service of their masters," approved February twelve, seventeen hundred and ninety-three, and the provisions of the act entitled "An act to amend, and supplementary to, the aforesaid act," approved September eighteen, eighteen hundred and fifty, be, and the same are hereby, declared to extend to and be in full force within the limits of said Territory of Nebraska.

SEC. 11. *And be it further enacted*, That there shall be appointed an Attorney for said Territory, who shall continue in office for four years, and until his successor shall be appointed and qualified, unless sooner removed by the President, and who shall receive the same fees and salary as the Attorney of the United States for the present Territory of Utah. There shall also be a Marshal for the Territory appointed, who shall hold his office for four years, and until his successor shall be appointed and qualified, unless sooner removed by the President, and who shall execute all processes issuing from the said courts when exercising their jurisdiction as Circuit and District Courts of the United States; he shall perform the duties, be subject to the same regulation and penalties, and be entitled to the same fees, as the Marshal of the District Court of the United States for the present Territory of Utah, and shall, in

addition, be paid two hundred dollars annually as a compensation for extra services.

SEC. 12. *And be it further enacted*, That the Governor, Secretary, Chief Justice, and Associate Justices, Attorney and Marshal, shall be nominated, and, by and with the advice and consent of the Senate, appointed by the President of the United States. The Governor and a Secretary to be appointed as aforesaid, shall, before they act as such, respectively take an oath or affirmation before the District Judge or some Justice of the Peace in the limits of said Territory, duly authorized to administer oaths and affirmations by the laws now in force therein, or before the Chief Justice, or some Associate Justice of the Supreme Court of the United States, to support the Constitution of the United States, and faithfully to discharge the duties of their respective offices, which said oaths, when so taken, shall be certified by the person by whom the same shall have been taken; and such certificates shall be received and recorded by the said Secretary among the Executive proceedings; and the Chief Justice and Associate Justices, and all other civil officers in said Territory, before they act as such, shall take a like oath or affirmation before the said Governor or Secretary, or some Judge or Justice of the Peace of the Territory, who may be duly commissioned and qualified, which said oath or affirmation shall be certified and transmitted by the person taking the same to the Secretary, to be by him recorded as aforesaid; and, afterwards, the like oath or affirmation shall be taken, certified, and recorded, in such manner and form as may be prescribed by law. The Governor shall receive an annual salary of two thousand five hundred dollars. The Chief Justice and Associate Justices shall each receive an annual salary of two thousand dollars. The Secretary shall receive an annual salary of two thousand dollars. The said salaries shall be paid quarter-yearly, from the dates of the respective appointments, at the Treasury of the United States; but no such payment shall be made until said officers shall have entered upon the duties of their respective appointments. The members of the Legislative Assembly shall be entitled to receive three dollars each per day during their attendance at the sessions thereof, and three dollars each for every twenty miles' travel in going to and returning from the said sessions, estimated according to the nearest usually travelled route; and an additional allowance of three dollars shall be paid to the presiding officer of each house for each day he shall so preside. And a chief clerk, one assistant clerk, a sergeant-at-arms, and doorkeeper, may be chosen for each house; and the chief clerk shall receive four dollars per day, and the said other officers three dollars per day, during the session of the Legislative Assembly; but no other officers shall be paid by the United States: *Provided*, That there shall be but one session of the legislature annually, unless, on an extraordinary occasion, the Governor shall think proper to call the legislature together. There shall be appropriated, annually, the usual sum, to be expended by the Governor, to defray the contingent expenses of the Territory, including the salary of a clerk of the Executive Department; and there shall also be appropriated, annually, a sufficient sum, to be expended by the Secretary of the Territory, and upon an estimate to be made by the Secretary of the Treasury of the United States, to defray the expenses of the Legislative Assembly, the printing of the laws, and other incidental expenses; and the Governor and Secretary of the Territory shall, in the disbursement of all moneys intrusted to them, be governed solely by the instructions of the Secretary of the Treasury of the United States, and shall, semi-annually, account to the said Secretary for the manner in which the aforesaid moneys shall have been expended; and no expenditure shall be made by said Legislative Assembly for objects not specially authorized by the acts of Congress, making the appropriations, nor beyond the sums thus appropriated for such objects.

SEC. 13. *And be it further enacted*, That the Legislative Assembly of the Territory of Nebraska shall hold its first session at such time and place in said Territory as the Governor thereof shall appoint and direct; and at said first session, or as soon thereafter as they shall deem expedient, the Governor and Legislative Assembly shall proceed to locate and establish the seat of government for said Territory at such place as they may deem eligible; which place, however, shall thereafter be subject to be changed by the said Governor and Legislative Assembly.

SEC. 14. *And be it further enacted*, That a delegate to the House of Representatives of the United States, to serve for the term of two years, who shall be a citizen of the United States, may be elected by the voters qualified to elect members of the Legislative Assembly, who shall be entitled to the same rights and privileges as are exercised and enjoyed by the delegates from the several other Territories of the United States to the said House of Representatives, but the delegate first elected shall hold his seat only during the term of the Congress to which he shall be elected. The first election shall be held at such time and places, and be conducted in such manner, as the Gov-

ernor shall appoint and direct; and at all subsequent elections the times, places, and manner of holding the elections, shall be prescribed by law. The person having the greatest number of votes shall be declared by the Governor to be duly elected; and a certificate thereof shall be given accordingly. That the Constitution, and all Laws of the United States which are not locally inapplicable, shall have the same force and effect within the said Territory of Nebraska as elsewhere within the United States, except the eighth section of the act preparatory to the admission of Missouri into the Union approved March sixth, eighteen hundred and twenty, which, being inconsistent with the principle of non-intervention by Congress with slaves in the States and Territories, as recognized by the legislation of eighteen hundred and fifty, commonly called the Compromise Measures, is hereby declared inoperative and void; it being the true intent and meaning of this act not to legislate slavery into any Territory or State, nor to exclude it therefrom, but to leave the people thereof perfectly free to form and regulate their domestic institutions in their own way, subject only to the Constitution of the United States: *Provided*, That nothing herein contained shall be construed to revive or put in force any law or regulation which may have existed prior to the act of sixth March, eighteen hundred and twenty, either protecting, establishing, prohibiting, or abolishing slavery.

SEC. 15. *And be it further enacted*, That there shall hereafter be appropriated, as has been customary for the Territorial governments, sufficient amount, to be expended under the direction of the said Governor of the Territory of Nebraska, not exceeding the sums heretofore appropriated for similar objects, for the erection of suitable public buildings at the seat of government, and for the purchase of a library, to be kept at the seat of government for the use of the Governor, Legislative Assembly, Judges of the Supreme Court, Secretary, Marshal, and Attorney of said Territory, and such other persons, and under such regulations as shall be prescribed by law.

SEC. 16. *And be it further enacted*, That when the lands in the said Territory shall be surveyed under the direction of the government of the United States, preparatory to bringing the same into market, section; numbered sixteen and thirty-six in each township in said Territory shall be, and the same are hereby, reserved for the purpose of being applied to schools in said Territory, and in the States and Territories hereafter to be erected out of the same.

SEC. 17. *And be it further enacted*, That, until otherwise provided by law, the Governor of said Territory may define the Judicial Districts of said Territory, and assign the judges who may be appointed for said Territory to the several districts; and also appoint the times and places for holding courts in the several counties or subdivisions in each of said Judicial Districts by proclamation, to be issued by him; but the Legislative Assembly, at their first or any subsequent session, may organize, alter, or modify such Judicial Districts, and assign the judges, and alter the times and places of holding the courts, as to them shall seem proper and convenient.

SEC. 18. *And be it further enacted*, That all officers to be appointed by the President, by and with the advice and consent of the Senate, for the Territory of Nebraska, who, by virtue of the provisions of any law now existing, or which may be enacted during the present Congress, are required to give security for moneys that may be intrusted with them for disbursement, shall give such security, at such time and place, and in such manner, as the Secretary of the Treasury may prescribe.

SEC. 19. *And be it further enacted*, That all that part of the Territory of the United States included within the following limits, except such portions thereof as are hereinafter expressly exempted from the operations of this act, to wit, beginning at a point on the western boundary of the State of Missouri, where the thirty-seventh parallel of north latitude crosses the same; thence west on said parallel to the eastern boundary of New Mexico; thence north on said boundary to latitude thirty-eight; thence following said boundary westward to the east boundary of the Territory of Utah, on the summit of the Rocky Mountains; thence northward on said summit to the fortieth parallel of latitude, thence east on said parallel to the western boundary of the State of Missouri; thence south with the western boundary of said State to the place of beginning, be, and the same is hereby, created into a temporary government by the name of the Territory of Kansas; and when admitted as a State or States, the said Territory, or any portion of the same, shall be received into the Union with or without slavery, as their Constitution may prescribe at the time of their admission: *Provided*, That nothing in this act contained shall be construed to inhibit the government of the United States from dividing said Territory into two or more Territories, in such manner and at such times as Congress shall deem convenient and proper, or from attaching any portion of said Territory to any other State or Territory of the United States: *Provided* further, That nothing in this act contained shall be construed to impair the rights of person or property now pertaining to the Indians in said Territory, so long as such rights shall remain unextinguished by treaty between the United States and such Indians, or to include any territory which, by treaty with any Indian tribe, is not, without the consent of said tribe, to be included within the territorial limits or jurisdiction of any State or Territory; but all such territory shall be excepted out of the boundaries, and constitute no part of the Territory of Kansas, until said tribe shall signify their assent to the President of the United States to be included within the said Territory of Kansas, or to affect the authority of the government of the United States to make any regulation respecting such Indians, their lands, property, or other rights, by treaty, law, or otherwise, which it would have been competent to the government to make if this act had never passed.

SEC. 20. *And be it further enacted*, That the executive power and authority in and over said Territory of Kansas shall be vested in a Governor, who shall hold his office for four years, and until his successor shall be appointed and qualified, unless sooner removed by the President of the United States. The Governor shall reside within said Territory, and shall be commander-in-chief of the militia thereof. He may grant pardons and respites for offences against the laws of said Territory, and reprieves for offences against the laws of the United States, until the decision of the President can be made known thereon; he shall commission all officers who shall be appointed to office under the laws of the said Territory, and shall take care that the laws be faithfully executed.

SEC. 21. *And be it further enacted*, That there shall be a Secretary of said Territory, who shall reside therein, and hold his office for five years, unless sooner removed by the President of the United States; he shall record and preserve all the laws and proceedings of the Legislative Assembly hereinafter constituted, and all the acts and proceedings of the Governor in his Executive Department; he shall transmit one copy of the laws and journals of the Legislative Assembly within thirty days after the end of each session, and one copy of the executive proceedings and official correspondence semi-annually, on the first days of January and July in each year, to the President of the United States, and two copies of the laws to the President of the Senate and to the Speaker of the House of Representatives, to be deposited in the libraries of Congress; and, in case of the death, removal, resignation, or absence of the Governor from the Territory, the Secretary shall be, and he is hereby, authorized and required to execute and perform all the powers and duties of the Governor during such vacancy or absence, or until another Governor shall be duly appointed and qualified to fill such vacancy.

SEC. 22. *And be it further enacted*, That the legislative power and authority of said Territory shall be vested in the Governor and a Legislative Assembly. The Legislative Assembly shall consist of a Council and House of Representatives. The Council shall consist of thirteen members, having the qualifications of voters, as hereinafter prescribed, whose term of service shall continue two years. The House of Representatives shall, at its first session, consist of twenty-six members possessing the same qualifications as prescribed for members of the Council, and whose term of service shall continue one year. The number of representatives may be increased by the Legislative Assembly, from time to time, in proportion to the increase of qualified voters: *Provided*, That the whole number shall never exceed thirty-nine. An apportionment shall be made, as nearly equal as practicable, among the several counties or districts, for the election of the Council and Representatives, giving to each section of the Territory representation in the ratio of its qualified voters as nearly as may be. And the members of the Council and of the House of Representatives shall reside in, and be inhabitants of, the district or county, or counties, for which they may be elected, respectively. Previous to the first election, the Governor shall cause a census, or enumeration of the inhabitants and qualified voters of the several counties and districts of the Territory, to be taken by such persons and in such mode as the Governor shall designate and appoint; and the persons so appointed shall receive a reasonable compensation therefor. And the first election shall be held at such time and places, and be conducted in such manner, both as to the persons who shall superintend such election and the returns thereof, as the Governor shall appoint and direct; and he shall at the same time declare the number of members of the Council and House of Representatives to which each of the counties or districts shall be entitled under this act. The persons having the highest number of legal votes in each of said Council Districts for members of the Council, shall be declared by the Governor to be duly elected to the Council; and the persons having the highest number of legal votes for the House of Representatives, shall be declared by the Governor to be duly elected members of said house: *Provided*, That in case two or more persons voted for

shall have an equal number of votes, and in case a vacancy shall otherwise occur in either branch of the Legislative Assembly, the Governor shall order a new election; and the persons thus elected to the Legislative Assembly shall meet at such place and on such day as the Governor shall appoint; but thereafter, the time, place, and manner of holding and conducting all elections by the people, and the apportioning the representation in the several counties or districts to the Council and House of Representatives, according to the number of qualified voters, shall be prescribed by law, as well as the day of the commencement of the regular sessions of the Legislative Assembly: *Provided*, That no session in any one year shall exceed the term of forty days, except the first session, which may continue sixty days.

SEC. 23. *And be it further enacted*, That every free white male inhabitant above the age of twenty-one years, who shall be an actual resident of said Territory, and shall possess the qualifications hereinafter prescribed, shall be entitled to vote at the first election, and shall be eligible to any office within the said Territory; but the qualifications of voters, and of holding office, at all subsequent elections, shall be such as shall be prescribed by the Legislative Assembly: *Provided*, That the right of suffrage and of holding office shall be exercised only by citizens of the United States, and those who shall have declared, on oath, their intention to become such, and shall have taken an oath to support the Constitution of the United States and the provisions of this act: And, provided further, That no officer, soldier, seaman, or marine, or other person in the army or navy of the United States, or attached to troops in the service of the United States, shall be allowed to vote or hold office in said Territory by reason of being on service therein.

SEC. 24. *And be it further enacted*, That the legislative power of the Territory shall extend to all rightful subjects of legislation consistent with the Constitution of the United States and the provisions of this act; but no law shall be passed interfering with the primary disposal of the soil; no tax shall be imposed upon the property of the United States; nor shall the lands or other property of non-residents be taxed higher than the lands or other property of residents. Every bill which shall have passed the Council and House of Representatives of the said Territory shall, before it become a law, be presented to the Governor of the Territory; if he approve, he shall sign it; but if not, he shall return it with his objections to the house in which it originated, who shall enter the objections at large on their journal, and proceed to reconsider it. If, after such reconsideration, two thirds of that house shall agree to pass the bill, it shall be sent, together with the objections, to the other house, by which, it shall likewise be reconsidered, and, if approved by two thirds of that house, it shall become a law. But in all such cases the votes of both houses shall be determined by yeas and nays, to be entered on the journal of each house, respectively. If any bill shall not be returned by the Governor within three days (Sundays excepted) after it shall have been presented to him, the same shall be a law in like manner as if he had signed it, unless the Assembly, by adjournment, prevent its return, in which case it shall not be a law.

SEC. 25. *And be it further enacted,* That all township, district, and; county officers, not herein otherwise provided for, shall be appointed or elected as the case may be, in such manner as shall be provided by the Governor and Legislative Assembly of the Territory of Kansas. The Governor shall nominate, and, by and with the advice and consent of the Legislative Council, appoint all officers not herein otherwise provided for; and, in the first instance, the Governor alone may appoint all said officers, who shall hold their offices until the end of the first session of the Legislative Assembly; and shall lay off the necessary districts for members of the Council and House of Representatives, and all other officers.

SEC. 26. *And be it further enacted,* That no member of the Legislative Assembly shall hold, or be appointed to, any office which shall have been created, or the salary or emoluments of which shall have been increased, while he was a member, during the term for which he was elected, and for one year after the expiration of such term; but this restriction shall not be applicable to members of the first Legislative Assembly; and no person holding a commission or appointment under the United States, except postmasters, shall be a member of the Legislative Assembly, or shall hold any office under the government of said Territory.

SEC. 27. *And be it further enacted,* That the judicial power of said Territory shall be vested in a supreme court, district courts, probate courts, and in justices of the peace. The Supreme Court shall Consist of chief justice and two associate justices, any two of whom shall constitute a quorum, and who shall hold a term at the seat of government of said Territory annually; and they shall hold their offices during the period of four years, and until their successors shall be appointed and qualified. The said Territory shall be divided into three judicial districts, and a dis-

trict court shall be held in each of said districts by one of the justices of the Supreme Court, at such times and places as may be prescribed by law; and the said judges shall, after their appointments, respectively, reside in the districts which shall be assigned them. The jurisdiction of the several courts herein provided for, both appellate and original, and that of the probate courts and of justices of the peace, shall be as limited by law: *Provided,* That justices of the peace shall not have jurisdiction of any matter in controversy when the title or boundaries of land may be in dispute, or where the debt or sum claimed shall exceed one hundred dollars; and the said supreme and district courts, respectively, shall possess chancery as well as common law jurisdiction. Said District Court, or the judge thereof, shall appoint its clerk, who shall also be the register in chancery, and shall keep his office at the place where the court may be held. Writs of error, bills of exception, and appeals shall be allowed in all cases from the final decisions of said district courts to the Supreme Court, under such regulations as may be prescribed by law; but in no case removed to the Supreme Court shall trial by jury be allowed in said court. The Supreme Court, or the justices thereof, shall appoint its own clerk, and every clerk shall hold his office at the pleasure of the court for which he shall have been appointed. Writs of error, and appeals from the final decisions of said supreme court, shall be allowed, and may be taken to the Supreme Court of the United States, in the same manner and under the same regulations as from the Circuit Courts of the United States, where the value of the property, or the amount in controversy, to be ascertained by the oath or affirmation of either party, or other competent witness, shall exceed one thousand dollars; except only that in all cases involving title to slaves, the said writ of error or appeals shall be allowed and decided by said supreme court, without regard to the value of the matter, property, or title in controversy; and except also that a writ of error or appeal shall also be allowed to the Supreme Court of the United States, from the decision of the said supreme court created by this act, or of any judge thereof, or of the district courts created by this act, or of any judge thereof, upon any writ of habeas corpus, involving the question of personal freedom: *Provided,* That nothing herein contained shall be construed to apply to or affect the provisions of the "act respecting fugitives from justice, and persons escaping from the service of their masters," approved February twelfth, seventeen hundred and ninety-three, and the "act to amend and supplementary to the aforesaid act," approved September eighteenth, eighteen hundred and fifty; and each of the said district courts shall have and exercise the same jurisdiction in all cases arising under the Constitution and laws of the United States as is vested in the Circuit and District Courts of the United States; and the said supreme and district courts of the said Territory, and the respective judges thereof, shall and may grant writs of habeas corpus in all cases in which the same are granted by the judges of the United States in the District of Columbia; and the first six days of every term of said courts, or so much thereof as may be neccssary, shall be appropriated to the trial of causes arising under the said Constitution and laws, and writs of error and appeal in all such cases shall-be made to the Supreme Court of said Territory, the same as in other cases. The said clerk shall receive the same fees in all such cases, which the clerks of the district courts of Utah Territory now receive for similar services.

SEC. 28. *And be it further enacted,* That the provisions of the act entitled "An act respecting fugitives from justice, and persons escaping from, the service of their masters," approved February twelfth, seventeen hundred and ninety-three, and the provisions of the act entitled "An act to amend, and supplementary to, the aforesaid act," approved September eighteenth, eighteen hundred and fifty, be, and the same are hereby, declared to extend to and be in full force within the limits of the said Territory of Kansas.

SEC. 29. *And be it further enacted,* That there shall be appointed an attorney for said Territory, who shall continue in office for four years, and until his successor shall be appointed and qualified, unless sooner removed by the President, and who shall receive the same fees and salary as the Attorney of the United States for the present Territory of Utah. There shall also be a marshal for the Territory appointed, who shall hold his office for four years, and until his successor shall be appointed and qualified, unless sooner removed by the President, and who shall execute all processes issuing from the said courts where exercising their jurisdiction as Circuit and District Courts of the United States; he shall perform the duties, be subject to the same regulations and penalties, and be entitled to the same fees, as the Marshal of the District Court of the United States for the present Territory of Utah, and shall, in addition, be paid two hundred dollars annually as a compensation for extra services.

SEC. 30. *And be it further enacted,* That the Governor, Secretary, Chief Justice, and Associate Justices, Attorney, and Marshal, shall be nominated, and, by and with the advice and consent of the Senate, appointed by the President of the United States. The Governor and Secretary to be appointed as aforesaid shall, before they act as such, respectively take an oath or affirmation before the district judge or some justice of the peace in the limits of said Territory, duly authorized to administer oaths and affirmations by the laws now in force therein, or before the Chief Justice or some Associate Justice of the Supreme Court of the United States, to support the Constitution of the United States, and faithfully to discharge the duties of their respective offices, which said oaths, when so taken, shall be certified by the person by whom the same shall have been taken; and such certificates shall be received and recorded by the said secretary among the executive proceedings; and the Chief Justice and Associate Justices, and all other civil officers in said Territory, before they act as such, shall take a like oath or affirmation before the said Governor or Secretary, or some Judge or Justice of the Peace of the Territory who may be duly commissioned and qualified, which said oath or affirmation shall be certified and transmitted by the person taking the same to the Secretary, to be by him recorded as aforesaid; and, afterwards, the like oath or affirmation shall be taken, certified, and recorded, in such manner and form as may be prescribed by law. The Governor shall receive an annual salary of two thousand five hundred dollars. The Chief Justice and Associate Justices shall receive As an annual salary of two thousand dollars. The Secretary shall receive an annual salary of two thousand dollars. The said salaries shall be paid quarter-yearly, from the dates of the respective appointments, at the Treasury of the United States; but no such payment shall be made until said officers shall have entered upon the duties of their respective appointments. The members of the Legislative Assembly shall be entitled to receive three dollars each per day during their attendance at the sessions thereof, and three dollars each for every twenty miles' travel in going to and returning from the said sessions, estimated according to the nearest usually travelled route; and an additional allowance of three dollars shall be paid to the presiding officer of each house for each day he shall so preside. And a chief clerk, one assistant clerk, a sergeant at-arms, and door-keeper, may be chosen for each house; and the chief clerk shall receive four dollars per day, and the said other officers three dollars per day, during the session of the Legislative Assembly; but no to other officers shall be paid by the United States: *Provided,* That there shall be but one session of the Legislature annually, unless, on an extraordinary occasion, the Governor shall think proper to call the Legislature together. There shall be appropriated, annually, the usual sum, to be expended by the Governor, to defray the contingent expenses of the Territory, including the salary of a clerk of the Executive Department and there shall also be appropriated, annually, a sufficient sum, to be expended by the Secretary of the Territory, and upon an estimate to be made by the Secretary of the Treasury of the United States, to defray the expenses of the Legislative Assembly, the printing of the laws, and other incidental expenses; and the Governor and Secretary of the Territory shall, in the disbursement of all moneys intrusted to them, be governed solely by the instructions of the secretary of the Treasury of the United States, and shall, semi-annually, account to the said secretary for lit the manner in which the aforesaid moneys shall have been expended; and no expenditure shall be made by said Legislative Assembly for objects not specially authorized by the acts of Congress making the appropriations, nor beyond the sums thus appropriated for such objects.

SEC. 31. *And be it further enacted*, That the seat of government of said Territory is hereby located temporarily at Fort Leavenworth; and that such portions of the public buildings as may not be actually used and needed for military purposes, may be occupied and used, under the direction of the Governor and Legislative Assembly, for such public purposes as may be required under the provisions of this act.

SEC. 32. *And be it further enacted*, That a delegate to the House of Representatives of the United States, to serve for the term of two years, who shall be a citizen of the United States, may be elected by the voters qualified to elect members of the Legislative Assembly, who shall be entitled to the same rights and privileges as are exercised and enjoyed by the delegates from the several other Territories of the United States to the said House of Representatives, but the delegate first elected shall hold his seat only during the term of the Congress to which he shall be elected. The first election shall be held at such time and places, and be conducted in such manner, as the Governor shall appoint and direct; and at all subsequent elections, the times, places, and manner of holding the elections shall be prescribed by law. The person having the greatest number of votes shall be declared by the Governor to be duly elected, and a certificate thereof shall be given accordingly. That the Constitution, and all laws of the United States which are not locally inapplicable, shall have the same force and effect within the said Territory of

Kansas as elsewhere within the United States, except the eighth section of the act preparatory to the admission of Missouri into the Union, approved March sixth, eighteen hundred and twenty, which, being inconsistent with the principle of non-intervention by Congress with slavery in the States and Territories, as recognized by the legislation of eighteen hundred and fifty, commonly called the Compromise Measures, is hereby declared inoperative and void; it being the true intent and meaning of this act not to legislate slavery into any Territory or State, nor to exclude it therefrom, but to leave the people thereof perfectly free to form and regulate their domestic institutions in their own way, subject only to the Constitution of the United States: *Provided*, That nothing herein contained shall be construed to revive or put in force any law or regulation which may have existed prior to the act of sixth of March, eighteen hundred and twenty, either protecting, establishing, prohibiting, or abolishing slavery.

SEC. 33. *And be it further enacted*, That there shall hereafter be appropriated, as has been customary for the territorial governments, a sufficient amount, to be expended under the direction of the said Governor of the Territory of Kansas, not exceeding the sums heretofore appropriated for similar objects, for the erection of suitable public buildings at the seat of government, and for the purchase of a library, to be kept at the seat of government for the use of the Governor, Legislative Assembly, Judges of the Supreme Court, Secretary, Marshal, and Attorney of said Territory, and such other persons, and under such regulations, as shall be prescribed by law.

SEC. 34. *And be it further enacted*, That when the lands in the said Territory shall be surveyed under the direction of the government of the United States, preparatory to bringing the same into market, sections numbered sixteen and thirty-six in each township in said Territory shall be, and the same are hereby, reserved for the purpose of being applied to schools in said Territory, and in the States and Territories hereafter to be erected out of the same.

SEC. 35. *And be it further enacted*, That, until otherwise provided by law, the Governor of said Territory may define the Judicial Districts of said Territory, and assign the judges who may be appointed for said Territory to the several districts; and also appoint the times and places forholding courts in the several counties or subdivisions in each of said judicial districts by proclamation, to be issued by him; but the Legislative Assembly, at their first or any subsequent session, may organize, alter, or modify such judicial districts, and assign the judges, and alter the times and places of holding the courts as to them shall seem proper and convenient.

SEC. 36. *And be it further enacted*, That all officers to be appointed by the President, by and with the advice and consent of the Senate, for the Territory of Kansas, who, by virtue of the provisions of any law now existing, or which may be enacted during the present Congress, are required to give security for moneys that may be intrusted with them for disbursement, shall give such security, at such time and place, and in such manner as the Secretary of the Treasury may prescribe.

SEC. 37. *And be it further enacted*, That all treaties, laws, and other engagements made by the government of the United States with the Indian tribes inhabiting the territories embraced within this act, shall be faithfully and rigidly observed, notwithstanding any thing contained in this act; and that the existing agencies and superintendencies of said Indians be continued with the same powers and duties which are now prescribed by law, except that the President of the United States may, at his discretion, change the location of the office of superintendent.

Approved, May 30, 1854.

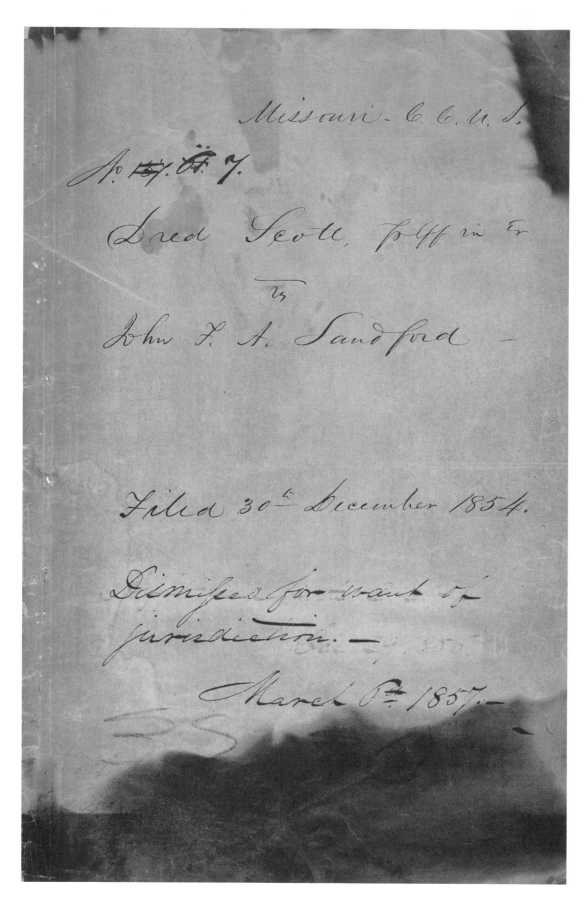

Missouri – C. C. U. S.

No. 17. O. 7.

Dred Scott, plff in Er

vs

John F. A. Sandford –

Filed 30th December 1854.

Dismissed for want of jurisdiction. –

March 6th 1857. –

Dred Scott v. Sandford (National Archives and Records Administration)

DRED SCOTT V. SANDFORD

"[African Americans] are not included, and were not intended to be included, under the word 'citizens' in the Constitution."

Overview

In March 1857 Chief Justice Roger B. Taney announced the opinion of the U.S. Supreme Court in *Dred Scott v. John F. A. Sandford*, which was the Court's most important decision ever issued on slavery. The decision had a dramatic effect on American politics as well as law. The case involved a Missouri slave named Dred Scott who claimed to be free because his master had taken him to what was then the Wisconsin Territory and is today the state of Minnesota. In the Missouri Compromise (also known as the Compromise of 1820), Congress has declared that there would be no slavery north of the state of Missouri. Thus, Scott claimed to be free because he had lived in a federal territory where slavery was not allowed. In an opinion that was more than fifty pages long, Chief Justice Taney held that Scott was still a slave, that the Missouri Compromise was unconstitutional, and that Congress had no power to ban slavery from a federal territory. In a part of the decision that shocked many northerners, Chief Justice Taney also held that blacks could never be citizens of the United States and that they had no rights under the Constitution. With notorious bluntness, Taney declared that blacks were "so far inferior, that they had no rights which the white man was bound to respect." The decision was criticized by many northerners and led many to support the new Republican Party. While it is an exaggeration to say the case caused the Civil War, Chief Justice Taney's decision certainly inflamed sectional tensions. It also helped lead to the nomination and election of Abraham Lincoln in 1860, which in turn led to secession and the war.

Context

In the Northwest Ordinance of 1787 the Congress, under the Articles of Confederation, banned slavery from all of the territories north and west of the Ohio River. This area, known as the Northwest Territory, would ultimately become the states of Ohio, Indiana, Illinois, Michigan, and Wisconsin. At the time, the western boundary of the Unit-

ed States was the Mississippi River. The territory west of the Mississippi belonged to Spain.

In 1802 Spain ceded its territories north of Mexico to France, and in 1803 the United States acquired all this land through the Louisiana Purchase. Most of the Louisiana Purchase territory was directly west of the Ohio River and north of the point where the Ohio flowed into the Mississippi. In 1812 Louisiana entered the Union as a slave state without any controversy. In 1818 when Missouri sought admission to the Union as a slave state, however, a number of members of Congress from the North objected on the ground that Missouri should be governed by the Northwest Ordinance. This led to a protracted two-year debate over the status of slavery in Missouri. In the end Congress accepted a compromise developed by Representative Henry Clay of Kentucky. Known as the Missouri Compromise, the law allowed Missouri to enter the Union as a slave state and admitted Maine as a free state. The law also prohibited slavery north and west of Missouri.

At the time of these debates Dred Scott was a slave in Virginia. In 1830 his master, Peter Blow, moved to St. Louis, taking Dred Scott with him. In 1832 Peter Blow died, and shortly after that Dred Scott was sold to Captain John Emerson, a U.S. Army surgeon. In 1833 Emerson was sent to Fort Armstrong, which was located on the site of the modern-day city of Rock Island, Illinois. Scott might have claimed his freedom while at Fort Armstrong, because Illinois was a free state. Under the accepted rule of law at the time, slaves could usually become free if their masters voluntarily brought them to a free state. Indeed, as early as 1824 the Missouri Supreme Court had freed a slave named Winny because her master had taken her to Illinois. In 1836 the Missouri Supreme Court freed another slave woman, Rachel, because her master, who was in the army, had taken her to forts in present-day Michigan and Minnesota. However, Scott, who was illiterate, probably did not know he could be freed, and he made no effort to gain his freedom at this time.

In 1836 the army sent Emerson to Fort Snelling in what is today the city of St. Paul, Minnesota. At the time, this area was called the Wisconsin Territory, and slavery was illegal there under the Missouri Compromise. Once again, Scott might have claimed his freedom because of his resi-

Time Line

1795–1800
- Dred Scott is born in Virginia. The exact date and year are unknown.

1821
- Missouri enters the Union as a slave state under the Missouri Compromise, which bans slavery north and west of Missouri.

1830
- Peter Blow moves to St. Louis with his slave Dred Scott.

1831
- **January 1**
  In Boston the abolitionist William Lloyd Garrison begins to publish the *Liberator*, the first successful abolitionist newspaper in the United States.

- **August 21**
  In Southampton County, Virginia, Nat Turner leads the bloodiest slave rebellion in American history, leaving white southerners deeply shaken as more than fifty whites and about one hundred blacks die.

1832–1833
- Peter Blow, Dred Scott's owner, dies in St. Louis in 1832.

- Captain John Emerson, a U.S. Army surgeon, purchases Dred Scott from the estate of Peter Blow.

1833
- **December 1**
  Emerson is assigned to Fort Armstrong, on the present-day site of Rock Island, Illinois. He brings Dred Scott with him.

1836
- **May 4**
  Emerson transfers to Fort Snelling, bringing Dred Scott with him.

1837
- **November**
  Emerson transfers to Fort Jessup in Louisiana, but he leaves Dred Scott and his wife at Fort Snelling, where they are rented out.

---

dence in a free jurisdiction, but he did not. From 1836 to 1840 Scott lived at Fort Snelling, at Fort Jessup in Louisiana, and then again at Fort Snelling. During this time he married a slave named Harriet, who was then owned by Lawrence Taliaferro, the Indian agent at Fort Snelling. Taliaferro either sold or gave Harriet to Emerson so the newly married couple could be together. In 1838 Emerson married Irene Sanford.

In 1840 Captain Emerson left the Scotts and their two daughters in St. Louis while he went to Florida during the Second Seminole War. In 1842 Emerson left the army and moved to Iowa, a free territory, but he left his slaves and his wife in St. Louis. In 1843 Dr. Emerson died, and ownership of the Scotts passed to Irene Sanford Emerson.

At this point Dred Scott attempted to purchase his freedom with the help of the sons of his former master, Peter Blow. However, Irene Emerson refused to allow Scott to buy his freedom. Thus, in 1846 a lawyer—the first of five who volunteered to help Scott—filed a suit in St. Louis Circuit Court, claiming that he had become free while living in both Illinois and the Wisconsin Territory (Minnesota) and that once free he could not be reenslaved when he returned to Missouri. By this time there had been numerous cases on the issue in the Missouri courts, and usually slaves who had lived in free states or territories were declared free. For technical reasons, however, Dred Scott did not get his hearing until 1850, about four years after he first sued for freedom. At that point a jury of twelve white men, sitting in the slave state of Missouri, declared Scott and his family to be free.

This should have ended the case, but Irene Emerson appealed to the Missouri Supreme Court in an effort to retain her property. The Scotts were a valuable asset. In addition, while the case had been pending, the Court had hired out the Scotts and kept their wages in an account. Thus, Irene Emerson was trying to keep four slaves plus the wages of Dred and Harriet for the previous four years.

Under the existing precedents Irene Emeson should not have held out much hope that she would win her case. However, a recent amendment to the Missouri Constitution provided for the election of the state supreme court, and in 1851 a new court took office. Two of the new justices were adamantly proslavery. It therefore seemed like the right time for Mrs. Emerson to challenge the decisions that had led to Scott's freedom.

In 1852 the Missouri Supreme Court, by a two-to-one vote, reversed the decision freeing Dred Scott. Reflecting his proslavery sentiments and his hostility to the growing antislavery movement in the North, Justice William Scott (who was not related to Dred Scott) declared that the state would no longer follow its own precedents on slavery. This decision revolutionized Missouri law, but it was consistent with decisions in some Deep South states, which had also abandoned the idea that slaves could become free if they were brought to free states.

Dred Scott's quest for freedom should have ended here, because there was no higher court where he could appeal the decision. Under American law at the time, Scott had no grounds for appealing to the U.S. Supreme Court because no constitutional issue had been raised in the case. The federal courts did not have jurisdiction over the status of slaves within the states.

By this time, however, Mrs. Emerson had moved east and married another physician, Dr. Calvin Chaffee of Springfield, Massachusetts. She could not take her slaves with her because slavery was illegal in Massachusetts. Moreover, her new husband was a firm opponent of slavery, and any discussion of her property interest in the Scotts might have undermined her new marriage. Thus, she either gave or sold the Scotts to her brother, John F. A. Sanford, who lived in New York City but had business interests in both St. Louis and New York. (He spelled his last name Sanford, but the clerk of the U.S. Supreme Court would add an extra "d" to his name, and thus the case would be known as *Dred Scott v. Sandford*.)

Sanford's residence in New York opened up the possibility that Dred Scott could now reopen his case in a federal court. Under the Constitution citizens of one state are allowed to sue citizens of another state. This is known as diversity jurisdiction, because there is a diversity (or difference) in the state citizenship of the people involved in the lawsuit. The framers of the Constitution believed that it was necessary for federal courts to be able to hear suits between citizens of different states because otherwise the people would fear that the courts of one state would favor the state's own citizens. The federal courts presumably would be neutral.

Thus, in 1853 Scott's newest lawyer filed a suit in federal court against John Sanford. Scott alleged that he was a "citizen" of Missouri and sued Sanford for assault and battery, asking for $10,000 in damages. Sanford responded with something called a plea in abatement. In this response Sanford argued that the court should abate (stop) the case immediately because, as Sanford argued, Dred Scott "was not a citizen of the State of Missouri, as alleged in his declaration, being a negro of African descent, whose ancestors were of pure African blood, and who were brought into this country and sold as slaves." In essence, Sanford argued that no black person could be a citizen of Missouri, so even if Dred Scott was free, the federal court did not have jurisdiction to hear the case.

In 1854 U.S. District Judge Robert Wells rejected this argument. He held that *if* Dred Scott was free, then he should be considered a citizen for the purpose of diversity jurisdiction. This was the first and only victory Dred Scott had in the federal courts. After hearing all the evidence, Wells decided that Scott's status had to be determined by applying the law of Missouri. Since the Missouri Supreme Court had already held that Scott was not free, Judge Wells ruled against Scott. This set the stage for the case to go to the U.S. Supreme Court. In the December 1855 term the Supreme Court heard arguments in the case, but in the spring of 1856, with a presidential election looming, the Court declined to decide the case and instead asked for new arguments in the next term, beginning in December 1856, which was after the election.

Time Line

1838

■ **February 6**
Emerson marries Irene Sanford and brings the Scotts to Louisiana.

■ **July**
Emerson is reassigned to Fort Snelling, and the Scotts accompany him.

1840

■ Emerson is reassigned to Florida, and the Scotts are left in St. Louis with Irene Emerson.

1843

■ **December**
Emerson dies, and ownership of Scotts passes to Irene Emerson.

1846

■ Dred Scott files suit to gain freedom in St. Louis Circuit Court; he loses the suit on a technicality.

1848

■ The Missouri Supreme Court grants Dred Scott the right to have a new trial to test his freedom.

■ **February 2**
Treaty of Guadalupe Hidalgo ends Mexican-American War.

1850

■ A jury of twelve white men in St. Louis, Missouri, declares Dred Scott free, based on his residence in Illinois and at Fort Snelling.

■ Congress passes a series of statutes collectively known as the Compromise of 1850.

■ **November**
Irene Emerson marries Dr. Calvin Chafee of Springfield, Massachusetts. Her brother, John F. A. Sanford, continues to defend her claim to Dred Scott.

1852

■ In *Scott v. Emerson* the Missouri Supreme Court overturns nearly three decades of precedents and reverses Dred Scott's victory in the lower court.

1853

■ Dred Scott initiates a new suit, against John F. A. Sanford, in the U.S. Circuit Court for Missouri.

1854

■ U.S. Judge Robert Wells allows Dred Scott to sue in federal court but then rules against him. Scott remains a slave.

1856

■ December
U.S. Supreme Court hears arguments in Dred Scott case.

1857

■ March 4
James Buchanan is inaugurated as president. In his address he urges all Americans to support the outcome of the pending case on slavery in the territories (the Dred Scott case).

■ March 6
Chief Justice Taney announces his decision in *Dred Scott v. Sandford*.

■ May 26
Taylor Blow, the son of Peter Blow, formally manumits the Scotts, having purchased them from John Sanford after the Supreme Court decision.

1858

■ September 17
Dred Scott dies in St. Louis from tuberculosis.

While Dred Scott's case was making its way through the courts, slavery had emerged as the central issue of American politics. In 1820 the Missouri Compromise had settled the issue of slavery in the territories. Starting in 1836, however, the Republic of Texas requested to become part of the United States. Presidents Andrew Jackson and Martin Van Buren resisted accepting Texas because they knew that bringing Texas into the Union would reopen the issue of slavery in the West and probably would lead to a war with Mexico. In late 1844 President John Tyler, who was coming to the end of his term, managed to get Congress to accept Texas, which entered the Union in 1845. This immediately let to a confrontation with Mexico, which had never recognized Texas independence. In April 1846 American and Mexican troops clashed, and by May the two nations were at war. The war ended in September 1847, when General Zachary Taylor entered Mexico City. In the Treaty of Guadalupe Hidalgo, signed on February 2, 1848,

Mexico recognized the Texas annexation and ceded all of its northern lands, which included all or part of the present-day states of California, Arizona, New Mexico, Nevada, Utah, and Colorado.

The acquisition of this territory, known as the Mexican Cession, led to a crisis in the Union as the nation debated the status of slavery in the new territories. Congress finally broke the deadlock with a series of statutes collectively known as the Compromise of 1850. These laws allowed slavery in the new territories but admitted California as a free state. This compromise did not satisfy the South, which wanted to repeal the restrictions on slavery in the Missouri Compromise. This was accomplished in 1854 with the passage of the Kansas-Nebraska Act. This law allowed the creation of territorial governments in the territories west and northwest of Missouri—including the present-day states of Kansas, Nebraska, South Dakota, and North Dakota—without regard to slavery. The law allowed the settlers of these territories to decide for themselves whether or not to allow slavery.

The Kansas-Nebraska Act had two immediate results. First was a revolution in politics and the emergence of a new political organization that became the Republican Party. By 1856 it was the dominant party in the North. Its main goal was to prevent the spread of slavery into the territories. Meanwhile, in Kansas a small civil war broke out between supporters and opponents of slavery. Known as Bleeding Kansas, the conflict claimed more than fifty lives in 1855 and 1856.

In 1856 the new Republican Party nominated John C. Frémont for the presidency. Frémont, nicknamed "the Pathfinder," was a national hero for his explorations in the West and his role in securing California during the Mexican-American War. Running on a slogan of "Free Soil, Free Labor, Free Speech, Free Men," Frémont and the new party carried eleven northern states. This was not enough to win but was nevertheless a very impressive showing for a brand-new party. The winning candidate, James Buchanan, was a Pennsylvanian but strongly sympathetic to the South and slavery. He supported opening all of the territories to slavery. In his inaugural address Buchanan declared that the issue of slavery in the territories was a question for the judicial branch and urged Americans to accept the outcome of the Court's pending ruling in the Dred Scott case. Buchanan could so confidently take this position because two justices on the court, Robert C. Grier and John Catron, had told him how the case would be decided. Two days later Chief Justice Taney announced the decision. Rather than settling the issue of slavery in the territories, the decision only made it more troublesome and controversial.

About the Author

Roger Brooke Taney (pronounced Tawnee) had a long and distinguished career in American politics and law. He was born in 1777 into a wealthy slaveholding family on the eastern shore of Maryland. He served in the Maryland legislature as a Federalist, but in the 1820s he became a supporter of Andrew Jackson. He was attorney general in Jackson's administration and drafted what became Jackson's famous veto in 1831 of the bill to recharter the Second Bank of the United States. As a young lawyer he freed his own slaves because he had no use for them, but he never opposed slavery or favored abolition. As attorney general he prepared a detailed opinion for President Jackson asserting that free blacks were not entitled to passports and could never be considered citizens of the United States. Taney served briefly as secretary of the treasury, overseeing the removal of deposits from the Bank of the United States.

In 1837 Taney became chief justice of the United States, a position he held until 1864, longer than any other chief justice except John Marshall. As chief justice he was a staunch supporter of slavery and the interests of the southern states. By 1857, when he delivered his opinion in Dred Scott's case, Taney was deeply hostile to abolitionism and vigorously proslavery. In 1860 and 1861 he tacitly supported secession and opposed all of President Lincoln's efforts to maintain the Union, suppress the insurrection, and end slavery. When Taney died in 1864, the U.S. Senate refused to authorize a statue for him, as it had for other deceased justices. In arguing against the proposal for a statue, Senator Charles Sumner of Massachusetts declared that Taney had "administered justice at last wickedly, and degraded the judiciary of the country, and degraded the age." He predicted that "the name is to be hooted down the pages of history" (rpt. in Finkelman, 1997, p. 222).

Explanation and Analysis of the Document

All nine justices wrote an opinion in this case. The opinions range in length from Justice Robert C. Grier's half-page concurrence to Justice Benjamin R. Curtis's seventy-page dissent. Chief Justice Taney's "Opinion of the Court" is fifty-four pages long. The nine opinions, along with a handful of pages summarizing the lawyers' arguments, consume 260 pages of United States Supreme Court Reports. In his opinion Chief Justice Taney declared that the Missouri Compromise was unconstitutional. This was only the second Supreme Court decision to strike down a federal law. The only other antebellum decision to strike down a federal act—Marbury v. Madison (1803)—held unconstitutional a minor portion of the Judiciary Act of 1789. Here the Court struck down a major statute.

In his opinion Chief Justice Taney discusses three issues: black citizenship, the constitutionality of the Missouri Compromise, and the power of Congress to ban slavery from the territories. First he examines whether the question of citizenship is legitimately before the Court. The lower federal court had assumed that if Dred Scott was free, he was a citizen of the state where he lived, and he had a right to sue a citizen of another state in federal court. Taney rejects this conclusion. Since the 1830s he had believed that blacks could never be citizens of the United States. Now he had a chance to make his views the law.

An 1887 engraving of Dred Scott (Library of Congress)

Taney bases his argument entirely on race. In a very inaccurate history of the founding period, which ignored the fact that free blacks had voted in a number of states at the time of the ratification of the Constitution, Taney asserts that at the founding of the nation blacks, whether enslaved or free, were without any political or legal rights. He declares that blacks

are not included, and were not intended to be included, under the word "citizens" in the Constitution, and can therefore claim none of the rights and privileges which that instrument provides for and secures to citizens of the United States. On the contrary, they were at that time [1787] considered as a subordinate and inferior class of beings, who had been subjugated by the dominant race, and, whether emancipated or not, yet remained subject to their authority, and had no rights or privileges but such as those who held the power and the Government might choose to grant them.

In one of the most notoriously racist statement in American law, Taney declares that blacks are "so far inferior, that they had no rights which the white man was bound to respect." He therefore concludes that blacks could never be citizens of the United States, even if they were born in the country and considered to be citizens of the states in which they live.

Justice Roger B. Taney wrote the Court's majority opinion in **Dred Scott v. Sandford.** (Library of Congress)

Taney then turns to the issue of slavery in the territories. Here he discusses the constitutionality of the Missouri Compromise and the status of slavery in the territories. His goal was to settle, in favor of the South, the status of slavery in the territories. To do this Taney had to overcome two strong arguments in favor of congressional power over slavery in the territories. First was the clause in the Constitution that explicitly gave Congress the power to regulate the territories. Second was the political tradition, dating from the Northwest Ordinance, that Congress had such a power. Taney accomplished this through an examination of two separate provisions of the Constitution: the territories clause and the Fifth Amendment.

The territories clause of the Constitution, Article IV, Section 3, Paragraph 2, provides that "Congress shall have Power to dispose of and make all needful Rules and Regulations respecting the Territory or other Property belonging to the United States." Congress had used this clause to govern the territories, prohibiting slavery in some territories and allowing it in others. As recently as 1854 Congress had passed the Kansas-Nebraska Act, allowing the settlers of a territory to allow or ban slavery as they wished. Almost all Americans assumed that Congress had the power to prohibit slavery in the territories. One American who did not was Chief Justice Taney.

In his opinion Taney interprets the territories clause to apply only to those territories the United States had owned in 1787. Taney writes that the clause is

confined, and was intended to be confined, to the territory which at that time belonged to, or was claimed by, the United States, and was within their boundaries as settled by the treaty with Great Britain, and can have no influence upon a territory afterwards acquired from a foreign Government. It was a special provision for a known and particular territory, and to meet a present emergency, and nothing more.

Few scholars today find this argument even remotely plausible. This was also true in 1857. Justice John Catron, who agreed with Taney on almost every other point, dissented from the claim that Congress could not pass laws to regulate the territories. Nevertheless, Taney asserts that Congress has only the power to provide a minimal government in the territories, but nothing beyond that. Taney implies that allowing Congress to actually govern the territories would be equivalent to "establish[ing] or maintain[ing] colonies bordering on the United States or at a distance, to be ruled and governed at its own pleasure." Taney's argument here was absurd. By 1857 the United States had held some territory (what later became the eastern tip of Minnesota) for the entire period since the adoption of the Constitution without making it a state or treating it as a colony.

The weakness of his argument did not stop Taney, who was determined, as few justices have been, to reach a specific result. His goal was to prohibit the congressional regulation of slavery in the territories, and any argument, it seemed, would do the trick. However, if Congress could not govern the territories, then they would be governed by the settlers. What would happen if the settlers, such as those in Kansas, voted to prohibit slavery? Taney found an answer to this question in the Fifth Amendment to the U.S. Constitution, which prohibits the government from taking private property without due process of law.

Thus, Taney argues that forbidding slavery in the territories violates the due process clause of the Fifth Amendment, which declares that under federal law no person could "be deprived of life, liberty, or property without due process of law." Taney asserts that "an act of Congress which deprives a citizen of the United States of his liberty or property, merely because he came himself or brought his property into a particular Territory of the United States, and who had committed no offence against the laws, could hardly be dignified with the name of due process of law."

This led Taney to assert that slavery was a special form of property with special constitutional protection. Thus he writes:

the right of property in a slave is distinctly and expressly affirmed in the Constitution. The right to traffic in it, like an ordinary article of merchandise and property, was guaranteed to the citizens of the United States, in every State that might desire it, for twenty years. And the Government in express terms is pledged to protect it in all future time, if the slave escapes from

"No one, we presume, supposes that any change in public opinion or feeling, in relation to this unfortunate race, in the civilized nations of Europe or in this country, should induce the court to give to the words of the Constitution a more liberal construction in their favor than they were intended to bear when the instrument was framed and adopted."

(Chief Justice Roger Taney, Majority Opinion)

"They [African Americans] are not included, and were not intended to be included, under the word 'citizens' in the Constitution, and can therefore claim none of the rights and privileges which that instrument provides for and secures to citizens of the United States. On the contrary, they were at that time [1787] considered as a subordinate and inferior class of beings, who had been subjugated by the dominant race, and, whether emancipated or not, yet remained subject to their authority, and had no rights or privileges but such as those who held the power and the Government might choose to grant them."

(Chief Justice Roger Taney, Majority Opinion)

"The right of property in a slave is distinctly and expressly affirmed in the Constitution. The right to traffic in it, like an ordinary article of merchandise and property, was guaranteed to the citizens of the United States, in every State that might desire it, for twenty years. And the Government in express terms is pledged to protect it in all future time, if the slave escapes from his owner."

(Chief Justice Roger Taney, Majority Opinion)

"At the time of the ratification of the Articles of Confederation, all free native-born inhabitants of the States of New Hampshire, Massachusetts, New York, New Jersey, and North Carolina, though descended from African slaves, were not only citizens of those States, but such of them as had the other necessary qualifications possessed the franchise of electors, on equal terms with other citizens."

(Justice Benjamin R. Curtis, Dissenting Opinion)

his owner. This is done in plain words—too plain to be misunderstood. And no word can be found in the Constitution which gives Congress a greater power over slave property, or which entitles property of that kind to less protection than property of any other description. The only power conferred is the power coupled with the duty of guarding and protecting the owner in his rights.

This was perhaps Chief Justice Taney's strongest argument. The Constitution of 1787 clearly protected slavery in a number of places. It was an important and unique kind of property, and thus it needed to be protected. Moreover, Taney's argument that all citizens should be able to bring their property with them into every federal territory was not wholly wrong. Indeed, the heart of Taney's argument was that slavery was an important part of American society, therefore slave owners had to have equal access to federal lands.

Chief Justice Taney thus declared that any prohibition on slavery in the territories violated the Fifth Amendment. Even the people of a territory could not ban slavery through the territorial legislature. Taney writes, "And if Congress itself cannot do this—if it is beyond the powers conferred on the Federal Government—it will be admitted, we presume, that it could not authorize a Territorial Government to exercise them. It could confer no power on any local Government, established by its authority, to violate the provisions of the Constitution." Like the Missouri Compromise, under Taney's interpretation of the Constitution, popular sovereignty also was unconstitutional.

Six other justices agreed with all or some of Taney's decision. Four were from the South, and two, Samuel Nelson of New York and Robert C. Grier of Pennsylvania, were northern Democrats with southern sympathies. Two justices, John McLean of Ohio and Benjamin R. Curtis of Massachusetts, issued stinging dissents. Both pointed out, at great length, that Taney's history was wrong and that blacks voted in a number of states at the time of the country's founding. Both justices pointed out that since African Americans voted for the ratification of the Constitution in 1787, it was hard to argue that they could not be considered citizens of the nation they helped to create. The dissenters also stressed that since 1787 no one had doubted that Congress could regulate the territories and ban slavery in them. On both grounds they may have had the better historical arguments but not the votes on the Court.

Audience

The main audience for this law was the people of the United States, and particularly the Congress. Chief Justice Taney hoped this decision would forever settle the question of slavery in the territories and stop Congress from trying to ban slavery. He also hoped it would end the conflict in Kansas over slavery, because under this decision the Kansas territorial government could not prohibit slavery.

Impact

Few cases have had such a huge impact on American politics. Most southerners cheered the decision. So did President Buchanan, who hoped the decision would bring peace to Kansas and destroy the Republican Party, since its main platform was prohibiting slavery in the territories. It also undercut Buchanan's rival in the Democratic Party, Senator Stephen A. Douglas. He had been the leading proponent of popular sovereignty in the territories, which would have allowed the settlers in the territories to decide for themselves whether they wanted slavery. This had been the basis of the Kansas-Nebraska Act, which Douglas sponsored. Under *Dred Scott*, however, popular sovereignty was unconstitutional because the territorial governments were prohibited from banning slavery. Douglas would give tacit support for the decision, but it undermined his political strength in the North.

Republicans around the nation attacked the decision. Horace Greeley, the Republican editor of the *New York Tribune*, responded to the decision with outrage, calling Taney's opinion "wicked," "atrocious," and "abominable" and a "collation of false statements and shallow sophistries." The paper's editor thought Taney's decision had no more validity than the opinions that might be expressed in any "Washington bar-room" (Fehrenbacher, 1978, p. 417). The *Chicago Tribune* declared that Taney's statements on black citizenship were "inhuman dicta" (Fehrenbacher, 1978, p. 417). The black abolitionist Frederick Douglass called it a "devilish decision—this judicial incarnation of wolfishness!" (rpt. in Finkelman, 1997, p. 174). He also believed, however, that the decision would lead more people to oppose slavery. In 1858 Abraham Lincoln, in his "House Divided" Speech, attacked the decision and warned that if Republicans were not elected to office, the "next Dred Scott decision" would lead to the nationalization of slavery. Lincoln predicted, "We shall *lie down* pleasantly dreaming that the people of *Missouri* are on the verge of making their state *free*; and we shall *awake* to the *reality*, instead that the *Supreme* Court has made *Illinois* a *slave* state." Lincoln was convinced that the "logical conclusion" of Taney's opinion was that "what one master might lawfully do with Dred Scott, in the free state of Illinois, every master might lawfully do with any other *one*, or *one thousand* slaves in Illinois, or in any other free state" (Finkelman, 1997, pp. 185–195).

The decision helped make Abraham Lincoln a national figure and led to his nomination and election as president in 1861. The nation would overrule *Dred Scott* with the adoption of the Thirteenth Amendment to the Constitution in 1865, which ended all slavery in the United States, and the Fourteenth Amendment in 1868, which made all people born in the United States citizens of the United States.

Related Documents

Lincoln, Abraham. "House Divided Speech." In *Created Equal? The Complete Lincoln-Douglas Debates of 1858*, ed. Paul M.

Angle. Chicago: University of Chicago Press, 1958. In accepting the Republican nomination to run for the Senate in 1858, Lincoln focused most of his speech on the *Dred Scott* decision, arguing that it was part of a vast conspiracy to nationalize slavery. Lincoln considered his senatorial opponent, Stephan A. Douglas, to be one of the political leaders, along with Chief Justice Taney and President Buchanan, who were trying to nationalize slavery.

Bibliography

■ Books

Ehrlich, Walter. *They Have No Rights: Dred Scott's Struggle for Freedom* Westport, Conn.: Greenwood Press, 1979.

Fehrenbacher, Don E. *The Dred Scott Case: Its Significance in American Law and Politics.* New York: Oxford University Press, 1978.

——. *The Slaveholding Republic: An Account of the United States Government's Relations to Slavery.* New York: Oxford University Press, 2001.

Finkelman, Paul. *An Imperfect Union: Slavery, Federalism, and Comity.* Chapel Hill: University of North Carolina Press, 1981.

——. *Slavery in the Courtroom: An Annotated Bibliography of American Cases.* Washington, D.C.: Government Printing Office, 1985.

——. *Dred Scott v. Sandford: A Brief History with Documents.* Boston: Bedford Books, 1997.

— By Paul Finkelman

Questions for Further Study

1. While most Americans find Taney's decision morally wrong, do any of his arguments make sense?

2. Why do you think Dred Scott did not try to gain his freedom when he lived in Illinois or at Fort Snelling?

3. What are the legacies of the decision today? Are there ways in which the ideas of Chief Justice Taney might still be alive in our culture?

Glossary

jurisdiction	the power or right of a court to hear a case
mulatto	a person of mixed European and African ancestry; technically, a mulatto was considered half European and half African, but the term was more loosely used to describe all people with some African and some European ancestry

DRED SCOTT V. SANDFORD

Mr. Chief Justice Taney delivered the opinion of the court.

This case has been twice argued. After the argument at the last term, differences of opinion were found to exist among the members of the court; and as the questions in controversy are of the highest importance, and the court was at that time much pressed by the ordinary business of the term, it was deemed advisable to continue the case, and direct a re-argument on some of the points, in order that we might have an opportunity of giving to the whole subject a more deliberate consideration. It has accordingly been again argued by counsel, and considered by the court; and I now proceed to deliver its opinion. There are two leading questions presented by the record: 1. Had the Circuit Court of the United States jurisdiction to hear and determine the case between these parties? And 2. If it had jurisdiction, is the judgment it has given erroneous or not? The plaintiff in error, who was also the plaintiff in the court below, was, with his wife and children, held as slaves by the defendant, in the State of Missouri; and he brought this action in the Circuit Court of the United States for that district, to assert the title of himself and his family to freedom. The declaration is in the form usually adopted in that State to try questions of this description, and contains the averment necessary to give the court jurisdiction; that he and the defendant are citizens of different States; that is, that he is a citizen of Missouri, and the defendant a citizen of New York. The defendant pleaded in abatement to the jurisdiction of the court, that the plaintiff was not a citizen of the State of Missouri, as alleged in his declaration, being a negro of African descent, whose ancestors were of pure African blood, and who were brought into this country and sold as slaves. To this plea the plaintiff demurred, and the defendant joined in demurrer. The court overruled the plea, and gave judgment that the defendant should answer over.

And he thereupon put in sundry pleas in bar, upon which issues were joined; and at the trial the verdict and judgment were in his favor. Whereupon the plaintiff brought this writ of error. Before we speak of the pleas in bar, it will be proper to dispose of the questions which have arisen on the plea in abatement. That plea denies the right of the plaintiff to sue in a court of the United States, for the reasons therein stated. If the question raised by it is legally before us, and the court should be of opinion that the facts stated in it disqualify the plaintiff from becoming a citizen, in the sense in which that word is used in the Constitution of the United States, then the judgment of the Circuit Court is erroneous, and must be reversed. It is suggested, however, that this plea is not before us; and that as the judgment in the court below on this plea was in favor of the plaintiff, he does not seek to reverse it, or bring it before the court for revision by his writ of error; and also that the defendant waived this defence by pleading over, and thereby admitted the jurisdiction of the court. But, in making this objection, we think the peculiar and limited jurisdiction of courts of the United States has not been adverted to. This peculiar and limited jurisdiction has made it necessary, in these courts, to adopt different rules and principles of pleading, so far as jurisdiction is concerned, from those which regulate courts of common law in England, and in the different States of the Union which have adopted the common-law rules.

In these last-mentioned courts, where their character and rank are analogous to that of a Circuit Court of the United States; in other words, where they are what the law terms courts of general jurisdiction; they are presumed to have jurisdiction, unless the contrary appears. No averment in the pleadings of the plaintiff is necessary, in order to give jurisdiction. If the defendant objects to it, he must plead it specially, and unless the fact on which he relies is found to be true by a jury, or admitted to be true by the plaintiff, the jurisdiction cannot be disputed in an appellate court.

Now, it is not necessary to inquire whether in courts of that description a party who pleads over in bar, when a plea to the jurisdiction has been ruled against him, does or does not waive his plea; nor whether upon a judgment in his favor on the pleas in bar, and a writ of error brought by the plaintiff, the question upon the plea in abatement would be open for revision in the appellate court. Cases that may have been decided in such courts, or rules that may have been laid down by common-law pleaders, can have no influence in the decision in this court. Because, under the Constitution and laws of the United States, the rules which govern the pleadings in its courts, in questions of jurisdiction, stand on different principles and are regulated by different laws.

This difference arises, as we have said, from the peculiar character of the Government of the United States. For although it is sovereign and supreme in its appropriate sphere of action, yet it does not possess all the powers which usually belong to the sovereignty of a nation. Certain specified powers, enumerated in the Constitution, have been conferred upon it; and neither the legislative, executive, nor judicial departments of the Government can lawfully exercise any authority beyond the limits marked out by the Constitution. And in regulating the judicial department, the cases in which the courts of the United States shall have jurisdiction are particularly and specifically enumerated and defined; and they are not authorized to take cognizance of any case which does not come within the description therein specified. Hence, when a plaintiff sues in a court of the United States, it is necessary that he should show, in his pleading, that the suit he brings is within the jurisdiction of the court, and that he is entitled to sue there. And if he omits to do this, and should, by any oversight of the Circuit Court, obtain a judgment in his favor, the judgment would be reversed in the appellate court for want of jurisdiction in the court below. The jurisdiction would not be presumed, as in the case of a common-law English or State court, unless the contrary appeared. But the record, when it comes before the appellate court, must show, affirmatively, that the inferior court had authority, under the Constitution, to hear and determine the case. And if the plaintiff claims a right to sue in a Circuit Court of the United States, under that provision of the Constitution which gives jurisdiction in controversies between citizens of different States, he must distinctly aver in his pleading that they are citizens of different States; and he cannot maintain his suit without showing that fact in the pleadings.

This point was decided in the case of *Bingham v. Cabot*, (in 3 Dall., 382,) and ever since adhered to by the court. And in *Jackson v. Ashton*, (8 Pet., 148,) it was held that the objection to which it was open could not be waived by the opposite party, because consent of parties could not give jurisdiction.

It is needless to accumulate cases on this subject. Those already referred to, and the cases of *Capron v. Van Noorden*, (in 2 Cr., 126,) and *Montalet v. Murray*, (4 Cr., 46,) are sufficient to show the rule of which we have spoken. The case of *Capron v. Van Noorden* strikingly illustrates the difference between a common-law court and a court of the United States.

If, however, the fact of citizenship is averred in the declaration, and the defendant does not deny it, and put it in issue by plea in abatement, he cannot offer evidence at the trial to disprove it, and consequently cannot avail himself of the objection in the appellate court, unless the defect should be apparent in some other part of the record. For if there is no plea in abatement, and the want of jurisdiction does not appear in any other part of the transcript brought up by the writ of error, the undisputed averment of citizenship in the declaration must be taken in this court to be true. In this case, the citizenship is averred, but it is denied by the defendant in the manner required by the rules of pleading, and the fact upon which the denial is based is admitted by the demurrer. And, if the plea and demurrer, and judgment of the court below upon it, are before us upon this record, the question to be decided is, whether the facts stated in the plea are sufficient to show that the plaintiff is not entitled to sue as a citizen in a court of the United States. We think they are before us. The plea in abatement and the judgment of the court upon it, are a part of the judicial proceedings in the Circuit Court, and are there recorded as such; and a writ of error always brings up to the superior court the whole record of the proceedings in the court below. And in the case of the *United States v. Smith*, (11 Wheat., 172,) this court said, that the case being brought up by writ of error, the whole record was under the consideration of this court. And this being the case in the present instance, the plea in abatement is necessarily under consideration; and it becomes, therefore, our duty to decide whether the facts stated in the plea are or are not sufficient to show that the plaintiff is not entitled to sue as a citizen in a court of the United States.

This is certainly a very serious question, and one that now for the first time has been brought for decision before this court. But it is brought here by those who have a right to bring it, and it is our duty to meet it and decide it.

The question is simply this: Can a negro, whose ancestors were imported into this country, and sold as slaves, become a member of the political community formed and brought into existence by the Constitution of the United States, and as such become entitled to all the rights, and privileges, and immunities, guarantied by that instrument to the citizen? One of which rights is the privilege of suing in a court of the United States in the cases specified in the Constitution.

It will be observed, that the plea applies to that class of persons only whose ancestors were negroes of the African race, and imported into this country, and sold and held as slaves. The only matter in issue before the court, therefore, is, whether the descendants of such slaves, when they shall be emancipated, or who are born of parents who had become free before their birth, are citizens of a State, in the sense in which the word citizen is used in the Constitution of the United States. And this being the only matter in dispute on the pleadings, the court must be understood as speaking in this opinion of that class only, that is, of those persons who are the descendants of Africans who were imported into this country, and sold as slaves.

The situation of this population was altogether unlike that of the Indian race. The latter, it is true, formed no part of the colonial communities, and never amalgamated with them in social connections or in government. But although they were uncivilized, they were yet a free and independent people, associated together in nations or tribes, and governed by their own laws. Many of these political communities were situated in territories to which the white race claimed the ultimate right of dominion. But that claim was acknowledged to be subject to the right of the Indians to occupy it as long as they thought proper, and neither the English nor colonial Governments claimed or exercised any dominion over the tribe or nation by whom it was occupied, nor claimed the right to the possession of the territory, until the tribe or nation consented to cede it. These Indian Governments were regarded and treated as foreign Governments, as much so as if an ocean had separated the red man from the white; and their freedom has constantly been acknowledged, from the time of the first emigration to the English colonies to

the present day, by the different Governments which succeeded each other. Treaties have been negotiated with them, and their alliance sought for in war; and the people who compose these Indian political communities have always been treated as foreigners not living under our Government. It is true that the course of events has brought the Indian tribes within the limits of the United States under subjection to the white race; and it has been found necessary, for their sake as well as our own, to regard them as in a state of pupilage, and to legislate to a certain extent over them and the territory they occupy. But they may, without doubt, like the subjects of any other foreign Government, be naturalized by the authority of Congress, and become citizens of a State, and of the United States; and if an individual should leave his nation or tribe, and take up his abode among the white population, he would be entitled to all the rights and privileges which would belong to an emigrant from any other foreign people.

We proceed to examine the case as presented by the pleadings.

The words "people of the United States" and "citizens" are synonymous terms, and mean the same thing. They both describe the political body who, according to our republican institutions, form the sovereignty, and who hold the power and conduct the Government through their representatives. They are what we familiarly call the "sovereign people," and every citizen is one of this people, and a constituent member of this sovereignty. The question before us is, whether the class of persons described in the plea in abatement compose a portion of this people, and are constituent members of this sovereignty? We think they are not, and that they are not included, and were not intended to be included, under the word "citizens" in the Constitution, and can therefore claim none of the rights and privileges which that instrument provides for and secures to citizens of the United States. On the contrary, they were at that time considered as a subordinate and inferior class of beings, who had been subjugated by the dominant race, and, whether emancipated or not, yet remained subject to their authority, and had no rights or privileges but such as those who held the power and the Government might choose to grant them.

It is not the province of the court to decide upon the justice or injustice, the policy or impolicy, of these laws. The decision of that question belonged to the political or law-making power; to those who formed the sovereignty and framed the Constitution. The duty of the court is, to interpret the instrument they have framed, with the best lights we can obtain on the subject, and to administer it as we find it, according to its true intent and meaning when it was adopted.

In discussing this question, we must not confound the rights of citizenship which a State may confer within its own limits, and the rights of citizenship as a member of the Union. It does not by any means follow, because he has all the rights and privileges of a citizen of a State, that he must be a citizen of the United States. He may have all of the rights and privileges of the citizen of a State, and yet not be entitled to the rights and privileges of a citizen in any other State. For, previous to the adoption of the Constitution of the United States, every State had the undoubted right to confer on whomsoever it pleased the character of citizen, and to endow him with all its rights. But this character of course was confined to the boundaries of the State, and gave him no rights or privileges in other States beyond those secured to him by the laws of nations and the comity of States. Nor have the several States surrendered the power of conferring these rights and privileges by adopting the Constitution of the United States. Each State may still confer them upon an alien, or any one it thinks proper, or upon any class or description of persons; yet he would not be a citizen in the sense in which that word is used in the Constitution of the United States, nor entitled to sue as such in one of its courts, nor to the privileges and immunities of a citizen in the other States. The rights which he would acquire would be restricted to the State which gave them. The Constitution has conferred on Congress the right to establish an uniform rule of naturalization, and this right is evidently exclusive, and has always been held by this court to be so. Consequently, no State, since the adoption of the Constitution, can by naturalizing an alien invest him with the rights and privileges secured to a citizen of a State under the Federal Government, although, so far as the State alone was concerned, he would undoubtedly be entitled to the rights of a citizen, and clothed with all the rights and immunities which the Constitution and laws of the State attached to that character.

It is very clear, therefore, that no State can, by any act or law of its own, passed since the adoption of the Constitution, introduce a new member into the political community created by the Constitution of the United States. It cannot make him a member of this community by making him a member of its own. And for the same reason it cannot introduce any person, or description of persons, who were not intended to be embraced in this new political family, which the Constitution brought into existence, but were intended to be excluded from it.

The question then arises, whether the provisions of the Constitution, in relation to the personal rights and privileges to which the citizen of a State should be entitled, embraced the negro African race, at that time in this country, or who might afterwards be imported, who had then or should afterwards be made free in any State; and to put it in the power of a single State to make him a citizen of the United States, and endue him with the full rights of citizenship in every other State without their consent? Does the Constitution of the United States act upon him whenever he shall be made free under the laws of a State, and raised there to the rank of a citizen, and immediately clothe him with all the privileges of a citizen in every other State, and in its own courts?

The court think the affirmative of these propositions cannot be maintained. And if it cannot, the plaintiff in error could not be a citizen of the State of Missouri, within the meaning of the Constitution of the United States, and, consequently, was not entitled to sue in its courts.

It is true, every person, and every class and description of persons, who were at the time of the adoption of the Constitution recognised as citizens in the several States, became also citizens of this new political body; but none other; it was formed by them, and for them and their posterity, but for no one else. And the personal rights and privileges guaranteed to citizens of this new sovereignty were intended to embrace those only who were then members of the several State communities, or who should afterwards by birthright or otherwise become members, according to the provisions of the Constitution and the principles on which it was founded. It was the union of those who were at that time members of distinct and separate political communities into one political family, whose power, for certain specified purposes, was to extend over the whole territory of the United States. And it gave to each citizen rights and privileges outside of his State which he did not before possess, and placed him in every other State upon a perfect equality with its own citizens as to rights of person and rights of property; it made him a citizen of the United States.

It becomes necessary, therefore, to determine who were citizens of the several States when the Constitution was adopted. And in order to do this, we must recur to the Governments and institutions of the thirteen colonies, when they separated from Great Britain and formed new sovereignties, and took their places in the family of independent nations. We must inquire who, at that time, were recognised as the people or citizens of a State, whose rights and liberties had been outraged by the English Government; and who declared their independence, and assumed the powers of Government to defend their rights by force of arms.

In the opinion of the court, the legislation and histories of the times, and the language used in the Declaration of Independence, show, that neither the class of persons who had been imported as slaves, nor their descendants, whether they had become free or not, were then acknowledged as a part of the people, nor intended to be included in the general words used in that memorable instrument.

It is difficult at this day to realize the state of public opinion in relation to that unfortunate race, which prevailed in the civilized and enlightened portions of the world at the time of the Declaration of Independence, and when the Constitution of the United States was framed and adopted. But the public history of every European nation displays it in a manner too plain to be mistaken.

They had for more than a century before been regarded as beings of an inferior order, and altogether unfit to associate with the white race, either in social or political relations; and so far inferior, that they had no rights which the white man was bound to respect; and that the negro might justly and lawfully be reduced to slavery for his benefit. He was bought and sold, and treated as an ordinary article of merchandise and traffic, whenever a profit could be made by it. This opinion was at that time fixed and universal in the civilized portion of the white race. It was regarded as an axiom in morals as well as in politics, which no one thought of disputing, or supposed to be open to dispute; and men in every grade and position in society daily and habitually acted upon it in their private pursuits, as well as in matters of public concern, without doubting for a moment the correctness of this opinion.

And in no nation was this opinion more firmly fixed or more uniformly acted upon than by the English Government and English people. They not only seized them on the coast of Africa, and sold them or held them in slavery for their own use; but they took them as ordinary articles of merchandise to every country where they could make a profit on them, and were far more extensively engaged in this commerce than any other nation in the world.

The opinion thus entertained and acted upon in England was naturally impressed upon the colonies they founded on this side of the Atlantic. And, accordingly, a negro of the African race was regarded by them as an article of property, and held, and bought and sold as such, in every one of the thirteen colonies which united in the Declaration of Independence, and afterwards formed the Constitution of the United States. The slaves were more or less numerous in the different colonies, as slave labor was found more or less profitable. But no one seems to have doubted the correctness of the prevailing opinion of the time.

The legislation of the different colonies furnishes positive and indisputable proof of this fact.

It would be tedious, in this opinion, to enumerate the various laws they passed upon this subject. It will be sufficient, as a sample of the legislation which then generally prevailed throughout the British colonies, to give the laws of two of them; one being still a large slaveholding State, and the other the first State in which slavery ceased to exist.

The province of Maryland, in 1717, (ch. 13, s. 5,) passed a law declaring "that if any free negro or mulatto intermarry with any white woman, or if any white man shall intermarry with any negro or mulatto woman, such negro or mulatto shall become a slave during life, excepting mulattoes born of white women, who, for such intermarriage, shall only become servants for seven years, to be disposed of as the justices of the county court, where such marriage so happens, shall think fit; to be applied by them towards the support of a public school within the said county. And any white man or white woman who shall intermarry as aforesaid, with any negro or mulatto, such white man or white woman shall become servants during the term of seven years, and shall be disposed of by the justices as aforesaid, and be applied to the uses aforesaid."

The other colonial law to which we refer was passed by Massachusetts in 1705, (chap. 6.) It is entitled "An act for the better preventing of a spurious and mixed issue," &c.; and it provides, that "if any negro or mulatto shall presume to smite or strike any person of the English or other Christian nation, such negro or mulatto shall be severely whipped, at the discretion of the justices before whom the offender shall be convicted."

And "that none of her Majesty's English or Scottish subjects, nor of any other Christian nation, within this province, shall contract matrimony with any negro or mulatto; nor shall any person, duly authorized to solemnize marriage, presume to join any such in marriage, on pain of forfeiting the sum of fifty pounds; one moiety thereof to her Majesty, for and towards the support of the Government within this province, and the other moiety to him or them that shall inform and sue for the same, in any of her Majesty's courts of record within the province, by bill, plaint, or information."

We give both of these laws in the words used by the respective legislative bodies, because the language in which they are framed, as well as the provisions contained in them, show, too plainly to be misunderstood, the degraded condition of this unhappy race. They were still in force when the Revolution began, and are a faithful index to the state of feeling towards the class of persons of whom they speak, and of the position they occupied throughout the thirteen colonies, in the eyes and thoughts of the men who framed the Declaration of Independence and established the State Constitutions and Governments. They show that a perpetual and impassable barrier was intended to be erected between the white race and the one which they had reduced to slavery, and governed as subjects with absolute and despotic power, and which they then looked upon as so far below them in the scale of created beings, that intermarriages between white persons and negroes or mulattoes were regarded as unnatural and immoral, and punished as crimes, not only in the parties, but in the person who joined them in marriage. And no distinction in this respect was made between the free negro or mulatto and the slave, but this stigma, of the deepest degradation, was fixed upon the whole race.

We refer to these historical facts for the purpose of showing the fixed opinions concerning that race, upon which the statesmen of that day spoke and acted. It is necessary to do this, in order to determine whether the general terms used in the Constitution of the United States, as to the rights of man and the rights of the people, was intended to include them, or to give to them or their posterity the benefit of any of its provisions.

The language of the Declaration of Independence is equally conclusive:

It begins by declaring that, "when in the course of human events it becomes necessary for one people to dissolve the political bands which have connected them with another, and to assume among the powers of the earth the separate and equal station to which the laws of nature and nature's God entitle them, a decent respect for the opinions of mankind requires that they should declare the causes which impel them to the separation."

It then proceeds to say: "We hold these truths to be self-evident: that all men are created equal; that they are endowed by their Creator with certain unalienable rights; that among them is life, liberty, and the pursuit of happiness; that to secure these rights, Governments are instituted, deriving their just powers from the consent of the governed."

The general words above quoted would seem to embrace the whole human family, and if they were used in a similar instrument at this day would be so understood. But it is too clear for dispute, that the enslaved African race were not intended to be included, and formed no part of the people who framed and adopted this declaration; for if the language, as understood in that day, would embrace them, the conduct of the distinguished men who framed the Declaration of Independence would have been utterly and flagrantly inconsistent with the principles they asserted; and instead of the sympathy of mankind, to which they so confidently appealed, they would have deserved and received universal rebuke and reprobation.

Yet the men who framed this declaration were great men—high in literary acquirements—high in their sense of honor, and incapable of asserting principles inconsistent with those on which they were acting. They perfectly understood the meaning of the language they used, and how it would be understood by others; and they knew that it would not in any part of the civilized world be supposed to embrace the negro race, which, by common consent, had been excluded from civilized Governments and the family of nations, and doomed to slavery. They spoke and acted according to the then established doctrines and principles, and in the ordinary language of the day, and no one misunderstood them. The unhappy black race were separated from the white by indelible marks, and laws long before established, and were never thought of or spoken of except as property, and when the claims of the owner or the profit of the trader were supposed to need protection.

This state of public opinion had undergone no change when the Constitution was adopted, as is equally evident from its provisions and language.

The brief preamble sets forth by whom it was formed, for what purposes, and for whose benefit and protection. It declares that it is formed by the people of the United States; that is to say, by those who were members of the different political communities in the several States; and its great object is declared to be to secure the blessings of liberty to themselves and their posterity. It speaks in general terms of the people of the United States, and of citizens of the several States, when it is providing for the exercise of the powers granted or the privileges secured to the citizen. It does not define what description of persons are intended to be included under these terms, or who shall be regarded as a citizen and one of the people. It uses them as terms so well understood, that no further description or definition was necessary.

But there are two clauses in the Constitution which point directly and specifically to the negro race as a separate class of persons, and show clearly that they were not regarded as a portion of the people or citizens of the Government then formed.

One of these clauses reserves to each of the thirteen States the right to import slaves until the year 1808, if it thinks proper. And the importation which it thus sanctions was unquestionably of persons of the race of which we are speaking, as the traffic in slaves in the United States had always been confined to them. And by the other provision the States pledge themselves to each other to maintain the right of property of the master, by delivering up to him any slave who may have escaped from his service, and be found within their respective territories. By the first above-mentioned clause, therefore, the right to purchase and hold this property is directly sanctioned and authorized for twenty years by the people who framed the Constitution. And by the second, they pledge themselves to maintain and uphold the right of the master in the manner specified, as long as the Government they then formed should endure. And these two provisions show, conclusively, that neither the description of persons therein referred to, nor their descendants, were embraced in any of the other provisions of the Constitution; for certainly these two clauses were not intended to confer on them or their posterity the blessings of liberty, or any of the personal rights so carefully provided for the citizen.

No one of that race had ever migrated to the United States voluntarily; all of them had been brought here as articles of merchandise. The number that had been emancipated at that time were but few in comparison with those held in slavery; and they were identified in the public mind with the race to which they belonged, and regarded as a part of the slave population rather than the free. It is obvious that they were not even in the minds of the framers of the Constitution when they were conferring special rights and privileges upon the citizens of a State in every other part of the Union.

Indeed, when we look to the condition of this race in the several States at the time, it is impossible to believe that these rights and privileges were intended to be extended to them.

It is very true, that in that portion of the Union where the labor of the negro race was found to be unsuited to the climate and unprofitable to the master, but few slaves were held at the time of the Declaration of Independence; and when the Constitution was adopted, it had entirely worn out in one of them, and measures had been taken for its gradual abolition in several others. But this change had not been produced by any change of opinion in relation to this race; but because it was discovered, from experience, that slave labor was unsuited to the climate and productions of these States: for some of the States, where it had ceased or nearly ceased to exist, were actively engaged in the slave trade, procuring cargoes on the coast of Africa, and transporting them for sale to those parts of the Union where their labor was found to be profitable, and suited to the climate and productions. And this traffic was openly carried on, and fortunes accumulated by it, without reproach from the people of the States where they resided. And it can hardly be supposed that, in the States where it was then countenanced in its worst form—that is, in the seizure and transportation—the people could have regarded those who were emancipated as entitled to equal rights with themselves.

And we may here again refer, in support of this proposition, to the plain and unequivocal language of the laws of the several States, some passed after the Declaration of Independence and before the Constitution was adopted, and some since the Government went into operation.

We need not refer, on this point, particularly to the laws of the present slaveholding States. Their statute books are full of provisions in relation to this class, in the same spirit with the Maryland law which we have before quoted. They have continued to treat them as an inferior class, and to subject them to strict police regulations, drawing a broad line of distinction between the citizen and the slave races, and legislating in relation to them upon the same principle which prevailed at the time of the Declaration of Independence. As relates to these States, it is too plain for argument, that they have never been regarded as a part of the people or citizens of the State, nor supposed to possess any political rights which the dominant race might not withhold or grant at their pleasure. And as long ago as 1822, the

Court of Appeals of Kentucky decided that free negroes and mulattoes were not citizens within the meaning of the Constitution of the United States; and the correctness of this decision is recognized, and the same doctrine affirmed, in 1 Meigs's Tenn. Reports, 331.

And if we turn to the legislation of the States where slavery had worn out, or measures taken for its speedy abolition, we shall find the same opinions and principles equally fixed and equally acted upon.

Thus, Massachusetts, in 1786, passed a law similar to the colonial one of which we have spoken. The law of 1786, like the law of 1705, forbids the marriage of any white person with any negro, Indian, or mulatto, and inflicts a penalty of fifty pounds upon any one who shall join them in marriage; and declares all such marriage absolutely null and void, and degrades thus the unhappy issue of the marriage by fixing upon it the stain of bastardy. And this mark of degradation was renewed, and again impressed upon the race, in the careful and deliberate preparation of their revised code published in 1836. This code forbids any person from joining in marriage any white person with any Indian, negro, or mulatto, and subjects the party who shall offend in this respect, to imprisonment, not exceeding six months, in the common jail, or to hard labor, and to a fine of not less than fifty nor more than two hundred dollars; and, like the law of 1786, it declares the marriage to be absolutely null and void. It will be seen that the punishment is increased by the code upon the person who shall marry them, by adding imprisonment to a pecuniary penalty.

So, too, in Connecticut. We refer more particularly to the legislation of this State, because it was not only among the first to put an end to slavery within its own territory, but was the first to fix a mark of reprobation upon the African slave trade. The law last mentioned was passed in October, 1788, about nine months after the State had ratified and adopted the present Constitution of the United States; and by that law it prohibited its own citizens, under severe penalties, from engaging in the trade, and declared all policies of insurance on the vessel or cargo made in the State to be null and void. But, up to the time of the adoption of the Constitution, there is nothing in the legislation of the State indicating any change of opinion as to the relative rights and position of the white and black races in this country, or indicating that it meant to place the latter, when free, upon a level with its citizens. And certainly nothing which would have led the slaveholding States to suppose,

that Connecticut designed to claim for them, under the new Constitution, the equal rights and privileges and rank of citizens in every other State.

The first step taken by Connecticut upon this subject was as early as 1774, wen it passed an act forbidding the further importation of slaves into the State. But the section containing the prohibition is introduced by the following preamble:

> "And whereas the increase of slaves in this State is injurious to the poor, and inconvenient."

This recital would appear to have been carefully introduced, in order to prevent any misunderstanding of the motive which induced the Legislature to pass the law, and places it distinctly upon the interest and convenience of the white population—excluding the inference that it might have been intended in any degree for the benefit of the other.

And in the act of 1784, by which the issue of slaves, born after the time therein mentioned, were to be free at a certain age, the section is again introduced by a preamble assigning a similar motive for the act. It is in these words:

> "Whereas sound policy requires that the abolition of slavery should be effected as soon as may be consistent with the rights of individuals, and the public safety and welfare"—showing that the right of property in the master was to be protected, and that the measure was one of policy, and to prevent the injury and inconvenience, to the whites, of a slave population in the State.

And still further pursuing its legislation, we find that in the same statute passed in 1774, which prohibited the further importation of slaves into the State, there is also a provision by which any negro, Indian, or mulatto servant, who was found wandering out of the town or place to which he belonged, without a written pass such as is therein described, was made liable to be seized by any one, and taken before the next authority to be examined and delivered up to his master—who was required to pay the charge which had accrued thereby. And a subsequent section of the same law provides, that if any free negro shall travel without such pass, and shall be stopped, seized, or taken up, he shall pay all charges arising thereby. And this law was in full operation when the Constitution of the United States was adopted, and was not repealed till 1797. So that up to that time free negroes and mulattoes were associated with servants and slaves in the police regulations established by the laws of the State.

And again, in 1833, Connecticut passed another law, which made it penal to set up or establish any school in that State for the instruction of persons of the African race not inhabitants of the State, or to instruct or teach in any such school or institution, or board or harbor for that purpose, any such person, without the previous consent in writing of the civil authority of the town in which such school or institution might be.

And it appears by the case of *Crandall v. The State*, reported in 10 Conn. Rep., 340, that upon an information filed against Prudence Crandall for a violation of this law, one of the points raised in the defence was, that the law was a violation of the Constitution of the United States; and that the persons instructed, although of the African race, were citizens of other States, and therefore entitled to the rights and privileges of citizens in the State of Connecticut. But Chief Justice Dagget, before whom the case was tried, held, that persons of that description were not citizens of a State, within the meaning of the word citizen in the Constitution of the United States, and were not therefore entitled to the privileges and immunities of citizens in other States.

The case was carried up to the Supreme Court of Errors of the State, and the question fully argued there. But the case went off upon another point, and no opinion was expressed on this question.

We have made this particular examination into the legislative and judicial action of Connecticut, because, from the early hostility it displayed to the slave trade on the coast of Africa, we may expect to find the laws of that State as lenient and favorable to the subject race as those of any other State in the Union; and if we find that at the time the Constitution was adopted, they were not even there raised to the rank of citizens, but were still held and treated as property, and the laws relating to them passed with reference altogether to the interest and convenience of the white race, we shall hardly find them elevated to a higher rank anywhere else.

A brief notice of the laws of two other States, and we shall pass on to other considerations.

By the laws of New Hampshire, collected and finally passed in 1815, no one was permitted to be enrolled in the militia of the State, but free white citizens; and the same provision is found in a subsequent collection of the laws, made in 1855. Nothing could more strongly mark the entire repudiation of

the African race. The alien is excluded, because, being born in a foreign country, he cannot be a member of the community until he is naturalized. But why are the African race, born in the State, not permitted to share in one of the highest duties of the citizen? The answer is obvious; he is not, by the institutions and laws of the State, numbered among its people. He forms no part of the sovereignty of the State, and is not therefore called on to uphold and defend it. Again, in 1822, Rhode Island, in its revised code, passed a law forbidding persons who were authorized to join persons in marriage, from joining in marriage any white person with any negro, Indian, or mulatto, under the penalty of two hundred dollars, and declaring all such marriages absolutely null and void; and the same law was again re-enacted in its revised code of 1844. So that, down to the last-mentioned period, the strongest mark of inferiority and degradation was fastened upon the African race in that State.

It would be impossible to enumerate and compress in the space usually allotted to an opinion of a court, the various laws, marking the condition of this race, which were passed from time to time after the Revolution, and before and since the adoption of the Constitution of the United States. In addition to those already referred to, it is sufficient to say, that Chancellor Kent, whose accuracy and research no one will question, states in the sixth edition of his *Commentaries*, (published in 1848, 2 vol., 258, note b,) that in no part of the country except Maine, did the African race, in point of fact, participate equally with the whites in the exercise of civil and political rights.

The legislation of the States therefore shows, in a manner not to be mistaken, the inferior and subject condition of that race at the time the Constitution was adopted, and long afterwards, throughout the thirteen States by which that instrument was framed; and it is hardly consistent with the respect due to these States, to suppose that they regarded at that time, as fellow-citizens and members of the sovereignty, a class of beings whom they had thus stigmatized; whom, as we are bound, out of respect to the State sovereignties, to assume they had deemed it just and necessary thus to stigmatize, and upon whom they had impressed such deep and enduring marks of inferiority and degradation; or, that when they met in convention to form the Constitution, they looked upon them as a portion of their constituents, or designed to include them in the provisions so carefully inserted for the security and protection of the liberties and rights of their citizens. It cannot be supposed that they intended to secure to them rights, and privileges, and rank, in the new political body throughout the Union, which every one of them denied within the limits of its own dominion. More especially, it cannot be believed that the large slaveholding States regarded them as included in the word citizens, or would have consented to a Constitution which might compel them to receive them in that character from another State. For if they were so received, and entitled to the privileges and immunities of citizens, it would exempt them from the operation of the special laws and from the police regulations which they considered to be necessary for their own safety. It would give to persons of the negro race, who were recognised as citizens in any one State of the Union, the right to enter every other State whenever they pleased, singly or in companies, without pass or passport, and without obstruction, to sojourn there as long as they pleased, to go where they pleased at every hour of the day or night without molestation, unless they committed some violation of law for which a white man would be punished; and it would give them the full liberty of speech in public and in private upon all subjects upon which its own citizens might speak; to hold public meetings upon political affairs, and to keep and carry arms wherever they went. And all of this would be done in the face of the subject race of the same color, both free and slaves, and inevitably producing discontent and insubordination among them, and endangering the peace and safety of the State.

It is impossible, it would seem, to believe that the great men of the slaveholding States, who took so large a share in framing the Constitution of the United States, and exercised so much influence in procuring its adoption, could have been so forgetful or regardless of their own safety and the safety of those who trusted and confided in them.

Besides, this want of foresight and care would have been utterly inconsistent with the caution displayed in providing for the admission of new members into this political family. For, when they gave to the citizens of each State the privileges and immunities of citizens in the several States, they at the same time took from the several States the power of naturalization, and confined that power exclusively to the Federal Government. No State was willing to permit another State to determine who should or should not be admitted as one of its citizens, and entitled to demand equal rights and privileges with their own people, within their own territories. The right of naturalization was therefore, with one accord, surrendered by the States, and confided to the Federal Government. And this power granted to Congress to establish an uniform rule of naturalization is, by the well-understood meaning of the word, confined to persons born in a foreign country, under a foreign Government. It is not a power to raise to the rank of a citizen any one born in the United States, who, from birth or parentage, by the laws of the country, belongs to an inferior and subordinate class. And when we find the States guarding themselves from the indiscreet or improper admission by other States of emigrants from other countries, by giving the power exclusively to Congress, we cannot fail to see that they could never have left with the States a much more important power—that is, the power of transforming into citizens a numerous class of persons, who in that character would be much more dangerous to the peace and safety of a large portion of the Union, than the few foreigners one of the States might improperly naturalize. The Constitution upon its adoption obviously took from the States all power by any subsequent legislation to introduce as a citizen into the political family of the United States any one, no matter where he was born, or what might be his character or condition; and it gave to Congress the power to confer this character upon those only who were born outside of the dominions of the United States. And no law of a State, therefore, passed since the Constitution was adopted, can give any right of citizenship outside of its own territory.

A clause similar to the one in the Constitution, in relation to the rights and immunities of citizens of one State in the other States, was contained in the Articles of Confederation. But there is a difference of language, which is worthy of note. The provision in the Articles of Confederation was, "that the free inhabitants of each of the States, paupers, vagabonds, and fugitives from justice, excepted, should be entitled to all the privileges and immunities of free citizens in the several States."

It will be observed, that under this Confederation, each State had the right to decide for itself, and in its own tribunals, whom it would acknowledge as a free inhabitant of another State. The term free inhabitant, in the generality of its terms, would certainly include one of the African race who had been manumitted. But no example, we think, can be found of his admission to all the privileges of citizenship in any State of the Union after these Articles were formed, and while they continued in force. And, notwithstanding the generality of the words "free inhabitants," it is very clear that, according to their accepted meaning in that day, they did not include the African race, whether free or not: for the fifth section of the ninth article provides that Congress should have the power "to agree upon the number of land forces to be raised, and to make requisitions from each State for its quota in proportion to the number of white inhabitants in such State, which requisition should be binding."

Words could hardly have been used which more strongly mark the line of distinction between the citizen and the subject; the free and the subjugated races. The latter were not even counted when the inhabitants of a State were to be embodied in proportion to its numbers for the general defence. And it cannot for a moment be supposed, that a class of persons thus separated and rejected from those who formed the sovereignty of the States, were yet intended to be included under the words "free inhabitants," in the preceding article, to whom privileges and immunities were so carefully secured in every State.

But although this clause of the Articles of Confederation is the same in principle with that inserted in the Constitution, yet the comprehensive word inhabitant, which might be construed to include an emancipated slave, is omitted; and the privilege is confined to citizens of the State. And this alteration in words would hardly have been made, unless a different meaning was intended to be conveyed, or a possible doubt removed. The just and fair inference is, that as this privilege was about to be placed under the protection of the General Government, and the words expounded by its tribunals, and all power in relation to it taken from the State and its courts, it was deemed prudent to describe with precision and caution the persons to whom this high privilege was given—and the word citizen was on that account substituted for the words free inhabitant. The word citizen excluded, and no doubt intended to exclude, foreigners who had not become citizens of some one of the States when the Constitution was adopted; and also every description of persons who were not fully recognised as citizens in the several States. This, upon any fair construction of the instruments to which we have referred, was evidently the object and purpose of this change of words.

To all this mass of proof we have still to add, that Congress has repeatedly legislated upon the same construction of the Constitution that we have given. Three laws, two of which were passed almost immediately after the Government went into operation, will be abundantly sufficient to show this. The two first are particularly worthy of notice, because many of the men who assisted in framing the Constitution,

and took an active part in procuring its adoption, were then in the halls of legislation, and certainly understood what they meant when they used the words "people of the United States" and "citizen" in that well-considered instrument.

The first of these acts is the naturalization law, which was passed at the second session of the first Congress, March 26, 1790, and confines the right of becoming citizens "to aliens being free white persons."

Now, the Constitution does not limit the power of Congress in this respect to white persons. And they may, if they think proper, authorize the naturalization of any one, of any color, who was born under allegiance to another Government. But the language of the law above quoted, shows that citizenship at that time was perfectly understood to be confined to the white race; and that they alone constituted the sovereignty in the Government.

Congress might, as we before said, have authorized the naturalization of Indians, because they were aliens and foreigners. But, in their then untutored and savage state, no one would have thought of admitting them as citizens in a civilized community. And, moreover, the atrocities they had but recently committed, when they were the allies of Great Britain in the Revolutionary war, were yet fresh in the recollection of the people of the United States, and they were even then guarding themselves against the threatened renewal of Indian hostilities. No one supposed then that any Indian would ask for, or was capable of enjoying, the privileges of an American citizen, and the word white was not used with any particular reference to them.

Neither was it used with any reference to the African race imported into or born in this country; because Congress had no power to naturalize them, and therefore there was no necessity for using particular words to exclude them.

It would seem to have been used merely because it followed out the line of division which the Constitution has drawn between the citizen race, who formed and held the Government, and the African race, which they held in subjection and slavery, and governed at their own pleasure.

Another of the early laws of which we have spoken, is the first militia law, which was passed in 1792, at the first session of the second Congress. The language of this law is equally plain and significant with the one just mentioned. It directs that every "free able-bodied white male citizen" shall be enrolled in the militia. The word white is evidently used to exclude the African race, and the word "citizen" to exclude unnaturalized foreigners; the latter forming no part of the sovereignty, owing it no allegiance, and therefore under no obligation to defend it. The African race, however, born in the country, did owe allegiance to the Government, whether they were slave or free; but it is repudiated, and rejected from the duties and obligations of citizenship in marked language.

The third act to which we have alluded is even still more decisive; it was passed as late as 1813, (2 Stat., 809,) and it provides: "That from and after the termination of the war in which the United States are now engaged with Great Britain, it shall not be lawful to employ, on board of any public or private vessels of the United States, any person or persons except citizens of the United States, or persons of color, natives of the United States." Here the line of distinction is drawn in express words. Persons of color, in the judgment of Congress, were not included in the word citizens, and they are described as another and different class of persons, and authorized to be employed, if born in the United States.

And even as late as 1820, (chap. 104, sec. 8,) in the charter to the city of Washington, the corporation is authorized "to restrain and prohibit the nightly and other disorderly meetings of slaves, free negroes, and mulattoes," thus associating them together in its legislation; and after prescribing the punishment that may be inflicted on the slaves, proceeds in the following words: "And to punish such free negroes and mulattoes by penalties not exceeding twenty dollars for any one offence; and in case of the inability of any such free negro or mulatto to pay any such penalty and cost thereon, to cause him or her to be confined to labor for any time not exceeding six calendar months." And in a subsequent part of the same section, the act authorizes the corporation "to prescribe the terms and conditions upon which free negroes and mulattoes may reside in the city."

This law, like the laws of the States, shows that this class of persons were governed by special legislation directed expressly to them, and always connected with provisions for the government of slaves, and not with those for the government of free white citizens. And after such an uniform course of legislation as we have stated, by the colonies, by the States, and by Congress, running through a period of more than a century, it would seem that to call persons thus marked and stigmatized, "citizens" of the United States, "fellow-citizens," a constituent part of the sovereignty, would be an abuse of terms, and not calculated to exalt the character of an American citizen in the eyes of other nations.

The conduct of the Executive Department of the Government has been in perfect harmony upon this subject with this course of legislation. The question was brought officially before the late William Wirt, when he was the Attorney General of the United States, in 1821, and he decided that the words "citizens of the United States" were used in the acts of Congress in the same sense as in the Constitution; and that free persons of color were not citizens, within the meaning of the Constitution and laws; and this opinion has been confirmed by that of the late Attorney General, Caleb Cushing, in a recent case, and acted upon by the Secretary of State, who refused to grant passports to them as "citizens of the United States."

But it is said that a person may be a citizen, and entitled to that character, although he does not possess all the rights which may belong to other citizens; as, for example, the right to vote, or to hold particular offices; and that yet, when he goes into another State, he is entitled to be recognised there as a citizen, although the State may measure his rights by the rights which it allows to persons of a like character or class resident in the State, and refuse to him the full rights of citizenship.

This argument overlooks the language of the provision in the Constitution of which we are speaking.

Undoubtedly, a person may be a citizen, that is, a member of the community who form the sovereignty, although he exercises no share of the political power, and is incapacitated from holding particular offices. Women and minors, who form a part of the political family, cannot vote; and when a property qualification is required to vote or hold a particular office, those who have not the necessary qualification cannot vote or hold the office, yet they are citizens.

So, too, a person may be entitled to vote by the law of the State, who is not a citizen even of the State itself. And in some of the States of the Union foreigners not naturalized are allowed to vote. And the State may give the right to free negroes and mulattoes, but that does not make them citizens of the State, and still less of the United States. And the provision in the Constitution giving privileges and immunities in other States, does not apply to them.

Neither does it apply to a person who, being the citizen of a State, migrates to another State. For then he becomes subject to the laws of the State in which he lives, and he is no longer a citizen of the State from which he removed. And the State in which he resides may then, unquestionably, determine his status or condition, and place him among the class of persons who are not recognised as citizens, but belong to an inferior and subject race; and may deny him the privileges and immunities enjoyed by its citizens.

But so far as mere rights of person are concerned, the provision in question is confined to citizens of a State who are temporarily in another State without taking up their residence there. It gives them no political rights in the State, as to voting or holding office, or in any other respect. For a citizen of one State has no right to participate in the government of another. But if he ranks as a citizen in the State to which he belongs, within the meaning of the Constitution of the United States, then, whenever he goes into another State, the Constitution clothes him, as to the rights of person, will all the privileges and immunities which belong to citizens of the State. And if persons of the African race are citizens of a State, and of the United States, they would be entitled to all of these privileges and immunities in every State, and the State could not restrict them; for they would hold these privileges and immunities under the paramount authority of the Federal Government, and its courts would be bound to maintain and enforce them, the Constitution and laws of the State to the contrary notwithstanding. And if the States could limit or restrict them, or place the party in an inferior grade, this clause of the Constitution would be unmeaning, and could have no operation; and would give no rights to the citizen when in another State. He would have none but what the State itself chose to allow him. This is evidently not the construction or meaning of the clause in question. It guaranties rights to the citizen, and the State cannot withhold them. And these rights are of a character and would lead to consequences which make it absolutely certain that the African race were not included under the name of citizens of a State, and were not in the contemplation of the framers of the Constitution when these privileges and immunities were provided for the protection of the citizen in other States.

The case of *Legrand v. Darnall* (2 Peters, 664) has been referred to for the purpose of showing that this court has decided that the descendant of a slave may sue as a citizen in a court of the United States; but the case itself shows that the question did not arise and could not have arisen in the case.

It appears from the report, that Darnall was born in Maryland, and was the son of a white man by one of his slaves, and his father executed certain instruments to manumit him, and devised to him some landed property in the State. This property Darnall afterwards sold to Legrand, the appellant, who gave his notes for the purchase-money. But becoming afterwards apprehensive that the appellee had not been emancipated according to the laws of Maryland, he refused to pay the notes until he could be better satisfied as to Darnall's right to convey. Darnall, in the mean time, had taken up his residence in Pennsylvania, and brought suit on the notes, and recovered judgment in the Circuit Court for the district of Maryland.

The whole proceeding, as appears by the report, was an amicable one; Legrand being perfectly willing to pay the money, if he could obtain a title, and Darnall not wishing him to pay unless he could make him a good one. In point of fact, the whole proceeding was under the direction of the counsel who argued the case for the appellee, who was the mutual friend of the parties, and confided in by both of them, and whose only object was to have the rights of both parties established by judicial decision in the most speedy and least expensive manner.

Legrand, therefore, raised no objection to the jurisdiction of the court in the suit at law, because he was himself anxious to obtain the judgment of the court upon his title. Consequently, there was nothing in the record before the court to show that Darnall was of African descent, and the usual judgment and award of execution was entered. And Legrand thereupon filed his bill on the equity side of the Circuit Court, stating that Darnall was born a slave, and had not been legally emancipated, and could not therefore take the land devised to him, nor make Legrand a good title; and praying an injunction to restrain Darnall from proceeding to execution on the judgment, which was granted. Darnall answered, averring in his answer that he was a free man, and capable of conveying a good title. Testimony was taken on this point, and at the hearing the Circuit Court was of opinion that Darnall was a free man and his title good, and dissolved the injunction and dismissed the bill; and that decree was affirmed here, upon the appeal of Legrand.

Now, it is difficult to imagine how any question about the citizenship of Darnall, or his right to sue in that character, can be supposed to have arisen or been decided in that case. The fact that he was of African descent was first brought before the court upon the bill in equity. The suit at law had then passed into judgment and award of execution, and the Circuit Court, as a court of law, had no longer any authority over it. It was a valid and legal judgment, which the court that rendered it had not the power to reverse or set aside. And unless it had jurisdiction as a court of equity to restrain him from using its process as a court of law, Darnall, if he thought proper, would have been at liberty to proceed on his judgment, and compel the payment of the money, although the allegations in the bill were true, and he was incapable of making a title. No other court could have enjoined him, for certainly no State equity court could interfere in that way with the judgment of a Circuit Court of the United States.

But the Circuit Court as a court of equity certainly had equity jurisdiction over its own judgment as a court of law, without regard to the character of the parties; and had not only the right, but it was its duty—no matter who were the parties in the judgment—to prevent them from proceeding to enforce it by execution, if the court was satisfied that the money was not justly and equitably due. The ability of Darnall to convey did not depend upon his citizenship, but upon his title to freedom. And if he was free, he could hold and convey property, by the laws of Maryland, although he was not a citizen. But if he was by law still a slave, he could not. It was therefore the duty of the court, sitting as a court of equity in the latter case, to prevent him from using its process, as a court of common law, to compel the payment of the purchase-money, when it was evident that the purchaser must lose the land. But if he was free, and could make a title, it was equally the duty of the court not to suffer Legrand to keep the land, and refuse the payment of the money, upon the ground that Darnall was incapable of suing or being sued as a citizen in a court of the United States. The character or citizenship of the parties had no connection with the question of jurisdiction, and the matter in dispute had no relation to the citizenship of Darnall. Nor is such a question alluded to in the opinion of the court.

Besides, we are by no means prepared to say that there are not many cases, civil as well as criminal, in which a Circuit Court of the United States may exercise jurisdiction, although one of the African race is a party; that broad question is not before the court. The question with which we are now dealing is, whether a person of the African race can be a citizen of the United States, and become thereby entitled to a special privilege, by virtue of his title to that character, and which, under the Constitution, no one but a citizen can claim. It is manifest that the case of Legrand and Darnall has no bearing on that question, and can have no application to the case now before the court.

This case, however, strikingly illustrates the consequences that would follow the construction of the Constitution which would give the power contended for to a State. It would in effect give it also to an individual. For if the father of young Darnall had manumitted him in his lifetime, and sent him to reside in a State which recognised him as a citizen, he might have visited and sojourned in Maryland when he pleased, and as long as he pleased, as a citizen of the United States; and the State officers and tribunals would be compelled, by the paramount authority of the Constitution, to receive him and treat him as one of its citizens, exempt from the laws and police of the State in relation to a person of that description, and allow him to enjoy all the rights and privileges of citizenship, without respect to the laws of Maryland, although such laws were deemed by it absolutely essential to its own safety.

The only two provisions which point to them and include them, treat them as property, and make it the duty of the Government to protect it; no other power, in relation to this race, is to be found in the Constitution; and as it is a Government of special, delegated, powers, no authority beyond these two provisions can be constitutionally exercised. The Government of the United States had no right to interfere for any other purpose but that of protecting the rights of the owner, leaving it altogether with the several States to deal with this race, whether emancipated or not, as each State may think justice, humanity, and the interests and safety of society, require. The States evidently intended to reserve this power exclusively to themselves.

No one, we presume, supposes that any change in public opinion or feeling, in relation to this unfortunate race, in the civilized nations of Europe or in this country, should induce the court to give to the words of the Constitution a more liberal construction in their favor than they were intended to bear when the instrument was framed and adopted. Such an argument would be altogether inadmissible in any tribunal called on to interpret it. If any of its provisions are deemed unjust, there is a mode prescribed in the instrument itself by which it may be amended; but while it remains unaltered, it must be construed now as it was understood at the time of its adoption. It is not only the same in words, but the same in meaning, and delegates the same powers to the Government, and reserves and secures the same rights and privileges to the citizen; and as long as it continues to exist in its present form, it speaks not only in the same words, but with the same meaning and intent with which it spoke when it came from the hands of its framers, and was voted on and adopted by the people of the United States. Any other rule of construction would abrogate the judicial character of this court, and make it the mere reflex of the popular opinion or passion of the day. This court was not created by the Constitution for such purposes. Higher and graver trusts have been confided to it, and it must not falter in the path of duty.

What the construction was at that time, we think can hardly admit of doubt. We have the language of the Declaration of Independence and of the Articles of Confederation, in addition to the plain words of the Constitution itself; we have the legislation of the different States, before, about the time, and since, the Constitution was adopted; we have the legislation of Congress, from the time of its adoption to a recent period; and we have the constant and uniform action of the Executive Department, all concurring together, and leading to the same result. And if anything in relation to the construction of the Constitution can be regarded as settled, it is that which we now give to the word "citizen" and the word "people."

And upon a full and careful consideration of the subject, the court is of opinion, that, upon the facts stated in the plea in abatement, Dred Scott was not a citizen of Missouri within the meaning of the Constitution of the United States, and not entitled as such to sue in its courts; and, consequently, that the Circuit Court had no jurisdiction of the case, and that the judgment on the plea in abatement is erroneous.

We are aware that doubts are entertained by some of the members of the court, whether the plea in abatement is legally before the court upon this writ of error; but if that plea is regarded as waived, or out of the case upon any other ground, yet the question as to the jurisdiction of the Circuit Court is presented on the face of the bill of exception itself, taken by the plaintiff at the trial; for he admits that he and his wife were born slaves, but endeavors to make out his title to freedom and citizenship by showing that they were taken by their owner to certain places, hereinafter mentioned, where slavery could not by law exist, and that they thereby became free, and upon their return to Missouri became citizens of that State.

Now, if the removal of which he speaks did not give them their freedom, then by his own admission he is still a slave; and whatever opinions may be entertained in favor of the citizenship of a free person of the African race, no one supposes that a slave is a citizen of the State or of the United States. If, therefore, the acts done by his owner did not make them free persons, he is still a slave, and certainly incapable of suing in the character of a citizen.

The principle of law is too well settled to be disputed, that a court can give no judgment for either party, where it has no jurisdiction; and if, upon the showing of Scott himself, it appeared that he was still a slave, the case ought to have been dismissed, and the judgment against him and in favor of the defendant for costs, is, like that on the plea in abatement, erroneous, and the suit ought to have been dismissed by the Circuit Court for want of jurisdiction in that court.

But, before we proceed to examine this part of the case, it may be proper to notice an objection taken to the judicial authority of this court to decide it; and it has been said, that as this court has decided against the jurisdiction of the Circuit Court on the plea in abatement, it has no right to examine any question presented by the exception; and that anything it may say upon that part of the case will be extra-judicial, and mere obiter dicta.

This is a manifest mistake; there can be no doubt as to the jurisdiction of this court to revise the judgment of a Circuit Court, and to reverse it for any error apparent on the record, whether it be the error of giving judgment in a case over which it had no jurisdiction, or any other material error; and this, too, whether there is a plea in abatement or not.

The objection appears to have arisen from confounding writs of error to a State court, with writs of error to a Circuit Court of the United States. Undoubtedly, upon a writ of error to a State court, unless the record shows a case that gives jurisdiction, the case must be dismissed for want of jurisdiction in this court. And if it is dismissed on that ground, we have no right to examine and decide upon any question presented by the bill of exceptions, or any other part of the record. But writs of error to a State court, and to a Circuit Court of the United States, are regulated by different laws, and stand upon entirely different principles. And in a writ of error to a Circuit Court of the United States, the whole record is before this court for examination and decision; and if the sum in controversy is large enough to give jurisdiction, it is not only the right, but it is the judicial duty of the court, to examine the whole case as presented by the record; and if it appears upon its face that any material error or errors have been committed by the court below, it is the duty of this court to reverse the judgment, and remand the case. And certainly an error in passing a judgment upon the merits in favor of either party, in a case which it was not authorized to try, and over which it had no jurisdiction, is as grave an error as a court can commit.

The plea in abatement is not a plea to the jurisdiction of this court, but to the jurisdiction of the Circuit Court. And it appears by the record before us, that the Circuit Court committed an error, in deciding that it had jurisdiction, upon the facts in the case, admitted by the pleadings. It is the duty of the appellate tribunal to correct this error; but that could not be done by dismissing the case for want of jurisdiction here—for that would leave the erroneous judgment in full force, and the injured party without remedy. And the appellate court therefore exercises the power for which alone appellate courts are constituted, by reversing the judgment of the court below for this error. It exercises its proper and appropriate jurisdiction over the judgment and proceedings of the Circuit Court, as they appear upon the record brought up by the writ of error.

The correction of one error in the court below does not deprive the appellate court of the power of examining further into the record, and correcting any other material errors which may have been committed by the inferior court. There is certainly no rule of law—nor any practice—nor any decision of a court—which even questions this power in the appellate tribunal. On the contrary, it is the daily practice of this court, and of all appellate courts where they reverse the judgment of an inferior court for error, to correct by its opinions whatever errors may appear on the record material to the case; and they have always held it to be their duty to do so where the silence of the court might lead to misconstruction or future controversy, and the point has been relied on by either side, and argued before the court.

In the case before us, we have already decided that the Circuit Court erred in deciding that it had jurisdiction upon the facts admitted by the pleadings. And it appears that, in the further progress of the case, it acted upon the erroneous principle it had decided on the pleadings, and gave judgment for the defendant, where, upon the facts admitted in the exception, it had no jurisdiction.

We are at a loss to understand upon what principle of law, applicable to appellate jurisdiction, it can be supposed that this court has not judicial authority to correct the last-mentioned error, because they had before corrected the former; or by what process of reasoning it can be made out, that the error of an inferior court in actually pronouncing judgment for one of the parties, in a case in which it had no jurisdiction, cannot be looked into or corrected by this court, because we have decided a similar question presented in the pleadings. The last point is distinctly presented by the facts contained in the plaintiff's own bill of exceptions, which he himself brings here by this writ of error. It was the point which chiefly occupied the attention of the counsel on both sides in the argument—and the judgment which this court must render upon both errors is precisely the same. It must, in each of them, exercise jurisdiction over the judgment, and reverse it for the errors committed by the court below; and issue a mandate to the Circuit Court to conform its judgment to the opinion pronounced by this court, by dismissing the case for want of jurisdiction in the Circuit Court. This is the constant and invariable practice of this court, where it reverses a judgment for want of jurisdiction in the Circuit Court.

It can scarcely be necessary to pursue such a question further. The want of jurisdiction in the court below may appear on the record without any plea in abatement. This is familiarly the case where a court of chancery has exercised jurisdiction in a case where the plaintiff had a plain and adequate remedy at law, and it so appears by the transcript when brought here by appeal. So also where it appears that a court of admiralty has exercised jurisdiction in a case belonging exclusively to a court of common law. In these cases there is no plea in abatement. And for the same reason, and upon the same principles, where the defect of jurisdiction is patent on the record, this court is bound to reverse the judgment, although the defendant has not pleaded in abatement to the jurisdiction of the inferior court.

The cases of *Jackson v. Ashton* and of *Capron v. Van Noorden*, to which we have referred in a previous part of this opinion, are directly in point. In the last-mentioned case, Capron brought an action against Van Noorden in a Circuit Court of the United States, without showing, by the usual averments of citizenship, that the court had jurisdiction. There was no plea in abatement put in, and the parties went to trial upon the merits. The court gave judgment in favor of the defendant with costs. The plaintiff thereupon brought his writ of error, and this court reversed the judgment given in favor of the defendant, and remanded the case with directions to dismiss it, because it did not appear by the transcript that the Circuit Court had jurisdiction.

The case before us still more strongly imposes upon this court the duty of examining whether the court below has not committed an error, in taking jurisdiction and giving a judgment for costs in favor of the defendant; for in *Capron v. Van Noorden* the judgment was reversed, because it did not appear that the parties were citizens of different States. They might or might not be. But in this case it does appear that the plaintiff was born a slave; and if the facts upon which he relies have not made him free, then it appears affirmatively on the record that he is not a citizen, and consequently his suit against Sandford was not a suit between citizens of different States, and the court had no authority to pass any judgment between the parties. The suit ought, in this view of it, to have been dismissed by the Circuit Court, and its judgment in favor of Sandford is erroneous, and must be reversed.

It is true that the result either way, by dismissal or by a judgment for the defendant, makes very little, if any, difference in a pecuniary or personal point of view to either party. But the fact that the result would be very nearly the same to the parties in either form of judgment, would not justify this court in sanctioning an error in the judgment which is patent on the record, and which, if sanctioned, might be drawn into precedent, and lead to serious mischief and injustice in some future suit.

We proceed, therefore, to inquire whether the facts relied on by the plaintiff entitled him to his freedom. The case, as he himself states it, on the record brought here by his writ of error, is this:

The plaintiff was a negro slave, belonging to Dr. Emerson, who was a surgeon in the army of the United States. In the year 1834, he took the plaintiff from the State of Missouri to the military post at Rock Island, in the State of Illinois, and held him there as a slave until the month of April or May, 1836. At the time last mentioned, said Dr. Emerson removed the plaintiff from said military post at Rock Island to the military post at Fort Snelling, situate on the west bank of the Mississippi river, in the Territory known as Upper Louisiana, acquired by the United States of France, and situate north of the latitude of thirty-six degrees thirty minutes north, and north of the State of Missouri. Said Dr. Emerson held the plaintiff in slavery at said Fort Snelling, from said last-mentioned date until the year 1838.

In the year 1835, Harriet, who is named in the second count of the plaintiff's declaration, was the negro slave of Major Taliaferro, who belonged to the army of the United States. In that year, 1835, said Major Taliaferro took said Harriet to said Fort Snelling, a military post, situated as hereinbefore stated, and kept her there as a slave until the year 1836, and then sold and delivered her as a slave, at said Fort Snelling, unto the said Dr. Emerson here-inbefore named. Said Dr. Emerson held said Harriet in slavery at said Fort Snelling until the year 1838.

In the year 1836, the plaintiff and Harriet inter-married, at Fort Snelling, with the consent of Dr. Emerson, who then claimed to be their master and owner. Eliza and Lizzie, named in the third count of the plaintiff's declaration, are the fruit of that marriage. Eliza is about fourteen years old, and was born on board the steamboat Gipsey, north of the north line of the State of Missouri, and upon the river Mississippi. Lizzie is about seven years old, and was born in the State of Missouri, at the military post called Jefferson Barracks.

In the year 1838, said Dr. Emerson removed the plaintiff and said Harriet, and their said daughter Eliza, from said Fort Snelling to the State of Missouri, where they have ever since resided.

Before the commencement of this suit, said Dr. Emerson sold and conveyed the plaintiff, and Harriet, Eliza, and Lizzie, to the defendant, as slaves, and the defendant has ever since claimed to hold them, and each of them, as slaves.

In considering this part of the controversy, two questions arise: 1. Was he, together with his family, free in Missouri by reason of the stay in the territory of the United States hereinbefore mentioned? And 2. If they were not, is Scott himself free by reason of his removal to Rock Island, in the State of Illinois, as stated in the above admissions?

We proceed to examine the first question.

The act of Congress, upon which the plaintiff relies, declares that slavery and involuntary servitude, except as a punishment for crime, shall be forever prohibited in all that part of the territory ceded by France, under the name of Louisiana, which lies north of thirty-six degrees thirty minutes north latitude, and not included within the limits of Missouri. And the difficulty which meets us at the threshold of this part of the inquiry is, whether Congress was authorized to pass this law under any of the powers granted to it by the Constitution; for if the authority is not given by that instrument, it is the duty of this court to declare it void and inoperative, and incapable of conferring freedom upon any one who is held as a slave under the have of any one of the States.

The counsel for the plaintiff has laid much stress upon that article in the Constitution which confers on Congress the power "to dispose of and make all needful rules and regulations respecting the territory or other property belonging to the United States;" but, in the judgment of the court, that provision has no bearing on the present controversy, and the power there given, whatever it may be, is confined, and was intended to be confined, to the territory which at that time belonged to, or was claimed by, the United States, and was within their boundaries as settled by the treaty with Great Britain, and can have no influence upon a territory afterwards acquired from a foreign Government. It was a special provision for a known and particular territory, and to meet a present emergency, and nothing more.

A brief summary of the history of the times, as well as the careful and measured terms in which the article is framed, will show the correctness of this proposition.

It will be remembered that, from the commencement of the Revolutionary war, serious difficulties existed between the States, in relation to the disposition of large and unsettled territories which were included in the chartered limits of some of the States. And some of the other States, and more especially Maryland, which had no unsettled lands, insisted that as the unoccupied lands, if wrested from Great Britain, would owe their preservation to the common purse and the common sword, the money arising from them ought to be applied in just proportion among the several States to pay the expenses of the war, and ought not to be appropriated to the use of the State in whose chartered limits they might happen to lie, to the exclusion of the other States, by whose combined efforts and common expense the territory was defended and preserved against the claim of the British Government.

These difficulties caused much uneasiness during the war, while the issue was in some degree doubtful, and the future boundaries of the United States yet to be defined by treaty, if we achieved our independence.

The majority of the Congress of the Confederation obviously concurred in opinion with the State of Maryland, and desired to obtain from the States which claimed it a cession of this territory, in order that Congress might raise money on this security to carry on the war. This appears by the resolution passed on the 6th of September, 1780, strongly urging the States to cede these lands to the United States, both for the sake of peace and union among themselves, and to maintain the public credit; and this was followed by the resolution of October 10th, 1780, by which Congress pledged itself, that if the lands were ceded, as recommended by the resolution above mentioned, they should be disposed of for the common benefit of the United States, and be settled and formed into distinct republican States, which should become members of the Federal Union, and

have the same rights of sovereignty, and freedom, and independence, as other States.

But these difficulties became much more serious after peace took place, and the boundaries of the United States were established. Every State, at that time, felt severely the pressure of its war debt; but in Virginia, and some other States, there were large territories of unsettled lands, the sale of which would enable them to discharge their obligations without much inconvenience; while other States, which had no such resource, saw before them many years of heavy and burdensome taxation; and the latter insisted, for the reasons before stated, that these unsettled lands should be treated as the common property of the States, and the proceeds applied to their common benefit.

The letters from the statesmen of that day will show how much this controversy occupied their thoughts, and the dangers that were apprehended from it. It was the disturbing element of the time, and fears were entertained that it might dissolve the Confederation by which the States were then united.

These fears and dangers were, however, at once removed, when the State of Virginia, in 1784, voluntarily ceded to the United States the immense tract of country lying northwest of the river Ohio, and which was within the acknowledged limits of the State. The only object of the State, in making this cession, was to put an end to the threatening and exciting controversy, and to enable the Congress of that time to dispose of the lands, and appropriate the proceeds as a common fund for the common benefit of the States. It was not ceded, because it was inconvenient to the State to hold and govern it, nor from any expectation that it could be better or more conveniently governed by the United States.

The example of Virginia was soon afterwards followed by other States, and, at the time of the adoption of the Constitution, all of the States, similarly situated, had ceded their unappropriated lands, except North Carolina and Georgia. The main object for which these cessions were desired and made, was on account of their money value, and to put an end to a dangerous controversy, as to who was justly entitled to the proceeds when the lands should be sold. It is necessary to bring this part of the history of these cessions thus distinctly into view, because it will enable us the better to comprehend the phraseology of the article in the Constitution, so often referred to in the argument.

Undoubtedly the powers of sovereignty and the eminent domain were ceded with the land. This was essential, in order to make it effectual, and to accomplish its objects. But it must be remembered that, at that time, there was no Government of the United States in existence with enumerated and limited powers; what was then called the United States, were thirteen separate, sovereign, independent States, which had entered into a league or confederation for their mutual protection and advantage, and the Congress of the United States was composed of the representatives of these separate sovereignties, meeting together, as equals, to discuss and decide on certain measures which the States, by the Articles of Confederation, had agreed to submit to their decision. But this Confederation had none of the attributes of sovereignty in legislative, executive, or judicial power. It was little more than a congress of ambassadors, authorized to represent separate nations, in matters in which they had a common concern.

It was this Congress that accepted the cession from Virginia. They had no power to accept it under the Articles of Confederation. But they had an undoubted right, as independent sovereignties, to accept any cession of territory for their common benefit, which all of them assented to; and it is equally clear, that as their common property, and having no superior to control them, they had the right to exercise absolute dominion over it, subject only to the restrictions which Virginia had imposed in her act of cession. There was, as we have said, no Government of the United States then in existence with special enumerated and limited powers. The territory belonged to sovereignties, who, subject to the limitations above mentioned, had a right to establish any form of government they pleased, by compact or treaty among themselves, and to regulate rights of person and rights of property in the territory, as they might deem proper. It was by a Congress, representing the authority of these several and separate sovereignties, and acting under their authority and command, (but not from any authority derived from the Articles of Confederation,) that the instrument usually called the ordinance of 1787 was adopted; regulating in much detail the principles and the laws by which this territory should be governed; and among other provisions, slavery is prohibited in it. We do not question the power of the States, by agreement among themselves, to pass this ordinance, nor its obligatory force in the territory, while the confederation or league of the States in their separate sovereign character continued to exist.

This was the state of things when the Constitution of the United States was formed. The territory ceded by Virginia belonged to the several confederated States as common property, and they had united in establishing in it a system of government and jurisprudence, in order to prepare it for admission as States, according to the terms of the cession. They were about to dissolve this federative Union, and to surrender a portion of their independent sovereignty to a new Government, which, for certain purposes, would make the people of the several States one people, and which was to be supreme and controlling within its sphere of action throughout the United States; but this Government was to be carefully limited in its powers, and to exercise no authority beyond those expressly granted by the Constitution, or necessarily to be implied from the language of the instrument, and the objects it was intended to accomplish; and as this league of States would, upon the adoption of the new Government, cease to have any power over the territory, and the ordinance they had agreed upon be incapable of execution, and a mere nullity, it was obvious that some provision was necessary to give the new Government sufficient power to enable it to carry into effect the objects for which it was ceded, and the compacts and agreements which the States had made with each other in the exercise of their powers of sovereignty. It was necessary that the lands should be sold to pay the war debt; that a Government and system of jurisprudence should be maintained in it, to protect the citizens of the United States who should migrate to the territory, in their rights of person and of property. It was also necessary that the new Government, about to be adopted, should be authorized to maintain the claim of the United States to the unappropriated lands in North Carolina and Georgia, which had not then been ceded, but the cession of which was confidently anticipated upon some terms that would be arranged between the General Government and these two States. And, moreover, there were many articles of value besides this property in land, such as arms, military stores, munitions, and ships of war, which were the common property of the States, when acting in their independent characters as confederates, which neither the new Government nor any one else would have a right to take possession of, or control, without authority from them; and it was to place these things under the guardianship and protection of the new Government, and to clothe it with the necessary powers, that the clause was inserted in the Constitution which give Congress the power "to dispose of and make all needful rules and regulations respecting the territory or other property belonging to the United

States." It was intended for a specific purpose, to provide for the things we have mentioned. It was to transfer to the new Government the property then held in common by the States, and to give to that Government power to apply it to the objects for which it had been destined by mutual agreement among the States before their league was dissolved. It applied only to the property which the States held in common at that time, and has no reference whatever to any territory or other property which the new sovereignty might afterwards itself acquire.

The language used in the clause, the arrangement and combination of the powers, and the somewhat unusual phraseology it uses, when it speaks of the political power to be exercised in the government of the territory, all indicate the design and meaning of the clause to be such as we have mentioned. It does not speak of any territory, nor of Territories, but uses language which, according to its legitimate meaning, points to a particular thing. The power is given in relation only to the territory of the United States—that is, to a territory then in existence, and then known or claimed as the territory of the United States. It begins its enumeration of powers by that of disposing, in other words, making sale of the lands, or raising money from them, which, as we have already said, was the main object of the cession, and which is accordingly the first thing provided for in the article. It then gives the power which was necessarily associated with the disposition and sale of the lands—that is, the power of making needful rules and regulations respecting the territory. And whatever construction may now be given to these words, every one, we think, must admit that they are not the words usually employed by statesmen in giving supreme power of legislation. They are certainly very unlike the words used in the power granted to legislate over territory which the new Government might afterwards itself obtain by cession from a State, either for its seat of Government, or for forts, magazines, arsenals, dock yards, and other needful buildings.

And the same power of making needful rules respecting the territory is, in precisely the same language, applied to the other property belonging to the United States—associating the power over the territory in this respect with the power over movable or personal property—that is, the ships, arms, and munitions of war, which then belonged in common to the State sovereignties. And it will hardly be said, that this power, in relation to the last-mentioned objects, was deemed necessary to be thus specially given to the new Government, in order to authorize it to make needful rules and regulations respecting the ships it might itself build, or arms and munitions of war it might itself manufacture or provide for the public service.

No one, it is believed, would think a moment of deriving the power of Congress to make needful rules and regulations in relation to property of this kind from this clause of the Constitution. Nor can it, upon any fair construction, be applied to any property but that which the new Government was about the receive from the confederated States. And if this be true as to this property, it must be equally true and limited as to the territory, which is so carefully and precisely coupled with it—and like it referred to as property in the power granted. The concluding words of the clause appear to render this construction irresistible; for, after the provisions we have mentioned, it proceeds to say, "that nothing in the Constitution shall be so construed as to prejudice any claims of the United States, or of any particular State."

Now, as we have before said, all of the States, except North Carolina and Georgia, had made the cession before the Constitution was adopted, according to the resolution of Congress of October 10, 1780. The claims of other States, that the unappropriated lands in these two States should be applied to the common benefit, in like manner, was still insisted on, but refused by the States. And this member of the clause in question evidently applies to them, and can apply to nothing else. It was to exclude the conclusion that either party, by adopting the Constitution, would surrender what they deemed their rights. And when the latter provision relates so obviously to the unappropriated lands not yet ceded by the States, and the first clause makes provision for those then actually ceded, it is impossible, by any just rule of construction, to make the first provision general, and extend to all territories, which the Federal Government might in any way afterwards acquire, when the latter is plainly and unequivocally confined to a particular territory; which was a part of the same controversy, and involved in the same dispute, and depended upon the same principles. The union of the two provisions in the same clause shows that they were kindred subjects; and that the whole clause is local, and relates only to lands, within the limits of the United States, which had been or then were claimed by a State; and that no other territory was in the mind of the framers of the Constitution, or intended to be embraced in it. Upon any other construction it would be impossible to account for the insertion of the last provision in the place where it is found, or to comprehend why, or for what object, it was associated with the previous provision.

This view of the subject is confirmed by the manner in which the present Government of the United States dealt with the subject as soon as it came into existence. It must be borne in mind that the same States that formed the Confederation also formed and adopted the new Government, to which so large a portion of their former sovereign powers were surrendered. It must also be borne in mind that all of these same States which had then ratified the new Constitution were represented in the Congress which passed the first law for the government of this territory; and many of the members of that legislative body had been deputies from the States under the Confederation—had united in adopting the ordinance of 1787, and assisted in forming the new Government under which they were then acting, and whose powers they were then exercising. And it is obvious from the law they passed to carry into effect the principles and provisions of the ordinance, that they regarded it as the act of the States done in the exercise of their legitimate powers at the time. The new Government took the territory as it found it, and in the condition in which it was transferred, and did not attempt to undo anything that had been done. And, among the earliest laws passed under the new Government, is one reviving the ordinance of 1787, which had become inoperative and a nullity upon the adoption of the Constitution. This law introduces no new form or principles for its government, but recites, in the preamble, that it is passed in order that this ordinance may continue to have full effect, and proceeds to make only those rules and regulations which were needful to adapt it to the new Government, into whose hands the power had fallen. It appears, therefore, that this Congress regarded the purposes to which the land in this Territory was to be applied, and the form of government and principles of jurisprudence which were to prevail there, while it remained in the Territorial state, as already determined on by the States when they had full power and right to make the decision; and that the new Government, having received it in this condition, ought to carry substantially into effect the plans and principles which had been previously adopted by the States, and which no doubt the States anticipated when they surrendered their power to the new Government. And if we regard this clause of the Constitution as pointing to this Territory, with a Territorial Government already established in it, which had been ceded to the States for the purposes hereinbefore mentioned—

every word in it is perfectly appropriate and easily understood, and the provisions it contains are in perfect harmony with the objects for which it was ceded, and with the condition of its government as a Territory at the time. We can, then, easily account for the manner in which the first Congress legislated on the subject—and can also understand why this power over the territory was associated in the same clause with the other property of the United States, and subjected to the like power of making needful rules and regulations. But if the clause is construed in the expanded sense contended for, so as to embrace any territory acquired from a foreign nation by the present Government, and to give it in such territory a despotic and unlimited power over persons and property, such as the confederated States might exercise in their common property, it would be difficult to account for the phraseology used, when compared with other grants of power—and also for its association with the other provisions in the same clause.

The Constitution has always been remarkable for the felicity of its arrangement of different subjects, and the perspicuity and appropriateness of the language it uses. But if this clause is construed to extend to territory acquired by the present Government from a foreign nation, outside of the limits of any charter from the British Government to a colony, it would be difficult to say, why it was deemed necessary to give the Government the power to sell any vacant lands belonging to the sovereignty which might be found within it; and if this was necessary, why the grant of this power should precede the power to legislate over it and establish a Government there; and still more difficult to say, why it was deemed necessary so specially and particularly to grant the power to make needful rules and regulations in relation to any personal or movable property it might acquire there. For the words, other property necessarily, by every known rule of interpretation, must mean property of a different description from territory or land. And the difficulty would perhaps be insurmountable in endeavoring to account for the last member of the sentence, which provides that "nothing in this Constitution shall be so construed as to prejudice any claims of the United States or any particular State," or to say how any particular State could have claims in or to a territory ceded by a foreign Government, or to account for associating this provision with the preceding provisions of the clause, with which it would appear to have no connection.

The words "needful rules and regulations" would seem, also, to have been cautiously used for some definite object. They are not the words usually employed by statesmen, when they mean to give the powers of sovereignty, or to establish a Government, or to authorize its establishment. Thus, in the law to renew and keep alive the ordinance of 1787, and to re-establish the Government, the title of the law is: "An act to provide for the government of the territory northwest of the river Ohio." And in the Constitution, when granting the power to legislate over the territory that may be selected for the seat of Government independently of a State, it does not say Congress shall have power "to make all needful rules and regulations respecting the territory;" but it declares that "Congress shall have power to exercise exclusive legislation in all cases whatsoever over such District (not exceeding ten miles square) as may, by cession of particular States and the acceptance of Congress, become the seat of the Government of the United States."

The words "rules and regulations" are usually employed in the Constitution in speaking of some particular specified power which it means to confer on the Government, and not, as we have seen, when granting general powers of legislation. As, for example, in the particular power to Congress "to make rules for the government and regulation of the land and naval forces, or the particular and specific power to regulate commerce;" "to establish an uniform rule of naturalization;" "to coin money and regulate the value thereof." And to construe the words of which we are speaking as a general and unlimited grant of sovereignty over territories which the Government might afterwards acquire, is to use them in a sense and for a purpose for which they were not used in any other part of the instrument. But if confined to a particular Territory, in which a Government and laws had already been established, but which would require some alterations to adapt it to the new Government, the words are peculiarly applicable and appropriate for that purpose. The necessity of this special provision in relation to property and the rights or property held in common by the confederated States, is illustrated by the first clause of the sixth article. This clause provides that "all debts, contracts, and engagements entered into before the adoption of this Constitution, shall be as valid against the United States under this Government as under the Confederation." This provision, like the one under consideration, was indispensable if the new Constitution was adopted. The new Government was not a mere change in a dynasty, or in a form of government, leaving the nation or sovereignty the same, and clothed with all the rights, and

bound by all the obligations of the preceding one. But, when the present United States came into existence under the new Government, it was a new political body, a new nation, then for the first time taking its place in the family of nations. It took nothing by succession from the Confederation. It had no right, as its successor, to any property or rights of property which it had acquired, and was not liable for any of its obligations. It was evidently viewed in this light by the framers of the Constitution. And as the several States would cease to exist in their former confederated character upon the adoption of the Constitution, and could not, in that character, again assemble together, special provisions were indispensable to transfer to the new Government the property and rights which at that time they held in common; and at the same time to authorize it to lay taxes and appropriate money to pay the common debt which they had contracted; and this power could only be given to it by special provisions in the Constitution. The clause in relation to the territory and other property of the United States provided for the first, and the clause last quoted provided for the other. They have no connection with the general powers and rights of sovereignty delegated to the new Government, and can neither enlarge nor diminish them. They were inserted to meet a present emergency, and not to regulate its powers as a Government.

Indeed, a similar provision was deemed necessary, in relation to treaties made by the Confederation; and when in the clause next succeeding the one of which we have last spoken, it is declared that treaties shall be the supreme law of the land, care is taken to include, by express words, the treaties made by the confederated States. The language is: "and all treaties made, or which shall be made, under the authority of the United States, shall be the supreme law of the land."

Whether, therefore, we take the particular clause in question, by itself, or in connection with the other provisions of the Constitution, we think it clear, that it applies only to the particular territory of which we have spoken, and cannot, by any just rule of interpretation, be extended to territory which the new Government might afterwards obtain from a foreign nation. Consequently, the power which Congress may have lawfully exercised in this Territory, while it remained under a Territorial Government, and which may have been sanctioned by judicial decision, can furnish no justification and no argument to support a similar exercise of power over territory afterwards acquired by the Federal Government. We put aside, therefore, any argument, drawn from precedents, showing the extent of the power which the General Government exercised over slavery in this Territory, as altogether inapplicable to the case before us.

But the case of the *American and Ocean Insurance Companies v. Canter* (1 Pet., 511) has been quoted as establishing a different construction of this clause of the Constitution. There is, however, not the slightest conflict between the opinion now given and the one referred to; and it is only by taking a single sentence out of the latter and separating it from the context, that even an appearance of conflict can be shown. We need not comment on such a mode of expounding an opinion of the court. Indeed it most commonly misrepresents instead of expounding it. And this is fully exemplified in the case referred to, where, if one sentence is taken by itself, the opinion would appear to be in direct conflict with that now given; but the words which immediately follow that sentence show that the court did not mean to decide the point, but merely affirmed the power of Congress to establish a Government in the Territory, leaving it an open question, whether that power was derived from this clause in the Constitution, or was to be necessarily inferred from a power to acquire territory by cession from a foreign Government. The opinion on this part of the case is short, and we give the whole of it to show how well the selection of a single sentence is calculated to mislead.

The passage referred to is in page 542, in which the court, in speaking of the power of Congress to establish a Territorial Government in Florida until it should become a State, uses the following language:

"In the mean time Florida continues to be a Territory of the United States, governed by that clause of the Constitution which empowers Congress to make all needful rules and regulations respecting the territory or other property of the United States. Perhaps the power of governing a Territory belonging to the United States, which has not, by becoming a State, acquired the means of self-government, may result, necessarily, from the facts that it is not within the jurisdiction of any particular State, and is within the power and jurisdiction of the United States. The right to govern may be the inevitable consequence of the right to acquire territory. Whichever may be the source from which the power is derived, the possession of it is unquestionable."

It is thus clear, from the whole opinion on this point, that the court did not mean to decide whether the power was derived from the clause in the Constitution, or was the necessary consequence of the right to acquire. They do decide that the power in Congress is unquestionable, and in this we entirely concur, and nothing will be found in this opinion to the contrary. The power stands firmly on the latter alternative put by the court—that is, as "the inevitable consequence of the right to acquire territory."

And what still more clearly demonstrates that the court did not mean to decide the question, but leave it open for future consideration, is the fact that the case was decided in the Circuit Court by Mr. Justice Johnson, and his decision was affirmed by the Supreme Court. His opinion at the circuit is given in full in a note to the case, and in that opinion he states, in explicit terms, that the clause of the Constitution applies only to the territory then within the limits of the United States, and not to Florida, which had been acquired by cession from Spain. This part of his opinion will be found in the note in page 517 of the report. But he does not dissent from the opinion of the Supreme Court; thereby showing that, in his judgment, as well as that of the court, the case before them did not call for a decision on that particular point, and the court abstained from deciding it. And in a part of its opinion subsequent to the passage we have quoted, where the court speak of the legislative power of Congress in Florida, they still speak with the same reserve. And in page 546, speaking of the power of Congress to authorize the Territorial Legislature to establish courts there, the court say: "They are legislative courts, created in virtue of the general right of sovereignty which exists in the Government, or in virtue of that clause which enables Congress to make all needful rules and regulations respecting the territory belonging to the United States."

It has been said that the construction given to this clause is new, and now for the first time brought forward. The case of which we are speaking, and which has been so much discussed, shows that the fact is otherwise. It shows that precisely the same question came before Mr. Justice Johnson, at his circuit, thirty years ago—was fully considered by him, and the same construction given to the clause in the Constitution which is now given by this court. And that upon an appeal from his decision the same question was brought before this court, but was not decided because a decision upon it was not required by the case before the court.

There is another sentence in the opinion which has been commented on, which even in a still more striking manner shows how one may mislead or be misled by taking out a single sentence from the opinion of a court, and leaving out of view what precedes and follows. It is in page 546, near the close of the opinion, in which the court say: "In legislating for them," (the territories of the United States,) "Congress exercises the combined powers of the General and of a State Government." And it is said, that as a State may unquestionably prohibit slavery within its territory, this sentence decides in effect that Congress may do the same in a Territory of the United States, exercising there the powers of a State, as well as the power of the General Government.

The examination of this passage in the case referred to, would be more appropriate when we come to consider in another part of this opinion what power Congress can constitutionally exercise in a Territory, over the rights of person or rights of property of a citizen. But, as it is in the same case with the passage we have before commented on, we dispose of it now, as it will save the court from the necessity of referring again to the case. And it will be seen upon reading the page in which this sentence is found, that it has no reference whatever to the power of Congress over rights of person or rights of property—but relates altogether to the power of establishing judicial tribunals to administer the laws constitutionally passed, and defining the jurisdiction they may exercise.

The law of Congress establishing a Territorial Government in Florida, provided that the Legislature of the Territory should have legislative powers over "all rightful objects of legislation; but no law should be valid which was inconsistent with the laws and Constitution of the United States."

Under the power thus conferred, the Legislature of Florida passed an act, erecting a tribunal at Key West to decide cases of salvage. And in the case of which we are speaking, the question arose whether the Territorial Legislature could be authorized by Congress to establish such a tribunal, with such powers; and one of the parties, among other objections, insisted that Congress could not under the Constitution authorize the Legislature of the Territory to establish such a tribunal with such powers, but that it must be established by Congress itself; and that a sale of cargo made under its order, to pay salvors, was void, as made without legal authority, and passed no property to the purshaser. It is in disposing of this objection that the sentence relied on occurs, and the court begin that part of the opinion

by stating with great precision the point which they are about to decide.

They say: "It has been contended that by the Constitution of the United States, the judicial power of the United States extends to all cases of admiralty and maritime jurisdiction; and that the whole of the judicial power must be vested 'in one Supreme Court, and in such inferior courts as Congress shall from time to time ordain and establish.' Hence it has been argued that Congress cannot vest admiralty jurisdiction in courts created by the Territorial Legislature."

And after thus clearly stating the point before them, and which they were about to decide, they proceed to show that these Territorial tribunals were not constitutional courts, but merely legislative, and that Congress might, therefore, delegate the power to the Territorial Government to establish the court in question; and they conclude that part of the opinion in the following words: "Although admiralty jurisdiction can be exercised in the States in those courts only which are established in pursuance of the third article of the Constitution, the same limitation does not extend to the Territories. In legislating for them, Congress exercises the combined powers of the General and State Governments."

Thus it will be seen by these quotations from the opinion, that the court, after stating the question it was about to decide in a manner too plain to be misunderstood, proceeded to decide it, and announced, as the opinion of the tribunal, that in organizing the judicial department of the Government in a Territory of the United States, Congress does not act under, and is not restricted by, the third article in the Constitution, and is not bound, in a Territory, to ordain and establish courts in which the judges hold their offices during good behaviour, but may exercise the discretionary power which a State exercises in establishing its judicial department, and regulating the jurisdiction of its courts, and may authorize the Territorial Government to establish, or may itself establish, courts in which the judges hold their offices for a term of years only; and may vest in them judicial power upon subjects confided to the judiciary of the United States. And in doing this, Congress undoubtedly exercises the combined power of the General and a State Government. It exercises the discretionary power of a State Government in authorizing the establishment of a court in which the judges hold their appointments for a term of years only, and not during good behaviour; and it exercises the power of the General Government in investing that court with admiralty jurisdiction, over which the General Government had exclusive jurisdiction in the Territory.

No one, we presume, will question the correctness of that opinion; nor is there anything in conflict with it in the opinion now given. The point decided in the case cited has no relation to the question now before the court. That depended on the construction of the third article of the Constitution, in relation to the judiciary of the United States, and the power which Congress might exercise in a Territory in organizing the judicial department of the Government. The case before us depends upon other and different provisions of the Constitution, altogether separate and apart from the one above mentioned. The question as to what courts Congress may ordain or establish in a Territory to administer laws which the Constitution authorizes it to pass, and what laws it is or is not authorized by the Constitution to pass, are widely different—are regulated by different and separate articles of the Constitution, and stand upon different principles. And we are satisfied that no one who reads attentively the page in Peters's Reports to which we have referred, can suppose that the attention of the court was drawn for a moment to the question now before this court, or that it meant in that case to say that Congress had a right to prohibit a citizen of the United States from taking any property which he lawfully held into a Territory of the United States.

This brings us to examine by what provision of the Constitution the present Federal Government, under its delegated and restricted powers, is authorized to acquire territory outside of the original limits of the United States, and what powers it may exercise therein over the person or property of a citizen of the United States, while it remains a Territory, and until it shall be admitted as one of the States of the Union.

There is certainly no power given by the Constitution to the Federal Government to establish or maintain colonies bordering on the United States or at a distance, to be ruled and governed at its own pleasure; nor to enlarge its territorial limits in any way, except by the admission of new States. That power is plainly given; and if a new State is admitted, it needs no further legislation by Congress, because the Constitution itself defines the relative rights and powers, and duties of the State, and the citizens of the State, and the Federal Government. But no power is given to acquire a Territory to be held and governed permanently in that character.

And indeed the power exercised by Congress to acquire territory and establish a Government there,

according to its own unlimited discretion, was viewed with great jealousy by the leading statesmen of the day. And in the Federalist, (No. 38,) written by Mr. Madison, he speaks of the acquisition of the Northwestern Territory by the confederated States, by the cession from Virginia, and the establishment of a Government there, as an exercise of power not warranted by the Articles of Confederation, and dangerous to the liberties of the people. And he urges the adoption of the Constitution as a security and safeguard against such an exercise of power.

We do not mean, however, to question the power of Congress in this respect. The power to expand the territory of the United States by the admission of new States is plainly given; and in the construction of this power by all the departments of the Government, it has been held to authorize the acquisition of territory, not fit for admission at the time, but to be admitted as soon as its population and situation would entitle it to admission. It is acquired to become a State, and not to be held as a colony and governed by Congress with absolute authority; and as the propriety of admitting a new State is committed to the sound discretion of Congress, the power to acquire territory for that purpose, to be held by the United States until it is in a suitable condition to become a State upon an equal footing with the other States, must rest upon the same discretion. It is a question for the political department of the Government, and not the judicial; and whatever the political departent of the Government shall recognise as within the limits of the United States, the judicial department is also bound to recognise, and to administer in it the laws of the United States, so far as they apply, and to maintain in the Territory the authority and rights of the Government, and also the personal rights and rights of property of individual citizens, as secured by the Constitution. All we mean to say on this point is, that, as there is no express regulation in the Constitution defining the power which the General Government may exercise over the person or property of a citizen in a Territory thus acquired, the court must necessarily look to the provisions and principles of the Constitution, and its distribution of powers, for the rules and principles by which its decision must be governed.

Taking this rule to guide us, it may be safely assumed that citizens of the United States who migrate to a Territory belonging to the people of the United States, cannot be ruled as mere colonists, dependent upon the will of the General Government, and to be governed by any laws it may think proper to impose. The principle upon which our Governments rest, and upon which alone they continue to exist, is the union of States, sovereign and independent within their own limits in their internal and domestic concerns, and bound together as one people by a General Government, possessing certain enumerated and restricted powers, delegated to it by the people of the several States, and exercising supreme authority within the scope of the powers granted to it, throughout the dominion of the United States. A power, therefore, in the General Government to obtain and hold colonies and dependent territories, over which they might legislate without restriction, would be inconsistent with its own existence in its present form. Whatever it acquires, it acquires for the benefit of the people of the several States who created it. It is their trustee acting for them, and charged with the duty of promoting the interests of the whole people of the Union in the exercise of the powers specifically granted.

At the time when the Territory in question was obtained by cession from France, it contained no population fit to be associated together and admitted as a State; and it therefore was absolutely necessary to hold possession of it, as a Territory belonging to the United States, until it was settled and inhabited by a civilized community capable of self-government, and in a condition to be admitted on equal terms with the other States as a member of the Union. But, as we have before said, it was acquired by the General Government, as the representative and trustee of the people of the United States, and it must therefore be held in that character for their common and equal benefit; for it was the people of the several States, acting through their agent and representative, the Federal Government, who in fact acquired the Territory in question, and the Government holds it for their common use until it shall be associated with the other States as a member of the Union.

But until that time arrives, it is undoubtedly necessary that some Government should be established, in order to organize society, and to protect the inhabitants in their persons and property; and as the people of the United States could act in this matter only through the Government which represented them, and the through which they spoke and acted when the Territory was obtained, it was not only within the scope of its powers, but it was its duty to pass such laws and establish such a Government as would enable those by whose authority they acted to reap the advantages anticipated from its acquisition, and to gather there a population which would enable it to

assume the position to which it was destined among the States of the Union. The power to acquire necessarily carries with it the power to preserve and apply to the purposes for which it was acquired. The form of government to be established necessarily rested in the discretion of Congress. It was their duty to establish the one that would be best suited for the protection and security of the citizens of the United States, and other inhabitants who might be authorized to take up their abode there, and that must always depend upon the existing condition of the Territory, as to the number and character of its inhabitants, and their situation in the Territory. In some cases a Government, consisting of persons appointed by the Federal Government, would best subserve the interests of the Territory, when the inhabitants were few and scattered, and new to one another. In other instances, it would be more advisable to commit the powers of self-government to the people who had settled in the Territory, as being the most competent to determine what was best for their own interests. But some form of civil authority would be absolutely necessary to organize and preserve civilized society, and prepare it to become a State; and what is the best form must always depend on the condition of the Territory at the time, and the choice of the mode must depend upon the exercise of a discretionary power by Congress, acting within the scope of its constitutional authority, and not infringing upon the rights of person or rights of property of the citizen who might go there to reside, or for any other lawful purpose. It was acquired by the exercise of this discretion, and it must be held and governed in like manner, until it is fitted to be a State.

But the power of Congress over the person or property of a citizen can never be a mere discretionary power under our Constitution and form of Government. The powers of the Government and the rights and privileges of the citizen are regulated and plainly defined by the Constitution itself. And when the Territory becomes a part of the United States, the Federal Government enters into possession in the character impressed upon it by those who created it. It enters upon it with its powers over the citizen strictly defined, and limited by the Constitution, from which it derives its own existence, and by virtue of which alone it continues to exist and act as a Government and sovereignty. It has no power of any kind beyond it; and it cannot, when it enters a Territory of the United States, put off its character, and assume discretionary or despotic powers which the Constitution has denied to it. It cannot create for itself a new character separated from the citizens of the United States, and the duties it owes them under the provisions of the Constitution. The Territory being a part of the United States, the Government and the citizen both enter it under the authority of the Constitution, with their respective rights defined and marked out; and the Federal Government can exercise no power over his person or property, beyond what that instrument confers, nor lawfully deny any right which it has reserved.

A reference to a few of the provisions of the Constitution will illustrate this proposition.

For example, no one, we presume, will contend that Congress can make any law in a Territory respecting the establishment of religion, or the free exercise thereof, or abridging the freedom of speech or of the press, or the right of the people of the Territory peaceably to assemble, and to petition the Government for the redress of grievances.

Nor can Congress deny to the people the right to keep and bear arms, nor the right to trial by jury, nor compel any one to be a witness against himself in a criminal proceeding.

These powers, and others, in relation to rights of person, which it is not necessary here to enumerate, are, in express and positive terms, denied to the General Government; and the rights of private property have been guarded with equal care. Thus the rights of property are united with the rights of person, and placed on the same ground by the fifth amendment to the Constitution, which provides that no person shall be deprived of life, liberty, and property, without due process of law. And an act of Congress which deprives a citizen of the United States of his liberty or property, merely because he came himself or brought his property into a particular Territory of the United States, and who had committed no offence against the laws, could hardly be dignified with the name of due process of law.

So, too, it will hardly be contended that Congress could by law quarter a soldier in a house in a Territory without the consent of the owner, in time of peace; nor in time of war, but in a manner prescribed by law. Nor could they by law forfeit the property of a citizen in a Territory who was convicted of treason, for a longer period than the life of the person convicted; nor take private property for public use without just compensation.

The powers over person and property of which we speak are not only not granted to Congress, but are in express terms denied, and they are forbidden to exercise them. And this prohibition is not confined to the States, but the words are general, and extend to the whole territory over which the Constitution gives it power to legislate, including those portions of it remaining under Territorial Government, as well as that covered by States. It is a total absence of power everywhere within the dominion of the United States, and places the citizens of a Territory, so far as these rights are concerned, on the same footing with citizens of the States, and guards them as firmly and plainly against any inroads which the General Government might attempt, under the plea of implied or incidental powers. And if Congress itself cannot do this—if it is beyond the powers conferred on the Federal Government—it will be admitted, we presume, that it could not authorize a Territorial Government to exercise them. It could confer no power on any local Government, established by its authority, to violate the provisions of the Constitution.

It seems, however, to be supposed, that there is a difference between property in a slave and other property, and that different rules may be applied to it in expounding the Constitution of the United States. And the laws and usages of nations, and the writings of eminent jurists upon the relation of master and slave and their mutual rights and duties, and the powers which Governments may exercise over it, have been dwelt upon in the argument.

But in considering the question before us, it must be borne in mind that there is no law of nations standing between the people of the United States and their Government, and interfering with their relation to each other. The powers of the Government, and the rights of the citizen under it, are positive and practical regulations plainly written down. The people of the United States have delegated to it certain enumerated powers, and forbidden it to exercise others. It has no power over the person or property of a citizen but what the citizens of the United States have granted. And no laws or usages of other nations, or reasoning of statesmen or jurists upon the relations of master and slave, can enlarge the powers of the Government, or take from the citizens the rights they have reserved. And if the Constitution recognises the right of property of the master in a slave, and makes no distinction between that description of property and other property owned by a citizen, no tribunal, acting under the authority of the United States, whether it be legislative, executive, or judicial, has a right to draw such a distinction, or deny to it the benefit of the provisions and guarantees which have been provided for the protection of private property against the encroachments of the Government.

Now, as we have already said in an earlier part of this opinion, upon a different point, the right of property in a slave is distinctly and expressly affirmed in the Constitution. The right to traffic in it, like an ordinary article of merchandise and property, was guarantied to the citizens of the United States, in every State that might desire it, for twenty years. And the Government in express terms is pledged to protect it in all future time, if the slave escapes from his owner. This is done in plain words—too plain to be misunderstood. And no word can be found in the Constitution which gives Congress a greater power over slave property, or which entitles property of that kind to less protection that property of any other description. The only power conferred is the power coupled with the duty of guarding and protecting the owner in his rights.

Upon these considerations, it is the opinion of the court that the act of Congress which prohibited a citizen from holding and owning property of this kind in the territory of the United States north of the line therein mentioned, is not warranted by the Constitution, and is therefore void; and that neither Dred Scott himself, nor any of his family, were made free by being carried into this territory; even if they had been carried there by the owner, with the intention of becoming a permanent resident.

We have so far examined the case, as it stands under the Constitution of the United States, and the powers thereby delegated to the Federal Government.

But there is another point in the case which depends on State power and State law. And it is contended, on the part of the plaintiff, that he is made free by being taken to Rock Island, in the State of Illinois, independently of his residence in the territory of the United States; and being so made free, he was not again reduced to a state of slavery by being brought back to Missouri.

Our notice of this part of the case will be very brief; for the principle on which it depends was decided in this court, upon much consideration, in the case of *Strader et al. v. Graham*, reported in 10th Howard, 82. In that case, the slaves had been taken from Kentucky to Ohio, with the consent of the owner, and afterwards brought back to Kentucky. And this court held that their status or condition, as free or slave, depended upon the laws of Kentucky, when they were brought back into that State, and not of Ohio; and that this court had no jurisdiction to revise the judgment of a State court upon its own laws. This was the point directly before the court, and the decision that this court had not jurisdiction turned upon it, as will be seen by the report of the case.

So in this case. As Scott was a slave when taken into the State of Illinois by his owner, and was there held as such, and brought back in that character, his status, as free or slave, depended on the laws of Missouri, and not of Illinois.

It has, however, been urged in the argument, that by the laws of Missouri he was free on his return, and that this case, therefore, cannot be governed by the case of *Strader et al. v. Graham*, where it appeared, by the laws of Kentucky, that the plaintiffs continued to be slaves on their return from Ohio. But whatever doubts or opinions may, at one time, have been entertained upon this subject, we are satisfied, upon a careful examination of all the cases decided in the State courts of Missouri referred to, that it is now firmly settled by the decisions of the highest court in the State, that Scott and his family upon their return were not free, but were, by the laws of Missouri, the property of the defendant; and that the Circuit Court of the United States had no jurisdiction, when, by the laws of the State, the plaintiff was a slave, and not a citizen.

Moreover, the plaintiff, it appears, brought a similar action against the defendant in the State court of Missouri, claiming the freedom of himself and his family upon the same grounds and the same evidence upon which he relies in the case before the court. The case was carried before the Supreme Court of the State; was fully argued there; and that court decided that neither the plaintiff nor his family were entitled to freedom, and were still the slaves of the defendant; and reversed the judgment of the inferior State court, which had given a different decision. If the plaintiff supposed that this judgment of the Supreme Court of the State was erroneous, and that this court had jurisdiction to revise and reverse it, the only mode by which he could legally bring it before this court was by writ of error directed to the Supreme Court of the State, requiring it to transmit the record to this court. If this had been done, it is too plain for argument that the writ must have been dismissed for want of jurisdiction in this court. The case of *Strader and others v. Graham* is directly in point; and, indeed, independent of any decision, the language of the 25th section of the act of 1789 is too clear and precise to admit of controversy.

But the plaintiff did not pursue the mode prescribed by law for bringing the judgment of a State court before this court for revision, but suffered the case to be remanded to the inferior State court, where it is still continued, and is, by agreement of parties, to await the judgment of this court on the point. All of this appears on the record before us, and by the printed report of the case.

And while the case is yet open and pending in the inferior State court, the plaintiff goes into the Circuit Court of the United States, upon the same case and the same evidence, and against the same party, and proceeds to judgment, and then brings here the same case from the Circuit Court, which the law would not have permitted him to bring directly from the State court. And if this court takes jurisdiction in this form, the result, so far as the rights of the respective parties are concerned, is in every respect substantially the same as if it had in open violation of law entertained jurisdiction over the judgment of the State court upon a writ of error, and revised and reversed its judgment upon the ground that its opin-ion upon the question of law was erroneous. It would ill become this court to sanction such an attempt to evade the law, or to exercise an appellate power in this circuitous way, which it is forbidden to exercise in the direct and regular and invariable forms of judicial proceedings.

Upon the whole, therefore, it is the judgment of this court, that it appears by the record before us that the plaintiff in error is not a citizen of Missouri, in the sense in which that word is used in the Constitution; and that the Circuit Court of the United States, for that reason, had no jurisdiction in the case, and could give no judgment in it. Its judgment for the defendant must, consequently, be reversed, and a mandate issued, directing the suit to be dismissed for want of jurisdiction.

An 1860 lithograph of Abraham Lincoln (Library of Congress)

ABRAHAM LINCOLN'S "HOUSE DIVIDED" SPEECH

1858

"A house divided against itself cannot stand."

Overview

On June 16, 1858, the Republican Party of Illinois convened at Springfield to nominate its candidate for the U.S. Senate. Taking a first step toward the popular election of U.S. senators, the convention bypassed the state legislature and unanimously nominated Abraham Lincoln as its candidate. Anticipating his nomination, Lincoln had been preparing his acceptance speech a month before the convention, writing out parts on scraps of paper and depositing them in his stovepipe hat. It would be known to history as the "House Divided" Speech.

The threat of slavery spreading into new territories had impelled Lincoln in 1854 to join the new Republican Party, which existed for one purpose: to prevent the further expansion of slavery. By 1857 the Supreme Court's *Dred Scott v. Sandford* decision had convinced him that unless stopped, slavery would eventually become legal throughout the United States. This possibility persuaded Lincoln to run for the federal Senate in the election of 1858.

Lincoln's opponent, Stephen Douglas, was a leading Democratic senator. A special sense of urgency gripped Lincoln as the convention approached. Important leaders of the Republican Party urged support for Douglas in Illinois. They believed that allying with Douglas could forge an antislavery majority, but Lincoln thought that Douglas was not committed to stopping slavery. He entered the Senate race determined to expose Douglas's weakness on slavery and to restore the moral vision of the Republican Party.

Context

Between 1848 and 1854 the United States added the West Coast and the Southwest to its national domain and began the settlement of the Great Plains of Kansas and Nebraska. Even before the cessation of hostilities with Mexico, the question of whether this massive area would be open to slavery was posed. The Wilmot Proviso, which prohibited slavery in the lands of the Mexican Cession, passed the House of Representatives in 1846 but failed in the southern-dominated Senate.

By 1848 three positions on the future of these lands had emerged: 1) slavery should be allowed, 2) slavery should be prohibited, and 3) slavery should be decided by popular sovereignty. Popular sovereignty left the question of slavery to the residents of the territories themselves. By 1849 sectional tensions over slavery in the territories threatened to spark secession. Hoping to restore the national consensus on the slavery question, Henry Clay of Kentucky and Stephen Douglas of Illinois cobbled together a package of bills that tried to conciliate all three positions. These bills, collectively known as the Compromise of 1850, admitted California as a free state, outlawed the slave trade in the nation's capital, enacted a stiffer fugitive slave law, and left the future of slavery in the New Mexico and Utah territories to popular sovereignty. The compromise pleased no one, however. The new fugitive slave law enraged antislavery northerners, the admission of California as a free state angered southerners, and leaving the territories to popular sovereignty stoked anxieties on both sides.

In 1854 Douglas introduced the Kansas-Nebraska Act, which organized the Kansas-Nebraska territories based on popular sovereignty and began an explosive argument over what the settlers were constitutionally empowered to do. Letting settlers decide whether to allow slavery in these territories invalidated the Missouri Compromise of 1820. The prospect of slavery invading the free-labor North ignited a firestorm among Free-Soilers. This fear fed the growing belief in the existence of a "slave power" conspiracy to expand slavery. When the renewed sectional division split the Whig Party, Free-Soil forces united to form the Republican Party in 1854 based on opposition to the expansion of slavery.

Lincoln personally believed that slavery was morally evil, violated the ideals of the Declaration of Independence, and threatened free labor everywhere. While he was convinced that if it were allowed to expand, slavery would imperil the existence of the United States as a popular government, he also believed that the Constitution protected slavery where it existed. Fearing a trend toward the spread of slavery, Lincoln joined the Republicans and became a party leader in Illinois.

By 1856 a bitter war raged in Kansas. "Bleeding Kansas," as the divided state was called, dominated the news when the Republicans nominated John C. Frémont for president in 1856. Frémont lost a close race to James Buchanan.

1820

■ **March 6**
President James Monroe signs the Missouri Compromise, which admits Missouri as a slave state and Maine as a free state and bars slavery north of the parallel 36°30' north.

1846

■ **August 8**
Wilmot Proviso is proposed in the House of Representatives.

1848

■ **February 2**
Treaty of Guadalupe Hidalgo is signed, giving the United States new territory in the Southwest.

1850

■ **September 17**
The final bills constituting the Compromise of 1850 are signed into law by President Millard Fillmore.

1853

■ **March 4**
Franklin Pierce is inaugurated as president.

1854

■ **May 30**
Pierce signs the Kansas-Nebraska Act into law.

1857

■ **March 4**
James Buchanan is inaugurated as president.

■ **March 6**
Dred Scott v. Sandford endorses southern views on race and slavery.

1858

■ **June 16**
Upon his nomination for the Senate, Lincoln delivers the "House Divided" Speech.

1859

■ **October 16–18**
John Brown's raid takes place at Harpers Ferry, West Virginia.

1860

■ **November 6**
Lincoln is elected president.

In 1857 Supreme Court Justice Roger Taney issued the *Dred Scott v. Sandford* decision. Taney ruled that as chattel property, slaves remained slaves whether they resided in slave states or free states. Taney also nullified the Missouri Compromise of 1820 by ruling that Congress lacked the authority to ban slavery anywhere in the national domain.

In the winter of 1858 a proslavery minority in Kansas met in Lecompton and drafted a constitution, which it then submitted to Congress. President Buchanan embraced the Lecompton Constitution and urged Congress to admit Kansas as the sixteenth slave state.

Douglas opposed the Lecompton Constitution as the product of an undemocratic process. Elated at Douglas's opposition to the proslavery constitution, eastern Republicans such as *New York Tribune* editor Horace Greeley and William H. Seward urged Illinois Republicans to support Douglas in the upcoming Senate race. A stunned Lincoln responded with letters of protest while preparing to battle the "Douglas revolt" in his party in the upcoming Senate race. On June 16, 1858, the Illinois Republican Party staged a revolt of its own by unanimously nominating Abraham Lincoln for the U.S Senate.

About the Author

Abraham Lincoln was born on February 12, 1809, in a one-room log cabin in Hardin County, Kentucky, to Thomas Lincoln and Nancy Hanks. Lincoln's parents belonged to a Baptist church that opposed slavery. Young Lincoln was exposed to slavery when an influx of planters moved into central Kentucky. Unable to compete with the slave-owning planters and bested in court battles with competing land claimants, Thomas Lincoln took his family across the Ohio River into Spencer County, Indiana, in 1816. Two years later Lincoln's mother died, and Thomas married a Kentucky widow, Sarah Bush Johnston. Emotionally distant from his father, Lincoln gave his affections to Sarah, whom he called "Mother" for the rest of his life.

Regarded as a diligent farmworker, Lincoln spent his leisure time reading, a trait that earned him a reputation as a dreamy bookworm. In 1828, with another youth, he guided a flatboat loaded with farm produce 1,200 miles down the Ohio and the Mississippi rivers to New Orleans. In New Orleans, Lincoln saw large numbers of slaves and probably witnessed a slave auction. In March 1830 Lincoln's father moved to central Illinois. At age twenty-two, Lincoln left home, canoeing down the Sangamon River to the village of New Salem in Sangamon County, Illinois.

Lincoln received a minimal education at local "subscription schools," where pupils paid a fee to study rudimentary arithmetic and reading. An avid reader, Lincoln sought out books wherever he could. He read the Bible, John Bunyan's *Pilgrim's Progress*, and William Shakespeare's plays. His favorite book was Parson Weems's *Life of George Washington*, a romanticized account of the lives of the Founding Fathers. He also read and memorized the Declaration of Independence, the Constitution, and writings about the Federalist period. He revered the Founding Fathers and documents of the early republic. His favorite Founding Father was the economic nationalist Alexander Hamilton. The hardship and poverty of rural life made Lincoln a natural Whig. The "American System" of the Whig politician Henry Clay, which called for federal support for internal improvements like roads and canals, advocacy of protective tariffs to foster domestic industry, and support for a national bank, appealed to Lincoln's belief in an activist government.

Lincoln ran unsuccessfully for the Illinois Assembly in 1832 on a Whig program to make the Sangamon River navigable for steamboats. He was elected to the Illinois state legislature two years later. While serving on this legislature, he discovered the eighteenth-century English jurist William Blackstone's *Commentaries on the Laws of England*, which he committed to memory. Deciding to pursue a career in law, Lincoln taught himself Chitty's *Pleadings* and Judge Story's *Equity*. Admitted to the bar in 1837, Lincoln moved to Springfield and began a partnership with John Todd Stuart. Lincoln was a generalist who argued cases from small property disputes to large railroad suits to capital murder. An expert at cross-examination, summary argument, and jury pleading, he gradually built a prosperous legal practice. Serving four terms in the state legislature, Lincoln emerged as an Illinois Whig Party leader. He made his first antislavery speech from the floor of the Illinois House in 1837. In 1844 he formed a partnership with a fellow Whig, William "Billy" Herndon, that lasted until Lincoln departed for Washington in 1861.

In 1839 Lincoln met Mary Todd, the daughter of prominent Kentucky slaveholders. They married in 1842 and had four sons: Robert Todd Lincoln (1843–1926), Edward Baker Lincoln (1846–1850), William Wallace Lincoln (1850–1862), and Thomas "Tad" Lincoln (1853–1871). Only Robert survived into adulthood. Lincoln lost many loved ones during his life: His mother, Nancy, died when he was nine; his brother, Thomas, died in infancy; and his sister, Sarah, died with her stillborn child.

Lincoln served a single term in the U.S. House of Representatives (1847–1849). He opposed the war with Mexico as an unconstitutional threat to expand slavery into new western territories. He challenged President Polk's justification for the war that American troops had been fired on while within their own territory. From the floor of Congress, Lincoln peppered Polk with a torrent of speeches called the "spot resolutions." Knowing that American troops had been in disputed territory south of the Texas border, Lincoln demanded that Polk designate the "spot" where the fighting had occurred.

The war with Mexico was popular in Illinois, and Lincoln's attacks on Polk were turned against him. He chose not to run for reelection in order to concentrate on building his legal practice. In 1854 the Kansas-Nebraska Act "awakened" him. By voiding the Missouri Compromise and threatening to spread slavery to new territories, the act rekindled old sectional divisions and destroyed the Whig Party. Lincoln joined with Conscience Whigs and former Free-Soil Party and Liberty Party members to form the

Time Line

1861

■ **March 4**
Lincoln gives his First Inaugural Address.

1863

■ **January 1**
The Emancipation Proclamation takes effect.

■ **November 19**
Lincoln gives the Gettysburg Address.

1865

■ **March 4**
Lincoln delivers his Second Inaugural Address.

■ **April 9**
Confederate general Robert E. Lee surrenders at Appomattox, Virginia.

■ **April 14**
Lincoln is assassinated.

Republican Party in 1854. In 1858, jumping at the chance to directly confront Douglas as an abettor of slavery, Lincoln ran for the U.S. Senate. The campaign featured the "House Divided" Speech and the Lincoln-Douglas debates. Lincoln lost the election, but the campaign vaulted him to a leadership position in the Republican Party nationally and led indirectly to his presidential nomination in 1860.

Lincoln carried all the northern states in the election of 1860. Months before his inauguration, the seven cotton states of the lower South seceded. In his First Inaugural Address on March 4, 1861, Lincoln reassured the South that he had no intention of interfering with slavery where it existed and urged the seceded states to rejoin the Union. He swore to honor his constitutional duty to preserve the Union while making it clear that he would not tolerate secession. Lincoln's hand was forced in April 1861 when Fort Sumter in Charleston Harbor was made to surrender to Confederate forces. He called for seventy-five thousand troops to retake federal forts, protect the capital, and preserve the Union, which in his view remained intact in the face of an internal rebellion. The resulting state of war forced North Carolina, Virginia, Tennessee, and Arkansas to join the Confederacy.

Until September 1862 Lincoln's aim was to restore the states in rebellion to the Union. By summer 1862 the North's poor showing on the battlefield and its limited war aims combined to push France and Great Britain to the edge of recognizing the Confederacy. At the same time, radicals in his own party insisted that the war could not be won without striking at the South's massive slave-labor force, which kept the rebel armies fed and provisioned. On September 22, 1862, Lincoln issued the preliminary Emancipation Proclamation, declaring that as of New Year's Day, 1863, all slaves in states still in rebellion would be free. The Emancipation Proclamation changed the overall aims of the war from preserving the Union to ending slavery. No European power would side with a rebellion to preserve slavery. In spring 1863 Lincoln issued a call to enlist black troops to fight for the Union. These moves enraged the slave South and moralized the North. By war's end, more than 186,000 blacks, both free and slave, would serve in the U.S. military. The shift in the overall aims of the war disrupted production in the South, as slaves received word that their freedom was at stake and began to desert the plantations. Lincoln's Gettysburg Address, delivered on November 19, 1863, is the clearest statement of Lincoln's changing views on the aims of the war. The address joined a recommitment to the ideal of the Declaration of Independence that all men are created equal with a novel emphasis on a "new birth of freedom," referring to the abolition of slavery ("Collected Works of Abraham Lincoln," http://quod.lib.umich.edu/l/lincoln).

In July 1863 Union victories at Gettysburg in the East and Vicksburg on the Mississippi River turned the tide of the war. The emergence of Ulysses S. Grant and William Tecumseh Sherman as aggressive Union generals and the shift in the war aims from reunion to reconstructing the Union without slavery combined to provide light at the tunnel's end. When Grant's forces bogged down in bloody fighting around Petersburg, Virginia, and Sherman stalled at the gates of Atlanta, however, war weariness demoralized the North. By late August 1864, Lincoln was secretly conceding the upcoming election to the Democratic challenger, General George B. McClellan. Then news broke that Atlanta had fallen, giving Sherman a direct path to the sea and into South Carolina, and Lincoln's fortunes changed. He was easily reelected to a second term in November 1864.

With the war's end in view, Lincoln's Second Inaugural Address on March 4, 1865, captured the change in Lincoln that took place during the four years of war. In tones echoing John Brown, Lincoln cast the war in the light of divine retribution visited upon the nation, both North and South, for the mortal sin of slavery. At the same time, he invoked a vision of a peace without vindictiveness. On April 9, 1865, General Lee surrendered at Appomattox Court House in Virginia, and Joseph E. Johnston's army in North Carolina quickly followed suit. The Articles of Surrender made no mention of treason or punishment and helped to assure that there was no continuing guerrilla warfare.

On Friday, April 14, 1865, Lincoln was fatally shot at Ford's Theatre in Washington while attending a performance of *Our American Cousin* with his wife and two guests. He died of a head wound the next day. The assassin was the well-known actor and Confederate sympathizer John Wilkes Booth. The task of framing a policy for reconstructing the former slave states would be left to Lincoln's successors.

Explanation and Analysis of the Document

Lincoln's "House Divided" Speech is divided into three parts. The opening of the speech discusses the crisis of a nation torn apart by slavery. The second part details the involvement of northern Democrats in a scheme to nationalize slavery. The closing section opposes Douglas as leader of the antislavery forces.

Early in the speech Lincoln blames the Kansas-Nebraska Act and its author, Stephen Douglas, for opening the door to the extension of slavery. Rather than "putting an end to slavery agitation," notes Lincoln, the act opened a Pandora's box of proslavery agitation. Lincoln's premise is that if Douglas's Kansas-Nebraska Act and popular sovereignty had not opened the door, the winds of slavery would not have become the raging storm that threatens the Union.

While predicting neither partition nor secession, Lincoln states that the Union will not be divided by slavery forever. Lincoln foresees two possibilities: 1) Either slavery's opponents will contain slavery where the Constitution places it until its eventual extinction, or 2) slavery will spread until it encompasses the entire country. The "house divided" metaphor in the fifth sentence (the quote is taken from the Gospels of Mark and Matthew in the Bible) along with the three sentences that follow contain the most controversial words of the speech:

> "A house divided against itself cannot stand." I believe this government cannot endure, permanently half *slave* and half *free*. I do not expect the Union to be *dissolved*—I do not expect the house to *fall*—but I *do* expect it will cease to be divided. It will become *all* one thing, or *all* the other.

Lincoln's supporters cautioned him against using this language, but he assumed that his audience of Illinois Republicans would be familiar with the biblical metaphor. His reference to the extinction of slavery was rooted in a shared understanding that the Founding Fathers considered slavery a temporary evil that would cease to exist at some indefinite point in the future. Southerners, however, heard a threat to extinguish slavery. Many came to view the speech as a precursor of William H. Seward's "irrepressible conflict" speech given just five months later. Lincoln chose the house-divided metaphor to attack two ideas simultaneously: that there could be a common ground between slavery and freedom and that the Republican Party shared common ground with Douglas, the facilitator of slavery. Lincoln's objective in the speech is to prevent the Republican Party from making a tactical change that would make it the tail on the Douglas kite, thus abandoning its own moral foundation.

Lincoln begins the second part of the speech by charging that a conspiracy has been working to establish the legal mechanisms to nationalize slavery. In support of his claim, Lincoln refers to the historical record. He points to the "history of its construction," from which "the evidences of design, and concert of action, among its chief bosses" could be traced. Lincoln cites three main points as benchmarks in erecting the mechanisms needed to nationalize slavery.

The first point "was … gained" when Douglas, with the support of President Franklin Pierce, introduced the Kansas-

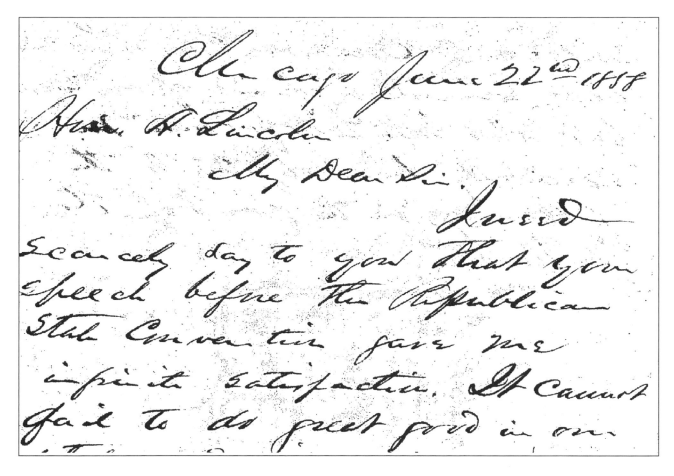

"I need scarcely say to you that your speech before the Republican State Convention gave me infinite satisfaction."
John L. Scripps, letter to Abraham Lincoln, June 22, 1858. (Library of Congress)

Nebraska Act. When Douglas was asked on the Senate floor whether he thought the people of a territory could legally exclude slavery, "the latter answers, 'That is a question for the Supreme Court.'" Lincoln claims that the *Dred Scott* decision was deferred until James Buchanan's election was secured and the Republican Frémont defeated. The election of the proslavery Buchanan was "the *second* point gained." A few days before Roger Taney's decision, Buchanan exhorted the public to accept the decision, in Lincoln's words, "*whatever it might be.*" When the decision was announced, Douglas made a speech in Springfield endorsing it. By this time in the speech, Lincoln has linked Douglas to slavery in the territories, to the proslavery Democrats Pierce and Buchanan, and to Chief Justice Taney.

Having linked Douglas with Buchanan, Lincoln then turns to the dispute over the Lecompton Constitution and Kansas. Lincoln reduces Douglas's struggle over the Lecompton Constitution to "a squabble" over a "*mere* question of *fact*"—whether the people of Kansas had democratically voted for the Constitution. But on the question of slavery, "he *cares* not whether slavery be voted *down* or voted *up.*" Lincoln argues that after the Taney court ruled that slavery could not be legislated out of a territory, popular sovereignty became simply a doctrine of a people's

"right … to make their own constitution." It was upon this simple Democratic point that Douglas and the Republicans agreed and nothing more.

In subsequent lines Lincoln points to the *Dred Scott* decision as the final "point gained." By depriving slaves and their descendants of the right to citizenship and by denying Congress the power to exclude slavery from the territories, Chief Justice Taney allowed slave owners to "*fill up* the territories with slaves" as protected property. By reducing slaves to the legal status of portable property, the decision increased the prospect that "the institution" could be made permanent anywhere in the United States. Lincoln sums up the decision by arguing that just as Dred Scott's master was free to keep him as a slave in the free state of Illinois, any slave owner may be free to bring "*one*, or one *thousand* slaves" into Illinois or "any other free State."

Lincoln then argues that the effect of the trajectory from Kansas-Nebraska to *Dred Scott* was to "*mould* public opinion, at least *Northern* public opinion, to not *care* whether slavery is voted *down* or voted *up.*" The "not care" wording alluded to Douglas's attitude that he "doesn't care" whether or not the people of Kansas voted to legalize slavery.

Lincoln subsequently concedes that he cannot prove the existence of a conspiracy. He bases his claim on a build-

> "'A house divided against itself cannot stand.'"
>
> (Paragraph 5)

> "I believe this government cannot endure, permanently half slave and half free."
>
> (Paragraph 6)

> "We shall lie down pleasantly dreaming that the people of Missouri are on the verge of making their State free; and we shall awake to the reality, instead, that the Supreme Court has made Illinois a slave State."
>
> (Paragraph 58)

> "They remind us that he is a very great man, and that the largest of us are very small ones. Let this be granted. But, 'a living dog is better than a dead lion.'"
>
> (Paragraph 63)

> "How can he oppose the advances of slavery? He don't care anything about it."
>
> (Paragraph 63)

ing metaphor familiar to any Illinois farmer, in the process referring to four workmen who have the names Stephen, Franklin, Roger, and James. Just as the workmen Stephen, Franklin, Roger, and James planned their building together and built its scaffolding with only one piece missing, implies Lincoln, Senator Stephen Douglas, Presidents Franklin Pierce and James Buchanan, and Chief Justice Roger Taney worked together to build a structure needing only one more piece to nationalize slavery. That last piece of timber was the anticipated "Second Dred Scott," which would allow masters to own and work slaves anywhere in the Union. Far from speculating, Lincoln was well aware that such a case (*Lemmon v. The People*) was making its way through the New York courts.

In the last part of the speech, Lincoln turns to the hopes of the eastern wing of the Republican Party for a coalition with Douglas. He disparages Douglas's suitability as an antislavery leader, referring to him as a "*caged* and *toothless*" "*dead* lion" who wouldn't oppose the advance of slavery, which "he don't *care* anything about." He concludes with an appeal to the conscience of the Republican Party

to oppose slavery on moral grounds, saying that if they "stand firm … sooner or later the victory is *sure* to come."

Audience

Lincoln's immediate audience was the Illinois Republican Party, especially the thousand-plus delegates at the state nominating convention. The metaphor of the house divided, the savaging of their longtime foe Stephen Douglas, and the invocation of a conspiracy to spread slavery found receptive ears among the assembled party activists. The speech's logical structure and hard-hitting rhetoric impressed Douglas as well, who realized that Lincoln was a force to be reckoned with.

In a larger sense, Lincoln sent a clear message to the Republican Party, particularly to its eastern powerbrokers like Greeley and Seward in New York, that he would make Illinois the arena for a fight against Douglas. The speech galvanized the attention of voters regardless of party affiliation. Lincoln was less conscious of the audience south of the Mason-Dixon Line, however, who heard in the speech a threat to slavery emanating from the Republicans after *Dred Scott*. Southern hotspurs called this orientation "black Republicanism," a form of political abolitionism. Lincoln's speech also heightened the awareness of northern Democrats that the Republicans were becoming a forceful sectional party that would have to be dealt with in the election of 1860. No Democrat realized this more than Stephen Douglas, as he prepared to answer Lincoln with countercharges of his own.

Impact

Following Lincoln's "House Divided" Speech, the table was set for the most famous battle in the history of American Senate campaigns. Douglas agreed to a series of seven debates, which became known as the "Lincoln-Douglas Debates." The debate trail covered over four thousand miles and drew tens of thousands of spectators. Each debate, printed in major newspapers outside the South, riveted public attention across the nation. The contrast between Lincoln, who was six feet, four inches tall and had the persistent logical manner of a prosecuting attorney, and the foot-shorter "little giant" with the booming voice, truculent mien, and well-honed theatrical oratory, could not have been starker.

Although Lincoln received more votes than Douglas, the Illinois apportionment system, biased toward the conservative southern half of the state, worked to return Douglas to the Senate. Lincoln accomplished his goal of breaking the Republican Party from its illusions in Douglas, however. Douglas's race-baiting rhetoric, his painting the moderate Lincoln as a "black Republican," and his defense of southern expansionism led eastern Republicans to back Lincoln. Greeley's *New York Herald Tribune* denounced Douglas's "squatter sovereignty" principle, his opposition to civil rights of any kind for free blacks, and his willingness to let slavery grow.

By spring 1860 the debates had been published in book form. Selling for fifty cents a copy, the first run of thirty thousand copies quickly sold out, and subsequent printings also sold quickly. While it is too much to attribute Lincoln's nomination for the presidency to the debates, the speech and the subsequent debates advertised Lincoln throughout the North and made his name a household word.

Related Documents

Finkelman, Paul. Dred Scott v. Sanford: *A Brief History with Documents*. Boston: Bedford Press, 1997. This book contains the opinions of all justices of the Taney Court, newspaper responses to the decision, Frederick Douglass's response, the Lincoln-Douglas Debates, and congressional debates.

Hay, John, and John G. Nicolay, eds. *Abraham Lincoln: Complete Works, Comprising His Speeches, Letters, State Papers, and Miscel-laneous Writings*. New York: Century Co., 1894. Nicolay and Hay, two of Lincoln's secretaries during his presidency, compiled Lincoln's writings for this 1894 publication. Included are texts from the Lincoln-Douglas debates of 1858.

Basler, Roy P., ed. *Abraham Lincoln: His Speeches and Writings*. Cleveland: World Pub. Co., 1946. This book contains useful analytical notes by Basler and a preface by the Lincoln biographer Carl Sandburg.

Fitzhugh, George. *Cannibals All! Or, Slaves without Masters*. Cambridge: Belknap Press of Harvard University Press, 1960. This work is a defense of slavery versus free labor by the Virginia sociologist George Fitzhugh, who argues that slavery is a superior social and economic system to free labor capitalism and ought to be extended to the North to include enslavement of free workers.

Bibliography

■ Books

Donald, David Herbert. *Lincoln*. New York: Simon & Schuster, 1995.

Fehrenbacher, Don Edward. *Prelude to Greatness: Lincoln in the 1850s*. Stanford, Calif.: Stanford University Press, 1962.

Foner, Eric. *Free Soil, Free Labor, Free Men: The Ideology of the Republican Party before the Civil War*. New York: Oxford University Press, 1995.

Goodwin, Doris Kearns. *Team of Rivals: The Political Genius of Abraham Lincoln*. New York: Simon & Schuster, 2005.

Jaffa, Harry V. *Crisis of the House Divided: An Interpretation of the Issues in the Lincoln-Douglas Debates*. New York: Doubleday, 1959.

———. *A New Birth of Freedom: Abraham Lincoln and the Coming of the Civil War*. Oxford, England: Rowman & Littlefield, 2000.

McPherson, James M. *Abraham Lincoln and the Second American Revolution*. New York: Oxford University Press, 1990.

Oates, Stephen B. *With Malice toward None: The Life of Abraham Lincoln*. New York: New American Library, 1978.

■ Web Sites

"The Abraham Lincoln Papers at the Library of Congress." Library of Congress "American Memory" Web site.
   http://memory.loc.gov/ammem/alhtml/malhome.html. Accessed on July 17, 2007.

"American President, An Online Reference Resource: Abraham Lincoln (1809–1865)." Miller Center of Public Affairs, University of Virginia Web site.
   http://www.millercenter.virginia.edu/academic/americanpresident/lincoln. Accessed on July 14, 2007.

"The Collected Works of Abraham Lincoln." Abraham Lincoln Association Web site.
http://quod.lib.umich.edu/l/lincoln/. Accessed on July 21, 2007.

VandeCreek, Drew E. "Lincoln's Biography." Lincoln/Net Web site.
http://lincoln.lib.niu.edu/abio.html. Accessed on July 21, 2007.

—By Robert R. Montgomery

Questions for Further Study

1. In the "House Divided" Speech, Lincoln outlined a conspiracy to spread slavery throughout the United States. Douglas ridiculed the conspiracy theory in his response, and even Lincoln admitted he could not prove that a conspiracy existed. Do you think Lincoln used the idea of conspiracy as a rhetorical device to persuade and move his audience as he would summarize a case in a courtroom? Or, considering the case he does make, do you think that Lincoln really believed there was sufficient evidence for a reasonable person to infer the existence of a conspiracy?

2. Lincoln held that the Union could not remain divided and would eventually become either all slave or all free. He insisted that he never suggested that slavery could be abolished by government action. When Douglas asked Lincoln how he proposed to prevent the spread of slavery after the *Dred Scott* decision, Lincoln answered that he did not know. Was Lincoln sincere and honest, or was he staking out a political position? In other words, do you think that Lincoln actually was prepared in his own mind for the possibility of a secession crisis and possible civil war or not?

3. Lincoln has been mythologized at different times depending on the climate of opinion. He has been cast as an inveterate foe of slavery and the "Great Emancipator" of black people. Conversely, he has been seen as a cynical politician who actually cared nothing about slaves and merely used the issue for his own purposes. Considering what you know of Lincoln from his speeches, actions, and personal history, evaluate these two views. What is your own opinion about Lincoln and the question of slavery and race?

4. Assume that rather than issuing a call for troops after the fall of Fort Sumter and going to war to preserve the Union, Lincoln had simply let the seven states of the Deep South secede. In your opinion, what would have been the result? More than one scenario is possible. For instance, consider the fate of the eight slave states of the upper South. What about the future of the Confederate States of America?

5. It has been remarked that before the Civil War it was said that "the United States are," while after the war it was said that "the United States is." This refers to the triumph of a national meaning of federalism over a "states rights" meaning. The states rights interpretation of federalism held that individual states were sovereign powers. Proponents of this view, from Thomas Jefferson to John C. Calhoun, argued that individual states could reject or nullify federal laws that they deemed to be unconstitutional. To what extent was the sectional crisis of the 1850s, which led to the Civil War, a reflection of these conflicting philosophies? Another way to think about this is to ask yourself whether the sectional crisis was more about slavery and freedom and less about the nature of the Union or vice versa.

acquiesce	to consent or comply passively or without protest
augmented	added to or made greater in amount or number or strength
concert	a plan or arrangement made by mutual agreement
mortices	rectangular cavities in a piece of wood, stone, or other material, prepared to receive a tenon and thus form a joint
mould	a frame or model around or on which something is formed or shaped
scaffolding	a system or arrangement of materials used to form a raised platform or supporting framework
tenon	a projection on the end of a piece of wood shaped for insertion into a mortise to make a joint

www.milestonedocuments.com

ABRAHAM LINCOLN'S "HOUSE DIVIDED" SPEECH

Mr. President and Gentlemen of the Convention.

If we could first know *where* we are, and *whither* we are tending, we could then better judge *what* to do, and *how* to do it.

We are now far into the *fifth* year, since a policy was initiated, with the *avowed* object, and *confident* promise, of putting an end to slavery agitation.

Under the operation of that policy, that agitation has not only, *not ceased*, but has *constantly augmented*.

In *my* opinion, it *will* not cease, until a *crisis* shall have been reached, and passed.

"A house divided against itself cannot stand."

I believe this government cannot endure, permanently half *slave* and half *free*.

I do not expect the Union to be *dissolved*—I do not expect the house to *fall*—but I *do* expect it will cease to be divided.

It will become *all* one thing, or *all* the other.

Either the *opponents* of slavery, will arrest the further spread of it, and place it where the public mind shall rest in the belief that it is in course of ultimate extinction; or its *advocates* will push it forward, till it shall become alike lawful in *all* the States, *old* as well as *new*—North as well as South.

Have we no *tendency* to the latter condition?

Let any one who doubts, carefully contemplate that now almost complete legal combination—piece of *machinery* so to speak—compounded of the Nebraska doctrine, and the Dred Scott decision. Let him consider not only *what work* the machinery is adapted to do, and *how well* adapted; but also, let him study the *history* of its construction, and trace, if he can, or rather *fail*, if he can, to trace the evidences of design, and concert of action, among its chief bosses, from the beginning.

But, so far, *Congress* only, had acted; and an *indorsement* by the people, *real* or apparent, was indispensable, to *save* the point already gained, and give chance for more.

The new year of 1854 found slavery excluded from more than half the States by State Constitutions, and from most of the national territory by Congressional prohibition.

Four days later, commenced the struggle, which ended in repealing that Congressional prohibition.

This opened all the national territory to slavery; and was the first point gained.

This necessity had not been overlooked; but had been provided for, as well as might be, in the notable argument of "*squatter sovereignty*," otherwise called "*sacred right of self government*," which latter phrase, though expressive of the only rightful basis of any government, was so perverted in this attempted use of it as to amount to just this: That if any *one* man, choose to enslave *another*, no *third* man shall be allowed to object.

That argument was incorporated into the Nebraska bill itself, in the language which follows: "*It being the true intent and meaning of this act not to legislate slavery into any Territory or state, nor to exclude it therefrom; but to leave the people thereof perfectly free to form and regulate their domestic institutions in their own way, subject only to the Constitution of the United States.*"

Then opened the roar of loose declamation in favor of "Squatter Sovereignty," and "Sacred right of self government."

"But," said opposition members, "let us be more *specific*—let us *amend* the bill so as to expressly declare that the people of the territory *may* exclude slavery." "Not we," said the friends of the measure; and down they voted the amendment.

While the Nebraska bill was passing through congress, a *law case*, involving the question of a negroe's freedom, by reason of his owner having voluntarily taken him first into a free state and then a territory covered by the congressional prohibition, and held him as a slave, for a long time in each, was passing through the U.S. Circuit Court for the District of Missouri; and both Nebraska bill and law suit were brought to a decision in the same month of May, 1854. The negroe's name was "Dred Scott," which name now designates the decision finally made in the case.

Before the *then* next Presidential election, the law case came *to*, and was argued *in* the Supreme Court of the United States; but the *decision* of it was deferred until *after* the election. Still, *before* the election, Senator Trumbull, on the floor of the Senate, requests the leading advocate of the Nebraska bill to state *his opinion* whether the people of a territory can constitutionally exclude slavery from their limits; and the latter answers, "That is a question for the Supreme Court."

The election came. Mr. Buchanan was elected, and the *indorsement*, such as it was, secured. That was the *second* point gained. The indorsement, however, fell short of a clear popular majority by nearly four hundred thousand votes, and so, perhaps, was not overwhelmingly reliable and satisfactory.

The *outgoing* President, in his last annual message, as impressively as possible *echoed back* upon the people the *weight* and *authority* of the indorsement.

The Supreme Court met again; *did not* announce their decision, but ordered a re-argument.

The Presidential inauguration came, and still no decision of the court; but the *incoming* President, in his inaugural address, fervently exhorted the people to abide by the forthcoming decision, *whatever it might be*.

Then, in a few days, came the decision.

The reputed author of the Nebraska bill finds an early occasion to make a speech at this capitol indorsing the Dred Scott Decision, and vehemently denouncing all opposition to it.

The new President, too, seizes the early occasion of the Silliman letter to *indorse* and strongly *construe* that decision, and to express his *astonishment* that any different view had ever been entertained.

At length a squabble springs up between the President and the author of the Nebraska bill, on the *mere* question of *fact*, whether the Lecompton constitution was or was not, in any just sense, made by the people of Kansas; and in that squabble the latter declares that all he wants is a fair vote for the people, and that he *cares* not whether slavery be voted *down* or voted *up*. I do not understand his declaration that he cares not whether slavery be voted down or voted up, to be intended by him other than as an *apt definition* of the *policy* he would impress upon the public mind—the *principle* for which he declares he has suffered much, and is ready to suffer to the end.

And well may he cling to that principle. If he has any parental feeling, well may he cling to it. That principle, is the only *shred* left of his original Nebraska doctrine. Under the Dred Scott decision, "squatter sovereignty" squatted out of existence, tumbled down like temporary scaffolding—like the mould at the foundry served through one blast and fell back into loose sand—helped to carry an election, and then was kicked to the winds. His late *joint* struggle with the Republicans, against the Lecompton Constitution, involves nothing of the original Nebraska doctrine. That struggle was made on a point, the right of a people to make their own constitution, upon which he and the Republicans have never differed.

The several points of the Dred Scott decision, in connection with Senator Douglas' "care not" policy, constitute the piece of machinery, in its *present* state of advancement. This was the third point gained.

The *working* points of that machinery are:

First, that no negro slave, imported as such from Africa, and no descendant of such slave can ever be a *citizen* of any State, in the sense of that term as used in the Constitution of the United States.

This point is made in order to deprive the negro, in every possible event, of the benefit of this provision of the United States Constitution, which declares that—

"The citizens of each State shall be entitled to all privileges and immunities of citizens in the several States."

Secondly, that "subject to the Constitution of the United States," neither *Congress* nor a *Territorial Legislature* can exclude slavery from any United States territory.

This point is made in order that individual men may *fill up* the territories with slaves, without danger of losing them as property, and thus to enhance the chances of *permanency* to the institution through all the future.

Thirdly, that whether the holding a negro in actual slavery in a free State, makes him free, as against the holder, the United States courts will not decide, but will leave to be decided by the courts of any slave State the negro may be forced into by the master.

This point is made, not to be pressed *immediately*; but, if acquiesced in for a while, and apparently *indorsed* by the people at an election, *then* to sustain the logical conclusion that what Dred Scott's master might lawfully do with Dred Scott, in the free State of Illinois, every other master may lawfully do with any other *one*, or one *thousand* slaves, in Illinois, or in any other free State.

Auxiliary to all this, and working hand in hand with it, the Nebraska doctrine, or what is left of it, is to *educate* and *mould* public opinion, at least *Northern* public opinion, to not *care* whether slavery is voted *down* or voted *up*.

This shows exactly where we now *are*; and *partially* also, whither we are tending.

It will throw additional light on the latter, to go back, and run the mind over the string of historical facts already stated. Several things will *now* appear less *dark* and *mysterious* than they did *when* they were transpiring. The people were to be left "perfectly free" "subject only to the Constitution." What the *Constitution* had to do with it, outsiders could not *then* see. Plainly enough *now*, it was an exactly fitted *niche*, for the Dred Scott decision to afterwards come in, and declare the *perfect freedom* of the people, to be just no freedom at all.

Why was the amendment, expressly declaring the right of the people to exclude slavery, voted down? Plainly enough *now*, the adoption of it, would have spoiled the niche for the Dred Scott decision.

Why was the court decision held up? Why, even a Senator's individual opinion withheld, till *after* the Presidential election? Plainly enough *now*, the speaking out *then* would have damaged the *"perfectly free"* argument upon which the election was to be carried.

Why the *outgoing* President's felicitation on the indorsement? Why the delay of a reargument? Why the incoming President's *advance* exhortation in favor of the decision?

These things *look* like the cautious *patting* and *petting* a spirited horse, preparatory to mounting him, when it is dreaded that he may give the rider a fall.

And why the hasty after indorsements of the decision by the President and others?

We can not absolutely *know* that all these exact adaptations are the result of preconcert. But when we see a lot of framed timbers, different portions of which we know have been gotten out at different times and places and by different workmen—Stephen, Franklin, Roger and James, for instance—and when we see these timbers joined together, and see they exactly make the frame of a house or a mill, all the tenons and mortices exactly fitting, and all the lengths and proportions of the different pieces exactly adapted to their respective places, and not a piece too many or too few—not omitting even scaffolding—or, if a single piece be lacking, we can see the place in the frame exactly fitted and prepared to yet bring such piece in—in *such* a case, we find it impossible to not *believe* that Stephen and Franklin and Roger and James all understood one another from the beginning, and all worked upon a common *plan* or *draft* drawn up before the first lick was struck.

It should not be overlooked that, by the Nebraska bill, the people of a *State* as well as *Territory*, were to be left *"perfectly free"* *"subject only to the Constitution."*

Why mention a *State*? They were legislating for *territories*, and not *for* or *about* States. Certainly the people of a State *are* and *ought to be* subject to the Constitution of the United States; but why is mention of this *lugged* into this merely *territorial* law? Why are the people of a *territory* and the people of a *state* therein *lumped* together, and their relation to the Constitution therein treated as being *precisely* the same?

While the opinion of *the Court*, by Chief Justice Taney, in the Dred Scott case, and the separate opinions of all the concurring Judges, expressly declare that the Constitution of the United States neither permits Congress nor a Territorial legislature to exclude slavery from any United States territory, they all *omit* to declare whether or not the same Constitution permits a *state*, or the people of a State, to exclude it.

Possibly, this was a mere *omission*; but who can be *quite* sure, if McLean or Curtis had sought to get into the opinion a declaration of unlimited power in the people of a *state* to exclude slavery from their limits, just as Chase and Macy sought to get such declaration, in behalf of the people of a territory, into the Nebraska bill—I ask, who can be quite *sure* that it would not have been voted down, in the one case, as it had been in the other.

The nearest approach to the point of declaring the power of a State over slavery, is made by Judge Nelson. He approaches it more than once, using the precise idea, and *almost* the language too, of the Nebraska act. On one occasion his exact language is, "except in cases where the power is restrained by the Constitution of the United States, the law of the State is supreme over the subject of slavery within its jurisdiction."

In what *cases* the power of the *states is* so restrained by the U.S. Constitution, is left an *open* question, precisely as the same question, as to the restraint on the power of the *territories* was left open in the Nebraska act. Put *that* and *that* together, and we have another nice little niche, which we may, ere long, see filled with another Supreme Court decision, declaring that the Constitution of the United States does not permit a *state* to exclude slavery from its limits.

And this may especially be expected if the doctrine of "care not whether slavery be voted *down* or voted *up*," shall gain upon the public mind sufficiently to give promise that such a decision can be maintained when made.

Such a decision is all that slavery now lacks of being alike lawful in all the States.

Welcome or unwelcome, such decision *is probably coming, and will soon be upon us, unless the power of the present political dynasty shall be met and overthrown*.

We shall *lie down* pleasantly dreaming that the people of *Missouri* are on the verge of making their State *free*; and we shall *awake* to the *reality*, instead, that the *Supreme* Court has made *Illinois* a *slave* State.

To meet and overthrow the power of that dynasty, is the work now before all those who would prevent that consummation.

That is *what* we have to do.

But *how* can we best do it?

There are those who denounce us *openly* to their *own* friends, and yet whisper *us softly*, that *Senator Douglas* is the *aptest* instrument there is, with which to effect that object. *They* do *not* tell us, nor has *he* told us, that he *wishes* any such object to be effected. They wish us to *infer* all, from the facts, that he now has a little quarrel with the present head of the dynasty; and that he has regularly voted with us, on a single point, upon which, he and we, have never differed.

They remind us that *he* is a very *great man*, and that the largest of *us* are very small ones. Let this be granted. But "a *living dog* is better than a *dead lion*." Judge Douglas, if not a *dead* lion *for this work*, is at least a *caged* and *toothless* one. How can he oppose the advances of slavery? He don't *care* anything about it. His avowed *mission is impressing* the "public heart" to *care* nothing about it.

A leading Douglas Democratic newspaper thinks Douglas' superior talent will be needed to resist the revival of the African slave trade.

Does Douglas believe an effort to revive that trade is approaching? He has not said so. Does he *really* think so? But if it is, how can he resist it? For years he has labored to prove it a *sacred right* of white men to take negro slaves into the new territories. Can he possibly show that it is *less* a sacred right to *buy* them where they can be bought cheapest? And, unques-

tionably they can be bought *cheaper in Africa* than in *Virginia*.

He has done all in his power to reduce the whole question of slavery to one of a mere *right of property*; and as such, how can *he* oppose the foreign slave trade—how can he refuse that trade in that "property" shall be "perfectly free"—unless he does it as a *protection* to the home production? And as the home *producers* will probably not *ask* the protection, he will be wholly without a ground of opposition.

Senator Douglas holds, we know, that a man may rightfully be *wiser to-day* than he was *yesterday*—that he may rightfully *change* when he finds himself wrong.

But, can we for that reason, run ahead, and *infer* that he *will* make any particular change, of which he, himself, has given no intimation? Can we *safely* base *our* action upon any such *vague* inference?

Now, as ever, I wish to not *misrepresent* Judge Douglas' *position*, question his *motives*, or do ought that can be personally offensive to him.

Whenever, *if ever*, he and we can come together on *principle* so that *our great cause* may have assistance from *his great ability*, I hope to have interposed no adventitious obstacle.

But clearly, he is not *now* with us—he does not *pretend* to be—he does not *promise* to *ever* be.

Our cause, then, must be intrusted to, and conducted by its own undoubted friends—those whose hands are free, whose hearts are in the work—who *do care* for the result.

Two years ago the Republicans of the nation mustered over thirteen hundred thousand strong.

We did this under the single impulse of resistance to a common danger, with every external circumstance against us.

Of *strange, discordant*, and even, *hostile* elements, we gathered from the four winds, and *formed* and fought the battle through, under the constant hot fire of a disciplined, proud, and pampered enemy.

Did we brave all *then*, to *falter* now?—*now*—when that same enemy is *wavering*, dissevered and belligerent?

The result is not doubtful. We shall not fail—if we stand firm, we shall not fail.

Wise councils may *accelerate* or *mistakes delay* it, but, sooner or later the victory is *sure* to come.

This engraving from 1860 shows a mass meeting organized to support the call of the South Carolina legislature for a state convention to discuss possible secession from the Union. (Library of Congress)

"A geographical line has been drawn across the Union."

Overview

The Declaration of Causes of Secession, adopted on December 24, 1860, represented South Carolina's statement to the South, the nation, and the world that it was compelled to secede from the Union. In a detailed explanation, South Carolina presented the southern theory of the Union and the nature of the U.S. Constitution, aired its grievances against the North, and justified its decision to secede. It left no doubt that the precipitating factor behind its withdrawal from the Union was the election of Abraham Lincoln to the presidency.

South Carolina's decision to secede encouraged secessionists elsewhere to intensify their opposition to the Union and, in rapid fashion, to persuade their states to follow suit. The justifications for secession were grounded in the compact theory of the Constitution, the view that sovereign states had created the Union and, therefore, in the exercise of their sovereignty, could withdraw from the Union at their pleasure. The declaration sought legitimacy, moreover, through its reference to the causes that impelled the American colonists to declare their independence from England: The rights of the people had been violated by a government grown tyrannical. Those conditions in 1776 and 1860, South Carolina argued, justified the right of the people to create their own government. For South Carolinians, tyranny emerged in the form of Abraham Lincoln, who, they declared, intended to destroy slavery, in violation of southerners' property rights in their slaves. The arguments aroused the passions of the lower southern states and soon put the nation on a war footing. As a result, the United States would never be the same.

Context

The election of Abraham Lincoln to the presidency in 1860 proved to be the tipping point for South Carolina. Fearful that Lincoln would place the law of slavery on a path toward its extinction, as he had indicated in 1858 in his famous "House Divided" Speech, secessionists in South Carolina, on the very day that Lincoln was elected—November 6—called for a convention to remove their state from the Union.

Although Lincoln's election triggered secession in South Carolina and, within six weeks, in six other states in the Lower South, the decision to secede did not necessarily reflect the best interests of the South. Indeed, it has been widely perceived as a blunder of historic proportions. Nor was it one that required immediacy. In fact, while Lincoln's victory unleashed great fears throughout the region, it did not engender a uniform response.

Three different positions developed in response to Lincoln's election. The first, held by the "fire-eaters," argued for immediate secession. Members of this camp, the most radical of the three, believed that each state should secede without waiting for a decision from other states. Its members expressed great concern about the threat posed to slavery and, somewhat more generally, to the status of white supremacy. The second group, known as the "cooperationists," argued that states should not act individually, but collectively, in response to Lincoln's victory. The third position, that of the "unconditional unionists," reflected clear opposition to the idea of secession. Proponents of this position lived principally in the border states: Maryland, Kentucky, Delaware, and Missouri. It is likely that the cooperationists held the dominant position in the Lower South, and this may have caused the North to believe as a result that the South was not inclined to secede. But the North's confusion of cooperationism with unionism ignored the fact that the cooperationists subscribed to the belief that states possessed the right to secede. The real issue for that camp involved determinations of timing and tactics.

Apart from divisions on issues of methods and timing, the Lower South was united by its belief in state sovereignty and states' rights, its insistence on a constitutional property right to slaves, and its considerable fear of northern intentions. Lincoln's election unleashed a panoply of fears. South Carolinian secessionists hammered away at a grim future under Lincoln and the Republicans, who, they believed, meant to abolish slavery. Secessionists, for example, pointed to the impact on the South of Republican opposition to the extension of slavery in the western territories. The net result, they argued, would be the incorpora-

1860

■ **November 6**
Abraham Lincoln is elected as the sixteenth president. In response to Lincoln's election, the South Carolina state legislature calls for a convention to withdraw from the Union.

■ **December 3**
In his annual message, President James Buchanan declares secession illegal.

■ **December 20**
South Carolina, by a vote of 169–0, becomes the first state to secede from the Union.

■ **December 24**
South Carolina adopts the Declaration of the Immediate Causes Which Induce and Justify the Secession of South Carolina from the Federal Union.

1861

■ **January 9**
Mississippi secedes by a vote of 85–15.

■ **January 10**
Florida secedes by a vote of 62–7.

■ **January 11**
Alabama secedes by a vote of 61–39.

■ **January 19**
Georgia secedes by a vote of 208–89.

■ **January 26**
Louisiana secedes by a vote of 113–17.

■ **February 1**
Texas secedes by a vote of 166–8.

■ **February 4**
Confederate states send delegates to a constitutional convention in Montgomery, Alabama.

■ **February 7**
The Alabama convention adopts a provisional constitution for the Confederate States of America

■ **February 9**
Jefferson Davis is elected provisional president.

tion in the Union of additional free states, which would easily outnumber southern states in Congress. Congress would repeal the Fugitive Slave Act, and slaves would engage in a mass migration to the North, depriving the South of its labor pool. Lincoln, it was charged, would appoint Republicans to the U.S. Supreme Court, and the institution that had been long controlled by Southern justices would become a tool of the North. Finally, Congress might employ means of abolishing slavery altogether. In sum, the southern way of life was jeopardized by the ascension of Lincoln. In this context, the secessionists won converts, and South Carolina withdrew from the Union.

About the Author

Following Abraham Lincoln's election to the presidency, Christopher Gustavus Memminger, a member of the South Carolina statehouse, became a forceful advocate of secession. As author of the Declaration of the Immediate Causes Which Induce and Justify the Secession of South Carolina from the Federal Union, Memminger asserted the reasons for the state's secession. Memminger was also selected to represent South Carolina as a delegate to the provisional congress that established the Confederate States of America. He served, moreover, as chairman of the twelve-man committee that wrote the provisional constitution in just four days.

Memminger was born on January 9, 1803, in Württemberg, Germany. After his father was killed in combat, Memminger immigrated with his mother to Charleston, South Carolina. After his mother died from yellow fever in 1807, young Christopher was sent to an orphanage. He was soon taken into the home of Thomas Bennett, later a governor of South Carolina. Memminger graduated from South Carolina College in 1819 and, after studying law, opened in 1825 what became a highly successful law practice in Charleston. In 1832, he married Mary Wilkinson.

Memminger plunged into the world of politics in 1836 when he won a seat in the South Carolina legislature, where he served until 1852. He returned to the legislature and served from 1854 to 1860. His career in the legislature was distinguished by his efforts as chair of the finance committee to reform state finances and the practices of the banking community and by his commitment to education. In 1855 he embarked on a thirty-year career as Charleston's commissioner of schools, marked by his efforts to establish a city public school system. For thirty-two years, moreover, he held a position on the board of South Carolina College.

Throughout his political career, Memminger defended slavery. While viewed as moderate among secessionists, at least until Lincoln's election, he boldly asserted the need for South Carolina to secede and even declared that his state may have to drag others with it. In 1861 the Confederate president Jefferson Davis appointed Memminger secretary of the treasury. The effort to successfully fund the Civil War was probably doomed from the start. Despite his creative efforts to raise money, Memminger was helpless in the face of the depreciation of the currency and the ultimate collapse of Confederate credit, for which he was nonetheless held responsible.

In 1864 he resigned from his post under intense public pressure. He received a presidential pardon from President Andrew Johnson in 1866 for his role in the war and retired to Flat Rock, North Carolina, a year later, where he resumed the practice of law. He spent his retirement in service of public education for blacks and whites. He died in Charleston on March 7, 1888.

Explanation and Analysis of the Document

The South Carolina document explains and justifies the state's secession from the Union. In moving and even passionate terms, the state airs its view of the Union, the location of sovereignty within the United States, and its understanding of the nature of the Constitution. The declaration, moreover, represents a distillation of some of South Carolina's principal grievances against the North, and it explains, in the end, why the state had no choice but to secede. Whatever one's view of the document might be, it provides a window into a theory that ultimately destroyed the Union.

The Civil War constituted the gravest crisis in American constitutional history. The fact that the legal crisis stemmed principally from the debate on the repository of sovereignty in the United States brings the South Carolina document center stage, since it articulates a theory of state sovereignty. The first two paragraphs express South Carolina's frustration with the federal government. The government, it asserts, has frequently violated the Constitution of the United States, particularly in its encroachments on the rights of states. In fact, South Carolina had come perilously close to seceding from the Union in 1852, the declaration states, but out of respect to sister states, and with hope for improvement, elected to stay in the Union. Still, after years of usurpations and abuses of power, South Carolina had reached the end of its patience. It now had little choice but to secede. It is an exercise of respect for other states, and even for other nations, that it believes it has the duty to identify and explain the causes that have compelled its secession.

In paragraphs 3–7, the South Carolina document reviews the fundamental principles that characterized the Declaration of Independence. It distills two cornerstones from the colonists' appeal: "the right of a State to govern itself; and the right of a people to abolish a Government when it becomes destructive of the ends for which it was instituted." The first principle—that of self-government—was unassailable. The whole question, at least in the context of South Carolina's invocation of the fundamental right, involved the exercise of its power. What if a state, in the exercise of self-governance, were to abuse its powers? That state, by definition, would be tyrannical and thus vulnerable to revolution. Indeed, such behavior would invite the second great principle adduced by the colonists and embraced by South Carolina: the right of a people to abolish government when it violates the very tenets that gave birth to it in the first place.

South Carolina's invocation of the "Spirit of '76" raises vexing questions. For example, was secession legal, or was it an exercise in rebellion? Revolutions and rebellions typically are illegal, yet many secessionists argued that withdrawal was not illegal but fully constitutional. Of course, the American colonists had no legal or constitutional right to rebel against England. The Patriots in 1776 relied on the rhetoric of natural or inalienable rights, particularly found in the right to "abolish" government when it becomes destructive of just ends. Would South Carolina abandon the constitutional argument in favor of a natural right to revolt against the Union? The model of 1776 was not as useful if South Carolina had a legal right to secede, and disregard of the rationale for independence in 1776 deprived South Carolinians of the '76 model. Which fork in the road to take?

Most South Carolinians believed that secession was constitutionally protected. They held this ground by adducing the "compact theory," which maintained that the states were sovereign. At the time of the ratification of the Constitution, the sovereign states had opted to join the Union; it followed that they could leave the Union when they preferred to do so. The theory had its roots in the early Republic and had been manifested at various junctures in American history, including a role in the formation of the Virginia and Kentucky Resolutions of 1798. These resolutions, drafted by James Madison (Virginia) and Thomas Jefferson (Kentucky), advanced the compact theory and the right of the states to judge the constitutionality of federal measures, in this case, the dreaded Alien and Sedition Acts of 1798, which punished speech that damaged the reputation of the government. The argument claims that the sovereign states had delegated some parcel of authority to the federal government to act as their agent. Since sovereignty was undelegable and indivisible, the states retained it. Under this view, states might leave the Union and create a new one at their discretion. That is what South Carolina and other secessionist states proceeded to do in their creation of the Confederate States of America.

Other secessionists contended that their action was both legal and revolutionary. They saw no conflict between the two positions. They claimed that secession was constitutionally permissible on the basis of the compact theory and, at the same time, saw no reason why a people might not abolish a government that was encroaching on their

Time Line

1861

■ March 4
Abraham Lincoln assumes the office of the presidency.

■ April 12
Confederate soldiers fire upon Fort Sumter, starting the Civil War.

www.milestonedocuments.com

rights, as the Union was encroaching on the rights of Confederates. The right of secession was a legal right; the right to abolish government was an exercise of an inalienable right, as claimed by the American colonists. But many southerners invoked the model of 1776 in a highly selective and indeed arbitrary manner. The willingness to invoke the principle of self-government was not accompanied by a willingness to invoke the other high-minded principles of the Declaration of Independence, including liberty and equality. Critics of the South, including Republicans and abolitionists, were quick to point out the inconsistency and hypocrisy of the southern position.

The allure of legitimacy drew the South Carolinians to a conservative position on the question of the legality of secession. They preferred to rest on the compact theory and the right to withdraw. It was their aim, therefore, to portray the federal government as revolutionary, since it was violating the rights of the southerners, particularly their property rights in slaves. They cite, for example, the failure of the North to enforce the Fugitive Slave Act, the passage by northern states of personal liberty laws for blacks, and opposition to the expansion of slavery in the territories. In their depictions, the Union has become the menace to liberty, just as Great Britain had threatened the colonists' liberty a century before.

In paragraphs 8–11, the South Carolina declaration spells out the compact theory of the Constitution. The Constitution, it is argued, was submitted to "the states" for ratification. The sovereign states entered into a contract, or compact, with each other, which limited the powers of the federal government. In addition, the powers not granted to the federal government were, by virtue of the Tenth Amendment, reserved to the states. Sovereignty was retained by the states.

The compact theory hinges on the viability of the claim that the Constitution was submitted to the states as states. The historical evidence refutes that proposition. In the Constitutional Convention of 1787, the framers decided to submit the proposed Constitution to specifically held state-ratifying conventions. As James Madison explained it, the proposed Constitution could be evaluated only by a body that possessed higher authority than the proposed Constitution. States that would be created if and when the Constitution was adopted could hardly sit in judgment of the document that breathed life into them. The framers, as Madison explained, submitted the proposed Constitution to the people, who, as the sovereign entity in America, possessed the singular authority to approve or reject the document.

The question of the location of sovereignty in America represented the principal constitutional issue of the Civil War. The issue had seemingly been resolved in the Constitutional Convention. In 1819, in the landmark case of *McCulloch v. Maryland,* Chief Justice John Marshall had rejected the claim of state sovereignty. The people, he observed, were sovereign, not the states. His emphasis on the language in the preamble of the Constitution should have settled the question: "We the People of the United States, in order to form a more perfect Union … do ordain and establish this Constitution for the United States of America." The "peo-

ple," not the "states," he pointed out, had ratified the Constitution. If the state legislatures had ratified the Constitution, then they would have ordained it, but the people ratified it in special conventions to which delegates were elected to evaluate the proposed Constitution.

If the compact theory failed to explain the nature of the Constitution, then the concept of state sovereignty would be inadequate to justify secession. If secession were not lawful, then South Carolina would be forced to seek justication in the model of 1776, in the right, that is, to abolish government when it becomes destructive to the purposes for which it was established. It is in paragraphs 12–18 that South Carolina states its case that its right to slave property had been violated by the North. Under that scenario, the right to secede from the Union for the purpose of creating a new government is in play.

But the North, and specifically, Abraham Lincoln, denied that the property rights of the Confederate States has been violated. Indeed, in his First Inaugural Address in 1861, President Lincoln was at pains to assure southerners that the Union would not interfere with slavery where it existed. He emphasized, moreover, that as president he would enforce the provisions of the Fugitive Slave Act. At every turn, Lincoln sought to allay southern anxieties over the future of slavery. It was not enough, of course; no assurance would have been sufficient, since the South sought to expand slavery into the territories. If the Union maintained that it would protect the property rights of the Confederates and the South claimed that secession was protected under the Constitution, which side was promoting a "more perfect Union"?

The issue of the Union's attack on slavery is addressed in paragraph has 19–23. South Carolina contends that the Union has violated the provisions of the Constitution that maintain slavery, including the duty of states to comply with the Fugitive Slave Act. Since the Union has failed to adhere to its obligations in the Constitution to maintain a "more perfect Union," South Carolina is within its rights to secede. But Lincoln reacted with a sharp rebuke. He reminded the South that dissolution of the Union undermines the Union. The Union cannot be perfect, he argued, if it is destroyed by southern states.

The South Carolina declaration pointedly refers, in paragraph 22, to the election of Lincoln as the precipitating factor in its decision to withdraw from the Union. The document assails Lincoln, without naming him, as "a man" who is hostile to slavery and determined to terminate its existence. In the face of such hostility, South Carolina claims (in paragraph 25), states will no longer have equal rights, and the "guaranties of the Constitution will then no longer exist"; states will lose both their rights of self -government and self-protection; and the "Federal Government will have become their enemy." With that grim future, South Carolina declares, it is forced to secede from the Union. The decision was a great blunder. If South Carolina had stayed in Congress, it might have been able to temper legislation and programs, and it might have avoided the greatest tragedy in American history.

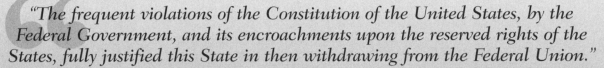

> *"The frequent violations of the Constitution of the United States, by the Federal Government, and its encroachments upon the reserved rights of the States, fully justified this State in then withdrawing from the Federal Union."*
>
> (Paragraph 1)

> *"A geographical line has been drawn across the Union, and all the States north of that line have united in the election of a man to the high office of President of the United States, whose opinions and purposes are hostile to slavery."*
>
> (Paragraph 22)

> *"We, therefore, the People of South Carolina, by our delegates in Convention assembled, appealing to the Supreme Judge of the world for the rectitude of our intentions, have solemnly declared that the Union heretofore existing between this State and the other States of North America, is dissolved."*
>
> (Paragraph 27)

Audience

The South Carolina declaration targeted four audiences: the people of South Carolina, the southern states, the northern states, and the rest of the world. South Carolina harbored great ambitions. It intended to persuade all four groups that the state had the legal right to secede from the Union and that it was entitled to exercise that right. After all, the federal government had encroached on its rights for many years, and the future looked particularly grim in light of Lincoln's election to the presidency. Of course, its statement to sister states in the South was meant to encourage further secession, and in this bid it enjoyed some success. Its declaration also represented a justification of its intended direction, and this conveyed to the North the most solemn disrespect for the Union that any state might convey. In addressing the nations of the world, South Carolina sought to increase its standing and assume the legal status of any nation.

Impact

The South Carolina document was incendiary. It fully intended to encourage other states to secede from the Union, and in this aim, it enjoyed mixed success. Its influence in the Lower South was very high. Within six weeks of its own secession, six other states followed suit. Of course, the justifications for secession adduced in the document were embraced in other southern states, which was to be expected, since they reflected a by-then generally understood proposition that states were sovereign entities and that they might withdraw from the Union at their pleasure.

The assertion in the document, moreover, of the compact theory linked the past, the present, and the future. Earlier generations had embraced a similar doctrine, and subsequent generations of Americans would embrace it as well to advance state interests against a powerful federal government. Of course, the concept of the compact theory, like its previous and subsequent iterations, had the potential for ugly and frightening application, as seen in the reaction of southern states to the efforts of civil rights advocates and marchers in the 1950s and 1960s.

In the end, the fact that the compact theory failed to explain the origin and nature of the Constitution retains a high degree of satisfaction. Indeed, if the secessionists had succeeded in their quest, the theory would have produced a volatile political climate in the United States. Different states in different regions would have possessed authority to come and go as they please. That would be a recipe for disaster, and it would disrupt the essence of democratic government—compromise. States would have issued ultimatums, and little good could have been accomplished in the nation. Fortunately, the South Carolina document did not have that impact.

Related Documents

"The Declaration of Independence." In *The American Constitution: Its Origins and Development*, ed. Alfred H. Kelly, Winfred A. Harbison, and Herman Belz. 2 vols. 7th ed. New York: W. W. Norton, 1991. Readers should compare the language of the Declaration of Independence with the South Carolina declaration.

Farrand, Max, ed. *The Records of the Federal Convention of 1787.* 4 vols. New Haven, Conn.: Yale University Press, 1966. These volumes provide an understanding of the views of the framers of the Constitution on the issue of sovereignty, and the general relationship between the federal government and the state governments.

Johnson, Michael P., ed. *Abraham Lincoln, Slavery and the Civil War: Selected Writings and Speeches.* New York: St. Martin's Press, 2001. This volume is a collection of important writings and speeches of Abraham Lincoln. Reading these works will provide insight into Lincoln's views on secession and the compact theory of the Constitution.

McCulloch v. Maryland, 17 U.S. 316 (1819). Readers will profit from reading Chief Justice Marshall's opinion for the U.S. Supreme Court, particularly for his views on the issue of sovereignty.

Bibliography

■ Books

Catton, Bruce. *The Coming Fury.* Vol. 1. Garden City, N.Y.: Doubleday, 1961.

Farber, Daniel. *Lincoln's Constitution.* Chicago: University of Chicago Press, 2003.

Hyman, Harold M., and William M. Wiecek. *Equal Justice under Law: Constitutional Development, 1835–1875.* New York: Harper & Row, 1982.

McPherson, James M. *Ordeal by Fire: The Civil War and Reconstruction.* New York: Knopf, 1982.

Potter, David M. *The Impending Crisis, 1848–1861.* New York: Harper & Row, 1976.

Stampp, Kenneth M. *The Imperiled Union: Essays on the Background of the Civil War.* New York: Oxford University Press, 1980.

—By David Gray Adler

Questions for Further Study

1. Historians and other scholars are fond of pondering great "what if" questions. Allow your mind to range broadly over the potential outcomes of the Civil War. What if the South had won the war? What does your vision of the United States say about a southern triumph?

2. What are the strengths and weaknesses of the compact theory? Does the theory support secession?

3. Did South Carolina express adequate justification for its secession from the Union? If not, how might it have strengthened its case?

4. Did the Union encroach on the rights of South Carolina, as asserted in the document?

5. Were South Carolina's fears of Abraham Lincoln justified? Why or why not?

burthening	placing a burden, responsibility, or duty upon
eloign	to remove or carry away, as to conceal
evinced	shown or demonstrated clearly
forbearance	the act of refraining or resisting
General Government	national or federal government
insurrection	the act of rebellion against civil authority
material	relevant
rendition	the act of surrendering a person to another jurisdiction
secession	the act of withdrawing from an organization or union or political entity
sovereignty	the location or repository of the supreme power in a country or political entity

www.milestonedocuments.com

SOUTH CAROLINA DECLARATION OF CAUSES OF SECESSION

The people of the State of South Carolina, in Convention assembled, on the 26th day of April, A.D., 1852, declared that the frequent violations of the Constitution of the United States, by the Federal Government, and its encroachments upon the reserved rights of the States, fully justified this State in then withdrawing from the Federal Union; but in deference to the opinions and wishes of the other slaveholding States, she forbore at that time to exercise this right. Since that time, these encroachments have continued to increase, and further forbearance ceases to be a virtue.

And now the State of South Carolina having resumed her separate and equal place among nations, deems it due to herself, to the remaining United States of America, and to the nations of the world, that she should declare the immediate causes which have led to this act.

In the year 1765, that portion of the British Empire embracing Great Britain, undertook to make laws for the government of that portion composed of the thirteen American Colonies. A struggle for the right of self-government ensued, which resulted, on the 4th of July, 1776, in a Declaration, by the Colonies, "that they are, and of right ought to be, FREE AND INDEPENDENT STATES; and that, as free and independent States, they have full power to levy war, conclude peace, contract alliances, establish commerce, and to do all other acts and things which independent States may of right do."

They further solemnly declared that whenever any "form of government becomes destructive of the ends for which it was established, it is the right of the people to alter or abolish it, and to institute a new government." Deeming the Government of Great Britain to have become destructive of these ends, they declared that the Colonies "are absolved from all allegiance to the British Crown, and that all political connection between them and the State of Great Britain is, and ought to be, totally dissolved."

In pursuance of this Declaration of Independence, each of the thirteen States proceeded to exercise its separate sovereignty; adopted for itself a Constitution, and appointed officers for the administration of government in all its departments—Legislative, Executive and Judicial. For purposes of defense, they united their arms and their counsels; and, in 1778, they entered into a League known as the Articles of Confederation, whereby they agreed to entrust the administration of their external relations to a common agent, known as the Congress of the United States, expressly declaring, in the first Article "that each State retains its sovereignty, freedom and independence, and every power, jurisdiction and right which is not, by this Confederation, expressly delegated to the United States in Congress assembled."

Under this Confederation the war of the Revolution was carried on, and on the 3rd of September, 1783, the contest ended, and a definite Treaty was signed by Great Britain, in which she acknowledged the independence of the Colonies in the following terms: "ARTICLE 1—His Britannic Majesty acknowledges the said United States, viz: New Hampshire, Massachusetts Bay, Rhode Island and Providence Plantations, Connecticut, New York, New Jersey, Pennsylvania, Delaware, Maryland, Virginia, North Carolina, South Carolina and Georgia, to be FREE, SOVEREIGN AND INDEPENDENT STATES; that he treats with them as such; and for himself, his heirs and successors, relinquishes all claims to the government, propriety and territorial rights of the same and every part thereof."

Thus were established the two great principles asserted by the Colonies, namely: the right of a State to govern itself; and the right of a people to abolish a Government when it becomes destructive of the ends for which it was instituted. And concurrent with the establishment of these principles, was the fact, that each Colony became and was recognized by the mother Country a FREE, SOVEREIGN AND INDEPENDENT STATE.

In 1787, Deputies were appointed by the States to revise the Articles of Confederation, and on 17th September, 1787, these Deputies recommended for the adoption of the States, the Articles of Union, known as the Constitution of the United States.

The parties to whom this Constitution was submitted, were the several sovereign States; they were to agree or disagree, and when nine of them agreed the compact was to take effect among those concurring; and the General Government, as the common agent, was then invested with their authority.

If only nine of the thirteen States had concurred, the other four would have remained as they then were—separate, sovereign States, independent of any of the provisions of the Constitution. In fact, two of the States did not accede to the Constitution until long after it had gone into operation among the other eleven; and during that interval, they each exercised the functions of an independent nation.

By this Constitution, certain duties were imposed upon the several States, and the exercise of certain of their powers was restrained, which necessarily implied their continued existence as sovereign States. But to remove all doubt, an amendment was added, which declared that the powers not delegated to the United States by the Constitution, nor prohibited by it to the States, are reserved to the States, respectively, or to the people. On the 23d May, 1788, South Carolina, by a Convention of her People, passed an Ordinance assenting to this Constitution, and afterwards altered her own Constitution, to conform herself to the obligations she had undertaken.

Thus was established, by compact between the States, a Government with definite objects and powers, limited to the express words of the grant. This limitation left the whole remaining mass of power subject to the clause reserving it to the States or to the people, and rendered unnecessary any specification of reserved rights.

We hold that the Government thus established is subject to the two great principles asserted in the Declaration of Independence; and we hold further, that the mode of its formation subjects it to a third fundamental principle, namely: the law of compact. We maintain that in every compact between two or more parties, the obligation is mutual; that the failure of one of the contracting parties to perform a material part of the agreement, entirely releases the obligation of the other; and that where no arbiter is provided, each party is remitted to his own judgment to determine the fact of failure, with all its consequences.

In the present case, that fact is established with certainty. We assert that fourteen of the States have deliberately refused, for years past, to fulfill their constitutional obligations, and we refer to their own Statutes for the proof.

The Constitution of the United States, in its fourth Article, provides as follows: "No person held to service or labor in one State, under the laws thereof, escaping into another, shall, in consequence of any law or regulation therein, be discharged from such service or labor, but shall be delivered up, on claim of the party to whom such service or labor may be due."

This stipulation was so material to the compact, that without it that compact would not have been made. The greater number of the contracting parties held slaves, and they had previously evinced their estimate of the value of such a stipulation by making it a condition in the Ordinance for the government of the territory ceded by Virginia, which now composes the States north of the Ohio River.

The same article of the Constitution stipulates also for rendition by the several States of fugitives from justice from the other States.

The General Government, as the common agent, passed laws to carry into effect these stipulations of the States. For many years these laws were executed. But an increasing hostility on the part of the non-slaveholding States to the institution of slavery, has led to a disregard of their obligations, and the laws of the General Government have ceased to effect the objects of the Constitution. The States of Maine, New Hampshire, Vermont, Massachusetts, Connecticut, Rhode Island, New York, Pennsylvania, Illinois, Indiana, Michigan, Wisconsin and Iowa, have enacted laws which either nullify the Acts of Congress or render useless any attempt to execute them. In many of these States the fugitive is discharged from service or labor claimed, and in none of them has the State Government complied with the stipulation made in the Constitution. The State of New Jersey, at an early day, passed a law in conformity with her constitutional obligation; but the current of anti-slavery feeling has led her more recently to enact laws which render inoperative the remedies provided by her own law and by the laws of Congress. In the State of New York even the right of transit for a slave has been denied by her tribunals; and the States of Ohio and Iowa have refused to surrender to justice fugitives charged with murder, and with inciting servile insurrection in the State of Virginia. Thus the constituted compact has been deliberately broken and disregarded by the non-slaveholding States, and the consequence follows that South Carolina is released from her obligation.

The ends for which the Constitution was framed are declared by itself to be "to form a more perfect union, establish justice, insure domestic tranquility, provide for the common defence, promote the general welfare, and secure the blessings of liberty to ourselves and our posterity."

These ends it endeavored to accomplish by a Federal Government, in which each State was recognized as an equal, and had separate control over its own institutions. The right of property in slaves was recognized by giving to free persons distinct political rights, by giving them the right to represent, and burthening them with direct taxes for three-fifths of their slaves; by authorizing the importation of slaves for twenty years; and by stipulating for the rendition of fugitives from labor.

We affirm that these ends for which this Government was instituted have been defeated, and the Government itself has been made destructive of them by the action of the non-slaveholding States. Those States have assume the right of deciding upon the propriety of our domestic institutions; and have denied the rights of property established in fifteen of the States and recognized by the Constitution; they have denounced as sinful the institution of slavery; they have permitted open establishment among them of societies, whose avowed object is to disturb the peace and to eloign the property of the citizens of other States. They have encouraged and assisted thousands of our slaves to leave their homes; and those who remain, have been incited by emissaries, books and pictures to servile insurrection.

For twenty-five years this agitation has been steadily increasing, until it has now secured to its aid the power of the common Government. Observing the *forms* of the Constitution, a sectional party has found within that Article establishing the Executive Department, the means of subverting the Constitution itself. A geographical line has been drawn across the Union, and all the States north of that line have united in the election of a man to the high office of President of the United States, whose opinions and purposes are hostile to slavery. He is to be entrusted with the administration of the common Government, because he has declared that that "Government cannot endure permanently half slave, half free," and that the public mind must rest in the belief that slavery is in the course of ultimate extinction.

This sectional combination for the submersion of the Constitution, has been aided in some of the States by elevating to citizenship, persons who, by the supreme law of the land, are incapable of becoming citizens; and their votes have been used to inaugurate a new policy, hostile to the South, and destructive of its beliefs and safety.

On the 4th day of March next, this party will take possession of the Government. It has announced that the South shall be excluded from the common territory, that the judicial tribunals shall be made sectional, and that a war must be waged against slavery until it shall cease throughout the United States.

The guaranties of the Constitution will then no longer exist; the equal rights of the States will be lost. The slaveholding States will no longer have the power of self-government, or self-protection, and the Federal Government will have become their enemy.

Sectional interest and animosity will deepen the irritation, and all hope of remedy is rendered vain, by the fact that public opinion at the North has invested a great political error with the sanction of more erroneous religious belief.

We, therefore, the People of South Carolina, by our delegates in Convention assembled, appealing to the Supreme Judge of the world for the rectitude of our intentions, have solemnly declared that the Union heretofore existing between this State and the other States of North America, is dissolved, and that the State of South Carolina has resumed her position among the nations of the world, as a separate and independent State; with full power to levy war, conclude peace, contract alliances, establish commerce, and to do all other acts and things which independent States may of right do.

Adopted December 24, 1860

Jefferson Davis (Library of Congress)

JEFFERSON DAVIS'S INAUGURAL ADDRESS TO THE CONFEDERACY

"A reunion with the States from which we have separated is neither practicable nor desirable."

Overview

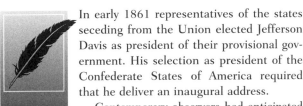

In early 1861 representatives of the states seceding from the Union elected Jefferson Davis as president of their provisional government. His selection as president of the Confederate States of America required that he deliver an inaugural address.

Contemporary observers had anticipated that South Carolina would lead the way to secession and drag along other Deep South states. They were correct. South Carolina's secession on December 20, 1860, created a chain reaction, as one Deep South state after another passed ordinances of secession. When Davis delivered his Inaugural Address on February 18, the six additional Deep South states (Georgia, Florida, Alabama, Mississippi, Louisiana, and Texas) had followed the lead of South Carolina and withdrawn from the Union. In February 1861, as Davis spoke, contemporaries waited to see what Virginia would do; they anticipated that Virginia's response to secession would determine the response of other slaveholding states: Maryland, Delaware, Kentucky, Missouri, Arkansas, North Carolina, Tennessee, and Arkansas. Their prediction was not entirely true, for when Virginia exited the Union, only Arkansas, North Carolina, and Tennessee followed suit.

Davis's speech occurred in a curious interregnum in American history. While some of the states that would form the Confederate States of America had left the Union, others had not. Abraham Lincoln, the newly elected president of the United States, would not take the oath of office until early March. War seemed uncertain. So, too, did the future of the nation. The nation assumed a wait-and-see attitude toward the slaveholding states, and the seceding states pondered their next move, too. Davis's Inaugural Address pointed toward a tentative plan for the seceding states' future.

Context

The states that constituted the United States had been mired in a "sectional conflict" since the debate over the U.S. Constitution in 1789. Throughout the long sectional conflict, the status of slavery served as the sole issue defin-

ing the conflict, and compromise had proved to be the only successful way to address sectional tensions. Prior to 1820, sectional concerns appeared intermittently in American politics. During the Constitutional Convention, for example, delegates debated how to count enslaved humans when determining the number of representatives to be seated by each state in Congress. Heated debate led to a compromise that counted each slave as the equivalent of three-fifths of one citizen.

In the first generations of the Republic's existence, most southern politicians publicly proclaimed slavery a necessary evil. In 1820, however, during debate over the admission of Missouri into the Union as a slave state, southerners in Congress began to extol only the virtues of slavery. Among the virtues, they said, was the wealth the labor of slaves provided the South and the nation; they also trumpeted the "civilizing" influence to which slavery exposed generations of Africans. According to the former president Thomas Jefferson, the debate over the Compromise of 1820 (or the Missouri Compromise) signified that the argument over slavery had taken a drastic turn and that turn should serve as a warning that the nation dangerously approached self-destruction. Over the next two decades, Jefferson's prediction seemed clairvoyant. National politics, as they played out in the South, tended exclusively to turn on the question of which candidate might most vigorously defend slavery, and a significant abolition movement took shape in the nonslaveholding states.

The Mexican-American War (1845–1847) heightened sectional tensions. Southern enthusiasm for the war and northern reluctance to embrace the cause of territorial acquisition in the Southwest ensured that the war would be characterized as one designed to expand the political influence of slaveholders. Soon after the war began, the U.S. Congress debated a resolution—the Wilmot Proviso—that declared slavery would be prohibited from any territory acquired during the war. Although the proviso never passed in Congress, the debate over the measure illustrated the differences between the sections. In 1850, when California sought to enter the Union as a free territory, southern politicians such as Jefferson Davis viewed the move as an effort to apply the Wilmot Proviso. However, as had often happened in the past, the debate over the status

Time Line

1860

■ **November 6**
Abraham Lincoln is elected president.

■ **December 20**
South Carolina secedes from the Union.

1861

■ **January**
Mississippi secedes from the Union.

■ **January 21**
Jefferson Davis resigns his seat in the U.S. Senate.

■ **February 9**
Jefferson Davis is selected on the fourth ballot as president of the provisional Confederate government.

■ **February 18**
In Montgomery, Alabama, Davis delivers his Inaugural Address.

■ **March 4**
Abraham Lincoln is inaugurated as president of the United States.

■ **April 12**
The Confederacy bombards the federal military installation at Fort Sumter located in Charleston Harbor.

■ **April 17**
The state of Virginia secedes from the Union.

■ **May 20**
Arkansas, the last state to secede from the Union, announces its secession.

territory and during which northern states passed personal liberty laws to undermine the abuses of the Fugitive Slave Act of 1850.

In the 1850s, as the South increasingly felt itself a persecuted minority within the nation, the establishment of the Republican Party in 1854 alarmed southern politicians as much as any other political event. The party, which arose in the wake of the collapse of the Whig Party, defined itself as a party of liberty for all. More important, because the party found a toehold only in nonslaveholding states, southerners regarded it as the vanguard of an impending wholesale assault on slavery. They promised that if a Republican president were elected without support from southern states, then the South would secede. When the second Republican nominee for president, Abraham Lincoln, won election to the White House in November 1860, southern states began withdrawing from the Union.

About the Author

Born on June 3, 1808, Jefferson Davis lived his early life in southwestern Kentucky near the Tennessee border. He was the last of the ten children of Samuel and Jane Davis. In 1812 Davis's father, a veteran of the American Revolution, moved his family to Wilkinson County, Mississippi, though soon afterward the elder Davis sent his youngest son back to Kentucky to attend school. At the age of ten, Jefferson Davis returned to Mississippi to attended Jefferson College near Natchez, which was hardly a college by modern standards, and then he attended Transylvania University in Lexington, Kentucky. He entered the U.S. Military Academy at West Point, New York, in 1824 and graduated four years later. Most of his early military career was spent in the upper Midwest, but he also served briefly as a first lieutenant in the cavalry in Indian Territory.

In 1835 Davis married Sarah Knox Taylor, the daughter of his former colonel, Zachary Taylor, but their marriage was short-lived. Sarah Davis died three months after their wedding. Devastated by her death, Davis removed to rural Mississippi, near Vicksburg, where next to his brother Joseph's plantation he carved out a plantation of his own, which he named Brierfield. After establishing the plantation, Davis won election to the U.S. House of Representatives in 1844, and he married Varina Howell the following year. Before his term in office ended, however, Davis resigned to raise a volunteer regiment, the Mississippi Rifles, which participated in the Mexican-American War with Davis as colonel of the unit. Davis distinguished himself during the war as a brave and wily leader. At the conclusion of the war, his military record and the fame it brought him prompted the governor of Mississippi to appoint Davis to an unfilled U.S. Senate seat. Shortly afterward, the state legislature elected Davis in his own right to the post. Once again, however, Davis did not remain until the end of his term.

Davis became embroiled in the bitter debate that eventually led to the passage of the Compromise of 1850. He

of California resulted in a compromise—the Compromise of 1850—which established the principle of popular sovereignty. Popular sovereignty meant that territories, rather than the federal government, could determine whether slavery could exist within territorial boundaries.

Southern opposition to the Compromise of 1850 led to the convening of state conventions. Even though opposition to the compromise provided the impetus for convening conventions, all southern states adopted some form of the "Georgia Platform." The Georgia Platform, with its guarantees of popular sovereignty and a more robust fugitive slave law, was intended to be the final compromise. Efforts by northern states and politicians to breach the compromise would provoke secession, the conventions implied. That promise lasted a scant ten years, an epoch during which popular sovereignty was bloodily contested in the Kansas viewed the compromise as a purposeful attack on white southerners' right to move slaves into the territory gained from Mexico during the late war. Anticipating that Mississippi and other southern states might leave the Union in 1850 or 1851 to protest the compromise, Davis resigned his Senate seat to run for governor against his fellow senator, Henry Stuart Foote, who had worked to pass the compromise. As governor of Mississippi, Davis thought, he could shape the debate about secession and the compromise. Although Davis cannot be labeled a fire-eater (a rabid proponent of secession from the Union), he campaigned against the enforcement of the compromise and looked forward to a state convention that would rebuke the compromise. However, by a scant 999 votes, Davis lost his 1851 bid to be governor of Mississippi. For two years, he remained out of office and devoted himself to the Brierfield plantation. Then, in 1853, the newly inaugurated president, Franklin Pierce, named Davis secretary of war. His term as secretary was marked by two interesting achievements, both of which testified to the realities of American expansion westward. First, he authored a report that proposed routes of a transcontinental railroad, and, second, he imported camels to the U.S. Army stationed in the Southwest, so that troops could better negotiate the arid terrain.

When Pierce lost the Democratic Party nomination for a second term, Davis sought election to the U.S. Senate. From 1857 until January 1861 Davis assumed his former seat, but he resigned from the Senate as soon as Mississippi seceded from the Union. Less than a month later, representatives of seven seceding Confederate states elected him president of the provisional government. In November 1861 the remaining seceding states elected him to a six-year term as president.

After the Civil War, Davis was arrested and imprisoned at Fort Monroe, Virginia. Soon, he was indicted for treason, yet at the urging of famous citizens from northern states, the prosecution dropped the case. Davis devoted the remainder of his life to writing *The Rise and Fall of the Confederate Government* and other works. In late 1889 he died in New Orleans, Louisiana.

Explanation and Analysis of the Document

Jefferson Davis's brief, twelve-paragraph Inaugural Address was intended to capture the imaginations of his immediate audience in Montgomery, Alabama, and also to offer border states cause to join the new Confederacy. Through his repeated appeals to American history, he hoped as well to assuage northern sentiment, which was aligning against the seceding states.

In the first paragraph, Davis offers his listeners what many would expect on such an occasion: a declaration of humility, a statement of his dependence on others for guidance, and "an abiding faith in the virtue and patriotism of the people." Reflecting the sentiment of many white southerners, Davis obliquely refers to the fact that the new nation felt like a persecuted minority while it was part of the United States. His reference to the moral superiority of the southern cause iterated a widely held belief that through the establishment of the Confederacy and because of its willingness to face all challengers, the South was providentially blessed and guaranteed to succeed. Put another way, in one simple turn of phrase, Davis captures the South's belief that secession was necessary to protect slavery and ultimately to protect Western civilization from the eccentricity and dangerous liberalism of the North. By placing himself and the southern people at the head of the conservative revolution to save Western civilization, Davis indicates his commitment to the cause. Finally, Davis plainly anticipates opposition to establishment of the Confederacy, but he notes that the South's "physical power," its determination, and providence promise long-term success for the Confederacy.

The second and third paragraphs represent efforts to link the new Confederacy to the mainstream of American history. By far, they are the most significant and complicated sections of the speech. Davis correctly characterizes the peaceful inauguration of the southern states as unique in world history. Never before had a minority of political entities withdrawn from a larger group without precipitating violence. Certainly, the United States, when it declared independence from Great Britain, did not achieve its aims free of revolutionary conflict. Davis asserts that the peaceful establishment of the Confederacy is owed to the American political theory that consent of the governed is required for the existence of government. Therefore, the people possess the right to withdraw from one government and form another. In a convoluted sentence more than a hundred words long, Davis references the stated goals of the Declaration of Independence signed in the early days of the American Revolution. When the national government ceased to deal justly with the South, provide domestic peace, and protect slavery and the interests of slaveholding societies, then the people assumed the right to remove themselves from the national union. Such references to the American Revolution and the Founding Fathers were a favorite rhetorical device of U.S. politicians, especially in the mid-nineteenth century. Davis confidently calls on history to judge whether or not the southern states acted in an effort to preserve the principles that motivated the Revolutionary generation to act.

Continuing his argument about the faithfulness of the Confederacy to national principles, Davis, in the third paragraph of his speech, argues that the actions of the southern states are not revolutionary. Rather, the southern states seek to return to the principles that moved a previous generation to declare independence and to establish an independent republic. The Confederacy consists of individual states, all of which continue to embrace equal protection before the law of whites and their property. Here, Davis makes his point to ensure foreign governments and investors that the southern states will continue to engage in commerce with all nations. He points out as well that the relations that southern states and businesses have enjoyed with international firms will not be changed by the inauguration of the Confederacy. Instead, the Confederacy will seek peace and free trade. Should proclamations of peaceful intentions fail to produce the desired results, Davis again invites history to judge the Confederacy's intentions as peaceable. His appeal to foreign governments remarkably includes an appeal to the United States. In an effort to extend an olive branch to the nonslaveholding states, Davis suggests that the dissolution of the Union need not dissolve commercial relations between the North and South. At the same time, Davis seems certain that war cannot be avoided, if only because of anticipated action by the U.S. government.

The fourth paragraph briefly reiterates points made in the preceding two paragraphs. In essence, the paragraph serves as a transition to the more practical concerns addressed in the fifth paragraph. In that paragraph, Davis outlines the specific branches of the executive branch of government that the Confederacy needs still to form. Although content to rely upon a militia for the protection of the Confederacy over the short term, Davis advocates establishment of a national army and a navy.

Complimenting the officers who wrote a constitution for the provisional government, Davis argues that the document maintains the significant features of the U.S. Constitution. Among such features is the provision that other states might join the Confederacy. Pointing out the availability of such an option, Davis invites other like-minded states to join the Confederacy. He also implies that he doubts the Confederacy would permit a reunion with nonslaveholding states, because the Confederacy requires homogeneity of thought. He need only to point to the difference of opinion about slavery that distinguishes the northern and southern states to make his point about the importance of single-minded devotion to the widely accepted common good.

In the seventh paragraph, Davis accurately predicts that the U.S. government will attempt in the future to block commerce between the seceding states and the rest of the world. The wartime blockade of southern ports conducted by the U.S. Navy proved his point. Again appealing to international industrial interests, Davis argues that such a blockade would be "unjust" and injurious to foreign trading partners. If such a disruption in trade were to occur, Davis assures his international listeners that they will not be able to trace the cause of the disruption to the southern states, which, he says, will continue to produce staple crops, even if confronted by warfare, just as they had always done. In the following paragraph, Davis adds that if commerce between the South and the rest of the world is shut down by the U.S. government, the world will lose the employment of millions of individuals and starvation will ensue.

The ninth paragraph indicates that the speech is returning to its first theme: the inadequacy of the new president. Proclaiming that he will make mistakes, he will never be accused of lacking enthusiasm for the Confederacy's cause of independence. The remainder of the speech returns to familiar themes. Boldly and explicitly, Davis declares that the Confederacy has revealed by its actions and in its constitution the intended meaning of the Founding Fathers when they penned the U.S. Constitution. Fortified by the proper interpretation, Davis asserts that a strict construction of the central government's authority will determine future action. Noting that his term in office will be limited to six years, he begs his audience to forgive his missteps and prays that upon his retirement the people of the Confederacy will continue to regard him warmly. Finally, Davis asserts the virtue of the citizens of the Confederacy and the justice of their cause and remarks that the favor of the deity will ensure the young nation's future success.

Audience

Elected by representatives from seven Deep South states to assume the role of president of the provisional government, Davis delivered his Inaugural Address to an audience of government officials and members of society of Montgomery, Alabama. Among the government officials present was Alexander Stephens of Georgia, who had been elected vice-president of the provisional government. Davis, who spent a full day writing the speech, especially directed its contents to his immediate audience.

Unlike the impromptu speeches that Davis had delivered as he traveled from Vicksburg to western Georgia and then on to Montgomery, the Inaugural Address was intended for a broader audience, too. Like many of Davis's prepared speeches, the Inaugural Address was designed to serve several audiences. He informed the seceding states of his support for their cause, yet at the same time offered to slaveholding states that had not yet seceded a justification for doing so. To northern states, those states firmly aligned with the government of the soon-to-be-inaugurated president, Abraham Lincoln, he offered the olive branch of peace and a chiding justification for the South's conservative revolution. He even addressed international businessmen and governments when he stated that the Confederacy intended to continue to sell its staple crops overseas.

Impact

The direct impact of Davis's speech was limited. Its influence over the conduct of the U.S. government, nonslaveholding states that had not yet seceded, and the international community cannot be measured by any subsequent event. Still, the document remains significant, for in it Davis encapsulated several decades of thinking about the sectional crisis, the defense of slavery, and southern arguments in favor of secession. He also spoke directly to the immediate goals of the new nation and plainly expressed concern about the ability of the Confederacy to exist in peace. Thus, his speech must be viewed as a synopsis of the past used to justify the present and a tentative plan for the future and less as a speech that shaped subsequent behavior.

Nonetheless, Davis did attempt in a concrete fashion to extend an olive branch to the U.S. government. He sent a

"*Sustained by the consciousness that the transition from the former Union to the present Confederacy has not proceeded from a disregard on our part of just obligations, or any failure to perform every constitutional duty, moved by no interest or passion to invade the rights of others, anxious to cultivate peace and commerce with all nations, if we may not hope to avoid war, we may at least expect that posterity will acquit us of having needlessly engaged in it.*"

(Paragraph 3)

"*If, however, passion or lust of dominion should cloud the judgment or inflame the ambition of those States [the states of the Union], we must prepare to meet the emergency and maintain, by the final arbitrament of the sword, the position which we have assumed among the nations of the earth.*"

(Paragraph 3)

"*For this your Constitution makes adequate provision; but beyond this, if I mistake not the judgment and will of the people, a reunion with the States from which we have separated is neither practicable nor desirable.*"

(Paragraph 6)

"*To increase the power, develop the resources, and promote the happiness of the Confederacy, it is requisite that there should be so much of homogeneity that the welfare of every portion shall be the aim of the whole.*"

(Paragraph 6)

delegation—the Peace Commission—to Washington, D.C., with the goal of purchasing federal forts and facilities located in the Confederacy. President Lincoln refused the overture. He did correctly predict that the flexibility of the Confederate constitution would permit other states to join. After the Confederate bombardment of Union-occupied Fort Sumter in April 1861, four other southern states abandoned the Union to unite with the Confederacy.

Additionally, Davis sent emissaries to European powers to help maintain the tide of financial and diplomatic support for the Confederacy to bring to life his vision of a financially independent nation. But the efforts of the emissaries never produced the desired results. Incorrectly, Davis had predicted that even if war visited the South, the pro-

duction of staple crops would continue unabated. Pinning his faith on the ability of the slaveholding states to continue trade with foreign businesses, Davis committed a grave error. In an age in which the producers of raw materials would soon fall victim to the demands of big business, he and the South miscalculated the significance of staple crops to American and Western commerce.

In the end, the conservative revolution that Davis advocated failed. The Confederacy became weighted down by internal political struggles that mirrored those engaged in while the South remained a part of the Union, including debates over the rights and responsibilities of states and the rights and responsibilities of the central government. Sadly, that the Confederacy survived four years of war to abort its birth testified to the commitment to slavery broadly shared among white southerners more than it testified to the virtue of its cause.

Related Documents

"Confederate States of America—Constitution for the Provisional Government." The Avalon Project at Yale Law School Web site. http://www.yale.edu/lawweb/avalon/csa/csapro.htm. Accessed on January 8, 2008. In his Inaugural Address, Davis refers to the constitution of the provisional government. The document represents the first attempt by the Confederate States of America to provide a framework of government.

"Confederate States of America: Declaration of the Immediate Causes Which Induce and Justify the Secession of South Carolina from the Federal Union." The Avalon Project at Yale Law School Web site. http://www.yale.edu/lawweb/avalon/csa/scarsec.htm. Accessed on January 8, 2008. The South Carolina Ordinance of Secession recounts, in part, the same history as Davis's Inaugural Address. The treatment of the past and the causes of secession in the two documents bear analysis.

"Confederate States of America: Mississippi Secession." The Avalon Project at Yale Law School Web site. http://www.yale.edu/lawweb/avalon/csa/missec.htm. Accessed on January 8, 2008. The Mississippi Ordinance of Secession was intended for a Mississippi audience, while Davis's Inaugural Address was meant for broader consumption. The documents use facts differently in interesting ways to justify the positions of their authors.

"First Inaugural Address of Abraham Lincoln." The Avalon Project at Yale Law School Web site. http://www.yale.edu/lawweb/avalon/presiden/inaug/lincoln1.htm. Accessed on January 8, 2008. Lincoln delivered his First Inaugural Address shortly after Davis delivered his. They responded to same exigencies, though they did so from a vastly different perspective.

"Inaugural Address of John F. Kennedy." The Avalon Project at Yale Law School Web site. http://www.yale.edu/lawweb/avalon/presiden/inaug/kennedy.htm. Accessed on January 8, 2008. Kennedy's Inaugural Address, though delivered in a time of tumult and uncertainty, offers a strikingly different tone than that found in Davis's address.

"Jefferson Davis's Resignation Speech from the U.S. Senate." In William J. Cooper, Jr., ed., *Jefferson Davis: The Essential Writings*. New York: Random House, 2003. Davis's resignation speech covers many of the same points as his Inaugural Address, though the differences between the tone—especially as related to the rhetoric—should be examined.

Bibliography

■ **Books**

Cooper, William J., Jr. *Jefferson Davis, American*. New York: Alfred A. Knopf, 2000.

Davis, William C. *Jefferson Davis: The Man and His Hour*. New York: HarperCollins, 1991.

Strode, Hudson. *Jefferson Davis: An American Patriot, 1806–1861*. New York: Harcourt, Brace, 1955.

Thomas, Emory M. *The Confederate Nation, 1861–1865*. New York: Harper & Row, 1979.

■ **Web Sites**

"Davis, Jefferson (1808–1889)." Biographical Directory of the United States Congress Web site.
  http://bioguide.congress.gov/scripts/biodisplay.pl?index=D0001 13. Accessed on December 13, 2007.

Olden, Sam. "Mississippi and the U.S.-Mexican War, 1846–1848." Mississippi HistoryNow Web site.
  http://mshistory.k12.ms.us/index.php?id=202. Accessed on December 13, 2007.

Williams, Clay. "The Road to War (1846–1860)," Mississippi HistoryNow Web site.
  http://mshistory.k12.ms.us/index.php?id=206. Accessed on December 13, 2007.

—By Bradley G. Bond

Questions for Further Study

1. Compare and contrast the Inaugural Address of Jefferson Davis and the First Inaugural Address of Abraham Lincoln. What themes do the documents share? Where do they diverge?

2. Examine Jefferson Davis's 1861 speech resigning his seat in the U.S. Senate. How does the tone of the speech differ from the Inaugural Address? How do the speeches resemble each other? What accounts for the similarities or differences?

3. Compare the ordinance of secession adopted by the state of South Carolina or by the state of Mississippi to Jefferson Davis's Inaugural Address. What themes do the documents share? Did Davis's address reflect the facts, fears, and hope of the secession ordinance? Explain how.

4. Presidential inaugural speeches are at once articulations of one person's vision and diplomatic overtures to citizens as well as to the international community. Another president, who assumed office during a turbulent era, John F. Kennedy, offered the world a famous inaugural address. How do Kennedy's address and Davis's address differ? What broad themes do they share?

Glossary

homogeneity	uniformity in shape, interest, and thought
perverted	altered or changed, especially for nefarious reasons
rectitude	moral uprightness or virtue
retard	to slow or hold back progress
sovereign	in this case, independent and supreme
vindicate	to deliver or set free

Jefferson Davis's Inaugural Address to the Confederacy

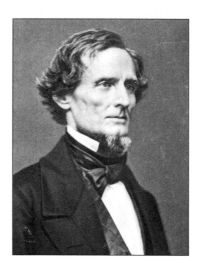

February 18, 1861

Gentlemen of the Congress of the Confederate States of America, Friends, and Fellow-citizens: Called to the difficult and responsible station of Chief Magistrate of the Provisional Government which you have instituted, I approach the discharge of the duties assigned to me with humble distrust of my abilities, but with a sustaining confidence in the wisdom of those who are to guide and aid me in the administration of public affairs, and an abiding faith in the virtue and patriotism of the people. Looking forward to the speedy establishment of a permanent government to take the place of this, which by its greater moral and physical power will be better able to combat with many difficulties that arise from the conflicting interests of separate nations, I enter upon the duties of the office to which I have been chosen with the hope that the beginning of our career, as a Confederacy, may not be obstructed by hostile opposition to our enjoyment of the separate existence and independence we have asserted, and which, with the blessing of Providence, we intend to maintain.

Our present political position has been achieved in a manner unprecedented in the history of nations. It illustrates the American idea that governments rest on the consent of the governed, and that it is the right of the people to alter or abolish them at will whenever they become destructive of the ends for which they were established. The declared purpose of the compact of the Union from which we have withdrawn was to "establish justice, insure domestic tranquillity, provide for the common defense, promote the general welfare, and secure the blessings of liberty to ourselves and our posterity"; and when, in the judgment of the sovereign States composing this Confederacy, it has been perverted from the purposes for which it was ordained, and ceased to answer the ends for which it was established, a peaceful appeal to the ballot box declared that, so far as they are concerned, the Government created by that compact should cease to exist. In this they merely asserted the right which the Declaration of Independence of July 4, 1776, defined to be "inalienable." Of the time and occasion of its exercise they as sovereigns were the final judges, each for itself. The impartial and enlightened verdict of mankind will vindicate the rectitude of our conduct; and He who knows the hearts of men will judge of the sincerity with which we have labored to preserve the Government of our fathers in its spirit.

The right solemnly proclaimed at the birth of the United States, and which has been solemnly affirmed and reaffirmed in the Bills of Rights of the States subsequently admitted into the Union of 1789, undeniably recognizes in the people the power to resume the authority delegated for the purposes of government. Thus the sovereign States here represented have proceeded to form this Confederacy; and it is by abuse of language that their act has been denominated a revolution. They formed a new alliance, but within each State its government has remained; so that the rights of person and property have not been disturbed. The agent through which they communicated with foreign nations is changed, but this does not necessarily interrupt their international relations. Sustained by the consciousness that the transition from the former Union to the present Confederacy has not proceeded from a disregard on our part of just obligations, or any failure to perform every constitutional duty, moved by no interest or passion to invade the rights of others, anxious to cultivate peace and commerce with all nations, if we may not hope to avoid war, we may at least expect that posterity will acquit us of having needlessly engaged in it. Doubly justified by the absence of wrong on our part, and by wanton aggression on the part of others, there can be no cause to doubt that the courage and patriotism of the people of the Confederate States will be found equal to any measure of defense which their honor and security may require. An agricultural people, whose chief interest is the export of commodities required in every manufacturing country, our true policy is peace, and the freest trade which our necessities will permit. It is alike our interest and that of all those to whom we would sell, and from whom we would buy, that there should be the fewest practicable restrictions upon the interchange of these commodities. There can, however, be but little rivalry between ours and any manufacturing or navigating community, such as the Northeastern States of the American Union. It must follow, therefore, that mutual interest will invite to good will and kind offices on both parts. If, however, passion or lust of dominion should cloud the judgment or inflame the ambition of those States, we must prepare to meet the emergency and maintain, by the final arbitrament of the sword, the position which we have assumed among the nations of the earth.

We have entered upon the career of independence, and it must be inflexibly pursued. Through many years of controversy with our late associates of the Northern States, we have vainly endeavored to secure tranquillity and obtain respect for the rights to which we were entitled. As a necessity, not a choice, we have resorted to the remedy of separation, and henceforth our energies must be directed to the conduct of our own affairs, and the perpetuity of the Confederacy which we have formed. If a just perception of mutual interest shall permit us peaceably to pursue our separate political career, my most earnest desire will have been fulfilled. But if this be denied to us, and the integrity of our territory and jurisdiction be assailed, it will but remain for us with firm resolve to appeal to arms and invoke the blessing of Providence on a just cause.

As a consequence of our new condition and relations, and with a view to meet anticipated wants, it will be necessary to provide for the speedy and efficient organization of branches of the Executive department having special charge of foreign intercourse, finance, military affairs, and the postal service. For purposes of defense, the Confederate States may, under ordinary circumstances, rely mainly upon the militia; but it is deemed advisable, in the present condition of affairs, that there should be a well-instructed and disciplined army, more numerous than would usually be required on a peace establishment. I also suggest that, for the protection of our harbors and commerce on the high seas, a navy adapted to those objects will be required. But this, as well as other subjects appropriate to our necessities, have doubtless engaged the attention of Congress.

With a Constitution differing only from that of our fathers in so far as it is explanatory of their well-known intent, freed from sectional conflicts, which have interfered with the pursuit of the general welfare, it is not unreasonable to expect that States from which we have recently parted may seek to unite their fortunes to ours under the Government which we have instituted. For this your Constitution makes adequate provision; but beyond this, if I mistake not the judgment and will of the people, a reunion with the States from which we have separated is neither practicable nor desirable. To increase the power, develop the resources, and promote the happiness of the Confederacy, it is requisite that there should be so much of homogeneity that the welfare of every portion shall be the aim of the whole. When this does not exist, antagonisms are engendered which must and should result in separation.

Actuated solely by the desire to preserve our own rights, and promote our own welfare, the separation by the Confederate States has been marked by no aggression upon others, and followed by no domestic convulsion. Our industrial pursuits have received no check, the cultivation of our fields has progressed as heretofore, and, even should we be involved in war, there would be no considerable diminution in the production of the staples which have constituted our exports, and in which the commercial world has an interest scarcely less than our own. This common interest of the producer and consumer can only be interrupted by exterior force which would obstruct the transmission of our staples to foreign markets—a course of conduct which would be as unjust, as it would be detrimental, to manufacturing and commercial interests abroad.

Should reason guide the action of the Government from which we have separated, a policy so detrimental to the civilized world, the Northern States included, could not be dictated by even the strongest desire to inflict injury upon us; but, if the contrary should prove true, a terrible responsibility will rest upon it, and the suffering of millions will bear testimony to the folly and wickedness of our aggressors. In the meantime there will remain to us, besides the ordinary means before suggested, the well-known resources for retaliation upon the commerce of an enemy.

Experience in public stations, of subordinate grade to this care and disappointment are the price of official elevation. You will see many errors to forgive, many deficiencies to tolerate; but you shall not find in me either want of zeal or fidelity to the cause that is to me the highest in hope, and of most enduring affection. Your generosity has bestowed upon me an undeserved distinction, one which I neither sought nor desired. Upon the continuance of that sentiment, and upon your wisdom and patriotism, I rely to direct and support me in the performance of the duties required at my hands.

We have changed the constituent parts, but not the system of government. The Constitution framed by our fathers is that of these Confederate States. In their exposition of it, and in the judicial construction it has received, we have a light which reveals its true meaning.

Thus instructed as to the true meaning and just interpretation of that instrument, and ever remembering that all offices are but trusts held for the people, and that powers delegated are to be strictly construed, I will hope by due diligence in the performance of my duties, though I may disappoint your expectations, yet to retain, when retiring, something of the good will and confidence which welcome my entrance into office.

It is joyous in the midst of perilous times to look around upon a people united in heart, where one purpose of high resolve animates and actuates the whole; where the sacrifices to be made are not weighed in the balance against honor and right and liberty and equality. Obstacles may retard, but they cannot long prevent, the progress of a movement sanctified by its justice and sustained by a virtuous people. Reverently let us invoke the God of our fathers to guide and protect us in our efforts to perpetuate the principles which by his blessing they were able to vindicate, establish, and transmit to their posterity. With the continuance of his favor ever gratefully acknowledged, we may hopefully look forward to success, to peace, and to prosperity.

In compliance with a custom as old as the government itself, I appear before you to address you briefly, and to take, in your presence, the oath prescribed by the Constitution of the United States, to be taken by the President "before he enters on the execution of his office."

The more modern custom of electing a Chief Magistrate upon a previously declared platform of principles, supercedes, in a great measure, the necessity of re-stating those principles in an address of this sort. Upon the plainest grounds of good faith, one so elected is not at liberty to shift his position. It is necessarily implied, if not expressed, that, in his judgment, the platform which he thus accepts, binds him to nothing either unconstitutional or inexpedient.

Having been so elected upon the Chicago Platform, and while I would repeat noth~~ing in it, of opposition or without a question of action against any man or party, I~~ hold myself bound by duty, as well as impelled by inclination to follow, within the executive sphere, the principles therein declared. By no other course could I meet the reasonable expectations of the country.

I do not consider it necessary at present for me to say more than I have, in relation to those matters of administration, about which there is no special excitement.

Apprehension seems to exist among the people of the Southern States, that by the accession of a Republican Administration, their property, and _____ and personal security, are to be endangered. Th_____ _____ for such apprehension _____ while existed _____ b'ished _____ eeches _____ right _____ d me _____ ar declarations, _____ than this, they placed in the platform, for _____ and as a law to themselves, and to me, the clear and emphatic resolution which I now read:

"_Resolved_, That the maintenance inviolate of the rights of the States, and especially to its own judgment exclusively, is essential to that balance of power on which the perfection and endurance of our political fabric depend; and we denounce the lawless invasion by armed force of the soil of any State or Territory, no matter under what pretext, as among the gravest of crimes."

I do not consider it necessary, at present, for me to discuss those matters of administration about which there is no special anxiety, or excitement.

The final printed version of Lincoln's First Inaugural Address is shown here with an earlier draft by him of part of the address. (Library of Congress)

ABRAHAM LINCOLN'S FIRST INAUGURAL ADDRESS

*"The mystic chords of memory ...
will yet swell the chorus of the Union."*

Overview

On March 4, 1861, Abraham Lincoln addressed his fellow citizens, as was the custom of presidents taking the oath of office. His main purpose was to allay the anxieties of the southern states that their property, peace, and personal security were endangered because a Republican administration was taking office. Thus, Lincoln reiterated his promise not to interfere with the institution of slavery. Indeed, he affirmed the rights of states to order and determine their own institutions. To do otherwise, he noted, would violate the U.S. Constitution. Furthermore, he vowed to enforce the federal Fugitive Slave Act, which stipulated that slaves escaping from southern masters be returned to their owners. At the same time, Lincoln argued that the U.S. Constitution was "perpetual," which is to say indissoluble. In effect, he was denying such states as South Carolina the right to secede. The Constitution could be amended, but the Union could not be broken. Thus he tempered his message of reconciliation with the admonition that under no circumstances would the federal government under his administration tolerate secession.

Context

By the time Lincoln was nominated for president in the spring of 1860, the issue of slavery had become a test of wills between the North and South. Abolitionists in the North were uncompromising, declaring slavery immoral. They agitated for immediate emancipation, or freeing, of slaves. Proslavery elements in the South not only defended their "peculiar institution" but also saw it as superior to the wage slavery of northern factories. In their view, slavery was a paternalistic institution, not the moral evil antislavery agitators deemed it. Between these extreme positions, many southerners and northerners looked for some way to preserve the Union that would not threaten the South but would limit the spread of slavery to the new territories in the West.

The new Republican Party, committed to opposing the spread of slavery, also sought ways to reach an accommodation with the South—although certain radicals in the party had ties to militant abolitionists, who rejected any compromise that would leave the institution of slavery intact. Passage on September 18, 1850, of the Fugitive Slave Act, a part of the Compromise of 1850 assuring the South that escaped slaves, when apprehended, would be returned to their owners, did little to appease southerners, even though Republicans such as Lincoln supported it. Like the Missouri Compromise of 1820, the Compromise of 1850 attempted to strike a balance between free-soil and slave states, ensuring that as a slave state entered the Union, so, too, would a free-soil state.

But tensions arose in such territories as Kansas and Nebraska, where free-soil and slave-state advocates clashed. In May 1856, John Brown, a militant abolitionist, slaughtered five proslavery advocates in the Kansas-Nebraska territory. Brown later inflamed passions over the slavery issue when he attacked Harpers Ferry, Virginia, in 1859 in an effort to foment a slave uprising that would ultimately overturn the institution of slavery itself. Although Brown's raid failed and he was executed, southerners concluded that sooner or later the federal government would enact measures that signaled the end of slavery.

In the Lincoln–Douglas debates of 1858, Douglas propounded the doctrine of "popular sovereignty," which meant that each state or territory could determine its position on slavery, which the federal government could not countermand. To Lincoln, however, providing this latitude destroyed the concept of a central government with nationally enforceable laws. But all he had to offer the South was the undertaking that under his administration the federal government would not hinder the already established institution of slavery.

In part, then, Lincoln was confronting a political crisis involving two sections of a nation striving to maintain their place in the balance of power. He presumed that as long as the federal government enacted no laws that interfered with the right to own slaves in the southern states, extremist calls for secession would ultimately dissipate through the kinds of compromises that had been formulated in 1820 and 1850. Unfortunately, Lincoln miscalculated, for he failed to see that the argument over slavery was, in the minds of many southerners, an issue striking directly at

1820
- Missouri Compromise stipulates that new states and territories in the Louisiana Purchase territory north of the southern boundary of Missouri, except Missouri, would be free, and those below that line would be slave.

1850
- Compromise of 1850 continues the principle of the Missouri Compromise, maintaining a balance of power between free and slave states, while the Fugitive Slave Act mandates that escaped slaves must be returned to their owners.

1856
- **May 24**
John Brown's followers murder five proslavery advocates near Pottawatomie Creek, Kansas.

1858
- **August 21–October 15**
Lincoln–Douglas debates take place.

1859
- **October 16**
John Brown attacks the arsenal at Harpers Ferry, Virginia.

1860
- **May 18**
Republican convention nominates Lincoln for president.

- **November 6**
Lincoln is elected president.

1860–1861
- **December 20, 1860–February 23, 1861**
South Carolina, Mississippi, Florida, Alabama, Georgia, Louisiana, and Texas secede. Convention of secessionist states establishes a constitution and elects Jefferson Davis as its first president.

1861
- **March 4**
Lincoln is inaugurated as president.

their own liberties and way of life. They viewed the Union as an organization of sovereign states that had the right to secede. Lincoln, on the other hand, interpreted the U.S. Constitution as implicitly forming a Union that could not be dissolved. As he put it in his First Inaugural Address, what government has ever stipulated that process by which it can be destroyed? Denying, then, this fundamental right to secede, Lincoln's efforts to reconcile with the South proved, in retrospect, to be of no avail.

About the Author

Abraham Lincoln, born on February 12, 1809, in a one-room log cabin in southeastern Kentucky, grew up in a frontier environment. He had little formal education but was a prodigious reader, favoring the Bible, Shakespeare, and biographies. As a young man he studied law. At age twenty-three he ran unsuccessfully for a seat in the General Assembly of Illinois, to which state his family had moved when he was nine. He served briefly in the Black Hawk War before being elected to the state legislature in 1834. Admitted to the bar in 1837, Lincoln proved to be a successful attorney, admired for his ability to argue on his feet in court cases.

In 1842 Lincoln married Mary Todd, the daughter of a prominent southern family. The couple had four children, but only one, Robert, survived into adulthood. Quarrelsome but proud of her husband, Mary supported Lincoln's political ambitions. He was elected for one term in the U.S. House of Representatives and made a notable speech opposing the Mexican-American War; the speech proved unpopular, however, and he did not run for reelection. Indeed, Lincoln's political career then seemed over not only because of his own politics but also because he had linked his future with that of the Whig Party, which steadily lost ground to the Democrats in the 1850s.

Lincoln's political prospects rose in 1854 when a new party, the Republicans, took control of the Illinois legislature. Lincoln was the Republican candidate for senator in the famous 1858 election, when he debated Stephen Douglas, the incumbent Democratic senator and a politician with a national profile and the ambition to be president. Although Lincoln's outstanding performance in the debates drew national attention, his party lost the statewide election, and Douglas retained his seat as senator.

While Lincoln was no abolitionist (as he did not favor immediate emancipation of the slaves), his public speeches clearly demonstrated that he thought slavery was evil. A prudent politician, he professed no desire to eliminate slavery in the South. Still, his opposition to the spread of slavery in the western territories signaled to the South that its power—sooner or later—would be curtailed as more states were added to the Union.

Even though Lincoln's position on slavery was not radical, the southern states made clear that they would not remain in the Union should Lincoln be elected president. This threat of secession notwithstanding, Lincoln was genuinely surprised when the South made good on its warning. Even after South Carolina seceded, Lincoln held out hope for some sort of compromise. He did not believe that it was in the economic interests of the South to secede, and thus he seriously underestimated that region's pride in its traditions and its fear that a northern-dominated federal government would eventually outlaw slavery and weaken the South's position in the Union. Lincoln did not understand that a majority of southerners considered his election a direct assault on their liberties.

After the fall of Fort Sumter, South Carolina, however, Lincoln could no longer doubt that war was at hand. His objective then was to prosecute a war that would preserve the Union. Not until relatively late in the war, beginning in 1863 with the Emancipation Proclamation, did the president make the freeing of the slaves a political and moral priority of a Union victory. Lincoln's steadfast reliance on General Grant—even in the face of mounting Union casualties—brought the war to a definitive end, enabling Lincoln to focus on plans for a generous reconstruction of the South, plans that, unfortunately, were aborted in the aftermath of his assassination on April 14, 1865.

Explanation and Analysis of the Document

Lincoln begins his First Inaugural Address by noting that he is following a custom as old as the government itself by addressing his fellow citizens with brief remarks before taking the oath of office and beginning his term as president. Setting aside routine matters of governmental administration that do not deserve comment, Lincoln in paragraph 3 addresses the southern states, assuring them they should have no concerns about their property, peace, and personal security. He does not believe there ever has been a reason for such concerns, since he has made his pacific intentions clear in a number of speeches, one of which he quotes to the effect that he does not intend to interfere with slavery and that such interference would be unlawful.

Lincoln notes in paragraph 5 that he has campaigned consistently on this pledge not to hinder slavery and that this was part of the Republican Party platform he accepted as a presidential candidate. Thus, in paragraph 6, he cites the platform resolution that acknowledges the "inviolate … rights of the states" and emphasizes that such states' rights are essential to the balance of power in the Union, so that no state can be invaded or its domestic institutions impeded without committing the gravest crime. Lincoln is at pains to establish the full and unwavering record of his support of the notion that the South's prerogatives cannot be taken away. His words are not just a way to placate the South but reflect a policy he has never recanted.

In paragraph 7, Lincoln renews his devotion to his long-held views, which are now the federal government's policy. He makes a point of saying that he will "cheerfully" extend the federal government's protection to all sections, states, and territories of the United States. At this point, the new president is establishing a tone of friendliness and accommo-

www.milestonedocuments.com

Time Line

1861

■ **April 13**
Fort Sumter, in South Carolina, surrenders to Confederate forces, beginning the Civil War.

1864

■ **November 8**
Lincoln is reelected.

1865

■ **April 9**
Robert E. Lee surrenders to Ulysses S. Grant, and the Civil War is ended.

■ **April 14**
John Wilkes Booth assassinates Lincoln.

dation to the very people he understands have opposed his election. In paragraphs 8 to 12, Lincoln takes up the issue of the Fugitive Slave Act, a part of the Compromise of 1850 meant to reassure the South that slavery would remain intact as an institution. The law was unpopular among antislavery groups in the North because it required the return of escaped slaves to their owners. Thus, to those who viewed slavery as immoral, the North was forced to condone the very southern institution that northern states had outlawed.

In paragraph 9 Lincoln cites the exact wording of the law, making it evident that he intends to abide by its provisions and emphasizing that the fugitive slaves must be regarded as property returnable to their owners. No other reading of this law is possible, Lincoln asserts, which is his way of saying that he will not shirk his duty in enforcing it. Since all members of Congress swear to uphold the law—the whole Constitution—they must obey the injunctions of the law in order to uphold their oaths of office. Whether it is the state or the federal government that returns the fugitive slave is not important. Rather, it is respect for carrying out the law that matters in this case, Lincoln concludes in paragraph 11. No state can decide the matter differently, since, as Lincoln points out in paragraph 12 (quoting the Constitution): "the citizens of each State shall be entitled to all privileges and immunities of citizens in the several States."

Lincoln declares in paragraph 13 that he will uphold the constitutionality of the nation's laws and not apply "hypercritical rules"—scruples about certain laws that others may deem unconstitutional. No one in either official or private positions has the right to disobey laws that they deem unconstitutional as long as those laws are not repealed.

Noting in paragraph 14 that the country has survived for seventy-two years under fifteen presidents and that it has confronted many perils and difficulties, Lincoln points out that his inauguration is different: For the first time the "disruption of the Federal Union, heretofore only menaced, is now formidably attempted." He is alluding to South Car-

The scene at Abraham Lincoln's First Inaugural Address, March 4, 1861 (Library of Congress)

olina, which has been joined by five other southern states that established their own constitution and confederacy.

Secession, however, is not an option. The Union is perpetual, Lincoln asserts in paragraph 15. That much is implied in the formation of any national government. No government includes in its creation the method by which it would dissolve itself. Lincoln regards this point as a "universal law." Only some force acting outside its laws and constitutions can destroy the Union. The only other way to break up the Union would be for all the states to agree to do so. But they are all parties to a contract, and Lincoln demonstrates in paragraph 16 that just because one party (state) decides not to honor the contract does not mean that the contract is unenforceable.

But Lincoln's unionist argument is not based solely on the U.S. Constitution. On the contrary, he observes in paragraph 17 that the Union is older than the Constitution, and thus the Union has a history of its own. Both the Declaration of Independence and the Articles of Confederation signify a maturing notion of the Union, or what the Constitution itself refers to as a "more perfect Union." Thus, in paragraph 18 Lincoln holds that if one or more states can lawfully declare the Union broken, then that is the same as denying the intent of the Constitution and treating the Union as "less perfect" than it was before the Constitution was ratified.

The consequences of Lincoln's logic are clear in paragraph 19: South Carolina and the other southern states have no right to secede, and the very act of declaring secession is an act against the federal government that has to be deemed insurrectionary or revolutionary, depending on how the secession is pursued. The laws of the Union, therefore, will be enforced in all the states, Lincoln announces in paragraph 20. Meaning to issue no threats, Lincoln says, he

must nevertheless assert that he will preserve and protect the Union as part of his "simple duty." Only the American people (his masters) can decide otherwise.

Lincoln hastens to add in paragraph 21 that he does not envision a violent defense of the Union unless he is faced with no other choice. He has no plans to invade any state or to resort to force. He even goes so far as to suggest that he will not impose federal officeholders where they are opposed. He is referring here to the patronage of the federal government under a Republican administration. In effect, he is promising not to foist Republican officeholders on the South. In other words, he will go out of his way not to antagonize those who fear the encroachment of the federal government. In paragraph 22, Lincoln reinforces his claim to flexibility, suggesting that problems with the federal government can been worked out on a state-by-state basis in a peaceful manner.

Realizing in paragraph 23 that he cannot sway any who might already have turned against the Union, Lincoln addresses those who "love the Union" but who may have seen "ills" (as he says in paragraph 24) where there are none or who face the hazard of flying to ills that are greater than the one that troubles them now. Lincoln asks in paragraph 25: Have any Constitutional rights been violated? A revolution might be in order, he concedes, if it could be demonstrated that any parts of the Constitution have been violated. But this is not the case. Of more concern to Lincoln is that the Constitution is silent on certain vital matters, which he puts as a series of questions: "Shall fugitives from labor be surrendered by national or by State authority? The Constitution does not expressly say. May Congress prohibit slavery in the Territories? The Constitution does not expressly say. Must Congress protect slavery in the Territories? The Constitution does not expressly say."

But secession is not the answer to differences of opinion about how to interpret or amend the Constitution. Those who secede will merely encourage others to secede and produce chaos, Lincoln predicts in paragraph 26. Government is about the business of compromise, in which majorities may give way to minorities and vice versa. Otherwise the idea of government itself ceases. In paragraph 27, Lincoln wonders: How can yet another new union of states achieve a harmony greater than the one already established? How can there ever be such "perfect identity of interests"?

Lincoln equates secession with anarchy in paragraph 28. A nation must be government by a majority, which is itself under certain checks and limitations. It is not possible for everyone to agree—unless unity is enforced through despotism. Lest he be thought of as setting himself up as the sole arbiter of what is constitutional, Lincoln describes in paragraph 29 the vital role of the Supreme Court. The Court is fallible and can make wrong decisions, but such decisions have only limited impact and can be overturned later. That the Court's decisions can be used for political advantage is undeniable, Lincoln admits, but that in itself is no argument against the Court's efforts to determine the constitutionality of the nation's laws. Yet he also expresses reservations about the Supreme Court as the ultimate

www.milestonedocuments.com

> "*I have no purpose, directly or indirectly, to interfere with the institution of slavery in the States where it exists. I believe I have no lawful right to do so, and I have no inclination to do so.*"
>
> (Paragraph 4)

> "*A disruption of the Federal Union, heretofore only menaced, is now formidably attempted.*"
>
> (Paragraph 14)

> "*In your hands, my dissatisfied fellow-countrymen, and not in mine, is the momentous issue of civil war.*"
>
> (Paragraph 37)

> "*The mystic chords of memory, stretching from every battlefield and patriot grave to every living heart and hearthstone all over this broad land, will yet swell the chorus of the Union, when again touched, as surely they will be, by the better angels of our nature.*"
>
> (Paragraph 38)

interpreter of the nation's will, preferring—as he would say later in the speech—that the voice of the people be heard concerning the ultimate fate of slavery.

Lincoln suggests in paragraph 30 that while two sections of the country, North and South, disagree over slavery, breaking up the Union would only make matters worse. On the one hand, the suppression of the slave trade could no longer be enforced; on the other, the return of fugitive slaves would no longer be possible if the two sections were split into separate nations. But Lincoln does not deny the remaining problem: what to do about slavery in the territories, given that one section of the country wants to stop the spread of slavery while the other actively promotes it.

Lincoln also views the breaking of the Union as a physical impossibility; it is not like a divorce in which the spouses do not have to live together, he notes in paragraph 31. The same issues that bedevil the Union would only get worse if North and South were two countries that had to negotiate treaties about the same contentious problems. Thus, Lincoln's legal and moral arguments segue into considerations of the impracticality of secession among people who share a common history. The proper route to change, Lincoln concludes in paragraph 32, is through amending

the Constitution. Although Lincoln refrains from recommending amendments, he prefers that the people themselves, in conventions, formulate the amendments. Amendments proposed to them are not likely to express with enough discrimination the popular will. Still, he does express some support for an amendment, specifying what he believes is already implicit in the Constitution: The federal government has no right to interfere in the domestic institutions of the states.

Lincoln affirms in paragraph 33 that as president, his duty is to carry out the law, not to make the law, and that is why in paragraph 34 he asks that the people themselves be seen as the final arbiters of the constitutional issues that are dividing one section from another. The American people themselves are a great tribunal. Because the people are sovereign, he is certain that no elected official can "injure the Government in the short space of four years." In effect, Lincoln is attempting to diffuse the South's fear that he is a demagogue, or dictator, who will suppress their rights and take away their property. He has no such power, and what power he commands is of limited duration.

Above all, Lincoln's speech has been intended to slow down those eagerly bent on secession. He pleads in paragraph 35 for them to take time to consider their actions calmly when the new administration has no "immediate power" to change the relationship between the sections of the country. Nearing the end of his speech, Lincoln declares: "In your hands, my dissatisfied fellow-countrymen, and not in mine, is the momentous issue of civil war." It is the first time he has used the term "civil war," and in this context it is meant to put the onus on the South. Lincoln has clearly rejected any responsibility for fomenting a sectional conflict, and he insists there are measures that can be taken within the law of the land to settle his fellow citizens' concerns. The new president will not be the aggressor.

Pulling away from a defense of himself and a characterization of his opponents, Lincoln appeals in a final paragraph to a common heritage, stretching back to the Revolution—a sacred event he heralds with the phrase "mystic chords of memory," which modulates into sounds of a Union, a chorus of voices, a sense of unison that derives from the "better angels of our nature." The Union, he suggests, speaks to the very ideals of what it means to be an American. Devotion to the Union brings out the best ("the better angels") of his fellow citizens. In the end, it is the nobility of the vision that the Union represents that strengthens Lincoln in his resolve to protect it.

Audience

Although Lincoln was addressing his fellow citizens, most of his speech, in fact, was directed explicitly to the southern states, four of which had already followed South Carolina's decision to secede. Nearly every sentence in the First Inaugural Address is aimed at emphasizing Lincoln's efforts to placate the South. He understood that he had already been demonized in the southern press, and so he made every effort to seem as reasonable and moderate as possible. He planned to take no military action and simply pointed out why the efforts to secede could not succeed. At the same time, he wanted to assure the entire nation that he understood the grave nature of the crisis and that he took the secessionist movement seriously.

Lincoln was also indirectly addressing those northerners and southerners still in favor of the Union, although there were elements in his northern audience that were willing to see the South secede rather than risk war, just as there were elements in the South that wavered in their support of the South Carolina secessionists. Virginia, for example, had not yet seceded. Lincoln clearly noted that while he was not preparing for war, he would not shirk from a military solution if the South continued with its determination to leave the Union. Other northerners wanted essentially to capitulate to southern demands— again to avoid a war. But Lincoln was just as adamant about the role of the federal government, which could not, in certain respects, be nullified by individual states. Lincoln spoke to both audiences—North and South—in the closing paragraph of his speech, attempting to find a language that would persuade both sides that they shared a heritage that bound them together much more than any issues that divided them.

Impact

Lincoln hoped that his address would strengthen the southern unionists. But his assertion of federal authority only angered many southerners and did nothing to hinder the drive toward secession. Although Lincoln had heeded advice to end his speech on an affectionate note, his words were quickly rejected, and by March 15, 1861, rebel batteries surrounded Fort Sumter, still flying a Union flag.

Some northern opposition newspapers (those supporting the Democratic Party) treated Lincoln's first inaugural respectfully, while others found him bellicose. The favorable notices mentioned his friendly tone and that he specifically disavowed any effort to coerce the southern states. Not surprisingly members of Lincoln's own party praised his firm but pacific purpose.

Predictably, southern newspapers, especially in the Lower South, where certain states had already seceded, resented Lincoln's effort to portray them as the aggressors. In the end, it was clear to them that Lincoln was offering no concessions. The *Charleston Mercury* called the inaugural the "tocsin of battle," and the *Richmond Dispatch* announced that the address "inaugurates civil war" (Donald, p. 284).

If the immediate impact of Lincoln's address could not retard, let alone stop, the drive toward secession, his closing words have continued to reverberate in a reunified nation, especially his notion of "mystic chords of memory," an invocation of a people's memory of their own struggles for freedom and that the very idea of the Union is an ennobling inspiration.

Related Documents

"Second Inaugural Address of Abraham Lincoln." The Avalon Project at Yale Law School Web site. http://www.yale.edu/lawweb/avalon/presiden/inaug/lincoln2.htm. Accessed on December 13, 2007. In his Second Inaugural Address, Lincoln explains the causes of the war and the attitude that should be adopted with a war in progress.

"Transcript of Constitution of the United States (1787)." 100 Milestone Documents Web site. http://www.ourdocuments.gov/doc.php?doc=9&page=transcript. Accessed on December 13, 2007. Lincoln notes that the U.S. Constitution does not expressly provide instruction on how to deal with several controversies concerning slavery.

"Transcript of Declaration of Independence (1776)." 100 Milestone Documents Web site. http://www.ourdocuments.gov/doc.php?doc=2&page=transcript. Accessed on December 13, 2007. Lincoln relies on the Declaration of Independence to establish that the United States as a union existed before the creation of the Constitution.

Bibliography

■ Books

Carwardine, Richard. *Lincoln: A Life of Purpose and Power*. New York: Alfred A. Knopf, 2006.

Donald, David Herbert. *Lincoln*. New York: Simon & Schuster, 1995.

Gienapp, William E. *Abraham Lincoln and Civil War America: A Biography*. New York: Oxford University Press, 2002.

Goodwin, Doris Kearns. *Team of Rivals: The Political Genius of Abraham Lincoln*. New York: Simon & Schuster, 2005.

Guelzo, Allen C. *Abraham Lincoln: Redeemer President*. Grand Rapids, Mich.: W. B. Eerdmans, 1999.

Handlin, Oscar, and Lilian Handlin. *Abraham Lincoln and the Union*. Boston: Atlantic Monthly Press, 1980.

Keneally, Thomas. *Abraham Lincoln*. New York: Lipper/Viking, 2003.

Kunhardt, Philip B., Jr. *A New Birth of Freedom: Lincoln at Gettysburg*. Boston: Little, Brown, 1983.

Miller, William Lee. *Lincoln's Virtues: An Ethical Biography*. New York: Knopf, 2002.

Neely, Mark E., Jr. *The Last Best Hope of Earth: Abraham Lincoln and the Promise of America*. Cambridge, Mass.: Harvard University Press, 1993.

Oates, Stephen B. *With Malice toward None: The Life of Abraham Lincoln*. New York: Harper & Row, 1977.

Paludan, Phillip Shaw. *The Presidency of Abraham Lincoln*. Lawrence: University Press of Kansas, 1994.

Thomas, Benjamin P. *Abraham Lincoln: A Biography*. New York: Knopf, 1952.

■ Web Sites

"Abraham Lincoln." The White House Web site. http://www.whitehouse.gov/history/presidents/al16.html. Accessed on December 13, 2007.

Abraham Lincoln Research Site Web site. http://members.aol.com/RVSNorton/Lincoln2.html. Accessed on December 13, 2007.

"Suggested Lincoln Sources." History Now Web site. http://www.historynow.org/12_2005/ask2b.html. Accessed on December 13, 2007.

—By Carl Rollyson

Questions for Further Study

1. Analyze Lincoln's First Inaugural Address in the context of the events leading up to the Civil War.

2. Compare Lincoln's First Inaugural Address and Second Inaugural Address. How did the Civil War change his attitude toward slavery and his conception of the Union?

3. Discuss Lincoln's interpretation of the Declaration of Independence and the U.S. Constitution in his First Inaugural Address.

4. Explain why Lincoln's assurances to the South did not allay southern anxieties and why his policies could not prevent the coming of a Civil War.

Glossary

accession	the assumption of an important position, usually a position of power
construe	To interpret or understand the meaning of a word, gesture, or action
enjoins	commands somebody to do something or behave in a certain way
exigency	something that a situation demands or makes urgently necessary and that puts pressure on the people involved
impunity	exemption from penalty or harm
insurrectionary	rebellious against the government or rulers of a country, often taking the form of armed conflict
jurisprudence	a body of laws
ordinances	laws or rules made by a government authority
pretext	a misleading or untrue reason given for doing something in an attempt to conceal the real reason
recanted	denied believing in something or repudiated what has been previously said or believed.
requisite	necessary or indispensable
resolves	formally expressed opinions of a group or governmental body
secession	the withdrawal from the Union of eleven southern states in 1860–1861 that led to the formation of the Confederacy and the beginning of the Civil War

ABRAHAM LINCOLN'S FIRST INAUGURAL ADDRESS

Fellow-Citizens of the United States:

In compliance with a custom as old as the Government itself, I appear before you to address you briefly and to take in your presence the oath prescribed by the Constitution of the United States to be taken by the President before he enters on the execution of this office.

I do not consider it necessary at present for me to discuss those matters of administration about which there is no special anxiety or excitement.

Apprehension seems to exist among the people of the Southern States that by the accession of a Republican Administration their property and their peace and personal security are to be endangered. There has never been any reasonable cause for such apprehension. Indeed, the most ample evidence to the contrary has all the while existed and been open to their inspection. It is found in nearly all the published speeches of him who now addresses you. I do but quote from one of those speeches when I declare that—

I have no purpose, directly or indirectly, to interfere with the institution of slavery in the States where it exists. I believe I have no lawful right to do so, and I have no inclination to do so.

Those who nominated and elected me did so with full knowledge that I had made this and many similar declarations and had never recanted them; and more than this, they placed in the platform for my acceptance, and as a law to themselves and to me, the clear and emphatic resolution which I now read:

Resolved, That the maintenance inviolate of the rights of the States, and especially the right of each State to order and control its own domestic institutions according to its own judgment exclusively, is essential to that balance of power on which the perfection and endurance of our political fabric depend; and we denounce the lawless invasion by armed force of the soil of

any State or Territory, no matter what pretext, as among the gravest of crimes.

I now reiterate these sentiments, and in doing so I only press upon the public attention the most conclusive evidence of which the case is susceptible that the property, peace, and security of no section are to be in any wise endangered by the now incoming Administration. I add, too, that all the protection which, consistently with the Constitution and the laws, can be given will be cheerfully given to all the States when lawfully demanded, for whatever cause—as cheerfully to one section as to another.

There is much controversy about the delivering up of fugitives from service or labor. The clause I now read is as plainly written in the Constitution as any other of its provisions:

No person held to service or labor in one State, under the laws thereof, escaping into another, shall in consequence of any law or regulation therein be discharged from such service or labor, but shall be delivered up on claim of the party to whom such service or labor may be due.

It is scarcely questioned that this provision was intended by those who made it for the reclaiming of what we call fugitive slaves; and the intention of the lawgiver is the law. All members of Congress swear their support to the whole Constitution—to this provision as much as to any other. To the proposition, then, that slaves whose cases come within the terms of this clause "shall be delivered up" their oaths are unanimous. Now, if they would make the effort in good temper, could they not with nearly equal unanimity frame and pass a law by means of which to keep good that unanimous oath?

There is some difference of opinion whether this clause should be enforced by national or by State authority, but surely that difference is not a very material one. If the slave is to be surrendered, it can be of but little consequence to him or to others by which authority it is done. And should anyone in any case be content that his oath shall go unkept on a merely unsubstantial controversy as to how it shall be kept?

Again: In any law upon this subject ought not all the safeguards of liberty known in civilized and humane jurisprudence to be introduced, so that a free man be not in any case surrendered as a slave? And might it not be well at the same time to provide by law for the enforcement of that clause in the Constitution which guarantees that "the citizens of each State shall be entitled to all privileges and immunities of citizens in the several States?"

I take the official oath today with no mental reservations and with no purpose to construe the Constitution or laws by any hypercritical rules; and while I do not choose now to specify particular acts of Congress as proper to be enforced, I do suggest that it will be much safer for all, both in official and private stations, to conform to and abide by all those acts which stand unrepealed than to violate any of them trusting to find impunity in having them held to be unconstitutional.

It is seventy-two years since the first inauguration of a President under our National Constitution. During that period fifteen different and greatly distinguished citizens have in succession administered the executive branch of the Government. They have conducted it through many perils, and generally with great success. Yet, with all this scope of precedent, I now enter upon the same task for the brief constitutional term of four years under great and peculiar difficulty. A disruption of the Federal Union, heretofore only menaced, is now formidably attempted.

I hold that in contemplation of universal law and of the Constitution the Union of these States is perpetual. Perpetuity is implied, if not expressed, in the fundamental law of all national governments. It is safe to assert that no government proper ever had a provision in its organic law for its own termination. Continue to execute all the express provisions of our National Constitution, and the Union will endure forever, it being impossible to destroy it except by some action not provided for in the instrument itself.

Again: If the United States be not a government proper, but an association of States in the nature of contract merely, can it, as acontract, be peaceably unmade by less than all the parties who made it? One party to a contract may violate it—break it, so to speak—but does it not require all to lawfully rescind it?

Descending from these general principles, we find the proposition that in legal contemplation the Union is perpetual confirmed by the history of the Union itself. The Union is much older than the Constitution. It was formed, in fact, by the Articles of Association in 1774. It was matured and continued by the Declaration of Independence in 1776. It was further matured, and the faith of all the then thirteen States expressly plighted and engaged that it should be perpetual, by the Articles of Confederation in 1778. And finally, in 1787, one of the declared objects for ordaining and establishing the Constitution was "to form a more perfect Union."

But if destruction of the Union by one or by a part only of the States be lawfully possible, the Union is less perfect than before the Constitution, having lost the vital element of perpetuity.

It follows from these views that no State upon its own mere motion can lawfully get out of the Union; that resolves and ordinances to that effect are legally void, and that acts of violence within any State or States against the authority of the United States are insurrectionary or revolutionary, according to circumstances.

I therefore consider that in view of the Constitution and the laws the Union is unbroken, and to the extent of my ability, I shall take care, as the Constitution itself expressly enjoins upon me, that the laws of the Union be faithfully executed in all the States. Doing this I deem to be only a simple duty on my part, and I shall perform it so far as practicable unless my rightful masters, the American people, shall withhold the requisite means or in some authoritative manner direct the contrary. I trust this will not be regarded as a menace, but only as the declared purpose of the Union that it will constitutionally defend and maintain itself.

In doing this there needs to be no bloodshed or violence, and there shall be none unless it be forced upon the national authority. The power confided to me will be used to hold, occupy, and possess the property and places belonging to the Government and to collect the duties and imposts; but beyond what may be necessary for these objects, there will be no invasion, no using of force against or among the people anywhere. Where hostility to the United States in any interior locality shall be so great and universal as to prevent competent resident citizens from holding the Federal offices, there will be no attempt to force obnoxious strangers among the people for that object. While the strict legal right may exist in the Government to enforce the exercise of these offices, the attempt to do so would be so irritating and so nearly impracticable withal that I deem it better to forego for the time the uses of such offices.

The mails, unless repelled, will continue to be furnished in all parts of the Union. So far as possible the people everywhere shall have that sense of perfect security which is most favorable to calm thought and reflection. The course here indicated will be followed unless current events and experience shall show a modification or change to be proper, and in every case and exigency my best discretion will be exercised, according to circumstances actually existing and with a view and a hope of a peaceful solution of the national troubles and the restoration of fraternal sympathies and affections.

That there are persons in one section or another who seek to destroy the Union at all events and are glad of any pretext to do it I will neither affirm nor deny; but if there be such, I need address no word to them. To those, however, who really love the Union may I not speak?

Before entering upon so grave a matter as the destruction of our national fabric, with all its benefits, its memories, and its hopes, would it not be wise to ascertain precisely why we do it? Will you hazard so desperate a step while there is any possibility that any portion of the ills you fly from have no real existence? Will you, while the certain ills you fly to are greater than all the real ones you fly from, will you risk the commission of so fearful a mistake?

All profess to be content in the Union if all constitutional rights can be maintained. Is it true, then, that any right plainly written in the Constitution has been denied? I think not. Happily, the human mind is so constituted that no party can reach to the audacity of doing this. Think, if you can, of a single instance in which a plainly written provision of the Constitution has ever been denied. If by the mere force of numbers a majority should deprive a minority of any clearly written constitutional right, it might in a moral point of view justify revolution; certainly would if such right were a vital one. But such is not our case. All the vital rights of minorities and of individuals are so plainly assured to them by affirmations and negations, guaranties and prohibitions, in the Constitution that controversies never arise concerning them. But no organic law can ever be framed with a provision specifically applicable to every question which may occur in practical administration. No foresight can anticipate nor any document of reasonable length contain express provisions for all possible questions. Shall fugitives from labor be surrendered by national or by State authority? The Constitution does not expressly say. May Congress prohibit slavery in the Territories? The Constitution does not expressly say. Must Congress protect slavery in the Territories? The Constitution does not expressly say.

From questions of this class spring all our constitutional controversies, and we divide upon them into majorities and minorities. If the minority will not acquiesce, the majority must, or the Government must cease. There is no other alternative, for continuing the Government is acquiescence on one side or the other. If a minority in such case will secede rather than acquiesce, they make a precedent which in turn will divide and ruin them, for a minority of their own will secede from them whenever a majority refuses to be controlled by such minority. For instance, why may not any portion of a new confederacy a year or two hence arbitrarily secede again, precisely as portions of the present Union now claim to secede from it? All who cherish disunion sentiments are now being educated to the exact temper of doing this.

Is there such perfect identity of interests among the States to compose a new union as to produce harmony only and prevent renewed secession?

Plainly the central idea of secession is the essence of anarchy. A majority held in restraint by constitutional checks and limitations, and always changing easily with deliberate changes of popular opinions and sentiments, is the only true sovereign of a free people. Whoever rejects it does of necessity fly to anarchy or to despotism. Unanimity is impossible. The rule of a minority, as a permanent arrangement, is wholly inadmissible; so that, rejecting the majority principle, anarchy or despotism in some form is all that is left.

I do not forget the position assumed by some that constitutional questions are to be decided by the Supreme Court, nor do I deny that such decisions must be binding in any case upon the parties to a suit as to the object of that suit, while they are also entitled to very high respect and consideration in all parallel cases by all other departments of the Government. And while it is obviously possible that such decision may be erroneous in any given case, still the evil effect following it, being limited to that particular case, with the chance that it may be overruled and never become a precedent for other cases, can better be borne than could the evils of a different practice. At the same time, the candid citizen must confess that if the policy of the Government upon vital questions affecting the whole people is to be irrevocably fixed by decisions of the Supreme Court, the instant they are made in ordinary litigation between parties in personal actions the people will have ceased to be their own rulers, having to that extent practically resigned their Government into the hands of that eminent tribunal. Nor is there in this view any assault upon the court or the judges. It is a duty from which they may not shrink to decide cases properly brought before them, and it is no fault of theirs if others seek to turn their decisions to political purposes.

One section of our country believes slavery is right and ought to be extended, while the other believes it is wrong and ought not to be extended. This is the only substantial dispute. The fugitive-slave clause of the Constitution and the law for the suppression of the foreign slave trade are each as well enforced, perhaps, as any law can ever be in a community where the moral sense of the people imperfectly supports the law itself. The great body of the people abide by the dry legal obligation in both cases, and a few break over in each. This, I think, can not be perfectly cured, and it would be worse in both cases after the separation of the sections than before. The foreign slave trade, now imperfectly suppressed, would be ultimately revived without restriction in one section, while fugitive slaves, now only partially surrendered, would not be surrendered at all by the other.

Physically speaking, we can not separate. We can not remove our respective sections from each other nor build an impassable wall between them. A husband and wife may be divorced and go out of the presence and beyond the reach of each other, but the different parts of our country can not do this. They can not but remain face to face, and intercourse, either amicable or hostile, must continue between them. Is it possible, then, to make that intercourse more advantageous or more satisfactory after separation than before? Can aliens make treaties easier than friends can make laws? Can treaties be more faithfully enforced between aliens than laws can among friends? Suppose you go to war, you can not fight always; and when, after much loss on both sides and no gain on either, you cease fighting, the identical old questions, as to terms of intercourse, are again upon you.

This country, with its institutions, belongs to the people who inhabit it. Whenever they shall grow weary of the existing Government, they can exercise their constitutional right of amending it or their revolutionary right to dismember or overthrow it. I can not be ignorant of the fact that many worthy and patriotic citizens are desirous of having the National Constitution amended. While I make no recommendation of amendments, I fully recognize the rightful authority of the people over the whole subject, to be exercised in either of the modes prescribed in the instrument itself; and I should, under existing circumstances, favor rather than oppose a fair opportunity being afforded the people to act upon it. I will venture to add that to me the convention mode seems preferable, in that it allows amendments to originate with the people themselves, instead of only permitting them to take or reject propositions originated by others, not especially chosen for the purpose, and which might not be precisely such as they would wish to either accept or refuse. I understand a proposed amendment to the Constitution—which amendment, however, I have not seen—has passed Congress, to the effect that the Federal Government shall never interfere with the domestic institutions of the States, including that of persons held to service. To avoid misconstruction of what I have said, I depart from my purpose not to speak of particular amendments so far as to say that, holding such a provision to now be implied constitutional law, I have no objection to its being made express and irrevocable.

The Chief Magistrate derives all his authority from the people, and they have referred none upon him to fix terms for the separation of the States. The people themselves can do this if also they choose, but the Executive as such has nothing to do with it. His duty is to administer the present Government as it came to his hands and to transmit it unimpaired by him to his successor.

Why should there not be a patient confidence in the ultimate justice of the people? Is there any better or equal hope in the world? In our present differences, is either party without faith of being in the right? If the Almighty Ruler of Nations, with His eternal truth and justice, be on your side of the North, or on yours of the South, that truth and that justice will surely prevail by the judgment of this great tribunal of the American people.

By the frame of the Government under which we live this same people have wisely given their public servants but little power for mischief, and have with equal wisdom provided for the return of that little to their own hands at very short intervals. While the people retain their virtue and vigilance no Administration by any extreme of wickedness or folly can very seriously injure the Government in the short space of four years.

My countrymen, one and all, think calmly and well upon this whole subject. Nothing valuable can be lost by taking time. If there be an object to hurry any of you in hot haste to a step which you would never take deliberately, that object will be frustrated by taking time; but no good object can be frustrated by it. Such of you as are now dissatisfied still have the old Constitution unimpaired, and, on the sensitive point, the laws of your own framing under it; while the new Administration will have no immediate power, if it would, to change either. If it were admitted that you who are dissatisfied hold the right side in the dispute, there still is no single good reason for precipitate action. Intelligence, patriotism, Christianity, and a firm reliance on Him who has never yet forsaken this favored land are still competent to adjust in the best way all our present difficulty.

In your hands, my dissatisfied fellow-countrymen, and not in mine, is the momentous issue of civil war. The Government will not assail you. You can have no conflict without being yourselves the aggressors. You have no oath registered in heaven to destroy the Government, while I shall have the most solemn one to "preserve, protect, and defend it."

I am loath to close. We are not enemies, but friends. We must not be enemies. Though passion may have strained it must not break our bonds of affection. The mystic chords of memory, stretching from every battlefield and patriot grave to every living heart and hearthstone all over this broad land, will yet swell the chorus of the Union, when again touched, as surely they will be, by the better angels of our nature.

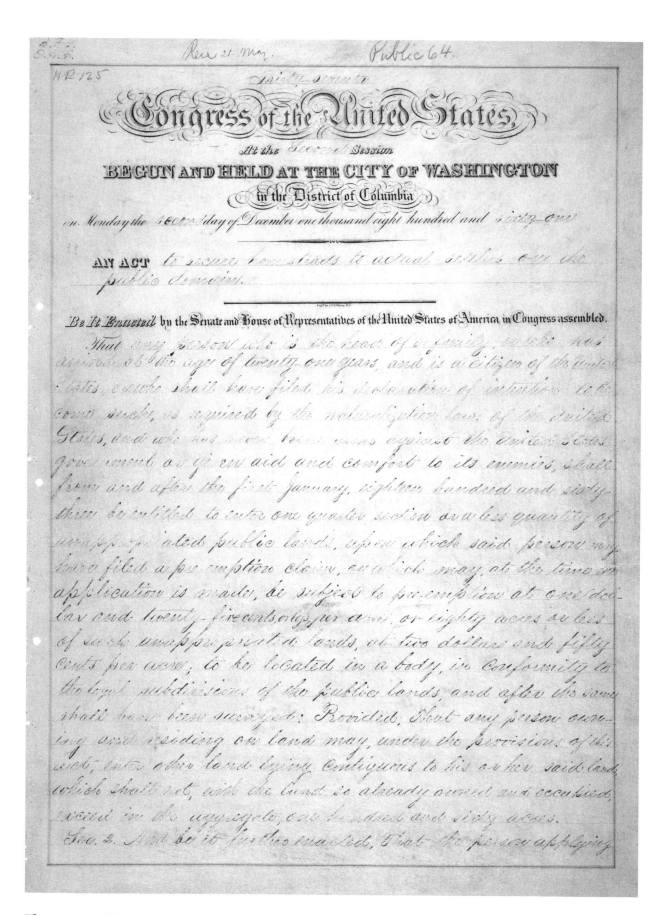

The Homestead Act (National Archives and Records Administration)

"Any person who is the head of a family ... shall ... be entitled to enter one quarter section."

Overview

On May 20, 1862, Abraham Lincoln, the U.S. president from the prairie state of Illinois, signed the Homestead Act into law. He enacted one of the most liberal land laws in history, a policy that theoretically gave free land to actual settlers. The act granted adult heads of families 160 acres of surveyed public land, given five years of continuous residence on the land and payment of a government filing fee. The law's passage was the culmination of almost eighty years of debate. Homesteading symbolized many of the aspirations of Jeffersonian republicanism. From the opening years of the American republic, policy makers including Thomas Jefferson had sought to devise a rational federal land policy with the twin goals of generating much-needed revenue for the national treasury and transferring public lands into private hands. They believed an effective federal land policy also would facilitate the orderly westward expansion and settlement of citizens and the spread of agrarianism and republican democracy. These efforts were predicated upon the persistent, aggressive dispossession of the Native American peoples of their land base.

The movement for free land had many champions and several unsuccessful but notable bill authors prior to 1862, including Felix Grundy McConnell, the congressman from Alabama; Andrew Johnson, the congressman, senator, and later U.S. president from Tennessee; Stephen A. Douglas, the senator from Illinois; and Samuel Houston, the senator from Texas. Despite defeats and entanglements with divisive issues such as slavery and immigration, the homestead principle possessed remarkable resilience. With the secession of the southern states in the prelude to the Civil War came the elimination of the primary opposition. Passage of a homestead bill became more likely, especially in the politically skilled hands of the popular Pennsylvanian Republican (and former Democrat) Galusha A. Grow, a persistent if not passionate advocate of free land for actual settlers and the author of his own House bill. More than any other politician, Grow is credited with being the father of the Homestead Act.

Context

Early land-disposal policies met policy makers' objectives with varying degrees of success and failure. Major legislation was passed as the Land Ordinance of 1785, the Northwest Ordinance of 1787 (which concerned the governance of new territories and their progression toward statehood, an important assurance to prospective land buyers), and subsequent revised land acts in 1796, 1800, and 1820. This series of land policies reflected Congress's recognition of the need to reform and liberalize citizens' access to land, with the goal of transferring as much public land into private ownership as possible. The earliest land policies offered large tracts of land for sale, which tended to favor speculators over individual purchasers (actual settlers), who could neither afford nor farm that much land. Yet western migration and settlement during this period often was made by a group seeking a large tract of land.

The Land Act of 1800 was a considerably more liberal land policy that was specifically geared toward the typical farmer. It offered the equivalent of four years of credit, a reduced minimum purchase tract of 320 acres at the price of $2 per acre, and closer western land office districts; it also gave the government the ability to compete for sales against major land companies that were selling to farmers. The act was crafted by William Henry Harrison, the Northwest Territory's congressional delegate and later the U.S. president, and Albert Gallatin, the congressman from Pennsylvania and soon-to-be treasury secretary, who had spearheaded an earlier land reform that had resulted in the 1796 act. The Harrison Land Act of 1800 succeeded well in stimulating sales, yet the experiment with land sales on credit had a ruinous effect on the economy, as evidenced by the Panic of 1819. The Land Act of 1820 was a corrective measure that ended credit sales but also reduced the minimum purchase tract size to eighty acres and the price to $1.25 per acre. Not surprisingly, without the option for credit, land sales plummeted. The land-policy historian Roy Robbins contends that the 1820 act "brought the whole population of the frontier to the brink of ruin" (p. 38).

Continued land-policy revision also was aimed at thwarting the many speculators or land monopolists as well as squatters. The illegal presence of squatters ahead of offi-

1785

■ **May 20**
Land Ordinance is signed; in 1784, Thomas Jefferson, the chairman of the committee to study the disposition of the western lands, submits first draft of the ordinance but is appointed the U.S. ambassador to France before the final version is passed.

1787

■ **July 13**
Northwest Ordinance is adopted by the Continental Congress, establishing rules for statehood.

1796

■ **May 18**
Land Act of 1796 is passed.

1800

■ **May 10**
Land Act of 1800 (Harrison Land Act) is passed, offering land sales on credit.

1819

■ The nation's first major economic depression, or "panic," occurs.

1820

■ **April 24**
Land Act of 1820 is passed, ending credit sales.

1830

■ **May 29**
Preemption Act of 1830 is passed, the first such act, though it is temporary by design.

1837

■ The nation's second major economic depression, or "panic," occurs.

1841

■ **September 4**
Preemption Act of 1841 is passed, offering more lasting protection of squatters' rights.

1850

■ **September 27**
Donation Land Claim Act is passed, providing donation grants of land.

1860

■ **June 22**
President Buchanan vetoes a homestead bill that overwhelmingly passed both the House and the Senate.

cial land surveys frequently provoked Indian hostilities, created chaos in legitimating land titles, and theoretically robbed the U.S. Treasury of prospective sales. But as the noted land-policy historian Paul Gates has observed, squatters significantly influenced land policy by constantly forcing the matter of preemption (a squatter's right of first purchase at the government price when land came up for sale at public auction) in front of Congress. In 1830 the Preemption Act was passed. This tentative, temporary legislation had to be renewed periodically to remain in effect. In 1841 a more comprehensive preemption law was passed to offer some protection of squatters' rights, signaling a major ideological turning point in U.S. land law policy.

Another reform dealt with the graduation of land prices, which was meant to address the problem of less desirable lands that remained unsold because the government minimum prices were too high; potentially workable, productive land was staying unimproved, untaxed, and unsettled. Between 1820 and 1854 the graduation issue repeatedly appeared before Congress, usually at the urging of its chief proponent, Thomas Hart Benton, the Democratic senator from Missouri. The Graduation Act was eventually passed in 1854 and specified that the price of public land that had been on the market for ten years, with some exceptions, would be valued at graduated (reduced) levels. For example, the price for land that had been unsold for ten to fifteen years would now be valued at $1.00 per acre and valued lower, at $0.75 per acre, if it remained unsold for fifteen to twenty years.

During the 1840s and 1850s national expansionism, the prolonged aftermath of the Panic of 1837, and the Mexican War (1846–1848) led to a rising call to grant free land to actual settlers. The immediate antecedents to the 1862 Homestead Act were expansionist-driven settlement bills that functioned much like the practice of awarding military land bounties (free grants of land to soldiers). To attract settlers to then-remote territories such as East Florida, Oregon, Washington, and New Mexico, Congress began offering "donation lands" to heads of households willing to reside on and cultivate 160, 320, or 640 acres, depending on the location of the donation grant. For example, in the Donation Land Claim Act of 1850, the original residence requirement to obtain the land title was four years, but this was later reduced to two years because of the apparent hardship experienced by the settlers. Here was the first inkling that free land might actually exact a heavy cost. These settlement laws also included terms for commutation—the homesteader's ability to commute the remainder of time owed on the residency requirement into a cash payment worth $1.25 per acre. Similar terms became an important provision in the 1862 Homestead Act.

One of the most prominent voices for land reform was the *New York Tribune* editor Horace Greeley. The enduring economic dislocations caused by the Panic of 1837 prompted Greeley and others to tout westward migration to those struggling in the East. (Greeley popularized the phrase "Go west, young man," which was originally written by John Soule of Indiana in an 1851 editorial.) Their urgings kept up the public pressure on Congress to produce and enact a homestead measure, but the Mexican War and the resulting Mexican Cession altered the political landscape: Land reform was overshadowed by the brewing sectional storm over slavery and expansion. However, other factors kept pushing forward the idea of meaningful land reform. Increasing foreign immigration rates and the discovery of gold in California led to greater western migration. Ongoing development toward a complete transcontinental railroad, which required huge tracts of surveyed public land, also meant potential settlers would have easier access to the new territories.

Congressional movement toward a homestead bill became intertwined with sectionalism and the disintegration of the Whig and Democratic parties. In 1847–1848, a cross-party group of politicians formed the Free-Soil Party, which opposed extending slavery into the new territories ceded by Mexico and supported enactment of a homestead law. Proslavery Democrats came to believe that legislation offering free land would mean the spread of an antislavery ideology and reality, threatening the South's way of life. Several land bills were introduced in the late 1840s and into the 1850s, but they received strong opposition under the Democratic presidencies of Franklin Pierce (1853–1857) and James Buchanan (1857–1861). The passage of the Kansas-Nebraska Act in 1854, which let the territories' settlers vote on whether to allow slaves, had a chilling effect upon land reform. However, the resulting formation of the Republican Party (and death of the Whigs) meant land laws were not completely absent from the congressional agenda.

The tide began to change in January 1859 when Congressman Grow, now a Republican, introduced a homestead bill in the House. It was immediately opposed by Alexander Stephens of Georgia, yet it passed by a vote of 120 to 76, without any debate. In the Senate, southern opposition succeeded in tabling the bill. Undeterred, Grow introduced the bill in the House again in February 1860, where again it passed. This time, the Senate endeavored to put forth its own homestead bill, but the process broke down when an attempt was made to substitute Grow's bill for the Senate bill, provoking southern charges that the bill was actually an abolitionist measure. Even so, a compromise bill passed both houses in June—only to be vetoed by President Buchanan. Buchanan's veto was a bitter pill for reformers like Greeley, who remarked prophetically, "Does any one suppose that Abraham Lincoln would ever veto such a bill?" (Robbins, p. 182).

Indeed, Lincoln did not. His victory in the 1860 presidential election gave clear ascendancy to the Republicans, the antislavery party, and prompted southern states to secede from the Union, inaugurating the Civil War era. Grow correctly perceived that, with southern opposition removed, the time was right to reintroduce the homestead bill, which he did in February 1862. After the bill passed both houses, President Lincoln signed the Homestead Act on May 20, 1862. Within a few months, Congress passed the Pacific Railway Act and the Morrill Act, which offered

Time Line

1862

■ **May 15**
The Department of Agriculture is created.

■ **May 20**
Homestead Act is signed into law by President Lincoln.

■ **July 1**
Pacific Railway Act is passed, granting public lands for the building of a transcontinental railroad.

■ **July 2**
Morrill Act is passed, granting public lands to the western states to establish agricultural colleges.

1864

■ **March 21**
Amended Homestead Act is passed, allowing soldiers who have served for two years to secure a homestead after only one year's residence.

1866

■ **June 21**
Southern Homestead Act is passed for states formerly in rebellion.

1870

■ **July 15**
Amended Homestead Act is passed, allowing soldiers who have served ninety days in the U.S. forces to enter 160 acres of premium reserved public lands along the railroads or anywhere in the public domain.

1872

■ **April 4**
Amended Homestead Act is passed, allowing soldiers to deduct up to four years of military service from their residency requirements.

1936

■ **March 19**
President Franklin D. Roosevelt signs legislation creating the Homestead National Monument.

1976

■ **October 21**
The Federal Land Policy and Management Act is passed, repealing the Homestead Act.

land grants to the western states to establish agricultural colleges. Taken together, these three pieces of legislation formed a blueprint for modern America. The western half of the United States was soon imprinted with homesteads, railroads, and colleges, a fundamentally important triad that shaped the region's identity for years to come.

About the Author

Galusha Grow was born in Windham County, Connecticut, in 1823, the second youngest of six children. Grow was four years old when his father died, and he went to live with his grandfather, a hotel owner and a Revolutionary War veteran. In 1834 his mother decided they should migrate westward, along with several other families, to try farming in Susquehanna County, Pennsylvania. The farming world there was harsher than he had seen in more prosperous Connecticut. Rural poverty seemed the norm, and this circumstance greatly influenced his future views on land reform issues. Like many families, the Grows supplemented farming with other enterprises, including owning a general store and participating in the lumber trade, both of which were adversely affected by the Panic of 1837. Young Grow's lumber-selling trips took him into the Upper South, where his encounters with plantations and slavery left a negative impression and led to his later opposition to the expansion of slavery into U.S. territories.

In the fall of 1840 Grow became a student at Amherst College in Massachusetts, where he distinguished himself as an outstanding orator with serious interests in law and land surveying. Following his graduation in 1844, he returned home to Pennsylvania to read law, was admitted to the bar in 1847, and opened a law office—but politics held a greater fascination. By the late 1840s, national and local party politics were ripe with explosive issues, namely expansionism involving Texas, Oregon, and California and the related issue of slavery. Both the Whig and Democratic parties suffered from internal dissension. Pennsylvania's Twelfth Congressional District, Grow's home, was strongly Democratic, and it was with this party that he initially identified himself. In political philosophy he was a Democrat in the tradition of Thomas Jefferson and Andrew Jackson, sometimes with a radical reputation. His district also was home to David Wilmot, a fellow Democrat and the author of the 1846 Wilmot Proviso, which urged the exclusion of slavery in the territories purchased from Mexico. Grow and Wilmot became lifelong friends as a result of their common northern Pennsylvania roots and interests in western development.

Grow's professional political career and Free-Soil ideology put him at the center of the intensifying sectionalism that immediately preceded the secession of southern states after Lincoln won the 1860 presidential election. Grow served in six consecutive Congresses (March 4, 1851, to March 3, 1863); he was elected as a Democrat to the first three and as a Republican to the last three. He served as the chairman of the Committee on Territories for two terms and as the Speaker of the House during his final term. More than anything, Grow historically has been identified as being the primary champion and mover of the homestead bill that became law in 1862. His homestead ideology linked national economic development to the settlement of the West—with actual settlers—by way of a liberal land policy. After May 1862, Grow continued to be active in his political career as a delegate to the Republican National Convention (1864, 1884, and 1892) and as a Republican congressman again in five consecutive Congresses (February 26, 1894, to March 3, 1903). He died in Pennsylvania in 1907.

Explanation and Analysis of the Document

◆ Section 1

In the first section, the act's basic premises are laid out: who is eligible, when the act takes effect, what is being offered, and where a homestead claim may be made. In establishing who is eligible, Grow includes a number of important references. The act stipulates that "any person," a head of a family or one who is twenty-one years or older, is entitled to enter a claim to one quarter section (160 acres) or less. The gender-neutral description of "any person" is highly significant for the 1860s and is underscored in Section 2 with several references to "he or she." This wording notably opens the way for women who meet either criterion to enter a claim on their own. In addition, the potential homesteader must be a citizen of the United States or have filed a declaration of his or her intention to become naturalized, a point included in anticipation of the great interest on the part of foreign immigrants. The final eligibility requirement reveals the sociopolitical context of the Civil War as a backdrop to the act: Only those who have "never borne arms against the United States Government or given aid and comfort to its enemies" may take up a homestead.

Although the Homestead Act was signed in May 1862, it states that it will not take effect until January 1863. At that time, a homesteader can make a claim on surveyed, "unappropriated public lands." The act allows that the person may have already filed for preemption on the homestead claim. However, the homesteader is restricted from acquiring more than 160 acres of contiguous land. With this limit, Congress sought to prevent land speculators and monopolists from amassing large land holdings while stopping actual potential settlers from homesteading.

◆ Section 2

Section 2 contains the provisions for formalizing the homestead claim into a legal title or patent, known as "proving up." Central to this process is an affidavit, with two credible witnesses, made before the land register or receiver. The affidavit attests to three points: (1) that the applicant ("he or she") is the head of a family, is at least twenty-one years old, or has served in the U.S. military; (2) that he has never taken up arms against the U.S. government or assisted its enemies; and (3) that the homestead application is for the sole use, benefit, and purpose of "actual settlement and cultivation" and not in any way for the benefit of anyone else. The third point is intended to thwart not only land monopolists but also the proliferation of dummy entries to achieve this same end.

Along with the affidavit, a homesteader must submit payment of a $10 filing fee, after which he or she will be permitted to officially "enter" the quantity of land making up the claim into record. The final patent will not be issued until five years from the original filing. In other words, filers are expected to commit to no less than five years of homesteading (residing or cultivating) their claim. In the case where the filer has died in the interim, the surviving spouse or heirs are entitled to the claim, after proving their five-year residence on the land and their citizenship. At no time can homesteaders "alienate" part of their claim.

◆ Sections 3 to 5

Sections 3 to 5 are brief, further refinements of the previous sections. The land register is directed to record all entries and forward all paperwork to the General Land Office. There is also the reminder that no homestead lands can be used to satisfy debts that were contracted before being given a patent. Finally, the claim can be lost or denied. If, before the five-year period expires, it can be shown that the filer either relocated to another residence or abandoned the claim for more than six months at any time, the prospective homestead will revert back to the government.

◆ Sections 6 to 8

The provisions detailed in Sections 6 to 8 are primarily concerned with clarifying what the act does not imply or allow. Section 6 states that no one is permitted to acquire title to more than one quarter section (160 acres), nor should the act's wording be construed as to interfere with existing preemption rights, including those deriving from a preemption filing made prior to the Homestead Act's passage. It also authorizes the commissioner of the General Land Office to prepare such rules as will be necessary to carry out all of these provisions. Moreover, land registers and receivers are entitled to the same compensation they had been receiving when the equivalent amount of land had been entered and paid with money. But that was all. A final provision is aimed at soldiers: No person who has served or may yet serve in the U.S. military for at least fourteen days as a regular or volunteer during a period of war, domestic or foreign, shall be denied the benefits of this act.

Section 7 is an affirmation of the authority to require that all requested oaths, affirmations, and affidavits be provided in accordance with the act's provisions. Section 8, the final section, is known as the commutation clause. Namely, nothing in the act shall be interpreted as preventing the homesteader from being able to pay the minimum price for the land entered before the end of the five-year requirement has passed, thus commuting his or her time remaining into a cash payment in order to get title to the land.

Horace Greeley was a leading voice for westward expansion in the period up to the passage of the Homestead Act. (Library of Congress)

Audience

The Homestead Act of 1862 was conceived, written, and passed with the national audience in mind, although urban residents in the East and secessionist southerners were the least connected to it. Like many other land-policy reformers, Congressman Grow was intellectually rooted both in the agricultural worldview of his Pennsylvania district and in the larger dynamics of mid-nineteenth-century America. His politics were informed by a widely held belief in the independence and virtues associated with Jeffersonian agrarianism. The end result was a straightforward piece of legislation that, in granting relatively easy access to land to actual settlers, remapped the western half of the United States and transformed its landscape.

Impact

As the historian Gates has concluded, despite the country's traditionally weak, "incongruent" land legislation, the federal land system can be judged a success; the home-

> "That any person who is the head of a family, or who has arrived at the age of twenty-one years, and is a citizen of the United States, or who shall have filed his declaration of intention to become such, ... shall ... be entitled to enter one quarter section or a less quantity of unappropriated public lands."
>
> (Section 1)

> "That nothing in this act shall be so construed as to prevent any person who has availed him or herself of the benefits of the first section of this act, from paying the minimum price ... for the quantity of land so entered at any time before the expiration of the five years, and obtaining a patent therefore from the government ... on making proof of settlement and cultivation as provided by existing laws granting preemption rights."
>
> (Section 8)

> "In regard to the homestead bill, ... I am in favor of settling the wild lands into small parcels so that every poor man may have a home."
>
> (Abraham Lincoln, February 13, 1861; qtd. in Villard, p. 81)

steading settlers of the environmentally challenging Great Plains and Far West regions would perhaps not be so generous in their overall assessment. Still, as a result of the Homestead Act, Jefferson's vision of small owner-operated (as opposed to tenant or corporate) farms across the Republic was made possible and eventually evident. Setting aside the southern states, Gates notes that more than 1.7 million such farms had been established by 1880. By 1900 public land states contained more than 2.4 million farms, of which 70 percent were still owner-operated enterprises. According to the National Archives Web site, more than 270 million acres were transferred from public to private ownership. Yet Robbins points to discrepancies that suggest the difficulty of homesteading. For example, in a twenty-year period beginning in 1862, from 552,112 original entries only 194,488 final entries were made. Numerous autobiographical accounts of the homesteading experience attest to its hardships. By way of commemoration, in 1936 the Department of the Interior recognized Daniel Freeman, a Union Army scout, as the first to make a claim under the Homestead Act (on January 1, 1863, the day it took effect) and created a monument on his homestead in Beatrice, Nebraska.

The launching of the homesteading era also inaugurated new philosophies about land reform, which led to the passage of several amendments to the 1862 Homestead Act.

Because the act had been passed on the heels of southern secession, the end of the Civil War in 1865 forced the question of extending provisions to former Confederate states with public lands. The Southern Homestead Act was passed in June 1866 and was repealed ten years later. Congress also passed a series of soldiers' homestead acts (1864, 1870, and 1872) that granted special privileges, such as allowing soldiers to deduct their time of military service from the residence requirement. A growing realization that not all land could or should be brought under the plow led to new (not always well-reasoned) legislation. The Timber Culture Act (1873) was designed to promote the growth of otherwise scarce timber on the western prairies, while the Desert Land Act (1877) unwisely encouraged the settlement and cultivation of what was deemed "desert" (land west of the one-hundredth meridian). It was not until 1976, when the Federal Land Policy and Management Act was passed, that the Homestead Act was repealed in the lower forty-eight states (with a ten-year extension granted to claims in Alaska).

The 1862 Homestead Act was layered with meaning about national identity and character. Many homesteaders—male, female, American born, and foreign born—were so affected by their consuming and often bitterly disappointing experiences, which forced them to endure hardships beyond reason, that they were moved to write about homesteading. These varied perspectives include those of Norwegian immigrants (Ole Edvart Rölvaag's *Giants in the Earth*), women (Willa Cather's *O Pioneers!* and Edith Kohl's *Land of the Burnt Thigh*), African Americans (Nell Irvin Painter's *Exodusters*), and families (Laura Ingalls Wilder's *Little House* series). Many of these experiences also have been turned into films for television and theater audiences. By the beginning of the twenty-first century, America's farm population had shrunk to about 2 percent of the national population. However, the historical grit, achievements, and drama associated with homesteading continue to offer lessons related to cultural, regional, and national identify; land use, land policy, and the environment; and immigrant, African American, and women's history.

Related Documents

American State Papers, 1789–1838. Series 3, Finance, and series 8, Public Lands. Buffalo, N.Y.: W. S. Hein, 1998. Library of Congress "American Memory" Web site. http://memory.loc.gov/ammem/amlaw/lwsp.html. Accessed on December 31, 2007. First published in 1832–1861 by Gales and Seaton, this thirty-eight-volume set includes all of Congress's key executive and legislative documents from 1789 to 1838. The volumes are divided into ten class or series titles, with documents most relevant to the Homestead Act included in the Finance and Public Lands series.

Bibliography

■ Articles
Gates, Paul Wallace. "The Homestead Law in an Incongruous Land System." *American Historical Review* 41 (July 1936): 652–681.

■ Books
Cross, Coy F. *Go West, Young Man!: Horace Greeley's Vision for America.* Albuquerque: University of New Mexico Press, 1995.

Dick, Everett. *The Lure of the Land: A Social History of the Public Lands from the Articles of Confederation to the New Deal.* Lincoln: University of Nebraska Press, 1970.

———. *The Sod-House Frontier, 1854–1890: A Social History of the Northern Plains from the Creation of Kansas and Nebraska to the Admission of the Dakotas.* Lincoln: University of Nebraska Press, 1979.

Gates, Paul Wallace. *History of Public Land Law Development.* Washington, D.C.: U.S. Government Printing Office, 1968.

Hibbard, Benjamin Horace. *A History of the Public Land Policies.* Madison: University of Wisconsin Press, 1965.

Ilisevich, Robert D. *Galusha A. Grow: The People's Candidate.* Pittsburgh: University of Pittsburgh Press, 1988.

Ise, John. *Sod and Stubble.* Lawrence: University Press of Kansas, 1996.

Kohl, Edith Eudora. *Land of the Burnt Thigh.* Saint Paul: Minnesota Historical Society Press, 1986.

Opie, John. *The Law of the Land: Two Hundred Years of American Farmland Policy.* Lincoln: University of Nebraska Press, 1994.

Painter, Nell Irvin. *Exodusters: Black Migration to Kansas after Reconstruction.* Lawrence: University Press of Kansas, 1986.

Robbins, Roy M. *Our Landed Heritage: The Public Domain, 1776–1970.* Lincoln: University of Nebraska Press, 1976.

Rölvaag, O. E. *Giants in the Earth: A Saga of the Prairie.* New York: Harper and Row, 1965.

Shannon, Fred A. *The Farmer's Last Frontier: Agriculture, 1860–1897.* Armonk, N.Y.: M. E. Sharpe, 1989.

Stewart, Elinore Pruitt. *Letters of a Woman Homesteader.* Mineola, N.Y.: Dover Publications, 2006.

Villard, Henry. *Lincoln on the Eve of '61: A Journalist's Story.* New York: Knopf, 1941.

Wilder, Laura Ingalls. *A Little House Treasury.* New York: HarperCollins, 2006.

■ Web Sites
"Homestead Act." Library of Congress "Primary Documents in American History" Web site.
    http://www.loc.gov/rr/program/bib/ourdocs/Homestead.html. Accessed on November 18, 2007.

"Homestead Act (1862)." 100 Milestone Documents Web site.
    http://www.ourdocuments.gov/doc.php?flash=true&doc=31. Accessed on November 18, 2007.

"The Homestead Act of 1862." The National Archives "Teaching with Documents" Web site.
    http://www.archives.gov/education/lessons/homestead-act/. Accessed on November 18, 2007.

"Homestead National Monument of America." National Park Service, U.S. Department of the Interior, Web site.
    http://www.nps.gov/home/heritagecenter.htm. Accessed on November 18, 2007.

"The Northern Great Plains, 1880–1920." Library of Congress "American Memory" Web site.
    http://memory.loc.gov/ammem/award97/ndfahtml/ngphome.html. Accessed on November 18, 2007.

—By Ginette Aley

Questions for Further Study

1. Laura Ingalls Wilder's captivating portrayal of growing up in a pioneering family, in the shadow of the Homestead Act, has become part of America's popular cultural tradition, both in terms of literature (the *Little House* series) and television (*Little House on the Prairie*). Compare and contrast Wilder's portrayal of homesteading in either format with that of her daughter, Rose Wilder Lane, who wrote the novel *Free Land* as a corrective. How might you account for the differing perceptions?

2. The Homestead Act has become an iconic American symbol of grit and determination, independence, virtuous agrarianism, and democracy. But who really profited from this movement toward western homesteads? Who did not profit, and why? Given that ultimately much undesirable land was brought under cultivation, what environmental implications does this suggest?

3. Contemporaries often considered that the Homestead Act represented a bet on the government's part that settlers could not reside on, improve, and prove up their 160-acre claims within five years. The title to the land and the filing fee were at stake. Whether male or female, is homesteading a challenge you would have undertaken? Why? Given the historical context, what would you have hoped to gain?

Glossary

affidavit	a sworn written statement
alienated	transferred or sold
claim	implied right of ownership of a location-specific tract of land, which becomes legitimated by an official title once all filings and fees have been processed, a certain number of years have passed, and specified improvements have been made
commutation	procedure by which a claimant is allowed to secure title to land sooner than the specified years by commuting the remaining time to a lump-sum purchase
preemption	principle and established customary assertion of a first right to a claim on public land, on the basis of prior residence and improvement

HOMESTEAD ACT

CHAP. LXXV. —*An Act to secure Homesteads to actual Settlers on the Public Domain.*

Be it enacted by the Senate and House of Representatives of the United States of America in Congress assembled, That any person who is the head of a family, or who has arrived at the age of twenty-one years, and is a citizen of the United States, or who shall have filed his declaration of intention to become such, as required by the naturalization laws of the United States, and who has never borne arms against the United States Government or given aid and comfort to its enemies, shall, from and after the first January, eighteen hundred and. sixty-three, be entitled to enter one quarter section or a less quantity of unappropriated public lands, upon which said person may have filed a preemption claim, or which may, at the time the application is made, be subject to preemption at one dollar and twenty-five cents, or less, per acre; or eighty acres or less of such unappropriated lands, at two dollars and fifty cents per acre, to be located in a body, in conformity to the legal subdivisions of the public lands, and after the same shall have been surveyed: Provided, That any person owning and residing on land may, under the provisions of this act, enter other land lying contiguous to his or her said land, which shall not, with the land so already owned and occupied, exceed in the aggregate one hundred and sixty acres.

SEC. 2. And be it further enacted, That the person applying for the benefit of this act shall, upon application to the register of the land office in which he or she is about to make such entry, make affidavit before the said register or receiver that he or she is the head of a family, or is twenty-one years or more of age, or shall have performed service in the army or navy of the United States, and that he has never borne arms against the Government of the United States or given aid and comfort to its enemies, and that such application is made for his or her exclusive

use and benefit, and that said entry is made for the purpose of actual settlement and cultivation, and not either directly or indirectly for the use or benefit of any other person or persons whomsoever; and upon filing the said affidavit with the register or receiver, and on payment of ten dollars, he or she shall thereupon be permitted to enter the quantity of land specified: Provided, however, That no certificate shall be given or patent issued therefor until the expiration of five years from the date of such entry; and if, at the expiration of such time, or at any time within two years thereafter, the person making such entry; or, if he be dead, his widow; or in case of her death, his heirs or devisee; or in case of a widow making such entry, her heirs or devisee, in case of her death; shall. prove by two credible witnesses that he, she, or they have resided upon or cultivated the same for the term of five years immediately succeeding the time of filing the affidavit aforesaid, and shall make affidavit that no part of said land has been alienated, and that he has borne rue allegiance to the Government of the United States; then, in such case, he, she, or they, if at that time a citizen of the United States, shall be entitled to a patent, as in other cases provided for by law: And provided, further, That in case of the death of both father and mother, leaving an Infant child, or children, under twenty-one years of age, the right and fee shall ensure to the benefit of said infant child or children; and the executor, administrator, or guardian may, at any time within two years after the death of the surviving parent, and in accordance with the laws of the State in which such children for the time being have their domicil, sell said land for the benefit of said infants, but for no other purpose; and the purchaser shall acquire the absolute title by the purchase, and be entitled to a patent from the United States, on payment of the office fees and sum of money herein specified.

SEC. 3. And be it further enacted, That the register of the land office shall note all such applications on the tract books and plats of, his office, and keep a register of all such entries, and make return thereof to the General Land Office, together with the proof upon which they have been founded.

SEC. 4. And be it further enacted, That no lands acquired under the provisions of this act shall in any event become liable to the satisfaction of any debt or debts contracted prior to the issuing of the patent therefor.

SEC. 5. And be it further enacted, That if, at any time after the filing of the affidavit, as required in the second section of this act, and before the expiration of the five years aforesaid, it shall be proven, after due notice to the settler, to the satisfaction of the register of the land office, that the person having filed such affidavit shall have actually changed his or her residence, or abandoned the said land for more than six months at any time, then and in that event the land so entered shall revert to the government.

SEC. 6. And be it further enacted, That no individual shall be permitted to acquire title to more than one quarter section under the provisions of this act; and that the Commissioner of the General Land Office is hereby required to prepare and issue such rules and regulations, consistent with this act, as shall be necessary and proper to carry its provisions into effect; and that the registers and receivers of the several land offices shall be entitled to receive the same compensation for any lands entered under the provisions of this act that they are now entitled to receive when the same quantity of land is entered with money, one half to be paid by the person making the application at the time of so doing, and the other half on the issue of the certificate by the person to whom it may be issued; but this shall not be construed to enlarge the maximum of

compensation now prescribed by law for any register or receiver: Provided, That nothing contained in this act shall be so construed as to impair or interfere in any manner whatever with existing preemption rights: And provided, further, That all persons who may have filed their applications for a preemption right prior to the passage of this act, shall be entitled to all privileges of this act: Provided, further, That no person who has served, or may hereafter serve, for a period of not less than fourteen days in the army or navy of the United States, either regular or volunteer, under the laws thereof, during the existence of an actual war, domestic or foreign, shall be deprived of the benefits of this act on account of not having attained the age of twenty-one years.

SEC. 7. And be it further enacted, That the fifth section of the act entitled "An act in addition to an act more effectually to provide for the punishment of certain crimes against the United States, and for other purposes," approved the third of March, in the year eighteen hundred and fifty-seven, shall extend to all oaths, affirmations, and affidavits, required or authorized by this act.

SEC. 8. And be it further enacted, That nothing in this act shall be construed as to prevent any person who has availed him or herself of the benefits of the first section of this act, from paying the minimum price, or the price to which the same may have graduated, for the quantity of land so entered at any time before the expiration of the five years, and obtaining a patent therefor from the government, as in other cases provided by law, on making proof of settlement and cultivation as provided by existing laws granting preemption rights.

APPROVED, May 20, 1862.

Recd 20 Jun

Public 108.

Thirty-Seventh Congress of the United States of America;

At the — Second — Session,

Begun and held at the city of Washington, on Monday, the — Second — day of December, one thousand eight hundred and sixty-one

AN ACT

Donating public lands to the several States and Territories which may provide colleges for the benefit of agriculture and the Mechanic arts.

Be it enacted by the Senate and House of Representatives of the United States of America in Congress assembled, **That** there be granted to the several States for the purposes hereinafter mentioned an amount of public land to be apportioned to each State a quantity equal to thirty thousand acres for each Senator and representative in Congress to which the States are respectively entitled by the apportionment under the census of eighteen hundred and sixty: Provided, That no mineral lands shall be selected or purchased under the provisions of this act. Sec. 2 And be it further enacted, That the land aforesaid, after being surveyed, shall be apportioned to the several States in sections or subdivisions of sections, not less than one quarter of a section, and whenever there are public lands in a State, subject to sale at private entry at one dollar and twenty-five cents per acre, the quantity to which said State shall be entitled shall be selected from such lands within the limits of such State and the Secretary of the Interior is hereby directed to issue to each of the states in which there is not the quantity of public lands subject to sale at private entry at one dollar and twenty five cents per acre to which said State may be entitled under the provisions of this act, land scrip to the amount in acres for the deficiency of its distributive share: said scrip to be sold by said States and the proceeds thereof applied to the uses and purposes prescribed in this act and for no other use or purpose whatsoever: Provided That in no case shall any State to which land scrip may thus be issued, be allowed to locate the same within the limits of any other State, or any Territory of the United States, but their assignees may thus locate said land scrip upon any of the unappropriated lands of the United States subject to sale at private entry at one dollar and twenty-five cents or less per acre. And provided further, that not more than one million acres shall be located by such assignees in any one of the States, And provided further that no such location shall be made before

The Morrill Act (National Archives and Records Administration)

"The moneys so invested shall constitute a perpetual fund ... in order to promote the liberal and practical education of the industrial classes."

Overview

The Morrill Act of July 2, 1862, also referred to as the Morrill Land Grant Act or the Land Grant Colleges Act, laid the foundation for state universities. The act bears the name of its creator, the Vermont Republican representative Justin Smith Morrill. Passed during the Civil War, the act marked the beginning of the federal government's involvement in public higher education. With it, Congress gave each state thirty thousand acres of federal land for each of its congressional districts to promote public education in agriculture, engineering, and military science. The land or the income from its sale was to be used to create or support educational institutions that fulfilled the aims of Congress. The legislation eventually led to the creation of sixty-nine colleges and universities, although it also promoted a certain degree of speculation. As some states were hard-pressed to meet wartime expenses, they sold their land cheaply to wealthy entrepreneurs, yet this should not overshadow the importance of the act in promoting the education of larger numbers of students and encouraging colleges to establish practical courses in agricultural, technical, and industrial subjects to attract students from the working classes.

The Morrill Act, first proposed in 1857, was passed by Congress in 1859, but President James Buchanan vetoed it. In 1861 Morrill resubmitted the act, including military tactics among the subjects the funded institutions should teach. As the country was heading toward secession and the Civil War, this was a crucial inclusion, and President Abraham Lincoln signed the act on July 2, 1862. As the first Morrill Act excluded the seceded southern states from its benefits, a second Morrill Act was created after the end of the Civil War to fund southern institutions that could prove that race was not a criterion for admission.

Context

The passage of the Morrill Act took place against the dramatic events of the Civil War. War production helped heavy industries in the North and strengthened the complementary relationship that already existed between agriculture and industry. Although the mechanization of agriculture had begun before the war, military recruitment and conscription gave farmers an added reason to buy machinery that could replace human labor, at least in part. As Benjamin F. Quillian has pointed out, "The young republic was highly dependent on agriculture, but American farming was inefficient and lacking in scientific knowledge and technology" (p. 93). With the growing of eastern cities and the opening up of European markets, American agriculture was gradually changing from its immediate purpose of feeding farmers' families into a commercial agriculture. This new commercial dimension required an educational system that could introduce newer and more advanced farming methods. The Morrill Act, from the very title, declared itself instrumental to this transition.

During the nineteenth century, debates on the institution of slavery had become increasingly prominent. The positions of free northern states and slaveholding southern states were becoming increasingly polarized and difficult to reconcile. In 1820 the Missouri Compromise had prohibited slavery in the former Louisiana Territory north of the parallel 36°30' north, except in the proposed state of Missouri. Particularly from the mid-1840s, with the expansion of the nation westward and the settlement of the Great Plains, Americans were confronted with the complex issue of whether new states and territories should be free or slaveholding, a thorny problem the Missouri Compromise failed to address.

This question eventually proved too divisive for an effective compromise. Factional interests with political parties and church denominations gradually replaced the tendency toward compromise for the national well-being. Northern Republicans were especially concerned that Democrats were planning to take over federal institutions and make slavery legal throughout the Union. They believed that slavery violated the principle of the free labor of free men, which they thought should be the guiding tenet for the country's development. These antislavery northerners were not necessarily antiracist; on the contrary, it was possible to oppose slavery and still be racist. Fears of so-called slave power, the idea that a slaveholding oligarchy was expanding

1854

■ **May 30**
Congress passes the Kansas-Nebraska Act.

1856

■ **November 4**
Democrat James Buchanan is elected fifteenth president of the United States.

1857

■ **March 6**
Chief Justice Roger Taney delivers the majority opinion of the Supreme Court in *Dred Scott v. Sandford*.

1859

■ **October 16**
The radical abolitionist John Brown leads an attack against the federal arsenal at Harpers Ferry, Virginia, to encourage a slave rebellion.

1860

■ **November 6**
Abraham Lincoln is elected sixteenth president of the United States.

■ **December 20**
South Carolina declares its independence from the Union, beginning the process of secession of southern states.

1861

■ **February 18**
Jefferson Davis is sworn in as the president of the Confederate States of America.

■ **April 12**
Confederate forces attack the federal garrison at Fort Sumter in Charleston Harbor, effectively starting the American Civil War.

1862

■ **July 2**
Congress passes the Morrill Act.

■ **September 22**
President Lincoln issues the Emancipation Proclamation, stating that on January 1, 1863, all slaves in the states in rebellion against the Union would be emancipated.

its political control over the whole country, were encouraging the growth of a larger antislavery movement, and slavery was increasingly seen as endangering the rights of white men to obtain jobs in slaveholding states.

On the other hand, southern Democratic leaders defended slavery and invoked the Constitution, claiming that the enslavement of African Americans was based on the Bible and above moral criticism. According to the southern proslavery thinker John C. Calhoun, the new territories added to the Union belonged to all states, including slaveholding ones. Thus, Calhoun invoked the constitutional right of slaveholders to take their slaves anywhere in the new territories. Another prominent southerner, the sociologist George Fitzhugh, declared slavery morally superior to wage labor, as factory owners did not take care of their sick workers and simply exploited their work. On the contrary, paternalistic southern slaveholders looked after their aged slaves.

The polarizing effects of the debate over slavery became apparent in the election of 1856. Fought immediately after the bitter and violent controversies surrounding the Kansas-Nebraska Act (1854), which had opened the two states to slavery, the election witnessed the victory of the Democratic candidate James Buchanan, the former ambassador to Britain. Buchanan had been selected as a candidate precisely because his role as ambassador had left him out of the territorial disputes over the extension of slavery to the new territories. The support of southern states was decisive for Buchanan's victory. The new president was elected without the support of eleven free states that would remain adverse to the Democratic Party for decades. John C. Frémont, the Republican candidate, won those states, making his party the dominant political force in the North.

Buchanan did not fully grasp the widening rift that slavery was causing in American society and was persuaded that he could keep the nation united if the American people accepted the interpretations of the Constitution by the Supreme Court. Yet following the *Dred Scott v. Sandford* Supreme Court ruling in 1857, northern concerns over the threat of slave power all but increased. Dred Scott was a Missouri slave who had decided to sue his owner for his freedom. Scott claimed that he should be freed because his owner had taken him to Illinois, a free state, for several years before moving to the Wisconsin Territory, where slavery was also barred because of the 1820 Missouri Compromise. Far from limiting itself to the case of Scott, the majority opinion, which ruled against the slave's claim, also declared the 1820 Missouri Compromise unconstitutional. With the Scott ruling, slave power seemed to have won a major constitutional victory, as the verdict came close to an endorsement of Calhoun's ideas.

Republican politicians used the growing fears of a possible takeover by slave power to strengthen their diverse coalition, which also included racists who felt that slavery could endanger their interests. Abraham Lincoln emerged as the party's nominee for the 1860 election. While Lincoln denied that Republicans intended to interfere with slavery where it existed, the party also stood firm against the extension of the institution into the new territories. In the meantime, the Democratic Party was becoming increasingly divided over the issue of slavery, and, as compromise failed, Democrats presented two nominees: Stephen A. Douglas for the northern wing and Vice President John C. Breckinridge for the South. This fragmentation helped Lincoln to win the vote in the Electoral College, although the sum of his opponents' votes exceeded Lincoln's.

Shortly after Lincoln's victory, the southern states, starting with South Carolina, began to secede from the Union. By February 1861, Mississippi, Florida, Alabama, Georgia, Louisiana, and Texas had joined South Carolina and created the Confederate States of America with Jefferson Davis as their president and a new government based in Montgomery, Alabama. Military hostilities between the Union and the Confederacy broke out when, in April 1861, Lincoln notified South Carolina authorities that he was sending a ship to resupply the federal garrison of Fort Sumter in Charleston Harbor. The Confederate government refused to recognize Lincoln's authority, as they realized they could not claim to head a sovereign nation if their ports were under the Union's control. When the garrison refused to surrender, Confederate forces attacked and, after two days, the garrison did surrender. Union troops were allowed to leave unharmed, but the Civil War had effectively begun.

About the Author

Justin Smith Morrill was born on April 14, 1810, in Strafford, Vermont. He attended the Thetford and Randolph Academies but ended his formal education at age fifteen to work as a merchant's clerk, an event that probably influenced his commitment to democratize the American educational system. Although he never attended a university, Morrill was awarded an honorary degree from the University of Pennsylvania in 1884.

After a career as a local businessman, Morrill became interested in politics in the 1850s. In 1852, he was elected as a Whig representative to the Thirty-fourth Congress and as a Republican to the five succeeding Congresses. Morrill helped found the Republican Party in Vermont, and as a political leader he worked to maintain harmony within the party. During his twelve years as a representative, he was the author of the Tariff of 1861, usually referred to as the Morrill Tariff, as well as of the Land Grant Colleges Act. Both acts became strongly associated with their creator. The Tariff of 1861 was consistent with Morrill's fiscal conservatism and introduced high import duties to protect American industry from overseas competition. Morrill opposed resorting to paper money during and after the U.S. Civil War and various proposals for the use of silver as a monetary standard.

Because the Land Grant Colleges Act helped to establish institutions that introduced agricultural and technical subjects in higher education, Morrill has become known as

Time Line

1863

■ July 1–3
The Union wins the battle of Gettysburg.

1864

■ November 8
Lincoln is reelected president.

1865

■ April 9
Robert E. Lee surrenders his Confederate army at Appomattox Court House, effectively ending the Civil War.

■ April 14
President Lincoln is shot at Ford's Theatre in Washington by the southern sympathizer John Wilkes Booth. The president dies the next day. Andrew Johnson becomes president.

■ December 18
Congress ratifies the Thirteenth Amendment banning slavery in the United States.

"the Father of the Agricultural Colleges." Because of his crucial contribution to higher education, many colleges established under the act have a Morrill Hall in his honor. In the Thirty-ninth Congress, Morrill served as chairman of the Committee on Ways and Means. During his years as a representative, Morrill also sponsored the Anti-Bigamy Act of 1862, which outlawed the Mormon practice of plural marriages and limited church ownership in any territory of the United States to $50,000. This second restriction also targeted the Mormons, trying to limit their ownership in Utah. Although Lincoln signed the act, no funds were allocated for its enforcement.

In 1866 Morrill was elected as a Republican to the Senate, where he was reelected five consecutive times. He remained in the Senate for almost thirty-one years, until his death. He established a record for longevity, serving in both houses for forty-three years. He also acted as chairman of the Committee on Public Buildings and Grounds, where he played a major role in obtaining the current Library of Congress main building through his work on the Joint Select Committee on Additional Accommodations for the Library. He also served on the Committee on Finance, as regent of the Smithsonian Institution (1883–1898), and as trustee of the University of Vermont (1865–1898). He died in Washington, D.C., on December 28, 1898. He is buried in the City Cemetery in Strafford, Vermont. In 1999 the U.S. Postal Service released a 55-cent postage stamp that paid homage to his role in establishing the land-grant colleges, the forerunners of many state universities.

Justin Smith Morrill (Library of Congress)

Explanation and Analysis of the Document

The full title of the Morrill Act is An Act Donating Public Lands to the Several States and Territories Which May Provide Colleges for the Benefit of Agriculture and the Mechanic Arts. This long title expresses one of the two governing principles of the act: practical knowledge and equality of opportunity.

The first section of the Act enunciates that Congress will give each state thirty thousand acres of federal land for each of its representatives and senators to promote public education in agriculture and the mechanical arts. This first section thus explicitly establishes the beginning of the federal government's direct involvement in public education. The second section allows the states to sell the donated land to private parties and use the income for the purposes expressed in the first section. Although the Morrill Act had a revolutionary impact on American education, eventually contributing to the establishment of more than sixty colleges and universities, this part of the legislation had the immediate effect of enriching a few major speculators. Businessmen and entrepreneurs were able to exploit the states' need to meet wartime expenses and could buy the land cheaply. The large supply meant that most states received very little for their land. Kentucky, for example, received only fifty cents per acre. Some states were able to keep their allotment for several years and eventually sell it at a much higher price. The land given to Cornell University was sold for over $5.50 per acre.

The second section of the document also maintains that if the federal land within a state was insufficient to meet that state's land grant, the state was issued "scrip" that authorized the state to select federal lands in other states to fund its institution. The third section makes clear that "all the expenses of management, superintendence, and taxes" previous to the sale of the land should be paid by the treasuries of the states to the federal treasury without being deducted from the proceeds of the sale. Thus, the entire income from the sale of the land should be devoted to the support of higher education in the agricultural and technical sectors.

Section 4 contains the core principles of the Morrill Act. It establishes that the money obtained from the sale of the land should be invested in "stocks of the United States, or of the States, or some other safe stocks." Such investment should constitute "a perpetual fund" for "the endowment, support, and maintenance" of at least one college where teaching would focus on agriculture, the mechanic arts, and military strategy. The inclusion of military strategy was instrumental in engineering the passage of the act during the Civil War. The section also makes clear that the focus on a practical curriculum is intended to promote the education of "the industrial classes." It reflects the growing need for agricultural and technical education in wartime America. As higher education was still largely unavailable to many agricultural and industrial workers, the Morrill Act aimed to provide a broader segment of the American people with a practical curriculum that was relevant to their daily lives.

Section 5 lists seven conditions for the granting of the land to the states. The states should maintain the fund's stability, reintegrating any sum that is lost. As an exception to this first condition, a maximum of 10 percent of the fund can be used to establish experimental farms authorized by the legislature. This type of activity would be allocated special funds with the Hatch Act of 1887, which authorized direct payment of federal grant funds to each state to establish an agricultural experiment station in connection with the state's land-grant institution.

The second condition forbids using the income from the sale of the land to construct or maintain buildings. The third condition gives each state five years to begin its support of at least one higher education institution promoting studies in agriculture and the technical arts. The fourth condition requires the states to produce an annual report on the institutions' progress. The fifth condition determines that if the state selects lands whose price has doubled because of a railroad grant, the acres of land should be proportionally diminished.

The sixth condition is one of the most important for the historical context of the document, for it forbids states in rebellion against the U.S. government to benefit from the act. This is a clear reference to the southern states that had seceded from the Union. After the war, the act was extended to the former Confederacy, and a second Morrill Act was passed in 1890, aimed specifically at the southern states.

"The moneys so invested shall constitute a perpetual fund ... to the endowment, support, and maintenance of at least one college where the leading object shall be, without excluding other scientific and classical studies, and including military tactics, to teach such branches of learning as are related to agriculture and the mechanic arts ... in order to promote the liberal and practical education of the industrial classes in the several pursuits and professions in life."

(Section 4)

"No State while in a condition of rebellion or insurrection against the government of the United States shall be entitled to the benefit of this act."

(Section 5, sixth condition)

"When any Territory shall become a State and be admitted into the Union, such new State shall be entitled to the benefits of the said act of July two, eighteen hundred and sixty-two, by expressing the acceptance therein required within three years from the date of its admission into the Union, and providing the college or colleges within five years after such acceptance, as prescribed in this act."

(Section 5, seventh condition)

This second act provided cash rather than lands to the institutions of southern states that could prove that race was not a criterion for admission. Those states for which race was a criterion for selection could still benefit from the second Morrill Act if they had a separate land-grant institution for people of color.

Finally, as a seventh and last condition, a state could benefit from the act if it accepted the law within three years of July 23, 1866. As an exception to this last condition, the document allows the territories that would become part of the Union to benefit from the act if they ratified it within three years from their admission.

The last three sections of the Morrill Act deal with land scrip. The document states that any land scrip issued as a result of the act should not be subjected to location before January 1, 1863. It also fixes the compensation for the land officers who locate the land scrip. Finally, the act requires the governors of the states that were issued land scrip to write an annual report on the sales of the scrip, their amounts, and the appropriations made as a result.

Audience

As with many government acts, the document was intended for a vast audience, for its benefits would be felt by the entire wartime American society. The Morrill Act was of crucial importance for the states, which could receive for the first time considerable material aid from the federal government for education. A particularly important segment of the act's audience was American farmers and industrial workers, who, until then, had no access to higher education. The legislation was intended to provide easier access to higher education and to supply them with the technical skills required by the new American industrial developments. The document thus encouraged the working classes to seek admission to the new institutions that would be created. The fifth section of the act, with its exclusion of the states in rebellion against the Union, indirectly addressed the people of the southern states, showing them the benefits they could have if they were part of the United States. The section also sounds as a warning for wavering Union states not to change their allegiance.

Impact

Since the founding of the nation, colleges and universities have been important institutions of higher learning, and their curricula have always been at the center of significant debate. In the late eighteenth century, such debates focused on whether the university curriculum should be based on the study of classics or should include more practical subjects. On the one hand, the advocates of a classical curriculum suggested the inclusion of Latin and Greek and courses in the natural sciences, English literature, and European history. These subjects were thought to be the best preparation to provide the political and cultural leadership for the future of American democracy. On the other hand, opponents of a classical focus claimed that higher education should become more practical and directly related to the pupils' vocational aspirations. The Morrill Act was a victory by this latter faction, for it provided funding for state institutions of higher education that included agriculture and mechanical arts in their curricula. As a result, the impact of the act on American education was twofold: It favored a more practical focus in higher education and opened academic institutions to the working classes. Many states transformed their agricultural colleges into universities, and prestigious institutions such as New York's Cornell University were founded thanks to the Morrill Act.

The Morrill Act, together with the Civil War, also had an impact on the education of women and African Americans. Until the 1860s and 1870s few institutions of higher education had admitted women and African Americans. American educational leaders began to think that colleges should form a class of African American professionals and that they should prepare women for suitable jobs or for marriage. The Morrill Act and the Civil War encouraged the admission of women to colleges such as Wisconsin (since 1867) and Minnesota (1869). The act also favored the founding of women's colleges such as Wellesley and Smith. By the 1880s women constituted a third of all college and university students in the United States. Several historically black colleges and universities, such as Alabama A&M University, Atlanta University, Howard University, Lincoln University, Tuskegee University, Delaware State University, Virginia State University, Tennessee State University, and South Carolina State University, to mention but a few, were established thanks to the Morrill Acts. Their curricula conformed to the racial and gender conventions of the nineteenth century. Thus, women were expected to become nurturers, and most women graduates followed a teaching career. Women and African Americans still encountered many obstacles in higher education, which were not removed until the 1960s. For example, campus rules restricted women's access to libraries, and even African American institutions mainly employed whites for academic and administrative jobs.

Many scholars have continued to praise the Morrill Act into the twenty-first century. It is usually credited for setting a revolutionary precedent that laid the foundation for state universities, for more democratic higher-education institu-

tions, and for the establishment of a more practical college curriculum. Yet some voices have risen in dissent. For example, Terry S. Reynolds has challenged the idea that antebellum colleges were hostile to practical subjects and that they made little attempt to develop programs of a concrete nature that could aid the economic growth of the country.

Related Documents

Hatch Act, U.S. *Statutes at Large* 24 (1887): 440–442. The act gave federal land grants to the states to create a series of agricultural experiment stations.

Memorial Addresses on the Life and Character of Justin S. Morrill. Washington, D.C.: Government Printing Office, 1899. The volume collects tributes to Justin Morrill by his congressional colleagues.

Servicemen's Readjustment Act, U.S. *Statutes at Large* 58 (1944): 284. Popularly known as the GI Bill, this act offered soldiers returning from World War II college or vocational education, thus promoting higher education for an increasingly larger number of students.

Smith-Lever Act, U.S. *Statutes at Large* 38 (1914): 372. The act establishes a network of cooperative extension services connected to land-grant universities to disseminate information on developments in agriculture, home economics, and related issues.

Bibliography

■ Articles
Reynolds, Terry S. "The Education of Engineers in America before the Morrill Act of 1862." *History of Education Quarterly* 32, no. 4 (Winter 1992): 459–482.

■ Books
Cross, Coy F. *Justin Smith Morrill: Father of the Land-Grant Colleges.* Lansing: Michigan State University Press, 1999.

The Land-Grant Tradition. Washington, D.C.: National Association of State Universities and Land-Grant Colleges, 1995.

Morrison, Toni. *The Bluest Eye.* London: Chatto & Windus, 1970.

Nevins, Allan. *The Origins of the Land-Grant Colleges and Universities.* Washington, D.C.: Civil War Centennial Commission, 1962.

Parker, William Belmont. *The Life and Public Services of Justin Smith Morrill.* Boston: Houghton Mifflin, 1924.

Quillian, Benjamin F. "Regaining the Trust in Higher Education." In *The New Balancing Act in Higher Education*, eds. Robert Louis Clark and Madeleine D'Ambrosio. Northampton, Mass.: Edward Elgar, 2006.

Ross, Earle D. *Democracy's College: The Land-Grant Movement in the Formative Stage.* Ames: Iowa State College Press, 1942.

■ **Web Sites**

"Justin Smith Morrill Homestead." Vermont State Historic Sites Web site.

   http://historicvermont.org/morrill/. Accessed on December 15, 2007.

"Shrine to Justin Smith Morrill." Tom Isern Home Page, North Dakota State University Web site.

   http://www.ndsu.nodak.edu/instruct/isern/morrill.htm. Accessed on December 15, 2007.

—By Luca Prono

Questions for Further Study

1. In The Origins of the Land-Grant Colleges and Universities, Allan Nevins writes that "the most important idea in the genesis of the land-grant colleges and state universities was that of democracy. … A fundamental emotion gave force to the principle that every child should have free opportunity for as complete an education as his tastes and abilities warranted. … No restrictions of class, or fortune, or sex, or geographical position—no restrictions whatsoever—should operate" (quoted at http://www.ndsu.nodak.edu/instruct/isern/morrill.htm). Assess the accuracy of Nevins's statement.

2. The Morrill Act witnessed an intervention of the federal government into education. Nowadays a clear majority of U.S. colleges and universities are private, but most students choose public institutions. Discuss the advantages and disadvantages of both types of institutions.

3. In this passage from her novel *The Bluest Eye*, the African American author Toni Morrison describes the oppressive effects of education on African Americans with direct reference to land-grant institutions: "They go to land-grant colleges, normal schools, and learn the white man's work with refinement: home economics to prepare his food; teacher education to instruct black children in obedience; music to soothe the weary master and entertain his blunted soul. Here they learn … how to behave. … In short, how to get rid of funkiness" (p. 64). To what extent does education reproduce and/or fight the inequalities in our society?

4. Imagine that you work at an institution that is developing a new curriculum involving a variety of accelerated courses for high-performing students. Write an essay either in favor of or against the proposal, focusing in particular on how it can interact with gender, race, and class inequalities.

Glossary

aforesaid	mentioned earlier
apportioned	divided and assigned according to proportions
appropriated	assigned a sum of money for a particular cause
hereinafter	at a later point within a piece of writing
hereinbefore	at an earlier point within a piece of writing
scrip	substitute for currency
therein	in that thing or place
thereof	from that circumstance

MORRILL ACT

Chap. CXXX.—*An Act Donating Public Lands to the several States and Territories which may provide Colleges for the Benefit of Agriculture and Mechanic Arts.*

Be it enacted by the Senate and House of Representatives of the United States of America in Congress assembled, That there be granted to the several States, for the purposes hereinafter mentioned, an amount of public land, to be apportioned to each State a quantity equal to thirty thousand acres for each senator and representative in Congress to which the States are respectively entitled by the apportionment under the census of eighteen hundred and sixty: *Provided*, That no mineral lands shall be selected or purchased under the provisions of this Act.

SEC. 2. *And be it further enacted*, That the land aforesaid, after being surveyed, shall be apportioned to the several States in sections or subdivisions of sections, not less than one quarter of a section; and whenever there are public lands in a State subject to sale at private entry at one dollar and twenty-five cents per acre, the quantity to which said State shall be entitled shall be selected from such lands within the limits of such State, and the Secretary of the Interior is hereby directed to issue to each of the States in which there is not the quantity of public lands subject to sale at private entry at one dollar and twenty-five cents per acre, to which said State may be entitled under the provisions of this act, land scrip to the amount in acres for the deficiency of its distributive share: said scrip to be sold by said States and the proceeds thereof applied to the uses and purposes prescribed in this act, and for no other use or purpose whatsoever: *Provided*, That in no case shall any State to which land scrip may thus be issued be allowed to locate the same within the limits of any other State, or of any Territory of the United States, but their assignees may thus locate said land scrip upon any of the unappropriated lands of the United States subject to sale at private entry at one dollar and twenty-five cents, or less, per acre: *And provided, further*, That not more than one million acres shall be located by such assignees in any one of the States: *And provided, further*, That no such location shall be made before one year from the passage of this Act.

SEC. 3. *And be it further enacted*, That all the expenses of management, superintendence, and taxes from date of selection of said lands, previous to their sales, and all expenses incurred in the management and disbursement of the moneys which may be received therefrom, shall be paid by the States to which they may belong, out of the Treasury of said States, so that the entire proceeds of the sale of said lands shall be applied without any diminution whatever to the purposes hereinafter mentioned.

SEC. 4. *And be it further enacted*, That all moneys derived from the sale of the lands aforesaid by the States to which the lands are apportioned, and from the sales of land scrip hereinbefore provided for, shall be invested in stocks of the United States, or of the States, or some other safe stocks, yielding not less than five per centum upon the par value of said stocks; and that the moneys so invested shall constitute a perpetual fund, the capital of which shall remain forever undiminished, (except so far as may be provided in section fifth of this act,) and the interest of which shall be inviolably appropriated, by each State which may take and claim the benefit of this act, to the endowment, support, and maintenance of at least one college where the leading object shall be, without excluding other scientific and classical studies, and including military tactics, to teach such branches of learning as are related to agriculture and the mechanic arts, in such manner as the legislatures of the States may respectively prescribe, in order to promote the liberal and practical education of the industrial classes in the several pursuits and professions in life.

SEC. 5. *And be it further enacted*, That the grant of land and land scrip hereby authorized shall be made on the following conditions, to which, as well as to the provisions hereinbefore contained, the previous assent of the several States shall be signified by legislative acts:

First. If any portion of the fund invested, as provided by the foregoing section, or any portion of the interest thereon, shall, by any action or contingency, be diminished or lost, it shall be replaced by the State to which it belongs, so that the capital of the fund shall remain forever undiminished; and the annual interest shall be regularly applied without diminution to the purposes mentioned in the fourth section of this act, except that a sum, not exceeding ten per centum upon the amount received by any State under the provisions of this act may be expended for the purchase of lands for sites or experimental farms, whenever authorized by the respective legislatures of said States.

Second. No portion of said fund, nor the interest thereon, shall be applied, directly or indirectly, under any pretence whatever, to the purchase, erection, preservation, or repair of any building or buildings.

Third. Any State which may take and claim the benefit of the provisions of this act shall provide, within five years from the time of its acceptance as provided in subdivision seven of this section, at least not less than one college, as described in the fourth section of this act, or the grant to such State shall cease; and said State shall be bound to pay the United States the amount received of any lands previously sold; and that the title to purchasers under the State shall be valid.

Fourth. An annual report shall be made regarding the progress of each college, recording any improvements and experiments made, with their cost and results, and such other matters, including State industrial and economical statistics, as may be supposed useful; one copy of which shall be transmitted by mail [free] by each, to all the other colleges which may be endowed under the provisions of this act, and also one copy to the Secretary of the Interior.

Fifth. When lands shall be selected from those which have been raised to double the minimum price, in consequence of railroad grants, they shall be computed to the States at the maximum price, and the number of acres proportionally diminished.

Sixth. No State while in a condition of rebellion or insurrection against the government of the United States shall be entitled to the benefit of this act.

Seventh. No State shall be entitled to the benefits of this act unless it shall express its acceptance thereof by its legislature within three years from July 23, 1866:

Provided, That when any Territory shall become a State and be admitted into the Union, such new State shall be entitled to the benefits of the said act of July two, eighteen hundred and sixty-two, by expressing the acceptance therein required within three years from the date of its admission into the Union, and providing the college or colleges within five years after such acceptance, as prescribed in this act.

SEC. 6. *And be it further enacted*, That land scrip issued under the provisions of this act shall not be subject to location until after the first day of January, one thousand eight hundred and sixty-three.

SEC. 7. *And be it further enacted*, That the land officers shall receive the same fees for locating land scrip issued under the provisions of this act as is now allowed for the location of military bounty land warrants under existing laws: *Provided*, their maximum compensation shall not be thereby increased.

SEC. 8. *And be it further enacted*, That the Governors of the several States to which scrip shall be issued under this act shall be required to report annually to Congress all sales made of such scrip until the whole shall be disposed of, the amount received for the same, and what appropriation has been made of the proceeds.

By the President of the United States of America.

A Proclamation.

Whereas, on the twenty-second day of September, in the year of our Lord one thousand eight hundred and sixty-two, a proclamation was issued by the President of the United States, containing, among other things, the following, to wit:

"That on the first day of January, in the "year of our Lord one thousand eight hundred "and sixty-three, all persons held as slaves within "any State or designated part of a State, the people "whereof shall then be in rebellion against the "United States, shall be then, thenceforward, and "forever free; and the Executive Government of the "United States, including the military and naval "authority thereof, will recognize and maintain "the freedom of such persons, and will do no act "or acts to repress such persons, or any of them,

The Emancipation Proclamation (National Archives and Records Administration)

EMANCIPATION PROCLAMATION

"Upon this act, sincerely believed to be an act of justice, warranted by the Constitution, ...

I invoke the considerate judgment of mankind, and the gracious favor of Almighty God."

Overview

The Emancipation Proclamation freed all slaves in the states that constituted the Confederacy. The document emphasizes that this action was a "war measure," taken, in part, to protect the slaves who were being offered refuge in Union forts, garrisons, and vessels. The proclamation was also offered as a moral statement, as an "act of justice" in accordance with the U.S. Constitution, and as a "military necessity." That President Abraham Lincoln was addressing not merely his countrymen and the rebels but the world and his maker as well is clear from the document's parting statement: "I invoke the considerate judgment of mankind, and the gracious favor of Almighty Lord."

Context

Lincoln issued the Emancipation Proclamation on September 22, 1862 (the proclamation would take effect on January 1, 1863), freeing forever those slaves in Confederate states. At this time the Civil War, begun in the spring of 1861, had yet to turn decisively in the North's favor, although Lincoln was beginning to envisage victory at long last after the Union army's success in the battle of Antietam. He had been elected to office pledging to keep the Union together, and when the South seceded, his main task became that of reuniting his nation. Although he was opposed to slavery and its extension into new states and territories, Lincoln never advocated complete, let alone immediate, abolition of what was known as the "peculiar institution." During the early stages of the war, he successfully kept border slave states like Maryland and Missouri in the Union by not issuing statements that might have driven them toward the Confederacy. Even with this proclamation, slaves in the border states within the Union remained the property of their owners.

Pressure on Lincoln to issue this proclamation had been building for some time. He had not been opposed to emancipation in principle once the war was in progress, but he thought the timing of such an act would be crucial; it would have to come at a time when it would foster respect and inspire his troops. Lincoln had rescinded an earlier proclamation of emancipation issued by John Frémont, one of the Union's commanders, in Missouri. Not only did Lincoln view Frémont's proclamation as premature, but it was also insubordinate, since it was the commander in chief's duty to make such a declaration. Moreover, Lincoln wanted to issue a very carefully worded document that would limit the scope of emancipation. Indeed, fervent abolitionists criticized Lincoln for not going so far as to liberate all slaves.

Lincoln's aim, however, was to cause disruption behind Confederate lines. He hoped that his proclamation would inspire slaves to desert their masters and join the Union cause. He also hoped that the dramatic act would prevent England and France from recognizing the legitimacy of the Confederacy and supporting rebel forces. While the Emancipation Proclamation was primarily a political and diplomatic document as well as a military measure, it nevertheless acquired enormous symbolic meaning because for the first time it made slavery itself one of the primary issues of the war. The ideological precedent this document set led to the enlistment of something like 200,000 soldiers and sailors in the Union army and navy.

About the Author

Abraham Lincoln, born on February 12, 1809, in a one-room log cabin in southeastern Kentucky, grew up in a frontier environment. He had little formal education but was a prodigious reader, favoring the Bible, Shakespeare, and biographies. As a young man he studied law. At age twenty-three he ran unsuccessfully for a seat in the Illinois General Assembly, to which state his family had moved when he was nine. He served briefly in the Black Hawk War before being elected to the state legislature in 1834. Admitted to the bar in 1837, Lincoln proved to be a successful attorney, admired for his ability to argue on his feet in court cases.

In 1842 Lincoln married Mary Todd, daughter of a prominent southern family. The couple had four children, but only one, Robert, survived into adulthood. Quarrelsome but proud of her husband, Mary supported Lincoln's political ambitions. He was elected for one term in the U.S.

Time Line

1860

■ **November 6**
Abraham Lincoln is elected president.

■ **December 20**
South Carolina becomes the first southern state to secede following the election of Abraham Lincoln as president.

1861

■ **March 4**
Lincoln is inaugurated as president.

■ **April 13**
Fort Sumter, in South Carolina, surrenders to Confederate forces, beginning the Civil War.

■ **April 17**
Virginia secedes.

■ **April 19**
Lincoln declares blockade of southern coast.

■ **May 16–June 8**
Arkansas, North Carolina, and Tennessee secede.

■ **August 6**
Congress approves first Confiscation Act, declaring Confederate slaves seized by the Union army to be free.

■ **August 30**
John C. Frémont, then commander of the Western Department, stationed in Missouri, proclaims the slaves in this state "forever free." Lincoln promptly rescinds Frémont's proclamation.

1862

■ **July 17**
Congress approves second Confiscation Act, declaring slaves taking refuge behind Union lines to be freed.

■ **September 17**
Union victory at Antietam.

■ **September 22**
Lincoln issues Emancipation Proclamation, to take effect in 100 days.

1863

■ **January 1**
Emancipation Proclamation takes effect.

■ **July 1–3**
Battle of Gettysburg; Robert E. Lee's invasion of the North fails.

House of Representatives and made a notable speech opposing the Mexican War; the speech proved unpopular, however, and he did not run for reelection. Indeed, Lincoln's political career then seemed over not only because of his own politics but also because he had linked his future with that of the Whig Party, which steadily lost ground to the Democrats in the 1850s.

Lincoln's political prospects actually rose in 1854 when a new party, the Republicans, took control of the Illinois legislature. Lincoln was the Republican candidate for senator in the famous 1858 election, when he debated Stephen Douglas, the incumbent Democratic senator and a politician with a national profile and the ambition to be president. Although Lincoln's outstanding performance in the debates drew national attention, his party lost the statewide election, and Douglas retained his seat as senator.

During those debates, Lincoln enunciated his position on the sensitive issue of slavery. Douglas attempted to portray Lincoln as supporting equality for blacks and whites, knowing full well that the electorate would reject such a position. Douglas himself advocated "popular sovereignty"—that is, allowing each state to vote on whether to accept or reject slavery. Lincoln objected, making no attempt to hide his rejection of slavery but promising not to oppose the institution where it already existed. Lincoln did emphasize that he opposed the "slave power"—that is, those states intent on spreading slavery to the territories in the West—as he wanted to contain the peculiar institution within its current southern borders.

Even though Lincoln's position on slavery was not radical, the southern states made clear that they would not remain in the Union should he be elected president. This threat of secession notwithstanding, Lincoln was genuinely surprised when the South made good on its warning; his objective then was to prosecute a war that would preserve the Union. In fact, Lincoln wished to prioritize the Union even if that meant retaining slavery in the South, although he also intended to consider abolition or partial emancipation if those actions would have the effect of reuniting the country. Lincoln's role as a symbol of northern dominance that secessionists could not abide culminated in his assassination by the southern sympathizer John Wilkes Booth.

Explanation and Analysis of the Document

In the summer of 1862, Lincoln concluded that freeing the slaves was essential if the Union was to emerge victorious from the war. Up until then, Lincoln had opposed the national government's interference with the present institution of slavery. He had only reluctantly signed into law the two Confiscation Acts. He was concerned about the seizure of property without due legal process, but he decided that the acts were temporary measures taken in time of war, and the Supreme Court declared the acts constitutional.

Radical Republicans like William Graham Sumner had been urging the president to free the slaves—an act he could then take because the Union was at war with the

Confederacy. In addition to Frémont's proclamation freeing the slaves, General David Hunter, in command of the Military Department of the South, proclaimed that "slavery and martial law in a free country are altogether incompatible" and declared that slaves in Florida, Georgia, and South Carolina were "forever free" (Donald, p. 363). Lincoln voided both decrees, asserting that only he, as commander in chief, could order such sweeping action; he did also note that he saw no constitutional reason why he could not issue an emancipation proclamation.

As early as July 1862, Lincoln began to draft the wording of just such an emancipation edict. He proceeded cautiously, uncertain as to whether the restrained document he proposed to his cabinet would have the desired effect of bolstering the Union's fortunes in the war. One early draft offered compensation to Confederate states if the they would cease their rebellion. But subsequent drafts deleted such conciliatory language and focused specifically on the fate of slaves in the rebellious states.

The final draft of the Emancipation Proclamation reads like a legal document that Lincoln the lawyer drafted. It is a carefully couched, formal piece of writing devoid of most of the president's gift for somber yet inspiring rhetoric. Because Lincoln was taking a momentous step in American history, he was extraordinarily mindful of setting limits upon what would be denoted by the word *emancipation*, which means, of course, "setting free or the condition of being free." The primary thrust of Lincoln's decree was that he was liberating only those slaves in the areas engaged in rebellion; he was setting them free from their southern masters.

The first paragraph of the document provides the date and the authority under which the proclamation is being made. The formal language harkens back to the earliest proclamations in history—the kind that were announced in the Roman forum, although the phrase "in the year of our Lord" emphasizes that this historic declaration is occurring in the Christian era. The effort to be absolutely precise and measured is one of the hallmarks of this edict.

The next paragraph states the main purpose of the document, which is to announce that on January 1, 1863, all slaves in the rebellious areas "shall be, then, thenceforward, and forever free." The wording is essential, because late in the Civil War certain slave states were considering liberating slaves who would agree to fight for the Confederacy. With Lincoln's proclamation, however, freedom was not contingent; southern slaves needed do nothing in particular in order to gain their freedom. In other words, whatever else might have been stated in the document, it extended an unequivocal grant of freedom to a certain segment of slaves. Moreover, this grant of freedom was not merely a matter of words, as the proclamation specifies that the U.S. government, including its military organizations, would be obligated not only to recognize but also to "maintain" that freedom. Thus, Lincoln set the precedent for the federal government's being responsible for the security of the freed men and women. He also added the proviso that the "military and naval"

Time Line

1865

■ **April 9**
Lee surrenders to Ulysses S. Grant, and the Civil War is ended.

■ **April 14**
John Wilkes Booth shoots Lincoln; the president dies the following day.

■ **December 18**
Thirteenth Amendment abolishes slavery.

authorities would do nothing to "repress" the efforts of former slaves to secure their "actual freedom." Commanders in the battlefield, engaged in occupying enemy territory, would be prohibited from taking any actions that would make it harder for "such persons" to escape bondage. In being used as a term referring to slaves and former slaves, the word "persons" accorded a measure of respect for a group that had been so fully repressed, to the extent that each slave was counted as three-fifths of a person in the U.S. Constitution. Still, Lincoln stopped short of ordering the armed forces to actively secure the freedom of "such persons." In many cases, Union commanders had already deliberately assisted and even proclaimed the liberation of slaves, but the president held back from making such actions an explicit war aim.

In the midst of the war Lincoln could not be sure which states or groups of states might be in rebellion as of January 1, 1863. That is why in the third paragraph he stipulates that the executive (Lincoln himself) will proclaim on a certain date which areas remain in rebellion. Thus, Lincoln left open the possibility that states in rebellion as of September 22, 1862, might return to the Union before January 1, 1863. Provided that a majority of the qualified voters in such states elected representatives to Congress, and that no "strong countervailing testimony" indicated that the states had not fully determined to rejoin the Union, the executive would no longer consider them in rebellion. The implications of this statement are striking: In effect, Lincoln suggested that southern slave states might return to the Union and keep their slaves. The likelihood at that point of a Confederate state returning to the Union was remote, but in the 100 days leading up to January 1, 1863, the fortunes of war might have brought some surprises. Indeed, Lincoln was leaving open a way for the rebellious states to return to the Union without sacrificing what they considered their property—that is, the slaves. Passages like this one constitute one reason why the Emancipation Proclamation disappointed some abolitionists and was attacked by others.

The fourth paragraph, like the first, states Lincoln's formal authority as commander in chief to issue the Emancipation Proclamation. He emphasizes that his declaration is a "fit and necessary war measure" and that it was undertak-

An engraving copied from an 1864 painting, done at the White House, titled "The First Reading of the Emancipation Proclamation before the Cabinet." (Library of Congress)

en only because of the exigencies of an "armed rebellion." Lincoln knew full well that the North would have offered little support for the unequivocal, absolute, and immediate liberation of all slaves, and he did not want his efforts to win the arduous, costly, and tragic war to be conflated with the agitations of abolitionists. An announcement of the complete abolition of slavery everywhere in the North and South alike would have signaled a drastic change in Lincoln's objectives in fighting the war—and might have caused border states with slaves to secede from the Union.

Paragraph 5 names the states in rebellion but also specifies "excepted parts" of those states (like the parishes in Louisiana) that were under Union control. In those parts no longer considered in rebellion, the proclamation would have no effect; they would be left "precisely as if this proclamation were not issued." The sixth paragraph reiterates in legal language that the slaves in the states and parts of states named in the fifth paragraph are now liberated "for the purpose aforesaid" (that is, as a war measure), and the freedom of "said persons" is to be recognized and maintained by military and naval authorities.

Lincoln addresses the former slaves in the seventh paragraph, enjoining them not to take up violence, except for their own protection, and to work "faithfully for reasonable wages." This curious statement was the result of discussions about what would happen to the masses of

people who would suddenly be freed. How would they defend themselves? How would they find employment and be paid for it? Before the Civil War, considerable public argument took place over how slave labor depressed the wages of free men, and Lincoln's statement here seems to allude to that concern. The newly freed slaves, in other words, were to make sure not to be exploited, such as by working for unreasonably low wages offered by employers seeking to take advantage of a cheap—and impoverished—new labor pool.

Lincoln broke new ground in paragraph 8, stipulating that former slaves could become part of the war effort, though only in a supportive capacity at garrisons, in forts, aboard ships, and so on. In other words, conspicuously absent from this declaration is an invitation to former slaves to enlist in the army and navy as combatants. Doubts existed that slaves could make effective frontline soldiers, particularly that they would stand up to enemy fire. Lincoln had also needed to consider the fact that northern troops might object to serving beside former slaves. Regardless of the aims of the war, the idea of equality between whites and African Americans was not one that the majority of whites entertained. Even Lincoln himself, at this point, was not prepared to acknowledge such equality, let alone put it into practice by integrating former slaves into the armed forces. Nevertheless, this paragraph

> *"That on the first day of January, in the year of our Lord one thousand eight hundred and sixty-three, all persons held as slaves within any State or designated part of a State, the people whereof shall then be in rebellion against the United States, shall be then, thenceforward, and forever free."*
>
> (Paragraph 2)

> *"And I hereby enjoin upon the people so declared to be free to abstain from all violence, unless in necessary self-defence; and I recommend to them that, in all cases when allowed, they labor faithfully for reasonable wages."*
>
> (Paragraph 7)

> *"And upon this act, sincerely believed to be an act of justice, warranted by the Constitution, upon military necessity, I invoke the considerate judgment of mankind, and the gracious favor of Almighty God."*
>
> (Paragraph 10)

represents a step forward in Lincoln's thinking, as he envisions an enlarged role for the freed slaves. In fact, they would eventually be recruited to fight on the front lines of the war.

Although Lincoln repeats in paragraph 10 that the proclamation is an act of "military necessity," that phrase is encircled by his assertion that it is an "act of justice" and that he invokes the "considerate judgment of mankind, and the gracious favor of Almighty God." In cloaking the largely political and military action with moral and even religious terms—and however painstakingly he dressed the document up as a legal one forged for limited purposes in a time of war—Lincoln made his proclamation a symbolic statement. Acts of justice, in other words, are far more than matters of "military necessity," and Lincoln is looking not only to the opinions of his fellow Americans but also to the considerate (that is, mindful or thoughtful) judgment of humankind as well as to the blessing of his creator. This note of humility—of subjecting himself to the verdict of history, so to speak, and to God's approval—is Lincoln's way of transforming his deed into an act of universal significance.

Lincoln ends the proclamation by noting that he has had the seal of the United States affixed to the document and by again specifying the date and the fact that it represents the eighty-seventh year of the country's independence. Thusly, Lincoln reaffirms his faith in the Union without explicitly saying so.

Secretary of State William H. Seward, at one time Lincoln's rival for the presidency, witnesses the document. Seward was sympathetic to the abolitionists but became a trusted and shrewd adviser to the president. Although he worried that the proclamation might cause deep divisions in the North and a slave rebellion in the South that would complicate the war effort, he backed Lincoln's strategy, and most of Lincoln's cabinet did so as well. The appearance of Seward's name on the proclamation surely communicated a message to those who wanted the complete abolition of slavery; in witnessing the document, Seward was implying that this measure was as much as could be expected at that point in the war.

Given its limited scope, the Emancipation Proclamation certainly could not have been the last word on the abolition of slavery. Lincoln understood as much, but as a politician and war leader he believed that the document was as bold a declaration as he could then make. He undoubtedly realized that pressures to accomplish more, such as to more fully involve the former slaves in the war—even to grant them citizenship—had to be withstood; further issues would have to be confronted in the near future. Lincoln believed that for the present, a temporizing message was as much as he—and the nation—could countenance. Although critics might have deemed the proclamation indecisive or evasive, Lincoln saw it as a way to come to terms with the current state of public opinion, to gain time, and to advance the state of public consciousness about a controversial issue.

Audience

Although Lincoln's intended audience actually was not blacks or former slaves, he was acutely consciousness of the profound significance of the Emancipation Proclamation for the people who would be freed from bondage. Shortly after signing the document, he gave it to an associate to read to a group of blacks assembled on Pennsylvania Avenue near the White House. As they listened to the words, they shouted, clapped, and sang in a robust demonstration of their approval.

Lincoln's proclamation was aimed primarily at northern soldiers and voters who would see in the edict a strengthening of their moral authority and at the southern nonslave populace as well as governments abroad that might hesitate to declare support for a Confederacy that remained a slave power. After all, the British nation had abolished slavery, and although members of the British government might have held a certain sympathy for the traditional, quasi-aristocratic South, Lincoln's "act of justice" would make it difficult for them to take sides against the Union.

Impact

The first wave of response to the Emancipation Proclamation varied by population but was generally favorable, drawing positive comments from observers such as the prominent abolitionist leader William Lloyd Garrison, the former slave and fellow abolitionist leader Frederick Douglass, and the writer Ralph Waldo Emerson. Lincoln's political party, the Republicans, likewise welcomed the proclamation. Democrats, on the other hand, denounced Lincoln's decree as unconstitutional and later nominated General George McClellan to oppose Lincoln in the 1864 presidential election; McClellan vowed not to fight a war to free slaves. Southerners, meanwhile, charged Lincoln with fomenting a slave revolt. Abroad, the response was mixed, with some British newspapers hailing Lincoln's humanitarian action and others supporting the South and criticizing the proclamation. Regardless of such criticism, the British government delayed consideration of a proposal to recognize the Confederacy, which meant that Lincoln had gained his objective of buying time with the proclamation.

A second wave of response to the document turned quite negative. In November 1862, northern voters returned Democratic majorities in several states that had voted for Lincoln in 1860, although Lincoln's party still held a slim majority in Congress. In the words of the historian Thomas Keneally, Lincoln's critics pointed out that all he had done was "liberate the slaves his armies had not so far encountered. He realized that this could leave the proclamation open to mockery, and some abolitionists at one end of the scale, and many Democratic newspapers and orators at the other, obliged him" (Keneally, p. 127).

While many historians emphasize that northern public opinion was against making the abolition of slavery a war issue, the biographer Richard Carwardine notes that the proclamation had a profound impact on Union soldiers. Many felt their moral conviction strengthened by the decree; they indeed believed that they were fighting for a just cause.

The historian Doris Kearns Goodwin notes that the proclamation "superseded legislation on slavery and property rights that had guided policy in eleven states for nearly three-quarters of a century. Three and a half million blacks who had lived enslaved for generations were promised freedom" (Goodwin, p. 464). Although Lincoln worried over the immediate reactions to the proclamation, he had his eye on posterity, noting that his place in history would likely be due to the Emancipation Proclamation. He considered the decree the crowning achievement of his administration.

Related Documents

"Civil War Harper's Weekly, September 14, 1861: Fremont's Slave Proclamation." Civil War Web site. http://www.sonofthesouth.net/leefoundation/civil-war/1861/september/slave-proclamation.htm. Accessed on January 9, 2008. This issue of *Harper's Weekly* contains text from General Frémont's proclamation of emancipation as well as an interpretation of its purposes and its legality.

"First Inaugural Address." Abraham Lincoln Online Web site. http://showcase.netins.net/web/creative/lincoln/speeches/1inaug.htm. Accessed on January 9, 2008. In his First Inaugural Address, Lincoln promises not to interfere with slavery where it exists.

McRae, Bennie J. "Major Generals John C. Fremont and David Hunter versus President Abraham Lincoln." Lest We Forget Web site. http://www.coax.net/people/lwf/FHL_POL.HTM. Accessed on January 9, 2008. This site presents General David Hunter's declaration of emancipation.

"Second Inaugural Address." The Avalon Project at Yale Law School Web site. http://www.yale.edu/lawweb/avalon/presiden/inaug/lincoln2.htm. Accessed on January 9, 2008. In his Second Inaugural Address, Lincoln explains the causes of the war and the attitude that should be adopted with a war in progress.

"Speech on the Dred Scott Decision, June 26, 1857." Founders' Library Web site. http://www.founding.com/founders_library/page ID.2260/default.asp. Accessed on January 9, 2008. Lincoln delivered this speech in response to a speech about the *Dred Scott* decision and other matters delivered by Stephen Douglas two weeks earlier.

"Transcript of Dred Scott v. Sanford (1857)." National Archives "Our Documents" Web site. http://www.ourdocuments.gov/doc.php?doc=29&page=transcript. Accessed on January 9, 2008. In March 1857, Dred Scott, a slave brought to the North by his master, lost his bid for freedom, as seven out of nine justices on the Supreme Court declared that no slave or descendant of a slave could be a U.S. citizen or ever had been a U.S. citizen; as a noncitizen, the Court stated, Scott had no rights, could not sue in federal court, and must remain a slave.

Bibliography

■ Books

Carwardine, Richard. *Lincoln: A Life of Purpose and Power*. New York: Alfred A. Knopf, 2006.

Donald, David Herbert. *Lincoln*. New York: Simon & Schuster, 1995.

Gienapp, William E. *Abraham Lincoln and Civil War America: A Biography*. New York: Oxford University Press, 2002.

Goodwin, Doris Kearns. *Team of Rivals: The Political Genius of Abraham Lincoln*. New York: Simon & Schuster, 2005.

Guelzo, Allen C. *Abraham Lincoln: Redeemer President*. Grand Rapids, Mich.: W. B. Eerdmans, 1999.

Keneally, Thomas. *Abraham Lincoln*. New York: Lipper/Viking, 2003.

McClure, A. K. *Abraham Lincoln and Men of War-Times: Some Personal Recollections of War and Politics during the Lincoln Administration*. Lincoln: University of Nebraska Press, 1997.

Neely, Mark E., Jr. *The Last Best Hope of Earth: Abraham Lincoln and the Promise of America*. Cambridge, Mass.: Harvard University Press, 1993.

Oates, Stephen B. *With Malice toward None: The Life of Abraham Lincoln*. New York: Harper & Row, 1977.

Paludan, Phillip Shaw. *The Presidency of Abraham Lincoln*. Lawrence: University Press of Kansas, 1994.

Thomas, Benjamin P. *Abraham Lincoln: A Biography*. New York: Knopf, 1952.

■ Web Sites

"Suggested Lincoln Sources." History Now Web site. http://www.historynow.org/12_2005/ask2b.html. Accessed on January 9, 2008.

—By Carl Rollyson

Questions for Further Study

1. While drafting the Emancipation Proclamation, Lincoln replied to an editorial in the *New York Tribune* attacking him for paying too much deference to border states with slaves and arguing that he should act on emancipation. Lincoln responded by noting that his highest priority was to save the Union, not to free the slaves. He went on to say that if he could save the Union by freeing some slaves or by freeing all of them, he would do so. What do Lincoln's sentiments reveal about his state of mind and his political calculations, considering that he was trying to stay true to his principles as well as to take into account Northern attitudes toward blacks?

2. Some critics have described the Emancipation Proclamation as lacking the emotion and vigor of some of Lincoln's other writings and speeches. Allen Guelzo, however, explains why Lincoln did not publish a more comprehensive or inspiring document: A proclamation with broader scope—say, freeing all slaves in the North and South alike—would have been challenged by the Supreme Court, which was still headed by Chief Justice Roger Taney, a former slaveholder. Research Taney's infamous opinion in the case *Dred Scott v. John F. A. Sandford* (1857); then consider the political and moral issues that Lincoln had to confront and why he ultimately decided to offer the proclamation as a war measure.

3. Compare and contrast Lincoln's response to the decision in *Dred Scott v. Sandford* (1857) to his decision to issue the Emancipation Proclamation.

4. Compare and contrast Lincoln's position on slavery in his First and Second Inaugural Addresses.

Glossary

emancipation   the act of freeing, the act of setting free from certain restrictions, or the condition of being free.

proclamation   a formal government announcement.

EMANCIPATION PROCLAMATION

By the President of the United States of America:

A Proclamation.

Whereas, on the twenty-second day of September, in the year of our Lord one thousand eight hundred and sixty-two, a proclamation was issued by the President of the United States, containing, among other things, the following, to wit:

"That on the first day of January, in the year of our Lord one thousand eight hundred and sixty-three, all persons held as slaves within any State or designated part of a State, the people whereof shall then be in rebellion against the United States, shall be then, thenceforward, and forever free; and the Executive Government of the United States, including the military and naval authority thereof, will recognize and maintain the freedom of such persons, and will do no act or acts to repress such persons, or any of them, in any efforts they may make for their actual freedom.

"That the Executive will, on the first day of January aforesaid, by proclamation, designate the States and parts of States, if any, in which the people thereof, respectively, shall then be in rebellion against the United States; and the fact that any State, or the people thereof, shall on that day be, in good faith, represented in the Congress of the United States by members chosen thereto at elections wherein a majority of the qualified voters of such State shall have participated, shall, in the absence of strong countervailing testimony, be deemed conclusive evidence that such State, and the people thereof, are not then in rebellion against the United States."

Now, therefore I, Abraham Lincoln, President of the United States, by virtue of the power in me vested as Commander-in-Chief, of the Army and Navy of the United States in time of actual armed rebellion against the authority and government of the United States, and as a fit and necessary war measure for suppressing said rebellion, do, on this first day of January, in the year of our Lord one thousand eight

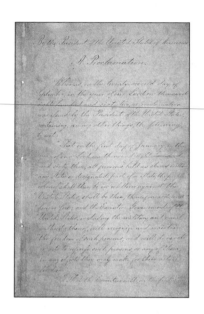

hundred and sixty-three, and in accordance with my purpose so to do publicly proclaimed for the full period of one hundred days, from the day first above mentioned, order and designate as the States and parts of States wherein the people thereof respectively, are this day in rebellion against the United States, the following, to wit:

Arkansas, Texas, Louisiana, (except the Parishes of St. Bernard, Plaquemines, Jefferson, St. John, St. Charles, St. James Ascension, Assumption, Terrebonne, Lafourche, St. Mary, St. Martin, and Orleans, including the City of New Orleans) Mississippi, Alabama, Florida, Georgia, South Carolina, North Carolina, and Virginia, (except the forty-eight counties designated as West Virginia, and also the counties of Berkley, Accomac, Northampton, Elizabeth City, York, Princess Ann, and Norfolk, including the cities of Norfolk and Portsmouth), and which excepted parts, are for the present, left precisely as if this proclamation were not issued.

And by virtue of the power, and for the purpose aforesaid, I do order and declare that all persons held as slaves within said designated States, and parts of States, are, and henceforward shall be free; and that the Executive government of the United States, including the military and naval authorities thereof, will recognize and maintain the freedom of said persons.

And I hereby enjoin upon the people so declared to be free to abstain from all violence, unless in necessary self-defence; and I recommend to them that, in all cases when allowed, they labor faithfully for reasonable wages.

And I further declare and make known, that such persons of suitable condition, will be received into the armed service of the United States to garrison forts, positions, stations, and other places, and to man vessels of all sorts in said service.

And upon this act, sincerely believed to be an act of justice, warranted by the Constitution, upon military necessity, I invoke the considerate judgment of mankind, and the gracious favor of Almighty God.

In witness whereof, I have hereunto set my hand and caused the seal of the United States to be affixed.

Done at the City of Washington, this first day of January, in the year of our Lord one thousand eight hundred and sixty three, and of the Independence of the United States of America the eighty-seventh.

By the President: ABRAHAM LINCOLN

WILLIAM H. SEWARD, Secretary of State.

GENERAL ORDERS, ⎰   WAR DEPARTMENT,
                                  ADJUTANT GENERAL'S OFFICE,
      No. 143. ⎱   *Washington, May* 22, 1863.

I..A Bureau is established in the Adjutant General's Office for the record of all matters relating to the organization of Colored Troops. An officer will be assigned to the charge of the Bureau, with such number of clerks as may be designated by the Adjutant General.

II..Three or more field officers will be detailed as Inspectors to supervise the organization of colored troops at such points as may be indicated by the War Department in the Northern and Western States.

III..Boards will be convened at such posts as may be decided upon by the War Department to examine applicants for commissions to command colored troops, who, on application to the Adjutant General, may receive authority to present themselves to the board for examination.

IV..No persons shall be allowed to recruit for colored troops except specially authorized by the War Department; and no such authority will be given to persons who have not been examined and passed by a board; nor will such authority be given any one person to raise more than one regiment.

V..The reports of Boards will specify the grade of commission for which each candidate is fit, and authority to recruit will be given in accordance. Commissions will be issued from the Adjutant General's Office when the prescribed number of men is ready for muster into service.

VI..Colored troops may be accepted by companies, to be afterwards consolidated in battalions and regiments by the Adjutant General. The regiments will be numbered *seriatim*, in the order in which they are raised, the numbers to be determined by the Adjutant General. They will be designated: "—— Regiment of U. S. Colored Troops."

VII..Recruiting stations and depôts will be established by the Adjutant General as circumstances shall require, and officers will be detailed to muster and inspect the troops.

War Department General Order 143 (National Archives and Records Administration)

WAR DEPARTMENT GENERAL ORDER 143

"No persons shall be allowed to recruit for colored troops except specially authorized by the War Department."

Overview

The U.S. War Department issued General Order 143 on May 22, 1863, to organize and provide uniform recruitment and governance of black troops. The order established the Bureau of U.S. Colored Troops, and after that date most existing and all newly recruited African American units were incorporated and administered with the bureau's supervision.

One of the biggest controversies during the American Civil War revolved around the role that African Americans should play in the Union war effort. From the onset of the conflict African Americans such as Frederick Douglass and other abolitionists urged President Abraham Lincoln to make ending slavery a war aim. African Americans also demanded a more active role in fighting the war. President Lincoln was hesitant to include black troops for several reasons. Racial prejudice was deep-seated in the northern states, and many, including Lincoln, feared that white soldiers would not fight side by side with African Americans. Many northerners held that African Americans were incapable of making good soldiers because they believed that blacks were too servile or cowardly.

Even before the Emancipation Proclamation brought slavery to the forefront of the conflict, blacks strove for inclusion in the ranks of the U.S. military despite the attitudes of northern whites. Both free blacks in the northern states and newly freed slaves in the southern areas under Union control were eager to contribute. Some Union generals began raising black units in southern occupied areas in 1862, but recruitment began in earnest after formal announcement of the Emancipation Proclamation on January 1, 1863. The first black units were organized as volunteer units of the states. General Order 143 formalized these efforts.'

Context

In April 1861, a mere few days after the Civil War had begun when the Confederates fired on Fort Sumter in the harbor at Charleston, South Carolina, a group of African Americans in Cleveland, Ohio, gathered to pledge their support for the Union cause. As they put it, "As colored citizens of Cleveland, desiring to prove our loyalty to the Government, [we] feel that we should adopt measures to put ourselves in a position to defend the government of which we claim protection." They continued: "That to-day, as in the times of '76, and the days of 1812, we are ready to go forth and do battle in the common cause of the country" (qtd. in McPherson, p. 20). Although African Americans had taken up arms during the American Revolution and during the War of 1812, federal law had prohibited the enlistment of blacks in state militias and the U.S. Army since 1792. At the beginning of the Civil War there were no black soldiers in the regular army, and most white northerners hoped to keep it that way.

African Americans recognized at the war's outset that this conflict had the potential to rid the United States of slavery, and they were eager to push for their inclusion in the fight. Abraham Lincoln's administration and the mainstream press were careful to declare that the war was about restoring the Union and emphatically denied that the issue of slavery had any role in the conflict. Northern public opinion, at least early in the war, was not prepared to consider challenging the racial balance that placed African Americans at the bottom of the social ladder. Prominent blacks and abolitionists, however, began pushing for the enlistment of black troops almost immediately, and many realized the implications of those fears. Perhaps Frederick Douglass most clearly outlined the fear of white northerners with regard to black military participation. In August 1861 he editorialized in his newspaper, *Douglass' Monthly*, "Once let the black man get upon his person the brass letters, U.S., let him get an eagle on his button, and a musket on his shoulder and bullets in his pocket, and there is no power on earth which can deny that he has earned the right to citizenship in the United States" (qtd. in McPherson, p. 163). Lincoln recognized that military service for blacks would indeed place African Americans in a position to demand the rights of citizenship, including suffrage. He also feared that the presence of black soldiers would discourage white enlistments. Another concern was maintaining the loyalty of the bor-

Time Line

1861

■ April 12
The Civil War begins following the firing on Fort Sumter at Charleston, South Carolina.

■ May
General Benjamin F. Butler declares escaped slaves to be the property of the Union and puts them to work behind Union lines.

■ August 6
Congress passes the first Confiscation Act authorizing the seizure of property, including slaves, used to aid the Confederate war effort.

1862

■ July 17
Congress passes the second Confiscation Act, authorizing federal courts to free the slaves of those fighting against the Union, and the Militia Act, authorizing President Abraham Lincoln to enroll African American troops in the Union army.

■ September 27
The First Louisiana Native Guards becomes the first black unit to be recognized by the War Department.

1863

■ January 1
The Emancipation Proclamation declares an end to slavery in the Confederate states under rebellion.

■ January
The First Kansas Volunteer Colored Infantry is mustered into service as the first regiment of African American troops raised in a northern state.

■ January
Governor John A. Andrew of Massachusetts is granted permission to raise an African American regiment, the Fifty-fourth Massachusetts Infantry.

■ May 22
The War Department issues General Order 143, creating the U.S. Colored Troops.

1864

■ June
Congress grants equal pay to soldiers in the U.S. Colored Troops.

---

der states, including Maryland, Kentucky, Missouri, and Delaware. Although these were slave states, they had not joined the Confederacy, and the president wanted them to remain part of the Union.

Despite these concerns, pressures to allow black military enlistment mounted from several directions. From early in the war the Confederate army employed free black and slave labor to perform much of the manual work required for the military. Eventually, the Confederate army requisitioned slaves from their masters in much the same way it appropriated food or other necessary supplies. Throughout the war African Americans not only raised much of the food that fed the Confederate troops but also built many of the fortifications and entrenchments that protected troops in the field. The Union general Benjamin F. Butler, in command of troops at Fortress Monroe in Virginia, was one of the earliest advocates of using African Americans in the Union cause. In May 1861 he declared escaped slaves who had labored on behalf of the Confederate war effort as "contraband of war" and refused to return them to their masters. Reasoning that returning the slaves to their masters would benefit the enemy, Butler put them to work behind Union lines. Although the policy was controversial, Lincoln allowed Butler's action to stand. Before the summer of 1861 ended, Congress would pass legislation to more clearly define how the Union army should treat the large numbers of slaves who sought freedom behind Union lines.

Realizing the importance of slave labor to the Confederacy, in August 1861 Congress passed the first Confiscation Act, permitting the seizure of any property, including slaves, used to aid the Confederate war effort. This provided legitimacy to Butler's ad hoc contraband policy, and over the duration of the war some 200,000 "contrabands" worked for the Union army. Although the act sidestepped the issue of emancipation, it did introduce the concept of manumission into federal policy. The same month, General John C. Frémont was bolder in declaring free the slaves of Confederates in Missouri. As commander in charge of the Department of the West in St. Louis, Frémont's emancipation declaration was a part of a larger plan to bring Missouri under closer control of the Union.

Alarmed that the action might lead Missouri and the other border states to join the Confederacy, Lincoln quickly rescinded the order and eventually removed Frémont from his post. Lincoln's action angered abolitionists such as the radical Parker Pillsbury, who condemned the president's act as "cowardly submission to southern and border slave state dictation" (qtd. in Smith, p. 12). Some prominent northern politicians, including Massachusetts governor John A. Andrew and Kansas senator James H. Lane, urged Lincoln to arm African Americans. Along with the generals John W. Phelps and David Hunter, they argued that blacks were eager to fight for the nation. Although Lincoln was not prepared to support a radical emancipation policy in 1861, by midyear 1862, at the urging of these men, he was beginning to see the value of including African Americans in the military. It was also becoming clear that emancipation would necessarily result if African Americans were allowed to enlist in the U.S. Army.

In July 1862 Congress passed two bills that tied emancipation to military enlistment. The second Confiscation Act authorized northern courts to free the slaves of those "engaged in rebellion" and authorized Lincoln to employ "as many persons of African descent as he may deem necessary and proper for the suppression of this rebellion, and for this purpose he may organize and use them in such manner as he may judge best for the public welfare" (qtd. in Smith, p. 14). The Militia Act granted freedom to slaves who worked for the U.S. Army and gave Lincoln the authority to "to receive into the service of the United States, for the purpose of constructing intrenchments, or performing camp service, or an other labor, or any military or naval service which they may be found competent, persons of African descent" (qtd. in Smith, p. 14). While Lincoln and many northerners remained skeptical about arming African Americans, Congress had clearly paved the way for the enlistment of blacks with these two acts. During the summer of 1862 Lincoln also began secretly drafting a proclamation that would emancipate slaves in the Confederate states that had not fallen under Union control.

The public would not learn of the Emancipation Proclamation until September 1862, when it was announced following the Union victory at the battle of Antietam. Not knowing Lincoln's plan, some northerners attacked his failure to fully execute the emancipation clause of the second Confiscation Act. Douglass proclaimed in an editorial, "The signs of the times indicate that the people will have to take this war into their own hands and dispense with the services of all who by their incompetency give aid and comfort to the destroyers of the country" (qtd. in McPherson, p. 47). Horace Greeley, editor of the *New York Tribune*, complained that Lincoln was too worried about the border states and urged him to enforce the new acts. In the summer and fall of 1862, as Lincoln cautiously danced around the full implementation of the second Confiscation Act, more radical military leaders in the field took it to heart.

The first African Americans to take up arms for the Union cause during the Civil War did so in the South. Empowered by the second Confiscation Act and the Militia Act, commanders in the field were willing and sometimes eager to begin enlisting black units. One of the first to do so was General Benjamin F. Butler, who by mid-1862 commanded occupation forces in Louisiana. As his earlier contraband policy might suggest, Butler had no problem employing African Americans to fill a shortfall in the number of Union soldiers available to defend New Orleans. On September 27 he mustered into service the First Louisiana Native Guards. Although blacks had been placed in defensive roles in several small units, this was the first sanctioned regiment of African American soldiers in the Union army. Pleased with the result, Butler organized two additional regiments, the Second and Third Louisiana Native Guards by November 1862. Other early African American regiments were raised in South Carolina, including the First South Carolina Volunteer Infantry (African Descent), commanded by the abolitionist

www.milestonedocuments.com

Time Line

1865
■ The Civil War ends in April, and in December the Thirteenth Amendment to the Constitution abolishes slavery in the United States.

1866
■ **July 28**
Congress authorizes two permanent African American regiments, the Ninth and Tenth United States Cavalry, who would gain renown as the Buffalo Soldiers.

Thomas Wentworth Higginson. In Kansas, before he had official authorization, Senator James H. Lane began recruiting for the First Kansas Volunteer Colored Infantry, which became the first black regiment recruited in the northern states. All African American units were headed by white commissioned officers, although eventually black soldiers could aspire to the rank of corporal or sergeant, and more than a hundred gained a commissioned rank. By the end of 1862 between three thousand and four thousand black men were serving in five regiments. When first recognized by the War Department, the soldiers in black regiments received $10 monthly pay, $3 less than their white counterparts.

Following the issuance of the final Emancipation Proclamation on January 1, 1863, black enlistment became a major priority and a central part of Lincoln's emancipation program. That month Massachusetts governor John A. Andrew was authorized to raise the Fifty-fourth Massachusetts Infantry, and prominent New England abolitionists rushed to help recruit. Secretary of War Edwin Stanton also authorized Rhode Island and Connecticut to begin recruiting black regiments. Black abolitionists, including Frederick Douglass, Martin R. Delany, Henry McNeal Turner, and John Mercer Langston, recruited broadly across the northern and midwestern states. In March 1863 the army's adjutant general, Lorenzo Thomas, was ordered to the South to head an enlistment drive.

Thomas's southern travels took him to the Mississippi Valley, where he was charged not only with recruiting African American troops but also with finding qualified officers to lead the newly forming regiments. The enlistment drive was successful, as Thomas found many freedmen eager to serve. Thomas's 1863 recruiting resulted in raising twenty black regiments but also pointed to the need for a more ordered system of recruitment and organization to govern the new troops. Issued on May 22, 1863, General Order 143 provided the mechanism for organizing all black regiments under the newly created Bureau of Colored Troops.

Assistant Adjutant General Charles W. Foster was appointed to lead the bureau, and he primarily supervised black enlistment and recruitment in both the North and South for the remainder of the war. Following the creation of the United States Colored Troops, African American reg-

Members of the 107th U.S. Colored Infantry, shown with musical instruments (Library of Congress)

iments with state names, with only a few exceptions, were renamed and designated units of the U.S. Colored Troops. Exceptions were made for a few regiments from Connecticut, Massachusetts, and Louisiana. The significance of renaming the First Kansas Colored Volunteer Infantry as the Seventy-ninth U.S. Colored Infantry or the First Louisiana Native Guards the Seventy-third U.S. Colored Infantry was that instead of being mustered into a state unit, the black soldiers became agents of the U.S. Army. In June 1864, a year after the creation of the Bureau of Colored Troops, Congress granted equal pay to African American soldiers. The Bureau of Colored Troops offered a professional, organized, and well-ordered chain of command and bureaucratic structure that enabled African Americans to gain a permanent place in the military and to stand and fight for the freedom guaranteed by the U.S. government.

About the Author

General Order 143 was a directive issued by the War Department and as such does not have an author of record. However, the army's adjutant general, Lorenzo Thomas, most likely had a hand in authoring the order. In March 1863, Secretary of War Edwin Stanton ordered Thomas to

the Mississippi Valley to recruit and muster regiments of African American troops.

Lorenzo Thomas was born in New Castle, Delaware, in 1804. An 1823 graduate of the U.S. Military Academy at West Point, Thomas was a career army officer who was appointed adjutant general of the army in the early months of the Civil War. In this post he was the person primarily responsible for recruitment and staffing of the army. It was under his watch that large-scale recruitment of black troops began. He was not known as an abolitionist or Radical Republican, who were critical of Lincoln's slowness in freeing the slaves and supporting their legal equality. Instead, as a moderate he was able to convince many of the necessity of enlisting African Americans in the army. Although Thomas did not favor black officers for the new regiments, he was a firm believer that the African American troops should not be relegated to general labor but rather should be given combat assignments. It was during his recruitment drive through Kentucky, Arkansas, Louisiana, Mississippi, and Tennessee in 1863 that Thomas came to realize that a new organizational system was required, resulting in General Order 143 creating the U.S. Colored Troops.

Following the Civil War, Thomas remained in the adjutant general's post, although his relationship with Secretary

> "*A Bureau is established in the Adjutant General's Office for the record of all matters relating to the organization of Colored Troops.*"
>
> (Section I)

> "*No persons shall be allowed to recruit for colored troops except specially authorized by the War Department.*"
>
> (Section IV)

> "*The non-commissioned officers of colored troops may be selected and appointed from the best men of their number in the usual mode of appointing non-commissioned officers.*"
>
> (Section VIII)

Stanton was somewhat tenuous and the secretary reportedly doubted Thomas's loyalty. Perhaps Stanton's concern had some foundation. In 1868, President Andrew Johnson briefly appointed Thomas interim secretary of war to replace Stanton. It was this action that led Congress to declare Johnson in violation of the Tenure of Office Act, resulting in his impeachment. During the impeachment proceedings both Thomas and Stanton claimed to be the secretary of war. After successfully avoiding conviction, Johnson failed to appoint Thomas permanently to the post. Thomas retired from the army with the rank of major general in February 1869. He died in 1875.

Explanation and Analysis of the Document

General Order 143 is divided into nine sections. Section I establishes a separate bureau within the War Department to administer and organize African American regiments, officially called Colored Troops. The order provides for an administrative officer and a number of supporting clerks to be appointed by the adjutant general.

Section II authorizes the appointment of three or more inspectors to oversee the organization of regiments within the U.S. Colored Troops. These inspectors could be sent anywhere within the northern states under the authorization of the War Department.

Section III attends to the recruitment of white commissioned officers to command units within the Colored Troops. The order authorizes an examining board or boards to evaluate and select among applicants for commissioned posts in command of the newly raised regiments.

Section IV restricts recruitment agents to those individuals authorized by the War Department. Recruiters were required to pass the evaluation of a specially created board, and each was permitted to raise only one regiment of Colored Troops.

Sections V and VI link an officer's rank to the number of troops he is authorized to recruit. Once the proscribed number of men was recruited, the adjutant general would grant the appropriate officer's commission. Recruitment could be into companies of about one hundred soldiers, which would then be incorporated into regiments that included up to ten companies. Instead of regiments bearing a number tied to their locus of recruitment, such as the Fifty-fourth Massachusetts, regiments of the U.S. Colored Troops would be numbered separately in the order in which they were raised. The first unit organized under General Order 143 would be the First U.S. Colored Troops, the next the Second U.S. Colored Troops, and so forth.

Section VII authorizes the establishment of recruiting depots and stations and provides for officers to oversee the inspection and mustering of the Colored Troops regiments.

Section VIII concerns the recruitment of noncommissioned officers, generally sergeants and corporals, from within the ranks of the African American members of each regiment. While the commanding commissioned officers of the Colored Troops were drawn from the white army population, African Americans could advance to noncommissioned officer status. An important distinction was made on the basis of responsibility. Commissioned officers enjoyed the responsibility of ultimate command of the regiment, but noncommissioned officers exercised more limited control over men within the unit. Noncommissioned officers were selected based on merit, and those that showed an aptitude for leading could be promoted, as from corporal to sergeant. Each company generally included four sergeants and four corporals, so opportunities to advance to officer status were not common.

The final section of the order establishes procedures for directing correspondence and inquiries regarding the Colored Troops. It directs that applications for officer appointments be made directly to the chief of the Bureau of Colored Troops.

Audience

General Order 143 is a military directive whose immediate audience was the Union army. It was especially aimed at those responsible for the administration and recruitment of African American troops. Those recruiting black enlistments outside the auspices of the army were another potential audience of the order. Ultimately, General Order 143 was aimed at the nation, as it laid the foundation for organizing and administering the participation of African American soldiers in the Union war effort. Beyond establishing procedures and an administrative structure, the order indicated clearly that African Americans would have a stake in American society.

Impact

By the end of the Civil War in April 1865, the Union army had recruited 178,975 African American soldiers into its ranks. Black troops made up 133 infantry regiments, four independent companies, seven cavalry regiments, twelve heavy artillery regiments, and ten companies of light infantry. Most of the black Union soldiers were former slaves, although a significant number were drawn from the ranks of the northern free black community. African Americans made up nearly 10 percent of all Union troops serving in the war.

The creation of the Bureau of Colored Troops had implications beyond the Civil War. In establishing a military bureau and administrative structure, General Order 143 set the precedent for permanent inclusion of African Americans in the military. By October 1865, the regiments of the U.S. Colored Troops began demobilizing, but this was not the end to black military participation. On July 28, 1866, Congress authorized the creation of two African American regiments for the regular army. The Ninth and Tenth U.S. Cavalry later gained recognition as the Buffalo Soldiers as they performed important service in the American West in the late 1800s. Although blacks would never again be denied entrance to the military, the U.S. Colored Troops also established the segregation of African Americans into separate units led by white commissioned officers. The U.S. military remained segregated through World War II. Racial separation in the military ended in July 1948 when President Harry S Truman signed Executive Order 9981 ending segregation in the armed forces.

Related Documents

Douglass, Frederick. "The Proclamation and a Negro Army." In *The Frederick Douglass Papers*, Series 1: *Speeches, Debates, and Interviews*, Vol. 3: *1855–63*, ed. John Blassingame and John R. McKivigan. New Haven, Conn.: Yale University Press, 1985. In this speech delivered in New York City on February 6, 1863, Douglass argued for the enlistment of black troops under identical terms with whites.

"The Emancipation Proclamation." National Archives and Records Administration "Featured Documents" Web site. http://www.archives.gov/exhibits/featured_documents/emancipation_proclamation/. Accessed on December 15, 2007. The Emancipation Proclamation granted freedom to slaves in areas of the Confederate states in rebellion against the Union.

Higginson, Thomas Wentworth. *Army Life in a Black Regiment*. *1870*. Reprint. New York: Collier Books, 1962. Higginson's memoir details the activities of the First South Carolina Volunteer Infantry, one of the first black regiments to be mustered in 1862.

Bibliography

■ Books
Fisher, Ernest F. *Guardians of the Republic: A History of the Noncommissioned Officer Corps of the U.S. Army*. New York: Stackpole Books, 2001.

McPherson, James M. *The Negro's Civil War: How American Blacks Felt and Acted during the War for the Union*. 1965. Reprint. New York: Ballantine Books, 1991.

Smith, John David, ed., *Black Soldiers in Blue: African American Troops in the Civil War Era*. Chapel Hill: University of North Carolina Press, 2002.

Trudeau, Noah Andre. *Like Men of War: Black Troops in the Civil War, 1862–1865*. Boston: Little, Brown, 1998.

■ Web Sites
"The Fight for Equal Rights: Black Soldiers in the Civil War." National Archives "Teaching with Documents" Web site.
   http://www.archives.gov/education/lessons/blacks-civil-war/. Accessed on December 9, 2007.

—By L. Diane Barnes

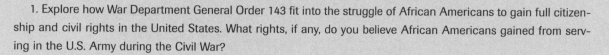

Questions for Further Study

1. Explore how War Department General Order 143 fit into the struggle of African Americans to gain full citizenship and civil rights in the United States. What rights, if any, do you believe African Americans gained from serving in the U.S. Army during the Civil War?

2. General Order 143 was issued several months after the Emancipation Proclamation. Explore the connection between these two documents. How did freeing slaves in the Confederate areas under rebellion tie to the recruitment of African American troops for the Union army?

3. African American troops complained about getting less pay than white soldiers until Congress granted pay equity in June 1864. What arguments were used to justify paying African Americans less? What arguments were used to support equal pay? Can you think of examples in today's society when certain groups or classes of people receive unequal compensation for equal work?

Glossary

adjutant general	the chief administrative officer of a military unit or army
regiment	unit of military organization including up to ten companies

WAR DEPARTMENT GENERAL ORDER 143

I—A Bureau is established in the Adjutant General's Office for the record of all matters relating to the organization of Colored Troops. An officer will be assigned to the charge of the Bureau, with such number of clerks as may be designated by the Adjutant General.

II—Three or more field officers will be detailed as Inspectors to supervise the organization of colored troops at such points as may be indicated by the War Department in the Northern and Western States.

III—Boards will be convened at such posts as may be decided upon by the War Department to examine applicants for commissions to command colored troops, who, on Application to the Adjutant General, may receive authority to present themselves to the board for examination.

IV—No persons shall be allowed to recruit for colored troops except specially authorized by the War Department; and no such authority will be given to persons who have not been examined and passed by a board; nor will such authority be given any one person to raise more than one regiment.

V—The reports of Boards will specify the grade of commission for which each candidate is fit, and authority to recruit will be given in accordance. Commissions will be issued from the Adjutant General's Office when the prescribed number of men is ready for muster into service.

VI—Colored troops maybe accepted by companies, to be afterward consolidated in battalions and regiments by the Adjutant General. The regiments will be numbered seriatim, in the order in which they are raised, the numbers to be determined by the Adjutant General. They will be designated: "—Regiment of U. S. Colored Troops."

VII—Recruiting stations and depots will be established by the Adjutant General as circumstances shall require, and officers will be detailed to muster and inspect the troops.

VIII—The non-commissioned officers of colored troops may be selected and appointed from the best men of their number in the usual mode of appointing non-commissioned officers. Meritorious commissioned officers will be entitled to promotion to higher rank if they prove themselves equal to it.

IX—All personal applications for appointments in colored regiments, or for information concerning them, must be made to the Chief of the Bureau; all written communications should be addressed to the Chief of the Bureau, to the care of the Adjutant General,

BY ORDER OF THE SECRETARY OF WAR:

E. D. TOWNSEND, Assistant Adjutant General.

GETTYSBURG ADDRESS

"This nation, under God, shall have a new birth of freedom — and ... government of the people, by the people, for the people, shall not perish from the earth."

Overview

On November 19, 1863, President Abraham Lincoln gave a short speech (lasting no more than two minutes) at the commemoration of a cemetery in Gettysburg, Pennsylvania, where more than fifty-one thousand Union and Confederate soldiers had died in a battle lasting three days, from July 1 to 3, 1863. This historic battle ended General Robert E. Lee's invasion of the North, but Lincoln chose to focus not on the Union victory but on the principles he believed the war had been fought over: liberty and equality as they had been defined in the Declaration of Independence. In a speech that is now considered the most eloquent ever delivered by an American president, he saw this battle and the war itself as leading toward a "new birth of freedom."

Context

Gettysburg was the most famous battle of the Civil War. It marked a turning point in the fortunes of the two sides. Until Gettysburg, Robert E. Lee seemed virtually invincible. He had defeated several Union generals in major battles on the Confederacy's home ground, driven Union forces back toward the U.S. capital, and now he was prepared to take the war to the North, hoping that with a decisive victory he could hasten the end of the war and secure the Confederacy's independence.

Gettysburg was of serious concern to President Lincoln because he had yet to find a commander who could aggressively pursue Lee and put him on the defensive. The war had gone so badly for the North at times that Lincoln confronted calls to sue for peace and to allow the southern states to secede. He also confronted a divided cabinet in which some members were severely critical of Lincoln's prosecution of the war. At one point, in an effort spearheaded by the cabinet member Salmon P. Chase, Lincoln had to meet with a delegation of Republican senators insisting on changes in his cabinet. Although Lincoln remained steadfast, maneuvering Chase into a resignation, Lincoln's reelection in 1864 was in doubt; significant num-

bers of voters seemed prepared to turn to a candidate who could offer a speedy resolution of the war.

Even after the battle of Gettysburg, Lincoln faced formidable obstacles. General George Meade had diminished but by no means destroyed Lee's aura of indomitability. Meade had failed to pursue Lee, and the Union still did not have a commander in the field who could match Lee's boldness and tactical genius, although General Ulysses S. Grant's victory at Vicksburg suggested that he might be the leader to galvanize Union forces east of the Mississippi River. Lincoln's war aims to preserve and protect the Union had become endangered by the Union army's failure to take the initiative. Calls by abolitionists to immediately free the slaves threatened to alienate Union supporters in border states that had slave populations. Moreover, large numbers of men in the North resisted military service, resulting public disaffection that erupted, for example, in the New York City draft riots in July 1863.

At Gettysburg cemetery, where thousands of hastily buried men were being reinterred in proper graves, Lincoln's task was no less than to remind the nation that its very existence was at stake, a cause for which hundreds of thousands of men were fighting and dying. Although his surprisingly brief speech seemed to have no immediate impact, and even Lincoln himself doubted the effectiveness of his address, the power of his concise and graceful prose gradually marked a turning point in public consciousness that confirmed Lincoln's faith in the prospects of democracy. He redefined the war, making it an inspiring quest for liberty and equality.

About the Author

Abraham Lincoln, born on February 12, 1809, in a one-room log cabin in southeastern Kentucky, grew up in a frontier environment. He had little formal education but was a prodigious reader, favoring the Bible, Shakespeare, and biographies. As a young man he studied law. At age twenty-three, he ran unsuccessfully for a seat in the General Assembly of Illinois, to which state his family had moved when he was nine. He served briefly in the Black Hawk War (1832) before being elected to the state legisla-

1861

■ **March 4**
Lincoln is inaugurated as president.

■ **April 14**
Fort Sumter, South Carolina, surrenders to Confederate forces, which begins the Civil War.

■ **July 21**
The Union loses a major battle at Bull Run.

1862

■ **November**
The Republican Party, Lincoln's party, loses congressional seats to Democrats.

■ **December 13**
The battle of Fredericksburg is a major Union defeat.

■ **December 16–20**
Lincoln is pressured to shake up his cabinet but prevails and accepts Salmon Chase's resignation.

1863

■ **January 1**
The Emancipation Proclamation takes effect.

■ **July 1–3**
The Battle of Gettysburg takes place; Lee's invasion of the North fails.

■ **July 4**
Grant captures Vicksburg.

■ **July 13–16**
Draft riots occur in New York City.

■ **November 19**
Lincoln delivers the Gettysburg Address.

1864

■ **March 9**
Lincoln names Grant a commanding general.

■ **November 8**
Lincoln is reelected.

1865

■ **April 9**
Lee surrenders to Grant, and the Civil War ends.

■ **April 14**
John Wilkes Booth shoots Lincoln; the president dies the following day.

---

ture in 1834. Lincoln was admitted to the bar in 1837 and proved to be a successful attorney, admired for his ability to argue on his feet in court cases.

In 1842 Lincoln married Mary Todd, the daughter of a prominent southern family. The couple had four children, but only one, Robert, survived into adulthood. Mary, quarrelsome but proud of her husband, supported Lincoln's political ambitions. He was elected for one term in the U.S. House of Representatives and made a notable speech opposing the Mexican War; the speech proved unpopular, however, and he did not run for reelection. Indeed, Lincoln's political career then seemed over not only because of his own politics but also because he had linked his future with that of the Whig Party, which steadily lost ground to the Democrats in the 1850s.

Lincoln's political prospects actually rose in 1854 when a new party, the Republicans, took control of the Illinois legislature. Lincoln was the Republican candidate for senator in the famous 1858 election, when he debated Stephen Douglas, the incumbent Democratic senator and a politician with a national profile and the ambition to be president. Although Lincoln's outstanding performance in the debates drew national attention, his party lost the statewide election, and Douglas retained his seat as senator.

Even though Lincoln's position on slavery was not radical, the southern states made clear that they would not remain in the Union should he be elected president. This threat of secession notwithstanding, Lincoln was genuinely surprised when the South made good on its warning; his objective then was to prosecute a war that would preserve the Union.

Lincoln had little military experience, however, and initially he had little understanding of how to conduct the war. He put the Union forces in the charge of General George McClellan, an able administrator beloved by his men but also a cautious field commander who consistently overestimated the Confederate army's strengths and avoided direct engagements with Lee's forces, thus delaying a vital showdown with the rebels. Contemptuous of Lincoln, who borrowed from the Library of Congress books about military strategy, McClellan did little to advance the Union cause, except for constantly parading and training his troops. Even worse, he was touted as a potential presidential candidate, putting Lincoln in the position of gingerly dealing with a man who considered himself less of a subordinate and more of a rival for the power Lincoln held. But McClellan's replacements (the generals Henry Halleck, Ambrose Burnside, and Joseph Hooker) could not do much to weaken Lee because they did not have his genius for strategy or his bold decisiveness. Not until Meade's holding action at Gettysburg and Grant's victories in the South and West did Union prospects brighten and Lincoln's leadership surmount the early disasters of his administration.

Lincoln's steadfast reliance on Grant, even in the face of mounting Union casualties, brought the war to a definitive end, enabling Lincoln to focus on plans for a generous reconstruction of the South, plans that, unfortunately, were curtailed in the aftermath of the president's assassination.

Lincoln's brief speech at Gettysburg was an unusual event during the Civil War. He had rarely traveled far from Washington, D.C. Moreover, the main speaker of the day was Edward Everett, a renowned orator, a classical scholar, former president of Harvard University, and governor of Massachusetts. The organizers of the event asked the president to make "a few appropriate remarks" (Donald, p. 460). Lincoln declined many such invitations to speak, so the press was surprised when he agreed to travel to Gettysburg. Here, however, was an opportunity to show how the battle of Gettysburg marked a defining moment in the war, and Lincoln had been looking for just such an opportunity to vindicate his handling of this national crisis. Lincoln did not confide in anyone his plans for the Gettysburg Address, but as the biographer David Donald observes, Lincoln realized that Everett, a former Whig, would issue a "conservative call for a return to 'the Union as it was'" (Donald, p. 462). In effect, this would mean reaffirming state sovereignty, which, in turn, could be taken as condoning a continuation of slavery. Thus Lincoln had to craft a speech that demonstrated why the Union could not return to its former state and why the war, in fact, was the fulfillment of the nation's first principles.

Although legend states that Lincoln improvised his famous speech from a few notes on an envelope, the historical record is clear that he left Washington with a draft of his remarks, which he went over on the train to Gettysburg and, after his arrival, the day before his address. By the morning of the event, he had made a clean copy of his speech from which he would read. Lincoln, not a very good extemporaneous speaker and prone to making indiscreet remarks, had learned that he would have to make every word count. In a day when presidents did not have speechwriters or a propaganda agency, Lincoln had to rely on his own genius to sway public opinion. On the evening of his arrival in Gettysburg, a crowd assembled, hoping to hear the president direct a few words to them. Lincoln declined their requests, however, wishing to say nothing that might disadvantage the well-wrought speech he would make the next day.

Lincoln arrived in time to tour the battlefield, observing the newly dug graves. More than one hundred seventy thousand soldiers had waged war against one another. Between nine thousand and fifteen thousand people, among them, family members of the fallen; the press; politicians, including cabinet members; and other notables as well as the curious and attention seekers gathered at this historic site. Lincoln sat and listened attentively as Everett spoke for two hours, vividly describing the battle and delivering what many contemporaries hailed as a magnificent oration, while others deplored it for its verbosity.

On this bright day, Lincoln arose, shook Everett's hand, warmly congratulated him, took his speech from his pocket, put on his steel-rimmed glasses, and began: "Four score and seven years ago our fathers brought forth, on this continent, a new nation, conceived in Liberty, and dedicated to the proposition that all men are created equal." The cadence of

An 1865 photograph of Abraham Lincoln (Library of Congress)

the words evokes the King James Bible. Counting back eighty-seven years refers to the birth of the nation—1776, the date of the Declaration of Independence.

The first paragraph contains one sentence of thirty words and frames the Civil War as dedicated to the purpose of freedom and equality. Rather than reiterating his determination to preserve the Union or, specifically, to end slavery, the president speaks to the American sense of identity; what Americans have in common is this devotion to an idea, a conception of liberty that had given birth to a new nation. In other words, the idea of America is born out of liberty, which, in turn, leads to the proposition of equality. Just how carefully Lincoln chooses not only these precise words but also their cadence is clear when they are compared with informal remarks he made on July 7, 1863, to more than one thousand people serenading him. From his White House balcony, he had asked, "How long is it— eighty odd years—since on the Fourth of July for the first time in the history of the world a nation by its representations, assembled and declared as a self-evident truth that 'all men are created equal'" (Donald, p. 459). The "eighty odd years" are replaced with the magisterial and biblical "[f]our score and seven," a phrase that is both more precise and awe inspiring, a formulation he designs to mark a moment in history. Also note the use of "our fathers," a way of describing the country's founding as a family matter, an ancestral achievement and one that spreads across a continent. Thus Lincoln, in one deftly turned and exquisitely modulated sentence, beginning with the first two rhyming words that are echoed in "fathers" and "forth," and in the alliteration of "new nation," fuses the present with the past, the moment with history. His measured prose reads almost like poetry but without any strained effort to sound poetic.

By invoking the Declaration of Independence, Lincoln emphasizes that the nation is older than its Constitution and the compromises that keep the Union together. Lincoln himself temporizes, announcing his willingness to condone slavery in the South so long as it does not spread to the new territories. He is personally opposed to slavery, but he nevertheless does not support the abolitionist call for the emancipation of the slaves everywhere in the United States. Now, however, Lincoln eschews any such distinctions, realizing the time for any sort of concession to Confederate demands is past. As David Donald observes, the president thus opposes those who are still calling for some kind of accommodation with the South, a negotiated peace that would return the country to the antebellum status quo.

In the second paragraph, Lincoln shifts to a direct discussion of the Civil War, suggesting that it is a test of the American experiment, whether any nation created out of a desire to ensure freedom and equality "can long endure." In other words, America stands for something more than itself; in effect, it stands for the very idea of liberty. The president repeats the word *dedication* twice in this paragraph (using it once in the first paragraph), which implies that the country is on a mission requiring devotion, commitment, enthusiasm, and perseverance. Lincoln implies that settling for anything less than the triumph of American principles would be a loss not only of the nation as its founders conceived it but also of the energy and conviction that inspired the world. Referring specifically to the Gettysburg battlefield that becomes a cemetery, the president says that the soldiers had died "here" so that the "nation might live." This perspective makes no distinction between Union and Confederate dead but rather suggests that their struggle is a confirmation of the country's core beliefs. Indeed, Lincoln never even uses the word *soldier*, emphasizing instead their commitment to a cause.

Although it is only proper to commemorate their deaths, as Lincoln remarks at the end of the second paragraph, he begins the third paragraph by taking exception to the assumption that any ceremony can "consecrate … this ground." The men who fought the battle have enacted their own consecration, he emphasizes, and words cannot do justice to their sacrifice, to the ground they have hallowed. Nothing we can say, Lincoln insists, can amplify or diminish their courageous actions. This is why he adds in one of his most famous statements that words alone are a "poor power" set beside actions: "The world will little note, nor long remember what we say here, but it can never forget what they did here." Paradoxically, Lincoln's confession

that words are incommensurate with the event's magnitude serves to enhance his own forensic authority. Unlike Everett, who tried to do justice to the battle in thousands of words, Lincoln confesses in twenty-one words that he has no vocabulary that could do justice to Gettysburg's significance. The "we," moreover, is not merely Lincoln but also everyone gathered to honor the men who have hallowed Gettysburg's ground. Thus the president speaks the words of a nation and not simply his own. Lincoln's use of the word *hallowed*, with its religious connotations, makes his presence and that of thousands of others a sacred commemoration of lives that have been spent in the service of nation, a nation that must endure in order to memorialize their sacrifice.

"It is for us the living," Lincoln observes, to carry on the unfinished work of those who have perished in liberty's cause. The way to honor them, in other words, is to dedicate and devote our lives to the noble work begun on the Gettysburg battlefield. It is this call to further action that inspires the president's vision that only the future can make good on the soldiers' sacrifices. In effect, Lincoln creates a kind of democratic saga, in which the dead at Gettysburg ensured the nation's life by stirring their fellow Americans to continue a cause that not only unites the country but also represents a "new birth of freedom," and a renewed resolve that "government of the people, by the people, for the people, shall not perish from the earth."

Implicitly, Lincoln defends the mission of his own administration, especially his stubborn refusal to consider any compromise that would jeopardize the Union, a continental entity devoted not merely to constitutional liberty but to the cause of equality as enunciated in the Declaration of Independence. This is not merely his policy but a sacred trust, "under God," as he notes in his closing sentence.

The Gettysburg Address is short, like a prayer, and devoid of rationalizations, partisan points, and any sort of defensive argumentation. Although the address can certainly be analyzed for its political implications, its rhetoric soars beyond the terms of its time. As Garry Wills points out in his book-length study of the speech and its ramifications, Lincoln changes the nature of public discourse by perfecting a manner that is both solemn and formal, yet direct, so that it seems he speaks not only for himself but indeed for the nation.

Audience

President Lincoln intended the Gettysburg Address for the whole nation. He was not commemorating a Union victory or denigrating the southern cause. He sought, on the contrary, to pay tribute to the nobility of the battle, implying that all concerned were fighting for a notion of freedom and equality. Thus, issues like slavery had to be excluded from the speech. Only, perhaps, in the phrase "new birth of freedom" could Lincoln's words be interpreted as obliquely referring to the liberation of African Americans, although even this phrase is abstract enough to encompass the notion

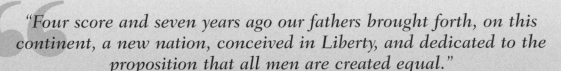

> "*Four score and seven years ago our fathers brought forth, on this continent, a new nation, conceived in Liberty, and dedicated to the proposition that all men are created equal.*"
>
> (Paragraph 1)

> "*The world will little note, nor long remember what we say here, but it can never forget what they did here.*"
>
> (Paragraph 2)

> "*It is rather for us to be here dedicated to the great task remaining before us—that from these honored dead we take increased devotion to that cause for which they here gave the last full measure of devotion—that we here highly resolve that these dead shall not have died in vain—that this nation, under God, shall have a new birth of freedom—and that government of the people, by the people, for the people, shall not perish from the earth.*"
>
> (Paragraph 3)

that the idea of freedom has been given new life on the Gettysburg site. By invoking the Declaration of Independence, Lincoln could build on principles that both sides in the Civil War revered, whatever their differences with respect to who could actually be considered free and equal.

More specifically, however, Lincoln's audience was composed of different factions: those who wanted a negotiated peace with the South, those who contemplated allowing the South to secede, and those who wanted to be reassured that Lincoln would persevere in pursuing the war until the South was defeated and brought back into the Union. Lincoln's aim was to rise above the political dissension of his day and affix the nation's attention to the universal implications of the Gettysburg battle and to the future generations who would bear the responsibility for fulfilling the cause of freedom and equality that these soldiers so nobly died to promote, not only for American citizens but also for the world.

Impact

The extreme brevity of Lincoln's address caught his audience by surprise. As Doris Kearns Goodwin reported, one eyewitness said, "[T]he assemblage stood motionless and silent" (Goodwin, p. 586). Although Lincoln seemed to doubt the success of his speech, Edward Everett, who later asked for a copy of the Gettysburg Address, wrote to the president, "I should be glad if I could flatter myself that I came as near to the central idea of the occasion, in two hours as you did in two minutes" (Goodwin, p. 586).

As biographer David Donald notes, Lincoln's speech gave an expansive view of the nation's future. Although many newspapers devoted major coverage to Everett's speech, gradually they turned attention to the president's remarks, sensing that he had delivered not merely a graceful speech but also one that "will live among the annals of man," the *Chicago Tribune* asserted (Donald, p. 465). "Heartfelt" and "felicitous" were the words of other articles in the press. The Gettysburg Address soon became the signature work of Lincoln's hand. He wrote at least five autograph copies (but others may have been lost).

The speech was not without its critics and not only in the South. Newspapers backing his opponents, the Democrats, denigrated Lincoln's effort, calling it silly and dishonest. The *New York World*, for example, attacked Lincoln's reliance on the Declaration of Independence and his discounting of the Constitution. Other newspapers saw in Lincoln's strategy a new war aim: the securing of equality. The war was no longer exclusively one to preserve the Union. Now the causes of Union and equality seemed to be indivisible: They were one cause.

If the Gettysburg Address also impressed impartial observers, it did nothing in the short term to enhance Lincoln's prestige or his power. The Union, even after Gettysburg, had yet to achieve the major victories that would ensure the triumph of Lincoln's vision. Thus, Lincoln's prospects for reelection remained doubtful well into 1864. If Lee had been checked in his advance north, his army in Virginia still threatened the U.S. capital, and voters across the nation, even in Illinois (Lincoln's home state), did not yet seem ready to embrace equality as a war objective.

The impact of Lincoln's speech has had far greater resonance than just as a document of his presidency or even of the Civil War, however. Garry Wills, for example, has compared the greatness of the address to the greatness of the classical speeches of the Greeks. Oscar and Lilian Handlin provide a close reading of the speech in terms that would be appropriate to a poem. They note the pause Lincoln creates with the conjunction "but" at the beginning of the third paragraph, which segues from a note of "somber reassurance" to a revival of energy, expressed in phrases that excite his audience to "increased devotion" as they contemplate the soldiers' "last full measure of devotion" (Handlin and Handlin, p. 162).

Countless commentators have noted that the Gettysburg Address could have been delivered at other battlefields and that Lincoln very carefully did not anchor his remarks in current events or even in the history of the war. Instead, his highly abstract wording is moving because of the skillful use of repetition, often of the simplest words, but recited in a precise and graceful order, so that they take on the inevitability of a perfect piece of music.

Related Documents

"First Inaugural Address." Abraham Lincoln Online Web site. http://showcase.netins.net/web/creative/lincoln/speeches/1inaug.htm. Accessed on November 21, 2007. In his First Inaugural Address, Lincoln promises not to interfere with slavery where it exists.

"Second Inaugural Address of Abraham Lincoln." The Avalon Project at Yale Law School Web site. http://www.yale.edu/lawweb/avalon/presiden/inaug/lincoln2.htm. Accessed on November 21, 2007. In his Second Inaugural Address, Lincoln explains the causes of the war and the attitude that should be adopted with a war in progress.

Bibliography

■ Books

Bullard, F. Lauriston. *"A Few Appropriate Remarks": Lincoln's Gettysburg Address*. Harrogate, Tenn.: Lincoln Memorial University, 1944.

Carwardine, Richard. *Lincoln: A Life of Purpose and Power*. New York: Alfred A. Knopf, 2006.

Donald, David Herbert. *Lincoln*. New York: Simon and Schuster, 1995.

Gienapp, William E. *Abraham Lincoln and Civil War America: A Biography*. New York: Oxford University Press, 2002.

Goodwin, Doris Kearns. *Team of Rivals: The Political Genius of Abraham Lincoln*. New York: Simon and Schuster, 2005.

Guelzo, Allen C. *Abraham Lincoln: Redeemer President*. Grand Rapids, Mich.: W. B. Eerdmans, 1999.

Handlin, Oscar, and Lilian Handlin. *Abraham Lincoln and the Union*. Boston: Atlantic Monthly Press, 1980.

Keneally, Thomas. *Abraham Lincoln*. New York: Lipper/Viking, 2003.

Kunhardt, Jr., Philip B. *A New Birth of Freedom: Lincoln at Gettysburg*. Boston: Little, Brown, 1983.

Neely, Mark E., Jr. *The Last Best Hope of Earth: Abraham Lincoln and the Promise of America*. Cambridge, Mass.: Harvard University Press, 1993.

Paludan, Phillip Shaw. *The Presidency of Abraham Lincoln*. Lawrence: University Press of Kansas, 1994.

Thomas, Benjamin P. *Abraham Lincoln: A Biography*. New York: Knopf, 1952.

Warren, Louis A. *Lincoln's Gettysburg Declaration: "A New Birth of Freedom"*. Fort Wayne, Ind.: Lincoln National Foundation, 1964.

Wills, Garry. *Lincoln at Gettysburg: The Words That Remade America*. New York: Simon and Schuster, 1992.

■ Web Sites

"Suggested Lincoln Sources." History Now Web site. http://www.historynow.org/12_2005/ask2b.html. Accessed on November 21, 2007.

"Transcript of Constitution of the United States." 100 Milestone Documents Web site. http://www.ourdocuments.gov/doc.php?doc=9&page=transcript. Accessed on November 21, 2007.

"Transcript of Declaration of Independence." 100 Milestone Documents Web site. http://www.ourdocuments.gov/doc.php?doc=2&page=transcript. Accessed on November 21, 2007.

"Transcript of Emancipation Proclamation." 100 Milestone Documents Web site. http://www.ourdocuments.gov/doc.php?flash=true&doc=34&page=transcript. Accessed on November 21, 2007.

—By Carl Rollyson

1. Five copies of Lincoln's Gettysburg Address survive in his own handwriting. He gave two copies to his secretaries, John Hay and John Nicolay, at the time he delivered the speech. Another copy was later sent to Edward Everett and two copies to the historian George Bancroft, one of which came into the possession of Colonel Anthony Bliss's family and has become known as the "Bliss copy," the one often used for facsimile reproductions of the Gettysburg Address. The Hay draft has editorial revisions in Lincoln's own hand. The Nicolay copy may be the first draft and perhaps even the one Lincoln read at Gettysburg, although newspaper accounts of Lincoln's speech differ slightly from the Nicolay copy. While the Hay copy includes phrasing quoted in contemporary newspaper accounts, it has missing words and seems to have been hastily copied. Most historians and biographers rely on the fifth copy, which Lincoln sent to Bancroft (the fourth copy being written on both sides of one paper and deemed unusable for a book the historian was planning to publish), because Lincoln signed the copy, gave it a title, and dated it. What do even slight changes and omissions reveal about Lincoln's style and purpose?

2. Compare the Gettysburg Address to the Emancipation Proclamation. The language of the two documents is quite different, reflecting Lincoln's different aims and purposes during the Civil War. What do these two documents reveal about Lincoln as a leader, writer, politician, and statesman?

3. Compare the Gettysburg Address to Lincoln's First and Second Inaugural Addresses. How do Lincoln's two inaugural addresses put the case for the Union? What special power does the brevity of the Gettysburg Address bring to Lincoln's political rhetoric? What does biographer Thomas Keneally mean when he calls the speech an example of Lincoln's "humble augustness" (Kenealy, p. 151)?

4. Compare the Declaration of Independence with the Gettysburg Address. What aspects of America's founding document does Lincoln emphasize? In what sense is his speech a second declaration of independence?

5. The battle of Gettysburg ended the day before the anniversary of the Declaration of Independence. How did Lincoln use this date to his advantage? How did phrases like a "new birth of freedom" reiterate what Lincoln saw as the national purpose?

6. Many commentators on the Gettysburg Address note that Lincoln uses the word *nation* five times. Why was this word especially useful for his purposes? What was Lincoln saying about the uniqueness of American nationhood?

7. The reception of Lincoln's speech depended on what listeners and readers made of his putting primary emphasis on the Declaration of Independence rather than on the U.S. Constitution. Lincoln seemed to be implying that the nation was more than the sum of its laws and political compromises. America stood for core principles that could not be understood without reference to the Declaration of Independence. Compare the Declaration to the Constitution. What aspects of American identity was Lincoln choosing to honor? What aspects did he decide not to acknowledge?

Glossary

score	twenty
consecrated	declared or set apart a building, area of ground, or specific spot as holy or sacred
hallow	make holy or keep for religious use; regard with great respect or reverence

GETTYSBURG ADDRESS

Four score and seven years ago our fathers brought forth, on this continent, a new nation, conceived in Liberty, and dedicated to the proposition that all men are created equal.

Now we are engaged in a great civil war, testing whether that nation, or any nation so conceived, and so dedicated, can long endure. We are met on a great battle-field of that war. We have come to dedicate a portion of that field, as a final resting place for those who here gave their lives, that that nation might live. It is altogether fitting and proper that we should do this.

But, in a larger sense, we can not dedicate—we can not consecrate—we can not hallow—this ground. The brave men, living and dead, who struggled here, have consecrated it far above our poor power to add or detract. The world will little note, nor long remember what we say here, but it can never forget what they did here. It is for us the living, rather, to be dedicated here to the unfinished work which they who fought here have thus far so nobly advanced. It is rather for us to be here dedicated to the great task remaining before us—that from these honored dead we take increased devotion to that cause for which they here gave the last full measure of devotion—that we here highly resolve that these dead shall not have died in vain—that this nation, under God, shall have a new birth of freedom—and that government of the people, by the people, for the people, shall not perish from the earth.

Fellow Countrymen.

At this second appearing to take the oath of the presidential office, there is less occasion for an extended address than there was at the first. Then a statement, somewhat in detail, of a course to be pursued, seemed fitting and proper. Now, at the expiration of four years, during which public declarations have been constantly called forth on every point and phase of the great contest which still absorbs the attention, and engrosses the energies of the nation, little that is new could be presented. The progress of our arms, upon which all else chiefly depends, is as well known to the public as to myself; and it is, I trust, reasonably satisfactory and encouraging to all. With high hope for the future, no prediction in regard to it is ventured.

On the occasion corresponding to this four years ago, all thoughts were anxiously di-

Abraham Lincoln's Second Inaugural Address (National Archives and Records Administration)

MILESTONE DOCUMENTS IN AMERICAN HISTORY

"With malice toward none; with charity for all ... let us strive on to finish the work we are in."

Overview

As one of the central texts in American history, Abraham Lincoln's Second Inaugural Address, delivered on March 4, 1865, defined the meaning of the Civil War and approached the task of Reconstruction with humility and compassion. By identifying slavery as the cause of war, the speech stands as testament to the transformative power of the Civil War—a war begun to defend the Union that became a war to end slavery. By focusing on God's presence and agency in the war, the speech stands as Lincoln's most definitive statement on the Civil War's meaning for the nation. Moving in its prose and striking in its clarity and brevity, the Second Inaugural Address, composed of a mere 703 words, has become, as Lincoln believed it would, one of his most important works.

Context

The year preceding Lincoln's Second Inaugural witnessed dramatic changes in public opinion throughout the North. Throughout most of 1864, it seemed likely that Lincoln would not be reelected. The nation was weary of war, and Democrats put forth as their candidate General George B. McClellan on a platform that called for peace negotiations. The Republican Party was divided, as it had been throughout the war. The issue of Reconstruction, or the process by which Confederate states would be returned to their proper relationship to the federal government, revealed splits within the party. Radicals wanted southern society refashioned, including legal equality for blacks, the possibility of black suffrage, and punitive measures against Confederates. Conservatives and moderates within the party balked at the revolutionary doctrines, favoring instead a plan for Reconstruction that secured emancipation without black voting rights and stripped leading Confederates of their political rights. In December 1863 Lincoln offered his own plan for Reconstruction, which called for loyal state governments to be organized when one-tenth of the voting population in 1860 took an oath of loyalty to the Union. Confederates would have to accept emancipation, but publicly Lincoln did not press for black suffrage, recognizing the limits of racial change among northern voters. Lincoln's political skill allowed him to thwart challenges from radicals within the party, and he secured the Republican nomination in June 1864.

Lincoln's prospects for reelection, however, hinged on military success. In 1864 the Union called for more volunteers, and Lincoln summoned General Ulysses S. Grant from the western theater to take command of the entire Union army as lieutenant general. In May, Grant began his Virginia offensive, which included the battle of the Wilderness and the battles at Spotsylvania and Cold Harbor. The northern public recoiled from the casualties, which included losses of sixty thousand in a single month of fighting. Lincoln called for more volunteers in July and announced a draft for September if districts failed to meet their quotas. Northern communities strained under the pressures of luring volunteers through bounties.

During the same period, radicals in Congress, dissatisfied when the reconstructed state of Louisiana failed to provide for black suffrage, offered their own plan for Reconstruction through the Wade-Davis bill. The legislation called for harsher measures for Reconstruction. Loyal state governments would be organized when a majority of voters had taken the oath of allegiance, rather than Lincoln's 10 percent. In addition, it required Confederates to take an ironclad oath maintaining that they had never aided the Confederacy and barred leading Confederates from holding office. The legislation also would have ended slavery. When the Wade-Davis bill passed Congress in July, Lincoln refused to act on it, rejecting Congress's authority over emancipation and desiring to uphold the loyal governments of Louisiana and Arkansas. He believed that his more lenient policy would undermine Confederate support and hasten the end of the war.

Facing criticism from both within and without, Lincoln believed he would be defeated in the November election. He also felt that he was bound to save the Union before his term expired and wrote as much in a private memorandum. When William Tecumseh Sherman captured Atlanta, however, public sentiment in the North began to change, as did Lincoln's prospects. While soldiers in the field had stead-

Time Line

1860

■ **November 6**
Lincoln is elected president.

■ **December 20**
South Carolina secedes from the Union.

1861

■ **January–February**
Remaining states of the Deep South secede.

■ **March 4**
Lincoln is inaugurated.

■ **April 12**
Fort Sumter is bombarded.

1862

■ **September 22**
Lincoln issues preliminary Emancipation Proclamation.

1863

■ **July 1–3**
Battle of Gettysburg.

■ **July 4**
Vicksburg is captured by the Union army

■ **October–November**
Republican success in state elections.

■ **November 19**
Lincoln gives Gettysburg Address.

■ **December 8**
Lincoln announces plan for Reconstruction.

1864

■ **March 9**
Lincoln names Ulysses S. Grant as commanding general.

■ **June–July**
Grant leads offensive in Virginia.

■ **June 8**
Lincoln is nominated to run for a second term.

■ **July 4**
Lincoln pocket vetoes Wade-Davis bill.

■ **September 2**
William Tecumseh Sherman captures Atlanta.

■ **November 8**
Lincoln is elected to a second term.

---

fastly supported Lincoln's candidacy, voters at home had increased confidence in the military prospects. Union forces controlled the Shenandoah Valley in Virginia, isolating Robert E. Lee from his supplies. Their votes in November reflected this change. Lincoln was reelected with 212 electoral votes to George B. McClellan's 21 and a majority of almost 400,000 votes. Lincoln captured almost 80 percent of soldiers' votes.

As Sherman's army marched through Georgia and the Carolinas, calls for retribution against a defeated South emanated from the northern press, pulpits, and politicians. Northerners seemed to revel in the destruction of private property waged by Sherman's soldiers and embraced the tenets of total warfare targeted against southern civilians.

Lincoln did not share in the mood of self-righteousness and vengeance. Following his election, he lobbied for the passage of the Thirteenth Amendment in Congress, which was accomplished on the last day of January 1865. In February he met Confederate delegates at Fort Monroe, Maryland, and defined peace terms: cessation of hostilities, acceptance of emancipation, and reunion. Nothing came of his efforts to negotiate an end to the war, but in his Second Inaugural Address, Lincoln would craft a document that defined the tenor, though not the specifics, of a reconstructed nation.

About the Author

Abraham Lincoln, the sixteenth president, was born in Hardin County, Kentucky, on February 12, 1809, to Thomas and Nancy Hanks Lincoln. His parents were Primitive Baptists, and Lincoln grew up in a home that subscribed to the doctrines of predestination and fatalism. Growing up in Indiana and later moving to Illinois, Lincoln was largely self-educated and had an abiding belief in the ability of an individual to shape his life through aspiration and hard work.

In 1834 Lincoln was elected to the Illinois General Assembly as a Whig and embarked on a career in law. Relocating to Springfield, Lincoln met and married Mary Todd, the daughter of a wealthy Kentucky slave owner. With the demise of the Whig Party, Lincoln moved toward the coalition party formed in opposition to the popular sovereignty doctrines of the Kansas-Nebraska Act. As a Republican, Lincoln ran against Democrat Stephen A. Douglas for Congress. His bid failed but produced the famed Lincoln-Douglas debates. It also provided Lincoln with national renown, which he enhanced when he gave his Cooper Union Address in New York City in February 1860. He used the speech to argue that Republicans were not a party of radical abolitionists but instead merely opposed slavery's expansion—a position, Lincoln stated in his speech, that the nation's founders held. The speech introduced him to eastern audiences and solidified his reputation as a moderate.

In May 1860, Lincoln's supporters secured his nomination for president over the radical William Seward of New York on the third ballot. In a four-way election in November, Lincoln defeated Democrat Stephen A. Douglas, Democrat John C. Breckenridge, and Constitutional Unionist John Bell, securing 180 electoral votes and a 900,000-vote margin of victory. Lincoln had not, however, secured a majority of popular votes and was elected by the northern states. In the wake of Lincoln's election, South Carolina seceded from the Union, and the Deep South states followed. In his First Inaugural Address, on March 4, 1861, Lincoln denied the right of secession but pledged that he would not interfere with slavery where it existed. The exigencies of war and Lincoln's evolving views on slavery altered this pledge, and on September 22, 1862, he issued the preliminary Emancipation Proclamation. When emancipation went into effect on January 1, 1863, it freed slaves in areas of rebellion.

On November 8, 1864, Lincoln was elected to a second term. When the Thirteenth Amendment passed Congress in January 1865, slavery was outlawed in the United States. When he addressed the nation and the world in his Second Inaugural Address in March 1865, Lincoln sought to find meaning in the war and define the course the nation would pursue upon its conclusion. Lincoln's vision was never fully articulated or realized, and he was shot by John Wilkes Booth on April 14, 1865, five days after the Confederate surrender. Lincoln died the following day.

Explanation and Analysis of the Document

The Second Inaugural Address begins slowly and rather unremarkably, as Lincoln notes that the second occasion of taking the oath of office warrants a less lengthy speech than the first. In the First Inaugural Address, he points out, it was appropriate to outline what course he would pursue. After four years of war, which included many public documents, Lincoln believes "little that is new could be presented." Referencing military affairs in 1864 and 1865, Lincoln observes that the army is making progress and believes it is "reasonably satisfactory and encouraging to all." While he could have followed that pronouncement with a list of accomplishments and victories, and a prediction of the end of the war, Lincoln chooses not to. Instead, he expresses "high hope" for the end of war but refuses to make any predictions.

In the second paragraph, Lincoln returns again to the occasion of the first inaugural, not to explain the challenges he faced in assuming office but to explain how the war occurred. He avows that "all dreaded it" and that everyone tried to prevent war. His next statement explains his meaning, noting that "insurgent agents" were in Washington, D.C., trying to negotiate a peaceful settlement and division of assets. By identifying these individuals as insurgents as well as labeling the Union and Confederacy as "parties" rather than countries, Lincoln underscores his legal position that secession was unlawful and that the war was a domestic rebellion rather than a war between belligerents. He also employs terms that allow for the idea that secession was caused by individuals and groups of influential people but not the entire population of the southern

Time Line

1865

- **January 31**
Thirteenth Amendment passes Congress.

- **February 3**
Lincoln attends Hampton Roads Peace Conference.

- **March 4**
Lincoln is inaugurated.

- **April 9**
Robert E. Lee surrenders.

- **April 11**
Lincoln's last speech addresses Reconstruction.

- **April 14**
Lincoln is shot; he dies the following day.

states. In the following sentence, he draws a sharp distinction, noting that one side would make war rather than allow the Union to exist and the other would accept it rather than see the Union destroyed. In an abrupt and powerful concluding sentence, Lincoln notes, "And the war came," marking a rhetorical shift in the speech and suggesting, through its passive voice, that something beyond human agency had brought on the war.

The third paragraph begins with what seems like a conventional accounting: One-eighth of the population was enslaved when the war began, and these slaves were in the southern states. Without defining the exact role that slavery played in the nation, Lincoln states that the slaves made up a "peculiar and powerful" interest, echoing the nineteenth-century idea that slavery was, as was often stated, the South's "peculiar institution," integral to the economy of the South as well as the nation. Everyone, Lincoln states, recognized that slavery had caused the war. In saying so, Lincoln marks the revolutionary change wrought by war; a war to preserve the Union, as he had characterized it in his First Inaugural Address, had become a war to end slavery. Identifying slavery as the cause of war, he singles out those insurgents who wanted to protect and expand the institution into the territories for attempting to tear the Union apart, carefully noting that the Union only wanted to prevent the expansion of slavery into the federal territories.

The following sentence signals a shift in the speech. Lincoln observes that neither side had anticipated the length or costs of the war or that the cause of the war—slavery—should end while the war would continue to rage. With these observations, Lincoln suggests that it was impossible for mere human agency to have brought about such a conflict. The speech arrives at it main topic: the relationship between God and war and its consequences for the nation. In a powerful sentence, signaling his shift to theological subjects, he observes that both the Union and Confederacy read the same Bible, pray to the same God,

An engraving depicting Abraham Lincoln taking the oath of office at his second inauguration. Chief Justice Salmon P. Chase administers the oath. (Library of Congress)

and ask for his blessing and aid in conquering the other. In the first of four references to the Bible, Lincoln describes slavery through Genesis 3:19, acknowledging that the Confederate appeal to God to aid them in "wringing their bread from the sweat of other men's faces" was "strange." He then invokes the Gospel of Matthew 7:1 and admonishes "judge not that we be not judged," suggesting that the North does not want to be judged by God because it shares in the guilt of slavery.

The second half of the third paragraph contains the central element of Lincoln's address—the truth, he would later write, that he thought needed to be told. Following an American tradition of Election Day sermons and jeremiads, Lincoln delivers the message that God's plan and intent were separate from that of either side and were impossible to discern. It was therefore impossible to claim for the Union God's divine sanction. In making this argument, Lincoln chastens his northern audience—who had, in varied forms, called for vengeance upon the South—and advocates a tenor of humility in the waning months of war. Lincoln observes that it was impossible for God to answer the prayers of both the North and the South and that the prayers of neither had been answered. The "Almighty," Lincoln maintains, has purposes that are unknown. He then invokes Matthew 18:7 to underscore the idea that a just God had given both the North and South the war as retribution.

Lincoln then returns to the cause of the war, slavery, and suggests that as the war continued even after God had chosen to end slavery, it was no more than the divine power

of a "Living God" at work—that is, a God that could both love and judge. Deeming the war a "scourge," in language that compared the pain of war to the pain of slaves whipped by the lash, Lincoln observes that all hope and pray for the war's end. Returning to the power of God's purposes, Lincoln allows that if God desires that the war continue until the profits of 250 years of slavery disappear and the blood drawn by the lash from slaves be paid in full by the blood drawn by the sword of war, it must be, as in Psalm 19:10, because God's judgments are righteous.

The fourth and closing paragraph is composed of a single sentence so poetic, so striking in its prose and use of starkly balanced polarity, that it has become the most emphasized portion of a speech, even while Lincoln's main point is contained in the preceding paragraph. The final paragraph points toward the future. The main clause of the sentence is to "strive on to finish the work we are in," turning toward the prospect of reconstruction. Lincoln brackets the simple admonition—reminiscent of the Gettysburg Address—with two related imperatives that stem from his belief that God had brought war to the nation—the entire nation—for his own purposes. The first is that the Union should approach the future with a lack of malice, with charity, and with a firm commitment to what right God allowed people to discern. Lincoln believed God was at work in the war, with designs that could not be identified by anyone, including a victorious people who vanquished a foe. The second imperative was for a nation to attend to those who suffered from war, regardless of the side they fought for, because to do so was to undertake action that would achieve a lasting and just peace, in the manner of God, expanding the vision beyond the United States toward other nations and the future.

Audience

The address was intended for a national and international audience. Thousands stood in inclement weather in Washington, D.C., to hear Lincoln's speech, which lasted approximately six minutes. Listeners included Frederick Douglass, slaves who had gained their freedom through the Emancipation Proclamation, and John Wilkes Booth. Millions more people read the address in newspapers throughout the Union and Confederacy and in countries throughout the world.

Lincoln's reference to the satisfactory progress of the military, an observer noted, was followed by a pause. A reporter for the *New York Herald* thought Lincoln anticipated applause, but the sentence was met with silence. The crowd offered applause when Lincoln noted that the Union would accept war before accepting secession and when he identified slavery as the cause of the war. Lincoln's reference to Genesis regarding slave owners' gaining their bread from the sweat of others was received as satire and prompted some laughter. For the remaining speech, the crowd was silent, with the exception of periodic praise to God offered by some African Americans in attendance. Frederick Douglass believed the speech was more a sermon than a state

> "Both read the same Bible, and pray to the same God; and each invokes His aid against the other. It may seem strange that any men should dare to ask a just God's assistance in wringing their bread from the sweat of other men's faces; but let us judge not that we be not judged. The prayers of both could not be answered. That of neither has been answered fully."
>
> (Paragraph 3)

> "With malice toward none; with charity for all; with firmness in the right, as God gives us to see the right, let us strive on to finish the work we are in; to bind up the nation's wounds; to care for him who shall have borne the battle, and for his widow, and his orphan—to do all which may achieve and cherish a just, and lasting peace, among ourselves, and with all nations."
>
> (Paragraph 4)

document and approved of it, but he observed that others in attendance were not as moved.

Throughout the North, response to the speech was tepid. The next morning, Western Union completed its connection from New York City to San Francisco, and Lincoln's speech was telegraphed to the coast. Newspapers that typically supported Lincoln, such as the *New York Times*, were disappointed that Lincoln had not celebrated Union achievements or affirmed that Confederate submission was the only term for peace. Others complained that Lincoln had defined slavery as the cause of the war but had failed to mention the Thirteenth Amendment, which would abolish slavery. Democratic newspaper editors found the effort entirely lacking and overly general as well. A comparatively few editorials in the northern press recognized the historic significance of the document. In the South, there were few newspapers altogether—only twenty-two continued to be published. Some of these dismissed the effort, while others were uncertain how to reconcile the theology of the address with their own belief in a Confederate nationalism that was explicitly Christian. In Europe the address was praised for its simplicity and modesty and for Lincoln's desire that the peace be lasting both among Americans and with other nations.

Lincoln, of course, recognized that his effort was met with much criticism. On March 15, nine days after his address, he wrote to Thurlow Reed, a New York Republican politician, thanking Reed for a complimentary letter, and acknowledged that his speech was not roundly praised. This, Lincoln believed, derived from its emphasis on religion—specifically his assertion that God's purpose may dif-

fer from men's, but he believed that people needed to be reminded that God governed the world. He believed that as president he could make such a statement and predicted the address would endure as well as any speech he had given.

Impact

In his prediction of the Second Inaugural Address's historic significance, Lincoln was prescient. While the Gettysburg Address has traditionally been seen as his greatest statement of the significance of the Civil War, recent scholarship argues that the Second Inaugural Address is the definitive statement of the war's meaning. Some observers thought as much. Charles Francis Adams, Jr., opined that it was, in its simplicity, "the historical keynote" of the war (White, p. 184). For those interested in Lincoln's religious beliefs, the speech is seen as his clearest statement of his theology, although biographers differ on whether it is best characterized as fatalism or Providence and whether it was shaped by his Primitive Baptist upbringing or Old Presbyterian worship. The final paragraph has also been used to articulate America's vision of itself as well as to highlight instances when the nation failed to live up to Lincoln's mandate.

Related Documents

"1864 State of the Union Address." PresidentialRhetoric.com Web site. http://www.presidentialrhetoric.com/historicspeeches/lincoln/stateoftheunion1864.html. Accessed on January 7, 2008. In his last address to Congress, Lincoln affirms his commitment to emancipation and considers the issue of Reconstruction.

"First Inaugural Address of Abraham Lincoln." The Avalon Project at Yale Law School Web site. http://www.yale.edu/lawweb/avalon/presiden/inaug/lincoln1.htm. Accessed on January 7, 2008. In this speech, written before he arrived in the capital and after the secession of seven southern states, Lincoln reaffirmed that he would not interfere with slavery where it existed but denied the right of secession.

"If Slavery Is Not Wrong, Nothing Is Wrong." American Treasures of the Library of Congress Web site. http://www.loc.gov/exhibits/treasures/trt027.html. Accessed on January 7, 2008. Lincoln wrote this letter to A. G. Hodges for publication, after outlining his views on emancipation in a meeting with Kentucky Unionists. In the letter, he claims that events have controlled him and points toward God's will in determining the end of slavery.

"Meditation on Divine Will." Abraham Lincoln Online Web site. http://showcase.netins.net/web/creative/lincoln/speeches/meditat.htm. Accessed on January 7, 2008. In this brief piece, Lincoln struggles with the will of God and its relationship to the war. Reasoning that God cannot support both sides, Lincoln posits that God has a purpose for the war, unclear as it may be to mortals. Because the piece anticipates the ideas of Lincoln's Second Inaugural Address, most historians attribute the writing to September 1862, while others believe it was written in 1864.

"Speech on Reconstruction." The History Place Web site. http://www.historyplace.com/lincoln/reconst.htm. Accessed on January 7, 2008. Lincoln gave this speech, his final one, from a White House window in response to crowds who had gathered upon Lee's surrender. In it, he suggests flexibility in approaching Reconstruction and raises the prospect of limited black suffrage.

Bibliography

■ Articles

Guelzo, Allen C. "Abraham Lincoln and the Doctrine of Necessity." *Journal of the Abraham Lincoln Association* 18, no. 1 (1997): 57–82.

Noll, Mark A. "'Both ... Pray to the Same God': The Singularity of Lincoln's Faith in the Era of the Civil War." *Journal of the Abraham Lincoln Association* 18, no. 1 (1997): 1–26.

Schwartz, Earl. "'A Poor Hand to Quote Scripture': Lincoln and Genesis 3:19." *Journal of the Abraham Lincoln Association* 23, no. 2 (2002): 37–49.

■ Books

Donald, David Herbert. *Lincoln*. New York: Simon & Schuster, 1995.

Gienapp, William E. *Abraham Lincoln and Civil War America: A Biography*. New York: Oxford University Press, 2002.

Guelzo, Allen C. *Abraham Lincoln: Redeemer President*. Grand Rapids, Mich.: W. B. Eerdmans, 1999.

Harris, William C. *With Charity for All: Lincoln and the Restoration of the Union*. Lexington: University Press of Kentucky, 1997.

Paludan, Phillip S. *The Presidency of Abraham Lincoln*. Lawrence: University Press of Kansas, 1994.

Peterson, Merrill D. *Lincoln in American Memory*. New York: Oxford University Press, 1994.

Schwartz, Barry. *Abraham Lincoln and the Forge of National Memory*. Chicago: University of Chicago Press, 2000.

Tackach, James. *Lincoln's Moral Vision: The Second Inaugural Address*. Jackson: University Press of Mississippi, 2002.

White, Ronald C. *Lincoln's Greatest Speech: The Second Inaugural*. New York: Simon & Schuster, 2002.

Wilson, Douglas L. *Lincoln's Sword: The Presidency and the Power of Words*. New York: Alfred A. Knopf, 2006.

Winger, Stewart. *Lincoln, Religion, and Romantic Cultural Politics*. DeKalb: Northern Illinois University Press, 2003.

Wolf, William J. *The Almost Chosen People: A Study of the Religion of Abraham Lincoln*. Garden City, N.Y.: Doubleday, 1959.

■ Web Sites

"Abraham Lincoln Papers." Library of Congress Web site. http://memory.loc.gov/ammem/alhtml/malhome.html. Accessed on December 12, 2007.

"Abraham Lincoln's Second Inaugural Address." Library of Congress "Primary Documents in American History" Web site. http://www.loc.gov/rr/program/bib/ourdocs/Lincoln2nd.html. Accessed on December 12, 2007.

The Collected Works of Abraham Lincoln. Abraham Lincoln Association Web site. http://quod.lib.umich.edu/l/lincoln/. Accessed on December 12, 2007.

—By Christine Dee

Questions for Further Study

1. According to Lincoln, who or what was to blame for the Civil War?

2. Did Lincoln strike a conciliatory tone? If so, how do you explain this?

3. What was the responsibility of the nation, according to Lincoln? What course was to be pursued upon achieving peace?

4. Compare Lincoln's First Inaugural Address and his Second Inaugural Address. What are the differences in the content, context, and tone of each speech? What accounts for these differences?

Glossary

deprecated	disapproved of
insurgents	those who revolt against a government but are not recognized as belligerents
rend	tear apart violently
territorial	pertaining to the unorganized territories of the United States
woe	misfortune or wretchedness
providence	the divine power that shapes human destiny
scourge	agent of punishment; literally, a whip
malice	the desire to see others suffer

ABRAHAM LINCOLN'S SECOND INAUGURAL ADDRESS

Fellow Countrymen:

At this second appearing to take the oath of the presidential office, there is less occasion for an extended address than there was at the first. Then a statement, somewhat in detail, of a course to be pursued, seemed fitting and proper. Now, at the expiration of four years, during which public declarations have been constantly called forth on every point and phase of the great contest which still absorbs the attention, and engrosses the enerergies [sic] of the nation, little that is new could be presented. The progress of our arms, upon which all else chiefly depends, is as well known to the public as to myself; and it is, I trust, reasonably satisfactory and encouraging to all. With high hope for the future, no prediction in regard to it is ventured.

On the occasion corresponding to this four years ago, all thoughts were anxiously directed to an impending civil-war. All dreaded it—all sought to avert it. While the inaugural address was being delivered from this place, devoted altogether to *saving* the Union without war, insurgent agents were in the city seeking to *destroy* it without war—seeking to dissol[v]e the Union, and divide effects, by negotiation. Both parties deprecated war; but one of them would *make* war rather than let the nation survive; and the other would *accept* war rather than let it perish. And the war came.

One eighth of the whole population were colored slaves, not distributed generally over the Union, but localized in the Southern part of it. These slaves constituted a peculiar and powerful interest. All knew that this interest was, somehow, the cause of the war. To strengthen, perpetuate, and extend this interest was the object for which the insurgents would rend the Union, even by war; while the government claimed no right to do more than to restrict the territorial enlargement of it. Neither party expected for the war, the magnitude, or the duration, which it has already

attained. Neither anticipated that the *cause* of the conflict might cease with, or even before, the conflict itself should cease. Each looked for an easier triumph, and a result less fundamental and astounding. Both read the same Bible, and pray to the same God; and each invokes His aid against the other. It may seem strange that any men should dare to ask a just God's assistance in wringing their bread from the sweat of other men's faces; but let us judge not that we be not judged. The prayers of both could not be answered; that of neither has been answered fully. The Almighty has His own purposes. "Woe unto the world because of offences! for it must needs be that offences come; but woe to that man by whom the offence cometh!" If we shall suppose that American Slavery is one of those offences which, in the providence of God, must needs come, but which, having continued through His appointed time, He now wills to remove, and that He gives to both North and South, this terrible war, as the woe due to those by whom the offence came, shall we discern therein any departure from those divine attributes which the believers in a Living God always ascribe to Him? Fondly do we hope—fervently do we pray—that this mighty scourge of war may speedily pass away. Yet, if God wills that it continue, until all the wealth piled by the bond-man's two hundred and fifty years of unrequited toil shall be sunk, and until every drop of blood drawn with the lash, shall be paid by another drawn with the sword, as was said three thousand years ago, so still it must be said "the judgments of the Lord, are true and righteous altogether."

With malice toward none; with charity for all; with firmness in the right, as God gives us to see the right, let us strive on to finish the work we are in; to bind up the nation's wounds; to care for him who shall have borne the battle, and for his widow, and his orphan—to do all which may achieve and cherish a just, and a lasting peace, among ourselves, and with all nations.

Articles of Agreement Relating to the Surrender of the Army of Northern Virginia
(National Archives and Records Administration)

ARTICLES OF AGREEMENT RELATING TO THE SURRENDER OF THE ARMY OF NORTHERN VIRGINIA

"By the South laying down their arms they will hasten that most desirable event."

Overview

The Articles of Agreement dictated by Union general Ulysses S. Grant and signed by Confederate general Robert E. Lee in April 1865 signaled that the American Civil War was nearly over. After Grant captured the Confederate capital of Richmond, Virginia, on April 3, 1865, Lee's army of fewer than thirty thousand straggling men was on the run and pressured on three sides by three times as many men. Lee's last hope to reach the food and provisions waiting at Appomattox Station was dashed when General Philip Sheridan's cavalry arrived first on April 8.

Realizing the futility of further resistance, Lee confided to his fellow officers in the early morning of April 9: "There is nothing left for me but to go and see Grant, and I would rather die a thousand deaths" (McPherson, p. 481). Lee sent out flags of truce and wrote a note to Grant requesting an interview to arrange the surrender of the Army of Northern Virginia. After a series of notes, the two leaders agreed to meet on April 9, 1865. Lee sent a subordinate to choose a meeting place in the village of Appomattox Court House. Ironically, the house chosen belonged to Mr Wilmer McLean, who had moved from Manassas Junction to Appomattox four years earlier, after the first battle of Bull Run, to get out of harm's way.

The meeting lasted approximately two and a half hours. Lee asked that the terms of surrender be formally written out. When Grant completed the finished copy, the two generals signed it. A little before four o'clock Lee shook hands with Grant, bowed to the other officers, and left the room. At the meeting's conclusion, the bloodiest conflict in the nation's history neared its end.

Context

By April 1865 the costs of the Civil War were staggering. About three million American men, one-third of all free males between the ages of fifteen and fifty-nine, had served in the war. Out of a population of 31 million people, total casualties exceeded one million. Six hundred and twenty thousand people were killed either in battle or by disease. The three hundred and fifty thousand Union dead represented 10 percent of all adult males of fighting age; the two hundred and sixty thousand Confederates represented 15–20 percent of all adults in the rebel states and a staggering 25 percent of white males between the ages of twenty and forty. The death toll exceeded that of deaths in all other U.S. wars from the Revolution through the Persian Gulf War. An additional seventy-five thousand died of war wounds after the war ended, and an estimated fifty thousand civilians died, totaling as many as seven hundred and fifty thousand dead because of the war. Approximately two hundred and seventy-five thousand on each side were maimed. Another four hundred and ten thousand spent time in unsanitary, overcrowded prison camps. Nearly 1.25 million of three million men who served in the Civil War were either killed or maimed. For the South alone, of a free white population of approximately five million, of which 1.4 million were draft-age males, over five hundred thousand men were either killed or maimed.

By 1865 Union forces permeated every corner of the Confederacy. William Tecumseh Sherman's army had cut a swath of destruction 425 miles long and 60 miles wide through Georgia and South Carolina. His forces had destroyed two-thirds of the value of all southern wealth. They had torn up two-thirds of its nine thousand railroad miles, and confiscated two-fifths of farm livestock. The planters had lost four billion dollars in slave property, and the worth of their lands had fallen to a fraction of their pre-war value. The Confederate currency was worthless. Farms choked on weeds, as conscripted small farmers had to leave their farms under the care of their wives and children.

In addition to the loss of 10 percent of its adult males, the North also had paid a heavy price for the war. The historian David Donald estimates that the total cost ran as high as ten billion dollars. Northerners had grown embittered as the war dragged on, not only by the mounting deaths and conscription but also by widely publicized news of atrocities like the massacre of black troops at Fort Pillow (Tennessee) by forces under the command of General Nathan Bedford Forrest and the starvation of thirteen thousand Union prisoners at Andersonville prison in Georgia.

Having staked all on its war for independence, the South had lost everything. All that remained was its honor

1864

■ **March 2**
Lincoln appoints Grant general in chief of all Union forces.

■ **May 4**
Grant sends Sherman through Georgia to the sea and Sheridan to the Shenandoah Valley and assumes command of Union forces north of Richmond.

■ **June 18**
Grant besieges Lee at Petersburg.

■ **September 2**
Sherman captures Atlanta.

■ **November 6**
Buoyed by Sherman's victory, Lincoln is reelected; Sherman starts the so-called March to the Sea through Georgia; Sheridan pursues Jubal Anderson Early in the Shenandoah.

1865

■ **February 3**
Hampton Roads Conference takes place; Lincoln rebuffs Confederate officials, insisting on unconditional surrender.

■ **March 4**
Lincoln's Second Inaugural Address appeals for a peace with "malice towards none."

■ **January–March 21**
Sherman drives through the Carolinas.

■ **March 28**
Lincoln meets with Grant and Sherman on the *River Queen* to discuss the military situation and the terms of the Confederate surrender.

■ **Spring**
Sherman drives north toward Johnston in North Carolina.

■ **April 2**
Grant breaks Lee's line; Lee evacuates Petersburg; Lee wires Davis to abandon Richmond, and Davis flees.

■ **April 5,**
Lincoln visits Richmond after Davis flees.

■ **April 7–9**
"Surrender Letters" are exchanged between Grant and Lee.

and the valor of its two major armies still in the field. Ruined and disconsolate at the prospect of surrendering to the hated Yankees, anger and resentment smoldered beneath surface resignation. The threat of prolonged guerrilla struggle loomed. If further provoked, the North was capable of vengefully turning on the South, whose treasonous responsibility for the war might have been punished by harsh occupation, trial and execution of the leaders of the rebellion, indemnification for northern losses, and political subjugation. The way in which the Civil War was concluded would determine the climate of opinion on both sides and be of decisive influence in shaping the possibilities for postwar reunion and reconstruction.

On February 3, 1864, Confederate President Jefferson Davis sent Vice President Alexander Stephens to confer with President Abraham Lincoln at Hampton Roads aboard the Union transport ship the *River Queen*. With Davis insisting on southern independence, Lincoln demanded unconditional surrender and sent the Confederate officials back to Richmond. In his Second Inaugural Address of March 4, 1864, Lincoln appealed to the nation for a peace without vengeance: "With malice towards none, with charity for all … let us strive on to finish the work we are in; to bind up the nation's wounds … to do all which may achieve and cherish a just and lasting peace." Lincoln signaled that he would see the struggle for reunion without slavery through to the end, but he was offering a peace free of retribution and vengeance.

On March 28 the generals George Gordon Meade, Sherman, and Grant and Admiral David Dixon Porter met with President Lincoln at City Point aboard the *River Queen* to discuss the military situation. According to Sherman's account of the meeting in his memoirs, when told that "one more bloody battle" remained to be fought, "the president exclaimed more than once, that there had been blood enough shed, and asked us if another battle could be avoided." Sherman asked, "What was to be done with the rebel armies when they were defeated?" Lincoln replied that "all he wanted was for us to defeat the opposing armies, and to get the men composing the Confederate armies back to their homes, at work on their farms and in their shops" (Sherman, pp. 811–813). Sherman would recollect that Lincoln's words echoed the Second Inaugural Address, which called for "charity." Both Sherman and Grant would later insist that the lenient surrender terms they offered were determined during this meeting with Lincoln.

When Union forces punched holes in the rebel line southwest of Petersburg, Virginia, on April 2, Lee decided to abandon the city and cabled Jefferson Davis to evacuate Richmond. Under the cover of darkness Lee crossed the Appomattox River, moving west and hoping to turn south to link up with General Joseph Johnston in North Carolina. On April 4 an exultant Lincoln visited Richmond. When Major General Godfrey Weitzel asked him what the army was supposed to do with the rebels, Lincoln responded, "If I were you I'd let 'em up easy" (Perret, p. 403). Lincoln feared that a political vacuum after the

Confederate surrender would lead to anarchy and years of guerrilla warfare.

After Sheridan's cavalry beat Lee to the food and provisions awaiting him at Appomattox Station, he knew that his starving army was trapped. Rejecting the suggestion of his fellow officers that he disperse his troops to fight as guerrillas, Lee prepared to surrender to Grant. Grant and Lee began an exchange of messages on April 7, known as the "Surrender Letters." Grant asked for the surrender of the Army of Northern Virginia. Hoping to negotiate an armistice rather than a surrender, Lee proposed a meeting to discuss peace terms. Grant appealed for Lee to lay down his arms without further loss of life. When Lee received word that General Meade was preparing to attack him, he stopped trying to negotiate and asked Grant to meet to discuss surrender terms. Lee had a subordinate choose Wilmer McLean's house in the town of Appomattox as the meeting place.

Expecting to be arrested, Lee donned his finest gray uniform. In sharp contrast, Grant wore his usual simple private's uniform. Following small talk about their mutual time in the Mexican-American War, Lee asked Grant for his surrender terms. Grant stated that his terms were the same as in his letter—Lee's men would simply turn in their arms and return home under parole. Eager to accept terms not mentioning arrest or imprisonment for his officers or men, Lee asked Grant to write the terms on paper. When Grant asked whether the terms were satisfactory, Lee replied, "It is more than I expected" (Hendrickson, p. 195). The last sentence was tantamount to a general amnesty for all Confederate troops— they would not have to worry about reprisals for having taken up arms against the government. Referring to the provision that his officers could keep their side arms, private horses, and baggage, Lee turned to Grant and said, "This will have a very happy effect upon my army" (Hendrickson, p. 195).

Continuing to press for concessions for his men, Lee noted that his cavalry and artillerymen owned their own horses, which the terms did not allow them to keep. Musing that these men would need their horses to plant crops to feed their hungry families, Grant stipulated that he would instruct the parole officers to let the men keep their horses. Grant went further, offering to provide transportation home for Lee's men. Mostly impassive to this point, Lee offered his appreciation at such unexpectedly generous terms by remarking, "This will have the best possible effect on the men. It will be very gratifying and do much to conciliating our people" (Hendrickson, p. 198).The meeting closed on a further note of conciliation when, after listening to Lee describe the famished state of his army, Grant asked, "Suppose I send over twenty-five thousand rations. Do you think that will be a sufficient supply?" Lee replied, "I think it will be ample and it will be a great relief I assure you" (Hendrickson, p. 200). After two and a half hours, Lee rose, bowed to Grant, and shook his hand before walking out of the house to meet his men and deliver the surrender terms.

Time Line

1865

- **April 9**
Lee surrenders the Army of Northern Virginia to Grant at Appomattox Court House.

- **April 14**
Lincoln is shot at Ford's Theatre by a Confederate sympathizer, John Wilkes Booth.

- **April 18**
Joseph Johnston surrenders to Sherman.

1868– 1876

- Grant serves two undistinguished terms as president.

1885

- **July 23**
Grant dies of cancer.

About the Author

The eldest of six children, Hiram Ulysses Grant was born in a two-room cabin on April 27, 1822, at Point Pleasant, Ohio, to Jesse Root Grant and Hannah Simpson. Called Ulysses by his father, Hiram grew up across the street from his father's tanning factory, with the stench of animal hides and tanning chemicals constantly in his nostrils. As a boy he did farm work, and at age sixteen he worked in his father's tannery. Grant, small in stature and of a sensitive nature, was a mediocre student, dubbed "Useless" by other students. His singular talent was his skill with horses and horsemanship.

He was mistakenly registered as "Ulysses S." when he was appointed to the U.S. Military Academy at West Point. Grant was an unexceptional cadet academically, but his superior horsemanship made him a candidate for the army's elite cavalry. When he was arrested for striking a horse, however, Grant's chances of a career in the cavalry were ruined. Graduating near the lower half of his class, he was posted to the infantry, where he would command common, rather than elite, soldiers.

Grant was posted to a St. Louis regiment along with his West Point roommate, Frederick Dent, who introduced Ulysses to his sister, Julia. The Dent family was wealthy, owning twenty slaves. Grant fought in the Mexican-American War, receiving two citations for bravery. After the war, he was redeployed as a brevet captain in Missouri, where he married Julia. Repelled by the Dent family's ownership of slaves, Grant's parents did not attend the wedding. Grant and Julia eventually had four children.

The routine of peacetime army life did not agree with Grant. He was constantly transferred to bases on the West Coast, far from his wife and children. To relieve his loneli-

Robert E. Lee (Library of Congress)

ness, he apparently turned to alcohol. Grant biographers differ on the circumstances of his departure from the army and on his drunkenness. The consensus view holds that Grant was a binge drinker who indulged episodically to relieve depression. Relations between Grant and his commander deteriorated, and Grant resigned from the army in 1854 and returned to his family in Missouri.

Over the next six years Grant tried and failed at several undertakings. His father-in-law gave him land to farm, but he could not make a go of it as a farmer. In 1858–1859 he worked briefly as a bill collector In 1861 the Civil War rescued Grant from a tedious job working in his brother's leather shop. The need for experienced officers was so great that the army accepted Grant's reenlistment despite his delinquent record. His first assignment was to organize an infantry unit out of the ragtag 21st Illinois Volunteer Infantry. After leading the regiment to success against guerrilla units in Missouri, Grant was promoted to brigadier general. His capture of Fort Henry and Fort Donelson on the Cumberland River in northern Tennessee in early 1862 marked the first significant military victories won by Union forces. His audacity in the West stood in sharp contrast to the methods of the defensive-minded generals in the East, especially George B. McLellan, who had bungled a chance to end the war with a force of over one hundred thousand men in the Peninsula campaign the previous summer. The contrast was not lost on Abraham Lincoln, who saw Grant as a possible replacement for the timid and prickly McLellan.

When Union forces suffered massive troop losses at Shilo, Grant's rivals and their political allies in Washington blamed him, claiming that he was drinking again. In response to demands that Grant be discharged, Lincoln is said to have retorted, "I can't spare this man; he fights!" (Donald, p. 171). By 1862 Lincoln had promoted the cigar-smoking Grant to major general. At Vicksburg in the early summer of 1862, Grant took his army across the Mississippi River, bypassing the fort's heavy artillery before doubling back to capture the garrison from the rear. The Vicksburg campaign gave the Union control of the Mississippi River, splitting the Confederacy in two. By early 1864 with the generals George Henry Thomas, Sheridan, and Sherman, Grant had captured eastern Tennessee, opening the Confederacy to a two-pronged assault from the West, which would ultimately lead to Lee's encirclement in Virginia.

Lincoln promoted Grant to lieutenant general and commander of all Union forces in March of 1864. Grant devised a coordinated offensive strategy to simultaneously strike the Confederacy from several directions. As an adjunct to the strategy, Grant formulated the doctrine of "total war." He broke with the conventional dictum that an army needed to maintain its supply lines or face starvation. Union forces penetrating deep into the South would rely on the enemy's own resource base, bringing the reality of war to the enemy population. As the army moved forward, it would make war on the enemy's means of making war by destroying railroads and bridges and by confiscating food supplies from the civilian population. Destroying the economic infrastructure that supplied the enemy armies was considered as important as tactical victories on the battlefield.

Grant placed General Sherman in command of forces in the West and moved his own command to Virginia to restart the long-stalled Union objective of destroying Lee's Army of Northern Virginia and capturing the Confederate capital at Richmond. Sherman would capture Atlanta and move over land to Savannah on the coast before turning north through South Carolina to engage and destroy Joe Johnston's army in North Carolina. Grant began his final campaign against Lee in May 1864, leading the Army of the Potomac across the Rapidan River. Grant and Lee fought two murderous battles in succession at the Wilderness and then at Spotsylvania Court House, with massive casualties on both sides. Despite casualty rates that would have driven previous Union commanders to retreat, Grant pledged in a legendary dispatch, "I propose to fight it out along this line if it takes all summer" (McPherson, p. 731). Caring little about winning individual battles, Grant's strategy was to exhaust Lee by hammering at him with superior force in a relentless succession of battles. This strategy forced Lee to fight a long, defensive battle rather than using the slashing counterattacks and surprise assaults he had used so effectively in the past. An expert in trench warfare, Lee had his outnumbered troops dig a continuously lengthening line around Petersburg, the gateway to Richmond. Grant took such enormous casualties in the long struggle around Petersburg that the opposition press in the North dubbed him "the butcher." The bloodiest carnage occurred at Cold Harbor on June 3. In his memoirs Grant conceded that the final third charge was a tactical error, but he continued to replenish his forces and press Lee.

Grant remained stalled before Petersburg through the summer of 1864, while Sherman was bogged down at Atlanta. As public patience in the North wore thin, the wisdom of Grant's strategy was increasingly challenged. By August, Lincoln confided to his aides that he expected to lose the upcoming election. Then, in September, Sherman took Atlanta, opinion in the North shifted, and Lincoln was easily reelected. In November, Sherman began his march through Georgia to Savannah and north to South Carolina.

By early April 1865 Grant's pressure forced Lee to overextend his lines. Eventually, Lee was forced to flee Petersburg, crossing the Appomattox River to the west. With the American flag flying over Richmond and no hope of breaking the Union containment to join Johnston in North Carolina, Lee sent surrender overtures to Grant. After a series of exchanges relating to the terms of surrender, Lee surrendered the Army of Northern Virginia at Appomattox Court House on April 9, 1865.

Despite being elected president twice, Grant's postwar career was anticlimactic. Grant opposed President Andrew Johnson's Reconstruction policy because he thought it was too lenient toward the former Confederates. This made him the choice of the radical wing of the Republican Party, who secured his nomination for president in the election of 1866. Grant's own policy was indecisive and inconsistent. As state after state was "redeemed" by conservative former Confederates, Grant stood by, claiming that defending black rights in the South should be left to local militias rather than to the U.S. Army. On the other hand, the Enforcement Acts of 1870–1871 broke the power of the Ku Klux Klan, and the Civil Rights Act of 1875 was an unprecedented attempt to extend federal protection to black civil rights in public accommodations.

In the ensuing years Grant's inexperience and his admiration of financially successful men led him into a series of scandals. In 1869, with the assistance of Grant's brothers-in-law the stock manipulators Jay Gould and Jim Fisk floated the rumor that the government would stop redeeming greenbacks, the paper currency issued during the war, for gold. In the resulting panic, the pair cornered the gold market, driving up the price of gold and bankrupting many legitimate businesses. When the president learned of the scheme, he belatedly intervened, directing the Treasury to sell four million dollars' worth of gold to lower the price. In 1872–1873 another scandal broke when it was revealed that Vice President Schuyler Colfax had been bribed with Crédit Mobilier stock in return for legislation favorable to western railroad companies. The 1874 Sanborn scandal involved tax farming by federal officials, while in the Whiskey Ring scandal treasury officials conspired with distillers to dodge excise taxes on whiskey. On top of the financial and graft scandals, speculation in railroad stock triggered the Panic of 1873, setting off a general economic depression for which the hapless Grant had no answer.

After returning from a celebrated world tour in the late 1870s, Grant was bankrupted by foolish investments in the

A lithograph depicting Robert E. Lee (right) formally surrendering to General Ulysses S. Grant at the Appomattox Court House on April 9, 1865 (Library of Congress)

fraudulent banking firm Grant & Ward. In a final act of courage and determination while dying of throat cancer, Grant kept himself alive long enough to finish writing his *Personal Memoirs.* Considered by critics a remarkable work of military memoir writing, Grant's memoirs earned enough money to pull his family out of debt. Grant died of throat cancer in 1885.

Explanation and Analysis of the Document

The five Articles of Agreement reflect the approach Lincoln had suggested aboard the *River Queen* in March. Considering that the officers of the Army of Northern Virginia and especially its commanding general, Robert E. Lee, were leaders of a bloody insurgency against the U.S. government and guilty of treason by any legal definition of the term, the conditions of surrender were remarkably generous. Lincoln wanted to offer Lee the most lenient terms consistent with unconditional surrender in order to remove his army from the battlefield and bring the Civil War to an end.

Article 1 is the most significant of the articles. The officers and men of the Army of Northern Virginia would not be

"The troops shall march by Brigades and Detachments to a designated point, stock their Arms, deposit their flags, Sabres, Pistols, etc. and from thence march to their homes under charge of their Officers."

(Article 1, Articles of Surrender of the Army of Northern Virginia)

"There is but one condition I would insist upon, namely: that the men and officers surrendered shall be disqualified for taking up arms again against the Government of the United States."

(Ulysses S. Grant to Robert E. Lee, April 8, 1865; Hendrickson, p. 177)

"By the South laying down their arms they will hasten that most desirable event, save thousands of human lives and hundreds of millions of property not yet destroyed."

(Ulysses S. Grant to Robert E. Lee, April 9, 1865; Hendrickson, p. 180)

held as prisoners of war or charged with treason. Article 1 simply requires the soldiers of the Army of Northern Virginia, marching in orderly formation, to stockpile their arms, flags, "Sabres, Pistols, etc." and continue marching home under charge of their own officers. According to previous agreement, they are "not to be disturbed by U.S. authority as long as they observe their paroles and the laws in force where they may reside" (McPherson, p. 849). This was an effective guarantee of immunity from prosecution for treason. The officers are allowed to retain their own sidearms.

Article 2 requires that all horses that are not the personal property of their riders and other "public property," be turned over to federal staff officers. Grant had originally insisted that Lee's troopers turn in their horses. When Lee requested that they be allowed to retain their horses because they needed them for farming, however, Grant readily assented. This was stipulated in Article 4: "Couriers and Wounded men of the artillery and Cavalry whose horses are their own private property will be allowed to retain them."

This spirit of generosity continues in the third article, granting former Confederate officers the right to use necessary means of transportation for their "Private baggage" for their trip home. The final article simply defines who is to be included in the agreement of surrender—basically, all officers and enlisted men serving with Lee when the negotiations actually commenced on the eighth of April. Cavalry that had escaped before that date and artillery units more than twenty miles away from Appomattox Court House are not included in the Articles of Agreement.

Audience

As commander of all Confederate forces and the most respected leader in the South, Robert E. Lee was Grant's primary audience. Lee's reaction to the surrender terms would determine how his own troops and the remaining Confederate forces in the field would view them. Despite their exhaustion and hunger, the rebel troops still under arms were battle-hardened veterans who would fight on at the slightest sign from their commander. In offering such generous surrender terms, Lincoln hoped to communicate to his former Whig allies throughout the South that they could convincingly promote the cause of reunion in their respective states and join him as allies in Reconstruction.

In a larger sense, the entire population of the southern states was the intended audience. With his own Upper South roots, Lincoln was well aware that a harsh peace stressing their treason would have stoked the fires of resentment and hatred burning beneath the surface. In a narrower political sense, Lincoln wanted to seize the initiative on Reconstruction from his radical adversaries, such as Secretary of War Edwin Stanton, by striking a conciliatory keynote at war's end.

Impact

The surrender terms served their immediate purpose of disarming the Army of Northern Virginia; by removing

Robert E. Lee from the battlefield, they effectively ended the Civil War. Nine days later, in Durham, North Carolina, General Johnston disregarded Jefferson Davis's plea for continued resistance and surrendered his thirty-seven thousand men to Sherman.

The leniency of the surrender terms definitely helped prevent transformation of the Civil War into a prolonged guerrilla war. Lee's lieutenants had urged that he take this course before the surrender, and Jefferson Davis favored this course as well. Such a decentralized war fought over the 500,000-plus square miles of the secessionist South would have been a long and bloody struggle reminiscent of the terror of "Bleeding Kansas" in the 1850s but on a grander scale. Lincoln had the foresight to see that this would have been the worst possible outcome. While the generous surrender terms did not produce a miracle of reconciliation, they succeeded in ending the bloodshed by demobilizing the rebel armies. With the armed conflict ended, the stage was set for a political and constitutional resolution of the underlying causes of the Civil War.

Related Documents

Chamberlain, Joshua Lawrence. *The Passing of the Armies: An Account of the Final Campaign of the Army of the Potomac.* Lincoln: University of Nebraska Press, 1998. The Bowdoin College professor and Gettysburg hero gives his account of the war's last days and the surrender at Appomattox.

Grant, Ulysses S. *Personal Memoirs.* New York: Modern Library, 1999. Grant's memoirs are useful for insight into Grant's personal data and his' strategic military thinking.

Lee, Robert E. *Lee's Dispatches; Unpublished Letters of General Robert E. Lee, C.S.A., to Jefferson Davis and the War Department of the Confederate States of America, 1862–65, from the Private Collections of Wymberley Jones De Renne.* New York: G. P. Putnam's Sons, 1915. Lee did not leave memoirs of the Civil War, but his views may be gleaned from his dispatches and letters to the Confederate president Jefferson Davis.

Sherman, William Tecumseh. *Memoirs of General W. T. Sherman* New York: Viking Press, 1990. Sherman's memoirs contain Admiral Porter's account of the meeting aboard the *River Queen* between Lincoln, Grant, and Sherman.

Bibliography

■ Books

Anderson, Nancy Scott, and Dwight Anderson. *The Generals: Ulysses S. Grant and Robert E. Lee.* New York: Random House, 1994.

Catton, Bruce. *Grant Takes Command.* Boston: Little, Brown, 1969.

———. *Never Call Retreat.* London: Phoenix, 2001.

Donald, David Herbert. *Liberty and Union: The Crisis of Popular Government 1830-1890* Boston: Little, Brown and Co., 1978.

Hendrickson, Robert. *The Road to Appomattox.* New York: John Wiley & Sons, 1998.

Marvel, William. *Lee's Last Retreat: The Flight to Appomattox.* Chapel Hill: University of North Carolina Press, 2002.

McFeely, William S. *Grant: A Biography.* New York: W. W. Norton, 1981.

McPherson, James M. *Ordeal by Fire: The Civil War and Reconstruction.* New York: Alfred A. Knopf, 1982.

———. *Battle Cry of Freedom: The Civil War Era.* New York: Oxford University Press, 1988.

Perret, Geoffrey. *Lincoln's War: The Untold Story of America's Greatest President as Commander in Chief.* New York: Random House, 2004.

Stern, Philip Van Doren. *An End to Valor: The Last Days of the Civil War.* Boston: Houghton Mifflin, 1958.

Wheeler, Richard. *Witness to Appomattox.* New York: Harper and Row, 1989.

Winik, Jay. *April, 1865: The Month That Saved America.* New York: HarperCollins Publishers, 2001.

■ Web Sites

"Appomattox Court House." National Park Service, U.S. Department of the Interior, Web site.
http://www.nps.gov/apco. Accessed on January 11, 2008.

"Second Inaugural Address of Abraham Lincoln." The Avalon Project at Yale Law School Web site.
http://www.yale.edu/lawweb/avalon/presiden/inaug/lincoln2.htm. Accessed on January 21, 2008.

"Ulysses Simpson Grant (1822–1885)." Miller Center of Public Affairs "American President: An Online Reference Resource" Web site.
http://www.millercenter.virginia.edu/academic/americanpresident/grant. Accessed on January 11, 2008.

Ulysses S. Grant Homepage Web site.
http://www.empirenet.com/~ulysses/index.htm. Accessed on January 11, 2008.

—By Robert Montgomery

1. The leniency of the "surrender terms" is credited with the avoidance of a guerrilla war by the defeated Confederacy. Given what you know about the conditions in the South by the spring of 1865 and considering Lee's opposition to continuing the war by unconventional means, how real was the threat of protracted guerrilla war? What do you think the rebel guerrilla outfits would have been like? To what extent do you think they would have enjoyed popular support?

2. Lincoln proposed to win the war and restore the Union first and then to reconstruct the Confederate states without slavery and with civil and political rights for the freedmen. To accomplish the first goal, he amnestied the leaders of the rebellion. By 1868 former Confederate officials were returned to the U.S. Congress under presidential Reconstruction. This rapid resurgence of the old antebellum elite is usually attributed to the laxity of President Andrew Johnson, a Democrat from Tennessee. Did the liberality of the surrender terms contribute to this outcome? Or did the onus lie exclusively with Johnson?

3. Many Civil War historians argue that the Emancipation Proclamation and the enlistment of black troops in 1863 transformed the conflict from a conservative effort to preserve the Union to a revolutionary struggle to overturn the social order of the slave South. Assuming they are right, how would you explain surrender terms that not only exempted the military leaders of the rebellion from treason charges but also even offered them assistance to return home to their families? Had Lincoln survived, how would he have responded to the charge that his surrender policy contradicted his Reconstruction goals?

4. After President Andrew Johnson rescinded Sherman's wartime distribution of land to former slaves and returned four hundred thousand slaves to their former owners, land redistribution was forgotten, and the hopes of the freed people for land were dashed. Despite its failures, Reconstruction did achieve gains for the freed people. Given what you know about Reconstruction, discuss what steps were taken to secure black rights. You might consider efforts in the areas of education and civil and political rights.

Glossary

Brigades	units of about three thousand men each, or three regiments
Corps	the largest units of an army, usually three divisions and an artillery brigade and comprising about thirty thousand men
construed	given meaning or explained
Couriers	messengers, especially those on official diplomatic business
Division	a unit of three brigades made up of about nine thousand men
Quarter Masters	officers responsible for the food, clothing, and equipment of troops
Side arms	firearms, such as pistols, that are held and fired with one hand

ARTICLES OF AGREEMENT RELATING TO THE SURRENDER OF THE ARMY OF NORTHERN VIRGINIA

Appomattox Court House Virginia

April 10, 1865

Agreement entered into this day in regard to the surrender of the Army of Northern Virginia to the United States Authorities.

1st The troops shall march by Brigades and Detachments to a designated point, stock their Arms, deposit their flags, Sabres, Pistols, etc. and from thence march to their homes under charge of their Officers, superintended by their respective Division and Corps Commanders, Officers, retaining their side Arms, and the authorized number of private horses.

2. All public horses and public property of all kinds to be turned over to Staff Officers designated by the United States Authorities.

3. Such transportation as may be agreed upon as necessary for the transportation of the Private baggage of Officers will be allowed to accompany the Officers, to be turned over at the end of the trip to the nearest U.S. Quarter Masters, receipts being taken for the same.

4. Couriers and Wounded men of the artillery and Cavalry whose horses are their own private property will be allowed to retain them.

5. The surrender of the Army of Northern Virginia shall be construed to include all the forces operating with that Army on the 8th inst., the date of commencement of negociation for surrender, except such bodies of Cavalry as actually made their escape previous to the surrender, and except also such forces of Artillery as were more than Twenty (20) miles from Appomattox Court House at the time of Surrender on the 9th inst.

Governor Benjamin Grubb Humphreys was responsible for pushing the Black Code through the Mississippi legislature. (Library of Congress)

BLACK CODE OF MISSISSIPPI

"Every freedman, free negro and mulatto shall ... have a lawful home or employment, and shall have written evidence thereof."

Overview

In 1865 the Mississippi state legislature passed a series of related laws known as the Black Code. These laws, written within months of the conclusion of the Civil War and styled after the state's antebellum slave code, represented the first effort by white Mississippians to define what freedom and citizenship would mean to recently freed slaves and others of African descent. As the Black Code reveals, the initial legal definition that whites offered suggests that they intended the condition of freedom for blacks to differ little from enslavement.

The Mississippi Black Code was the most extreme example of similar codes that sought to nullify the freedom of former slaves and to define their citizenship as virtual enslavement. The laws consequently offer an example of the attitudes of whites toward freed people and other people of African descent; they also testify to the persistence of those attitudes across time. Finally, the Black Code is significant because its existence proved to the United States Congress that southern states needed a more thoroughgoing reconstruction than that called for by President Andrew Johnson. A year after the passage of the Black Code, Congress assumed authority over Reconstruction in the southern states.

Context

In April 1865, after four years of fighting and deprivation, the Civil War ended. The cessation of fighting, however, did not firmly settle the end of their social system in white southerners' minds. The lack of commitment to black freedom in Washington, D.C., and among white southerners meant that former slaves could not easily acquire citizenship. By the conclusion of 1865, Mississippi, abetted by the U.S. president, offered firm evidence that white southerners, while reluctantly granting the abolition of slavery, refused to grant African Americans equality before the law.

An assassin took the life of President Abraham Lincoln within days of the war's end. Lincoln's generous plan for ensuring the return of the southern states to the Union fell into the hands of his successor, Andrew Johnson. The new president, a native of east Tennessee, significantly modified Lincoln's plan for Reconstruction by adding provisions intended to punish the elite planters of the South, whom he blamed for the secession crisis and the Civil War. In addition to depriving wealthy southerners and certain former Confederates of the right to citizenship, Johnson insisted that before southern states reenter the Union they repeal their secession ordinances and ratify the Thirteenth Amendment to the U.S. Constitution, which ended slavery.

Johnson's plan for Reconstruction, however, was ultimately undemanding. Even though he wished to punish certain Confederate officials and officers as well as wealthy planters, he refused to require that southern states embrace liberal notions of African American citizenship. In an August 1865 letter to Mississippi's provisional governor, William Sharkey, Johnson encouraged him to lead the state constitutional convention, which was meeting at the time, to grant the right to vote only to individuals who could read and write and to owners of property valued at a minimum of $250. Since few, if any, former slaves or African Americans living in Mississippi owned taxable property (real estate) of any sort and few could read and write, Johnson's vision of voting rights in the post-Emancipation era did not include extension of suffrage to more than a handful of blacks. Regarding suffrage, the 1865 constitutional convention chose to replicate the Constitution of 1832; it limited the right to vote to white males over the age of twenty-one.

Two other matters that the president demanded be addressed, the secession ordinance and the abolition of slavery, occupied the 1865 convention delegates. After much wrangling, the convention declared the ordinance of session "null and of no binding force" (*Journal of the Proceedings and Debates in the Constitutional Convention of the State of Mississippi, August, 1865*, p. 176). Convention delegates rejected other language that accomplished the same task, lest signers of the 1861 ordinance find themselves subject to prosecution as traitors. Delegates debated vigorously even the abolition of slavery. Foolishly hoping that the federal government might offer former slave owners compensation for the loss of their human property, the convention eventually declared that the state ended the institution of slavery not voluntarily but under duress.

1860

■ **December 20**
South Carolina secedes from the Union.

1861

■ **January 9**
Mississippi secedes from the Union.

■ **April 12**
The first shots of the Civil War are fired at Fort Sumter in the harbor at Charleston, South Carolina.

1865

■ **April 9**
Robert E. Lee surrenders the bulk of the Confederate army at Appomattox Court House, Virginia, effectively ending the Civil War.

■ **April 15**
President Abraham Lincoln dies after being shot the previous day, and Andrew Johnson becomes president.

■ **November 25**
The Mississippi legislature passes the Black Code.

1867

■ **March 26**
General E. O. C. Ord arrives in Mississippi as military governor, signaling the start of congressional Reconstruction in the state.

1875

■ **November 10**
The election of the Democrat John Marshal Stone signals the end of the Reconstruction in Mississippi and the beginning of a slow but certain retreat from the recognition of the fullness of African American citizenship.

Albert T. Morgan, a white northerner who went south during Reconstruction, rightly argued that through such language the delegates intended that their heirs know that "slavery had not been destroyed" (Morgan, pp. 204–205). Former slaves viewed the 1865 constitution in a similar manner. A group of former bondsmen meeting at Vicksburg predicted that soon the state of Mississippi would try to enslave blacks again or force them from the state.

At the conclusion of the constitutional convention, delegates filed a report with the newly elected state legislature. The report called for the body to withhold from former slaves "some unbridled privileges for the present." According to the report, "the wayward and vicious, idle and dishonest, the lawless and reckless, the wicked and improvident, the vagabond and meddler must be smarted, governed, reformed and guided by higher instincts, minds and morals higher and holier than theirs." Benjamin Grubb Humphreys, who was elected governor after the convention, embraced the convention report when he told the first postwar legislature: "The purity and progress of both races require that caste must be maintained" (Bond, pp. 158–159). Perhaps not surprisingly, the first Mississippi legislature to convene after the Civil War embraced the Black Code.

About the Author

A number of legislators contributed to the authorship of the Mississippi Black Code. While Governor Benjamin Grubb Humphreys probably did not write a word of the laws, he was singularly responsible for pushing the bill through the legislature. Debate over the code consumed an inordinate amount of time in the first postwar session of the legislature. The law was finally approved only when Humphreys offered a compromise between legislators, some of whom wanted to appease Republicans in Washington and thereby to avoid a more stringent Reconstruction process, and some of whom wished to ignore the demands of the federal government and the significance of the Confederacy's military defeat.

Humphreys (1808–1882) was a native of Claiborne County, Mississippi, and a brigadier general in the Confederate army. Before the war, he attended the U.S. Military Academy at West Point, though his participation in a rowdy demonstration, which led to a riot, caused him to be expelled. After his dismissal, he returned to Mississippi, where he became a cotton planter and politician in Sunflower County, the heart of the Mississippi Delta. In 1865 white Mississippians elected him governor, and in 1867 they reelected him. By that time, congressional Reconstruction had begun, and he resigned his office in 1868 soon after being sworn in, rather than operate under the supervision of a military governor. For almost ten years he worked for an insurance company in Jackson, Mississippi, before retiring back to his Sunflower County home.

Explanation and Analysis of the Document

The document consists of three parts: "An Act to Confer Civil Rights on Freedmen, and for Other Purposes"; "An Act to Regulate the Relation of Master and Apprentice, as Relates to Freedmen, Free Negroes, and Mulattoes"; and "An Act to Amend the Vagrant Laws of the State."

◆ **An Act to Confer Civil Rights on Freedmen, and for Other Purposes**

In this first section of the Black Code, African Americans are granted the right to buy and sell property other than real estate. By denying blacks the ability to own real property, the legislature attempts to ensure that they would remain dependent laborers. Indeed, Section 1 of the law permits blacks to rent property in cities and towns only if local government expressly allows them to. In this way, the legislature attempts to keep blacks in the country, close to agricultural labor, the only labor whites assume that blacks can perform.

Further attempts to control the labor of blacks appear in Sections 5 through 9. In those sections, African Americans are required to have a legally validated address and employment at the start of each new year, typically the same time that labor contracts are signed. Although blacks receive certain protections in the execution of contracts, they are not permitted to break their contracts with "good cause." Doing so would result in prosecution in the courts. The sections of the law addressing those who breach contracts resemble the sections of the separate act that regulated relations between masters and apprentices. By subjecting individuals who break their contracts to similar treatment and punishment as runaway apprentices, the legislature evinces its belief that African Americans could not be trusted to perform their labor.

The act also regulates the social rights of African Americans. While slaves never had the legal right to marry, the Black Code recognizes that they can marry as long as they marry someone of their own race. The code also allows former slaves who have lived with someone in a spousal relationship to record their relationship as married in the county records. To further clarify who classifies as black and is thus prohibited from marrying a white person, the law defines a mulatto as someone with a single "negro" great-grandparent.

Section 4 of the law says that former slaves and others of African descent can testify against other African Americans. In criminal proceedings, however, they can testify against a white person accused of committing a crime against a black person. The restriction on blacks' testimony in the court reflects restrictions that appear in the antebellum slave code.

◆ An Act to Regulate the Relation of Master and Apprentice, as Relates to Freedmen, Free Negroes, and Mulattoes

This section of the Mississippi Black Code may be the best known, as it provides ample evidence that lawmakers are reluctant to wholly abolish slavery. The first section of the law requires that officers of county courts twice annually file a report listing the names of African Americans under the age of eighteen who are orphans or whose parents cannot provide proper care for them. According to the law, juveniles who are listed on the report would be then apprenticed to a "competent and suitable person." Not only would the treatment provided to orphaned or neglected African Americans differ from the treatment provided to white orphans, former owners of orphaned or poorly cared for children would also be the preference when the court searches for a suitable master for the child. Apprenticed children would be subject to "moderate" corporal punishment and protected from cruel or inhumane treatment.

Gender determines the term of an orphaned or neglected child's indenture. Males are apprentices until they reach the age of twenty-one; females can achieve release from their indenture upon their eighteenth birthdays. Further, the law allowed the "recapture" of apprentices who flee before their term of service ends, and it permits punishment of apprentices who refuse to return to their masters. Apprentices could, however, challenge their masters' rights to retain them against their will. If a county court judges the apprentice to have good cause for desiring an end to his or her indenture, the court could release the apprentice and fine the master up to $100. Any fine collected would be used for the benefit of the apprentice.

This section of the law also prohibits any white person from helping an apprentice escape his or her master or from enticing an apprentice to accept employment. Individuals convicted of violating the law would be subject to punishment.

◆ An Act to Amend the Vagrant Laws of the State

This section of the law defines a broad swath of behavior, including juggling, gambling, and the habitual drinking of alcoholic beverages, as indicative of vagrancy. The law also classifies individuals (regardless of color) who do not work, misspend their money, and do not properly care for themselves or their dependents as vagrants. Prostitutes and gambling house operators, as well as all manner of citizens who obtain their income from illegal or immoral acts, are classified by the law as vagrants. Individuals who are convicted of vagrancy are fined up to $100 and may be sentenced to jail for up to ten days.

African Americans are subject to additional penalties for vagrancy, as are whites who are commonly associated with African Americans. Section 2 of the amendment clearly echoes Mississippi's antebellum slave code. Specifically, the section prohibits unemployed blacks from free assembly; it prohibits white males from assembling with African Americans or from having sexual relations with black women. Blacks who are convicted of vagrancy under Section 2 of the amendment are subject to a $50 fine and ten days in jail; white men are subject to a $200 fine and six months in jail.

If convicted, African Americans who cannot pay their fines are to be hired out by the county sheriff to labor until their fine is paid. If a black vagrant is too old or infirm to be hired out, then the sheriff can treat the vagrant as a pauper. According to the law, African Americans eighteen to sixty-five years old are required to pay a $1 poll tax to fund the "Freedman's Pauper Fund" in each county. (White paupers are cared for through other means of taxation, not a special pauper's tax.) Refusal or inability to pay the tax results in an African American being classified as a vagrant and being hired out to anyone who is willing to pay the tax for the vagrant.

Audience

Public laws are written, in part, to shape behavior. Consequently, the audience to whom the Mississippi Black

> "Every freedman, free negro and mulatto shall, on the second Monday of January, one thousand eight hundred and sixty-six, and annually thereafter, have a lawful home or employment, and shall have written evidence thereof."
>
> (Section 5, An Act to Confer Civil Rights on Freedmen, and for Other Purposes)

> "All rouges and vagabonds, idle and dissipated persons, beggars, jugglers, or persons practicing unlawful games or plays, runaways, common drunkards, common night-walkers, pilferers, lewd, wanton, or lascivious persons, in speech or behavior, common railers and brawlers, persons who neglect their calling or employment, misspend what they earn, or do not provide for the support of themselves or their families, or dependents, and all other idle and disorderly persons, including all who neglect all lawful business, habitually misspend their time by frequenting houses of ill-fame, gaming-houses, or tippling shops, shall be deemed and considered vagrants."
>
> (Section 1, An Act to Amend the Vagrant Laws of the State)

Code was addressed included all of Mississippi's residents and visitors. However, few Mississippians, including lawyers, law enforcement officials, and judges, would have read the actual text of the law.

Impact

Passage of the Black Code immediately provoked two reactions in the nation. In the South other state legislators emulated the Mississippi Black Code. Yet in the North the laws alerted Republicans in Congress to the fact that white southerners would not voluntarily embrace black liberty.

While testifying before Congress in 1865, Colonel Samuel Thomas, an official with the Bureau of Refugees, Freedmen, and Abandoned Lands, noted the persistence of such attitudes: "The whites esteem the blacks their property by natural right, and however much they may admit that the individual relations of masters and slaves have been destroyed by the war and the President's emancipation proclamation, they still have an ingrained feeling that the blacks at large belong to the whites at large, and whenever opportunity serves they treat the colored people just as their profit, caprice or passion may dictate" ("African American Voices," http://www.digitalhistory.uh.edu/black_voices/voices_display.cfm?id=82).

Taken together with President Andrew Johnson's alleged violation of laws and his disdain for Republican measures

directed toward ensuring the liberty of former slaves, Congress exerted its authority in 1866 and took over the reigns of Reconstruction. With a military governor placed in charge of Reconstruction in Mississippi, the state convened a new constitutional convention, a body elected in the first biracial, statewide election. The constitution that eventually emerged granted the full measure of citizenship to African Americans and thereby removed the Mississippi Black Code from the law books. Despite the code's brief life span, its impact reverberated broadly and throughout the course of Reconstruction.

Related Documents

Bond, Bradley G., ed. *Mississippi: A Documentary History*. Jackson: University Press of Mississippi, 2003. In this book, the chapter on antebellum includes replication of the antebellum slave code.

"Louisiana Black Codes." About.com "African-American History" Web site. http://afroamhistory.about.com/library/bllouisiana_black codes.htm. Accessed on January 18, 2008. This Web site posts an abbreviated version of the Louisiana Black Codes.

"Race, Racism, and the Law." University of Dayton School of Law Web site. http://academic.udayton.edu/race/02rights/jcrow02.htm. Accessed on January 18, 2008. This Web site includes examples of Jim Crow Laws passed in the late nineteenth and early twentieth centuries by a number of state legislatures.

Bibliography

■ Books

Bond, Bradley G. *Political Culture in the Nineteenth-Century South: Mississippi, 1830–1900.* Baton Rouge: Louisiana State University Press, 1995.

Harris, William C. *Presidential Reconstruction in Mississippi.* Baton Rouge: Louisiana State University Press, 1967.

———. *The Day of the Carpetbagger: Republication Reconstruction in Mississippi.* Baton Rouge: Louisiana State University Press, 1979.

Journal of the Proceedings and Debates in the Constitutional Convention of the State of Mississippi, August, 1865. Jackson, Miss., 1865.

Morgan, A. T. *Yazoo; or, On the Picket Line of Freedom in the South: A Personal Narrative.* 1884. Reprint. New York: Russell and Russell, 1968.

Wharton, Vernon Lane. *Negro in Mississippi, 1865–1890.* Chapel Hill: University of North Carolina Press, 1947.

■ Web Sites

"African American Voices." Digital History Web site. http://www.digitalhistory.uh.edu/black_voices/voices_display.cfm?id=82. Accessed on January 7, 2008

"Reconstruction in Mississippi, 1865–1876." Mississippi History Now Web site. http://teacherexchange.mde.k12.ms.us/MHNLP/reconstructionlp.htm. Accessed on January 7, 2008.

—By Bradley G. Bond

Questions for Further Study

1. Compare the Mississippi Black Code with the state's antebellum slave code.

2. How did the Mississippi Black Code differ from the Louisiana Black Code? How might those differences be explained?

3. Describe the restrictions placed upon African Americans by the Mississippi Black Code and by formal laws and ordinances enforced during the epoch of Jim Crow.

Glossary

freedmen	former slaves who had been emancipated at the conclusion of the Civil War
free negroes	blacks who had been emancipated by their owners, or the children of emancipated parents prior to the start of the Civil War
lewd	characterized by immorality or vulgarity
wanton	reflecting a lack of discipline or a refusal to submit to the formal or informal controls placed on individuals living in a civil society
lascivious	reflecting an inclination toward lust or lewdness
mulatto	a general term used to refer to people of mixed race, though it specifically refers to anyone who had at least one great-grandparent who was black
pauper	a term used mainly before the twentieth century to refer to poor or indigent people
tippling shops	businesses that sold liquor by either the glass or the bottle

BLACK CODE OF MISSISSIPPI

An Act to Confer Civil Rights on Freedmen, and for other Purposes

Section 1. All freedmen, free negroes and mulattoes may sue and be sued, implead and be impleaded, in all the courts of law and equity of this State, and may acquire personal property, and chooses in action, by descent or purchase, and may dispose of the same in the same manner and to the same extent that white persons may: Provided, That the provisions of this section shall not be so construed as to allow any freedman, free negro or mulatto to rent or lease any lands or tenements except in incorporated cities or towns, in which places the corporate authorities shall control the same.

Section 2. All freedmen, free negroes and mulattoes may intermarry with each other, in the same manner and under the same regulations that are provided by law for white persons: Provided, that the clerk of probate shall keep separate records of the same.

Section 3. All freedmen, free negroes or mulatoes who do now and have herebefore lived and cohabited together as husband and wife shall be taken and held in law as legally married, and the issue shall be taken and held as legitimate for all purposes; and it shall not be lawful for any freedman, free negro or mulatto to intermarry with any white person; nor for any person to intermarry with any freedman, free negro or mulatto; and any person who shall so intermarry shall be deemed guilty of felony, and on conviction thereof shall be confined in the State penitentiary for life; and those shall be deemed freedmen, free negroes and mulattoes who are of pure negro blood, and those descended from a negro to the third generation, inclusive, though one ancestor in each generation may have been a white person.

Section 4. In addition to cases in which freedmen, free negroes and mulattoes are now by law competent witnesses, freedmen, free negroes or mulattoes shall be competent in civil cases, when a party or parties to

the suit, either plaintiff or plaintiffs, defendant or defendants; also in cases where freedmen, free negroes and mulattoes is or are either plaintiff or plaintiffs, defendant or defendants. They shall also be competent witnesses in all criminal prosecutions where the crime charged is alleged to have been committed by a white person upon or against the person or property of a freedman, free negro or mulatto: Provided, that in all cases said witnesses shall be examined in open court, on the stand; except, however, they may be examined before the grand jury, and shall in all cases be subject to the rules and tests of the common law as to competency and credibility.

Section 5. Every freedman, free negro and mulatto shall, on the second Monday of January, one thousand eight hundred and sixty-six, and annually thereafter, have a lawful home or employment, and shall have written evidence thereof as follows, to wit: if living in any incorporated city, town, or village, a license from that mayor thereof; and if living outside of an incorporated city, town, or village, from the member of the board of police of his beat, authorizing him or her to do irregular and job work; or a written contract, as provided in Section 6 in this act; which license may be revoked for cause at any time by the authority granting the same.

Section 6. All contracts for labor made with freedmen, free negroes and mulattoes for a longer period than one month shall be in writing, and a duplicate, attested and read to said freedman, free negro or mulatto by a beat, city or county officer, or two disinterested white persons of the county in which the labor is to performed, of which each party shall have one: and said contracts shall be taken and held as entire contracts, and if the laborer shall quit the service of the employer before the expiration of his term of service, without good cause, he shall forfeit his wages for that year up to the time of quitting.

Section 7. Every civil officer shall, and every person may, arrest and carry back to his or her legal employer any freedman, free negro, or mulatto who shall have quit the service of his or her employer before the expiration of his or her term of service without good cause; and said officer and person shall be entitled to receive for arresting and carrying back every deserting employee aforesaid the sum of five dollars, and ten cents per mile from the place of arrest to the place of delivery; and the same shall be paid by the employer, and held as a set off for so much against the wages of said deserting employee: Provided, that said arrested party, after being so returned, may appeal to the justice of the peace or member of the board of police of the county, who, on notice to the alleged employer, shall try summarily whether said appellant is legally employed by the alleged employer, and has good cause to quit said employer. Either party shall have the right of appeal to the county court, pending which the alleged deserter shall be remanded to the alleged employer or otherwise disposed of, as shall be right and just; and the decision of the county court shall be final.

Section 8. Upon affidavit made by the employer of any freedman, free negro or mulatto, or other credible person, before any justice of the peace or member of the board of police, that any freedman, free negro or mulatto legally employed by said employer has illegally deserted said employment, such justice of the peace or member of the board of police issue his warrant or warrants, returnable before himself or other such officer, to any sheriff, constable or special deputy, commanding him to arrest said deserter, and return him or her to said employer, and the like proceedings shall be had as provided in the preceding section; and it shall be lawful for any officer to whom such warrant shall be directed to execute said warrant in any county in this State; and that said warrant may be transmitted without endorsement to any like officer of another county, to be executed and returned as aforesaid; and the said employer shall pay the costs of said warrants and arrest and return, which shall be set off for so much against the wages of said deserter.

Section 9. If any person shall persuade or attempt to persuade, entice, or cause any freedman, free negro or mulatto to desert from the legal employment of any person before the expiration of his or her term of service, or shall knowingly employ any such deserting freedman, free negro or mulato, or shall knowingly give or sell to any such deserting freedman, free negro or mulatto, any food, raiment, or other thing, he or she shall be guilty of a misdemeanor, and, upon conviction, shall be fined not less than twenty-five

dollars and not more than two hundred dollars and costs; and if the said fine and costs shall not be immediately paid, the court shall sentence said convict to not exceeding two months imprisonment in the county jail, and he or she shall moreover be liable to the party injured in damages: Provided, if any person shall, or shall attempt to, persuade, entice, or cause any freedman, free negro or mullatto to desert from any legal employment of any person, with the view to employ said freedman, free negro or mullato without the limits of this State, such costs; and if said fine and costs shall not be immediately paid, the court shall sentence said convict to not exceeding six months imprisonment in the county jail.

Section 10. It shall be lawful for any freedman, free negro, or mulatto, to charge any white person, freedman, free negro or mulatto by affidavit, with any criminal offense against his or her person or property, and upon such affidavit the proper process shall be issued and executed as if said affidavit was made by a white person, and it shall be lawful for any freedman, free negro, or mulatto, in any action, suit or controversy pending, or about to be instituted in any court of law equity in this State, to make all needful and lawful affidavits as shall be necessary for the institution, prosecution or defense of such suit or controversy.

Section 11. The penal laws of this state, in all cases not otherwise specially provided for, shall apply and extend to all freedman, free negroes and mulattoes....

An Act to Regulate the Relation of Master and Apprentice, as Relates to Freedmen, Free Negroes, and Mulattoes

Section 1. It shall be the duty of all sheriffs, justices of the peace, and other civil officers of the several counties in this State, to report to the probate courts of their respective counties semiannually, at the January and July terms of said courts, all freedmen, free negroes, and mulattoes, under the age of eighteen, in their respective counties, beats, or districts, who are orphans, or whose parent or parents have not the means or who refuse to provide for and support said minors; and thereupon it shall be the duty of said probate court to order the clerk of said court to apprentice said minors to some competent and suitable person on such terms as the court may direct, having a particular care to the interest of said minor: Provided, that the former owner of said minors shall have the preference when, in the opinion of the court, he or she shall be a suitable person for that purpose.

Section 2. The said court shall be fully satisfied that the person or persons to whom said minor shall be apprenticed shall be a suitable person to have the charge and care of said minor, and fully to protect the interest of said minor. The said court shall require the said master or mistress to execute bond and security, payable to the State of Mississippi, conditioned that he or she shall furnish said minor with sufficient food and clothing; to treat said minor humanely; furnish medical attention in case of sickness; teach, or cause to be taught, him or her to read and write, if under fifteen years old, and will conform to any law that may be hereafter passed for the regulation of the duties and relation of master and apprentice: Provided, that said apprentice shall be bound by indenture, in case of males, until they are twenty-one years old, and in case of females until they are eighteen years old.

Section 3. In the management and control of said apprentices, said master or mistress shall have the power to inflict such moderate corporeal chastisement as a father or guardian is allowed to infliction on his or her child or ward at common law: Provided, that in no case shall cruel or inhuman punishment be inflicted.

Section 4. If any apprentice shall leave the employment of his or her master or mistress, without his or her consent, said master or mistress may pursue and recapture said apprentice, and bring him or her before any justice of the peace of the county, whose duty it shall be to remand said apprentice to the service of his or her master or mistress; and in the event of a refusal on the part of said apprentice so to return, then said justice shall commit said apprentice to the jail of said county, on failure to give bond, to the next term of the county court; and it shall be the duty of said court at the first term thereafter to investigate said case, and if the court shall be of opinion that said apprentice left the employment of his or her master or mistress without good cause, to order him or her to be punished, as provided for the punishment of hired freedmen, as may be from time to time provided for by law for desertion, until he or she shall agree to return to the service of his or her master or mistress: Provided, that the court may grant continuances as in other cases: And provided further, that if the court shall believe that said apprentice had good cause to quit his said master or mistress, the court shall discharge said apprentice from said indenture,

and also enter a judgment against the master or mistress for not more than one hundred dollars, from the use and benefit of said apprentice, to be collected on execution as in other cases.

Section 5. If any person entice away any apprentice from his or her master or mistress, or shall knowingly employ an apprentice, or furnish him or her food or clothing without the written consent of his or her master or mistress, or shall sell or give said apprentice spirits without such consent, said person so offending shall be guilty of a misdemeanor, and shall, upon conviction there of before the county court, be punished as provided for the punishment of person enticing from their employer hired freedmen, free negroes or mulattoes.

Section 6. It shall be the duty of all civil officers of their respective counties to report any minors within their respective counties to said probate court who are subject to be apprenticed under the provisions of this act, from time to time as the facts may come to their knowledge, and it shall be the duty of said court from time to time as said minors shall be reported to them, or otherwise come to their knowledge, to apprentice said minors as hereinbefore provided.

Section 9. It shall be lawful for any freedman, free negro, or mulatto, having a minor child or children, as provided for by this act.

Section 10. In all cases where the age of the freedman, free negro, or mulatto cannot be ascertained by record testimony, the judge of the county court shall fix the age....

An Act to Amend the Vagrant Laws of the State

Section 1. All rogues and vagabonds, idle and dissipated persons, beggars, jugglers, or persons practicing unlawful games or plays, runaways, common drunkards, common night-walkers, pilferers, lewd, wanton, or lascivious persons, in speech or behavior, common railers and brawlers, persons who neglect their calling or employment, misspend what they earn, or do not provide for the support of themselves or their families, or dependents, and all other idle and disorderly persons, including all who neglect all lawful business, habitually misspend their time by frequenting houses of ill-fame, gaming-houses, or tippling shops, shall be deemed and considered vagrants, under the provisions of this act, and upon conviction thereof shall be fined not exceeding one hundred dollars, with all accruing costs, and be imprisoned, at the discretion of the court, not exceeding ten days.

Section 2. All freedmen, free negroes and mulattoes in this State, over the age of eighteen years, found on the second Monday in January, 1866, or thereafter, with no lawful employment or business, or found unlawful assembling themselves together, either in the day or night time, and all white persons assembling themselves with freedmen, Free negroes or mulattoes, or usually associating with freedmen, free negroes or mulattoes, on terms of equality, or living in adultery or fornication with a freed woman, freed negro or mulatto, shall be deemed vagrants, and on conviction thereof shall be fined in a sum not exceeding, in the case of a freedman, free negro or mulatto, fifty dollars, and a white man two hundred dollars, and imprisonment at the discretion of the court, the free negro not exceeding ten days, and the white man not exceeding six months.

Section 3. All justices of the peace, mayors, and aldermen of incorporated towns, counties, and cities of the several counties in this State shall have jurisdiction to try all questions of vagrancy in their respective towns, counties, and cities, and it is hereby made their duty, whenever they shall ascertain that any person or persons in their respective towns, and counties and cities are violating any of the provisions of this act, to have said party or parties arrested, and brought before them, and immediately investigate said charge, and, on conviction, punish said party or parties, as provided for herein. And it is hereby made the duty of all sheriffs, constables, town constables, and all such like officers, and city marshals, to report to some officer having jurisdiction all violations of any of the provisions of this act, and in case any officer shall fail or neglect any duty herein it shall be the duty of the county court to fine said officer, upon conviction, not exceeding one hundred dollars, to be paid into the county treasury for county purposes.

Section 4. Keepers of gaming houses, houses of prostitution, prostitutes, public or private, and all persons who derive their chief support in the employment's that militate against good morals, or against law, shall be deemed and held to be vagrants.

Section 5. All fines and forfeitures collected by the provisions of this act shall be paid into the county treasury of general county purposes, and in case of any freedman, free negro or mulatto shall fail for five days after the imposition of any or forfeiture upon him or her for violation of any of the provisions of this act to pay the same, that it shall be, and is hereby, made the duty of the sheriff of the proper county

to hire out said freedman, free negro or mulatto, to any person who will, for the shortest period of service, pay said fine and forfeiture and all costs: Provided, a preference shall be given to the employer, if there be one, in which case the employer shall be entitled to deduct and retain the amount so paid from the wages of such freedman, free negro or mulatto, then due or to become due; and in case freedman, free negro or mulatto cannot hire out, he or she may be dealt with as a pauper.

Section 6. The same duties and liabilities existing among white persons of this State shall attach to freedmen, free negroes or mulattoes, to support their indigent families and all colored paupers; and that in order to secure a support for such indigent freedmen, free negroes, or mulattoes, it shall be lawful, and is hereby made the duty of the county police of each county in this State, to levy a poll or capitation tax on each and every freedman, free negro, or mulatto, between the ages of eighteen and sixty years, not to exceed the sum of one dollar annually to each person so taxed, which tax, when collected, shall be paid into the county treasurer's hands, and constitute a fund to be called the Freedman's Pauper Fund, which shall be applied by the commissioners of the poor for the maintenance of the poor of the freedmen, free negroes and mulattoes of this State, under such regulations as may be established by the boards of county police in the respective counties of this State.

Section 7. If any freedman, free negro, or mulatto shall fail or refuse to pay any tax levied according to the provisions of the sixth section of this act, it shall be *prima facie* evidence of vagrancy, and it shall be the duty of the sheriff to arrest such freedman, free negro, or mulatto, or such person refusing or neglecting to pay such tax, and proceed at once to hire for the shortest time such delinquent taxpayer to any one who will pay the said tax, with accruing costs, giving preference to the employer, if there be one.

Section 8. Any person feeling himself or herself aggrieved by judgment of any justice of the peace, mayor, or alderman in cases arising under this act, may within five days appeal to the next term of the county court of the proper county, upon giving bond and security in a sum not less than twenty-five dollars nor more than one hundred and fifty dollars, conditioned to appear and prosecute said appeal, and abide by the judgment of the county court; and said appeal shall be tried *de novo* in the county court, and the decision of the said court shall be final.

Thirty-Eighth Congress of the United States of America;

At the Second Session,

Begun and held at the City of Washington, on Monday, the *fifth* day of December, one thousand eight hundred and sixty-four.

A RESOLUTION

Submitting to the legislatures of the several States a proposition to amend the Constitution of the United States.

Resolved by the Senate and House of Representatives of the United States of America in Congress assembled, (two-thirds of both houses concurring), that the following article be proposed to the legislatures of the several States as an amendment to the Constitution of the United States, which, when ratified by three-fourths of said Legislatures, shall be valid, to all intents and purposes, as a part of the said Constitution, namely: Article XIII. Section 1. Neither slavery nor involuntary servitude, except as a punishment for crime whereof the party shall have been duly convicted, shall exist within the United States, or any place subject to their jurisdiction. Section 2. Congress shall have power to enforce this article by appropriate legislation.

Schuyler Colfax
Speaker of the House of Representatives.

H. Hamlin
Vice President of the United States.
and President of the Senate.

Approved, February 1, 1865.

Abraham Lincoln

The Thirteenth Amendment (National Archives and Records Administration)

THIRTEENTH AMENDMENT TO THE U.S. CONSTITUTION

"Neither slavery nor involuntary servitude ...
shall exist within the United States."

Overview

The Thirteenth Amendment to the U.S. Constitution legally ended slavery in the United States. It was passed by Congress and ratified by the required three-fourths of the states in 1865. President Abraham Lincoln had issued the Emancipation Proclamation in 1862, declaring slaves in areas in rebellion against the government to be freed by executive decree. Afterward, Lincoln and many of his fellow Republicans had believed that more permanent legislation in the form of a constitutional amendment prohibiting slavery would be needed to ensure that the Emancipation Proclamation could not be subsequently ruled either unconstitutional or a temporary war measure. The Thirteenth Amendment was the first constitutional amendment to be adopted in over sixty years, and it initiated a series of subsequent amendments, including the Fourteenth and Fifteenth, with which it is often associated. Those two Reconstruction-era amendments guaranteed citizenship and voting rights to African Americans, and along with the Thirteenth Amendment they represented a crucial step in the broadening of the American legal definitions and conceptions of freedom and equality.

Context

Early in the Civil War, the North was divided on the issue of emancipation. The Republican Party and its leader, President Lincoln, opposed the expansion of slavery into the western territories but generally conceded that the Constitution protected the "peculiar institution" in the states where it already existed. A vocal minority of abolitionists within the party called for immediate emancipation, although they differed even among themselves about whether this desirable outcome could best be achieved by executive, legislative, or judicial action. The Democratic Party generally opposed emancipation, although as the war wore on many of its members grudgingly came to accept that the measure in some form might be necessary—to win the conflict, to remove the underlying cause and prevent its recurrence, and

to punish the recalcitrant southern slave owners for their continued, and immensely destructive, defiance.

During the "secession winter" of 1860–1861, before the outbreak of the war, Lincoln and other Republicans announced their support for a proposed amendment that would have guaranteed that the federal government could never abolish slavery in the southern states; Lincoln and his fellow Republicans were even willing to make this amendment unamendable in the future. Confederate leaders, convinced that secession and an independent southern nation would prove to be the best means of protecting slavery, scorned this offer. (Ironically for them, the true Thirteenth Amendment, which went into effect at the end of the war, took a form much less favorable to slave owners.) In July 1861 Congress passed, with overwhelming support, the Crittenden-Johnson Resolution, stating that the northern war aims would include the restoration of the Union but not the emancipation of southern slaves.

In the same cautious spirit, Lincoln resisted overt action against slavery in 1861 and for much of 1862. Concerned with maintaining support for the Union in the conflict-ridden border slave states (Maryland, Kentucky, Missouri, and tiny Delaware), the president overruled early emancipation declarations by General David Hunter in South Carolina and General John C. Frémont in Missouri. Lincoln encouraged the leaders of border states to adopt policies of voluntary, compensated emancipation, but without success. General Benjamin F. Butler adopted an effective expedient in May 1861 when he began refusing to return runaway slaves to their masters, characterizing them essentially as spoils of war. By thus treating slaves as property, he avoided the controversy associated with an announced policy of emancipation; while this did not entirely satisfy abolitionists, it was accepted by most northerners as a useful and clever compromise. The influx over Union lines of large numbers of African Americans fleeing slavery and seeking refuge put considerable additional pressure on government leaders to come up with a solution to this colossal problem, with huge moral and practical implications for the future of the nation's existence. Legislators were eventually bombarded with petitions and letters from constituents demanding action to end slavery. Congress essentially affirmed Butler's policy with the passage of the First Con-

1857

■ **March 6**
In the *Dred Scott* decision, the Supreme Court rules that Congress has no authority to prohibit slavery in the western territories.

1860

■ **December 20**
South Carolina becomes the first southern state to secede following the election of the northern Republican Abraham Lincoln as president.

1861

■ **April 12**
Confederate firing on Fort Sumter begins the American Civil War.

■ **March 2**
Congress passes a proposed amendment, which is never ratified, barring Congress from interfering with slavery in states where the institution exists.

1862

■ **April 16**
Slavery is abolished in the District of Columbia.

■ **September 22**
President Lincoln issues the Emancipation Proclamation.

1863

■ **January 1**
Emancipation Proclamation goes into effect.

1865

■ **January 31**
Congress proposes the Thirteenth Amendment to the states.

■ **April 9**
The Confederate general Robert E. Lee surrenders to the Union general Ulysses S. Grant, effectively ending the Civil War.

■ **December 18**
Secretary of State William H. Seward issues proclamation announcing that the Thirteenth Amendment has been ratified by the necessary three-quarters of the states.

1995

■ **March 6**
Mississippi ratifies the Thirteenth Amendment, 130 years after initially rejecting it.

fiscation Act in August 1861, authorizing representatives of the federal government to confiscate the slaves of disloyal citizens used in support of the rebellion.

The emancipation question was inseparable from the problem of precisely how to reconstruct southern state governments and oversee their restoration to the Union after the war. Ensuring that these states would be free of slavery seemed essential to many (though not all) northerners, but how to accomplish that aim was less obvious. Congress began to take more aggressive steps against slavery in 1862, while radicals like the Massachusetts senator Charles Sumner both publicly and privately maintained pressure on President Lincoln to use his war powers as commander in chief to do likewise. The Second Confiscation Act, of July 1862, provided for the forfeiture of slaves, as well as other property, belonging to those supporting the Confederacy. The lack of effective enforcement mechanisms along with doubts held by Lincoln and others regarding the act's constitutionality made the act somewhat irrelevant, but it did represent another tentative step toward a federal emancipation policy.

The most famous, though not the final, blow against American slavery was struck on September 22, 1862, when President Lincoln, shortly following the Union victory at the battle of Antietam, issued his famous Emancipation Proclamation, freeing all the slaves in areas of the South not occupied by federal troops as of the coming January 1. As this proclamation did not apply to the border slave states that had not seceded—and might ultimately have been regarded by the courts as a temporary war measure only—Lincoln and many of his fellow Republicans recognized that further action would be needed to end slavery and remove the root cause of the conflict between the North and the South. Although many Americans were reluctant to alter the text of the Constitution, which had not been amended for over sixty years and was widely regarded as permanent and sacred, an emancipation amendment seemed to offer the best and most definitive solution to this troublesome issue. As early as 1839 the staunch slavery opponent John Quincy Adams had introduced such a constitutional amendment to bring about abolition; although his proposal had made no headway at the time, the idea had been percolating among his successors in the political antislavery movement.

In December 1863 competing antislavery amendments were introduced in the House of Representatives by the Republican congressmen James M. Ashley, of Ohio, and James F. Wilson, of Iowa. Both men introduced their bills in the context of ongoing debate over how to reconstruct the southern states and bring them back into the Union. They advocated a constitutional amendment barring slavery as a means to ensure republican government in those states. Wilson's proposed amendment included an enforcement clause, empowering Congress to pass legislation to ensure compliance. In this session, however, the House passed neither an emancipation amendment nor any of the envisioned supplemental legislation intended to protect civil rights.

Charles Sumner initially took the lead in pushing for an abolition amendment in the Senate. He hoped not just to end slavery but also to ensure full legal and practical equality for African Americans. Even many fellow members of the Republican Party hesitated to push so far, worrying that the party's fragile wartime coalition of different ideological factions, as bolstered by an important bloc of Democrats who supported the war effort, might be damaged by overly radical legislation. On February 8, 1864, Sumner introduced a constitutional amendment outlawing slavery, hoping that it would be referred to a committee that he chaired on issues related to slavery and freedmen. Following standard legislative practice, however, the amendment was instead referred to the Judiciary Committee, chaired by Lyman Trumbull, of Illinois. Trumbull, a less radical Republican than Sumner, oversaw the crafting of a document with less explicit guarantees that former slaves would be granted full citizenship rights and protections.

Sumner's arrogant, humorless personality made it difficult for him to win colleagues over to his more radically egalitarian vision of the proposed amendment. Trumbull, meanwhile, insisted during debate that the more neutral language in his committee's version (much of it borrowed from the well-known Northwest Ordinance) would fully accomplish the same object of ensuring equality for all regardless of race. This claim was likely disingenuous, however. Trumbull and other Senate Republicans were hoping to avoid charges of favoring excessive and revolutionary social and political upheaval on the order of the French Revolution. One senator even expressed the fear that Sumner's amendment's promise that all individuals would be equal before the law could be applied to women, a measure that did not have widespread political support, at least among the men who held a monopoly on voting rights at the time.

The proposed antislavery amendment provoked extensive congressional debate, intended more to inspire supporters back in home districts who would later read published accounts of the speeches than to convince the fellow members, who rarely listened to colleagues' speeches in any event. As 1864 was an election year, the amendment was a particularly potent political issue, and with Lincoln's approval it became part of the Republican Party's campaign platform. The amendment passed the Senate on April 6, 1864, by a vote of 38 to 4; after a fierce struggle and considerable lobbying at the president's behest, it passed the House of Representatives on January 31, 1865, by a vote of 119 to 56, with enough Democrats joining with the Republican majority to ensure the measure's victory. Lincoln enthusiastically indicated his pleasure at this outcome by signing the amendment when it was presented to him, although he was not legally required to do so for it to go into effect.

One of the most difficult issues facing the supporters of the Thirteenth Amendment was that of ratification. Constitutional amendments needed to be ratified by three-quarters of the states in order to go into effect. Would the seceded states be counted toward this total? Most Republicans, following the lead of Lincoln, argued that secession was illegal and that the states had not technically left the Union. This presented a dilemma, as some southern states would then have to vote for the abolition amendment in order for it to go into effect. Charles Sumner proposed leaving the Confederate states out of the ratification calculations, but Trumbull and other Republicans successfully opposed this plan, as some worried that the amendment might seem to lack legitimacy if the southern states were not included in the ratification process. In one of his final speeches, only a few days before his assassination, Lincoln indicated that he agreed that all of the states must be allowed the opportunity to ratify the amendment. His successor, Andrew Johnson, implored conventions in the southern states to meet and voluntarily ratify the amendment, which indeed resulted in enough states ratifying the amendment for it to become law. Ominously, however, several of the ratification conventions in the former Confederate states warned that they did not accept the legitimacy of the clause giving Congress the right to pass supplemental legislation ensuring civil rights for African Americans. This significant distinction, generally overlooked by the administration and congressional leaders at the time, suggested that many southern whites were determined to prevent the establishment of equality for African Americans, despite the Thirteenth Amendment's promise of freedom.

About the Author

The Thirteenth Amendment had no single author. Some of its key congressional creators and supporters were James M. Ashley, James F. Wilson, Lyman Trumbull, and Charles Sumner.

James M. Ashley was born in Pennsylvania in 1824. The mostly self-educated young man moved west to Ohio in 1848, where he became the editor of a Democratic newspaper and a close political ally of the antislavery leader and future Supreme Court chief justice Salmon P. Chase. Ashley was first elected to Congress in 1858, representing the Republican Party. During the Civil War, he played a leading role in winning support for the emancipation of slaves in the District of Columbia before helping push for the Thirteenth Amendment. He would also favor a punitive Reconstruction policy, including confiscating the property of supporters of the Confederacy and taking away their political rights, which sometimes put him at odds with President Lincoln, who favored a more moderate and generous policy aimed at facilitating reconciliation and reunion. Ashley worked closely with Lincoln, however, in winning support among wavering members of both parties in order to ensure congressional passage of the Thirteenth Amendment. Following the war, Ashley was one of the leaders in the movement to impeach President Andrew Johnson for obstructing Reconstruction, and he aired wild accusations that Johnson had been complicit in Lincoln's murder. He later served as territorial governor of Montana and as a railroad president. He died in 1896.

James F. Wilson, born in Ohio in 1828, was a Republican congressman from Iowa during the Civil War. He had moved to Iowa and begun practicing law and involving

*Congressman James Mitchell Ashley's 1863 bill to
abolish slavery eventually evolved into the Thirteenth
Amendment.* (Library of Congress)

himself in politics in the early 1850s, and in 1856 he participated in the convention that revised the state's constitution. Wilson was first elected to Congress in 1861 when his district's former representative, Samuel R. Curtis, resigned to accept an appointment as a general in the Union Army. Once in the Republican-controlled House of Representatives, Wilson was appointed chairman of the Judiciary Committee despite the seniority of other party members on the committee, a compliment to Wilson's legal knowledge, ability, and work ethic. Like Ashley, he also helped win support for ending slavery in the District of Columbia. Following the Civil War, he served in both the Senate and the House of Representatives and as director of the Union Pacific Railroad. Wilson once reputedly turned down an offer of the prestigious position of secretary of state by President Ulysses S. Grant, possibly a wise move given the scandals and misfortune that tarnished the Grant cabinet. Wilson died in 1895, having occupied a

prominent place in the Iowa and national Republican leadership for forty years.

Lyman Trumbull, of Illinois, a Democrat turned Republican and one of the party's most forceful and respected national leaders during the Civil War era, was born in 1813. He was first elected to the Senate in 1855, triumphing over his rival, Abraham Lincoln, in one of the most bitter setbacks in the career of "Honest Abe." Although Lincoln and Trumbull had an uneasy personal relationship following this contest—and Mary Todd Lincoln afterward refused to speak to Trumbull's wife, Julia, her former friend—the two men put aside their differences to champion Republican policies, including the Thirteenth Amendment, during the Civil War. Fiesty and bespectacled, Trumbull broke with Radical Republicans over Reconstruction and voted against the impeachment of Andrew Johnson in 1868. Thereafter, he variously supported the short-lived Liberal Republican movement, returned to the Democratic fold, and even advocated the Populist Party (defending the socialist labor leader Eugene V. Debs at a trial for the appeal of his conviction for violating a federal antistrike injunction). Trumbull died in 1896.

Charles Sumner first took his seat as a senator from Massachusetts in 1851 at the age of forty, representing first the Free-Soil Party and subsequently the Republican Party. He gained fame for his scholarly oratory and zealous abolitionism as well as for suffering a savage beating from a stout cane wielded by the proslavery South Carolina congressman Preston Brooks on the floor of the Senate in 1856. This famous incident led Sumner to become, in the eyes of many northerners, a heroic symbol of freedom of speech and opponent of southern proslavery barbarism. Sumner did not return to take his Senate seat for several years, though his physical injuries healed relatively quickly. He exercised particular clout in foreign affairs issues owing to his knowledge and wide circle of acquaintances abroad, and he both chaired the Senate Foreign Affairs Committee and served as an adviser to Lincoln on international issues, often much to the annoyance of his long-time political rival Secretary of State William H. Seward. Sumner was one of the Thirteenth Amendment's first and most consistent advocates, and he remained committed to civil rights causes—often finding himself at odds with his fellow Republicans—until his death in 1874.

Explanation and Analysis of the Document

The Thirteenth Amendment announces that slavery will no longer be legally permitted in the United States or its territories, with the significant exception that "involuntary servitude" may be imposed on those who have been convicted of crimes. This loophole, to which Charles Sumner strongly objected, permitted those serving jail terms, often African Americans convicted on petty or false charges, to be used as a source of cheap, brutally coerced labor in

> "Neither slavery nor involuntary servitude, except as a punishment for crime whereof the party shall have been duly convicted, shall exist within the United States, or any place subject to their jurisdiction."
>
> (Section 1)

> "Congress shall have the power to enforce this article by appropriate legislation."
>
> (Section 2)

> "In passing this amendment we do not confer upon the negro the right to vote. We give him no right except his freedom, and leave the rest to the states."
>
> (Republican Senator John Henderson, *Congressional Globe*, April 6, 1864, p. 1438)

> "But this amendment is a king's cure-all for all the evils. It winds the whole thing up. He [Lincoln] would repeat that it was the fitting, if not the indispensable, adjunct to the consummation of the great game we are playing."
>
> (Nicolay, p. 475)

many southern states well into the twentieth century. The amendment does not specify what the legal status of the former slaves would be or if they would be fully entitled to the rights of American citizens.

The document also includes an enforcement clause, giving Congress the power to pass laws to enforce emancipation. Unfortunately, lack of political will and Supreme Court decisions leaving most issues of interpretation and enforcement to the states undermined the impact of this clause.

Audience

The Thirteenth Amendment was designed to appeal to northern Republicans and Democrats alike in order to keep both groups behind the war effort; partly for that reason, the authors avoided addressing controversial issues of enforcement, citizenship, and voting rights for the former slaves, which later amendments would address. As the amendment had to be ratified by some southern states as

well, its shapers had further incentive to keep its language and provisions as uncontroversial as possible. Too, the uncertain question of how it would be read and interpreted by the courts, then and in the future, loomed large.

President Lincoln, like other northern leaders during the Civil War, was also acutely conscious that steps to end slavery in America would be lauded and appreciated by another very meaningful audience: posterity. "We of this Congress and this administration will be remembered in spite of ourselves," he had assured legislators in his annual message to Congress of December 1, 1862. "In giving *freedom* to the *slave*, we *assure* freedom to the *free*—honorable alike in what we give, and what we preserve. ... The way is plain, peaceful, generous, just—a way which, if followed, the world will forever applaud, and God must forever bless" ("Annual Message to Congress," http://www.teachingamericanhistory.org/library/index.asp?document=1065). Indeed, the Thirteenth Amendment, like the Emancipation Proclamation, continues to garner laurels for those associated with it, as Lincoln hoped and expected it would.

The Thirteenth Amendment was widely hailed upon its passage and ratification for effectively ending slavery and bringing the United States into closer proximity to its ideals of freedom and democracy. The decree left open, however, the questions of whether former slaves would possess the full rights of citizenship and of what precisely those rights were. Lincoln's successor, Andrew Johnson, felt that no further federal civil rights legislation was necessary. On the other hand, congressional Republicans, who were displeased with the slow pace of change in the postwar southern states—and with those states' implementation of racist black codes in attempts to create slavery-like status for African Americans—increasingly used the enforcement clause of the Thirteenth Amendment to justify further action to ensure that slavery would be fully abolished. Among the first legislative efforts along these lines were the Freedmen's Bureau Acts, passed in 1865 and 1866, and the Civil Rights Act, passed in 1866, all aimed at ensuring that the former Confederate states did not violate the rights of African Americans. Johnson vetoed the two 1866 bills, breaking decisively with his former Republican allies on Reconstruction and civil rights, but Congress overrode both vetoes. The Civil Rights Act represented an attempt by Republicans to define just what the freedom they had offered the former slaves in the Thirteenth Amendment would look like. The Civil Rights Act defined all native-born Americans as citizens of the United States, negating the Supreme Court's suggestion in the 1857 *Dred Scott* case that African Americans could not lay claim to citizenship rights. These rights, as envisioned in the Civil Rights Act, did not necessarily include voting rights.

Subsequent constitutional amendments would go further to define the legal rights of African Americans. Ratified in 1868, the Fourteenth Amendment specified that as citizens, African Americans were entitled to due process and the equal protection of the law; ratified in 1870, the Fifteenth Amendment outlawed the use of race to disqualify citizens from voting. Together, the Thirteenth Amendment and its two successors were truly revolutionary, laying the foundation for a more egalitarian and democratic nation. Widespread resistance to implementing these amendments among white southerners—and their continued use of force, intimidation, and other extralegal methods of denying civil rights to African Americans—ultimately led to the collapse of the Reconstruction state governments in the South by 1877. Afterward came the gradual restoration of white supremacy in the form of a new system of discriminatory segregation. This Jim Crow era lasted for the better part of a century, with the promise of the Thirteenth Amendment left unfulfilled, until the civil rights movement of the 1950s and 1960s.

Indeed, for decades after its passage, as segregation was brutally imposed on African Americans, the Thirteenth Amendment was rarely cited by the courts. Generally, in the late nineteenth century the Supreme Court defined the freedom offered by the Thirteenth Amendment very narrowly and was reluctant to concede to the federal government sufficient power to enforce it. In 1872 the court ruled in *Blyew v. United States* that states could refuse to allow African Americans to deliver trial testimony. The 1873 Slaughter-House Cases ruling gave states virtually free rein in defining what the rights of state citizenship for African Americans consisted of, taking the teeth out of the Thirteenth and Fourteenth Amendments. The *Plessy v. Ferguson* decision of 1896 allowed segregation, in a notorious phrase, as long as the facilities offered to African Americans were "separate but equal." The ruling was ominously silent on how this "equality" would be determined and enforced. Further, in the 1906 case of *Hodges v. United States*, the Court averred that state courts would have the sole responsibility of identifying and addressing violations of the Thirteenth Amendment, a power that, needless to say, Jim Crow–era southern states were not aggressive in exercising.

Ultimately, a late-twentieth-century Supreme Court case resurrected the dormant amendment. In the *Jones v. Alfred H. Mayer Company* ruling of 1968, the Court insisted that the constitutional rights of an African American man had been violated when he was barred from buying property in a private housing development owing to his race. The Thirteenth Amendment, the Court ruled, had given African Americans freedom and the same status as all other Americans, making such discrimination illegal. Coming in the wake of other judicial and legislative civil rights rulings of the 1950s and 1960s, this case suggested that the full promise of the Thirteenth Amendment would finally be fulfilled.

Related Documents

Basler, Roy P., ed. *The Collected Works of Abraham Lincoln.* 9 vols. New Brunswick, N.J.: Rutgers University Press, 1953–1955. Lincoln's letters and speeches are essential for understanding the gradual—or slow, as many abolitionists saw it—evolution of his views on slavery and emancipation.

Berlin, Ira, et al., eds. *Freedom: A Documentary History of Emancipation, 1861–1867.* 4 vols. Cambridge, U.K.: Cambridge University Press, 1982–1993. This series is useful for understanding the critical role that slaves themselves played in bringing about emancipation, through practical efforts like running away from slaveholders and over Union lines during wartime as well as through political activity.

Blassingame, John W., et al., eds. *The Frederick Douglass Papers.* 5 vols. New Haven: Yale University Press, 1979–1992. The African American abolitionist orator, editor, author, and politician Douglass was one of the most articulate and influential leaders of the movement for emancipation.

Cox, Samuel S. *Eight Years in Congress, from 1857 to 1865.* New York: D. Appleton, 1865. A prominent congressional opponent of emancipation and the Thirteenth Amendment tells his side of the story.

Dana, Charles A. *Recollections of the Civil War: With the Leaders at Washington and in the Field in the Sixties.* New York: D. Appleton, 1898. This account by a member of the Lincoln administration contains an eye-opening and somewhat disillusioning account of the tactics used by the "Great Emancipator" to win congressional support for the Thirteenth Amendment.

Merrill, Walter M., ed. *The Letters of William Lloyd Garrison.* 6 vols. Cambridge, Mass.: Belknap Press of Harvard University Press, 1971–1981. Garrison regarded the passage of the Thirteenth Amendment as the culminating event of his three-decade career as an abolitionist editor, and he ceased publication of his newspaper the *Liberator* shortly following its passage in 1865.

Bibliography

■ Articles
Belz, Herman. "The Civil War Amendments to the Constitution: The Relevance of Original Intent." *Constitutional Commentary* 5 (1988): 115–141.

Plessy v. Ferguson, 163 U.S. (1896): 537.

Zuckert, Michael P. "Completing the Constitution: The Thirteenth Amendment." *Constitutional Commentary* 4 (1987): 259–284.

■ Books
Belz, Herman. *Abraham Lincoln, Constitutionalism, and Equal Rights in the Civil War Era.* New York: Fordham University Press, 1998.

Blight, David W., and Brooks D. Simpson, eds. *Union and Emancipation: Essays on Politics and Race in the Civil War Era.* Kent, Ohio: Kent State University Press, 1997.

Bogue, Allan G. *The Earnest Men: Republicans of the Civil War Senate.* Ithaca, N.Y.: Cornell University Press, 1981.

Du Bois, W. E. B. *Black Reconstruction in America: An Essay toward a History of the Part Which Black Folk Played in the Attempt to Reconstruct Democracy in America, 1860–1880.* New York: Russell and Russell, 1963.

Hyman, Harold M. *A More Perfect Union: The Impact of the Civil War and Reconstruction on the Constitution.* New York: Knopf, 1973.

Nicolay, John G. *A Short Life of Abraham Lincoln.* New York: Century, 1902.

Paludan, Phillip S. *A Covenant with Death: The Constitution, Law, and Equality in the Civil War Era.* Urbana: University of Illinois Press, 1975.

U.S. Congress. *Congressional Globe,* 38th Cong., 1st sess., 1864, 155.

Vorenberg, Michael. *Final Freedom: The Civil War, the Abolition of Slavery, and the Thirteenth Amendment.* Cambridge, U.K.: Cambridge University Press, 2001.

■ Web Sites
"Annual Message to Congress by Abraham Lincoln." December 1, 1862. Teaching American History Web site.
  http://www.teachingamericanhistory.org/library/index.asp?document=1065. Accessed on January 21, 2008.

"Documents from *Freedom: A Documentary History of Emancipation, 1861–1867.*" University of Maryland Web site.
  http://www.history.umd.edu/Freedmen/sampdocs.htm. Accessed on September 1, 2007.

"The End of Slavery: The Creation of the 13th Amendment." HarpWeek Web site.
  http://13thamendment.harpweek.com/. Accessed on September 1, 2007.

"From Slavery to Freedom: The African-American Pamphlet Collection, 1822–1909." Library of Congress "American Memory" Web site.
  http://memory.loc.gov/ammem/aapchtml/aapchome.html. Accessed on September 1, 2007.

—By Michael Thomas Smith

1. Why might some Americans have voted for the Thirteenth Amendment in 1865? Why might some have voted against it?

2. President Lincoln regarded the Thirteenth Amendment as a "king's cure-all for all the evils" of slavery, but following his death Congress passed two more amendments in an attempt to complete the work of ensuring freedom and equality for freedmen. Compare and contrast the Thirteenth Amendment with the Fourteenth and Fifteenth Amendments. Which do you think did the most to advance civil rights, and why do you think so?

3. Historians continue to argue about who should receive the most credit for ending slavery: President Lincoln, Congress, the army, or the slaves themselves. Which of these parties do you think played the most crucial role in this process, and why do you think so?

4. The great African American historian and political activist W. E. B. Du Bois wrote in his 1935 book *Black Reconstruction in America* that "slavery was not abolished even after the Thirteenth Amendment" (p. 188). To what extent and in what ways was this true? How was this possible, once the amendment had become law? What does this suggest about the power of the Constitution?

Glossary

jurisdiction	the right and power to interpret and apply the law.
slavery	the state of being bound in servitude as the property of a slaveholder.
whereof	of which.

THIRTEENTH AMENDMENT TO THE U.S. CONSTITUTION

AMENDMENT XIII

◆ **Section 1.**

Neither slavery nor involuntary servitude, except as a punishment for crime whereof the party shall have been duly convicted, shall exist within the United States, or any place subject to their jurisdiction.

◆ **Section 2.**

Congress shall have power to enforce this article by appropriate legislation.

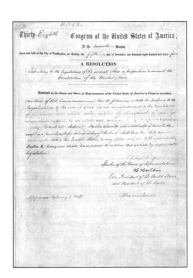

CHAP. XXXI. — *An Act to protect all Persons in the United States in their Civil Rights, and furnish the Means of their Vindication.*

April 9, 1866.

Be it enacted by the Senate and House of Representatives of the United States of America in Congress assembled, That all persons born in the United States and not subject to any foreign power, excluding Indians not taxed, are hereby declared to be citizens of the United States; and such citizens, of every race and color, without regard to any previous condition of slavery or involuntary servitude, except as a punishment for crime whereof the party shall have been duly convicted, shall have the same right, in every State and Territory in the United States, to make and enforce contracts, to sue, be parties, and give evidence, to inherit, purchase, lease, sell, hold, and convey real and personal property, and to full and equal benefit of all laws and proceedings for the security of person and property, as is enjoyed by white citizens, and shall be subject to like punishment, pains, and penalties, and to none other, any law, statute, ordinance, regulation, or custom, to the contrary notwithstanding.

Who are citizens of the United States,

their rights and obligations

SEC. 2. *And be it further enacted,* That any person who, under color of any law, statute, ordinance, regulation, or custom, shall subject, or cause to be subjected, any inhabitant of any State or Territory to the deprivation of any right secured or protected by this act, or to different punishment, pains, or penalties on account of such person having at any time been held in a condition of slavery or involuntary servitude, except as a punishment for crime whereof the party shall have been duly convicted, or by reason of his color or race, than is prescribed for the punishment of white persons, shall be deemed guilty of a misdemeanor, and, on conviction, shall be punished by fine not exceeding one thousand dollars, or imprisonment not exceeding one year, or both, in the discretion of the court.

Penalty for depriving any person of any right protected by this act, by reason of color or race, &c

SEC. 3. *And be it further enacted,* That the district courts of the United States, within their respective districts, shall have, exclusively of the courts of the several States, cognizance of all crimes and offences committed against the provisions of this act, and also, concurrently with the circuit courts of the United States, of all causes, civil and criminal, affecting persons who are denied or cannot enforce in the courts or judicial tribunals of the State or locality where they may be any of the rights secured to them by the first section of this act; and if any suit or prosecution, civil or criminal, has been or shall be commenced in any State court, against any such person, for any cause whatsoever, or against any officer, civil or military, or other person, for any arrest or imprisonment, trespasses, or wrongs done or committed by virtue or under color of authority derived from this act or the act establishing a Bureau for the relief of Freedmen and Refugees, and all acts amendatory thereof, or for refusing to do any act upon the ground that it would be inconsistent with this act, such defendant shall have the right to remove such cause for trial to the proper district or circuit court in the manner prescribed by the "Act relating to habeas corpus and regulating judicial proceedings in certain cases," approved March three, eighteen hundred and sixty-three, and all acts amendatory thereof. The jurisdiction in civil and criminal matters hereby conferred on the district and circuit courts of the United States shall be exercised and enforced in conformity with the laws of the United States, so far as such laws are suitable to carry the same into effect; but in all cases where such laws are not adapted to the object, or are deficient in the provisions necessary to furnish suitable remedies and punish offences against law, the common law, as modified and changed by the constitution and statutes of the State wherein the court having jurisdiction of the cause, civil or criminal, is held, so far as the

Courts of the United States to have jurisdiction of offences under this act.

Suits commenced in State courts may be removed on defendant's motion.

1865, ch. 90.
Vol. xiii. p. 507.

1863, ch. 87.
Vol. xii. p. 755.
Jurisdiction to be enforced according to the laws of the United States, or the common law, &c.

The Civil Rights Act of 1866 (Library of Congress)

CIVIL RIGHTS ACT OF 1866

"All persons born in the United States and not subject to any foreign power, excluding Indians not taxed, are hereby declared to be citizens of the United States."

Overview

On March 13, 1866, Congress passed the Civil Rights Act, its first civil rights measure, to establish the citizenship of blacks and to confer equality before the law with respect to the protection of the fundamental rights of person and property. Designed to enforce the Thirteenth Amendment's abolition of slavery, which was undermined by the passage of the Black Codes, the Civil Rights Act overturned the U.S. Supreme Court's ruling in *Dred Scott v. Sandford* (1857) that blacks were excluded from citizenship.

Section 1 of the act provided that all persons born in the United States and not subject to any foreign power, excluding Indians not taxed, were citizens of the United States. It declared that U.S. citizens "of every race and color ... shall have the same right, in every State and Territory in the United States, to make and enforce contracts, to sue, be parties, and give evidence, to inherit, purchase, lease, sell, hold, and convey real and personal property, and to full and equal benefit of all laws and proceedings for the security of person and property, as is enjoyed by white citizens." Violation of these rights, "under color of any law ... or custom," was subject to misdemeanor prosecution in federal courts. The concept of equality thus extended to civil and legal rights under state law but not to political rights.

Context

The Civil Rights Act transformed the protection of civil rights in the United States. Before its passage, the enforcement of civil rights was viewed as a state responsibility; afterward, it was increasingly perceived to be the responsibility of the federal government. It was, therefore, an integral part of the Reconstruction period, which changed the way the nation understood the Constitution.

The Civil Rights Act represented a direct response to the Black Codes. After the passage of the Thirteenth Amendment, which eliminated slavery and involuntary servitude but, more pointedly, the badges of slavery, a number of southern states enacted Black Codes to keep newly freed slaves in a subordinate status economically, politically, culturally, and legally. In essence, these codes reenacted and embraced elements of the law of slavery. Among other badges and shackles, the codes defined racial status, prohibited blacks from pursuing certain occupations, controlled the movements of blacks through a system of passes, prohibited the congregation of blacks and restricted their residence in certain areas, and specified an etiquette of deference to whites. Blacks, moreover, were excluded from jury duty, public office, and voting.

The Civil Rights Act was intended to curb the effects of the Black Codes, but it also foreshadowed the Fourteenth Amendment and, consequently, represented a bridge from the Thirteenth Amendment as part of a continued effort to bring legal equality to new freedmen, a defining pillar of the Reconstruction amendments. Supporters of the Thirteenth Amendment believed that it completed the Constitution and fulfilled the principles of the Declaration of Independence. Champions of the Fourteenth Amendment meant to constitutionalize the Civil Rights Act; indeed, the provisions of the act and Section 1 of the Fourteenth Amendment cover the same ground. The efforts by members of Congress, including the so-called Radical Republicans, to achieve this level of equality, however, were continually frustrated by President Andrew Johnson and his potent exercise of the presidential veto.

Johnson's traditional view of states' rights and his conception of racial hierarchy lay behind his repeated efforts to frustrate congressional efforts to elevate the legal status of black Americans. Before vetoing the Civil Rights Act, he vetoed a measure that would have expanded the Freedmen's Bureau and its aims to protect the rights of blacks. He denounced congressional efforts to impose citizenship for blacks in states that he believed were unrepresented, and he decried federal measures that would determine the scope of civil rights, a power, he believed, that belonged to the states. His antagonism toward blacks was further manifested in his opposition to the Fourteenth Amendment. The determination of Congress prevailed, as seen in its success in overriding Johnson's vetoes of both the Freedmen's Bureau Bill and the Civil Rights Act. Although Congress enjoyed victories in these and other battles with Johnson, genuine success proved elusive, since the United

Time Line

1857

■ **March 6**
The U.S. Supreme Court rules in *Dred Scott v. Sandford* that blacks are not citizens of the United States and thus have no capacity to bring lawsuits.

1865

■ **December 6**
The Thirteenth Amendment, which abolishes slavery and involuntary servitude, is ratified.

1866

■ **February 19**
Congress passes a bill that expands the Freedmen's Bureau; President Andrew Johnson immediately vetoes the bill.

■ **February 22**
On Washington's birthday, Johnson delivers a caustic denunciation of Republican leaders in Congress, widening the gap between the two branches.

■ **March 13**
Congress passes the Civil Rights Act.

■ **March 27**
Johnson vetoes the Civil Rights Act.

■ **April 9**
The Civil Rights Act becomes law after Congress overrides Johnson's veto.

■ **June 11**
Johnson vows to spend $20,000 of his own money and to use all of his influence to defeat the proposed Fourteenth Amendment.

■ **June 8 and 13**
The House and Senate approve the Fourteenth Amendment by the necessary two-thirds vote.

■ **July 9**
The Fourteenth Amendment is ratified.

About the Author

Lyman Trumbull, author of the Civil Rights Act of 1866, was born on October 12, 1813, in Colchester, Connecticut. He was educated at the prestigious Bacon Academy and began teaching at the age of sixteen. In 1834 he moved to Greenville, Georgia, where he studied law and opened a law practice. In 1837 he moved to Belleville, Illinois, where he resumed the practice of law.

Shortly after moving to Illinois, Trumbull entered politics. A man of strong conviction and principles, Trumbull exhibited a willingness to change political parties when party platforms and policies collided with his views and values. His plunge into political life began in 1840 when he was elected as a Democrat to the Illinois statehouse. He followed with a stint as Illinois secretary of state from 1841 to 1843 and then served as a justice on the Illinois Supreme Court from 1848 to 1853. Although he was elected to the U.S. House of Representatives in 1854, Trumbull never served because he was immediately elected to the U.S. Senate by the Illinois state senate.

Soon after his election to the U.S. Senate, Trumbull's opposition to slavery compelled him to resign from the Democratic Party to become a Republican. His three-term career in the Senate was distinguished by his commitment to the freedom of African Americans. He backed President Abraham Lincoln's Emancipation Proclamation of January 1, 1863, which freed slaves in states engaged in rebellion against the Union, but he believed in the need for emancipation of all slaves. Accordingly, he coauthored the Thirteenth Amendment, which, when ratified in 1865, abolished all slavery and involuntary servitude. His efforts on behalf of new freedmen resulted in a flurry of legislative activity. He authored the Freedmen's Bureau Bill, the Confiscation Acts, and the landmark Civil Rights Act of 1866, which he championed in his position as chair of the Senate Judiciary Committee.

In a courageous but costly decision, Trumbull broke party ranks, along with six other Republicans, in voting against the conviction of President Andrew Johnson during the president's impeachment trial in the Senate. Troubled by the procedural issues and the presentation of evidence during the trial, Trumbull exhibited an independence that had characterized his political career. His vote in the impeachment trial alienated him from the Republican Party. In 1872 he joined other liberal Republicans in supporting Horace Greeley's presidential campaign against the reelection bid of President Ulysses S. Grant.

At the end of his third term, Trumbull left Washington to return to his law practice, but he remained politically active until the end of his life. In 1880 he returned to the Democratic Party and campaigned unsuccessfully for the governorship of Illinois. In the 1890s he aligned himself with the Populist Party. Trumbull died in Chicago, on March 4, 1873.

The abolition of slavery triggered considerable debate about the legal status of new freedmen. Many northerners believed that the Thirteenth Amendment would provide an adequate solution: Having been freed and protected from further enslavement, blacks would simply assume the same status as whites. In particular, they would enjoy the same rights under the law possessed by other free persons. That optimistic view, however, was dashed by the rise of the Black Codes and the widespread violence visited upon blacks in various southern states.

In an ambitious undertaking, Congress attempted to protect blacks in terms that dramatically shifted the nation's understanding of civil rights enforcement. The Civil Rights Act establishes citizenship for blacks and provides for equality before the law in matters involving the protection of person and property. Section 1 of the act confers citizenship upon new freedmen in complete disregard of the Supreme Court's ruling in *Dred Scott v. Sandford* (1857), which excluded blacks from the ranks of citizenship.

The elevation of new freedmen to the class of American citizenship, an arrow in the heart of the racial discrimination inherent in the Black Codes, provides a seemingly effective means of ensuring security in the areas of life, liberty, and property. The declaration that blacks, as citizens, would possess "full and equal benefit of all laws … enjoyed by white persons" represents a quantum leap for a population that had been systematically denied every right afforded whites. The measure became all the more meaningful with the application of equality to the imposition of state court punishments, "any law, statute, ordinance, regulation, or custom, to the contrary notwithstanding." The concept of equal justice had not been remotely within the grasp of blacks at any point in American history. The concept is made clear by the declaration in Section 2 that the imposition of punishment on blacks that differs from that imposed on whites could be punished as a misdemeanor that carries with it a fine up to $1,000 and a one-year prison term.

Violators, moreover, would be tried in federal and not state courts. The provision in Section 3 that federal courts would have jurisdiction over all cases involving "crimes and offenses committed" against provisions of the act brought considerable assurance to blacks, who would justly lack confidence in state courts. The expanded jurisdiction of the federal courts also extends to appeals from state courts by persons unable to secure Section 1 rights.

Sections 4 through 9 specifically address the enforcement mechanisms of the Civil Rights Act. Chiefly, all federal law officers are authorized to initiate proceedings against violators. Federal judges are empowered to appoint commissioners for enforcement purposes. The president, moreover, is granted statutory authority to "employ" the army and navy as well as the militia to enforce the statute. Finally, Congress increases the appellate jurisdiction of the U.S. Supreme Court to include "questions of law" arising out of enforcement of the act.

Andrew Johnson (Library of Congress)

At bottom, the purpose of the Civil Rights Act is to protect the rights of blacks under state laws without distinction based on race. Enforcement of its provisions is assured by a national presence, armed with authority to punish those who would deny those rights. But the act is limited to the protection of civil and not political rights. Congress was not interested in full equality or in the prohibition of all forms of racial discrimination, governmental or private. This conclusion may be drawn from the refusal of the House of Representatives to adopt a measure that stated: "That there shall be no discrimination in civil rights or immunities among the inhabitants of any State or Territory of the United States on account of race, color, or previous condition of slavery" (Fairman, p. 1172). Enactment of this proposal would have placed Congress center stage in the enforcement of civil rights throughout the nation. Such a statute would have revolutionized the principles of federalism.

◆ **Johnson's Veto**

On March 27, 1866, President Andrew Johnson vetoed the Civil Rights Bill. In his veto message to congressional leaders, he cites political, policy, and constitutional concerns. He also reveals racist views.

Among other objections, Johnson denounces the legislation as interference with states' rights. He protests that the aim of Congress to confer citizenship upon new freedmen usurps what had long been considered a prerogative of the states. In addition, he notes, the decision of Congress to create citizens from a class of persons that had been excluded from citizenship also undercuts state authority. As a defender of state powers, moreover, he objects to a measure that affects states that, in his view, remains unrepresented in Congress. The southern states, he insists, have never been out of the Union. Rather, governmental authority has been temporarily seized by hostile forces. His emphasis on absolute state equality prohibits him from embracing legislation such as the Civil Rights Act, which imposes dramatic changes to which a southern state might not be able to object. Johnson also decries, on grounds of states' rights, the provision in the Civil Rights Act that transfers cases from state courts to federal courts.

Johnson also objects to the Civil Rights Act on policy grounds. He believes it unwise and unfair, for example, to bestow citizenship on a class of former slaves, newly freed, when foreigners worthy of citizenship are forced to wait five years to become naturalized citizens. He objects as well to the measure's interference in the relation of capital and labor. The guarantees of certain economic and property rights, he believes, represented poor economic policy.

Lurking behind Johnson's rationales for vetoing the Civil Rights Act is the ugly specter of his racism. Johnson had been on record as defending the supremacy of whites. He had derided blacks as inferior and incapable. In his message to Congress, moreover, he complains that the act is supplying protections for blacks that soar beyond those ever extended to whites. It is difficult to assess the degree to which Johnson's racism affected his view of the legislation, but there can be little doubt that it was significant.

Johnson's opposition to legislative efforts to improve the quality of life and legal standing for blacks was evident not merely in his veto of the Civil Rights Act but also in his earlier veto of legislation enacted to enhance protections for blacks in the subsequent Freedmen's Bureau Bill. The measure of his antagonism toward blacks may be seen as well in his stated determination to defeat the proposed Fourteenth Amendment, including the expenditure of $20,000 of his own money.

Audience

The Civil Rights Act of 1866, a landmark piece of legislation in every respect, enjoyed a nationwide audience. Indeed, the conferral by statute of citizenship upon the newly freed slaves and a catalog of their enumerated rights implied broad interest, for most Americans would be affected, directly or indirectly, by its terms. It is difficult to say which group—blacks who stood to benefit from the act or other citizens resentful of its terms because it represented a forceful response to the Black Codes—might have been more interested, but a measure that stood civil rights on its head enjoyed numerous and very attentive audiences.

The act signaled to black Americans that their lot in life stood a measurable chance of improvement. As a consequence, they constituted an audience of the first order. The repudiation of the repressive Black Codes demanded attention and with it the promise of new rights, privileges, and opportunities. Supporters of the Black Codes and repression of blacks watched the development and passage of the act

with great apprehension, since their lives were changing dramatically and they were powerless to prevent the changes.

Governmental officials in the executive and judicial branches of the federal government, as well as those in state government, were attentive students of the measure as well. The president was given specific enforcement authority. Federal judges, too, were armed with expanded jurisdiction and power to hear cases involving failure of officials to adhere to the terms of the act. State actors were highly attentive, since they were suddenly burdened with the obligation of implementing the newly established rights assigned to blacks, a compelling change for many officials.

Impact

The Civil Rights Act of 1866 represented the first effort of Congress to pass a civil rights bill. That the act conferred citizenship on former slaves, enumerated civil rights, supplied various methods of enforcement by both executive officials and judges, and imposed penalties and punishments on officials for failing to perform their duties speaks volumes for the effort of Congress to provide legal equality for blacks and whites under state laws. The act reversed the historic status of blacks before the law in clear and certain terms. At the creation of the Republic, blacks had been dealt their fate from the bottom of the deck. They were not legal persons and therefore had no legal rights. The act thus offered the promise of a monumental leap forward.

At a minimum, the Civil Rights Act was designed to destroy the repressive effects of the Black Codes. State officials would be barred by the terms of the statute from denying to black Americans the opportunity to exercise their newly granted rights to buy and sell property, negotiate and sign contracts, and initiate lawsuits, among others. But the act had limitations. It did not confer political rights; the franchise, for example was not extended on a national basis. That decision remained in the hands of the states. And, significantly, it did not apply to private action but only to state actors. Senator Lyman Trumbull, chair of the Senate Judiciary Committee and author of the bill, described its benefits for new freedmen as the "right to acquire property, the right to come and go at pleasure, the right to enforce rights, to make contracts" (Avins, p. 122).

The effectiveness of the Civil Rights Act was dampened, immediately, when President Andrew Johnson vetoed the measure. His opposition, on political, policy, and legal grounds, afforded southerners ammunition to attack the bill and curb its promise. Moreover, the reconstruction of the United States was fragile, and sea-changing provisions of the statute were not easily incorporated by a nation struggling to find its balance. The political climate in the South, moreover, was not conducive to effecting support for blacks. The Republican Party did not find success in the region, a failure that was in part attributable to Johnson's patronage and pardon policies, which were supportive of the Democrats. In truth, not all Republicans supported the efforts to promote equality. Racial animosity and violence

> "*That all persons born in the United States and not subject to any foreign power, excluding Indians not taxed, are hereby declared to be citizens of the United States.*"
>
> (Section 1)

> "*Such citizens, of every race and color, without regard to any previous condition of slavery or involuntary servitude ... shall have the same right, in every State and Territory in the United States ... to full and equal benefit of all laws and proceedings for the security of person and property, as is enjoyed by white citizens.*"
>
> (Section 1)

> "*That any person who, under color of any law, statute, ordinance, regulation, or custom, shall subject, or cause to be subjected, any inhabitant of any State or Territory to the deprivation of any right secured or protected by this act, or to different punishment, pains, or penalties ... than is prescribed for the punishment of white persons, shall be deemed guilty of a misdemeanor.*"
>
> (Section 2)

> "*That it shall be lawful for the President of the United States, or such person as he may empower for that purpose, to employ such part of the land or naval forces of the United States, or of the militia, as shall be necessary to prevent the violation and enforce the due execution of this act.*"
>
> (Section 9)

against blacks reflected in part the lectures and harangues from the Johnson White House that exploited the tensions surrounding the policies and fed the frustrations of citizens anxious about their own recovery. The violations of the rights of new freedmen largely went unpunished. The remedies were for the most part useless in a system in which the army, which might have aided blacks, was being hamstrung by a Justice Department that was controlled by the White House. At bottom, a statute that did not protect blacks against private acts was destined to be less than adequate. That lesson was seen as well in the failure of the Fourteenth Amendment, at least as far as the Supreme Court was concerned, to prevent private acts of racial dis-

crimination, the most far-reaching and notorious of actions undermining the cause of freedom for the former slaves.

The passage of the Civil Rights Act generated questions about whether it was constitutional. Some argued that it was a necessary and proper exercise of congressional power under the Thirteenth Amendment to eliminate slavery. Doubts were laid to rest, however, with the approval of the Fourteenth Amendment, widely viewed as constitutionalizing the Civil Rights Act, that is, incorporating or embodying its provisions in the amendment. Still, controversy surrounds the intentions of the framers of the Fourteenth Amendment, including heated debate on the question of whether it outlaws private acts of discrimination as well as the uncontested prohibition on discrimination by state actors.

The courts have transformed the Civil Rights Act into one of the nation's most important civil rights laws, far beyond its initial goal of undercutting the Black Codes. Over the years, the 1866 legislation has been revised and reenacted in different sections of the U.S. Code, but despite the legislative partitions, the original legislation has enjoyed a measure of vindication. For example, courts have divided on the issue of whether states might ban interracial marriages. Some courts found such marriages to be protected under Section 1 of the statute. It was not until 1967 that the Supreme Court, in *Loving v. Virginia*, held that interracial marriages were protected by the Fourteenth Amendment. In addition, some courts invoked Section 1 to strike down state laws that prohibited blacks from testifying against whites. In the 1870s, Section 1 lost much of its relevance, since issues involving its interpretation could be considered in light of the Fourteenth Amendment.

In what some critics have characterized as an exercise in judicial revisionism, the Supreme Court, in *Jones v. Alfred H. Mayer Co.* (1968), found that Congress did, under the 1866 act and the Thirteenth Amendment, outlaw private acts of racial discrimination. As a consequence, the Civil Rights Act became a powerful weapon in banning discrimination in the sale or lease of all housing, employment matters, schools, and virtually all contracts. Thus the impact and potential of the act were, perhaps, greater and more extensive than its architects had imagined.

Related Documents

"Civil Rights Act of 1875, 18 Stat. Part III, p. 335 (Act of Mar. 1, 1875)." University of Denver Sturm College of Law "American Legal History" Web site. http://www.law.du.edu/russell/lh/alh/docs/civrights1875.html. Readers should compare the provisions of the 1866 act with those of the 1875 act, in which Congress endeavored to prohibit racial discrimination in places of public accommodation.

Civil Rights Cases, 109 U.S. 3 (1883). The Supreme Court declared the Civil Rights Act of 1875 unconstitutional on the ground that Congress lacked authority to prohibit private acts of racial discrimination.

Fourteenth Amendment. The U.S. Constitution Online Web site. http://www.usconstitution.net/const.html#Am14. Readers will profit from a comparison of the provisions in Section 1 of the Civil Rights Act of 1866 with those in Section 1 of the Fourteenth Amendment, ratified on July 9, 1868.

Jones v. Alfred H. Mayer Co., 392 U.S. 409 (1968). The Supreme Court upheld congressional authority to prohibit private acts of racial discrimination under both the 1866 Civil Rights Act and the Thirteenth Amendment.

Bibliography

■ Articles

Kohl, Robert L. "The Civil Rights Act of 1866, Its Hour Come Round at Last: *Jones v. Alfred H. Mayer Co.*" *Virginia Law Review* 55, no. 2 (1969): 272–300.

Maltz, Earl M. "Reconstruction without Revolution: Republican Civil Rights Theory in the Era of the Fourteenth Amendment." *Houston Law Review* 24 (1987): 221–279.

■ Books

Avins, Alfred, ed. *The Reconstruction Amendments' Debates: The Legislative History and Contemporary Debates in Congress on the 13th, 14th, and 15th Amendments*. Richmond: Virginia Commission on Constitutional Government, 1967.

Belz, Herman. *A New Birth of Freedom: The Republican Party and Freedmen's Rights, 1861 to 1866*. Westport, Conn.: Greenwood Press, 1976.

Fairman, Charles. *Reconstruction and Reunion, 1864–88*. Vol. 1. New York: Macmillan, 1971.

Maltz, Earl. M. *Civil Rights, the Constitution, and Congress, 1863–1869*. Lawrence: University Press of Kansas, 1990.

Stryker, Lloyd Paul. *Andrew Johnson: A Study in Courage*. New York: Macmillan, 1929.

Trefousse, Hans L. *Andrew Johnson: A Biography*. New York: Norton, 1989.

—By David Gray Adler

Questions for Further Study

1. What was the meaning of "civil rights" in the 1866 Civil Rights Act?

2. How would you describe the relationship between the Civil Rights Act of 1866 and the Fourteenth Amendment? Describe their similarities and differences.

3. Compare and contrast the Civil Rights Act of 1868 and the Civil Rights Act of 1875. Did the later statute differ substantially from its predecessor? In what ways?

4. Suppose that Congress had extended the 1866 Civil Rights Act to the realm of private actions. Do you think that revised statute would have had a significant impact on the history of race relations in the United States?

5. How would you evaluate what some have characterized as judicial revisionism in the interpretation of the Civil Rights Act of 1866?

Glossary

civil rights	the protections and privileges of personal power granted by the Constitution
cognizance	jurisdiction to prosecute
custom	a set of practices that order social life
habeas corpus	the right of a person to obtain a legal order to appear in court, meant to protect against unlawful imprisonment
posse comitatus	a temporary police force, brought together typically to keep the peace or make an arrest

CIVIL RIGHTS ACT OF 1866

CHAP. XXXI.—*An Act to protect all Persons in the United States in their Civil Rights, and furnish the Means of their Vindication.*

Be it enacted by the Senate and House of Representatives of the United States of America in Congress assembled, That all persons born in the United States and not subject to any foreign power, excluding Indians not taxed, are hereby declared to be citizens of the United States; and such citizens, of every race and color, without regard to any previous condition of slavery or involuntary servitude, except as a punishment for crime whereof the party shall have been duly convicted, shall have the same right, in every State and Territory in the United States, to make and enforce contracts, to sue, be parties, and give evidence, to inherit, purchase, lease, sell, hold, and convey real and personal property, and to full and equal benefit of all laws and proceedings for the security of person and property, as is enjoyed by white citizens, and shall be subject to like punishment, pains, and penalties, and to none other, any law, statute, ordinance, regulation, or custom, to the contrary notwithstanding.

Sec. 2. *And be it further enacted,* That any person who, under color of any law, statute, ordinance, regulation, or custom, shall subject, or cause to be subjected, any inhabitant of any State or Territory to the deprivation of any right secured or protected by this act, or to different punishment, pains, or penalties on account of such person having at any time been held in a condition of slavery or involuntary servitude, except as a punishment for crime whereof the party shall have been duly convicted, or by reason of his color or race, than is prescribed for the punishment of white persons, shall be deemed guilty of a misdemeanor, and, on conviction, shall be punished by fine not exceeding one thousand dollars, or imprisonment not exceeding one year, or both, in the discretion of the court.

Sec. 3. *And be it further enacted,* That the district courts of the United States, within their respective districts, shall have, exclusively of the courts of the several States, cognizance of all crimes and offences committed against the provisions of this act, and also, concurrently with the circuit courts of the United States, of all causes, civil and criminal, affecting persons who are denied or cannot enforce in the courts or judicial tribunals of the State or locality where they may be any of the rights secured to them by the first section of this act; and if any suit or prosecution, civil or criminal, has been or shall be commenced in any State court, against any such person, for any cause whatsoever, or against any officer, civil or military, or other person, for any arrest or imprisonment, trespasses, or wrongs done or committed by virtue or under color of authority derived from this act or the act establishing a Bureau for the relief of Freedmen and Refugees, and all acts amendatory thereof, or for refusing to do any act upon the ground that it would be inconsistent with this act, such defendant shall have the right to remove such cause for trial to the proper district or circuit court in the manner prescribed by the "Act relating to habeas corpus and regulating judicial proceedings in certain cases," approved March three, eighteen hundred and sixty-three, and all acts amendatory thereof. The jurisdiction in civil and criminal matters hereby conferred on the district and circuit courts of the United States shall be exercised and enforced in conformity with the laws of the United States, so far as such laws are suitable to carry the same into effect; but in all cases where such laws are not adapted to the object, or are deficient in the provisions necessary to furnish suitable remedies and punish offences against law, the common law, as modified and changed by the constitution and statutes of the State wherein the court having jurisdiction of the cause, civil or criminal, is held, so far as the same is not inconsistent with the Constitution and laws of the United States, shall be extended to and govern said courts in the trial and disposition of such cause, and, if of a criminal nature, in the infliction of punishment on the party found guilty.

Sec. 4. *And be it further enacted*, That the district attorneys, marshals, and deputy marshals of the United States, the commissioners appointed by the circuit and territorial courts of the United States, with powers of arresting, imprisoning, or bailing offenders against the laws of the United States, the officers and agents of the Freedmen's Bureau, and every other officer who may be specially empowered by the President of the United States, shall be, and they are hereby, specially authorized and required, at the expense of the United States, to institute proceedings against all and every person who shall violate the provisions of this act, and cause him or them to be arrested and imprisoned, or bailed, as the case may be, for trial before such court of the United States or territorial court as by this act has cognizance of the offence. And with a view to affording reasonable protection to all persons in their constitutional rights of equality before the law, without distinction of race or color, or previous condition of slavery or involuntary servitude, except as a punishment for crime, whereof the party shall have been duly convicted, and to the prompt discharge of the duties of this act, it shall be the duty of the circuit courts of the United States and the superior courts of the Territories of the United States, from time to time, to increase the number of commissioners, so as to afford a speedy and convenient means for the arrest and examination of persons charged with a violation of this act; and such commissioners are hereby authorized and required to exercise and discharge all the powers and duties conferred on them by this act, and the same duties with regard to offences created by this act, as they are authorized by law to exercise with regard to other offences against the laws of the United States.

Sec. 5. *And be it further enacted*, That it shall be the duty of all marshals and deputy marshals to obey and execute all warrants and precepts issued under the provisions of this act, when to them directed; and should any marshal or deputy marshal refuse to receive such warrant or other process when tendered, or to use all proper means diligently to execute the same, he shall, on conviction thereof, be fined in the sum of one thousand dollars, to the use of the person upon whom the accused is alleged to have committed the offense. And the better to enable the said commissioners to execute their duties faithfully and efficiently, in conformity with the Constitution of the United States and the requirements of this act, they are hereby authorized and empowered, within their counties respectively, to appoint, in writing, under their hands, any one or more suitable persons, from time to time, to execute all such warrants and other process as may be issued by them in the lawful performance of their respective duties; and the persons so appointed to execute any warrant or process as aforesaid shall have authority to summon and call to their aid the bystanders or posse comitatus of the proper county, or such portion of the land or naval forces of the United States, or of the militia, as may be necessary to the performance of the duty with which they are charged, and to insure a faithful observance of the clause of the Constitution which prohibits slavery, in conformity with the provisions of this act; and said warrants shall run and be executed by said officers anywhere in the State or Territory within which they are issued.

Sec. 6. *And be it further enacted*, That any person who shall knowingly and willfully obstruct, hinder, or prevent any officer, or other person charged with the execution of any warrant or process issued under the provisions of this act, or any person or persons lawfully assisting him or them, from arresting any person for whose apprehension such warrant or process may have been issued, or shall rescue or attempt to rescue such person from the custody of the officer, other person or persons, or those lawfully assisting as aforesaid, when so arrested pursuant to the authority herein given and declared, or shall aid, abet, or assist any person so arrested as aforesaid, directly or indirectly, to escape from the custody of the officer or other person legally authorized as aforesaid, or shall harbor or conceal any person for whose arrest a warrant or process shall have been issued as aforesaid, so as to prevent his discovery and arrest after notice or knowledge of the fact that a warrant has been issued for the apprehension of such person, shall, for either of said offences, be subject to a fine not exceeding one thousand dollars, and imprisonment not exceeding six months, by indictment and conviction before the district court of the United States for the district in which said offense may have been committed, or before the proper court of criminal jurisdiction, if committed within any one of the organized Territories of the United States.

Sec. 7. *And be it further enacted*, That the district attorneys, the marshals, their deputies, and the clerks of the said district and territorial courts shall be paid for their services the like fees as may be allowed to them for similar services in other cases; and in all cases where the proceedings are before a commissioner, he shall be entitled to a fee of ten dollars in full for his services in each case, inclusive of all services incident to such arrest and examination. The person or persons authorized to execute the process to be issued by such commissioners for the arrest of offenders against the provisions of this act shall be entitled to a fee of five dollars for each person he or they may arrest and take before any such commissioner as aforesaid, with such other fees as may be deemed reasonable by such commissioner for such other additional services as may be necessarily performed by him or them, such as attending at the examination, keeping the prisoner in custody, and providing him with food and lodging during his detention, and until the final determination of such commissioner, and in general for performing such other duties as may be required in the premises; such fees to be made up in conformity with the fees usually charged by the officers of the courts of justice within the proper district or county, as near as may be practicable, and paid out of the Treasury of the United States on the certificate of the judge of the district within which the arrest is made, and to be recoverable from the defendant as part of the judgment in case of conviction.

Sec. 8. *And be it further enacted,* that whenever the President of the United States shall have reason to believe that offences have been or are likely to be committed against the provisions of this act within any judicial district, it shall be lawful for him, in his discretion, to direct the judge, marshal, and district attorney of such district to attend at such place within the district, and for such time as he may designate, for the purpose of the more speedy arrest and trial of persons charged with a violation of this act; and it shall be the duty of every judge or other officer, when any such requisition shall be received by him, to attend at the place and for the time therein designated.

Sec. 9. *And be it further enacted,* that it shall be lawful for the President of the United States, or such person as he may empower for that purpose, to employ such part of the land or naval forces of the United States, or of the militia, as shall be necessary to prevent the violation and enforce the due execution of this act.

Sec. 10. *And be it further enacted,* That upon all questions of law arising in any cause under the provisions of this act a final appeal may be taken to the Supreme Court of the United States.

SCHUYLER COLFAX, Speaker of the House of Representatives

LA FAYETTE S. FOSTER, President of the Senate, *pro tempore.*

◆ **In the Senate of the United States**

April 6, 1866.

The President of the United States having returned to the Senate, in which it originated, the bill entitled "An act to protect all persons in the United States in their civil rights, and furnish the means of their vindication," with his objections thereto, the Senate proceeded, in pursuance of the Constitution, to reconsider the same; and,

Resolved, That the said bill do pass, two-thirds of the Senate agreeing to pass the same.

Attest:

J.W. Forney, Secretary of the Senate.

◆ **In the House of Representatives U.S.**

April 9, 1866.

The House of Representatives having proceeded, in pursuance of the Constitution, to reconsider the bill entitled, "An act to protect all persons in the United States in their civil rights, and furnish the means of their vindication," returned to the Senate by the President of the United States, with his objections, and sent by the Senate to the House of Representatives, with the message of the President returning the bill:

Resolved, That the bill do pass, two-thirds of the House of Representatives agreeing to pass the same.

Attest:

Edward McPherson, Clerk,

by Clinton Lloyd, Chief Clerk.

FORTIETH CONGRESS, SECOND SESSION.

IN THE HOUSE OF REPRESENTATIVES UNITED STATES, *March 2, 1868.*

Articles exhibited by the House of Representatives of the United States, in the name of themselves and all the people of the United States, against Andrew Johnson, President of the United States, in maintenance and support of their impeachment against him for high crimes and misdemeanors in office.

ARTICLE I. That said Andrew Johnson, President of the United States, on the twenty-first day of February, in the year of our Lord one thousand eight hundred and sixty-eight, at Washington, in the District of Columbia, unmindful of the high duties of his office, of his oath of office, and of the requirement of the Constitution that he should take care that the laws be faithfully executed, did unlawfully, and in violation of the Constitution and laws of the United States, issue an order in writing for the removal of Edwin M. Stanton from the office of Secretary for the Department of War, said Edwin M. Stanton having been theretofore duly appointed and commissioned, by and with the advice and consent of the Senate of the United States, as such Secretary, and said Andrew Johnson, President of the United States, on the twelfth day of August, in the year of our Lord one thousand eight hundred and sixty-seven, and during the recess of said Senate, having suspended by his order Edwin M. Stanton from said office, and within twenty days after the first day of the next meeting of said Senate, that is to say, on the twelfth day of December in the year last aforesaid, having reported to said Senate such suspension with the evidence and reasons for his action in the case and the name of the person designated to perform the duties of such office temporarily until the next meeting of the Senate, and said Senate thereafterwards, on the thirteenth day of January, in the year of our Lord one thousand eight hundred and sixty-eight, having duly considered the evidence and reasons reported by said Andrew Johnson for said suspension, and having refused to concur in said suspension, whereby and by force of the provisions of an act entitled "An act regulating the tenure of certain civil offices," passed March second, eighteen hundred and sixty-seven. said Edwin M. Stanton did forthwith resume the functions of his office, whereof the said Andrew Johnson had then and there due notice, and said Edwin M. Stanton, by reason of the premises, on said twenty-first day of February, being lawfully entitled to hold said office of Secretary for the Department of War, which said order for the removal of said Edwin M. Stanton is in substance as follows, that is to say:

> EXECUTIVE MANSION,
> *Washington, D. C., February 21, 1868.*
>
> SIR: By virtue of the power and authority vested in me as President by the Constitution and laws of the United States, you are hereby removed from office as Secretary for the Department of War, and your functions as such will terminate upon the receipt of this communication.
>
> You will transfer to Brevet Major General Lorenzo Thomas, Adjutant General of the army, who has this day been authorized and empowered to act as Secretary of War *ad interim*, all records, books, papers, and other public property now in your custody and charge.
>
> Respectfully, yours,
>
> ANDREW JOHNSON.
>
> To the Hon. EDWIN M. STANTON, *Washington, D. C.*

The Articles of Impeachment of President Andrew Johnson (Library of Congress)

ARTICLES OF IMPEACHMENT OF ANDREW JOHNSON

"[He] did attempt to bring into disgrace, ridicule, hatred, contempt and reproach the Congress of the United States."

Overview

After the assassination of President Abraham Lincoln in April 1865, Vice President Andrew Johnson assumed the U.S. presidency. As Johnson was implementing his plans for Reconstruction after the Civil War, he encountered opposition from Republicans in Congress who did not agree with his lenient position toward southern radicals. As time passed, Johnson and Congress clashed on various acts related to Reconstruction. Johnson vetoed many bills and had many vetoes overridden by a hostile Congress. His most controversial action, however, was the removal of Secretary of War Edwin Stanton. Congress asserted that Johnson had disobeyed the Tenure of Office Act and, because of this and related crimes and misdemeanors, was therefore subject to impeachment.

The eleven Articles of Impeachment of Andrew Johnson were agreed upon by the House of Representatives in February 1868. The first eight deal with Johnson's dismissal of Stanton. Other articles address his alleged attempts to persuade others to violate the Constitution, to turn public opinion against Congress, and to deny Congress' lawful authority. The trial of Andrew Johnson, seventeenth president of the United States, began in March 1868. The impeachment attempt failed by a single vote on May 26, 1868.

Context

At the time of Lincoln's assassination, the country was just weeks from the end of the Civil War and beginning the initial steps of Reconstruction. While Lincoln also had problems with congressional Republicans, Johnson's were much worse: politically, he was a Democrat who opposed on principle many of the policies espoused by the Radical Republicans. Personally, he lacked both Lincoln's leadership ability and his willingness to compromise.

Within a month of assuming the presidency, Johnson decided to institute Lincoln's Reconstruction project. His timing coincided with Congressional recess, which was to last until December 1865, thus offending many members of Congress. Johnson invited Confederate states back into the Union, but his terms regarding former slaves infuriated Radical Republicans. Johnson wanted revolutionary southerners to maintain their political power, which entailed the further disenfranchisement of former slaves, in particular, their right to vote. Radical Republicans were in favor of giving freedmen voting privileges because they assumed they would vote for Lincoln's party, the Republican Party. This would ensure Republican power in the national government.

Johnson unilaterally readmitted the former Confederate states under terms that gave political power to leading Democrats, who did not want to give the newly freed slaves a role in their government. Once the southern states met the requirements Johnson established for their reintegration into the Union, they proceeded to hold their own elections and elected "Confederate heroes," who severely limited the rights of freedmen.

On March 2, 1867, Congress passed the Tenure of Office Act, forbidding the president to terminate any officer without the approval of the Senate. In the event the Senate was not in session, the president could suspend an officer only until the Senate could be heard. While Johnson vetoed the act, Congress had sufficient support to override his veto. The Tenure of Office Act was so vague that when it became law, questions still remained about its constitutionality and to whom it applied.

When Johnson tried to remove Stanton from his position as secretary of war and because of numerous disagreements, including Stanton's cooperation with Congressional Republicans and Stanton's refusal to implement Johnson's Reconstruction plans in the Confederate South, Congress considered impeaching Johnson—especially since Johnson not only suspended Stanton but also installed Ulysses S. Grant in the interim. When Congress returned to session in December, Johnson immediately provided its members with a justification for his removal of Stanton as secretary, as the Tenure of Office Act required. When the Senate reconvened, members decided that Johnson could not remove Stanton, and Stanton was thereby reinstated as secretary of war. When Johnson tried again to remove Stanton, Stanton "barricaded" himself inside the War Department (Solomon, p. 2922). At this point, the Radical Republicans sought more support for their opposition to the president.

1865

■ **March 4**
Johnson is inaugurated as vice president with Lincoln as president.

■ **April 14**
President Lincoln is shot at Ford's Theatre and dies the next morning.

■ **April 15**
Andrew Johnson becomes the seventeenth president of the United States.

■ **May 29**
Johnson pardons southerners.

1866

■ **January 25**
The Senate passes Freedmen's Bureau Bill.

■ **February 2**
The Civil Rights Bill is passed in the Senate.

■ **February 19**
The Freedmen's Bureau Bill is vetoed by Johnson.

■ **March 27**
The Civil Rights Bill is vetoed by Johnson.

■ **April 9**
The Civil Rights Bill is made law. This veto was the first ever to be passed over a presidential veto by Congress.

■ **July 16**
Johnson vetoes another version of the Freedmen's Bureau Bill.

■ **July 16**
The Freedmen's Bureau Bill is made law (passed despite second presidential veto).

1867

■ **March 2**
Congress votes to override Johnson's veto of the Tenure of Office Act; the Tenure of Office Act passes.

■ **June**
Congress rejects first impeachment attempt.

■ **August 12**
Johnson suspends Secretary of War Stanton and installs General Ulysses S. Grant in that post.

On February 24, 1868, the House voted to impeach President Johnson. The congressional decision to impeach Johnson was perhaps "the defensive response of a Congress faced by an aggressive executive using his presidential powers in a way that appeared to subvert the Constitution of the United States" (Benedict, p. 495). The actual Articles of Impeachment were drawn up and then adopted by the House on March 2–3. The Radical Republicans insisted on impeachment, whereas the conservative Republicans actually wanted to work with the new president.

Ultimately, the impeachment of Johnson failed. On May 17, 1868, the *New York Times* began its coverage of the trial as follows: "The great impeachment drama is practically at an end, and the President stands acquitted of the principal charge. Nineteen votes against thirty-five—just enough, and no more, to turn the scale of verdict. Twelve Democrats and seven Republicans—that magical number of seven—against thirty-five Republicans!" ("Impeachment. Final Vote in the Senate on the Eleventh Article," p. 1).

◆ **Key People**

The person most directly affected by the events leading up to impeachment was Secretary Edwin M. Stanton, who was initially appointed secretary of war by President Lincoln. He was removed by Johnson and replaced by Ulysses S. Grant. After Stanton was reinstated, Johnson attempted to remove him again and replace him with Adjutant General Lorenzo Thomas. Stanton refused to vacate his office the second time.

The Radical Republicans, led by Senator Charles Sumner (R-MA) and Congressman Thaddeus Stevens (R-PA), advocated impeachment. Other important Radical Republicans included James Ashley (R-OH), who presented the case against Johnson to the House; Benjamin F. Butler (R-MA), who delivered the opening remarks against Johnson; George S. Boutwell (R-MA), who chaired the committee responsible for writing the Articles of Impeachment; and John Covode (R-PA), who called for Johnson's impeachment the second time. Johnson was not without support, however, and both Timothy O. Howe (R-WI) and John Sherman (R-OH) were important voices opposing impeachment. Supreme Court Chief Justice Salmon P. Chase, who insisted on a proper trial, also indirectly helped Johnson's cause.

About the Author

When Thaddeus Stevens and John A. Bingham went to the Senate to inform them of the House's successful decision to impeach the president, they had not yet written any articles detailing precisely what crimes and misdemeanors President Johnson was accused of perpetrating. Instead, a committee was formed to write the articles after the vote to impeach Johnson was successful.

The committee charged with writing the Articles of Impeachment included the following men: John A. Bingham (R-OH), George S. Boutwell (R-MA), George W. Julian (R-IN), John A. Logan (R-IL), Thaddeus Stevens (R-PA), James

F. Wilson (R-IA), and Hamilton Ward (R-NY). Boutwell was the chair of the committee. Bingham and Wilson had once been moderates and were not in favor of impeachment; however, they approved John Covode's resolution to impeach the president and served on the committee. They were influenced, in part, by Johnson's breach of the Tenure of Office Act to join the ranks of those in favor of impeachment.

The committee began its work by conducting interviews with witnesses to Johnson's activities. After the interview process, the committee composed and agreed on ten articles of impeachment. These articles accused Johnson of crimes and misdemeanors regarding his attempted removal of Stanton and installation of Thomas as secretary of war, his disregard of the Tenure of Office Act, and his assertion that the Command of the Army Act (which required Johnson to issue orders through the general of the army, Ulysses S. Grant) was unconstitutional. The main problem with these accusations, however, was that they had all been debated before—the committee had not revealed anything about Johnson's conduct that was not already common knowledge. Wilson and Stevens worked together to write the eleventh article.

Explanation and Analysis of the Document

Before actually presenting these articles to the full Senate, a private conference was held to go over the articles on May 11. Article I was considered by the authors of the Articles of Impeachment to be the strongest argument for impeachment, but it was actually the weakest. Because Stanton was not removed from his post as secretary of war, Articles I, IV, V, and VI, which were also based on Stanton's removal, were therefore invalid and likely to fail. Furthermore, because of the weakness of this first article, it was presumed by influential senators that the remaining articles were equally weak. With the legitimacy of the first article in question, various Republican senators announced their plans to vote against other articles of impeachment as well. Some Republicans did not reveal their plans, making those leading the impeachment charge nervous. Thus, at the end of this meeting, eight of eleven articles were essentially abandoned. Those that remained were the second, third, and eleventh.

Senator John Sherman, representing Ohio, said that Articles I, IV, V, and VI, based upon Stanton's removal, must fail, because Stanton was not, in fact, illegally removed from the Department of War given that he had been appointed by Lincoln, not Johnson. Senator Sherman's opinion was influential, since he had been very much involved in drafting the text of the Tenure of Office Act. In the end, only three of the articles were actually voted upon by the Senate (II, III, and XI); the others had been debated and dismissed during meetings that preceded the trial.

◆ **Article I**

The first article of impeachment is a misdemeanor. The House asserts that President Johnson had disobeyed the

www.milestonedocuments.com

Time Line

1867

■ **December 6**
The first vote to proceed with impeachment of Johnson fails.

1868

■ **January 13**
The Senate rejects Johnson's bid to remove Stanton as secretary of war; Stanton is reinstated.

■ **February 21**
Johnson again suspends Stanton and appoints Lorenzo Thomas in his stead; Stanton refuses to leave office.

■ **February 24**
The House resolves to impeach Johnson on high crimes and misdemeanors by a vote of 126 to 47.

■ **February 27**
The House officially adopts eleven articles of impeachment to submit to the Senate.

■ **March 5**
The impeachment trial of President Johnson begins.

■ **May 11**
A Senate conference is held wherein senators make their intentions known regarding each article of impeachment. In fact, eight of the eleven articles are beaten in the conference.

■ **March 30**
Opening arguments in the trial begin and last until April 20.

■ **April 22**
The summary phase of the impeachment trial begins and ends on May 7.

■ **May 16**
The Senate gathers to consider the charges against President Johnson; it votes on Article XI only, which fails by one vote.

■ **May 26**
The Senate reassembles to finish voting on the Articles of Impeachment, beginning with the second article, which fails, as well as the third article, which also fails. At that point, the Senate adjourns the trial even though eight of the eleven articles have neither been discussed nor voted upon.

Secretary of War Edwin Stanton (Library of Congress)

Constitution and the Tenure of Office Act by calling, via letter, for the removal of Secretary of War Edwin M. Stanton. This action clearly violated the Tenure of Office Act, which stipulated that the president had to obtain approval from the Senate in order to dismiss cabinet officers.

This article was discarded because Stanton had been appointed by Lincoln, not Johnson. The Tenure of Office Act applied to the president who appointed the cabinet officer. That is, because Lincoln, not Johnson, had appointed Stanton, Johnson was well within his rights to dismiss Stanton in favor of Grant (the first time he dismissed Stanton) and Thomas (the second time he dismissed Stanton).

The failure of this particular article affected many of the remaining articles. Since this article was abandoned, segments of following articles were subsequently left out of consideration, such as the second element of the eleventh article.

◆ Article II

The second article is also a misdemeanor. This article deals with Johnson's second appointment to the secretary of war position, Lorenzo Thomas. This article references a letter penned by Johnson that advised Thomas of Stanton's removal from office, which also entailed giving all relevant documents of that office to Thomas. The second article was one of only three to be voted upon by the Senate, all of which failed. The others were the third article and the eleventh article.

◆ Article III

The third article is a misdemeanor, charging Johnson because he had appointed Thomas as secretary of war with-

out consulting the Senate about his actions—particularly since the Senate was in session at the time Johnson had attempted to appoint Thomas. The third article was one of only three articles to be voted upon by the Senate, and it failed. The others, which also failed, were the second article and the eleventh article.

◆ Article IV

The fourth article is the first of two crimes. It was not voted upon by the Senate during the trial. It charges Johnson with conspiring to dismiss Stanton with Thomas. It states that Johnson had conspired with Thomas and unnamed members of the House of Representatives to threaten and intimidate Stanton into leaving his post as secretary of war. Because the first article was found not to constitute a misdemeanor, Article IV was put aside and not subject to a vote.

◆ Article V

The fifth article is a misdemeanor and again involves Johnson's supposed conspiring with Thomas to defy the Tenure of Office Act with Stanton's dismissal. Again, Johnson was charged with conspiring with Thomas and unknown representatives to prevent the legal execution of the Tenure of Office Act. Because Article I was found not to constitute a misdemeanor, Article V was not voted upon.

◆ Article VI

The sixth article is a crime. Johnson is said to have conspired with Thomas to take the property of the United States, specifically from the Department of War, by force and seizure. Because Article I was found not to constitute a misdemeanor, Article VI was therefore also not voted upon.

◆ Article VII

Article VII is a misdemeanor that states that Johnson realized the unlawful nature of appropriating property belonging to the Department of War. This article was not voted upon by the Senate.

◆ Article VIII

Article VIII is also a misdemeanor. This article notes that Johnson had written a letter to Lorenzo Thomas informing him that he was to assume the office of secretary of war immediately. This article was not voted upon by the Senate.

◆ Article IX

Article IX is a misdemeanor. This article concerns Johnson's assertion that the standard requiring all orders to be passed through the general of the army was not only unconstitutional but also outside the general's responsibilities. This article was not voted upon by the Senate.

◆ Article X

Article X is a misdemeanor concerning Johnson's communication to the people about Congress' actions. This article asserts that Johnson had tried to disgrace Congress as well as various committees of that body. Furthermore, it alleges that Johnson had done so to deliberately garner support from the American people against Congress.

Article X is further broken down into three specifications. The first specification deals with statements Johnson had made two years earlier, saying that Congress represented only part of the states: those that had rejoined the Union. Johnson also had asserted that Congress may have appeared to be in favor of the Union but had acted such that disunion and discord between the states were the ultimate result.

The second specification deals with remarks Johnson had made in Cleveland, Ohio, where he had accused Congress of attempting to divide the government of the country. Furthermore, Johnson had stated that Congress had engaged in a propaganda campaign designed to turn the public sentiment against the president.

The third specification also regards statements made approximately two years previously and accuses Johnson of delivering speeches that were not only inappropriate but also subversive. Article X was never voted upon.

◆ Article XI

Article XI is a misdemeanor. Written to combine all charges and concerns of the previous ten articles, it was therefore essential to the case against Johnson.

The charges in the eleventh count are, first, that Congress could not issue amendments to the Constitution because Congress was not yet represented by all states. Johnson is also charged with accusing Congress of attempting to change the existing government and of planning a riot in New Orleans. The eleventh article was actually the first to be voted upon by the senators, on May 11. There were not enough guilty votes regarding this article for President Johnson to be impeached. Those who sought to impeach him were fairly certain it would pass and therefore devised no plan for action should it fail, which it did.

Thomas F. Williams (R-PA) then suggested that the group adjourn until the May 26. The hope was that the political scenario would change with the inclusion of more Republican senators from states not yet admitted into the Union, among other potential events. While the Senate recessed, the House reassembled to plan a better, more evidence-filled case against the president.

Voting in the Senate resumed on May 26 with consideration of the second article, which was soundly defeated. The third article was similarly defeated. Once the senators discovered that the impeachment would not be carried out owing to lack of support for the majority of the articles, they decided it would be better to drop the case and end the trial than to vote against impeachment. The eleventh article was one of only three articles to be voted upon by the Senate, all of which failed. The others were the second article and the third article.

Audience

The audience for the Articles of Impeachment of Andrew Johnson was primarily the members of the Senate

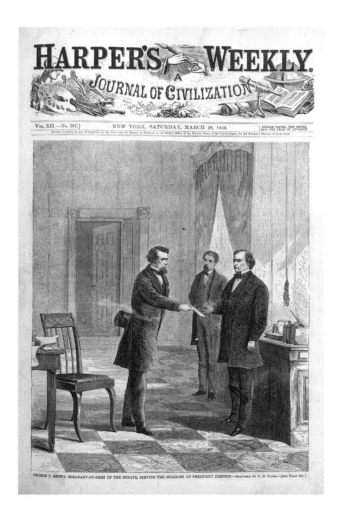

Andrew Johnson, attended by Col. W. G. Moore, being served impeachment summons in the White House by George T. Brown, sergeant-at-arms. (Library of Congress)

who would vote on Johnson's guilt or innocence of the charges advanced in the eleven articles. On a broader scale, however, the audience was the American public. In fact, the document begins as follows: "Articles exhibited by the House of Representatives of the United States, in the name of themselves and *all the people of the United States*, against Andrew Johnson, President of the United States, in maintenance and support of their impeachment against him for high crimes and misdemeanors" (emphasis added).

On February 25, 1868, the *New York Times* reported that visitors "rushed to the galleries" to witness the proceedings (p. 1). In fact, "the visitors' gallery filled and emptied according to the drama of the arguments" and "Johnson's presidency was picked apart in public" (Sachs, A22). The Senators did not debate the issue in front of the public assembled in the gallery. Instead, they went to the ladies' parlor adjacent to the Senate floor or asked that all visitors be escorted out so that they could discuss matters freely. Audience members had been observed applauding and hissing and were escorted out by police and ushers.

"That said Andrew Johnson ... unmindful of the high duties of his office and the dignity and proprieties thereof, and of the harmony and courtesies which ought to exist and be maintained between the executive and legislative branches ... did attempt to bring into disgrace, ridicule, hatred, contempt and reproach the Congress of the United States."

(Article X)

"Johnson as the Chief Magistrate of the United States, did make and declare, with a loud voice certain intemperate, inflammatory, and scandalous harangues, and therein utter loud threats and bitter menaces, as well against Congress."

(Article X)

"Never was a great malefactor so gently treated as Andrew Johnson."

(Thaddeus Stevens's speech on impeachment to the House of Representatives, *Harper's Weekly,* March 21, 1868)

"A man is not proved a villain because his views appear to be short-sighted and perilous."

(Editorial, *Harper's Weekly,* June 2, 1866)

Impact

As a result of the impeachment trial, the Founders and writers of the Constitution were once again praised for their invaluable insight. By restricting the vote to two-thirds of the Senate, the founders ensured that it would not be a simple task to remove a president. After Johnson's trial, the Republicans, particularly the Radical Republicans, had to regroup. Many worried that they had lost credibility with the American public, which would adversely affect the party. Others, of course, were adamant that the party would survive and would, in fact, grow stronger.

The long-term political impact of the impeachment was minimal. Johnson left office shortly after his trial, and the new president, Ulysses S. Grant, and the new Congress maintained amiable relations. All those involved in the impeachment were eager to put it behind them and focus on the pressing needs of the post-Civil War nation. As for Johnson, he was president for approximately nine more months after his acquittal. He returned to Tennessee, where he made an unsuccessful bid for the Senate in 1869. He tried again and won a Senate seat in 1874. He died not long thereafter, on July 31, 1875.

This was the first time an impeachment trial had been initiated against an American president. Because the grounds for trial were so clearly the result of policy disputes rather than actual misconduct, the impeachment effort failed. However, it did influence attitudes and behavior on presidential impeachment; no president was again tried until Bill Clinton in 1999.

Related Documents

An Act to Establish a Bureau for the Relief of Freedmen and Refugees. United States Statutes at Large 38th Congress, 2nd sess. (March 3, 1865). Library of Congress "American Memory" Web site. http://memory.loc.gov/cgi-bin/ampage?collId=llsl&fileName=013/llsl013.db&recNum=536. Accessed on January 21, 2008. This bill expanded the jurisdiction and capabilities of the Freedmen's Bureau, which provided welfare services to former slaves, by dividing the South into districts and adding new officers.

An Act Regulating the Tenure of Certain Civil Offices United States Statutes at Large 39th Congress, 2nd sess. (March 2, 1867). Library of Congress "American Memory" Web site. http://memory.loc.gov/cgi-bin/ampage?collId=llsl&fileName=014/llsl014.db&recNum=461. This act stipulated that the president could not remove any person, with the exception of cabinet members, who has been appointed to a civil office by the Senate without consulting and ultimately getting approval from the Senate.

"Rules of Procedure and Practice in the Senate When Sitting on the Trial of Impeachments." University of Missouri-Kansas City School of Law "Famous Trials" Web site. http://www.law.umkc.edu/faculty/projects/ftrials/impeach/rulesofimpeachment.html. Accessed on January 21, 2008. This document details the proper sequence of events (and precise times) for introducing the articles of impeachment to the Senate and explains how the managers from the House of Representatives are to present the articles to the Senate.

Trial of Andrew Johnson, President of the United States, before the Senate of the United States, on Impeachment by the House of Representatives for High Crimes and Misdemeanors. 2 vols. *Washington, D.C.: Government Printing Office, 1868.* These three volumes contain both the preliminary and the actual trial proceedings of the impeachment of President Andrew Johnson.

Bibliography

■ Articles

Benedict, Michael Les. "From Our Archives: A New Look at the Impeachment of Andrew Johnson." *Political Science Quarterly* 113, no. 3 (Fall 1998): 493–511.

Calabresi, Steven O., and Christopher S. Yoo. "The Unitary Executive during the Second Half-Century." *Harvard Journal of Law & Public Policy* 26, no. 3 (Summer 2003): 667–801.

"Impeachment. Final Vote in the Senate on the Eleventh Article. The President Acquitted of the Offences Charged. Adjournment of the Court without a Further Vote. An Investigation to be Made of the Bribery and Corruption Charges." *New York Times,* May 17, 1868.

"Impeachment. President Johnson Impeached before the Senate. Committees of Both Houses Appointed to Prepare the Case. The Forms to be Observed and Mode of Trial. Secretary Stanton Still at the War Office." *New York Times,* February 25, 1868.

Kaufhold, Jack. "Personality." *America's Civil War* 14, no. 2 (May 2001): 12–16.

Sachs, Susan. "The President's Trial: The Johnson Case; Once, Senate Impeachment Deliberations Defied Leaks for 131 Years. *New York Times,* February 10, 1999: A22.

Solomon, Burt. "Dethroning King Andy." *National Journal* 30, no. 50 (December 12, 1998): 2920–2924.

Tolson, Jay. "The 10 Worst Presidents." *U.S. News & World Report* 142, no. 7 (February 26, 2007): 40–53.

Trefousse, Hans L. "Impeached President Understood Power: Seventeenth President and the Press." *Media History Digest* 11, no. 2 (1991): 20–27.

Weisberger, Bernard A. "Impeachment Aftermath." *American Heritage* 50, no. 1 (February/March 1999): 22.

Zeitz, Joshua. "Impeach Johnson!" *New Republic* 220, no. 3 (January 18, 1999): 13–15.

■ Books

Hearn, Chester G. *The Impeachment of Andrew Johnson.* Jefferson, N.C.: McFarland & Company, 2000.

Means, Howard. *The Avenger Takes His Place: Andrew Johnson and the 45 Days That Changed the Nation.* Orlando, Fla.: Harcourt, 2006.

Trefousse, Hans L. *Impeachment of a President: Andrew Johnson, the Blacks, and Reconstruction.* New York: Fordham University Press, 1999.

■ Web Sites

Alexander, Richard. "High Crimes and Misdemeanors: The Constitutional and Historic Limits on Impeachment for Criminal Attacks upon State." Find Law Web site.
    http://library.findlaw.com/1998/Dec/1/127948.html. Accessed on July 30, 2007.

"Andrew Johnson." The State Library of North Carolina "Encyclopedia" Web site.
    http://statelibrary.dcr.state.nc.us/nc/bio/public/johnson.htm. Accessed on July 29, 2007.

"Editorial: Making Treason Odious," *Harper's Weekly,* June 2, 1866, p. 338. HarpWeek "Finding Precedent: The Impeachment of Andrew Johnson" Web site.
    http://www.impeach-andrewjohnson.com/05AJFirstVetoes/iiia-13a.htm. Accessed on January 21, 2008.

"Finding Precedent: The Impeachment of Andrew Johnson." HarpWeek Web site.
    http://www.impeach-andrewjohnson.com/default.htm. Accessed on July 29, 2007.

"History of the Impeachment of Andrew Johnson." Chapter X: A Conference Held and the First Vote Taken." The Avalon Project at Yale Law School Web site.
    http://www.yale.edu/lawweb/avalon/treatise/andrew_johnson/chap_10.htm. Accessed on July 30, 2007.

"History of the Impeachment of Andrew Johnson. Chapter XI: The Impeachers in a Maze—A Recess Ordered." The Avalon Project at Yale Law School Web site.
    http://www.yale.edu/lawweb/avalon/treatise/andrew_johnson/chap_10.htm. Accessed on July 30, 2007.

"House Document No. 108-222, Biographical Directory of the United States Congress 1774–2005: Fortieth Congress." GPO Access Web site. March 30, 2006.
http://a257.g.akamaitech.net/7/257/2422/26jan20061725/www.gpoaccess.gov/serialset/cdocuments/hd108-222/40th.pdf. Accessed on July 30, 2007.

"Jacksonian Democracy." Answers.com Web site.
http://www.answers.com/topic/jacksonian-democracy. Accessed on July 31, 2007.

"Johnson, Andrew." The New Book of Knowledge "The American Presidency" Web site.
http://ap.grolier.com/article?assetid=a2015580-h&template-name=/article/article.html. Accessed on July 29, 2007.

Linder, Douglas O. "Famous American Trials: The Andrew Johnson Impeachment Trial." Famous Trials Web site.
http://ap.grolier.com/article?assetid=a2015580-h&template-name=/article/article.html. Accessed on July 29, 2007.

"LLI Backgrounder on Impeachment." Legal Information Institute Web site.
http://www.law.cornell.edu/background/impeach/impeach.htm. Accessed on July 30, 2007.

"Mr. Steven's Last Speech on Impeachment," *Harper's Weekly*. HarpWeek "Finding Precedent: The Impeachment of Andrew Johnson" Web site.
http://www.impeach-andrewjohnson.com/09ImpeachmentAndAcquittal/vi-20.htm. Accessed on January 21, 2008.

"Research Guide on Impeachment: Historic Background on the Impeachment and Trial of President Andrew Johnson." The Library of Congress Web site.
http://memory.loc.gov/ammem/amlaw/Impeachment-Guide.html. Accessed on July 30, 2007.

"Proceedings of the Senate Sitting for the Trial of Andrew Johnson, President of the United States, on Articles of Impeachment Exhibited by the House of Representatives: Rules of Procedure and Practice in the Senate When Sitting on the Trial of Impeachments." Famous Trials Web site.
http://www.law.umkc.edu/faculty/projects/ftrials/impeach/rules-ofimpeachment.html. Accessed on September 5, 2007.

"Today in History: May 16. The Andrew Johnson Impeachment" Library of Congress "American Memory" Web site.
http://memory.loc.gov/ammem/today/may16.html#impeachment. Accessed on July 30, 2007.

"A Century of Lawmaking for a New Nation: U.S. Congressional Documents and Debates, 1774–1875. The Thirty-Ninth Congress, Sess. II, Ch. 153 and 154, 1867." Library of Congress "American Memory" Web site.
http://memory.loc.gov/cgi-bin/ampage?collId=llsl&fileName=014/llsl014.db&recNum=461. Accessed on July 30, 2007.

—By Kristina E. Curry and Mary E. Stuckey

Questions for Further Study

1. How does the impeachment of Andrew Johnson inform our opinions of the threatened impeachment of President Richard Nixon in 1974?

2. How does the impeachment of Andrew Johnson inform our opinions of the impeachment of President Bill Clinton in 1998?

3. The Radical Republicans have been portrayed by writers as both heroes and villains in their attack on President Johnson. How can both sides be justified?

4. What kinds of "high crimes and misdemeanors" should result in presidential impeachment?

5. Does the threat of impeachment help to ensure presidential honesty?

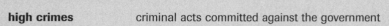

high crimes	criminal acts committed against the government
impeachment	Congressional procedure intended to unseat a public officer
misdemeanor	a lesser offense than "high crimes" but still a cause for impeachment and removal of a president
reconstruction	period ranging from approximately 1865 to 1877 when leaders debated ways in which to solve various social, economic, and political issues related to the eleven Confederate seceding states
An act regulating the tenure of certain civil office	act (also called simply the Tenure of Office Act) that was made law on March 2, 1867, even though it was vetoed by President Andrew Johnson; it attempted to prevent the president from removing members of his cabinet in whom he had no confidence and who are actually originally employed by Lincoln

ARTICLES OF IMPEACHMENT OF ANDREW JOHNSON

On Articles of Impeachment Exhibited by the House of Representatives

On Monday, February the 24th, 1868, the House of Representatives of the Congress of the United States resolved to impeach Andrew Johnson, President of the United States, of high crimes and misdemeanors, of which the Senate was apprised and arrangements were made for the trial. On Monday the 2d of March, articles of impeachment were agreed upon by the House of Representatives, and on the 4th they were presented to the Senate by the managers on the part of the House, who were accompanied by the House, the grand inquest of the nation, as a Committee of the Whole on the state of the Union. Mr. BINGHAM, chairman of the managers, read the articles as follows:

Articles exhibited by the House of Representatives of the United States, in the name of themselves and all the people of the United States, against Andrew Johnson, President of the United States, in maintenance and support of their impeachment against him for high crimes and misdemeanors.

◆ Article I.

That said Andrew Johnson, President of the United States, on the 21st day of February, in the year of our Lord, 1868, at Washington, in the District of Columbia, unmindful of the high duties of his office, of his oath of office, and of the requirement of the Constitution that he should take care that the laws be faithfully executed, did unlawfully and in violation of the Constitution and laws of the United States issue and order in writing for the removal of Edwin M. Stanton from the office of Secretary for the Department of War, said Edwin M. Stanton having been theretofore duly appointed and commissioned, by and with the advice and consent of the Senate of the United States, as such Secretary, and said

Andrew Johnson, President of the United States, on the 12th day of August, in the year of our Lord 1867, and during the recess of said Senate, having been suspended by his order Edwin M. Stanton from said office, and within twenty days after the first day of the next meeting of said Senate, that is to say, on the 12th day of December, in the year last aforesaid, having reported to said Senate such suspension, with the evidence and reasons for his action in the case and the name of the person designated to perform the duties of such office temporarily until the next meeting of the Senate, and said Senate thereafterward, on the 13th day of January, in the year of our Lord 1868, having duly considered the evidence and reasons reported by said Andrew Johnson for said suspension, and having been refused to concur in said suspension, whereby and by force of the provisions of an act entitled "An act regulating the tenure of certain civil offices," passed March 2, 1867, said Edwin M. Stanton did forthwith resume the functions of his office, whereof the said Andrew Johnson had then and there due notice, and said Edwin Stanton, by reason of the premises, on said 21st day of February, being lawfully entitled to hold said office of Secretary for the Department of War, which said order for the removal of said Edwin M. Stanton is, in substance, as follows, that is to say:

EXECUTIVE MANSION,
WASHINGTON, D.C., *February* 21, 1868

SIR: By virtue of the power and authority vested in me, as President by the Constitution and laws of the United States, you are hereby removed from the office of Secretary for the Department of War, and your functions as such will terminate upon receipt of their communication. You will transfer to Brevet Major-General L. Thomas, Adjutant-General of the Army, who has this day been authorized and empowered to act as Secretary of War ad interim, all books, paper and other public property now in your custody and charge.

Respectfully yours, ANDREW JOHNSON.

Hon. E. M. Stanton, Secretary of War

Which order was unlawfully issued, and with intent then are there to violate the act entitled "An act regulating the tenure of certain civil office," passed March 2, 1867; and, with the further intent contrary to the provisions of said act, and in violation thereof, and contrary to the provisions of the Constitution of the United States, and without the advice and consent of the Senate of the United States, the said Senate then and there being in session, to remove said Edwin M. Stanton from the office of Secretary for the Department of War, the said Edwin M. Stanton being then and there Secretary of War, and being then and there in the due and lawful execution of the duties of said office, whereby said Andrew Johnson, President of the United States, did then and there commit, and was guilty of a high misdemeanor in office.

◆ Article II.

That on the 21st day of February, in the year of our Lord 1868, at Washington, in the District of Columbia, said Andrew Johnson, President of the United States, unmindful of the high duties of his office, of his oath of office, and in violation of the Constitution of the United States, and contrary to the provisions of an act entitled "An act regulating the tenure of certain civil offices," passed March 2, 1867, without the advice and consent of the Senate of the United States, said Senate then and there being in session, and without authority of law, did, with intent to violate the Constitution of the United States and the act aforesaid, issue and deliver to one Lorenzo Thomas a letter of authority, in substance as follows, that is to say:

EXECUTIVE MANSION,
WASHINGTON, D.C., *February* 21, 1868
SIR: The Hon. Edwin M. Stanton having been this day removed from office as Secretary for the Department of War, you are hereby authorized and empowered to act as Secretary of War *ad interim*, and will immediately enter upon the discharge of the duties pertaining to that office.

Mr. Stanton has been instructed to transfer to you all the records, books, papers and other public property now in his custody and charge.

Respectfully yours, ANDREW JOHNSON

To Brevet Major-General Lorenzo Thomas, *Adjutant General United States Army, Washington, D.C.*

then and there being no vacancy in said office of Secretary for the Department of War: whereby said Andrew Johnson, President of the United States, did then and there commit, and was guilty of a high misdemeanor in office.

◆ Article III.

That said Andrew Johnson, President of the United States, on the 21st day of February, in the year of our Lord 1868, at Washington in the District of Columbia, did commit, and was guilty of a high misdemeanor in office, in this, that, without authority of law, while the Senate of the United States was then and there in session, he did appoint one Lorenzo Thomas to be Secretary for the Department of War, *ad interim*, without the advice and consent of the Senate, and with intent to violate the Constitution of the United States, no vacancy having happened in said office of Secretary for the Department of War during the recess of the Senate, and no vacancy existing in said office at the time, and which said appointment so made by Andrew Johnson, of said Lorenzo Thomas is in substance as follows, that is to say:

EXECUTIVE MANSION,
WASHINGTON, D.C., *February* 21, 1868
SIR: The Hon. Edwin M. Stanton having been this day removed from office as Secretary for the Department of War, you are hereby authorized and empowered to act as Secretary of War *ad interim*, and will immediately enter upon the discharge of the duties pertaining to that office.

Mr. Stanton has been instructed to transfer to you all the records, books, papers and other public property now in his custody and charge.

Respectfully yours, ANDREW JOHNSON

To Brevet Major-General Lorenzo Thomas, *Adjutant General United States Army, Washington, D.C.*

◆ Article IV.

That said Andrew Johnson, President of the United States, unmindful of the high duties of his office, and of his oath of office, in violation of the Constitution and laws of the United States, on the 21st day of February, in the year of our Lord 1868, at Washington, in the District of Columbia, did unlawfully conspire with one Lorenzo Thomas, and with other persons to the House of Representatives unknown, with intent by intimidation and threats unlawfully to hinder and prevent Edwin M. Stanton, then and there, the Secretary for the Department of War, duly appointed under the laws of the United States, from holding said office of Secretary for the Department of War, contrary to and in violation of the Constitution of the United States, and of the provisions of an act entitled "An act to define and punish certain conspiracies," approved July 31, 1861, whereby said Andrew Johnson, President of the United States, did then and there commit and was guilty of high crime in office.

◆ **Article V.**

That said Andrew Johnson, President of the United States, unmindful of the high duties of his office and of his oath of office, on the 21st of February, in the year of our Lord 1868, and on divers others days and time in said year before the 2d day of March, A.D. 1868, at Washington, in the District of Columbia, did unlawfully conspire with one Lorenzo Thomas, and with other persons in the House of Representatives unknown, to prevent and hinder the execution of an act entitled "An act regulating the tenure of certain civil office," passed March 2, 1867, and in pursuance of said conspiracy, did attempt to prevent Edwin M. Stanton, then and there being Secretary for the Department of War, duly appointed and commissioned under the laws of the United States, from holding said office, whereby the said Andrew Johnson, President of the United States, did then and there commit and was guilty of high misdemeanor in office.

◆ **Article VI.**

That said Andrew Johnson, President of the United States, unmindful of the high duties of his office and of his oath of office, on the 21st day of February, in the year of our Lord 1868, at Washington, in the District of Columbia, did unlawfully conspire with one Lorenzo Thomas, by force to seize, take, and possess the property of the United Sates in the Department of War, and then and there in the custody and charge of Edwin M. Stanton, Secretary for said Department, contrary to the provisions of an act entitled "An act to define and punish certain conspiracies," approved July 31, 1861, and with intent to violate and disregard an act entitled "An act regulating the tenure of certain civil offices," passed March 2, 1867, whereby said Andrew Johnson, President of the United States, did then and there commit a high crime in office.

◆ **Article VII.**

That said Andrew Johnson, President of the United States, unmindful of the high duties of his

office, and of his oath of office, on the 21st day of February, in the year of our Lord 1868, at Washington, in the District of Columbia, did unlawfully conspire with one Lorenzo Thomas with intent unlawfully to seize, take, and possess the property of the United States in the Department of War, in the custody and charge of Edwin M. Stanton, Secretary of said Department, with intent to violate and disregard the act entitled "An act regulating the tenure of certain civil offices," passed March 2, 1867, whereby said Andrew Johnson, President of the United States, did then and there commit a high misdemeanor in office.

◆ **Article VIII.**

That said Andrew Johnson, President of the United States, unmindful of the high duties of his office and of his oath of office, with intent unlawfully to control the disbursements of the moneys appropriated for the military service and for the Department of War, on the 21st day of February, in the year of our Lord 1868, at Washington, in the District of Columbia, did unlawfully and contrary to the provisions of an act entitled "An act regulating the tenure of certain civil offices," passed March 2, 1867, and in violation of the Constitution of the United States, and without the advice and consent of the Senate of the United States, and while the Senate was then and there in session, there being no vacancy in the office of Secretary for the Department of War, with intent to violate and disregard the act aforesaid, then and there issue and deliver to one Lorenzo Thomas a letter of authority in writing, in substance as follows, that is to say:

EXECUTIVE MANSION,
WASHINGTON, D.C., *February* 21, 1868
SIR: The Hon. Edwin M. Stanton having been this day removed from office as Secretary for the Department of War, you are hereby authorized and empowered to act as Secretary of War *ad interim*, and will immediately enter upon the discharge of the duties pertaining to that office.

Mr. Stanton has been instructed to transfer to you all the records, books, papers and other public property now in his custody and charge.

Respectfully yours, ANDREW JOHNSON

To Brevet Major-General Lorenzo Thomas, *Adjutant General United States Army, Washington, D.C.*

Whereby said Andrew Johnson, President of the United States, did then and there commit and was guilty of a high misdemeanor in office.

◆ Article IX.

That said Andrew Johnson, President of the United States, on the 22nd day of February, in the year of our Lord 1868, at Washington, in the District of Columbia, in disregard of the Constitution and the laws of the United States, duly enacted, as Commander-in-Chief of the Army of the United States, did bring before himself, then and there William H. Emory, a Major-General by brevet in the Army of the United States, actually in command of the department of Washington, and the military forces thereof, and did and there, as such Commander-in-Chief, declare to, and instruct said Emory, that part of a law of the United States, passed March 2, 1867, entitled "An act for making appropriations for the support of the army for the year ending June 30, 1868, and for other purposes," especially the second section thereof, which provides, among other things, that "all orders and instructions relating to military operations issued by the President or Secretary of War, shall be issued through the General of the Army, and, in case of his inability, through the next in rank," was unconstitutional, and in contravention of the commission of said Emory, and which said provision of law had been theretofore duly and legally promulgated by general order for the government and direction of the Army of the United States, as the said Andrew Johnson then and there well knew, with intent thereby to induce said Emory, in his official capacity as Commander of the department of Washington, to violate the provisions of said act, and to take and receive, act upon and obey such orders as he, the said Andrew Johnson, might make and give, and which should not be issued through the General of the Army of the United States, according to the provisions of said act, and with the further intent thereby to enable him, the said Andrew Johnson, to prevent the execution of an act entitled "An act regulating the tenure of certain civil offices," passed March 2, 1867, and to unlawfully prevent Edwin M. Stanton, then being Secretary for the Department of War, from holding said office and discharging the duties thereof, whereby said Andrew Johnson, President of the United States, did then and there commit, and was guilty of a high misdemeanor in office.

◆ Article X.

That said Andrew Johnson, President of the United States, unmindful of the high duties of his office and the dignity and proprieties thereof, and of the harmony and courtesies which ought to exist and be maintained between the executive and legislative branches of the Government of the United States, designing and intending to set aside the rightful authorities and powers of Congress, did attempt to bring into disgrace, ridicule, hatred, contempt and reproach the Congress of the United States, and the several branches thereof, to impair and destroy the regard and respect of all the good people of the United States for the Congress and legislative power thereof, (which all officers of the government ought inviolably to preserve and maintain,) and to excite the odium and resentment of all good people of the United States against Congress and the laws by it duly and constitutionally enacted; and in pursuance of his said design and intent, openly and publicly and before divers assemblages of citizens of the United States, convened in divers parts thereof, to meet and receive said Andrew Johnson as the Chief Magistrate of the United States, did, on the 18th day of August, in the year of our Lord 1866, and on divers other days and times, as well before as afterward, make and declare, with a loud voice certain intemperate, inflammatory, and scandalous harangues, and therein utter loud threats and bitter menaces, as well against Congress as the laws of the United States duly enacted thereby, amid the cries, jeers and laughter of the multitudes then assembled in hearing, which are set forth in the several specifications hereinafter written, in substance and effect, that it to say:

Specification First. In this, that at Washington, in the District of Columbia, in the Executive Mansion, to a committee of citizens who called upon the President of the United States, speaking of and concerning the Congress of the United States, heretofore, to wit: On the 18th day of August, in the year of our Lord, 1866, in a loud voice, declare in substance and effect, among other things, that is to say:

"So far as the Executive Department of the government is concerned, the effort has been made to restore the Union, to heal the breach, to pour oil into the wounds which were consequent upon the struggle, and, to speak in a common phrase, to prepare, as the learned and wise physician would, a plaster healing in character and co-extensive with the wound. We thought and we think that we had partially succeeded, but as the work progresses, as reconstruction seemed to be taking place, and the country was becoming reunited, we found a disturbing and moving element opposing it. In alluding to that element it shall go no further than your Convention, and the distinguished gentleman who has delivered the report of the proceedings, I shall make no reference that I do not believe, and the time and the occasion justify.

"We have witnessed in one department of the government every endeavor to prevent the restoration of peace, harmony and union. We have seen hanging upon the verge of the government, as it were, a body called or which assumes to be the Congress of the United States, while in fact it is a Congress of only part of the States. We have seen this Congress pretend to be for the Union, when its every step and act tended to perpetuate disunion and make a disruption of States inevitable.

"We have seen Congress gradually encroach, step by step, upon constitutional rights, and violate day after day, and month after month, fundamental principles of the government. We have seen a Congress that seemed to forget that there was a limit to the sphere and scope of legislation. We have seen a Congress in a minority assume to exercise power which, if allowed to be consummated, would result in despotism or monarchy itself."

Specification Second. In this, that at Cleveland, in the State of Ohio, heretofore to wit: On the third day of September, in the year of our Lord, 1866, before a public assemblage of citizens and others, said Andrew Johnson, President of the United States, speaking of and concerning the Congress of the United States, did, in a loud voice, declare in substance and effect, among other things, that is to say:

"I will tell you what I did do? I called upon your Congress that is trying to break up the Government."

"In conclusion, beside that Congress had taken much pains to poison the constituents against him, what has Congress done? Have they done anything to restore the union of the States? No: On the contrary, they had done everything to prevent it: and because he stood now where he did when the rebellion commenced, he had been denounced as a traitor. Who had run greater risks or made greater sacrifices than himself? But Congress, factions and domineering, had undertaken to poison the minds of the American people."

Specification Third. In this case, that at St. Louis, in the State of Missouri, heretofore to wit: On the 8th day of September, in the year of our Lord 1866, before a public assemblage of citizens and others, said Andrew Johnson, President of the United States, speaking of acts concerning the Congress of the United States, did, in a loud voice, declare in substance and effect, among other things, that is to say:

"Go on, perhaps if you had a word or two on the subject of New Orleans you might understand more about it than you do, and if you will go back and ascertain the cause of the riot at New Orleans, per-

haps you will not be so prompt in calling out 'New Orleans.' If you will take up the riot of New Orleans and trace it back to its source and its immediate cause, you will find out who was responsible for the blood that was shed there. If you will take up the riot at New Orleans and trace it back to the Radical Congress, you will find that the riot at New Orleans was substantially planned. If you will take up the proceedings in their caucuses you will understand that they knew that a convention was to be called which was extinct by its powers having expired; that it was said that the intention was that a new government was to be organized, and on the organization of that government the intention was to enfranchise one portion of the population, called the colored population, and who had been emancipated, and at the same time disfranchise white men. When you design to talk about New Orleans you ought to understand what you are talking about. When you read the speeches that were made, and take up the facts on the Friday and Saturday before that convention sat, you will find that speeches were made incendiary in their character, exciting that portion of the population? the black population? to arm themselves and prepare for the shedding of blood. You will also find that convention did assemble in violation of law, and the intention of that convention was to supersede the organized authorities in the State of Louisiana, which had been organized by the government of the United States, and every man engaged in that rebellion, in the convention, with the intention of superseding and upturning the civil government which had been recognized by the Government of the United States, I say that he was a traitor to the Constitution of the United States, and hence you find that another rebellion was commenced, having its origin in the Radical Congress.

"So much for the New Orleans riot. And there was the cause and the origin of the blood that was shed, and every drop of blood that was shed is upon their skirts and they are responsible. I could test this thing a little closer, but will not do it here to-night. But when you talk about the causes and consequences that resulted from proceedings of that kind, perhaps, as I have been introduced here and you have provoked questions of this kind, though it does not provoke me, I will tell you a few wholesome things that have been done by this Radical Congress in connection with New Orleans and the extension of the elective franchise.

"I know that I have been traduced and abused. I know it has come in advance of me here, as elsewhere, that I have attempted to exercise an arbitrary power in resisting laws that were intended to be forced upon the government; that I had exercised that power; that I had abandoned the party that elected me, and that I was a traitor, because I exercised the veto power in attempting, and did arrest for a time, that which was called a 'Freedmen's Bureau' bill. Yes, that I was a traitor. And I have been traduced; I have been slandered; I have been maligned; I have been called Judas Iscariot, and all that. Now, my countrymen, here to-night, it is very easy to indulge in epithets; it is easy to call a man a Judas, and cry out traitor, but when he is called upon to give arguments and facts he is very often found wanting. Judas Iscariot? Judas! There was a Judas, and he was one of the twelve Apostles. O, yes, the twelve Apostles had a Christ, and he never could have had a Judas unless he had twelve Apostles. If I have played the Judas who has been my Christ that I have played the Judas with? Was it Thad. Stevens? Was it Wendell Phillips? Was it Charles Sumner? They are the men that stop and compare themselves with the Savior, and everybody that differs with them in opinion, and tries to stay and arrest their diabolical and nefarious policy is to be denounced as a Judas."

"Well, let me say to you, if you will stand by me in this action, if you will stand by me in trying to give the people a fair chance? soldiers and citizens? to participate in these office, God be willing, I will kick them out. I will kick them out just as fast as I can.

"Let me say to you, in concluding, that what I have said is what I intended to say; I was not provoked into this, and care not for their menaces, the taunts and the jeers, I care not for threats, I do not intend to be bullied by enemies, nor erawed by my friends. But, God willing, with your help, I will veto their measures whenever any of them come to me."

Which said utterances, declarations, threats and harangues, highly censurable in any, are peculiarly indecent and unbecoming in the Chief Magistrate of the United States, by means whereof the said Andrew Johnson has brought the high office of the President of the United States into contempt, ridicule and disgrace, to the great scandal of all good citizens, whereby said Andrew Johnson, President of the United States, did commit, and was then and there guilty of a high misdemeanor in office.

◆ **Article XI.**

That the said Andrew Johnson, President of the United States, unmindful of the high duties of his office and of his oath of office, and in disregard of the Constitution and laws of the United States, did, heretofore, to wit: On the 18th day of August, 1866, at the city of Washington, and in the District of Columbia, by public speech, declare and affirm in substance, that the Thirty-Ninth Congress of the United States was not a Congress of the United States authorized by the Constitution to exercise legislative power under the same; but, on the contrary, was a Congress of only part of the States, thereby denying and intending to deny, that the legislation of said Congress was valid or obligatory upon him, the said Andrew Johnson, except in so far as he saw fit to approve the same, and also thereby denying the power of the said Thirty-Ninth Congress to propose amendments to the Constitution of the United States. And in pursuance of said declaration, the said Andrew Johnson, President of the United States, afterwards, to wit: On the 21st day of February, 1868, at the city of Washington, D.C., did, unlawfully and in disregard of the requirements of the Constitution that he should take care that the laws be faithfully executed, attempt to prevent the execution of an act entitled "An act regulating the tenure of certain civil office," passed March 2, 1867, by unlawfully devising and contriving and attempting to devise and contrive means by which he should prevent Edwin M. Stanton from forthwith resuming the functions of the office of Secretary for the Department of War, notwithstanding the refusal of the Senate to concur in the suspension therefore made by the said Andrew Johnson of said Edwin M. Stanton from said office of Secretary for the Department of War; and also by further unlawfully devising and contriving, and attempting to devise and contrive, means then and there to prevent the execution of an act entitled "An act making appropriations for the support of the army for the fiscal year ending June 30,1868, and for other purposes," approved March 2, 1867. And also to prevent the execution of an act entitled "An act to provide for the more efficient government of the rebel States," passed March 2, 1867. Whereby the said Andrew Johnson, President of the United States, did then, to wit: on the 21st day of February, 1868, at the city of Washington, commit and was guilty of a high misdemeanor in office.

<u>*Articles of a Treaty*</u> made and
concluded by and between Lieutenant General
William T. Sherman, General William S. Harney,
General Alfred H. Terry, General C. C. Augur,
J. B. Henderson, Nathaniel G. Taylor, John B.
Sanborn and Samuel F. Tappan, duly appointed
Commissioners on the part of the <u>United States</u> and
the different Bands of the <u>Sioux Nation</u> of Indians
by their Chiefs and Head men whose names are
hereto subscribed, they being duly authorized to act
in the premises.

<u>Article I</u>   From this day forward
all war between the parties to this agreement shall forever
cease. The Government of the United States desires peace
and its honor is hereby pledged to keep it. The Indians
desire peace and they now pledge their honor to maintain it.

    If bad men among the whites or among other
people, subject to the authority of the United States, shall commit
any wrong upon the person or property of the Indians, the United
States will, upon proof made to the Agent and forwarded to the
Commissioner of Indian Affairs at Washington City, proceed at once to
cause the offender to be arrested and punished according to the
laws of the United States and also reimburse the injured person
for the loss sustained.

    If bad men among the Indians shall commit a

The Treaty of Fort Laramie (National Archives and Records Administration)

TREATY OF FORT LARAMIE

"They will relinquish all right to occupy permanently the territory outside their reservations."

Overview

The Treaty of Fort Laramie (1868) was an agreement between the United States and various bands of Lakota Sioux, Yanktonai Sioux, Santee Sioux, and Arapaho. The treaty ended Red Cloud's War (1866–1867), established the boundaries of the Great Sioux Reservation, and protected Sioux hunting grounds and the sacred Black Hills from white encroachment. Other provisions of the treaty served as agents of assimilation by trying to induce the Indians to take up farming, wear non-Indian clothing, and educate their children.

The Treaty of Fort Laramie was one of the last great treaties signed between the American government and the Plains Indians. Despite the peaceful intentions of the treaty, the unwillingness of the federal government to live up to its stipulations and the inability of the signing tribes to enforce the treaty on all their members resulted in the Great Sioux War (also known as the Black Hills War) of 1876–1877 and the eventual removal of the Black Hills from Lakota ownership.

Context

By the time the Lakota signed the Treaty of Fort Laramie in 1868, the Great Plains were well on the way to being transformed from a land where the buffalo roamed freely and Native American tribes lived their traditional lifestyle. The United States acquired the Great Plains via the Louisiana Purchase of 1803. Various expeditions sponsored by the federal government during the first two decades of the nineteenth century concluded that the Great Plains were unfit for cultivation. As a consequence, the Great Plains became known as the Great American Desert, and the region was largely ignored until the 1840s. Beginning in the 1840s, however, overland emigrants began traveling through Plains Indian hunting grounds. The discovery of gold in California in 1848 opened the floodgates, and over the next few decades almost 500,000 people traversed the plains on their way to the Pacific Coast. The Plains Indians

felt this increased traffic through their hunting grounds in many ways. Timber was cut, watering holes were despoiled, forage was consumed, and game, particularly the bison, dispersed. More tragically, epidemic diseases such as cholera and smallpox were spread to the Plains Indians. Naturally, tribes such as the Lakota and Cheyenne attempted to protect their homeland.

To protect overland travelers, the military opened military posts such as Fort Laramie in Wyoming and Fort Kearny in Nebraska. To avoid warfare and guarantee the safe passage of overland emigrants, the government sought to make an agreement with the Plains tribes in 1851. On September 17, 1851, the United States signed the Treaty of Fort Laramie with the Sioux, Cheyenne, Arapaho, Crow, Shoshone, Assiniboine, Mandan, Hidatsa, and Arikara. The purpose of this first treaty was to bring peace to the Great Plains, assign a specific territory for each tribe, and keep the overland trails safe and open. In exchange for ending hostilities and allowing wagon trains safe passage through their territory, the Plains Indians were guaranteed an annual annuity worth $50,000 for fifty years. As would happen with future treaties, Congress reduced the annuity payment to ten years during the ratification process.

A brief period of peace ensued after the first Treaty of Fort Laramie, but in 1854 an unfortunate event near Fort Laramie would spark almost twenty-five years of intermittent warfare between the Plains Indians and the United States. Sometimes called the "Mormon cow incident" or the "Grattan massacre," the conflict erupted after a stray cow from a Mormon wagon train wandered off and was killed and eaten by a group of Brulé. With the intention of punishing the guilty party, Lieutenant John Grattan, along with twenty-nine soldiers and a civilian interpreter who was reportedly intoxicated, traveled from Fort Laramie to Chief Conquering Bear's village and demanded that the culprits be handed over. In the ensuing negotiations, shots were fired, and Conquering Bear was killed. Lakota warriors immediately pounced on Grattan's command, and within minutes every soldier and the interpreter lay dead or dying.

The following year, General William S. Harney was ordered to command a retaliatory expedition into Lakota territory. On September 3, 1855, Harney's six-hundred-man command surprised Little Thunder's Brulé Lakota at

Ash Hollow, Nebraska, on Blue Water Creek. When the shooting ceased, at least eighty-six Lakota, half of whom were women and children, were dead. Harney went on to occupy Fort Pierre (South Dakota) and then negotiated peace with the Lakota. Once again, the Lakota agreed not to interfere with the overland traffic. Harney's show of force began to create rifts in Lakota society. Some leaders, such as Spotted Tail, sought peaceful relations through diplomacy, while others, such as Crazy Horse, became more militant in protecting their homelands.

Large-scale warfare did not erupt again until the Civil War. Several conflicts not directly involving the Lakota would have an impact on relations between them and the United States. In 1862 the Santee Sioux launched a war against white settlers in Minnesota. When the U.S. military moved in to suppress the uprising, Santee refugees escaped to the Great Plains to seek refuge with their Lakota, Yankton, and Yanktonais cousins. Military expeditions pursued the Santee into the Plains and, in the battle of Whetstone Hill in September 1862 and at Killdeer Mountain in July 1863, inflicted heavy casualties on the Sioux. The long-term consequence of the these battles was a strengthened and united Lakota resistance to further American encroachments on their homeland.

Another Civil War–era conflict erupted during the fall of 1863 in Colorado when a military force commanded by Colonel John M. Chivington attacked a peaceful village of Cheyenne on Sand Creek in eastern Colorado. Although Chief Black Kettle was flying an American flag over the village and government officials promised that his village would be safe, Chivington attacked early in the morning, killing more than two hundred men, women, and children indiscriminately. The atrocity at Sand Creek sparked a wave of reprisals by the Cheyenne and their Lakota and Arapaho allies. War parties struck American settlements and wagon trains in Colorado, Kansas, and Nebraska, inflicting hundreds of casualties.

In 1865 war spread to the Powder River region in northeastern Wyoming and southeastern Montana. This region was the prized hunting grounds of the Plains Indians, but miners traveling to Montana via the Bozeman Trail began going through Lakota territory. Militants such as Red Cloud and Crazy Horse were determined to protect their land and began attacks on the overland travelers. Although the first Treaty of Fort Laramie guaranteed this territory for the Lakota, the military, rather than expelling the trespassers, built a series of forts along the Bozeman Trail to protect American citizens. The struggle to protect the Powder River country and the removal of the forts became known as Red Cloud's War.

Red Cloud's War comprised a series of small-scale skirmishes and one incredible Indian victory the Lakota remember as the Battle of the Hundred Slain. On December 21, 1866, Captain William J. Fetterman and eighty soldiers were led into an ambush by Crazy Horse and wiped out to the last man. During the summer of 1867, the Lakota continued harassing the American settlements, railroad construction crews, and the forts in the Powder River country. On August 1, a large Indian force attacked soldiers stationed at Fort C. F. Smith. Known as the Hayfield Fight, the battle ended without a clear victor. Just one day later, a sizable Lakota force led by Red Cloud fought soldiers from Fort Phil Kearny in what has become known as the Wagon Box Fight.

By the summer of 1867 American civilian and military authorities were at odds over what had become known as the "Indian problem." Military leaders such as General William Tecumseh Sherman firmly believed that the warring tribes must be militarily subdued and that only a thorough defeat of the Plains Indians would bring peace. On the other hand, an emerging reform movement that would evolve into President Ulysses S. Grant's "peace policy" began placing the blame for hostilities on the federal government and therefore sought a negotiated peace rather than the forced peace the military preferred. A government investigation into Indian affairs in the wake of the Fetterman massacre concluded that the recent hostilities were the result of flagrant treaty violations by the government. As a consequence, Congress interjected itself and created the Indian Peace Commission in July 1867. President Andrew Johnson ordered the commission to negotiate with the warring tribes, bring an end to hostilities, and concentrate the tribes on one of several large reservations in the western half of modern-day South Dakota and Oklahoma.

The commission was headed by the commissioner of Indian affairs Nathaniel G. Taylor, who was also a Methodist minister, lawyer, and close personal friend of President Johnson's. It would be his job to rein in the veteran military officers who also served on the commission: General Sherman along with the generals William S. Harney, Alfred H. Terry, and C. C. Auger. Other civilian members included Samuel F. Tappan, a leading reformer and former abolitionist; John B. Sanborn; and J. B. Henderson.

In September 1867 the Indian Peace Commission arrived on the Great Plains. After failed talks with bands of Oglala and Brulé Lakota at North Platte, Nebraska, and Fort Laramie, Wyoming, the commission headed south to Kansas to meet with Southern Plains tribes such as the Comanche, Kiowa, Arapaho, and Southern Cheyenne. The commission succeeded in signing the Treaty of Medicine Lodge Creek. This treaty, an almost mirror image of the Treaty of Fort Laramie, theoretically ended warfare and Indian opposition to the railroads, forts, and roads in exchange for a guaranteed reservation in Oklahoma and annual annuities.

After treating with the Southern Plains tribes, the commission moved back to negotiations with the Northern Plains tribes at Fort Laramie. On April 29, 1868, twenty-five chiefs and headmen of the Brulé Lakota signed the Treaty of Fort Laramie. A month later, thirty leaders among the Oglala also signed the treaty. Red Cloud, however, refused to come in and talk, and without his signature the work of the commission would have been considered a failure. Finally, when Red Cloud received word that the Bozeman Trail would be closed and the Powder River military

Time Line

1867

■ **October 21 and 28**
Southern Plains Indians sign the Treaty of Medicine Lodge Creek.

1868

■ **April 29**
Twenty-five chiefs and headmen (including Spotted Tail) of the Brulé Lakota become the first Indians to sign the Treaty of Fort Laramie.

■ **May 25**
Thirty chiefs and headmen of the Oglala Lakota (including Man Afraid of His Horses and American Horse) sign the treaty.

■ **November 6**
Red Cloud of the Oglala Lakota and various other bands sign the treaty.

1869

■ **February 16**
The U.S. Senate ratifies the Treaty of Fort Laramie.

1871

■ The Indian Appropriation Act ends treaty making, giving Congress much more say in Indian affairs.

1874

■ **July**
Gold is discovered in the Black Hills, leading to a number of treaty violations.

1876–1877

■ The Great Sioux War, including the Battle of the Little Bighorn, is fought on the Northern Plains.

1877

■ The Black Hills are removed from the Great Sioux Reservation.

1887

■ **February 8**
The Dawes Severalty Act is passed, allowing for Indian reservations to be allotted at the president's discretion

The Oglala Sioux chief Red Cloud (Library of Congress)

posts would be abandoned, he, along with Lakota chiefs from the Hunkpapa, Blackfeet, Cuthead, Two Kettle, and Sans Arc tribes signed the Treaty of Fort Laramie. Noticeably missing were the signatures of the staunch Lakota nationalists Crazy Horse of the Oglala and Sitting Bull of the Hunkpapa. The failure to obtain the signatures of all Lakota leaders would create friction in the near future.

About the Author

Members of the Indian Peace Commission most likely authored the Treaty of Fort Laramie. The commission was headed by Commissioner of Indian Affairs Nathaniel G. Taylor and included three other civilians: Samuel F. Tappan, a leading reformer and former abolitionist; John B. Sanborn; and J. B. Henderson. Sanborn stood out among the Sioux as being an important part of the treaty negotiations. The military was represented by four veteran officers: generals William T. Sherman, William S. Harney, Alfred H. Terry, and C. C. Auger. Harney was well known to the Lakota. Known as "Mad Bear" in Lakota culture, Harney had attacked Little Thunder's Brulé village in 1855.

Explanation and Analysis of the Document

◆ Article I

Article I ends Red Cloud's War. The treaty rather optimistically states that "war between the parties … shall for ever cease." Had the government lived up to the provisions of this treaty (protecting Sioux lands and the Black Hills from white encroachment) and had the signing tribes been able to enforce the treaty on all its members, warfare might have been avoided. Unfortunately, the discovery of gold in the Black Hills would spark warfare just eight years later.

In an attempt to guarantee peace, the United States agrees to arrest and prosecute any "bad men among the whites" who commit any wrongs against the person or property of the Indians. It is the government agent's duty to investigate and report to the commissioner of Indian affairs any crimes that might be committed. If it is proved that an Indian has been violated or his property damaged, the injured party would be reimbursed. How or who would pay the reparation is not clearly delineated. Likewise, if "bad men among the Indians" injure the person or property of a white man, the tribe is required to surrender the culprit to the government agent for prosecution. This clause obviously was addressing the issue that had led to the Grattan massacre fourteen years earlier. If an Indian is proved guilty, the injured party would be reimbursed through the Indians' annual annuity. In other words, if an Indian or Indians stole five horses from a white rancher and sufficient evidence was provided to the government agent, the annuity for that year would be reduced to pay reparations to the injured party. This clause was notoriously abused. Any time that livestock, crops, or any type of property was damaged or stolen, a white farmer or rancher could be reimbursed by reporting it to the government agent as an Indian depredation.

◆ Article II

Article II creates and delineates the boundaries of the Great Sioux Reservation. The original boundaries include all the territory west of the Missouri River in modern-day South Dakota. According to the treaty's wording, the reservation would be "set apart for the absolute and undisturbed use and occupation of the Indians." Non-Indians, except for government agents, civilian employees, and military officials in the discharge of duty, are prohibited from entering or settling on the reserve. Finally, the tribes signing this treaty agree to "relinquish all claims" to territories not outlined in Article II.

Creating the Great Sioux Reservation was part of a larger plan of the Indian Peace Commission. The plan called for the creation of a Southern and Northern Plains reservation for the purpose of concentrating the Plains Indians. The Treaty of Medicine Lodge Creek created a large southern reservation in western Oklahoma. The goal behind concentrating Indians in defined spaces was to open the Great Plains to white settlement and railroads. Realizing that other (non-Sioux) tribes would eventually need to settle on the reservation, Article II states that "friendly tribes or individual Indians" could be settled on the reserve.

◆ **Article III**

Article III provides for the expansion of the Great Sioux Reservation if not enough land is available for every qualified Indian to have 160 acres of tillable land.

◆ **Article IV**

In Article IV the federal government agrees to build a series of buildings to be used for agency administration. The government agrees to build at some place along the Missouri River, "where timber and water may be convenient," an agency warehouse for the Indians' annuities and trade goods, residences for the government agent and agency physician, and workshops for the blacksmith, miller, carpenter, farmer, and engineer. Other agency buildings includes a schoolhouse or mission building and a sawmill. In reality, these buildings became agents of assimilation and dispossession, as they aided in transforming the Plains Indians from nomadic bison hunters to settled farmers.

◆ **Article V**

Article V outlines the duties of the government agent. The agent is required to live full-time among the Indians and keep a home at the agency headquarters. In the event of depredations committed by or against the Indians, the agent is responsible for gathering evidence and sending it to the commissioner of Indian affairs for action. While a list of the agent's specific duties is not outlined in Article V, he is charged with carrying out the "faithful discharge of other duties enjoined on him by law." Having a full-time government agent who lived among the Indians and was responsible for distribution of annuities and investigation of conflicts among the Indians worked against traditional leadership by replacing the duties and responsibilities of the chiefs and headmen.

◆ **Article VI**

Article VI allows any head of family who "shall desire to commence farming" to select a 320-acre tract of land. This land would be removed from the communal holdings of the tribe and kept as private property of the allottee for as long as it is cultivated. Any Indian over the age of eighteen who is not the head of family can select eighty acres of land if he desires to commence farming. The government reserves the right to pass laws concerning the alienation, or transferring, of these allotments from one generation to the next.

Eliminating communally held land and turning Indians into private property owners was an important part of the assimilation process. The Dawes Act of 1887 would eventually force all Indians, whether they desired to become private property owners or not, to select a 160-acre allotment.

◆ **Article VII**

Although the Indian signers of the treaty probably did not think much about Article VII, it eventually became a contentious issue. "In order to insure the civilization of the Indians entering into this treaty," states Article VII, "the necessity of education is admitted." The federal government agrees to provide a school and teacher for every thirty children who can be "induced or compelled" to attend schools. Eventually, the Indians were induced to send their children to off-reservation boarding schools in faraway locales, such as Carlisle Indian Industrial School in Pennsylvania. The purpose of education was to seize Indian youth and mold them into American citizens before they could be infected by Indian culture. Indian schoolchildren were dressed like white Americans, were prohibited from speaking their native language, were given Christian names, and learned the basics of a grammar school education.

◆ **Article VIII**

Article VIII provides seed and agricultural implements for those who "in good faith" intend to begin "cultivating the soil." During the first year, Indian farmers would receive goods worth $100, and for the following three years goods valuing $25 would be provides. To further assist Indian farmers, Article VIII provides an agency farmer to instruct Indians in farming techniques. Moreover, once a hundred Indians begin farming, a second blacksmith would be available at the agency.

◆ **Article IX**

Article IX allows the federal government, after a ten-year period, to withdraw the services of the blacksmith, carpenter, engineer, farmer, miller, and physician. Once they were removed, the commissioner of Indian affairs, after "careful inquiry" into the conditions of the Indians, could spend up to $10,000 per year on their education and moral improvement. The hope of the federal government was that all Indians would eventually take allotments and begin farming. Once Indians were assimilated into American culture as the owners and cultivators of farms, the services of civilian employees, instructors, and teachers would be unnecessary.

◆ **Article X**

If the government expected Indians to give up their nomadic hunting culture, then regularly delivered annuities such as clothing and food would be necessary. Thus, the annuities to be received each year by the Indians are outlined in Article X. Every male over the age of eighteen would once a year receive a new set of clothing consisting of a wool coat and pants, flannel shirt, hat, and a pair of socks. Women over the age of twelve would receive a flannel skirt and twelve yards each of calico and cotton cloth.

Clothing was not all that was received. Under the discretion of the secretary of the interior, additional annuities would be distributed each year based on the following formula: $10 for each person who continues to "roam and hunt" and $20 for each person who farms. These annuities were to be provided for a period of thirty years (lowered to ten years during the ratification process). Finally, every Indian over four years of age who permanently settled on the reservation and abided by the treaty stipulations would receive one pound of meat and one pound of flour per day for a period of four years. Every lodge, or family, engaged in farming was entitled to receive one "good American cow"

William T. Sherman (Library of Congress)

and a pair of oxen broken for use in the field. To ensure that the proper goods arrived at the agency and were allotted properly, an army officer is required to be on site to supervise the distribution.

In what would become a contentious requirement outlined in Article X, the government agent is required to conduct an annual census. The government desired a census in order to provide an accurate count for annuity-distribution purposes. The Indians, however, viewed the census as a means to reduce their annuities. Conflicts regularly erupted over the yearly census, and Indians found clever ways to pad their numbers to increase the amount of annuities received.

◆ **Article XI**

Article XI is one of the most important, and misunderstood, parts of the treaty. The Indians signing the treaty agree to surrender their rights to all land outside the stipulated reservation boundaries. Indians did reserve the right to hunt in the unceded hunting grounds north of the North Platte River and east of the Bighorn Mountains. A carefully placed clause in Article XI, however, not recognized by the Indian signers, would eventually limit Indian territory to the reservation itself. Indians are permitted to hunt beyond reservation boundaries "so long as the buffalo may range thereon in such numbers as to justify the chase." What Indian signers did not foresee, and perhaps the federal government and particularly the military did, was that

the buffalo's days were numbered. With the buffalo all but extinct by the late 1870s, the Lakota became trapped within the boundaries of the reservation.

In signing the treaty, Indians also agree to withdraw all opposition to the transcontinental railroad being constructed through the Platte Valley and all future railroads, wagon roads, and mail stations. Furthermore, Indians agree to never kill or scalp a white man, kidnap white women or children, or attack any property belonging to the people of the United States. In the event that a future railroad or wagon road was to pass through the reservation, the government agrees to pay damages decided upon by "three disinterested commissioners," one of whom was a chief of the tribe.

Finally, the Indian signers agree to withdraw their opposition to the forts (establishments such as Fort Laramie, Fort McPherson, and Fort Kearny) and military roads south of the North Platte River.

◆ **Article XII**

Article XII would cause the federal government some misgivings in the future. This article requires that any future land cession would need the signatures of at least three-fourths of all adult Indian males. When the federal government wanted to remove the Black Hills from the Great Sioux Reservation in the aftermath of the Sioux War of 1876–1877, commissioners could not get the requisite number of signatures and, in fact, did not even try. Using graft, or simply ignoring Article XII, a federal commission obtained the signatures of several chiefs and headmen among the Oglala and Brulé Lakota bands and simply removed the Black Hills from the Great Sioux Reservation in 1877.

◆ **Article XIII**

In Article XII the federal government agrees to provide and fund for the agency the positions of blacksmith, carpenter, engineer, farmer, miller, teachers, and physician. The men and women who filled these positions were intended to introduce Indians to and teach them the necessary skills to become American citizens.

◆ **Article XIV**

Article XIV was used as an incentive to induce Indians to take up farming. Each year for a period of three years, $500 in presents would be distributed among the ten most productive farmers, as selected by the agent.

◆ **Article XV**

Article XV reinforces Article XI by stating that once the agency headquarters and related buildings were constructed, the Indians would consider the reservation their permanent home.

◆ **Article XVI**

Lakota leaders such as Red Cloud probably found Article XVI the most satisfying. One of Red Cloud's stipulations for ending the war and signing the treaty was that the military forts in the Powder River region and the Bozeman

Trail be abandoned. To get Red Cloud to sign the treaty, the federal government agreed that within ninety days of the signing of the treaty, all the military forts in this region and along the Bozeman Trail would be abandoned. In many ways, Article XVI recognizes the Lakota as victors in Red Cloud's War. They went to war with the United States with the purpose of closing emigration through the Powder River country and getting rid of the hated military posts. In this, Red Cloud and the Lakota succeeded. Many historians point to this victory as the only war won by Native Americans in the long history of Indian-American conflict.

Article XVI also reiterates the boundaries of the unceded hunting grounds. The land north of the North Platte River and east of the summits of the Bighorn Mountains (including the Black Hills) would be reserved as Indian hunting grounds. Moreover, all white persons are forbidden to enter this territory without the permission of Indians.

◆ Article XVII

Finally, Article XVII nullifies all existing treaty stipulations in relation to the payment of moneys, food, clothing, and annuities. The Treaty of Fort Laramie of 1868 supersedes all other agreements.

Audience

The Treaty of Fort Laramie was not written with any specific audience in mind. Rather, it was intended as a legally binding agreement between the United States and the Sioux Indians. By default, however, the Treaty of Fort Laramie outlined the federal government's plan to dispossess the Plains Indians of their traditional hunting culture: creating a reservation, limiting hunting grounds, transferring communal land holdings into privately owned farms, educating Indian children, and usurping the power of chiefs by having a government agent perform their traditional duties. Thus, the Treaty of Fort Laramie informed both the American public and the Plains Indians (who probably were not listening) of what to expect in the future.

Impact

The Treaty of Fort Laramie was doomed to fail before it was ever signed. Historians have outlined a number of problems that precluded a successful treaty. First, the United States tended to use treaties to attain short-term or immediate goals. In the case of the Treaty of Fort Laramie, the federal government wanted to end Red Cloud's War and protect American interests such as the transcontinental railroad. In order to get the required signatures, treaty commissioners agreed to provisions they never really intended to uphold. The government probably never intended that the Lakota Sioux would always own the entire Great Sioux Reservation. Thus, it was always necessary to break treaties or amend old treaties. In short, the federal government never viewed a treaty signed with Indi-

ans in the same way as it would a treaty signed with a foreign nation. The treaty was an agreement between unequals that could be changed, altered, or abrogated at the federal government's expediency.

Another problem is that many Indian treaty signers were apparently unaware of the specifics of the treaty. Red Cloud, for example, later claimed that he had never heard of the provision that required the agency headquarters to be housed along the Missouri River. Certainly most Lakota did not understand the boundaries of the Great Sioux Reservation or the limitations placed on their use of the unceded hunting grounds.

Another problem that stood in the way was the decentralized and individualistic nature of Plains Indian societies. Indian chiefs could speak only for their immediate bands. While the government viewed Red Cloud as an important leader, perhaps the leader of the Lakota, he really did not wield much power outside his particular band of Oglala Lakota. Moreover, any member of his band who did not support his signing of the treaty could remove himself from the band and join another. Thus, a number of militant Lakota never signed the treaty and did not feel obligated to live by its stipulations. Leaders such as Crazy Horse, Black Twin, Hump, and Sitting Bull vehemently opposed signing any treaty and therefore did not abide by the Treaty of Fort Laramie. This would cause misunderstandings, as the government believed that all Lakota should be bound by the treaty.

The 1874 discovery of gold in the Black Hills serves as an example of the failure of Indian treaties. When rumors of gold were confirmed, migrants swarmed into Lakota territory. The Treaty of Fort Laramie placed the Black Hills in the Great Sioux Reservation, and the federal government, according to Article II of the treaty, was obligated to keep non-Indians out. Both the federal government and the Lakota theoretically violated the treaty. The military failed to remove intruders and eventually pulled out of the Black Hills, leaving thousands of white miners occupying the Lakota's most sacred place. On the other hand, Lakota (though they were non-treaty-signing leaders such as Crazy Horse) began attacking and killing miners, a violation of Article XI. Technically, therefore, both sides violated the treaty.

Supporters of President Grant's peace policy demanded that the president enforce the Treaty of Fort Laramie. The military, western politicians and boosters, and most of the American public, however, wanted to see the Black Hills opened to mining and settlement. In an effort to avoid warfare, President Grant appointed a commission to negotiate the sale of the Black Hills. Led by Senator William Allison of Iowa, the commission offered to lease the Black Hills for $100,000 per year or buy the hills for $6,000,000. Of course the Lakota refused to sell this religiously and culturally significant territory.

The end result was the Great Sioux War of 1876–1877, the annihilation of George Custer's Seventh Cavalry at the battle of the Little Bighorn, the end of nomadic bison hunting, and the loss of the Black Hills. In the wake of victory in the Great Sioux War, Congress, which now had a voice in Indian affairs after the treaty-making process was

"*From this day forward all war between the parties to this agreement shall for ever cease. The government of the United States desires peace, and its honor is hereby pledged to keep it.*"

(Article I, Paragraph 1)

[The Great Sioux Reservation is] ... "*set apart for the absolute and undisturbed use and occupation of the Indians herein named.*"

(Article II)

"*If any individual belonging to said tribes of Indians ... being the head of a family, shall desire to commence farming, he shall have the privilege to select ... a tract of land ... not exceeding three hundred and twenty acres in extent.*"

(Article VI, Paragraph 1)

"*In order to insure the civilization of the Indians entering into this treaty, the necessity of education is admitted ... and they, therefore, pledge themselves to compel their children ... to attend school.*"

(Article VII, Paragraph 1)

"*The tribes who are parties to this agreement hereby stipulate that they will relinquish all right to occupy permanently the territory outside their reservations.*"

(Article XI, Paragraph 1)

"*[The Indians] reserve the right to hunt on any lands north of North Platte, and on the Republican Fork of the Smoky Hill river, so long as the buffalo may range thereon in such numbers as to justify the chase.*"

(Article XI, Paragraph 1)

"*They [Indians] will never kill or scalp white men, nor attempt to do them harm.*"

(Article XI, part 5)

nullified in 1871, moved to shave off the Black Hills from the Great Sioux Reservation. On August 15, 1876, Congress ordered that all annuities, including food, be withheld until the Lakota agreed to relinquish all of the unceded hunting grounds and the territory west of the 103rd meridian, a region that included the sacred Black Hills.

In order for this land to be relinquished, Article XII of the Treaty of Fort Laramie required the signatures of three-fourths of all Indian men. A commission led by the former commissioner of Indian affairs George Manypenny went to the Lakota and spelled out the demands: Surrender the Black Hills or starve to death. In the aftermath of their defeat in the Great Sioux War, with the bison herds all but extinct and Indians living on government rations, many Lakota chiefs and headmen, including Red Cloud, signed the agreement. Clearly violating Article XII, the commission returned to Washington, D.C., with a handful of signatures. The Black Hills, once protected by the Treaty of Fort Laramie, were removed from the Great Sioux Reservation.

In 1980, after a long legal battle, the U.S. Supreme Court judged that the government had violated Article XII of the Treaty of Fort Laramie and awarded the Lakota Sioux $105 million for the illegal taking of the Black Hills. The Lakota have refused to accept the monetary award because it would require surrendering all claims to their sacred Black Hills.

Related Documents

"Dawes Act." National Archives "Our Documents" Web site. http://www.ourdocuments.gov/doc.php?flash=true&doc=50&page=transcript. Accessed on January 22, 2008. Officially known as the General Allotment Act, the Dawes Severalty Act of 1887 authorized the president to select reservations for allotment. Reservation lands were surveyed, the land was allotted, and the remaining land was sold as public land. The goal of the Dawes Act was to detribalize Indians by transforming communally held land into private property holdings.

"Lakota Treaty of Fort Laramie 1851." Creighton University Web site. http://puffin.creighton.edu/lakota/1851_la.html. Accessed on January 22, 2008. The first Treaty of Fort Laramie, signed in 1851, attempted to bring peace to the Great Plains by guaranteeing the safe passage of overland travelers and by assigning each tribe specific territorial boundaries.

United States v. Sioux Nation of Indians 448 U.S. 371 (1980). On June 30, 1980, the U.S. Supreme Court ruled that the seizing of the Black Hills in 1877 had violated the Treaty of Fort Laramie. The Sioux were awarded $17.5 million (the market value of the Black Hills in 1877) and 5 percent interest for 103 years, adding an additional $105 million to the award. The Sioux have refused to accept the monetary award.

Bibliography

■ Articles

DeMallie, Raymond J. "Touching the Pen: Plains Indian Treaty Councils in Ethnohistorical Perspective." In *Ethnicity on the Great Plains,* ed. Frederick C. Luebke. Lincoln: University of Nebraska Press, 1980.

White, Richard. "The Winning of the West: The Expansion of the Western Sioux in the Eighteenth and Nineteenth Centuries." *Journal of American History* 65 (September 1978): 319–343.

■ Books

Hoig, Stan. *White Man's Paper Trail: Grand Councils and Treaty-Making on the Central Plains.* Boulder: University of Colorado Press, 2006.

Kappler, Charles J., ed. *Indian Treaties.* New York: Interland, 1972.

Olson, James C. *Red Cloud and the Sioux Problem.* Lincoln: University of Nebraska Press, 1965.

Ostler, Jeffrey. *The Plains Sioux and U.S. Colonialism from Lewis and Clark to Wounded Knee.* New York: Cambridge University Press, 2004.

Prucha, Francis Paul. *The Great Father: The United States Government and the American Indian.* 2 vols. Lincoln: University of Nebraska Press, 1995.

Weeks, Philip. *Farewell, My Nation: The American Indian and the United States, 1820–1890.* Arlington Heights, Ill.: Harlan Davidson, 1990.

Wunder, John R. *"Retained by the People": A History of American Indians and the Bill of Rights.* New York: Oxford University Press, 1994.

■ Web Sites

Kappler, Charles J., ed. "Indian Affairs: Laws and Treaties." Oklahoma State University Library Web site.
http://digital.library.okstate.edu/KAPPLER/index.htm. Accessed on December 16, 2007.

"New Perspectives on the West." Public Broadcasting System Web Site.
http://www.pbs.org/weta/thewest/. Accessed on December 16, 2007.

—By Mark R. Ellis

Questions for Further Study

1. By 1868 federal Indian policy was moving toward the assimilation of Native Americans. How did the federal government use the Treaty of Fort Laramie to dispossess the Plains Indians of their traditional way of life? In what ways were Indians to be transformed into American citizens?

2. Today some of the poorest counties in the nation are on the Sioux reservations in South Dakota. In what ways did the Treaty of Fort Laramie help contribute to the poverty that is so prevalent on Indian reservations today?

3. The opening line of the Treaty of Fort Laramie states that "war ... shall for ever cease." Just eight years later, however, warfare again erupted. Why was war between the Lakota and the United States inevitable? How did each side view the treaty and its stipulations?

Glossary

abrogating	repealing or canceling
alienation	the transference of property such as land to another
annulling	voiding, nullifying, or canceling
cession	the act of surrendering or transferring
Greenwich	Greenwich, England, located on the prime meridian
Land Book	a book held by the government agent that listed the legal boundaries of all allotments taken out by Indian farmers
lodge	a household or family unit among the Plains Indians
meridian	an imaginary line passing through the poles at right angles to the equator

Treaty of Fort Laramie

Articles of a Treaty Made and Concluded by and between

Lieutenant General William T. Sherman, General William S. Harney, General Alfred H. Terry, General O. O. Augur, J. B. Henderson, Nathaniel G. Taylor, John G. Sanborn, and Samuel F. Tappan, duly appointed commissioners on the part of the United States, and the different bands of the Sioux Nation of Indians, by their chiefs and headmen, whose names are hereto subscribed, they being duly authorized to act in the premises.

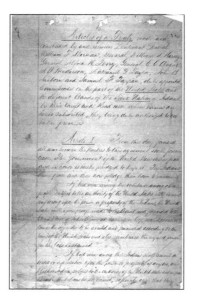

◆ Article I.

From this day forward all war between the parties to this agreement shall for ever cease. The government of the United States desires peace, and its honor is hereby pledged to keep it. The Indians desire peace, and they now pledge their honor to maintain it.

If bad men among the whites, or among other people subject to the authority of the United States, shall commit any wrong upon the person or property of the Indians, the United States will, upon proof made to the agent, and forwarded to the Commissioner of Indian Affairs at Washington city, proceed at once to cause the offender to be arrested and punished according to the laws of the United States, and also reimburse the injured person for the loss sustained.

If bad men among the Indians shall commit a wrong or depredation upon the person or property of nay one, white, black, or Indian, subject to the authority of the United States, and at peace therewith, the Indians herein named solemnly agree that they will, upon proof made to their agent, and notice by him, deliver up the wrongdoer to the United States, to be tried and punished according to its laws, and, in case they willfully refuse so to do, the person injured shall be reimbursed for his loss from the annuities, or other moneys due or to become due to them under this or other treaties made with the United States; and the President, on advising with the Commissioner of Indian Affairs, shall prescribe such rules and regulations for ascertaining damages under the provisions of this article as in his judgment may be proper, but no one sustaining loss while violating the provisions of this treaty, or the laws of the United States, shall be reimbursed therefor.

◆ Article II.

The United States agrees that the following district of country, to wit, viz: commencing on the east bank of the Missouri river where the 46th parallel of north latitude crosses the same, thence along low-water mark down said east bank to a point opposite where the northern line of the State of Nebraska strikes the river, thence west across said river, and along the northern line of Nebraska to the 104th degree of longitude west from Greenwich, thence north on said meridian to a point where the 46th parallel of north latitude intercepts the same, thence due east along said parallel to the place of beginning; and in addition thereto, all existing reservations of the east back of said river, shall be and the same is, set apart for the absolute and undisturbed use and occupation of the Indians herein named, and for such other friendly tribes or individual Indians as from time to time they may be willing, with the consent of the United States, to admit amongst them; and the United States now solemnly agrees that no persons, except those herein designated and authorized so to do, and except such officers, agents, and employees of the government as may be authorized to enter upon Indian reservations in discharge of duties enjoined by law, shall ever be permitted to pass over, settle upon, or reside in the territory described in this article, or in such territory as may be added to this reservation for the use of said Indians, and henceforth they will and do hereby relinquish all claims or right in and to any portion of the United States or Territories, except such as is embraced within the limits aforesaid, and except as hereinafter provided.

◆ Article III.

If it should appear from actual survey or other satisfactory examination of said tract of land that it contains less than 160 acres of tillable land for each person who, at the time, may be authorized to reside on it under the provisions of this treaty, and a very considerable number of such persons shall be disposed to commence cultivating the soil as farmers, the United States agrees to set apart, for the use of said Indians, as herein provided, such additional quantity of arable land, adjoining to said reservation, or as near to the same as it can be obtained, as may be required to provide the necessary amount.

◆ Article IV.

The United States agrees, at its own proper expense, to construct, at some place on the Missouri river, near the centre of said reservation where timber and water may be convenient, the following buildings, to wit, a warehouse, a store-room for the use of the agent in storing goods belonging to the Indians, to cost not less than $2,500; an agency building, for the residence of the agent, to cost not exceeding $3,000; a residence for the physician, to cost not more than $3,000; and five other buildings, for a carpenter, farmer, blacksmith, miller, and engineer-each to cost not exceeding $2,000; also, a school-house, or mission building, so soon as a sufficient number of children can be induced by the agent to attend school, which shall not cost exceeding $5,000.

The United States agrees further to cause to be erected on said reservation, near the other buildings herein authorized, a good steam circular saw-mill, with a grist-mill and shingle machine attached to the same, to cost not exceeding $8,000.

◆ Article V.

The United States agrees that the agent for said Indians shall in the future make his home at the agency building; that he shall reside among them, and keep an office open at all times for the purpose of prompt and diligent inquiry into such matters of complaint by and against the Indians as may be presented for investigation under the provisions of their treaty stipulations, as also for the faithful discharge of other duties enjoined on him by law. In all cases of depredation on person or property he shall cause the evidence to be taken in writing and forwarded, together with his findings, to the Commissioner of Indian Affairs, whose decision, subject to the revision of the Secretary of the Interior, shall be binding on the parties to this treaty.

◆ Article VI.

If any individual belonging to said tribes of Indians, or legally incorporated with them, being the head of a family, shall desire to commence farming, he shall have the privilege to select, in the presence and with the assistance of the agent then in charge, a tract of land within said reservation, not exceeding three hundred and twenty acres in extent, which tract, when so selected, certified, and recorded in the "Land Book" as herein directed, shall cease to be held in common, but the same may be occupied and held in the exclusive possession of the person selecting it, and of his family, so long as he or they may continue to cultivate it.

Any person over eighteen years of age, not being the head of a family, may in like manner select and cause to be certified to him or her, for purposes of cultivation, a quantity of land, not exceeding eighty acres in extent, and thereupon be entitled to the exclusive possession of the same as above directed.

For each tract of land so selected a certificate, containing a description thereof and the name of the person selecting it, with a certificate endorsed thereon that the same has been recorded, shall be delivered to the party entitled to it, by the agent, after the same shall have been recorded by him in a book to be kept in his office, subject to inspection, which said book shall be known as the "Sioux Land Book."

The President may, at any time, order a survey of the reservation, and, when so surveyed, Congress shall provide for protecting the rights of said settlers in their improvements, and may fix the character of the title held by each. The United States may pass such laws on the subject of alienation and descent of property between the Indians and their descendants as may be thought proper. And it is further stipulated that any male Indians over eighteen years of age, of any band or tribe that is or shall hereafter become a party to this treaty, who now is or who shall hereafter become a resident or occupant of any reservation or territory not included in the tract of country designated and described in this treaty for the permanent home of the Indians, which is not mineral land, nor reserved by the United States for special purposes other than Indian occupation, and who shall have made improvements thereon of the value of two hundred dollars or more, and continuously occupied the same as a homestead for the term of three years, shall be entitled to receive from the United States a patent for one hundred and sixty acres of land including his said improvements, the same to be in the form of the legal subdivisions of the surveys of the public lands. Upon application in writing, sustained by the proof of two disinterested witnesses, made to the register of the local land office when the land sought to be entered is within a land district, and when the tract sought to be entered is not in any land district, then upon said application and proof being made to the Commissioner of the General Land Office, and the right of such Indian or Indians to enter such tract or tracts of land shall accrue and be perfect from the date of his first improvements thereon, and shall continue as long as be continues his residence and improvements and no longer. And any Indian or Indians receiving a patent for land under the foregoing provisions shall thereby and from thenceforth become and be a citizen of the United States and be entitled to all the privileges and immunities of such citizens, and shall, at the same time, retain all his rights to benefits accruing to Indians under this treaty.

◆ Article VII.

In order to insure the civilization of the Indians entering into this treaty, the necessity of education is admitted, especially of such of them as are or may be settled on said agricultural reservations, and they, therefore, pledge themselves to compel their children, male and female, between the ages of six and sixteen years, to attend school, and it is hereby made the duty of the agent for said Indians to see that this stipulation is strictly complied with; and the United States agrees that for every thirty children between said ages, who can be induced or compelled to attend school, a house shall be provided, and a teacher competent to teach the elementary branches of an English education shall be furnished, who will reside among said Indians and faithfully discharge his or her duties as a teacher. The provisions of this article to continue for not less than twenty years.

◆ Article VIII.

When the head of a family or lodge shall have selected lands and received his certificate as above directed, and the agent shall be satisfied that he intends in good faith to commence cultivating the soil for a living, he shall be entitled to receive seeds and agricultural implements for the first year, not exceeding in value one hundred dollars, and for each succeeding year he shall continue to farm, for a peri-

od of three years more, he shall be entitled to receive seeds and implements as aforesaid, not exceeding in value twenty-five dollars. And it is further stipulated that such persons as commence farming shall receive instruction from the farmer herein provided for, and whenever more than one hundred persons shall enter upon the cultivation of the soil, a second blacksmith shall be provided, with such iron, steel, and other material as may be needed.

◆ Article IX.

At any time after ten years from the making of this treaty, the United States shall have the privilege of withdrawing the physician, farmer, blacksmith, carpenter, engineer, and miller herein provided for, but in case of such withdrawal, an additional sum thereafter of ten thousand dollars per annum shall be devoted to the education of said Indians, and the Commissioner of Indian Affairs shall, upon careful inquiry into their condition, make such rules and regulations for the expenditure of said sums as will best promote the education and moral improvement of said tribes.

◆ Article X.

In lieu of all sums of money or other annuities provided to be paid to the Indians herein named under any treaty or treaties heretofore made, the United States agrees to deliver at the agency house on the reservation herein named, on or before the first day of August of each year, for thirty years, the following articles, to wit:

For each male person over 14 years of age, a suit of good substantial woollen clothing, consisting of coat, pantaloons, flannel shirt, hat, and a pair of home-made socks.

For each female over 12 years of age, a flannel shirt, or the goods necessary to make it, a pair of woollen hose, 12 yards of calico, and 12 yards of cotton domestics.

For the boys and girls under the ages named, such flannel and cotton goods as may be needed to make each a suit as aforesaid, together with a pair of woollen hose for each.

And in order that the Commissioner of Indian Affairs may be able to estimate properly for the articles herein named, it shall be the duty of the agent each year to forward to him a full and exact census of the Indians, on which the estimate from year to year can be based.

And in addition to the clothing herein named, the sum of $10 for each person entitled to the beneficial effects of this treaty shall be annually appropriated for a period of 30 years, while such persons roam and hunt, and $20 for each person who engages in farming, to be used by the Secretary of the Interior in the purchase of such articles as from time to time the condition and necessities of the Indians may indicate to be proper. And if within the 30 years, at any time, it shall appear that the amount of money needed for clothing, under this article, can be appropriated to better uses for the Indians named herein, Congress may, by law, change the appropriation to other purposes, but in no event shall the amount of the appropriation be withdrawn or discontinued for the period named. And the President shall annually detail an officer of the army to be present and attest the delivery of all the goods herein named, to the Indians, and he shall inspect and report on the quantity and quality of the goods and the manner of their delivery. And it is hereby expressly stipulated that each Indian over the age of four years, who shall have removed to and settled permanently upon said reservation, one pound of meat and one pound of flour per day, provided the Indians cannot furnish their own subsistence at an earlier date. And it is further stipulated that the United States will furnish and deliver to each lodge of Indians or family of persons legally incorporated with the, who shall remove to the reservation herein described and commence farming, one good American cow, and one good well-broken pair of American oxen within 60 days after such lodge or family shall have so settled upon said reservation.

◆ Article XI.

In consideration of the advantages and benefits conferred by this treaty and the many pledges of friendship by the United States, the tribes who are parties to this agreement hereby stipulate that they will relinquish all right to occupy permanently the territory outside their reservations as herein defined, but yet reserve the right to hunt on any lands north of North Platte, and on the Republican Fork of the Smoky Hill river, so long as the buffalo may range thereon in such numbers as to justify the chase. And they, the said Indians, further expressly agree:

1st. That they will withdraw all opposition to the construction of the railroads now being built on the plains.

2d. That they will permit the peaceful construction of any railroad not passing over their reservation as herein defined.

3d. That they will not attack any persons at home, or travelling, nor molest or disturb any wagon trains,

coaches, mules, or cattle belonging to the people of the United States, or to persons friendly therewith.

4th. They will never capture, or carry off from the settlements, white women or children.

5th. They will never kill or scalp white men, nor attempt to do them harm.

6th. They withdraw all pretence of opposition to the construction of the railroad now being built along the Platte river and westward to the Pacific ocean, and they will not in future object to the construction of railroads, wagon roads, mail stations, or other works of utility or necessity, which may be ordered or permitted by the laws of the United States. But should such roads or other works be constructed on the lands of their reservation, the government will pay the tribe whatever amount of damage may be assessed by three disinterested commissioners to be appointed by the President for that purpose, one of the said commissioners to be a chief or headman of the tribe.

7th. They agree to withdraw all opposition to the military posts or roads now established south of the North Platte river, or that may be established, not in violation of treaties heretofore made or hereafter to be made with any of the Indian tribes.

◆ Article XII.

No treaty for the cession of any portion or part of the reservation herein described which may be held in common, shall be of any validity or force as against the said Indians unless executed and signed by at least three-fourths of all the adult male Indians occupying or interested in the same, and no cession by the tribe shall be understood or construed in such manner as to deprive, without his consent, any individual member of the tribe of his rights to any tract of land selected by him as provided in Article VI of this treaty.

◆ Article XIII.

The United States hereby agrees to furnish annually to the Indians the physician, teachers, carpenter, miller, engineer, farmer, and blacksmiths, as herein contemplated, and that such appropriations shall be made from time to time, on the estimate of the Secretary of the Interior, as will be sufficient to employ such persons.

◆ Article XIV.

It is agreed that the sum of five hundred dollars annually for three years from date shall be expended in presents to the ten persons of said tribe who in the judgment of the agent may grow the most valuable crops for the respective year.

◆ Article XV.

The Indians herein named agree that when the agency house and other buildings shall be constructed on the reservation named, they will regard said reservation their permanent home, and they will make no permanent settlement elsewhere; but they shall have the right, subject to the conditions and modifications of this treaty, to hunt, as stipulated in Article XI hereof.

◆ Article XVI.

The United States hereby agrees and stipulates that the country north of the North Platte river and east of the summits of the Big Horn mountains shall be held and considered to be unceded. Indian territory, and also stipulates and agrees that no white person or persons shall be permitted to settle upon or occupy any portion of the same; or without the consent of the Indians, first had and obtained, to pass through the same; and it is further agreed by the United States, that within ninety days after the conclusion of peace with all the bands of the Sioux nation, the military posts now established in the territory in this article named shall be abandoned, and that the road leading to them and by them to the settlements in the Territory of Montana shall be closed.

◆ Article XVII.

It is hereby expressly understood and agreed by and between the respective parties to this treaty that the execution of this treaty and its ratification by the United States Senate shall have the effect, and shall be construed as abrogating and annulling all treaties and agreements heretofore entered into between the respective parties hereto, so far as such treaties and agreements obligate the United States to furnish and provide money, clothing, or other articles of property to such Indians and bands of Indians as become parties to this treaty, but no further.

In testimony of all which, we, the said commissioners, and we, the chiefs and headmen of the Brule band of the Sioux nation, have hereunto set our hands and seals at Fort Laramie, Dakota Territory, this twenty-ninth day of April, in the year one thousand eight hundred and sixty-eight.

N. G. TAYLOR,
W. T. SHERMAN,
Lieutenant General
WM. S. HARNEY,

Brevet Major General U.S.A.
JOHN B. SANBORN,
S. F. TAPPAN,
C. C. AUGUR,
Brevet Major General
ALFRED H. TERRY,
Brevet Major General U.S.A.

Attest:
A. S. H. WHITE, Secretary.

Executed on the part of the Brule band of Sioux by the chiefs and headman whose names are hereto annexed, they being thereunto duly authorized, at Fort Laramie, D. T., the twenty-ninth day of April, in the year A.D. 1868.

MA-ZA-PON-KASKA, his X mark, Iron Shell.
WAH-PAT-SHAH, his X mark, Red Leaf.
HAH-SAH-PAH, his X mark, Black Horn.
ZIN-TAH-GAH-LAT-WAH, his X mark, Spotted Tail.
ZIN-TAH-GKAH, his X mark, White Tail.
ME-WAH-TAH-NE-HO-SKAH, his X mark, Tall Man.
SHE-CHA-CHAT-KAH, his X mark, Bad Left Hand.
NO-MAH-NO-PAH, his X mark, Two and Two.
TAH-TONKA-SKAH, his X mark, White Bull.
CON-RA-WASHTA, his X mark, Pretty Coon.
HA-CAH-CAH-SHE-CHAH, his X mark, Bad Elk.
WA-HA-KA-ZAH-ISH-TAH, his X mark, Eye Lance.
MA-TO-HA-KE-TAH, his X mark, Bear that looks behind.
BELLA-TONKA-TONKA, his X mark, Big Partisan.
MAH-TO-HO-HONKA, his X mark, Swift Bear.
TO-WIS-NE, his X mark, Cold Place.
ISH-TAH-SKAII, his X mark, White Eye.
MA-TA-LOO-ZAH, his X mark, Fast Bear.
AS-HAH-HAII-NAH-SHE, his X mark, Standing Elk.
CAN-TE-TE-KI-YA, his X mark, The Brave Heart.
SHUNKA-SHATON, his X mark, Day Hawk.
TATANKA-WAKON, his X mark, Sacred Bull.
MAPIA SHATON, his X mark, Hawk Cloud.
MA-SHA-A-OW, his X mark, Stands and Comes.
SHON-KA-TON-KA, his X mark, Big Dog.

Attest:
ASHTON S. H. WHITE, Secretary of Commission.
GEORGE B. WITHS, Phonographer to Commission.
GEO. H. HOLTZMAN.
JOHN D. HOWLAND.
JAMES C. O'CONNOR.
CHAR. E. GUERN, Interpreter.
LEON T. PALLARDY, Interpreter.
NICHOLAS JANIS, Interpreter.

Executed on the part of the Ogallalla band of Sioux by the chiefs and headmen whose names are hereto subscribed, they being thereunto duly authorized, at Fort Laramie, the 25th day of May, in the year A. D. 1868.

TAH-SHUN-KA-CO-QUI-PAH, his mark, Man-afraid-of-his-horses.

SHA-TON-SKAH, his X mark, White Hawk.

SHA-TON-SAPAH, his X mark, Black Hawk.

EGA-MON-TON-KA-SAPAH, his X mark, Black Tiger.

OH-WAH-SHE-CHA, his X mark, Bad Wound.

PAH-GEE, his X mark, Grass.

WAH-NON SAH-CHE-GEH, his X mark, Ghost Heart.

COMECH, his X mark, Crow.

OH-HE-TE-KAH, his X mark, The Brave.

TAH-TON-KAH-HE-YO-TA-KAH, his X mark, Sitting Bull.

SHON-KA-OH-WAH-MEN-YE, his X mark, Whirlwind Dog.

HA-KAH-KAH-TAH-MIECH, his X mark, Poor Elk.

WAM-BU-LEE-WAH-KON, his X mark, Medicine Eagle.

CHON-GAH-MA-HE-TO-HANS-KA, his X mark, High Wolf.

WAH-SECHUN-TA-SHUN-KAH, his X mark, American Horse.

MAH-KAH-MAH-HA-MAK-NEAR, his X mark, Man that walks under the ground.

MAH-TO-TOW-PAH, his X mark, Four Bears.

MA-TO-WEE-SHA-KTA, his X mark, One that kills the bear.

OH-TAH-KEE-TOKA-WEE-CHAKTA, his X mark, One that kills in a hard place.

TAH-TON-KAH-TA-MIECH, his X mark, The Poor Bull.

OH-HUNS-EE-GA-NON-SKEN, his X mark, Mad Shade.

SHAH-TON-OH-NAH-OM-MINNE-NE-OH-MINNE, his X mark, Whirling hawk.

MAH-TO-CHUN-KA-OH, his X mark, Bear's Back.

CHE-TON-WEE-KOH, his X mark, Fool Hawk.

WAH-HOH-KE-ZA-AH-HAH, his X mark.

EH-TON-KAH, his X mark, Big Mouth.

MA-PAH-CHE-TAH, his X mark, Bad Hand.

WAH-KE-YUN-SHAH, his X mark, Red Thunder.

WAK-SAH, his X mark, One that Cuts Off.

CHAH-NOM-QUI-YAH, his X mark, One that Presents the Pipe.

WAH-KE-KE-YAN-PUH-TAH, his X mark, Fire Thunder.

MAH-TO-NONK-PAH-ZE, his X mark, Bear with Yellow Ears.

CON-REE-TEH-KA, his X mark, The Little Crow.

HE-HUP-PAH-TOH, his X mark, The Blue War Club.

SHON-KEE-TOH, his X mark, The Blue Horse.

WAM-BALLA-OH-CONQUO, his X mark, Quick Eagle.

TA-TONKA-SUPPA, his X mark, Black Bull.

MOH-TOH-HA-SHE-NA, his X mark, The Bear Hide.

Attest:

S. E. WARD.

JAS. C. O'CONNOR.

J. M. SHERWOOD.

W. C. SLICER.

SAM DEON,

H. M. MATHEWS.

JOSEPH BISS.

NICHOLAS JANIS, Interpreter.

LEFROY JOTT, Interpreter.

ANTOINE JANIS, Interpreter.

Executed on the part of the Minneconjou band of Sioux by the chiefs and headmen whose names are hereunto subscribed, they being thereunto duly authorized.

HEH-WON-GE-CHAT, his X mark, One Horn.

OH-PON-AH-TAH-E-MANNE, his X mark, The Elk that Bellows Walking.

HEH-HO-LAH-ZEH-CHA-SKAH, his X mark, Young White Bull.

WAH-CHAH-CHUM-KAH-COH-KEEPAH, his X mark, One that is Afraid of Shield.

HE-HON-NE-SHAKTA, his X mark, The Old Owl.

MOC-PE-A-TOH, his X mark, Blue Cloud.

OH-PONG-GE-LE-SKAH, his X mark, Spotted Elk.

TAH-TONK-KA-HON-KE-SCHUE, his X mark, Slow bull.

SHONK-A-NEE-SHAH-SHAH-ATAH-PE, his X mark, The Dog Chief.

MA-TO-TAH-TA-TONK-KA, his X mark, Bull Bear.

WOM-BEH-LE-TON-KAH, his X mark, The Big Eagle.

MATOH, EH-SCHNE-LAH, his X mark, The Lone Bear.

MA-TOH-OH-HE-TO-KEH, his X mark, The Brave Bear.

EH-CHE-MA-KEH, his X mark, The Runner.

TI-KI-YA, his X mark, The Hard.

HE-MA-ZA, his X mark, Iron Horn.

Attest:

JAS. C O'CONNOR,

WM. D. BROWN,
NICHOLAS JANIS,
ANTOINE JANIS,
  Interpreters.

Executed on the part of the Yanctonais band of Sioux by the chiefs and headmen whose names are hereto subscribed, they being thereunto duly authorized:

MAH-TO-NON-PAH, his X mark, Two Bears.
MA-TO-HNA-SKIN-YA, his X mark, Mad Bear.
HE-O-PU-ZA, his X mark, Louzy.
AH-KE-CHE-TAH-CHE-KA-DAN, his X mark,
  Little Soldier.
MAH-TO-E-TAN-CHAN, his X mark, Chief Bear.
CU-WI-TO-WIA, his X mark, Rotten Stomach.
SKUN-KA-WE-TKO, his X mark, Fool Dog.
ISH-TA-SAP-PAH, his X mark, Black Eye.
IH-TAN-CHAN, his X mark, The Chief.
I-A-WI-CA-KA, his X mark, The One who Tells the
  Truth.
AH-KE-CHE-TAH, his X mark, The Soldier.
TA-SHI-NA-GI, his X mark, Yellow Robe.
NAH-PE-TON-KA, his X mark, Big Hand.
CHAN-TEE-WE-KTO, his X mark, Fool Heart.
HOH-GAN-SAH-PA, his X mark, Black Catfish.
MAH-TO-WAH-KAN, his X mark, Medicine Bear.
SHUN-KA-KAN-SHA, his X mark, Red Horse.
WAN-RODE, his X mark, The Eagle.
CAN-HPI-SA-PA, his X mark, Black Tomahawk.
WAR-HE-LE-RE, his X mark, Yellow Eagle.
CHA-TON-CHE-CA, his X mark, Small Hawk, or
  Long Fare.
SHU-GER-MON-E-TOO-HA-SKA, his X mark, Fall
  Wolf.
MA-TO-U-TAH-KAH, his X mark, Sitting Bear.
HI-HA-CAH-GE-NA-SKENE, his X mark, Mad Elk.

Arapahoes.
LITTLE CHIEF, his X mark.
TALL BEAR, his X mark.
TOP MAN, his X mark.
NEVA, his X mark.
THE WOUNDED BEAR, his X mark.
WHIRLWIND, his X mark.
THE FOX, his X mark.
THE DOG BIG MOUTH, his X mark.
SPOTTED WOLF, his X mark.
SORREL HORSE, his X mark.
BLACK COAL, his X mark.
BIG WOLF, his X mark.
KNOCK-KNEE, his X mark.

BLACK CROW, his X mark.
THE LONE OLD MAN, his X mark.
PAUL, his X mark.
BLACK BULL, his X mark.
BIG TRACK, his X mark.
THE FOOT, his X mark.
BLACK WHITE, his X mark.
YELLOW HAIR, his X mark.
LITTLE SHIELD, his X mark.
BLACK BEAR, his X mark.
WOLF MOCASSIN, his X mark.
BIG ROBE, his X mark.
WOLF CHIEF, his X mark.

  Witnesses:
  ROBERT P. MCKIBBIN,
Captain 4th Infantry, and Bvt. Lieut. Col. U. S. A.,
Commanding Fort Laramie.
WM. H. POWELL,
Brevet Major, Captain 4th Infantry.
HENRY W. PATTERSON,
Captain 4th Infantry.
THEO E. TRUE,
Second Lieutenant 4th Infantry.
W. G. BULLOCK.
FORT LARAMIE, WYOMING TERRITORY
 November 6, 1868.
MAH-PI-AH-LU-TAH, his X mark, Red Cloud.
WA-KI-AH-WE-CHA-SHAH, his X mark, Thunder
  Man.
MA-ZAH-ZAH-GEH, his X mark, Iron Cane.
WA-UMBLE-WHY-WA-KA-TUYAH, his X mark,
  High Eagle.
KO-KE-PAH, his X mark, Man Afraid.
WA-KI-AH-WA-KOU-AH, his X mark, Thunder
  Flying Running.

Witnessess:
W. MCE. DYE,
Brevet Colonel U. S. Army,
Commanding.
A. B. CAIN,
Captain 4th Infantry, Brevet Major U. S. Army.
ROBT. P. MCKIBBIN,
Captain 4th Infantry, Bvt. Lieut. Col. U. S. Army.
JNO. MILLER,
Captain 4th Infantry.
G. L. LUHN,
First Lieutenant 4th Infantry, Bvt. Capt. U. S.
  Army.
H. C. SLOAN,
Second Lieutenant 4th Infantry.

Read 16 June.

Thirty-ninth Congress of the United States, at the first Session, begun and held at the City of Washington, in the District of Columbia, on Monday the fourth day of December, one thousand eight hundred and sixty-five.

Joint Resolution proposing an amendment to the Constitution of the United States.

Be it resolved by the Senate and House of Representatives of the United States of America in Congress assembled, (two-thirds of both Houses concurring,) That the following article be proposed to the legislatures of the several States as an amendment to the Constitution of the United States, which, when ratified by three-fourths of said legislatures, shall be valid as part of the Constitution, namely:

Article XIV.

Section 1. All persons born or naturalized in the United States, and subject to the jurisdiction thereof, are citizens of the United States and of the State wherein they reside. No State shall make or enforce any law which shall abridge the privileges or immunities of citizens of the United States; nor shall any State deprive any person of life, liberty, or property, without due process of law; nor deny to any person within its jurisdiction the equal protection of the laws.

Section 2. Representatives shall be apportioned among the several States according to their respective numbers, counting the whole number of persons in each State, excluding Indians not taxed. But when the right to vote at any election for the choice of electors for President and Vice President of the United States, Representatives in Congress, the Executive and Judicial officers of a State, or the members of the Legislature thereof, is denied to any of the male inhabitants of such State, being twenty-one years of age, and citizens of the United States, or in any way abridged, except for participation in rebellion, or other crime, the basis of representation therein shall be reduced in the proportion which the

The Fourteenth Amendment (National Archives and Records Administration)

FOURTEENTH AMENDMENT TO THE U.S. CONSTITUTION

"No State shall make or enforce any law which shall abridge the privileges or immunities of citizens of the United States."

Overview

Even before the Civil War ended, President Abraham Lincoln wrestled with Congress over how to reconstruct the Union. After Lincoln's assassination, President Andrew Johnson initiated a minimalist program that offended many northerners. The Thirty-ninth Congress, after failing to reach a compromise with Johnson, proposed a constitutional amendment to solve the most pressing issues.

The Fourteenth Amendment extended citizenship and rights to the freed slaves and excluded many prominent former Confederates from government. It revised the formula for congressional reapportionment and settled the status of wartime debts. The Fourteenth Amendment, approved by Congress in June 1866, was pronounced ratified by the states on July 28, 1868. Although today three of its five sections are nonfunctional, the first section of the amendment has been used, especially since the mid-1900s, to expand significantly the rights of African Americans and other groups in society. Accompanying these developments, the powers of the Supreme Court and federal government have increased at the expense of the states. Debate rages to the present day about the ultimate boundaries of the Fourteenth Amendment.

Context

In 1861 the Lincoln administration and Congress declared that the goal of the Civil War was to restore the Union and that slavery was not to be disturbed. By mid-1862 President Lincoln had changed his mind, to the delight of abolitionists and the grudging acceptance of many frustrated northerners. His Emancipation Proclamation and the subsequent Thirteenth Amendment ended the institution. Nevertheless, with the capitulation of the Confederacy in the spring of 1865, the government faced numerous unprecedented questions that the Constitution was unable to answer. Foremost among the uncertainties were, first, the requirements and procedures for readmitting the Confederate states into the Union and, second, the

status of the freed slaves. The absence of the politically astute Abraham Lincoln complicated the resolution of these problems.

President Andrew Johnson certainly did not shy away from the task, but his stubbornness allowed for little consultation with Republican congressional leaders. The former Democrat from Tennessee demanded that southern states renounce their Confederate debts and ratify the Thirteenth Amendment. He had little interest in any other steps to assist the freed slaves and was content to leave their progress to state action. Johnson also used presidential pardons to restore some prominent Confederates to political life. He then permitted the obedient ex-Confederate states to elect state officials as well as representatives and senators to Congress.

The Republican-dominated Thirty-ninth Congress, which first met December 4, 1865, would have none of this. Individual southern states aggravated the situation by enacting so-called Black Codes, which significantly circumscribed the economic and social freedoms of former slaves. At this time political rights were not contemplated by many in the North or South. To counter the Black Codes, Congress passed the Freedmen's Bureau Bill and the Civil Rights Act in February 1866 to give the freed slaves educational and economic opportunities and to guarantee basic civil rights. Johnson vetoed both. Although Congress overrode both vetoes, Republican congressmen concluded that they needed to take a greater initiative to restore the Union and protect African Americans. A constitutional amendment (or series of amendments) seemed the most effective device to remedy the situation and to prevent future legislation from undermining their gains.

About the Author

The Fourteenth Amendment has many authors. It was legislation of the first session of the Thirty-ninth Congress following the recommendation of the Joint Committee on Reconstruction. In general, the Republican majority in Congress was responsible for its major features and success. The criticisms of the Democratic minority did little to reshape the amendment.

Time Line

1861

■ **April 12**
Fort Sumter is bombarded, beginning the Civil War.

1862

■ **September 17**
The battle of Antietam (Maryland) is a draw, but Robert E. Lee's Army of Northern Virginia is forced to retreat.

■ **September 22**
With the preliminary Emancipation Proclamation, Lincoln warns seceded states of the impending emancipation of slaves.

1863

■ **January 1**
Using his war powers to issue the Emancipation Proclamation, Lincoln frees the slaves in ten states.

1865

■ **April 9**
Lee surrenders at Appomattox, Virginia.

■ **April 14**
Lincoln is shot at Ford's Theatre in Washington, D.C., and dies the next morning.

■ **December 18**
The Thirteenth Amendment is ratified, ending slavery in the United States.

1866

■ **March 27**
President Johnson vetoes the Civil Rights Act.

■ **April 6–9**
The Senate and House of Representatives override the veto of the Civil Rights Act.

■ **June 8–13**
The Senate and House of Representatives pass the final version of the Fourteenth Amendment.

1868

■ **July 28**
The Fourteenth Amendment is pronounced ratified.

1869

■ **March 4**
Ulysses S. Grant is inaugurated as president.

John A. Bingham, a Republican representative from Ohio, is usually credited with the wording of the crucial first section of the Fourteenth Amendment. He was born in Mercer, Pennsylvania, on January 21, 1815. He attended Franklin College in Ohio and later studied law. Bingham was admitted to the bar in 1840 and served as district attorney for Tuscarawas County, Ohio from 1846 to 1849. He was known for his antislavery sentiments and had advocated for the rights of free blacks. In 1854, following the political turmoil of the Kansas-Nebraska Act, Bingham was elected to Congress. Although he was defeated in the 1862 congressional election, Lincoln employed Bingham's talents in the Bureau of Military Justice and then as solicitor in the U.S. Court of Claims. In the spring of 1865 he was a judge advocate in the commission that tried the Lincoln assassination conspirators. Bingham was returned to Congress, taking his seat in December 1865. In the Joint Committee on Reconstruction, Bingham played an active role, especially in composing draft after draft of what would become the Fourteenth Amendment. Ironically, he was one of the few Republicans who agreed with President Johnson that the Civil Rights Act of 1866 was unconstitutional. Bingham, however, felt that the true solution was a constitutional amendment legitimizing the federal government's protection of black rights. In 1868 Bingham was instrumental in the impeachment of President Johnson. He failed to get renominated in 1872. President Grant appointed the former congressman to be minister to Japan in 1873, where he served for twelve years. Bingham died in Cadiz, Ohio, on March 19, 1900.

Thaddeus Stevens, a Republican representative from Pennsylvania, led a vigorous opposition to President Johnson's Reconstruction program. His motion created the Joint Committee on Reconstruction to investigate whether southern congressmen should be seated and to propose guidelines for the states' restoration. Stevens, who served as cochair of the Joint Committee, strove to secure maximum punishment of the former Confederates and maximum rights for the freedmen. Born in Danville, Vermont, on April 4, 1792, Thaddeus Stevens graduated from Dartmouth College in 1814 and moved to Pennsylvania that same year. He was admitted to the bar in 1816 and established a law practice in Gettysburg and later in Lancaster. He defended many fugitive slaves without taking a fee. Stevens served in the Pennsylvania legislature and the convention to revise the state constitution. He refused to sign the constitution because it restricted suffrage to white men. From 1849 to 1853 Stevens served in Congress as a Whig who opposed the extension of slavery. He returned to the House of Representatives in March 1859 as a Republican and represented Pennsylvania there until his death on August 11, 1868.

Stevens was the leader of the Radical Republicans in the House during and after the war. He was a vocal critic of Lincoln's moderation on slavery and Reconstruction. He felt that the former Confederate states were conquered territories and that Congress had primary responsibility to supervise such territories. Stevens pushed as hard as he could to secure black suffrage and to disfranchise all Confederates whom he classified as traitors. Unlike some radicals, however, Stevens had a pragmatic streak. When leading the debate in favor of the passage of the Fourteenth Amendment, he responded to his fellow radicals that he was disappointed with the proposed amendment, but as to why he would "accept so imperfect a proposition? I answer, because I live among men and not among angels" (ctd. in Foner, p. 255). Stevens continued to advocate black suffrage as a condition of readmission to the Union. Two years later he demanded the impeachment of President Johnson, but he was fatally ill at the time and left the matter in the hands of others, including Bingham.

The members of the Joint Committee on Reconstruction conducted the early debates on the Fourteenth Amendment. In January 1866 alone they received more than fifty proposals for constitutional amendments. From the House, in addition to Stevens and Bingham, were Elihu B. Washburne of Illinois, Roscoe Conkling of New York, George S. Boutwell of Massachusetts, Justin S. Morrill of Vermont, Henry T. Blow of Missouri, Henry Grider of Kentucky, and Andrew J. Rogers of New Jersey. The Senate appointed as William Pitt Fessenden of Maine, James W. Grimes of Iowa, Jacob M. Howard of Michigan, Ira Harris of New York, George H. Williams of Oregon, and Reverdy Johnson of Maryland. Rogers, Grider, and Johnson were the only Democrats on the committee. Although he was often ill, Fessenden acted as a moderate counterbalance to Stevens's designs.

Explanation and Analysis of the Document

◆ Section 1

The least controversial part of section 1 is the first sentence, which makes it clear that the former slaves are now citizens of the United States and citizens of the states in which they live. National citizenship is thus defined for the first time. This pointedly overturns the *Dred Scott* decision of 1857. In that Supreme Court case, Chief Justice Roger Taney denied Dred Scott, a slave, his freedom in part on the ground that a black might be a citizen of a state but not of the United States. Therefore, Scott had no right to sue in a federal court. In 1866, however, Republicans wanted to prevent former slaves from slipping into a half-free position by explicitly granting them citizenship and at least the promise of federal protection.

The lengthy second sentence contains three distinctive clauses—the meaning of each remains controversial today. Each prohibits certain state actions. First the Fourteenth Amendment guarantees to each citizen privileges and immunities; second, all "persons" are protected from a loss of life, liberty, and property without "due process"; and, third, all are to enjoy the "equal protection of the laws." At a minimum, congressmen are determined to stop the southern states from enacting Black Codes that recreate a form of near-slavery. Many, including John Bingham, specifically declare that their intention is to constitutional-

Time Line

1870

■ July 15
Georgia is readmitted to the Union, becoming the final ex-Confederate state to be reconstructed.

1873

■ April 14
With their decision in the Slaughter-House Cases, the Supreme Court significantly restricts the scope of the Fourteenth Amendment.

1883

■ October 15
With their decision in the Civil Rights Cases, the Supreme Court limits enforcement of the Fourteenth Amendment by declaring the Civil Rights Act of 1875 unconstitutional.

1896

■ May 18
With the *Plessy v. Ferguson* decision, the Supreme Court permits "separate but equal" facilities for African Americans.

ize the Civil Rights Act of 1866. Former abolitionists have long wanted to extend to African Americans the natural rights that are celebrated in the Declaration of Independence. The vagueness of Section 1 emerges from "the difficulties inherent in any attempt to incorporate a natural law concept into a constitution or public law, especially in a federal system. No legal authorities supplied neat definitions of civil rights; none does today, or can" (Hyman and Wiecek, pp. 406–407).

John Bingham, the principal author of Section 1, takes the terms "privileges and immunities" from Article IV, Section 2, of the U.S. Constitution. He and Senator Jacob Howard argue that the phrase embraces not only the rights that the states created for its citizens but also the Bill of Rights. Many scholars today agree with Bingham that the federal government has the power to enforce the Bill of Rights on the states. This represents a huge expansion of federal power in the 1860s. Some of Bingham's colleagues and later scholars dispute this broad interpretation. They observe that privileges and immunities preceded the Bill of Rights, and the wording simply meant that citizens visiting from another state would enjoy the same rights as the citizens of that state. This might include freedom of movement, property rights, and freedom to make contracts. In essence, the privileges and immunities clause guarantees equality within a state. In the Slaughter-House Cases (1873) the Supreme Court declined to apply the privileges or immunities clause to a Louisiana state law. While most

MENDING THE FAMILY KETTLE.

In this 1866 engraving Andrew Johnson holds a leaking kettle, labeled "The Reconstructed South," towards a woman representing liberty and Columbia, carrying a baby representing the newly approved Fourteenth Amendment. (Library of Congress)

constitutional scholars see this as a poor decision, it would have the real effect of negating whatever meaning the phrase had.

Section 1 guarantees every person "due process of law." Bingham takes this phrase from the Fifth Amendment, which says that the federal government cannot deny due process. The Fourteenth Amendment dictates that a state may not do so either. The accepted interpretation of due process is simply that the legal rules, proceedings, and cus-

toms of a state are available to all persons in that state, again with an emphasis on equality for all. Later in the nineteenth century, the Supreme Court would expand the meaning of due process by examining how laws and regulations affected the life, liberty, or property of persons.

Finally, Section 1 restricts states from denying "to any person … the equal protection of the laws." In the 1860s this is another assertion of equal justice and that states cannot discriminate against groups of individuals by selectively enforcing its laws. As such, it is a subset of rights contained in the privileges and immunities clause. For decades the clause has little impact, to the point where Justice Oliver Wendell Holmes ridiculed it as "the last refuge of a lawyer with no other arguments to make" (Urofsky, p. 442). Again, in time, the meaning of the equal protection clause would change. Because of the confusion over what "privileges or immunities" means, the interpretation of what constitutes "equal laws" results in a vast expansion of rights and government-enforced toleration of minority groups in society.

◆ Section 2

The Thirteenth Amendment ended slavery, but it remained unclear how to apportion members of Congress in the absence of the three-fifths clause (Article I, Section 2, of the Constitution). On one level the Fourteenth Amendment's answer is not surprising; apportionment is based on the total number of people, excluding Native Americans on reservations and tribal areas. According to Section 2, if a state discriminates against any group of adult males by preventing them from voting for federal or state offices, the state would be punished by losing representation. The total number of people would be reduced in proportion to the group of voters that is excluded. In other words, a state cannot benefit with a full representation in Congress if they refuse to let some of their male citizens vote.

This section represents a complicated compromise. Radical Republicans like Thaddeus Stevens and Charles Sumner of Massachusetts demanded black suffrage. While most northerners wanted protection for African Americans in the South, they generally were not prepared to give them the right to vote in either the South or the North. On the other hand, if blacks were to be counted as full persons, not three-fifths persons, the southern states would gain approximately ten to twelve representatives. It seemed ironic that because of four years of bloodletting, white southerners would increase their presence in Congress without recognizing the needs and rights of the freedmen. At that time, northern states had small black populations, so excluding them made no difference in their congressional delegations. Senator James Grimes proposed the solution to forgo black suffrage but to prevent the increase of the southern delegation in the House of Representatives. If a former slave state wanted to grant its black male citizens the vote, then the apportionment would change. The Fifteenth Amendment granting suffrage to African Americans would make this section largely moot.

Despite the protests of Elizabeth Cady Stanton, Susan B. Anthony, and other leaders of the women's rights movement, the word male is used for the first time in the Constitution. There would be no penalty for denying women the right to vote.

◆ Section 3

The Fourteenth Amendment prevented some Confederates from serving in federal and state offices. This section was also a product of compromise. Radicals wanted to disfranchise anyone who aided the Confederacy, but this was seen as too draconian, if not impractical. If blacks were denied political rights, the former Confederate states would be in turmoil for decades. Instead, the Congress came up with a much milder punishment. If one held state or federal office before the Civil War but then renounced loyalty to the United States, that person was to be forbidden to hold federal or state office, with two exceptions. First, anyone who received a presidential pardon before the ratification of the Fourteenth Amendment could hold office. Second, the amendment allowed Congress to pardon, in effect, an individual by a two-thirds vote in each house.

Northerners were upset by two patterns in the months following the end of the war. First, President Johnson was increasingly lenient to wealthy former slaveholders who came to plead for mercy or who sent their spouses to do so. Second, as Johnson's approved state governments came into operation, former Confederate military officers and political leaders were filling positions in state government and being sent to Washington, D.C., to assume seats in Congress. The South's leaders were not showing sufficient sorrow for the death and destruction they had caused.

A substantial amount of the debate recorded in the *Congressional Globe* surrounds this section and its earlier drafts. Some like Stevens wanted severe penalties for all Confederates. Others wanted disfranchisement until 1870 or 1876. The compromise was to deny political power to as many established southern leaders as possible with the hope that new white leaders would emerge with more conciliatory views. As crucial as Section 1 was for the future, Stevens concluded one of his last speeches about the Fourteenth Amendment by exclaiming, "Give us the third section or give us nothing" (ctd. in James, 1956, p. 130).

◆ Section 4

The Fourteenth Amendment makes it clear that all the debts the United States incurred in prosecuting the war, including soldiers' bounties for enlisting and their pensions, war bonds, greenback currency, and other debts, are legitimate. All Confederate debts, including their paper money and bonds, are worthless. Furthermore, slave owners would not be reimbursed for the loss of their slaves.

This section is largely obvious to all. Some Radical Republicans tried to scare the northern public into thinking that if President Johnson had his way and if the Democratic Party gained control of Congress, northern creditors would not be paid in full but Confederates *would* be paid in full. This was nonsense, or perhaps this was just a ploy to get votes. This section, however, reassures the Union's backers—both foreign and domestic. British shipbuilders who financed and supplied Confederate blockade-runners, on the other hand, were out of luck. Finally, there was some concern that the Emancipation Proclamation and Thirteenth Amendment conflicted with the Fifth Amendment, since no one, even slaveholders, could have their property taken from them without due process of law. Section 4 resolves the issue by explicitly stating that slaveholders would not be compensated for freed slaves.

◆ Section 5

The single sentence repeats Section 2 of the Thirteenth Amendment almost verbatim. Congress would have the authority to defend the rights outlined in Section 1. When Congress passed the Freedmen's Bureau Bill and the Civil Rights Act, many Republicans felt they had the authority under this provision of the Thirteenth Amendment. President Johnson disagreed, and Republicans feared that the Supreme Court might back the president's interpretation. By reemphasizing Congress's authority in the Fourteenth Amendment, Republicans thought that the problem could be avoided. The Ku Klux Klan Act of 1871 (also called the Civil Rights Act of 1871) and the Civil Rights Act of 1875 are just two manifestations of that belief.

Audience

As an addition to the Constitution this legislation was addressed to the entire nation. Each supporter of the amendment in Congress had his own opinion as to how the balance of federal and state powers was changed to the advantage of the former. All agreed that the rights of all citizens were being expanded.

More specifically, the Fourteenth Amendment was a message to four distinct audiences who had very different interests. First, the amendment told President Johnson that Congress was taking charge of Reconstruction policy. If the southerners (with Johnson's silent consent) were not going to protect the lives and rights of African Americans, Congress would do so. Section 3 struck at Johnson's liberal pardoning policies. President Johnson, of course, would not accept this message and took on the Republicans as they campaigned for Congress in the fall of 1866.

Second, the Fourteenth Amendment was addressed to the former Confederate states. Southern whites were being told to heed Congress if they wished to reenter the Union. They would need a new political leadership, and their Black Codes were unacceptable. Originally, there was a provision that would have admitted a state's delegation to Congress upon its ratification of the Fourteenth Amendment. That measure was tabled. Here the Radical Republicans had their way. Tennessee quickly ratified the amendment and was readmitted, but this clearly did not set a precedent. It was presumed by many, however, that ratification would substantially advance the states toward readmission. Section 2 also prodded the southern states to adopt black suffrage. Unfortunately, President Johnson encouraged southerners to reject the amendment. With no clear promise of readmission and the drastic consequences of the amendment, white southerners balked.

Third, the message sent to northern voters was that Republicans in Congress, not the president, had their interests at heart. Although it is difficult to measure public opinion, it is safe to say that northerners wanted the South to pay and to express sorrow for what they had done. They also wanted some degree of protection for southern blacks. Johnson and white southerners had utterly disappointed

them. Republicans gave the northern electorate hope. By avoiding black suffrage directly, punishing Confederate leaders, and guaranteeing the payment of debts, the Fourteenth Amendment was a rallying issue for Republicans in the 1866 and succeeding elections.

Fourth, for oppressed southern blacks, struggling to make their way amidst a hostile and humiliated white population, the Fourteenth Amendment held much promise. Should they ever get the right to vote, the party of Lincoln would be their destination. In the meantime, southern blacks relied upon Congress for protection. The Joint Committee on Reconstruction published a report too late to be used by Congress, but it documented the plight of the freedmen and, of course, appealed to the northern public to aid them.

Impact

Politically the Fourteenth Amendment struck a positive chord with the northern electorate. Not surprisingly, President Johnson misjudged public sentiment. The congressional elections of 1866 produced decisive Republican majorities in both the Senate and the House. The North trusted Congress with the responsibility of Reconstruction, which President Johnson might resist at his own peril.

The Fourteenth Amendment required the ratification of twenty-eight of the thirty-seven states. Connecticut was the first to ratify (June 25, 1866), followed quickly by New Hampshire (July 6) and Tennessee (July 19). Ratification became complicated when, in early 1868, New Jersey and Ohio tried to rescind their approvals. By July 28, 1868, Secretary of State William Seward certified that twenty-eight states had ratified the Fourteenth Amendment, allowing it to go into operation.

The Fourteenth Amendment, and particularly Section 1, has had a complicated history. Supreme Court justices and constitutional scholars have read the intentions of its authors in different ways. The legal scholar Alexander Bickel concludes that Section 1 fulfilled the moderate Republicans' objective of striking down the Black Codes but speculates that perhaps there was a compromise to create language that "was sufficiently elastic to permit reasonable future advances" (p. 61). Thus, the debate about how far to stretch the Fourteenth Amendment continues to rage.

In the Slaughter-House Cases (1873), the Supreme Court pulled away from an expansive application of Section 1 of the Fourteenth Amendment. The state of Louisiana had the right to create "reasonable" laws, and "reasonable" was defined as applying equally to all. The federal government had no responsibility to supervise the states and should concern itself with fundamental rights. The Court's majority refused to explore the meaning of "privileges or immunities." In the Civil Rights Cases (1883), the Supreme Court struck down the Civil Rights Act of 1875, which prevented discrimination in public accommodations and by private individuals. The Court claimed that the Fourteenth Amendment dealt only with discrimination by state governments. Sadly, the Court's majority in *Plessy v.*

"No State shall make or enforce any law which shall abridge the privileges or immunities of citizens of the United States; nor shall any State deprive any person of life, liberty, or property, without due process of law; nor deny to any person within its jurisdiction the equal protection of the laws."

(Section 1)

"Representatives shall be apportioned among the several States according to their respective numbers, counting the whole number of persons in each State, excluding Indians not taxed."

(Section 2)

"No person shall be a Senator or Representative in Congress, or elector of President and Vice-President, or hold any office, civil or military, under the United States, or under any State, who, having previously taken an oath, as a member of Congress, or as an officer of the United States, or as a member of any State legislature, or as an executive or judicial officer of any State, to support the Constitution of the United States, shall have engaged in insurrection or rebellion against the same."

(Section 3)

Ferguson (1896) reached the conclusion that "separate but equal" facilities were constitutional.

The concept of due process evolved in important ways. In several cases the Supreme Court examined the substance of state laws to determine whether individuals' liberty and property were unfairly impinged. In *Munn v. Illinois* (1876) the Court declared that the state of Illinois could serve the public good by imposing maximum rates charged by grain-storage operators, even though those operators might lose profits. In *Santa Clara County v. Southern Pacific Railroad Company* (1886) the Court broadened the definition of person to include corporations, who then sought relief from state regulations as an infringement of their property under due process. The Supreme Court began to inspect the details of laws, not just the procedures. This is termed "substantive due process." Such an approach led to the striking down of state regulation of businesses, including laws setting maximum work hours or improving working conditions. *Lochner v. New York* (1905) is often cited as the classic statement of the doctrine. Amidst the massive distress caused by the Great Depression, applying substantive due process to eco-

nomic regulation was discredited. What is significant is that substantive due process shifted to the "equal protection of the laws" portion of the Fourteenth Amendment.

In the late 1930s Justice Hugo Black suggested that the equal protection clause meant that the federal government had the responsibility to impose the Bill of Rights on the states. The so-called doctrine of incorporation, whereby the Fourteenth Amendment incorporates the liberties in the Bill of Rights and allows the courts to apply them to state laws, is quite controversial. Cases involving gay rights and affirmative action rely on Section 1 of the Fourteenth Amendment. The Supreme Court in *Griswold v. Connecticut* (1965) said the Bill of Rights and the Fourteenth Amendment created a zone of privacy for individuals against government intrusion. As such, in *Roe v. Wade* (1973) the Supreme Court ruled that state laws forbidding abortion represented a violation of a woman's right to privacy and were unconstitutional.

In today's society Section 1 has made it clear that the ways in which states treat their own citizens is a question of federal law. The responsibility of interpreting the Fourteenth Amendment has fallen into the hands of the federal judiciary and has significantly shifted the balance of power in our federal system. The debate over what rights the Fourteenth Amendment protects and the extent of substantive due process to investigate state laws will continue well into the future.

The fates of the other sections of the Fourteenth Amendment were relatively anticlimactic. The Fifteenth Amendment, which allows black suffrage, largely supplanted Section 2. Furthermore, despite decades of regulations in southern states inhibiting black voting, Section 2 was never invoked. No attempt was made to diminish southern congressional delegations. By the late 1890s those former Confederates who were adversely affected by section 3 were either dead or had been pardoned by Congress. In a symbolic vote in 1978 Congress removed the political disability of Jefferson Davis and Robert E. Lee. With regard to Section 4 the status of the debts of the Union and Confederacy was never in doubt.

Related Documents

Kendrick, Benjamin B. *The Journal of the Joint Committee of Fifteen on Reconstruction, 39th Congress, 1865–1867*. Vol. 67. New York: Columbia University Studies in History, 1914. The Joint Committee was responsible for drafting the Fourteenth Amendment. The tinkering with the language and their discussions reveal the political interests of the moderate Republican, Radical Republican, and Democratic members.

U.S. Congress. *Congressional Globe*, 46 vols. Washington, D.C., 1834–1873. The debates and procedural maneuvering surrounding the approval of the Fourteenth Amendment are recorded in the discussions of the Thirty-ninth Congress, first session, 1865–1866. The evolution of the language of the amendment can be followed in the discussions of the Senate and House of Representatives.

Bibliography

■ Articles

Aynes, Richard L. "On Misreading John Bingham and the Fourteenth Amendment." *Yale Law Journal* 103, no. 1 (October 1993): 57–104.

Bickel, Alexander M. "The Original Understanding and the Segregation Decision." *Harvard Law Review* 69, no. 1 (November 1955): 1–65.

Harrison, John. "Reconstructing the Privileges or Immunities Clause." *Yale Law Journal* 101, no. 7 (May 1992): 1385–1474.

West, Robin. "Toward an Abolitionist Interpretation of the Fourteenth Amendment." *West Virginia Law Review* 94 (Fall 1991): 111–155.

■ Books

Benedict, Michael L. *The Blessings of Liberty: A Concise History of the Constitution of the United States*. 2nd ed. Boston: Houghton Mifflin, 2006.

Foner, Eric. *Reconstruction: America's Unfinished Revolution, 1863–1877*. New York: Harper and Row, 1988.

Hyman, Harold, and William M. Wiecek. *Equal Justice under Law: Constitutional Development, 1835–1875*. New York: Harper and Row, 1982.

James, Joseph B. *The Framing of the Fourteenth Amendment*. Urbana: University of Illinois Press, 1956.

———. *The Ratification of the Fourteenth Amendment*. Macon, Ga.: Mercer University Press, 1984.

Nelson, William. *The Fourteenth Amendment: From Political Principle to Judicial Doctrine*. Cambridge, Mass.: Harvard University Press, 1988.

Perry, Michael J. *We the People: The Fourteenth Amendment and the Supreme Court*. New York: Oxford University Press, 1999.

TenBroek, Jacobus. *The Antislavery Origins of the Fourteenth Amendment*. Berkeley: University of California Press, 1951.

Urofsky, Melvin I. *A March of Liberty: A Constitutional History of the United States*. New York: Alfred A. Knopf, 1988.

■ Web Sites

"14th Amendment to the U.S. Constitution." Library of Congress "Primary Documents in American History" Web site.
   http://www.loc.gov/rr/program/bib/ourdocs/14thamendment.html. Accessed on July 31, 2007.

—By M. Philip Lucas

Questions for Further Study

1. How does the Fourteenth Amendment respond to the concerns of President Johnson in his veto of the Civil Rights Act of 1866? To what extent are the goals of the Civil Rights Act contained in the Fourteenth Amendment?

2. Does the Fourteenth Amendment undermine the federal system set up by the Constitution by subverting the rights of the states? Does it delegate too much power to the central government? Has this readjustment of powers been taken too far in our current society?

3. Does the Fourteenth Amendment undermine democracy by overemphasizing equality at the expense of majority rule and the predominant values of American society?

4. Constitutional scholars and Supreme Court justices debate whether the Fourteenth Amendment incorporates the Bill of Rights. To what degree do the Bill of Rights conflict with or complement the intention of Section 1 of the Fourteenth Amendment?

Glossary

abridge	lessen or curtail
bounties	recruitment money for those volunteering for the army
due process of law	regular legal proceedings and customs
immunities	exemptions
jurisdiction	authority of a government power

FOURTEENTH AMENDMENT TO THE U.S. CONSTITUTION

Section 1.

All persons born or naturalized in the United States, and subject to the jurisdiction thereof, are citizens of the United States and of the State wherein they reside. No State shall make or enforce any law which shall abridge the privileges or immunities of citizens of the United States; nor shall any State deprive any person of life, liberty, or property, without due process of law; nor deny to any person within its jurisdiction the equal protection of the laws.

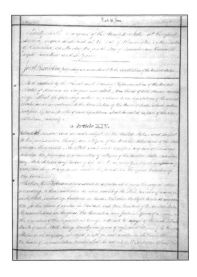

Section 2.

Representatives shall be apportioned among the several States according to their respective numbers, counting the whole number of persons in each State, excluding Indians not taxed. But when the right to vote at any election for the choice of electors for President and Vice-President of the United States, Representatives in Congress, the Executive and Judicial officers of a State, or the members of the Legislature thereof, is denied to any of the male inhabitants of such State, being twenty-one years of age, and citizens of the United States, or in any way abridged, except for participation in rebellion, or other crime, the basis of representation therein shall be reduced in the proportion which the number of such male citizens shall bear to the whole number of male citizens twenty-one years of age in such State.

Section 3.

No person shall be a Senator or Representative in Congress, or elector of President and Vice-President, or hold any office, civil or military, under the United States, or under any State, who, having previously taken an oath, as a member of Congress, or as an officer of the United States, or as a member of any State legislature, or as an executive or judicial officer of any State, to support the Constitution of the United States, shall have engaged in insurrection or rebellion against the same, or given aid or comfort to the enemies thereof. But Congress may by a vote of two-thirds of each House, remove such disability.

Section 4.

The validity of the public debt of the United States, authorized by law, including debts incurred for payment of pensions and bounties for services in suppressing insurrection or rebellion, shall not be questioned. But neither the United States nor any State shall assume or pay any debt or obligation incurred in aid of insurrection or rebellion against the United States, or any claim for the loss or emancipation of any slave; but all such debts, obligations and claims shall be held illegal and void.

Section 5.

The Congress shall have the power to enforce, by appropriate legislation, the provisions of this article.

Fortieth Congress of the United States of America;

At the *third* Session,

Begun and held at the city of Washington, on Monday, the *seventh* day of *December*, one thousand eight hundred and *sixty-eight*.

A RESOLUTION

Proposing an amendment to the Constitution of the United States.

Resolved by the Senate and House of Representatives of the United States of America in Congress assembled, (two-thirds of both Houses concurring) That the following article be proposed to the legislatures of the several States as an amendment to the Constitution of the United States, which, when ratified by three-fourths of said legislatures shall be valid as part of the Constitution, namely:

Article XV.

Section 1. The right of citizens of the United States to vote shall not be denied or abridged by the United States or by any State on account of race, color, or previous condition of servitude —

Section 2. The Congress shall have power to enforce this article by appropriate legislation.

Schuyler C. Fax
Speaker of the House of Representatives.

B. F. Wade
President of the Senate pro tempore.

Attest:
Edw. McPherson
Clerk of House of Representatives.

Geo. C. Gorham
Secy. of Senate U.S.

The Fifteenth Amendment (National Archives and Records Administration)

"The right ... to vote shall not be denied or abridged by the United States or by any State on account of race, color, or previous condition of servitude."

Overview

The Fifteenth Amendment (1870) was the third and last amendment adopted in the era immediate following the Civil War. For the first time in American history, it prohibited states from denying the right to vote to individuals on the basis of "race, color, or previous condition of servitude." Section 2 of the amendment further vested Congress with power to enforce it.

The Fifteenth Amendment bears elements of both continuity and discontinuity with earlier American history. Consistent with earlier history, it did not make voting an affirmative right for African Americans or other citizens, but rather it prohibited denying or abridging such groups the right to vote. Because it was the first specific prohibition to be incorporated into the Constitution, it served as a model for the Nineteenth Amendment (1920), which prohibited similar denials based on sex, and the Twenty-sixth Amendment (1971), which prohibited such denials to those who were eighteen years of age or older.

When Congress proposed the Fifteenth Amendment and the states ratified it, Congress was still attempting to "reconstruct" the southern states; this period of Reconstruction began in 1866 and ended in 1877. During this time, federal troops were posted in the South. Congress had forced states to adopt constitutions extending the right to vote to former slaves, and it had required southern states to ratify the Fourteenth Amendment as a condition for renewed representation in Congress.

Ironically, northern voters resisted some of the same requirements that they had imposed on the South. In his pathbreaking study of the Fifteenth Amendment, William Gillette observed that five jurisdictions rejected black suffrage in referendums in 1865. These votes, most of which were overwhelming, occurred in the Colorado territory in September, in Connecticut in October, in Wisconsin and Minnesota in November, and in the District of Columbia in December. Similar votes rejected such suffrage in the Nebraska Territory in June 1866, in Kansas and Ohio in 1867, in Michigan and Missouri in 1868, and in New York in 1869. Minnesota reversed itself in November 1868, which was the same year Iowa also accepted such suffrage, but these states remained exceptions to the general rule.

Context

The United States transformed from thirteen separate colonies into thirteen states united and independent from Great Britain. Even though they vested powers in a central government, first under the Articles of Confederation from 1781 to 1789 and then under the Constitution that they created in 1787, the states retained numerous rights. Delegates to the Constitutional Convention, rejecting calls to impose a national property qualification on voters, left voting qualifications to the states, simply specifying in Article I, Section 2, of the Constitution that "the Electors [voters] in each State shall have the Qualifications requisite for Electors of the most numerous Branch of the State Legislature." Over time, most states eliminated voting qualifications based on church membership and religious belief—a common requirement in the early colonies—or property ownership; because property was more freely available in America than elsewhere, this qualification had rarely disenfranchised large numbers of voters. American history is commonly portrayed as progressively democratic, but in retrospect the movement was not always as forward as some think. Although its supporters claimed that the presidential election of 1828 ushered in a period of Jacksonian democracy, the emphasis continued to be on universal white male suffrage rather than on universal suffrage. Indeed, because the U.S. Constitution apportioned representation in the U.S. House of Representatives not simply according to white population but also according to "three-fifths" of such "other persons [a euphemism for slaves]," southern whites who were otherwise losing population compared with northerners and westerners continued to be overrepresented there.

Over time, southerners who once defended slavery only as a "necessary evil" came to defend it as a positive good. The South justified slavery on theories of human inequality that contradicted the nation's earlier articulation in the Declaration of Independence that "all men are created equal"; leading southerners argued that slavery both lifted

Time Line

1776

■ **July 4**
Congress adopts the Declaration of Independence, which declares that "all men are created equal."

1828

■ **November 3**
Andrew Jackson's election to the presidency stands for the rise of the common man, which is often associated with universal white male suffrage.

1857

■ **March**
The U.S. Supreme Court declares in the *Dred Scott* decision that blacks are not and cannot be U.S. citizens.

1860

■ **November 6**
Abraham Lincoln is narrowly elected president.

1861

■ **April 12**
The Civil War begins when southerners fire on Fort Sumter in South Carolina.

1863

■ **January 1**
Lincoln issues his Emancipation Proclamation, proclaiming the freedom of black slaves behind Confederate lines.

1865

■ **April 18**
The Confederate army surrenders, ending the Civil War.

■ **December 6**
The states ratify the Thirteenth Amendment, ending slavery.

1866

■ **June 13**
Congress proposes the Fourteenth Amendment.

1868

■ **July 9**
The states ratify the Fourteenth Amendment.

■ **November 3**
Ulysses S. Grant is narrowly elected president.

---

what they regarded as the inferior race and provided leisure time for the superior race to cultivate itself. As southern attitudes hardened in justifying slavery, northern attitudes hardened against it. Not all northerners joined abolitionists in favoring immediate emancipation, but an increasing number concluded that the institution was morally wrong and would have to be eliminated.

As slave states continued to lose power vis-à-vis the North, southerners increasingly feared that northern states would eventually strike at their "peculiar institution" of slavery. After the Republican Abraham Lincoln was narrowly elected president in 1860, eleven southern states chose to secede. Lincoln felt duty-bound to preserve the Union, and in 1861 the nation's bloodiest conflict, the Civil War, began. By the end of the war in 1865 Lincoln, who had long regarded slavery as a moral evil, had transformed its objective from that of simply preserving the Union to that of freeing the slaves. His Emancipation Proclamation, which initially applied as a war measure only behind enemy lines, was eventually secured by the ratification of the Thirteenth Amendment, which abolished chattel slavery throughout the nation.

Southern states attempted to limit the freedom of the newly freed slaves through legislation restricting movement and limiting other rights, Congress responded again by proposing the Fourteenth Amendment, which the states ratified in 1868. It overturned the notorious Supreme Court decision in *Dred Scott v. Sandford* (1857) and declared that all persons including blacks "born or naturalized" within the United States were citizens entitled to the privileges and immunities of U.S. citizens and to due process and equal protection. Ironically, by abolishing slavery, the Thirteenth Amendment increased southern representation in the House of Representatives by invalidating the three-fifths clause; Republicans thought they had to act to insure that this increased southern representation did not actually work against African American rights. Section 2 of the Fourteenth Amendment, short of specifically prohibiting states from denying the vote to blacks, provided great anguish to advocates of woman's suffrage and allowed representation to be reduced in states that denied or abridged the right to vote to "any of the male inhabitants of such State, being twenty-one years of age, and citizens of the United States, except for rebellion, or other crime." Congress never reduced a state's representation based on this provision.

During the 1866 congressional elections President Andrew Johnson, who had become president in 1865 after John Wilkes Booth assassinated Lincoln, opposed ratification of the Fourteenth Amendment, which Congress had just proposed. Republicans picked up substantial support in this election, and Congress subsequently approved a bill over Johnson's veto on January 8, 1867, granting black suffrage in the District of Columbia. It followed up with a similar expansion of the franchise in the federal territories and required Nebraska to extend to blacks the right to vote as a condition of its admission into the Union. In the fifth section of the First Reconstruction Act of March 2, 1867, Congress further required southern states to enfranchise blacks as a condition of readmission into the Union and representation within Congress. Although the House of Representatives impeached President Johnson in 1868, the Senate fell a single vote shy of the two-thirds needed to convict him and remove him from office.

In the meantime, sentiment against African American voting outside the South continued to be strong, with Democrats picking up some seats that they had lost in 1866 in special elections. The Republican presidential platform that Ulysses S. Grant ran on in 1868 reflected the party's reluctance to extend the policies it had adopted in the South outside that region. Not surprisingly, Democrats praised President Johnson for opposing congressional Reconstruction and continued to advance the view that, despite the outcome of the Civil War, federalism left determination of the franchise to the states.

The Republican Ulysses S. Grant defeated the Democrat Horatio Seymour by only 300,000 votes in the 1868 election; he would have won the Electoral College but not the popular vote without the support of southern blacks whom Republicans had enfranchised. With most African Americans continuing to be grateful to Republicans for both their freedom and their civil and political rights, expanding the franchise to northern blacks presented a way to bolster Republican strength in the North.

Time Line

1869

■ **February 26**
Congress proposes the Fifteenth Amendment.

1870

■ **February 3**
The states ratify the Fifteenth Amendment

1965

■ **August 6**
President Lyndon B. Johnson signs the historic Voting Rights Act, which Congress later reaffirms and extends.

1966

■ **March 7 and June 13**
Relying largely on Section 2 of the Fifteenth Amendment, the U.S. Supreme Court upholds key provisions of the Voting Rights Act of 1965 in *South Carolina v. Katzenbach* and *Katzenbach v. Morgan*.

About the Author

Two-thirds majorities in both houses of Congress are needed to propose amendments, and approval by three-fourths of the states is needed to ratify them. When Congress proposed the Fifteenth Amendment, it followed the procedures used for all previous amendments, sending the amendment to state legislatures rather than to state conventions (as it would later do in the case of the Twenty-first Amendment, repealing national Prohibition on alcohol) for ratification. Some opponents of the amendment in Congress had sought to send the amendment to special state conventions.

The first version of the Fifteenth Amendment, which Republican Representative George S. Boutwell of Massachusetts authored in the House of Representatives, ended up being close to the final version. Ohio representatives Samuel Shellabarger and John A. Bingham, who was largely responsible for the wording of Section 1 of the Fourteenth Amendment, proposed more extensive amendments in the House. The initial version that the Senate considered, which was also broader than the one that Congress actually adopted, was largely the work of Henry Wilson, a Massachusetts Republican who would later serve as vice president under Ulysses S. Grant.

Ultimately, a congressional conference committee of six men proposed the existing Fifteenth Amendment. The committee focused not only on ironing out the differences between the House and Senate versions of the amendment but also on proposing language that was likely to gain the support of the necessary three-fourths of state legislatures.

Explanation and Analysis of the Document

The Fifteenth Amendment consists of two very brief sections. The first provides that "the right of citizens of the United States to vote shall not be denied or abridged by the United States or by any State on account of race, color, or previous condition of servitude." The second specifies that "Congress shall have the power to enforce this article by appropriate legislation." The scope of the Fifteenth Amendment is limited to U.S. citizens. Section 1 of the Fourteenth Amendment had established that all persons "born or naturalized in the United States" were citizens, but Congress had not yet extended such citizenship to Native Americans, and there was widespread opposition to naturalizing Chinese in the American West as well as to naturalizing Irish and other immigrants in other parts of the county. Whereas the Fourteenth Amendment extended some civil rights to all "persons," the Fifteenth Amendment intends to guard only "citizens" against deprivation of their votes.

In a continuation of federal principles, Section 1 of the Fifteenth Amendment does not positively confer the right to vote on anyone; it simply prohibits denying or abridging such rights based on "race, color, or previous condition of servitude." In contrast to this negative wording, Section 2 more positively vests Congress with enforcement powers, using language almost identical to that employed in Section 2 of the Thirteenth Amendment and Section 5 of the Fourteenth Amendment.

Given its brevity, the Fifteenth Amendment is best understood in the context of possible alternatives. The Republican representative Boutwell initially sought simul-

THE RESULT OF THE FIFTEENTH AMENDMENT.
And the Rise and Progress of the African Race in America and its final Accomplishment, and Celebration on May 19th A.D.1870.

This print from 1870 commemorates the celebration over the passage of the Fifteenth Amendment in Baltimore, Maryland (Library of Congress)

taneously to introduce both a bill and an amendment to enfranchise northern blacks, but rights secured by a bill were less secure than those achieved by an amendment, and the fact that Boutwell thought an amendment might be desirable suggested that legislation might exceed existing federal powers. The version of the amendment that Boutwell introduced in the House of Representatives was close to the final version. Ohio's Republican representative Shellabarger had proposed a more detailed and radical version, while fellow Ohio Republican John A. Bingham had offered a similar proposal, which allowed states to establish a one-year residency requirement.

In the Senate, Nevada Republican William M. Stewart introduced an amendment on January 28, 1869, that would also have protected the rights of African Americans to hold office. Republican Representative Jacob Howard of Michigan proposed a similar amendment, which the Senate defeated on February 8, that would have made it permissible to exclude naturalized Chinese or Irish from balloting. The next day the Senate also rejected a proposal by Henry Wilson that would have abolished restrictions on voting or office holding based on factors including race, color, property, and education and that would thus presumably have precluded literacy tests and poll taxes. Initially defeated, the Senate subsequently accepted a modified version of Wilson's amendment and an additional proposal by Indiana Senator Oliver P. Morton to reform the Electoral College.

The House considered the Senate amendment on February 15 but rejected it and requested a conference committee to resolve differences between the two proposals. The longtime abolitionist Wendell Phillips was among those who feared that the Senate's more utopian proposal stood little chance of ratification. Debate continued in both houses until they finally agreed to a conference committee consisting of House members Bingham, Boutwell,

and John A. Logan (Republican from Illinois) and Senate members Steward, Roscoe Conkling (Republican from New York), and George Edmunds (Republican from Vermont). This committee adopted the current version of the amendment. The House accepted this version by the necessary two-thirds vote on February 25, 1869, and the Senate agreed to it the next day. William Gillette, in his book on the subject, observes that the amendment sought two limited goals: "to enfranchise the northern Negro" and "to protect the southern Negro against disenfranchisement" (p. 77). He further attributed its passage largely to congressional moderates.

Nevada was the first state to ratify the amendment on March 1, 1869. During this process New York initially approved the amendment and then attempted to rescind its ratification, while Ohio first rejected it and then approved it. (Today's precedents, while still ambiguous, are more favorable to Ohio's actions than to New York's actions.) Congress required some southern states to approve it as a condition of resuming their place in Congress, and Secretary of State Hamilton Fish declared the amendment ratified on March 30, 1870. Southern states, dominated by Reconstruction governments, were most supportive of the amendment, which faced strong opposition in border states, tepid endorsement in the Middle Atlantic states, and considerable conflict in the Midwest. Kentucky, Delaware, California, Tennessee, Maryland, and Oregon all rejected ratification, although some later approved it.

Advocates of women's suffrage, who had called for women's suffrage at the Seneca Falls Convention of 1848 and who were already chaffing over the use of the word male to describe voters in Section 2 of the Fourteenth Amendment, were very disappointed by the adoption of the Fifteenth Amendment. Susan B. Anthony and Elizabeth Cady Stanton were among those who refused to endorse an amendment that extended suffrage to black men but not to women. When the American Equal Rights Association met in New York City in May 1869, it split into the National Woman Suffrage Association, led by Anthony and Stanton, and the American Woman Suffrage Association, led by Lucy Stone. These organizations continued to work apart until they were united in 1890 as the National American Woman Suffrage Association.

Audience

Once proposed and ratified by the required majorities, constitutional amendments join other parts of the Constitution as part of what Article VI of the Constitution calls "the supreme law of the land." The language of amendments thus speaks to the American people and to the world as a whole. Like the two previous amendments, the Fifteenth helped articulate American values and provide legal language that individuals can cite when they attempt to secure their rights in courts. Many Americans, including President Grant, who had favored its adoption, viewed it as the culmination of earlier provisions in the Thirteenth and Fourteenth Amend-

> "The right of citizens of the United States to vote shall not be denied or abridged by the United States or by any State on account of race, color, or previous condition of servitude."
>
> (Section 1)

> "If it be just, it should not be denied; if it be necessary, it should be adopted; if it be a punishment to traitors, they deserve it."
>
> (Thaddeus Stevens, qtd. in Gillette, p. 31)

> "I would sooner cut off my right hand than ask for the ballot for the black man and not for woman."
>
> (Susan B. Anthony, qtd. in McFeely, p. 266)

> "The question of suffrage is one which is likely to agitate the public so long as a portion of the citizens of the nation are excluded from its privileges in any State. It seems to be very desirable that this question should be settled now, and I entertain the hope and express the desire that it may be by the ratification of the fifteenth article of amendment to the Constitution."
>
> (Ulysses S. Grant, First Inaugural Address, March 4, 1869)

ments and as a practical implementation of the principles articulated in the Declaration of Independence.

The Fifteenth Amendment arguably carried different messages for North and South. It required states in the North, which had previously rejected black suffrage, to accept it, while attempting to assure that southern states, on which Congress had imposed such suffrage, would retain it. While the former hopes were largely fulfilled, the latter were dashed relatively quickly and did not reemerge for nearly a century.

Impact

Although the Fifteenth Amendment successfully enfranchised northern blacks, its long-term impact on African Americans in the South for its first one hundred years was negligible. Congress initially adopted Enforcement Acts between 1866 and 1875 designed to prevent obstruction to federal voting, but once northern troops left the South in 1877, whites who had once supported the

Confederacy struggled to regain their power. They effectively evaded the force of the Fifteenth Amendment through adoption of numerous stratagems left open when Congress omitted restrictions on property or educational qualifications. The Supreme Court decision in *Ex parte Yarbrough* (1884) was one of the few cases where the Court upheld federal laws restricting private actions aimed at denying African American voting rights.

Literacy tests, often administered in a highly discriminatory fashion, were used to keep both lower-class whites and blacks from voting. Many states further combined them with grandfather clauses, which the U.S. Supreme Court did not invalidate until *Guinn v. United States* (1915); such clauses exempted individuals whose grandfathers had voted—at a time when only whites could vote—from such literacy tests. States also adopted poll taxes, which they sometimes made cumulative so that individuals who wanted to vote had to pay the tax not only for that year but also for previous years in which they had not voted. Other states added additional obstacles to voter registration. In still others, racist groups like the Ku Klux Klan used physical violence to intimidate black voters. As the Democratic Party increasingly dominated the South (so that the winners of the Democratic primary almost always won in general elections), it, too, cooperated in black disenfranchisement by excluding blacks until the Supreme Court finally outlawed the practice in *Smith v. Allwright* (1944).

Although the nation never returned to chattel slavery, judicial interpretations of the Thirteenth, Fourteenth, and Fifteenth Amendments were extremely limited by the end of the nineteenth century. In the Civil Rights Cases of 1883 the Court decided that the amendments covered only state as opposed to private actions. By 1896 the Court used the doctrine of "separate but equal" to approve the developing system of racial segregation in *Plessy v. Ferguson*. The Court did not reverse course until its historic 1954 decision in *Brown v. Board of Education*, which finally began the long process of desegregation.

The Fifteenth Amendment proved so ineffective in its first century that Goldwin Smith, a British-born barrister who presented plans for reforming the Constitution in 1898, favorably cited a petition by Louisiana and other states to repeal it. Ironically, at about the same time, a number of attorneys unsuccessfully argued that the amendment had been so revolutionary and so contrary to American federalism that it had violated implicit constitutional limitations on the constitutional amending process.

However impotent it seemed, in time the amendment provided authority not only for some of the Supreme Court decisions that invalidated its evasions but also for congressional legislation. In 1957 Congress adopted the first of a number of civil rights acts designed to overcome the paucity of southern African American voters. These acts reached their high point with the adoption of the Voting Rights Act of 1965. Relying on congressional enforcement powers in Section 2 of the Fifteenth Amendment, this law suspended the use of literacy tests in seven southern states and used U.S. marshals to register voters. The law further prohibited states from adopting new laws that might restrict black suffrage without federal clearance. Justice Hugo Black was the only justice to object to this provision when the Supreme Court upheld this and other provisions in *South Carolina v. Katzenbach* (1966). Congress subsequently extended the Voting Rights Act in 1970, 1975, 1982, and 2006.

In 1964 the Twenty-fourth Amendment prohibited the imposition of poll taxes in federal elections. Relying chiefly on the equal protection clause of the Fourteenth Amendment, the Supreme Court subsequently extended this ban to state elections in *Harper v. Virginia Board of Elections* (1966).

Since the Supreme Court's decision in *Baker v. Carr* (1962) ruling that issues of state legislative apportionment are justiciable (that is, subject to judicial intervention), the Supreme Court has increasingly overseen state plans for legislative apportionment. In recent years, it has looked with increased suspicion at plans that used racial classifications to configure districts, sometimes even in cases where states used such plans to increase rather than to restrict minority representation. The Court has clearly

understood the Fifteenth Amendment as giving it a broad mandate to oversee voting issues.

Related Documents

"Dred Scott v. Sandford (1857)." Landmark Cases Web site. http://www.landmarkcases.org/dredscott/home.html. Accessed on August 6, 2007. This Web site contains selections from the Supreme Court's historic decision and other supporting information.

"Fifteenth Amendment to the Constitution." The Library of Congress "Primary Documents in American History" Web site. http://www.loc.gov/rr/program/bib/ourdocs/15thamendment.html. Accessed on August 6, 2007. This Web site allows one to search supporting documents pertaining to this amendment.

"Guinn & Beal v. United States (No. 96)." Cornell University "Supreme Court Collection" Web site. http://www.law.cornell.edu/supct/html/historics/USSC_CR_0238_0347_ZS.html. Accessed on August 6, 2007. The text of the U.S. Supreme Court decision that invalidated the grandfather clause.

Bibliography

■ Books

Amar, Akhil R. *America's Constitution: A Biography*. New York: Random House, 2005.

Bernstein, R. B. "Fifteenth Amendment." In *Constitutional Amendments: 1789 to the Present*, ed. Kris E. Palmer. Detroit: Gale Group, 2000.

Cogan, Neil H. *The Complete Reconstruction Amendments and Statutes*. 6 vols. New Haven, Conn.: Yale University Press, 2006.

Gillette, William. *The Right to Vote: Politics and the Passage of the Fifteenth Amendment*. Baltimore: Johns Hopkins Press, 1965.

Grimes, Alan P. *Democracy and the Amendments to the Constitution*. Lexington, Mass.: Lexington Books, 1978.

Keyssar, Alexander. *The Right to Vote: The Contested History of Democracy in the United States*. New York: Basic Books, 2000.

Kyvig, David E. *Explicit and Authentic Acts: Amending the U.S. Constitution, 1776–1995*. Lawrence: University Press of Kansas, 1996.

Mathews, John M. *Legislative and Judicial History of the Fifteenth Amendment*. Baltimore: Johns Hopkins Press, 1909.

McFeely, William S. *Frederick Douglass*. New York: W. W. Norton, 1991.

Pendergast, Tom, Sara Pendergast, and John Sousanis. *Constitutional Amendments: From Freedom of Speech to Flag Burning*. 3 vols. Detroit, Mich.: UXL, 2001.

Vile, John R. *Encyclopedia of Constitutional Amendments, Proposed Amendments, and Amending Issues, 1789–2002.* 2nd ed. Santa Barbara, Calif.: ABC-CLIO, 2003.

■ **Web Sites**

"First Inaugural Address of Ulysses S. Grant." The Avalon Project at Yale Law School Web site.
http://www.yale.edu/lawweb/avalon/presiden/inaug/grant1.htm. Accessed on January 15, 2008.

"Fourteenth Amendment." National Archives Experience, "Charters of Freedom" Web site.
http://www.archives.gov/national-archives-experience/charters/constitution_amendments_11-27.html. Accessed on January 15, 2008.

Stanton, Elizabeth Cady. "Declaration of Sentiments and Resolutions, Seneca Falls Convention, 1848." Furman University Web site.
http://facweb.furman.edu/~benson/seneca-falls.cmu. Accessed on August 6, 2007.

"The Voting Rights Act of 1965." U.S. Department of Justice Web site.
http://www.usdoj.gov/crt/voting/intro/intro_b.htm. Accessed on August 6, 2007.

"Voting Rights Act: Timeline." American Civil Liberties Union Web site.
http://www.votingrights.org/timeline/?year=1700. Accessed August 6, 2007.

—By John R. Vile

Questions for Further Study

1. When members of Congress debated the language of the Fifteenth Amendment, they had to decide whether to include protections for women as well as for African American men. Would it have been better for them to sponsor an amendment to protect the rights of both groups that might go down in defeat or for them to do what they chose to do? What do you think might have been the consequences of linking these two rights together?

2. Once federal troops withdrew in 1877 and southerners elected Democrats who opposed racial equality, the Fifteenth Amendment largely remained a virtual dead letter in the South. What, if anything, do you think the authors of the amendment might have done to preclude later evasions through literacy tests, all-white primaries, poll taxes, and the like?

3. Once the Nineteenth Amendment was adopted in 1920, women had few problems accessing the polls. How can you account for the relative success of the Nineteenth Amendment compared with the relative failure (especially in its early years) of the Fifteenth Amendment?

4. Literacy tests and poll taxes proved to be central obstacles to African American voting. Do you think it is possible to make a nonracist argument on behalf of one or both of these mechanisms? How would you make such an argument? Do you think it is convincing? Do you think literacy tests that are administered fairly might encourage people who would not otherwise do so to get an education?

5. Today laws restrict relatively few groups from voting. Restrictions vary from state to state, but they include limits on voting for felons, former felons, the mentally ill, noncitizens, and individuals under the age of eighteen. Do you think any of these restrictions should be lifted? If so, which ones? Explain.

6. The political landscape has changed considerably since the states ratified the Fifteenth Amendment in 1870. Do you think any existing state would seek to reimpose restrictions on African American voting if there was no such amendment today? Generally, do you think it more likely that the national government or the states might seek to restrict such rights? Explain.

7. Do you think it is permissible to apportion districts to maximize the likelihood that members of minority races will be able to elect members of their own race? Do you consider such apportionment essential similar to or qualitatively different from attempting to maximize party advantage? Explain.

Glossary

abridged	curtailed
servitude	slavery

FIFTEENTH AMENDMENT TO THE U.S. CONSTITUTION

A Resolution Proposing an amendment to the Constitution of the United States.

Resolved by the Senate and House of Representatives of the United States of America in Congress assembled, (two-thirds of both Houses concurring) that the following article be proposed to the legislature of the several States as an amendment to the Constitution of the United States which, when ratified by three-fourths of said legislatures shall be valid as part of the Constitution, namely:

◆ **Article XV.**

Section 1. The right of citizens of the United States to vote shall not be denied or abridged by the United States or by any State on account of race, color, or previous condition of servitude—

Section 2. The Congress shall have the power to enforce this article by appropriate legislation.

Forty-second Congress of the United States of America;

At the Second Session,

Begun and held at the City of Washington, on Monday, the Fourth day of December, one thousand eight hundred and seventy-one.

AN ACT

To set apart a certain tract of land lying near the head-waters of the Yellowstone River as a public park.

Be it enacted by the Senate and House of Representatives of the United States of America in Congress assembled,

That the tract of land in the Territories of Montana and Wyoming lying near the head-waters of the Yellowstone River, and described as follows, to wit, commencing at the junction of Gardiner's River with the Yellowstone River, and running east to the meridian passing ten miles to the eastward of the most eastern point of — Yellowstone Lake; thence south along said meridian to the parallel of latitude passing ten miles south of the most southern point of Yellowstone Lake; thence west along said parallel to the meridian passing fifteen miles west of the most western point of Madison Lake; thence north along said meridian to the latitude of the junction of the Yellowstone and Gardiner's Rivers; thence east to the place of beginning is hereby reserved and withdrawn from settlement, occupancy, or sale under the laws of the United States, and dedicated and set apart as a public park or pleasuring-ground for the benefit and enjoyment of the people; and all persons who shall locate or settle upon or occupy the same, or any part thereof, except as herein-after provided, shall be considered trespassers, and removed therefrom. Sec. 2 That said public park shall be under the exclusive control of the Secretary of the Interior, whose duty it shall be, as soon as practicable, to make and publish such rules and regulations as he may deem necessary or proper for the care and management of the same. Such reg-ulations shall provide for the preservation, from injury or spoliation, of all timber, mineral deposits, natural curiosities, or wonders within said park, and their retention in their natural condition. The Secretary may, in his discretion, grant leases for building pur-poses for terms not exceeding ten years, of small parcels of ground, at such places in said park as shall require the erection of buildings for the accommodation of visitors; all of the proceeds of said leases, and all other revenues that may be derived from any source connected with said park, to be expended under his direction in the management of the same, and the construction of roads and bridle-paths therein. He shall provide against the wanton destruction of the fish and game found within said park, and against their capture or destruction for the purposes of merchandise or profit. He shall also cause all persons trespassing upon the same

Act Establishing Yellowstone National Park (National Archives and Records Administration)

ACT ESTABLISHING YELLOWSTONE NATIONAL PARK

"The tract of land ... lying near the headwaters of the Yellowstone River ... is hereby ... set apart as a public park or pleasuring-ground."

Overview

The law to preserve and protect the Yellowstone environs was the first legislation to establish a national park. This area of some two million acres, about the size of Delaware and Rhode Island combined, stretched into what would become the states of Montana, Wyoming, and Idaho. In 1864 the federal government enacted the Yosemite Act to protect Yosemite Valley and its encircling peaks and the Mariposa Grove of Sierra redwoods; however, the state of California was given responsibility for the sites. When the U.S government passed a law in 1872 to protect Yellowstone on behalf of the entire country, it demonstrated the growing concern of many citizens that such a treasure be saved for future generations of Americans. As the world's first national park, Yellowstone was unique to America. With its erupting geysers, hot springs, and forest of petrified wood, Yellowstone was spectacular and enormous.

While America lacked historical monuments, castles, and medieval cities, it had vast wilderness and astounding natural sights. Yellowstone was created because Americans wanted to promote these sights and because they thought the land was worthless and not suitable for development. People also wanted to protect the area and restrict the number of leases to avoid creating the "carnival" atmosphere of Niagara Falls, with its souvenir shops and lack of free public access. Preserving the wilderness was a minor concern and protecting endangered species was not a consideration in forever setting aside the parklands. Yellowstone remained the country's only national park until 1890.

Context

In the United States in 1870 there were still wilderness to be explored and settlements to be established. Pioneers continued pushing westward to find homes. Both Montana and Wyoming were territories, and much of the area had not been explored. People had traveled through these territories, however, and passed along legends about what the area was like. Prehistoric peoples had settled there, and later tribes of Blackfoot, Crow, and Shoshone Indians lived and traveled through the area. Owing to the color of the rock, early trappers and traders, who were mostly French, called it Roche Jaune, which is French for "yellow rock." The first documented white man to visit Yellowstone was John Colter, a trapper and former member of the Lewis and Clark Expedition, who traveled over the region between 1807 and 1810 and witnessed what Washington Irving called the "hidden fires, smoking pits, and the all-pervading smell of brimstone" (qtd. in Bartlett, p. 99). The area was named "Colter's Hell," but many believed that Colter's tales were exaggerated. The mountain man Jim Bridger was noted for his tales about Yellowstone, but he was regarded as a colossal liar, a "Munchausen of the American West" (Haines, vol. 1, p. 53). People had reason to doubt Bridger's claims—whoever heard of mud that boils or streams of hot water shooting into the air? Bridger described the petrified forest and the erupting geysers, but few believed him.

Following the trappers and mountain men, prospectors searched the area for gold. Several mining expeditions visited the area, but the ore discovered was not the finest, and getting it out of the area was difficult. Yellowstone's future was determined by its inaccessibility. If the area's resources could not be inexpensively brought to market, the land was "worthless." In 1860 the first organized attempt to explore Yellowstone, led by Captain William F. Raynolds, an Army engineer, guided by Bridger, did not occur because of an early snow. Although Walter Washington De Lacy, a prospector and civil engineer, published the first reasonably accurate map of the Yellowstone region in 1865, the Civil War put further attempts to explore the area on hold. In 1869, however, the first of three major expeditions that eventually resulted in the Act Establishing Yellowstone National Park took place.

David E. Folsom, Charles W. Cook, and William Peterson, experienced frontiersmen who had prospected gold in Montana, explored Yellowstone (September 6–October 11, 1869). They saw the hot springs, climbed below Tower Falls, and measured the depth of the Grand Canyon of the Yellowstone River and the height of the falls. Cook later stated that settlers should be kept out of the area so that it could be "kept for the public some way" (qtd. in Haines, vol. 1, page 103). Folsom hoped that the government would

Time Line

1807–1808	■ Jim Colter is the first white man to travel through the Yellowstone area.
1860s	■ Prospectors look for gold.
1864	■ June 30 Yosemite Land Grant is passed.
1869	■ September 6–October 11 Folsom, Cooke, Peterson Expedition takes place.
1870	■ August 17–September 27 Washburn-Doane Expedition takes place. ■ September 19 Campfire discussion takes place concerning preserving the area as a national park.
1871	■ July 15–August 27 The Hayden Survey (also called the Hayden Expedition) takes place. ■ December 18 A bill to create Yellowstone National Park is introduced in both houses of Congress.
1872	■ March 1 Act Establishing Yellowstone National Park is signed into law by President Grant.
1883	■ March 3 Military assistance is authorized to protect the park.
1894	■ May 7 The National Park Protective Act (the Lacey Act) is passed to protect the birds and animals in Yellowstone. ■ August 3 The Hayes Act (also called Leases in the Yellowstone National Park) is passed, detailing specifications for leases within the park.
1916	■ August 25 The National Park Service Organic Act of 1916 establishes the National Park Service.

step in and prevent private settlement. The expedition produced an updated version of De Lacy's map and an article in the July 1870 *Western Monthly* magazine. However, when Folsom and Cook offered a collaborative diary of the expedition to the *New York Tribune, Harper's,* and *Scribner's Monthly,* the publications refused the manuscript. The editors of these publications considered the diary "unreliable material" (qtd. in Haines, vol. 1, p. 101) and worried that their reputation for publishing factual material might be tarnished if they printed it. Still, this first expedition generated enthusiasm in leading citizens from Montana to see the wonders for themselves.

Although rumors of trouble with Native Americans damped some of the public's keenness to visit the region, nineteen men mounted an expedition. The expedition, which lasted from August 17 to September 27, 1870, was led by Surveyor General Henry Dana Washburn, the politician and business promoter Nathaniel Pitt Langford, and the attorney Cornelius Hedges. Their military escort was led by Lieutenant Gustavus Cheney Doane. Unlike those on the first expedition, the men on this expedition, commonly known as the Washburn-Doane Expedition, suffered. They often went hungry, and one member, Truman C. Everts, became lost for thirty-seven days and nearly died. The men did make progress, however. They climbed several peaks and measured and analyzed some of the prominent natural features.

On the evening of September 19, at a campsite by the Gibbon and Firehole rivers near Madison Junction in what is now Wyoming, the explorers discussed the area's future. Some intended to file claims on the land around the geysers and waterfalls, anticipating demands by tourists to see them. Hedges proposed that instead of being divided among private speculators, the land be "set apart as a great National Park" (qtd. in Haines, vol. 1, p. 130). Langford felt that if Congress could be persuaded of the uniqueness of Yellowstone's natural attractions, such a reservation was possible. Over the years, there have been scholarly disputes over who first proposed the idea of preserving Yellowstone as a national park. What is clear is how the idea was made a reality. During the winter following the expedition, Langford lectured several times in the East, drumming up enthusiasm for the project. He also published two articles on Yellowstone, with engraved illustrations, in *Scribner's Monthly,* which had shifted its stance regarding the legitimacy of the claims. The public was interested, but some felt that such sights were not possible, harkening back to the disbelief over Colter's and Bridger's tales.

One person who heard Langford lecture in Washington, D.C., was intrigued and in a position to test the credibility of Langford's "tales." The geologist Ferdinand Vandiveer Hayden, director of the Geological and Geographical Survey of the Territories, had been leading scientific expeditions in the West and was determined to go to Yellowstone in 1871. With increasing public interest as the result of Langford's articles and lectures, Hayden felt the time was right to seek congressional funding for an official government exploration. Hayden had support from James G.

Blaine, Speaker of the House of Representatives, and Henry L. Dawes, an influential congressman from Massachusetts; both were supporters of the Northern Pacific Railroad, a company hoping to increase business through tourism and western exploration; through their efforts, in March 1871 Congress allotted forty thousand dollars for the survey.

Scientists and visual documentarians were included in the thirty-two-man party. The scientists measured, evaluated, and confirmed that the tall tales of bubbling mud and erupting geysers were facts. The photographer William Henry Jackson and the landscape artist Thomas Moran provided the visual evidence. Hayden was to prepare a geological map and send collected specimens of flora and fauna to the Smithsonian. The expedition arrived at Yellowstone around July 20, 1871, and departed around September 5. Hayden combined scientific analysis and excitement in his description of Yellowstone as "a mercurial Wonderland of beguiling attractions" (qtd. in Magoc, p. 16). His hope that the survey would produce "immediate practical results" (qtd. in Magoc, p. 17) was given a boost with a letter sent to him by A. B. Nettleton of the Northern Pacific Railroad Company, conveying the suggestion from Judge William D. Kelley, a longtime investor in the Northern Pacific, that Congress pass a bill reserving the Great Geyser Basin "as a public park forever" (qtd. in Haines, vol. 1, p. 155).

On December 18, 1871, the draft bill to create Yellowstone National Park, prepared by Montana Congressional Delegate William H. Clagett, was introduced in both houses of Congress. Senator Samuel Clarke Pomeroy of Kansas, chairman of the Committee on Public Lands, had asked the privilege of initiating the legislature; consequently, his bill S 392 appeared first, followed immediately by Clagett's introduction of an identical bill in the House as HR 764. Supporters of the bill began a campaign to promote its passage. Hayden arranged for a display of geological specimens brought back from the Yellowstone area and photographs by Jackson and sketches by Moran in the rotunda of the capitol. Copies of the May and June issues of *Scribner's Monthly* with Langford's two-part article "The Wonders of the Yellowstone" were distributed to all senators and representatives.

On January 22, 1872, Senator Pomeroy reported S 392 back from the Committee on Public Lands with the recommendation that it be passed. Although the necessity for such legislation was questioned, on January 30, S 392 was defended by senators Henry B. Anthony (Rhode Island), Thomas W. Tipton (Nebraska), George F. Edmunds (Vermont), and Lyman Trumbull (Illinois). The only objection was from Senator Cornelius Cole of California, who said that he did not see the reason for setting aside such a large tract of land for a public park when "there is an abundance of public park ground in the Rocky Mountains that will never be occupied" (qtd. in Haines, vol. 1, p. 170). After Trumbull assured Cole that the law could be repealed later "if it is anybody's way" (qtd. in Haines, vol. 1, p. 170), the bill was passed and sent to the House. There the favorable report of the Committee on Public Lands was presented by Representatives John B. Hawley (Illinois) and Mark Dunnell (Minnesota). Henry L. Dawes, a behind-the-scenes power in the House, spoke in favor of the immediate passage of the bill and assured the economy-minded Forty-Second Congress that creation of the park would put no additional strain on the Treasury. The roll-call vote recorded 115 ayes, 65 nays, and 60 as not voting. Having passed both houses, S 392 was sent to President Ulysses S. Grant, who signed it into law on March 1, 1872, creating the first national park.

About the Author

Although many men had a part in implementing this document, the question of authorship is a subject of scholarly debate. According to the scholar Alfred Runte, it was Henry Dawes who was primarily responsible for drafting the bill. Dawes took credit for writing the bill and in 1892 specifically stated that he had taken an interest in the park from the "day of its creation," going on to say that he "had the honor to write the bill which created it" (qtd. in Bartlett, p. 199). However, other scholars claim that William Clagett authored the bill. This allegation is seen as ridiculous by the park historian Aubrey Haines, who claims that Clagett did not write the document but simply altered the wording of the Yosemite Land Grant to fit the Yellowstone circumstances.

Explanation and Analysis of the Document

The Act Establishing Yellowstone National Park is similar to the Yosemite Land Grant of 1864. Both stress that the land be set apart for public use and recreation, although the Yosemite Land Grant clearly specifies "for all time," while the Yellowstone act does not mention time. For the Yosemite Land Grant, only the most "monumental" parcels were set aside, including forty square miles for the Yosemite Valley and only four square miles for Mariposa Grove; Hayden's concern that more "wonders" were yet undiscovered prompted the much larger dimensions of Yellowstone. Both documents include the granting of leases for ten-year terms and state that the income from the leases be used to improve and maintain the property. Yosemite was within the boundaries of California, and the state was given the responsibility for the area. However, Yellowstone was located in an area involving territories and was to be a national park with the U.S. government as caretaker. However, the omission of detailed instructions on how to preserve and protect the area and ambiguous language in the document created a scenario that would lead to problems during the early years of park operation.

The act has two distinct sections. Section 1 specifically states that a certain tract of land be set apart as a public park. Although the act created the world's first national park, the document uses the term *public park*. The document specifically details the area, 3,344 square miles, using physical landmarks in the territories of Montana and Wyoming, which were not yet states. (Montana became a state in 1889, and Wyoming became a state in 1890.) Both

The "Old Faithful" geyser in Yellowstone National Park
(Library of Congress)

territories were sparsely populated, and the land reserved for the park was viewed by many as worthless—a reason why the supporters of the park were able to set aside such a large area. When the question of the park's boundaries arose, legislators had referred to Hayden, whose suggestions for the park reflected his feeling that there might be other "decorations" (qtd. in Nash, p. 112) yet undiscovered. Hayden's report also noted that the region was a wasteland. Hayden reported that the severity of the winters made cultivation and raising stock impossible. The volcanic rock precluded successful mining. Consequently, setting aside the area would not interfere with the future of the West as a supplier of natural resources. There was also the belief at this time that the country still had vast territories for settlers heading west to occupy.

The act specifies that the area be used as a "public park or pleasuring-ground for the benefit and enjoyment of the people." This reflects the belief during this time that it was important to preserve natural wonders for the public to enjoy. Many were soured by the cupidity characterized by developers around Niagara Falls. In his report, Hayden warns that "persons are now waiting for the spring to … take possession of these remarkable curiosities, to make merchandise of these beautiful specimens, to fence in these rare wonders" (qtd. in Merrill, p. 208). Hayden stresses that Congress should not make the mistake of selling parts of the park for private interests because Yellowstone is for the benefit and enjoyment of

all people. But Yellowstone was to be a "pleasuring-ground" and not an amusement park. The benefit would come from visiting nature, simply enjoying the beauty provided by the mountains, the lake, the rivers, and the falls. (The concept of nature as providing solace and enlightenment was an idea that developed in England with the Romantic poets.)

An additional benefit could be medical. Hot springs are traditionally regarded as having health-giving powers. In its enthusiastic report on the Yellowstone bill having passed in the House, the *New York Times*, on February 29, 1872, stated "from the height of the land, and the salubrity of the atmosphere, physicians are of opinion that the Yellowstone Park will become a valuable resort for certain classes of invalids" and that "the mineral springs, with which the place abounds, possess various curative powers." The newspaper also suggests that Yellowstone may become the Baden of America, with strangers coming from all over the world to "drink the waters, and gaze on picturesque splendors only to be seen in the heart of the American Continent." Some predicted that Yellowstone Park would become a great international "Nervous Sanatorium" and that the "revolting mud-pools" would "do their part for the healing of mankind" (qtd. in Sears, p. 176).

The act also prohibits people from settling within the park, with the exception of those needed to maintain the park's safety and provide services to visitors. According to the act, anyone else attempting to create homes within the park would be removed.

Section 2 puts the park under the control of the secretary of the interior—at this time, Columbus Delano—who was to make and publish rules and regulations for the park "soon as practicable." It took years for such rules to be drafted. The rules and regulations were to promote the preservation and protection of the natural resources and the "natural curiosities, or wonders" within the park. Resources were to be retained "in their natural condition." Preservation requires planning, and the harm caused by the increasing numbers of tourists in the park could not be envisioned. The park was for people to enjoy, and, therefore, their needs had to be provided for. Ten-year leases for the erection of buildings to provide for the accommodation of visitors were spelled out. Income from the leases was to be used to operate the park and to build necessary roads and bridle paths. Future abuses were not imagined. In the 1870s annual visitors numbered about three hundred, but by 1965 two million people visited the park in one year, and by 2005 the number of visitors had increased to three million. In the provision against "wanton destruction of the fish and game," the term *wanton* was vague. In the early years of the park, visitors shot animals and birds indiscriminately. One tourist, having come across six bears near Yellowstone Falls, killed five of them. One winter, over four thousand elk were killed for their hides. Even with subsequent legislation, by 1930 the slaughter of animals resulted in the near eradication of certain species such as cougars and wolves. Looking to reestablish the original nature of the park, wolves were

> *"That the tract of land in the Territories of Montana and Wyoming, lying near the headwaters of the Yellowstone River ... is hereby reserved and withdrawn from settlement, occupancy, or sale ... and set apart as a public park or pleasuring-ground."*
>
> (Paragraph 1)

> *"Such regulations shall provide for the preservation, from injury or spoliation, of all timber, mineral deposits, natural curiosities, or wonders within said park, and their retention in their natural condition."*
>
> (Paragraph 2)

reintroduced in 1995, much to the anger of neighboring ranchers and farmers.

The secretary of the interior had the legal power to remove trespassers to prevent animals from being captured and sold, but there was no funding for him to carry out his duties or even to pay his salary. Initially, supporters of the park used the argument that the park could be managed for free, realizing that members of Congress had little interest in spending much time or money on a place so remote from mainstream America. Congress passed the bill to create the park based on the premise that it would cost nothing. However, protecting and managing such a large and diverse area could not be funded solely by the income from leases. It was not until 1878 that Congress appropriated ten thousand dollars for the fiscal year of 1879, a sum not nearly adequate to preserve and protect the park. No precedent existed for managing such a park. The first superintendent was Nathaniel Langford, who served from 1872 to 1877; he received no salary, had no budget or staff, and visited Yellowstone only twice during his five-year tenure. Unlike the Yosemite Land Grant, which made both the financing and the protection of the area the responsibility of the state of California, in the Act Establishing Yellowstone National Park, both elements were stipulated to be the responsibility of the national government.

The final statement of the act permits the secretary of the interior to have those destroying animals removed from the park. The vagueness of this statement led to numerous abuses of the park. The Sundry Civil Bill of 1883 enabled the secretary of the interior to call upon the secretary of war to provide troops to carry out the mandate against trespassers and those abusing the park's natural resources, including the wildlife. The 1894 National Park Protective Act (the Lacey Act) included more regulations concerning birds, fish, and animals in the park.

Audience

The primary audience for the act was those readers of the popular press, magazines such as *Scribner's Monthly* and *Harper's* that laid the foundation of the national park idea. Both Montana newspapers and the *New York Times* had articles spurring interest in the proposed park. Major segments of the audience were "pioneering sightseers" (Perrottet, p. 83), wealthy easterners, early conservationists, and nature-loving aristocrats from Europe. The act was also of great interest in cultured circles and among those inclined toward science. The audience was generally intrigued by the power, color, and spectacle of the exotic found in the park. The idea of seeing such sights was exciting, but only those "genteel" citizens who had the financial and leisure requirement to do so could visit this "wonderland.&rdquo

Impact

The reaction to the act establishing Yellowstone as a park for the people was universally positive. The *Nevada Territorial Enterprise* stated, "This will be the grandest park in the world" (qtd. in Magoc, p. 19). *Scribner's Monthly* described it as a "colossal sort of junketing place" (qtd. in Haines, vol. 1, p. 178). Initially it was a milestone in the history of tourism but has become a key document for conservation and environmental concerns. However, preserving wilderness was never anyone's plan for Yellowstone in the early days. The initial advocates for the park were more concerned with preventing private acquisition and exploitation of the geysers, hot springs, waterfalls, and other curiosities. Often the wilderness was viewed as frightening and not appealing, unlike the attraction provided by nature. In fact, one danger, aside from those naturally provided by the scalding hot geysers and the difficult mountain trails, was Native Americans. In 1877 a skirmish between tourists and Nez Perce warriors in Lower Geyser Basin resulted in fatalities. Two years later, all Native Americans were removed from the park.

Another danger was greed. Following the Civil War, the period of peace and increasing wealth stirred the avarice of developers. The completion of the Transcontinental Railroad in 1869 encouraged developers in the West. The Northern Pacific quietly established the Yellowstone Park Improvement Company to develop needed tourist services within park. In September 1882, Secretary of the Interior Henry M. Teller gave the company control over 4,400 acres, including sites such as Old Faithful, Lake Yellowstone, and the Grand Canyon of the Yellowstone. The company had control over the telegraph, all transportation, the use of timber and coal from the park as needed, and the exclusive right to build hotels. Under the lease agreement, it would pay two dollars per acre for 640-acre sections surrounding the park's most desirable sites. Members of the company also had the right to farm some of the park. All these rights were contrary to the intent and the actual language of the act. However, the activities of the company became public knowledge owing to the efforts of Lieutenant General Philip Sheridan and friends such as "Buffalo Bill" Cody, who wrote letters urging conservation. Articles, particularly those written by the early conservationist George Bird Grinnell, editor of *Forest and Stream* magazine, led to the Sundry Civil Bill of 1883 that halted the granting of monopoly rights. Other legislation protecting the park followed.

Initially, the park was praised as a "museum" where people could see the "freaks and phenomena of Nature" (qtd. in Nash, p. 113). *Scribner's Monthly* described the park as a place where "Yankee enterprise will dot the new Park with hostelries and furrow it with lines of travel" (qtd. in Nash, p. 113), but others felt the park was not needed. In 1883, during a debate for funding for the park, Senator John J. Ingalls of Kansas attacked Yellowstone, describing it as "an expensive irrelevancy" (qtd. in Nash, p. 113). He stated that the best thing the government could do with the park was to survey it and sell it. Senator George G. Vest of Missouri defended the park as esthetically important in counteracting America's increasing materialism. Looking at the future, Vest declared that the United States needed Yellowstone "as a great breathing-place for the national lungs" (qtd. in Nash, p. 114). Fortunately, Vest's point of view prevailed.

Over the years, other conflicts relating to the park occurred. One concerned providing a right of way for the railroad through the park. Grinnell, articles in his magazine, and other supporters of the park reminded the public that Yellowstone was the "people's park" (qtd. in Smith page 18). *Harper's* magazine joined the fight as well. The vote in Congress to permit the Northern Pacific spur to cut across the northeast corner of Yellowstone was turned down 107 to 65. Ironically, it was the Northern Pacific Railroad and its desire to promote tourism that sponsored the expedition of 1870 and financed Langford's lectures, which were critical in engaging support for the creation of the park.

The increasing popularity of the park for tourists escalated. Although the railroads never did obtain access routes into the park, automobiles did. Tourists traveling to Wonderland in cars and recreational vehicles have become a threat to what made the park unique. Since the National Park Service was established in 1916, it has attempted to balance the needs and desires of visitors with the preservation of Yellowstone. Fortunately, of the park's two million acres, only 2 percent are developed, and 99 percent of tourists do not stray from the main trails.

Yellowstone was the first in a series of fifty-eight national parks in the United States, and other countries followed suit in developing national parks. The difficulties in the early years of the park and the omissions and vague language of the original document were amended for Yellowstone and in the creation of the other parks. The creation of Yellowstone acknowledged the country's need to set aside land in the country that, at that time, seemed to be limitless. With no concept of future concerns, the park has evolved as people changed their focus from protecting sites to saving an ecosystem. Yellowstone is the protected core of the eighteen-million-acre Greater Yellowstone Ecosystem; its Lamar Valley is so rich in wildlife that it has been called the American Serengeti. To many, Yellowstone is an icon of what is the United States, a reminder of the past and a distinctively American monument.

Related Documents

Hayden, Ferdinand V. *Preliminary Report of the United States Geographical Survey of Montana and Portions of Adjacent Territories, Being a Fifth Annual Survey of Progress.* Washington, D.C.: Government Printing Office, 1872. This report validated much of the mystery associated with the area by measuring and analyzing the physical phenomena in the park as well as naming many of the sites.

"The Hayes Act." Congressional Acts Pertaining to Yellowstone Web site. http://www.yellowstone-online.com/history/yhfour.html. Accessed on January 18, 2008. This act, passed in 1894, was another act concerning leases in the park, specifying no premises to exclude the public from viewing certain sites. It repealed any aspect of the Sundry Civil Bill that conflicts with this document.

"The National Park Protective Act." Congressional Acts Pertaining to Yellowstone Web site. http://www.yellowstone-online.com/history/yhfour.html. Accessed on January 18, 2008. This 1894 act detailed protection of the birds and animals in the park. It specifies allowable fishing techniques. The act also provides for a commissioner to live in the park to have jurisdiction over all complaints and violations of the law and to enforce the rules and regulations of the park.

"Sundry Civil Bill for March 3, 1883." Congressional Acts Pertaining to Yellowstone Web site. http://www.yellowstone-online.com/history/yhfour.html. Accessed on January 18, 2008. This bill provided funding for the superintendent and employees and detailed leasing arrangements for hotels and "necessary outbuildings." The document also specifies the secretary of war, if requested by the secretary of the interior, may use troops to protect the park and prevent trespassers.

"Yosemite Land Grant of 1864." Yosemite National Park Web site. http://www.nps.gov/archive/yose/planning/documents/yoselandgrant.htm. Accessed on January 18, 2008. This act of Congress, on June 30, 1864, authorized a grant to the State of California of the Yosemite Valley and the "Mariposa Big Tree Grove" (commonly called the Mariposa Grove of Giant Sequoias) to be protected and managed by the state.

Bibliography

■ Articles

Hutton, Paul A. "Phil Sheridan's Crusade for Yellowstone." *American History Illustrated* (February 1985): 10–13.

Perrottet, Tony. "Yellowstone: In the Beginning." *Smithsonian* (May 2004): 80–85.

Rast, Raymond W. "Vistas, Visions, and Visitors: Creating the Myth of Yellowstone National Park, 1872–1915." *Journal of the West* 37, no. 2 (April 1998): 80–89.

Smith, Langdon. "The Contested Landscape of Early Yellowstone." *Journal of Cultural Geography* 22, no.1 (Fall/Winter 2004): 3–26.

"The Yellowstone Park Bill." *New York Times*, February 29, 1872.

■ Books

Barringer, Mark Daniel. *Selling Yellowstone: Capitalism and the Construction of Nature.* Lawrence: University Press of Kansas, 2002.

Bartlett, Richard A. *Nature's Yellowstone.* Albuquerque: University of New Mexico Press, 1974.

Chittenden, Hiram Martin. *The Yellowstone National Park, Historical and Descriptive.* Saint Paul, Minn.: J. E. Haynes, 1924.

Grusin, Richard A. *Culture, Technology, and the Creation of America's National Parks.* New York: Cambridge University Press, 2004.

Haines, Aubrey L. *The Yellowstone Story: A History of Our First National Park.* 2 vols. Yellowstone National Park, Wyo: Yellowstone Library and Museum Association, 1977.

Magoc, Chris J. *Yellowstone: The Creation and Selling of an American Landscape, 1870–1903.* Albuquerque: University of New Mexico Press, 1999.

Merrill, Marlene Deahl, ed. *Yellowstone and the Great West: Journals, Letters, and Images from the 1871 Hayden Expedition.* Lincoln: University of Nebraska Press, 1999.

Nash, Roderick. *Wilderness and the American Mind.* Rev. ed. New Haven, Conn.: Yale University Press, 1973.

Runte, Alfred. *National Parks: The American Experience.* Lincoln: University of Nebraska Press, 1979.

Schullery, Paul, and Lew Whittlesey. *Myth and History in the Creation of Yellowstone National Park.* Lincoln: University of Nebraska Press, 2003.

Sears, John F. *Sacred Places; American Tourist Attractions in the Nineteenth Century.* New York: Oxford University Press, 1989.

■ Web Sites

"A Century of Lawmaking for a New Nation: U.S. Congressional Documents and Debates, 1774–1875" Library of Congress "American Memory" Web site.
    http://memory.loc.gov/ammem/amlaw/. Accessed on June 15, 2007.

Macdonald, Jim. "Yellowstone History Guide." The Magic of Yellowstone Web site.
    http://www.yellowstone-online.com/history.html. Accessed on July 31, 2007.

"Yellowstone." National Park Service Web site.
    http://www.nps.gov/yell. Accessed on August 28, 2007.

—By Marcia B. Dinneen

1. How does the protection of a vast area such as a national park contribute to efforts to combat global warming?

2. Characterize Yellowstone National Park as a reflection of the cultural legacy of the development and expansion of the United States.

3. Review the history of Yellowstone before 1872. How are the myths and tall tales about the area confirmed by scientific evidence?

4. Jim Williams, former program manager at the Yellowstone Association Institute, stated that "Yellowstone is being very well managed—nothing bad is going to happen with the park. It's what will happen outside the park that will damage it" (qtd. in Perrottet, p. 85). Discuss this statement with reference to the land development surrounding the park.

Glossary

headwaters	waters from which a river arises
enacted	made into law
Territories	parts of the United States that are not admitted as a state
to wit	namely, that is to say
meridian	a great circle on the earth's surface passing through both geophysical poles
thence	from that place
pleasuring-ground	an area for public amusement
hereinafter	in the following part of this document
spoliation	the act of spoiling
said	named or mentioned before
bridle-paths	trails for riding horses
wanton	cruel and merciless; excessive

ACT ESTABLISHING YELLOWSTONE NATIONAL PARK

An Act to Set Apart a Certain Tract of Land Lying near the Headwaters of the Yellowstone River as a Public Park.

Be it enacted by the Senate and House of Representatives of the United States of America in Congress assembled, That the tract of land in the Territories of Montana and Wyoming, lying near the headwaters of the Yellowstone River, and described as follows, to wit, commencing at the junction of Gardiner's river with the Yellowstone river, and running east to the meridian passing ten miles to the eastward of the most eastern point of Yellowstone lake; thence south along said meridian to the parallel of latitude passing ten miles south of the most southern point of Yellowstone lake; thence west along said parallel to the meridian passing fifteen miles west of the most western point of Madison lake; thence north along said meridian to the latitude of the junction of Yellowstone and Gardiner's rivers; thence east to the place of beginning, is hereby reserved and withdrawn from settlement, occupancy, or sale under the laws of the United States, and dedicated and set apart as a public park or pleasuring-ground for the benefit and enjoyment of the people; and all persons who shall locate or settle upon or occupy the same, or any part thereof, except as hereinafter provided, shall be considered trespassers and removed therefrom.

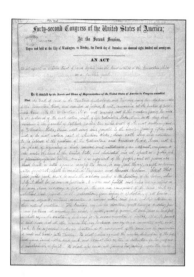

SEC 2. That said public park shall be under the exclusive control of the Secretary of the Interior, whose duty it shall be, as soon as practicable, to make and publish such rules and regulations as he may deem necessary or proper for the care and management of the same. Such regulations shall provide for the preservation, from injury or spoliation, of all timber, mineral deposits, natural curiosities, or wonders within said park, and their retention in their natural condition. The Secretary may in his discretion, grant leases for building purposes for terms not exceeding ten years, of small parcels of ground, at such places in said park as shall require the erection of buildings for the accommodation of visitors; all of the proceeds of said leases, and all other revenues that may be derived from any source connected with said park, to be expended under his direction in the management of the same, and the construction of roads and bridle-paths therein. He shall provide against the wanton destruction of the fish and game found within said park, and against their capture or destruction for the purposes of merchandise or profit. He shall also cause all persons trespassing upon the same after the passage of this act to be removed therefrom, and generally shall be authorized to take all such measures as shall be necessary or proper to fully carry out the objects and purposes of this act.

President Rutherford B. Hayes (Library of Congress)

RUTHERFORD B. HAYES'S INAUGURAL ADDRESS

"He serves his party best who serves the country best."

Overview

After a disputed presidential election, Rutherford B. Hayes recognized the depths of the division within the country and sought to calm the situation with his Inaugural Address, delivered on March 5, 1877. The United States had seemed to be on the verge of a second civil war during the winter of 1876–1877. The bitter dispute over the outcome of the election was finally resolved in favor of Hayes, the Republican candidate, yet many Americans remained convinced that the Democrat Samuel J. Tilden was the actual winner. As the date of Hayes's inauguration approached, even his supporters worried that he could never overcome the poisonous atmosphere that surrounded the contest. Talk of an armed invasion of Washington, D.C., to install Tilden in the White House was in the air. In his address, Hayes signaled his desire to move beyond the conflicts of Reconstruction toward a lasting reconciliation between the North and South.

Hayes sincerely hoped to find common ground between northern Republicans and southern Democrats. He also believed that he could persuade southern whites to respect the civil rights of former slaves. It was Hayes's vision that Americans could put aside their differences and agree upon certain universal principles: the rule of law, the need for honest government, the value of education. Unfortunately, these goals were only partially achieved. While his Inaugural Address was well received, it failed to lead to the southern political and social realignments he had advocated.

Context

American politics during the 1870s saw a weakening of the Republican Party's domination of the federal government. Scandals surrounding the presidency of Ulysses S. Grant, the onset of an economic depression, and doubts about Reconstruction policies in the South all contributed to a shift in the political situation. In the North, the Democratic Party began to recover from charges of disloyalty during the Civil War and showed renewed strength, winning control of the U.S. House of Representatives in 1874. In the South,

the Republican coalition of newly enfranchised blacks, moderate whites, and transplanted northerners ("carpetbaggers") began to lose control of state governments as Democrats returned to power under the banner of home rule and white supremacy. While Republican-backed Reconstruction governments were at least partially successful in securing civil rights for former slaves and reorganizing the southern economy, accounts of corruption and violence across the South helped to weaken support for them among northern voters. By 1876 it seemed likely that the Republicans would lose their grip on both Congress and the presidency.

The Democrats felt confident that their presidential candidate, New York's governor Samuel J. Tilden, would be swept into the White House by reform-minded voters. A wealthy attorney and veteran political strategist, Tilden had cleaned up corruption by both Democratic and Republican officeholders in his state and promised to do the same in Washington, D.C. For their part, the Republicans were divided into several factions, some demanding cleaner government and others favoring the status quo. At the Republican National Convention held in June 1876, the party passed over such well-known leaders as the former Speaker of the House James G. Blaine, New York's senator Roscoe Conkling, and the former secretary of the treasury Benjamin Bristow in favor of Ohio's governor Rutherford B. Hayes. A durable and well-liked figure in his home state, Hayes offended none of his party's factions and seemed an acceptable compromise choice. The general election campaign was hard fought and often venomous. The Democrats reminded voters of the scandals associated with Grant and his Republican allies in Congress and blamed them for the poor economic situation as well. The Republicans returned to their familiar tactic of "waving the bloody shirt" (recounting crimes against Union soldiers by the Confederacy) and equating the Democratic Party with treason.

On election night, the returns initially indicated that Tilden had defeated Hayes by carrying New York, Indiana, and other pivotal northern states along with the entire South. Several Republican-backed newspapers, though, claimed that Hayes had won Louisiana, South Carolina, and Florida (the only southern states still controlled by Republican governors) and was therefore elected. Both parties sent "visiting statesmen" to the South to represent

1822

■ **October 4**
Rutherford B. Hayes is born in Delaware, Ohio.

1861

■ **April 12**
Confederate troops fire on Fort Sumter, beginning the Civil War.

1864

■ **October 11**
Hayes is elected to the U.S. Congress while still serving in the Union army.

1865

■ **May 26**
Last Confederate troops surrender, ending the Civil War.

1867

■ **March 2**
U.S. Congress passes the Reconstruction Act over President Andrew Johnson's veto.

1868

■ **January 13**
Hayes begins first of three terms as governor of Ohio.

■ **November 3**
Republican Ulysses S. Grant is elected president of United States.

1876

■ **June 16**
Hayes is nominated for president by the Republican Party

■ **November 8**
Republicans challenge the Democratic claim that Samuel J. Tilden has defeated Hayes in presidential election vote.

1877

■ **January 18**
An electoral commission is proposed by Congress to solve election deadlock.

■ **March 2**
Congress completes electoral vote count, electing Hayes.

■ **March 5**
Hayes publicly takes oath of office and delivers presidential Inaugural Address.

their interests and engage in questionable dealings with local politicians. Rival election-return boards released conflicting vote totals, and rumors of bribery and fraud began to fly. Papers certifying the validity of rival Republican and Democratic electors were signed by opposing officials in the three contested states; there was no clearly defined constitutional method for determining which votes should be accepted as valid. Evidence indicates that black voters across the South were subject to intimidation and violence to prevent them from voting Republican. In turn, Republicans in power in the three contested southern states threw out Democratic ballots. It is fair to say that Democrats kept likely Republican voters from the polls, while Republicans destroyed or suppressed votes cast by Democrats.

As tempers rose, a joint congressional committee created an electoral commission consisting of five senators, five congressmen, and five U.S. Supreme Court Justices to choose between the conflicting sets of electoral votes. In February 1877, the Electoral Commission ruled in the Florida case that it could not examine the ballots. This favored Hayes, as did similar decisions in the Louisiana and South Carolina cases. House Democrats responded by threatening to delay indefinitely the final count by filibuster.

Meanwhile, behind-the-scenes discussions were taking place between Hayes's representatives and leading southern Democrats, who sought to gain concessions from Hayes in turn for their support. Also involved in these negotiations were powerful railroad interests seeking federal aid in building a line from the South to the Pacific Coast; they indicated that they would encourage southern Democrats in Congress to back Hayes if he favored their projects. For his part, Hayes indicated that he would withdraw military support from Republican carpetbag governments and back southern infrastructure projects and education efforts. On February 26, 1877, Republican representatives for Hayes met with southern Democrats at the Wormley Hotel in Washington to strike a final agreement. On March 2, House Democrats stopped the filibuster, allowing Hayes to be declared the winner by a single electoral vote. Hayes took the presidential oath of office privately the next day and was formally inaugurated two days later.

About the Author

Rutherford Birchard Hayes was born in Delaware, Ohio, on October 4, 1822. His father died two months before his birth; Sardis Birchard, his mother's bachelor uncle and a successful businessman, became his guardian. In 1838 he enrolled in Kenyon College, where he made friends who were later to be helpful in his political career. After graduating in 1842, he went on to earn a law degree from Harvard University and, in 1850, established a practice in Cincinnati. After surviving some lean years, he began to win praise for his legal skills through several high-profile criminal cases. In 1852, Hayes married Lucy Webb, a beautiful and accomplished young woman with a strong interest in abolition, temperance, and other social causes.

Hayes became more and more politically active in the 1850s. He supported the Whig Party before switching his allegiance to the Republican Party after its founding in 1854. In 1857 he declined a nomination for Congress; a year later, he was elected Cincinnati city solicitor. His political career was interrupted by the outbreak of the Civil War. Hayes was appointed major of a Union volunteer regiment and soon earned a reputation for valor under fire. Wounded four times during the war, he was promoted to brevet brigadier general after his heroic service in October 1864 at the battle of Cedar Creek. The following year, he was nominated to the U.S. House of Representatives by the Republicans and elected while still serving in the field. He resigned from the Union army in 1865 with the rank of brevet major general. Looking back, Hayes recalled his Civil War years as the most fulfilling of his life.

As a congressman, Hayes supported the Reconstruction policies of his party and visited the South to gain a firsthand impression of conditions there. Reelected in 1866, he resigned his seat to accept the Republican nomination for governor of Ohio. During the campaign, he supported a state constitutional amendment enfranchising blacks and opposed paying government bonds in greenbacks (a policy favored by "soft money" Democrats). After securing a narrow victory, Hayes spent his term promoting financial support for schools and charitable institutions, appointing judges, and sponsoring a state geological survey. Reelected in 1869 after another close contest, he was successful in reforming the juvenile justice system and establishing the college that eventually became Ohio State University. Hayes left office in 1871, ran unsuccessfully for Congress the following year, and was encouraged by his party to seek a third Ohio gubernatorial term in 1875. Defeating the incumbent Democrat William Allen, he once again stressed aid to public institutions and worked to reduce the state debt.

After becoming president in 1877, Hayes attempted to continue the same sort of fiscally conservative, moderately reformist spirit he had displayed as governor. But his efforts to depoliticize the civil service were fought by his fellow Republicans, while a Democratic-controlled Congress opposed his hard-money policies. His efforts to placate southern whites while preserving the civil rights of former slaves also met with mixed results. Journalists and congressional Democrats continued to question the legitimacy of Hayes's election; his foes branded him "His Fraudulency" and "Rutherfraud B. Hayes." Declining to seek a second term, Hayes left office in 1881 and devoted himself to promoting education, civil rights, and prison reform causes in private life. At the time of his death on January 17, 1893, Hayes was eulogized as a principled, fair-minded leader who worked to promote clean, nonpartisan government and unity between North and South.

Explanation and Analysis of the Document

In the opening paragraphs of his Inaugural Address, Hayes strikes a reasonable, conciliatory tone. The contro-

Time Line

1877
■ April 24
Hayes withdraws troops from the Louisiana statehouse, ending Reconstruction.

1881
■ March 4
Hayes ends his term as president.

1893
■ January 17
Hayes dies in Spiegel Grove, Ohio.

versial circumstances of his election victory form the background of his remarks. In a real sense, he is still making the case for his elevation to the presidency. He signals his willingness to adapt to conditions by loosely sketching out "certain important ends to be attained" during his term in office, guided by motives he hopes that the nation shares. By expressing his hope that "every motive for misrepresentation has passed away," Hayes both concedes the intense feeling surrounding the 1876 election and signals that he expects partisans to put aside their differences for the common national good. He asks citizens of whatever political affiliation to give him a fair hearing and "candidly" judge his words on their merits. To emphasize his consistency of principle (and to indirectly refute charges that he made deals to secure his office), he refers back to his letter accepting the Republican nomination in June 1876. He will do his best to act upon the principles mentioned in the letter, he says, though he acknowledges it will be a "grave and difficult task."

Hayes devotes the heart of his address (paragraphs 2–10) to discussing his views on southern self-government and race relations. He begins by stating that protecting the constitutional rights of all American citizens is the most important subject facing the country—a seemingly uncontroversial premise that actually contains a number of points in dispute. Hayes specifically says that agreement upon principles and laws that will secure the "permanent pacification of the country" are needed. The phrase is significant, considering that "permanent pacification" is mentioned in the 1876 Republican platform in terms of military enforcement of the Fourteenth and Fifteenth Amendments to the Constitution in the southern states. By discussing pacification in *national* rather than sectional terms, Hayes is signaling that his administration favors offering incentives to the South rather than relying on coercion to achieve its goals. He quickly goes on to admit that the "immeasurable benefits" that resulted from the defeat of the Confederacy have not been realized in the South and that Reconstruction has fallen short of success. In carefully balanced language, Hayes stresses that restoration of southern home rule is his goal—but only with the equal

A picture of the crowd at the inauguration of Rutherford B. Hayes (Library of Congress)

rights of whites and black citizens guaranteed. Obedience to the Constitution—including its new amendments dealing with civil rights—must be the basis for a post-Reconstruction South. Overall, the theme of national unity is stressed, underscoring that the problems of one section are the problems of all.

In pursuing this theme in paragraph 6, Hayes suggests that loyalty to a political party is unimportant compared with the reestablishment of sound constitutional government in the southern states. This is intended as an overture to elements within the southern Democratic Party to cooperate with his administration on certain issues. He frames the choices ahead in terms of peaceful social order versus "barbarism" and emphasizes that every citizen, Republican or Democrat, has a stake in the outcome. Moving beyond generalities in paragraph 7, he comes to grips with the racial issues that resulted from the abolition of slavery. Hayes acknowledges—with just a hint of irritation—that some Americans still resist the idea that emancipation was a positive thing for everyone. He reasserts the familiar Republican position that the federal government has a moral obligation to protect the civil rights of former slaves. But then, in paragraph 8, he quickly follows by stating that force is not enough; blacks and whites must find a way to work together to create positive change. To help foster this, Hayes again reaches past party lines toward conservative

southern whites by stating that the region's problems go beyond political questions. Specifically, he indicates that the economic development of the South will receive "the considerate care of the National Government," though he is careful to avoid specific proposals. (The ambiguity of this language was disappointing to those supporting internal improvements in the South, especially railroad promoters.)

In paragraph 9, Hayes takes up the theme of promoting education, an interest of his during his tenure as governor of Ohio. At the time, federal aid to state education was considered a radical idea. While the Freedmen's Bureau had aided efforts by private citizens to start schools for former slaves during the early days of Reconstruction, the federal government had been reluctant to directly fund education in the South (or elsewhere). Hayes's endorsement of federal support for state-funded schools is vaguely worded but significant nonetheless.

By tying his desire for cooperation and understanding between the races to the larger need for national reconciliation, Hayes returns to the grand theme of Union. He makes clear in paragraph 10 that his ultimate goal is the elimination of all divisions—be they racial or sectional—from American life.

Hayes turns his attention to civil service reform in paragraph 11. While both major parties had supported this goal in the 1876 election, the Republican Party carried the heavy burden of the rampant corruption within the Grant administration. Moreover, such Republican leaders as New York's senator Roscoe Conkling ridiculed civil service reformers and fought to keep the spoils system intact. Hayes owed his presidential nomination in part to his party's reform wing, though he was also indebted to other factions as well. He chooses to come down firmly on the side of the reformers in his address, stating that he intends that his efforts to cleanse civil service policies would be "thorough, radical and complete." Offices would not be granted as political favors, not even at the request of congressmen from his party. This was a direct challenge to Conkling, who soon became an active opponent of the Hayes administration.

The topic of civil service reform leads Hayes into the wider question of partisanship in government. In paragraph 12, he reflects that Democrats and Republicans alike had pledged themselves to civil service reform in the last election, recognizing its popularity across party lines. Taking this bipartisan theme further, Hayes notes that while he owes his election to a particular party, he is charged to represent more than the nation's Republicans. As an added measure for taking politics out of government, he advocates restricting the president of the United States to a single six-year term.

Financial questions are touched upon in paragraph 15. Hayes alludes to the financial crash of September 1973, which began in the banking industry and turned into a deep and sustained depression. He has little to say on the subject, other than to welcome signs of economic upturn. The much-debated issue of resumption—that is, deflating the currency and phasing out greenbacks in favor of specie (coin)—is dealt with briefly in the next paragraph. Hayes reaffirms his support of "safe paper currency" based firmly upon gold, a policy he supported as Ohio governor. Although he does not go into detail, his words express support for the monetary position of the Grant administration and for the Specie Payment Resumption Act, passed by the U.S. Congress in 1875 to restore paper money to the gold level.

Foreign relations are taken up in paragraphs 18–20. Alluding to such recent European conflicts as the Franco-Prussian War, Hayes reaffirms traditional American neutrality. His comments may also indirectly refer to President Grant's unsuccessful attempt to annex the Dominican Republic (an effort Hayes had opposed). He goes on to endorse Grant's policy of submitting disputes between the United States and foreign nations to impartial arbitration.

Hayes spends most of the remainder of his address discussing the presidential election dispute. He begins by downplaying the intense bitterness surrounding the contest, asserting that the "excitement" generated was no greater than in previous elections. The only unusual aspect, he claims, was the "uncertainty of the result"—a statement that sidesteps the charges of fraud and bribery hurled by Republican and Democratic partisans at each other. He concentrates instead on affirming the legal authority of the Electoral Commission to settle the dispute. Hayes praises the commissioners' ability and fairness but concedes that "human judgment is never unerring." Even

so, the decision to uphold the electoral vote count favorable to Hayes's cause should be accepted as final. In fact, all Americans should celebrate the fact that the controversy was settled without violence. This, he points out, is the first time in history that a nation as great as the United States has resolved such a political crisis through peaceful legal means. Americans should take pride in this fact, even if they have doubts about how the process of choosing the president was conducted. The American belief in the supremacy of law is one of the key themes of the address. With it, Hayes manages to link respect for the Constitution and its recent amendments with acceptance of the 1876 election results and the need for an honest civil service.

In his conclusion, Hayes calls upon the nation to rally around its shared principles, secured by democratic consent rather than by force. The final sentence of paragraph 27 is adapted from a prayer intended for legislative proceedings, found in *The Book of Common Prayer*, a well-known text in the United States during the nineteenth century, used by the Episcopal Church. Ending on this reassuring note reinforces the inclusive and forgiving tone of Hayes's address.

Audience

Hayes had several audiences in mind when he wrote his Inaugural Address. First, he wished to reassure the American people as a whole that his elevation to the presidency represented the triumph of law, not the outcome of political deal making. With firm yet restrained language, he signals to the country at large that the question of his election is settled and that armed resistance will not be tolerated. Beyond this, he speaks to the nation's collective desire for reconciliation between the sections and the demand for political reform. His insistence upon a gold-based currency is similarly aimed at a broad conservative constituency crossing partisan and sectional lines. By closing his address with lines from a prayer, he unites his audience in a benediction for the good of the country.

The address also contains appeals to specific segments of his audience. Moving beyond the "bloody shirt" rhetoric of his supporters during the presidential campaign, he reaches out to the South by stating that its problems can be solved only by peaceful rather than military means. Going further, he speaks of restoring local self-government and offering a degree of economic aid to the region. By mentioning that these issues transcend party interests, he indicates his desire to expand the Republican Party's base in the South. Hayes tempers these welcoming words with a warning that southern whites must respect the rights of former slaves and recognize that southern society has irrevocably changed. For African Americans in the South, he offers reassurance that their rights will not be tampered with (though he is vague on specific guarantees) and indicates his willingness to support education programs.

Finally, Hayes speaks to the politicians in his own party when he declares himself in favor of civil service reform. By

> "Only a local government which recognizes and maintains inviolate the rights of all is a true self-government."
>
> (Paragraph 4)

> "The evils which afflict the Southern States can only be removed or remedied by the united and harmonious efforts of both races, actuated by motives of mutual sympathy and regard."
>
> (Paragraph 8)

> "Universal suffrage should rest upon universal education."
>
> (Paragraph 9)

> "He serves his party best who serves the country best."
>
> (Paragraph 13)

> "The fact that two great political parties have in this way settled a dispute in regard to which good men differ as to the facts and the law no less than as to the proper course to be pursued in solving the question in controversy is an occasion for general rejoicing."
>
> (Paragraph 24)

advocating appointments to office based on merit rather than partisan service, he throws down the gauntlet before Republican congressional leaders. In the process, he signals to his primary audience—the American people—that he will correct the misdeeds of the Grant administration and oppose his fellow party leaders if necessary.

Impact

Overall, Hayes's Inaugural Address received a positive reaction. It calmed the mood of a fearful nation and laid out a blueprint for how the new president intended to govern. For the most part, Hayes followed the policies his address sketched out during his term of office.

Hayes quickly made good on his pledge to hasten the end of Reconstruction and restore southern home rule. By the end of April 1877, he had withdrawn federal troops from the statehouses of Louisiana and South Carolina,

allowing "Redeemer" Democrats to take power. (Redeemer Democrats pledged themselves to "redeem" the South from Reconstruction and reestablish white rule.) Hayes understood that the new governors would protect the civil rights of African Americans, particularly their right to vote, but it quickly became evident that southern Democrats were unable or unwilling to do so. Hayes criticized Louisiana and South Carolina for failing to live up to their pledges but took no real action. Many southern blacks as well as their northern white allies felt betrayed by Hayes's policy.

Initially, Hayes had hoped to bring moderate southern Democrats (particularly former Whig Party members) into the fold of the Republican Party. Toward that end, he appointed the Tennessee Democrat David M. Key as postmaster general. But an effort to gain southern Democratic support for the election of the Republican James A. Garfield as Speaker of the House failed, which in turn led northern Republicans to oppose Hayes administration policies seen as favorable to the South. Instead of weakening, political divisions between the sections grew stronger during Hayes's term.

The economic assistance hinted at in Hayes's address also did not materialize. Despite intimations he would do so, he failed to support efforts to subsidize the Texas & Pacific Railroad's ambitious construction plans. Hayes was unable to follow through on passing federal aid to education; in his last annual message to Congress, he made a final unsuccessful plea for assisting schools in the South.

Hayes had better success in advancing civil service reform. His appointment of Key and of the prominent reformer Carl Schulz to his cabinet indicated that he would seriously challenge the spoils system. He aroused the wrath of Roscoe Conkling by dismissing his ally Chester A. Arthur from his lucrative post as collector at the New York Custom House. After a fierce struggle, Hayes was able to get a replacement for Arthur confirmed by the Senate. While Congress thwarted his efforts at comprehensive civil service reform, his victory over Conkling had important symbolic value. It should also be noted that Hayes appointed to various federal positions a number of local politicians who had helped secure his victory in Louisiana.

Despite Hayes's assurances that prosperity was returning, economic difficulties persisted into his term. His response to workers' strikes in Pittsburgh, Philadelphia, and elsewhere during the summer of 1877 was to send in federal troops to restore order—an action he was no longer willing to take to enforce civil rights protection in the South. Hayes felt that "education" would improve management-labor relations. Years after his term ended, he expressed more sympathy for workers' rights and criticized the unregulated growth of industrial monopolies.

The hard-money policies outlined in Hayes's address were carried out, though not without a fight with congressional Democrats. In February 1878, the Bland-Allison Act authorizing coinage of silver passed both houses of Congress over Hayes's veto. He was also unable to stop the repeal of the Specie Payment Resumption Act. By 1879, however, there was enough specie in the U.S. Treasury to redeem all greenbacks in gold, which at least quieted the hard- versus soft-money debate for the moment.

Hayes's hopes that the country could put the 1876 election behind it were not realized. Newspapers that had backed Tilden continued to challenge Hayes's legitimacy. In 1878 a House committee chaired by the Democrat Clarkson N. Potter conducted investigations into Republican voter fraud in Louisiana and Florida. Evidence also came to light that Tilden's nephew had likewise attempted to bribe election officials. Although the Potter Committee issued a report concluding that Tilden had actually won the presidency, there was no move to unseat Hayes.

In the end, the lofty goals and good intentions of Hayes's Inaugural Address were only partially realized. While the tranquility of the country was largely secured, the fundamental shifts in social and political relations that his address outlined were not achieved. It can be said, though, that Hayes largely won the respect of the country for his efforts. He was at peace with how he had carried out his duties. "Nobody ever left the Presidency with less regret, less disappointment, fewer heartburns, or more general content with the result of his term," he wrote shortly before he retired from office (Trefousee, p. 126).

Related Documents

Hinsdale, Burke A., ed. *The Works of James Abram Garfield.* 2 vols. Boston: James R. Osgood & Company, 1883. Fellow Ohioan and future U.S. president Garfield represented Hayes in the South during the 1876 election dispute and served on the Electoral Commission. Included here are his closely reasoned speeches arguing Hayes's right to the presidency.

Williams, Charles Richard, ed. *The Diary and Letters of Rutherford Birchard Hayes, Nineteenth President of the United States.* 5 vols. Columbus, Ohio: Ohio State Archeological and Historical Society, 1922–1926. Hayes kept a diary from his childhood until his death. His private thoughts and personal correspondence shed considerable light on his values and motivations. The writings gathered in these volumes reveal Hayes to be a principled Victorian-era gentleman who loved his family and approached public service as a high calling.

Williams, T. Harry. *Hayes: The Diary of a President, 1875–1881.* New York: David McKay, 1964. This useful volume edits Hayes's diary entries from 1875 to 1881 into a clear, succinct narrative of the crucial events of the time. Williams's scholarly footnotes are helpful.

Bibliography

■ Books

Barnard, Harry. *Rutherford B. Hayes and His America.* Indianapolis, Ind.: Bobbs-Merrill, 1954.

Flick, Alexander C. *Samuel Jones Tilden: A Study in Political Sagacity.* New York: Dodd, Mead, 1939.

Foner, Eric. *Reconstruction: America's Unfinished Revolution, 1863–1877.* New York: Harper & Row, 1988.

Hoogenboom, Ari. *The Presidency of Rutherford B. Hayes.* Lawrence: University Press of Kansas, 1988.

———. *Rutherford B. Hayes: Warrior and President.* Lawrence: University Press of Kansas, 1995.

Jordan, David M. *Roscoe Conkling of New York: Voice in the Senate.* Ithaca, N.Y.: Cornell University Press, 1971.

Morgan, H. Wayne. *From Hayes to McKinley: National Party Politics, 1877–1896.* Syracuse, N.Y.: Syracuse University Press, 1969.

Morris, Roy, Jr. *Fraud of the Century: Rutherford B. Hayes, Samuel J. Tilden and the Stolen Election of 1876.* New York: Simon & Schuster, 2004.

Roseboom, Eugene H. *A History of Presidential Elections*. New York: Macmillan, 1970.

Trefousse, Hans L. *Rutherford B. Hayes*. New York: Times Books, 2002.

Woodward, C. Vann. *Reunion and Reaction: The Compromise of 1877 and the End of Reconstruction*. Boston: Little, Brown, 1951.

■ **Web Sites**

"Biography of Rutherford B. Hayes." Rutherford B. Hayes Presidential Center Web site.
http://www.rbhayes.org/hayes/president/. Accessed on December 22, 2007.

"Diary and Letters of Rutherford B. Hayes." Rutherford B. Hayes Presidential Center/Ohio Historical Society Web site.
http://www.ohiohistory.org/onlinedoc/hayes/index.cfm. Accessed on December 22, 2007.

"Rutherford B. Hayes," White House Web site.
http://www.whitehouse.gov/history/presidents/rh19.html. Accessed December 22, 2007.

—By Barry Alfonso

Questions for Further Study

1. Hayes's stated policy toward the South relied upon the goodwill of white-controlled governments to enforce protection of African American civil rights. By the end of the nineteenth century, segregation had become law across the South, and blacks had effectively lost the right to vote in most localities. Could this have been prevented? Should Reconstruction, including its military component, have remained in effect? Discuss what Hayes's options were.

2. Historians have drawn parallels between the 1876 and 2000 U.S. presidential elections. In both cases, a Republican candidate was ultimately declared the winner, even though his Democratic opponent had won more popular votes and the methods used for counting ballots were in dispute in at least one southern state. Based upon their words and actions, compare how Rutherford B. Hayes and George W. Bush attempted to overcome their controversial election victories and unite the country behind their administrations.

3. In his Inaugural Address, Hayes lists civil service reform as a major goal. His opponents countered that rewarding loyal party workers with government jobs reflected the will of the voters. Does the saying "To the victor belong the spoils" have any validity? Should elected leaders have the right to hire and fire as they see fit? Discuss this in light of recent controversies, such as the claim that in 2006 the Bush administration's Department of Justice dismissed U.S. attorneys for partisan reasons.

4. Hayes claims in his Inaugural Address that conditions in the South could be improved only by "united and harmonious efforts of both races, actuated by motives of mutual sympathy and regard." Is it possible for a government to encourage these feelings in its citizens, to actually change their hearts and minds? Are there recent examples of this?

Glossary

actuated	to incite or move to action
arbitration	the settlement of a dispute by a person or persons chosen to hear both sides and come to a nonpartisan decision
beneficent	showing the quality of being kind or doing good
prostration	complete physical exhaustion or helplessness
providential	as if decreed by a divine power
specie	coin, as distinguished from paper money
tribunal	a court of justice
tumults	noisy commotions; disturbances

RUTHERFORD B. HAYES'S INAUGURAL ADDRESS

Fellow-Citizens:

We have assembled to repeat the public ceremonial, begun by Washington, observed by all my predecessors, and now a time-honored custom, which marks the commencement of a new term of the Presidential office. Called to the duties of this great trust, I proceed, in compliance with usage, to announce some of the leading principles, on the subjects that now chiefly engage the public attention, by which it is my desire to be guided in the discharge of those duties. I shall not undertake to lay down irrevocably principles or measures of administration, but rather to speak of the motives which should animate us, and to suggest certain important ends to be attained in accordance with our institutions and essential to the welfare of our country.

At the outset of the discussions which preceded the recent Presidential election it seemed to me fitting that I should fully make known my sentiments in regard to several of the important questions which then appeared to demand the consideration of the country. Following the example, and in part adopting the language, of one of my predecessors, I wish now, when every motive for misrepresentation has passed away, to repeat what was said before the election, trusting that my countrymen will candidly weigh and understand it, and that they will feel assured that the sentiments declared in accepting the nomination for the Presidency will be the standard of my conduct in the path before me, charged, as I now am, with the grave and difficult task of carrying them out in the practical administration of the Government so far as depends, under the Constitution and laws on the Chief Executive of the nation.

The permanent pacification of the country upon such principles and by such measures as will secure the complete protection of all its citizens in the free enjoyment of all their constitutional rights is now the one subject in our public affairs which all thoughtful and patriotic citizens regard as of supreme importance.

Many of the calamitous efforts of the tremendous revolution which has passed over the Southern States still remain. The immeasurable benefits which will surely follow, sooner or later, the hearty and generous acceptance of the legitimate results of that revolution have not yet been realized. Difficult and embarrassing questions meet us at the threshold of this subject. The people of those States are still impoverished, and the inestimable blessing of wise, honest, and peaceful local self-government is not fully enjoyed. Whatever difference of opinion may exist as to the cause of this condition of things, the fact is clear that in the progress of events the time has come when such government is the imperative necessity required by all the varied interests, public and private, of those States. But it must not be forgotten that only a local government which recognizes and maintains inviolate the rights of all is a true self-government.

With respect to the two distinct races whose peculiar relations to each other have brought upon us the deplorable complications and perplexities which exist in those States, it must be a government which guards the interests of both races carefully and equally. It must be a government which submits loyally and heartily to the Constitution and the laws—the laws of the nation and the laws of the States themselves—accepting and obeying faithfully the whole Constitution as it is.

Resting upon this sure and substantial foundation, the superstructure of beneficent local governments can be built up, and not otherwise. In furtherance of such obedience to the letter and the spirit of the Constitution, and in behalf of all that its attainment implies, all so-called party interests lose their apparent importance, and party lines may well be permitted to fade into insignificance. The question we have to consider for the immediate welfare of those States of the Union is the question of government or no government; of social order and all the peaceful industries and the happiness that belongs to it, or a return to barbarism. It is a question in which every citizen of the nation is deeply interested, and with respect to which we ought not to be, in a partisan sense, either Republicans or Democrats, but fellow-citizens and fellowmen, to whom the interests of a common country and a common humanity are dear.

The sweeping revolution of the entire labor system of a large portion of our country and the advance of 4,000,000 people from a condition of servitude to that of citizenship, upon an equal footing with their former masters, could not occur without presenting problems of the gravest moment, to be dealt with by the emancipated race, by their former masters, and by the General Government, the author of the act of emancipation. That it was a wise, just, and providential act, fraught with good for all concerned, is not generally conceded throughout the country. That a moral obligation rests upon the National Government to employ its constitutional power and influence to establish the rights of the people it has emancipated, and to protect them in the enjoyment of those rights when they are infringed or assailed, is also generally admitted.

The evils which afflict the Southern States can only be removed or remedied by the united and harmonious efforts of both races, actuated by motives of mutual sympathy and regard; and while in duty bound and fully determined to protect the rights of all by every constitutional means at the disposal of my Administration, I am sincerely anxious to use every legitimate influence in favor of honest and efficient local self-government as the true resource of those States for the promotion of the contentment and prosperity of their citizens. In the effort I shall make to accomplish this purpose I ask the cordial cooperation of all who cherish an interest in the welfare of the country, trusting that party ties and the prejudice of race will be freely surrendered in behalf of the great purpose to be accomplished. In the important work of restoring the South it is not the political situation alone that merits attention. The material development of that section of the country has been arrested by the social and political revolution through which it has passed, and now needs and deserves the considerate care of the National Government within the just limits prescribed by the Constitution and wise public economy.

But at the basis of all prosperity, for that as well as for every other part of the country, lies the improvement of the intellectual and moral condition of the people. Universal suffrage should rest upon universal education. To this end, liberal and permanent provision should be made for the support of free schools by the State governments, and, if need be, supplemented by legitimate aid from national authority.

Let me assure my countrymen of the Southern States that it is my earnest desire to regard and promote their truest interest—the interests of the white and of the colored people both and equally—and to put forth my best efforts in behalf of a civil policy which will forever wipe out in our political affairs the color line and the distinction between North and South, to the end that we may have not merely a united North or a united South, but a united country.

I ask the attention of the public to the paramount necessity of reform in our civil service—a reform not merely as to certain abuses and practices of so-called official patronage which have come to have the sanction of usage in the several Departments of our Government, but a change in the system of appointment itself; a reform that shall be thorough, radical, and complete; a return to the principles and practices of the founders of the Government. They neither expected nor desired from public officers any partisan service. They meant that public officers should owe their whole service to the Government and to the people. They meant that the officer should be secure in his tenure as long as his personal character remained untarnished and the performance of his duties satisfactory. They held that appointments to office were not to be made nor expected merely as rewards for partisan services, nor merely on the nomination of members of Congress, as being entitled in any respect to the control of such appointments.

The fact that both the great political parties of the country, in declaring their principles prior to the election, gave a prominent place to the subject of reform of our civil service, recognizing and strongly urging its necessity, in terms almost identical in their specific import with those I have here employed, must be accepted as a conclusive argument in behalf of these measures. It must be regarded as the expression of the united voice and will of the whole country upon this subject, and both political parties are virtually pledged to give it their unreserved support.

The President of the United States of necessity owes his election to office to the suffrage and zealous labors of a political party, the members of which cherish with ardor and regard as of essential importance the principles of their party organization; but he should strive to be always mindful of the fact that he serves his party best who serves the country best.

In furtherance of the reform we seek, and in other important respects a change of great importance, I recommend an amendment to the Constitution prescribing a term of six years for the Presidential office and forbidding a reelection.

With respect to the financial condition of the country, I shall not attempt an extended history of the embarrassment and prostration which we have suffered during the past three years. The depression in all our varied commercial and manufacturing interests throughout the country, which began in September, 1873, still continues. It is very gratifying, however, to be able to say that there are indications all around us of a coming change to prosperous times.

Upon the currency question, intimately connected, as it is, with this topic, I may be permitted to repeat here the statement made in my letter of acceptance, that in my judgment the feeling of uncertainty inseparable from an irredeemable paper currency, with its fluctuation of values, is one of the greatest obstacles to a return to prosperous times. The only safe paper currency is one which rests upon a coin basis and is at all times and promptly convertible into coin.

I adhere to the views heretofore expressed by me in favor of Congressional legislation in behalf of an early resumption of specie payments, and I am satisfied not only that this is wise, but that the interests, as well as the public sentiment, of the country imperatively demand it.

Passing from these remarks upon the condition of our own country to consider our relations with other lands, we are reminded by the international complications abroad, threatening the peace of Europe, that our traditional rule of noninterference in the affairs of foreign nations has proved of great value in past times and ought to be strictly observed.

The policy inaugurated by my honored predecessor, President Grant, of submitting to arbitration grave questions in dispute between ourselves and foreign powers points to a new, and incomparably the best, instrumentality for the preservation of peace, and will, as I believe, become a beneficent example of the course to be pursued in similar emergencies by other nations.

If, unhappily, questions of difference should at any time during the period of my Administration arise between the United States and any foreign government, it will certainly be my disposition and my hope to aid in their settlement in the same peaceful and honorable way, thus securing to our country the great blessings of peace and mutual good offices with all the nations of the world.

Fellow-citizens, we have reached the close of a political contest marked by the excitement which usually attends the contests between great political parties whose members espouse and advocate with earnest faith their respective creeds. The circumstances were, perhaps, in no respect extraordinary save in the closeness and the consequent uncertainty of the result.

For the first time in the history of the country it has been deemed best, in view of the peculiar circumstances of the case, that the objections and questions in dispute with reference to the counting of the electoral votes should be referred to the decision of a tribunal appointed for this purpose.

That tribunal—established by law for this sole purpose; its members, all of them, men of long-established reputation for integrity and intelligence, and, with the exception of those who are also members of the supreme judiciary, chosen equally from both political parties; its deliberations enlightened by the research and the arguments of able counsel—was entitled to the fullest confidence of the American people. Its decisions have been patiently waited for, and accepted as legally conclusive by the general judgment of the public. For the present, opinion will widely vary as to the wisdom of the several conclusions announced by that tribunal. This is to be anticipated in every instance where matters of dispute are made the subject of arbitration under the forms of law. Human judgment is never unerring, and is rarely regarded as otherwise than wrong by the unsuccessful party in the contest.

The fact that two great political parties have in this way settled a dispute in regard to which good men differ as to the facts and the law no less than as to the proper course to be pursued in solving the question in controversy is an occasion for general rejoicing.

Upon one point there is entire unanimity in public sentiment—that conflicting claims to the Presidency must be amicably and peaceably adjusted, and that when so adjusted the general acquiescence of the nation ought surely to follow.

It has been reserved for a government of the people, where the right of suffrage is universal, to give to the world the first example in history of a great nation, in the midst of the struggle of opposing parties for power, hushing its party tumults to yield the issue of the contest to adjustment according to the forms of law.

Looking for the guidance of that Divine Hand by which the destinies of nations and individuals are shaped, I call upon you, Senators, Representatives, judges, fellow-citizens, here and everywhere, to unite with me in an earnest effort to secure to our country the blessings, not only of material prosperity, but of justice, peace, and union—a union depending not upon the constraint of force, but upon the loving devotion of a free people; "and that all things may be so ordered and settled upon the best and surest foundations that peace and happiness, truth and justice, religion and piety, may be established among us for all generations."

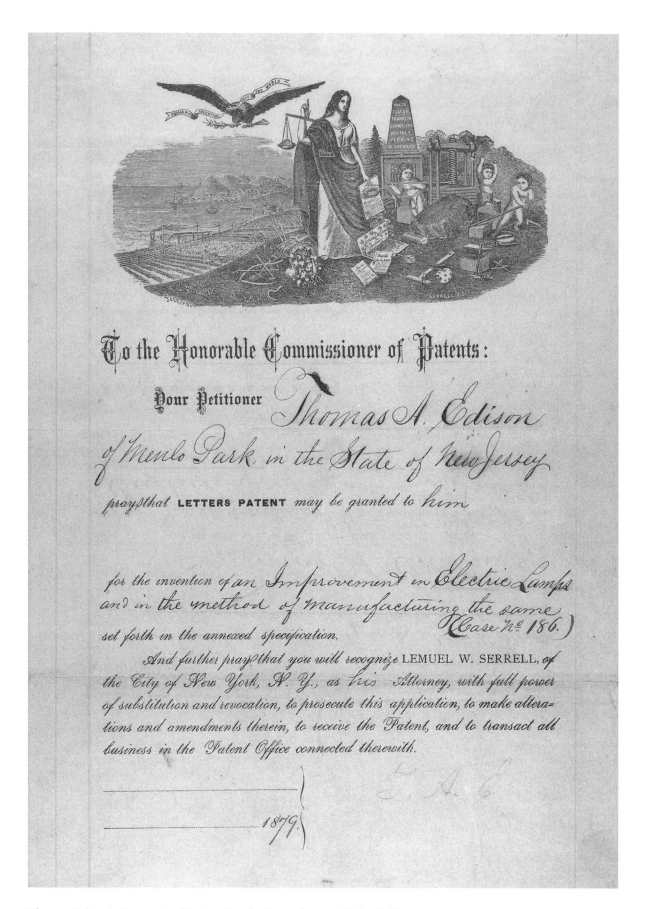

Thomas Edison's Patent Application for the Incandescent Light Bulb (National Archives and Records Administration)

Thomas Edison's Patent Application for the Incandescent Light Bulb

"I, Thomas Alva Edison, ...
have invented an improvement on Electric Lamps."

Overview

In the late 1870s gaslight was the primary means used to light residential homes and most businesses. Electric lighting had been conceived of decades earlier, but no one had been able to produce electric lighting in a safe, feasible, affordable manner. A number of inventors were working on this problem, but Thomas Edison was the first to develop a long-lasting, practical light bulb. His patent application for that light bulb was filed with the United States Patent Office on November 4, 1879, and his patent was granted on January 27, 1880.

Edison's patent on an "Improvement in Electric Lamps" gave him the right to exclude anyone else from making, using, or selling his improved light-bulb technology. As a practical matter, it also provided Edison with the opportunity to raise the funding necessary to develop the electric generation and distribution infrastructure necessary to power electric lighting. Power generation and electric lighting would develop hand in hand to light America, and the Edison Electric Light Company would eventually merge with other companies to become General Electric.

Context

Thomas Edison was the first person to apply the methods of mass production to the process of invention. He did so by creating what could be considered the first industrial research laboratory, employing many scientists and engineers, all of whom were engaged in continual research and development. Edison's research laboratory turned out many significant inventions, including the phonograph, the improved light bulb, and the moving motion picture.

Edison's research laboratory approach was critical to his improvement of the light bulb. The key challenge facing the development of a usable light bulb at the time was the creation of a long-lasting filament. Incandescent light works by passing an electric current through a filament. The filament heats up, causing it to emit photons, which generate light. While incandescent light bulbs had been invented around the turn of the nineteenth century, the light lasted only briefly—the best of them lasted several hours—because the filaments rapidly burned out as the result of oxidation. Electric arc lamps also existed in the early 1800s, but these lamps required a large amount of power, produced intensely bright light, and were dangerous for residential or small-scale use. Into the 1870s a practical electric light bulb continued to elude inventors, and gaslight remained the lighting technology of the day. Infrastructure to manufacture, distribute, and use gaslight was well established.

Edison became involved in light-bulb research and development in the 1870s and purchased the patents of earlier innovators on which to build his work. Edison put a team of about ten researchers to work in his laboratory to develop longer-lasting filaments for light bulbs. He founded the Edison Electric Light Company in 1878 with funding from J. P. Morgan, several of the Vanderbilts, and other investors. After experimenting with a variety of metals, the industry standard at that time, the team turned to carbonized plant fibers. Members of Edison's team tested every vegetable growth that they could get their hands on. Edison contacted biologists from around the world to have them send various plants for testing. Over six thousand vegetable growths were tested in Edison's laboratory. Edison may have been referring to this effort when he said, "Results! Why, man, I have gotten a lot of results. I know several thousand things that won't work" (Cook, p. 693).

Edison was in a race against several other inventors also attempting to improve the incandescent light. His first successful test of the incandescent light was on October 22, 1879, with a carbonized filament that lasted about twelve hours. Edison continued to improve the light bulb and filed his patent application on November 4, 1879, less than two weeks after the first successful experiment.

In addition to his improvements on the light bulb, Edison invented new and better power stations and means of electrical distribution. The combination of Edison's inventions reshaped American society. Although it would take decades, electric lighting became the norm in residential homes, significantly increasing the safety, quality, and availability of lighting. Business operations were affected even more dramatically as it became easy for workers to

Time Line

1802
- Sir Humphry Davy invents the first incandescent light, using a platinum filament.

1809
- Davy invents the first electric arc lamp.

1841
- Frederick de Moleyns receives the first patent on an incandescent lamp, using powdered charcoal filament.

1847
- **February 11**
Thomas Alva Edison is born in Milan, Ohio.

1850
- Joseph Swan begins experimenting with electric light bulbs with carbonized paper filaments.

1859
- **Winter**
Edison gets a job selling newspapers and candy for the Grand Trunk Railroad. He sets up a chemistry lab and a printing press on the train.

1860
- Swan obtains a British patent on a partial vacuum incandescent lamp with a carbon filament.

1863
- **Spring**
Edison becomes a telegraph operator and begins to experiment with improvements to the telegraph.

1868
- **October 28**
Edison files his first patent application, for an automatic vote recorder. The patent is granted the following year.

1869
- **April–May**
Edison leaves his position as a telegraph operator. He moves to New York City, begins to focus on inventive activities, and patents several telegraph advances.

work at night, which eventually led to around-the-clock work shifts. The development of the electric industry also led to the installation of electric infrastructure throughout the country—the power stations and distribution networks necessary to deliver electricity to homes and businesses. This infrastructure, in turn, made possible the development of home appliances and electronic business equipment that again transformed residential and work life in the middle of the twentieth century.

About the Author

Thomas Alva Edison was born in Milan, Ohio, on February 11, 1847. His family moved to Port Huron, Michigan, when a new train line bypassed Milan. Edison had only three months of formal schooling; the rest of his education came from his mother's homeschooling and learning on his own. When Edison was young, he saved the child of a station agent from being struck by a train. Out of gratitude, the station agent trained Edison as a telegraph operator, and efforts to improve the telegraph were the start of Edison's career as an inventor. Edison's first patent, which did not prove commercially successful, was for an electric vote recorder. Various inventions followed, but Edison's first major accomplishment was the invention of the quadruplex telegraph, which he was able to sell to Western Union for ten thousand dollars. These funds allowed Edison to develop a research laboratory.

On Christmas Day in 1871 Edison married sixteen-year-old Mary Stilwell. The couple had three children before Mary died in 1884. On February 24, 1886, Edison married Mina Miller, who was herself the daughter of an inventor. Edison and his second wife had three children. Their first son, Charles, became president of his father's company (which he ran until it was sold in 1959) and later served in the cabinet of President Franklin D. Roosevelt and as governor of New Jersey.

Edison first achieved popular fame with the invention of the phonograph in 1877. The phonograph stunned the public—it was the first invention to record and reproduce sound and was unlike anything that existed at the time. Edison soon became known as "the Wizard of Menlo Park." (Menlo Park, New Jersey, was the location of his laboratory.) In addition to the improved light bulb and related electrical advances, Edison later invented the moving motion picture.

Edison received 1,093 U.S. patents as well as many patents in various European countries, making him one of the most prolific inventors of all time. His greatest contribution, however, may have been the development of the first industrial research laboratory. He was the first person to apply the methods of mass production to the process of invention. Edison's laboratory brought together electrical and chemical research divisions within a machine shop to create a wide variety of products. An 1887 newspaper article describes his laboratory as containing "eight thousand kinds of chemicals, every kind of screw made, every size of needle, every kind of cord or wire, hair of humans, horses, hogs, cows, rabbits, goats, minx, camels … silk in every texture, cocoons, various kinds of hoofs, shark's teeth, deer horns, tortoise shell … cork, resin, varnish and oil, ostrich feathers, a peacock's tail, jet, amber, rubber, all ores" and more (qtd. in Shulman, pp. 158–160). Edison died on October 18, 1931.

Explanation and Analysis of the Document

The essence of the patent system is a relatively simple bargain: An inventor discloses to the world the nature of his or her new invention and how it works in exchange for the right to exclude others from practicing the invention for a specified time. The potential to exclude others creates incentives for inventors to invest research and development resources into invention in the hope of being able to profit from technological advances.

Obtaining a patent starts with drafting and filing an application with the United States Patent and Trademark Office. In Edison's time it was called simply the United States Patent Office. Each patent contains claims, written by the patent applicant, that define the subject matter (invention) to which the inventor is claiming intellectual property rights. A patent examiner, a representative of the patent office, reviews the patent application claims to determine whether they are worthy of a patent. In order to receive a patent at the time of Edison's light-bulb application, an invention had to be useful and novel, represent an inventive advance over previous technology, and be adequately disclosed. In 1952 Congress changed the judicially created inventive advance requirement to the current "non-obvious" requirement. Today an invention must be useful, new, "non-obvious," and adequately disclosed to receive a patent. The adequate disclosure requirement mandates that an inventor disclose enough information about the invention so that a person in the field could practice the invention. This requirement ensures that the public receives its reward from the patent system—understanding the new technology.

If the patent examiner determines that the patent claims satisfy the patent validity requirements, a patent is granted. The patent owner then has the right to exclude anyone else from making, using, or selling the patented subject matter for a certain time. In Edison's day, the patent term was seventeen years from the date of patent grant; today the term is twenty years from the date of patent application. If the patent examiner does not believe the patent validity requirements are met, the applicant may try to convince the examiner otherwise or revise the patent to receive a grant.

The patent owner's right to prohibit anyone else from making, using, or selling the patented subject matter potentially allows the patent owner to charge high prices for the invention or to license to others the right to make the invention. When Edison's Improvement in Electric Lamps patent was granted, it gave him monopoly control over the manufacture and sale of the incandescent light bulb he had invented.

Time Line

1870

- **February 15**
Edison moves to Newark, New Jersey, and opens a telegraph manufacturing and invention shop.

1875

- Edison separates his research laboratory from his manufacturing shop. He invents the electric pen (an early copying device) and various additional advances in the telegraph. Edison also announces the discovery of "etheric force." (He was actually observing the behavior of radio waves.) His claim is controversial and is not accepted by the scientific community.

- **March 23**
Edison applies for a patent on the quadruplex telegraph, which can transmit four messages simultaneously. He later sells his patent to Western Union for $10,000 (far more than he expected to receive).

1876

- **January–March**
Using the profits from the sale of quadruplex telegraph patent, Edison establishes the first full-scale industrial research laboratory, in Menlo Park, New Jersey. The laboratory combines electrical and chemical laboratories with an experimental machine shop.

1877

- Edison invents the phonograph and the carbon transmitter, an improvement in telephone technology.

1878

- **October 16**
Edison founds the Edison Electric Light Company.

1879

- **January**
Edison invents the direct-current generator for incandescent electric lighting.

- **October 22**
The first successful test of Edison's new carbon-filament light bulb is accomplished.

- **November 4**
Edison files his application on an improvement on the electric light bulb.

Time Line

1879

■ **December 31**
Edison demonstrates his light bulb publicly for the first time.

1880

■ **January 27**
Edison's light-bulb patent is granted.

■ **October 1**
Edison sets up a factory to manufacture electric light bulbs.

1882

■ **September 4**
Edison Electric Light Company's first electricity generation station begins operation, providing electricity to fifty-nine customers in Lower Manhattan.

1888

■ Edison engages in a "war of the currents" with George Westinghouse as Edison challenges the safety of the new alternating-current electric systems versus Edison's direct current electricity. Alternating current would eventually become dominant.

1889

■ **April 24**
The Edison Electric Light Company merges with several of Edison's other electricity generation and distribution companies to become the Edison General Electric Company.

1892

■ **April 15**
Edison General Electric merges with the Thomson-Houston Company. The combined companies become General Electric. Edison effectively leaves the electric operations business.

1893

■ **February**
Edison invents and demonstrates the motion-picture system.

1931

■ **October 18**
Edison dies. The nation dims its light bulbs for one minute on the day of his funeral.

The patent claimed an improvement in electric lamps covering "a carbon filament or strip coiled and connected ... to platina contact wires." His application described use of a carbon filament of "cotton and linen thread, wood splints, papers coiled in various ways, ... and carbon in various forms, mixed with tar and rolled out into wires of various lengths and diameters." Edison made the first public demonstration of his light bulb in Menlo Park, New Jersey, on New Year's Eve 1879 and proclaimed, "We will make electricity so cheap that only the rich will burn candles" (Evans, p. 323). Edison actually discovered the best-performing carbonized vegetable growths after his patent issued—several species of bamboo. The carbonized bamboo filaments could be used to create incandescent light bulbs that would burn for 1,200 hours, far beyond the existing state of technology and other carbonized fibers. Edison received a patent on his bamboo improvement in 1881.

Audience

Edison's patent application was written for an extremely small audience: the patent-examining corps at the United States Patent Office who would decide whether Edison would receive a patent. Edison's patent was also written with an eye toward competitors and the judicial system, as the patent claims would define his intellectual property rights, if granted.

Impact

The practical incandescent light bulb is one of the most transformative patented inventions of all time. Safe, effective lighting became generally affordable for widespread residential use for the first time. Business operations also changed dramatically as workers were able to work more easily at night, eventually leading to shifts that could operate around the clock. Edison did not invent the light bulb, though he is more appropriately credited with having "lit up the world."

Edison's and others' light-bulb patents were the subject of lengthy and costly patent litigation over rights to various incandescent light improvements. Edison's patent was invalidated by the United States Patent Office in 1883 based on prior inventions by William Sawyer but then reinstated in 1889 by a judge who held that Edison had a valid patent claim for the improvement of electric light with a high-resistance carbon filament. The judge reasoned that Edison "was the first to make a carbon of materials and by a process which was especially designed to impart high specific resistance to it; the first to make a carbon in the special form for the special purpose of imparting to it high total resistance; and the first to combine such a burner with the necessary adjuncts of lamp construction to prevent its disintegration and give it sufficiently long life" ("Edison's Patent Upheld," p. 2). Problematically from a patent law perspective, the judge's opinion was based on the advantages of a carbonized

"*To all whom it may concern: Be it known that I, Thomas Alva Edison, of Menlo Park, in the State of New Jersey, United States of America, have invented an improvement on Electric Lamps.*"

(Paragraph 1)

"*The object of this invention is to produce electric lamps giving light by incandescence, which lamps shall have high resistance, so as to allow of the practical subdivision of the electric light.*"

(Paragraph 1)

bamboo filament, which was not included in the patent claims in the relevant patent or invented by Edison until several months after his patent was granted.

Related light-bulb litigation concerned Edison's challenge to the patent on William Sawyer's aforementioned light-bulb invention, which was owned by Sawyer and Man Electric Company. Edison claimed that the Sawyer and Man patent was invalid, and this case went all the way to the U.S. Supreme Court. As noted in *Consolidated Electric Light Company v. McKeesport Light Company*, Sawyer and Man's patent claimed an "incandescing conductor for an electric lamp, of carbonized fibrous or textile material." Sawyer and Man had actually used carbonized paper in their particular incandescent lamp but claimed all "carbonized fibrous or textile material" in their patent. Edison argued that the Sawyer and Man patent was too broad, because they had not actually enabled the use of all the thousands of types of carbonized fibrous materials or a method for discovering which ones would work. In order to obtain a patent, part of the adequate disclosure requirement mandates that the patent application enable persons in the relevant field "to make and use" the invention. The core of Edison's argument was that carbonized bamboo was a type of carbonized fibrous material but that Sawyer and Man had not enabled the use of carbonized bamboo because others in the field would not know to use it. Edison's strong evidence on this point was that he needed to test over six thousand vegetable growths, gathered from around the world, to determine that bamboo worked best. In other words, Sawyer and Man had not taught and were not themselves aware of everything that they were trying to claim in their patent. Edison effectively was arguing that Sawyer and Man had invented only the use of carbonized paper as a filament and not a broad class of materials. The Supreme Court sided with Edison, holding Sawyer and Man's patent invalid for lack of enablement. As the Supreme Court explained, "If the description be so vague and uncertain that no one can tell, except by independent experiments, how to construct the patented device, the patent is void" (*Consolidated Electric Light Company v. McKeesport Light Company* [159 U.S. 465 (1895)]). This patent holding remains an important decision in patent law today.

Edison was less successful in Britain. His corresponding British light-bulb patent was defeated by Joseph Swan, who patented a similar light bulb in Britain several months before Edison's U.S. or British patent. Some credit Swan with having made the critical light-bulb improvements often attributed to Edison. After this decision, Edison and Swan merged their light companies in Britain, and Edison eventually purchased Swan's interest. As with most inventions, many inventors contributed to the development of the electric light. Edison's light-bulb contribution, contained partially in his patent, was the combination of a more effective filament with a better vacuum, which produced a much longer-lasting and less expensive incandescent light.

By the end of 1880, Edison had developed a sixteen-watt light bulb that could last for 1,500 hours. Later light-bulb improvements by others included the use of inert gas in the light bulb, which reduced the pressure on the bulb glass, and the use of tungsten as a filament. Edison had experimented with tungsten when his team was initially trying all varieties of filaments, but the tools necessary to work with it in the manner required did not yet exist. Edison's most important contribution to electric lighting actually may have been his development of a system of electricity distribution, including the invention of a new electric generator and better means of electricity distribution, which combined with the light bulb to produce commercially feasible lighting for the first time. Owning the light-bulb patent was critical to Edison's being able to secure investment for these continued advances. Edison was the one who put everything together to develop practical, affordable lighting.

Edison began to commercialize his light bulbs in 1881. His first electricity-generation station began operation in

A 1911 photograph of Thomas Edison (Library of Congress)

1882, providing electricity to fifty-nine customers in Lower Manhattan. The following year, the first incandescent lighting system using overhead wires started lighting Roselle, New Jersey. The continued high cost of electricity and its support infrastructure, however, meant that electrical development progressed slowly. By 1889, ten years after Edison's patent application, Edison Electric had more than one hundred power stations and more than seven hundred customers. Then costs came down, and development began to speed up. Ten years later, in 1899, there were more than three million electric customers. It would take about fifty years from the date of Edison's patent application for electric light to reach one-quarter of the U.S. population.

Edison was one of the foremost inventors of all time. His inventions not only transformed diverse aspects of all Americans' lives but also played a significant role in a period of extraordinary technological advance in the United States that led to America's becoming one of the world's superpowers. In 1889 the Edison Electric Light Company merged with several of Edison's other companies involved in electricity generation and distribution to become the Edison General Electric Company. Three years later, Edison General Electric merged with a large electric competitor, and the combined companies became General Electric. Owing to a disagreement, perhaps over Edison's name being dropped from the company name, Edison ended his general involvement with General Electric's operations and electric lighting development. Gen-

eral Electric is now the sixth-largest company in the United States, generating $168 billion in revenue annually. General Electric is the only company in the Dow Jones Industrial Index today that was also included in the original index in 1896.

Related Documents

Consolidated Electric Light Company v. McKeesport Light Company, 159 U.S. 465 (1895). The Supreme Court decision in which Edison's discovery of carbonized bamboo filaments served to invalidate a potentially competing electric light patent owned by Sawyer and Man Electric Company.

Edison, Thomas. *Improvement in Electric Lamps.* U.S. Patent 214,636, filed Nov. 4, 1879, and issued Jan. 27, 1880. Thomas Edison's first patent on electric lights.

———. *Carbon for Electric Lamps.* U.S. Patent 251,540, filed August 6, 1880, and issued Dec. 27, 1881. Edison's patent on the use of carbonized bamboo filaments, the advance that really increased the longevity of incandescent lamps.

Sawyer, William, and Albon Man. *Electric Light.* U.S. Patent 317,676, filed Jan. 9, 1880, and issued May 12, 1885. Sawyer and Man's patent unsuccessfully asserted against Edison's Improvement in Electric Lamps patent.

———. *Improvement in Electric Lamps.* U.S. Patent 205,144, filed May 16, 1888, and issued June 18, 1878. Sawyer and Man's patent on incandescent lights using "carbonized fibrous or textile material," which would eventually be invalidated by the U.S. Supreme Court in a challenge by Edison.

Bibliography

■ Articles
"Edison's Patent Upheld." *New York Times,* July 15, 1891.

■ Books
Baldwin, Neil. *Edison: Inventing the Century.* New York: Hyperion Books, 1995.

Collins, Theresa M., and Lisa Gitelman. *Thomas Edison and Modern America: A Brief History with Documents.* New York: Palgrave Macmillan, 2002.

Cook, John. *The Book of Positive Quotations.* 2nd edition. Minneapolis, Minn.: Fairview Press, 2007.

Evans, Harold. *They Made America: From the Steam Engine to the Search Engine: Two Centuries of Innovators.* New York: Little, Brown and Company, 2004.

Jonnes, Jill. *Empires of Light: Edison, Tesla, Westinghouse, and the Race to Electrify the World.* New York: Random House, 2003.

LIGHT THROWN ON A DARK SUBJECT.
(Which is Bad for the Gas Companies.)

In this drawing from 1878, Thomas Edison, with his newly invented electric light bulb, throws light on the gas company monopoly, personified by two men with monstrous gas-meter heads. (Library of Congress)

Josephson, Matthew. *Edison: A Biography.* Reprint. New York: John Wiley and Sons, 1992.

McCormick, Blaine. *At Work with Thomas Edison: 10 Business Lessons from America's Greatest Innovator.* Irvine, Calif.: Entrepreneur Press, 2001.

Shulman, Seth. *Owning the Future.* Boston: Houghton Mifflin, 1999.

Yenne, William, and Morton Grosser, eds. *100 Inventions That Shaped World History.* San Francisco: Bluewood Books, 1993.

■ **Web Sites**

"Consequences of Edison's Lamp." Smithsonian's National Museum of American History "Lighting a Revolution" Web site. http://americanhistory.si.edu/lighting/19thcent/consq19.htm. Accessed on August 3, 2007.

"Inventions Shape the Future." Edisonian Museum Web site. http://www.edisonian.com. Accessed on August 3, 2007.

"Light Bulb." The Great Idea Finder Web site. http://www.ideafinder.com/history/inventions/lightbulb.htm. Accessed on August 7, 2007.

Rutgers University "Edison Papers" Web site. http://edison.rutgers.edu/. Accessed on August 3, 2007.

"A Spark … of Brilliance." The Franklin Institute "Resources for Science Learning" Web site. http://sln.fi.edu/qa98/attic12/attic12.html. Accessed on August 3, 2007.

"Timeline of Thomas Edison's Life." PBS American Experience Web site. http://www.pbs.org/wgbh/amex/edison/timeline/index.html. Accessed on August 3, 2007.

—By Gregory N. Mandel

Questions for Further Study

1. Some reviews of the development of the incandescent light bulb conclude that there were more than twenty inventors outside Edison's laboratory who contributed to the development of the light bulb. Why do you think Edison is commonly credited as the inventor of the light bulb? Is it appropriate that Edison reaped substantial rewards if he was the one who made the final crucial advance? Is it appropriate that Edison reaped substantial rewards if he was the one who figured out how to provide the necessary infrastructure for practical incandescent light? Is it appropriate that Edison receives the public recognition as the inventor of the electric light?

2. If Edison had not invented the practical incandescent light or if the United States Patent Office had denied Edison's patent application, how do you think history would have been different?

3. Can you think of any other inventions that affected society to as great an extent as the practical incandescent light?

4. A patent is a functional document; it creates legal rights. Other fundamental documents in the history of the United States, such as the Constitution and its amendments and U.S. Supreme court decisions, are also functional. Many documents, however, are not functional, among them Patrick Henry's "Liberty or Death" Speech, the Federalist Papers, and Abraham Lincoln's First Inaugural Address. What are the similarities and differences between how functional and nonfunctional documents affect society?

Glossary

carbonized	converted or reduced to carbon, such as by partial burning
electric lamp	historic term for a light bulb
fibrous	made of fibers
filament	a thin fiber or wire that is heated to incandescence by passing an electric current through it
incandescent	producing radiation (light) through heating
moving motion picture	a movie
patent	a right to exclude others from making or using claimed technology
patent office	a government office that evaluates patent applications and grants patents
quadruplex telegraph	a telegraph machine that could send four messages at once, two in each direction.

Thomas Edison's Patent Application for the Incandescent Light Bulb

Electric Lamp: Specification Forming Part of Letters Patent No. 223,898, dated January 27, 1880. Application filed November 4, 1879.

To all whom it may concern:

Be it known that I, THOMAS ALVA EDISON, of Menlo Park, in the State of New Jersey, United Sates of America, have invented an Improvement in Electric Lamps, and in the method of manufacturing the same, (Case No. 186,) of which the following is a specification.

The object of this invention is to produce electric lamps giving light by incandescence, which lamps shall have high resistance, so as to allow of the practical subdivision of the electric light.

The invention consists in a light giving body of carbon wire or sheets coiled or arranged in such a manner as to offer great resistance to the passage of the electric current, and at the same time present but a slight surface from which radiation can take place.

The invention further consists in placing such burner of great resistance in a nearly perfect vacuum to prevent oxidation and injury to the conductor by the atmosphere. The current is conducted into the vacuum-bulb through platina wires sealed into the glass.

The invention further consists in the method of manufacturing carbon conductors of high resistance, so as to be suitable for giving light by incandescence, and in the manner of securing perfect contact between the metallic conductors or leading-wires and the carbon conductor.

Heretofore light by incandescence has been obtained from rods of carbon of one to four ohms resistance, placed in closed vessels, in which the atmospheric air has been replaced by gases that do not combine chemically with the carbon. The vessel holding the burner has been composed of glass cemented to a metallic base. The connection between the leading wires and the carbon has been obtained by clamping the carbon to the metal. The leading-wires have always been large, so that their

resistance shall be many times less than the burner, and, in general, the attempts of previous persons have been to reduce the resistance of the carbon rod. The disadvantages of following this practices are, that a lamp having but one to four ohms resistance cannot be worked in great numbers in multiple arc without the employment of main conductors of enormous dimensions; that, owing to the low resistance of the lamp, the leading-wires must be of large dimensions and good conductors, and a glass globe cannot be kept tight at the place where the wires pass in and are cemented; hence the carbon is consumed, because there must be almost a perfect vacuum to render the carbon stable, especially when such carbon is small in mass and high in electrical resistance.

The use of a gas in the receiver at the atmospheric pressure, although not attacking the carbon, serves to destroy it in time by "air-washing," or the attrition produced by the rapid passage of the air over the slightly-coherent highly-heated surface of the carbon. I have reversed this practice. I have discovered that even a cotton thread properly carbonized and placed in a sealed glass bulb exhausted to one-millionth of an atmosphere offers from one hundred to five hundred ohms resistance to the passage of the current, and that it is absolutely stable at very high temperatures; that if the thread be coiled as a spiral and carbonized, or if any fibrous vegetable substance which will leave a carbon residue after heating in a closed chamber be so coiled, as much as two thousand ohms resistance may be obtained without presenting a radiating-surface greater than three-sixteenths of an inch; that if such fibrous material be rubbed with a plastic composed of lamp-black and tar, its resistance may be made high or low, according to the amount of lamp-black placed upon it; that carbon filaments may be made by a combination of tar and lamp-black, the latter being previously ignited in a closed crucible for several hours and afterward moistened and kneaded until it assumes the consistency of thick putty. Small pieces of this material may be rolled out in the form of wire as small as seven one-thousandths of a inch in diameter and over a foot in length, and the same may be counted with a non-conducting non-carbonizing substance and wound on a bobbin, or as a spiral, and the tar carbonized in a closed chamber by subjecting it to high heat, the spiral after carbonization retaining its form.

All these forms are fragile and cannot be clamped to the leading wires with sufficient force to insure good contact and prevent beating. I have discovered that if platinum wires are used and the plastic lamp black and tar material be molded around it in the act of carbonization there is an intimate union by combination and by pressure between the carbon and platina, and nearly perfect contact is obtained without the necessity of clamps; hence the burner and the leading-wires are connected to the carbon ready to be placed in the vacuum-bulb.

When fibrous material is used the plastic lamp black and tar are used to secure it to the platina before carbonizing.

By using the carbon wire of such high resistance I am enabled to use fine platinum wires for leading-wires, as they will have a small resistance compared to the burner, and hence will not heat and crack the sealed vacuum-bulb. Platina can only be used as its expansion is nearly the same as that of glass.

By using a considerable length of carbon wire and coiling it the exterior, which is only a small portion of its entire surface, will form the principal radiating-surface; hence I am able to raise the specific heat of the whole of the carbon, and thus prevent the rapid reception and disappearance of the light, which on a plain wire is prejudicial, as it shows the least unsteadiness of the current by the flickering of the light; but if the current is steady the defect does not show.

I have carbonized and used cotton and linen thread, wood splints, papers coiled in various ways, also lamp-black, plumbago, and carbon in various forms, mixed with tar and kneaded so that the same may be rolled out into wires of various lengths and diameters. Each wire, however, is to be uniform in size throughout.

If the carbon thread is liable to be distorted during carbonization it is to be coiled between a helix of copper wire. The ends of the carbon or filament are secured to the platina leading-wires by plastic carbonizable material, and the whole placed in the carbonizing-chamber. The copper, which has served to prevent distortion of the carbon thread, is afterward eaten away by nitric acid, and the spiral soaked in water, and then dried and placed on the glass holder, and a glass bulb blown over the whole, with a leading-tube for exhaustion by a mercury-pump. This tube, when a high vacuum has been reached, is hermetically sealed.

With substances which are not greatly distorted in carbonizing, they may be coated with a non-conducting non-carbonizable substance, which allows one coil or turn of the carbon to rest upon and be supported by the other.

In the drawings, Figure 1 shows the lamp sectionally. a is the carbon spiral or thread. $c\ c'$ are the thickened ends of the spiral, formed of the plastic compound of lamp-black and tar. $d\ d'$ are the platina wires. $h\ h$ are the clamps, which serve to connect the platina wires, cemented in the carbon, with the leading-wires $x\ x$, sealed in the glass vacuum-bulb. $e\ e$ are copper wires, connected just outside the bulb to the wires $x\ x$. m is the tube (shown by dotted lines) leading to the vacuum-pump, which, after exhaustion, is hermetically sealed and the surplus removed.

Fig. 2 represents the plastic material before being wound into a spiral.

Fig. 3 shows the spiral after carbonization, ready to have a bulb blown over it.

I claim as my invention—

1. An electric lamp for giving light by incandescence, consisting of a filament of carbon of high resistance, made as described, and secured to metallic wires, as set forth.

2. The combination of carbon filaments with a receiver made entirely of glass and conductors passing through the glass, and from which receiver the air is exhausted, for the purposes set forth.

3. A carbon filament or strip coiled and connected to electric conductors so that only a portion of the surface of such carbon conductors shall be exposed for radiating light, as set forth.

The method herein described of securing the platina contact-wires to the carbon filament and carbonizing of the whole in a closed chamber, substantially as set forth.

Signed by me this 1st day of November, A.D. 1879.

THOMAS A. EDISON

Witnesses:

S. L. GEIFFIN, JOHN F. RANDOLPH

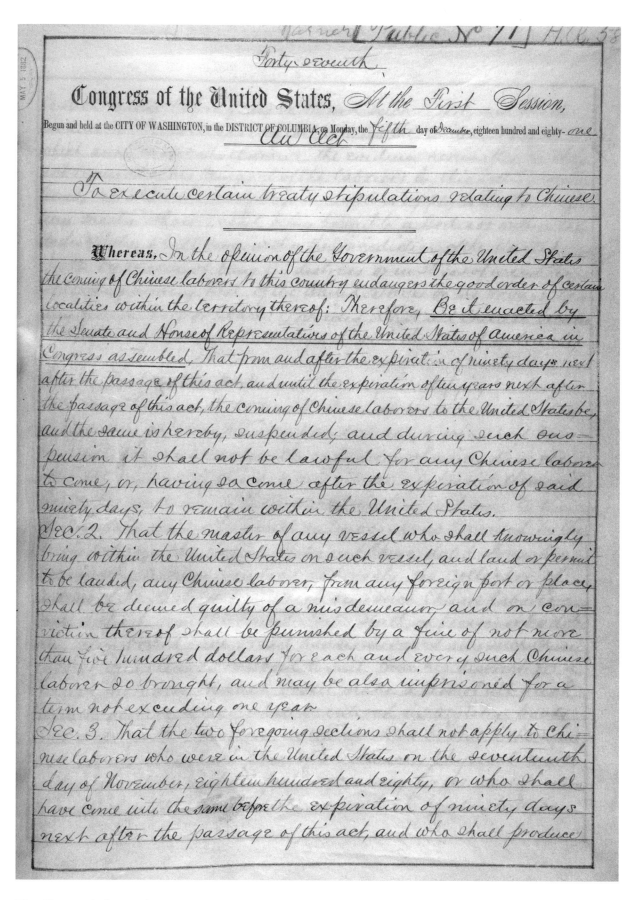

Forty-seventh

Congress of the United States, At the First Session,

Begun and held at the CITY OF WASHINGTON, in the DISTRICT OF COLUMBIA, on Monday, the *fifth* day of *December*, eighteen hundred and eighty-*one*

An Act

To execute certain treaty stipulations relating to Chinese.

Whereas, In the opinion of the Government of the United States the coming of Chinese laborers to this country endangers the good order of certain localities within the territory thereof: Therefore, Be it enacted by the Senate and House of Representatives of the United States of America in Congress assembled, That from and after the expiration of ninety days next after the passage of this act, and until the expiration of ten years next after the passage of this act, the coming of Chinese laborers to the United States be, and the same is hereby, suspended; and during such suspension it shall not be lawful for any Chinese laborer to come, or, having so come after the expiration of said ninety days, to remain within the United States.

SEC. 2. That the master of any vessel who shall knowingly bring within the United States on such vessel, and land or permit to be landed, any Chinese laborer, from any foreign port or place, shall be deemed guilty of a misdemeanor, and on conviction thereof shall be punished by a fine of not more than five hundred dollars for each and every such Chinese laborer so brought, and may be also imprisoned for a term not exceeding one year.

SEC. 3. That the two foregoing sections shall not apply to Chinese laborers who were in the United States on the seventeenth day of November, eighteen hundred and eighty, or who shall have come into the same before the expiration of ninety days next after the passage of this act, and who shall produce

The **Chinese Exclusion Act** (National Archives and Records Administration)

CHINESE EXCLUSION ACT

"The coming of Chinese laborers to this country endangers the good order of certain localities."

Overview

Whether or not the United States is a melting pot—a mixing of diverse racial and ethnic groups—has long been the subject of debate. One challenge to this metaphor arose in the late 1800s, when a movement developed to stop the influx of Chinese laborers. Congress responded by passing the Chinese Exclusion Act of 1882. This act and the ensuing legislation that lengthened and strengthened its provisions legitimated the exclusion of a particular group from this country based on race and ethnicity.

The Chinese had come to the United States to work. Disembarking on the West Coast, Chinese laborers helped build that part of the nation. They contributed their talents and energies, but a place in American society was not part of the bargain. As their numbers increased and as white workers felt pressure from an economic downturn, derision and violence were directed toward the Chinese. Congress acted not to protect the Chinese but to bar their entry to the United States.

Context

Among the many people flocking to California in the 1840s and onward were large numbers of Chinese immigrants who took the long voyage from Asia to the West Coast of the United States to find work. Immigrating at high rates throughout the decades ahead, these men (for the great majority of Chinese immigrants were male) worked in the mines, on railroad construction, as farmers, and in cities. They helped build the western states and territories.

In the 1870s economic hard times hit the nation. Chinese laborers became targets of hostile campaigns mounted by labor leaders, fanned by political candidates, and supported by white workers. The Chinese were perceived to work hard for low wages. In the eyes of white workers that made them the enemies of good wages and secure jobs. The Chinese were thought to embody alien ways of living, thinking, and worshipping, which made them unsuited for inclusion in American society. On editorial pages and in political speeches, Chinese laborers were ridiculed and reviled. In some places whites violently opposed the presence of Chinese workers.

A movement to exclude Chinese laborers from entering the United States began during these times and quickly gained momentum. In the late 1870s, Congress took up the issue by commissioning fact finding and by holding debates. Legislation was drafted, but, for a time, treaties already existing between the United States and China stood squarely in the way of attempts to legislatively exclude Chinese laborers. By 1882 treaty amendments had removed those impediments because of a favorable political climate and diplomatic arrangements permitting a law to keep a group of people out of the country whose industry and ways of life offended the dominant culture. In April, Congress passed the Chinese Exclusion Act. On May 6, 1882, President Chester Arthur signed into law a bill that denied entry to the United States on the basis of race and ethnicity.

About the Author

The Chinese Exclusion Act of 1882 was drafted, debated, and voted on in the early months of the first session of the Forty-seventh Congress. John F. Miller, a Republican from California serving his first term, introduced the bill in the Senate. It quickly passed in that chamber and then in the House. Following its veto by President Chester Arthur, the bill was amended to meet the president's objections, passed by the Senate and House again, and signed into law. The speedy passage of the bill and efficient response to the president's veto were the product of two prior developments contributing to the content of the act.

First, in prior sessions of Congress, the issue of Chinese exclusion was explored and debated in depth. In 1876 Congress had appointed a joint special committee to study Chinese immigration and dispatched its members to California to investigate the "Chinese question." Aaron A. Sargent, Republican Senator from California, authored the committee's report; its findings supported the campaign for Chinese exclusion. Second, treaty arrangements between the United States and China were changed in 1880 to permit the legislation. James B. Angell, a minister to China during

Time Line

1868

■ **July 28**
The Burlingame Treaty is signed, assuring Chinese the right to travel and reside in the United States.

1877

■ **February 27**
A report on Chinese immigration by the Joint Special Congressional Committee to Investigate Chinese Immigration is released, disparaging the presence of Chinese laborers in the United States.

1879

■ **March 1**
The Fifteen Passenger Bill, limiting the number of Chinese laborers on a ship coming to the United States, is vetoed by President Rutherford B. Hayes because it is inconsistent with the Burlingame Treaty.

1880

■ **November 17**
The Angell Treaty is signed, amending the Burlingame Treaty to permit the United States to limit the immigration of Chinese laborers.

1882

■ **May 6**
The Chinese Exclusion Act is signed by President Arthur; it suspends entry of Chinese laborers into United States for ten years and puts conditions on reentry of Chinese laborers who leave the United States.

1888

■ **October 1**
The Scott Act is signed by President Grover Cleveland and bars the reentry of Chinese laborers into the United States who have left the country.

1892

■ **May 5**
The Geary Act is signed by President Benjamin Harrison, extending the Chinese Exclusion Act of 1882 for ten years and strengthening its enforcement.

---

the Hayes administration, headed the commission that negotiated amendments to existing treaties. The resulting Angell Treaty allowed the United States to legislate limits on Chinese immigration.

Explanation and Analysis of the Document

◆ Background and Opening Section

To make possible the Chinese Exclusion Act of 1882 required Congress to bring into synch its legislation to exclude Chinese with treaty provisions between the nations. Treaties had to be changed to permit greater restriction on Chinese migration, and legislation to exclude the Chinese had to be tailored to match those changes. Only then could Congress successfully usher into law An Act to Execute Certain Treaty Stipulations relating to Chinese.

The Treaty of Tien-tsin, signed in 1858, had opened Chinese cities to U.S. diplomatic, trade, and Christian missionary efforts but gave few concessions to China in return. Negotiations to amend those arrangements, begun at China's behest, resulted in the Burlingame Treaty, negotiated and signed in 1868. Among its provisions was the assurance that "Chinese subjects visiting or residing in the United States shall enjoy the same privileges, immunities, and exemptions in respect to travel or residence, as may there be enjoyed by the citizens or subjects of the most favored nation" (Article VI).

This provision, argued Representative Edwin Meade of New York in 1876 during U.S. House debates concerning Chinese exclusion, precluded Congress from passing "laws prohibiting or restricting Chinese immigration … without first obtaining the concurrence of the Chinese Government itself" (Miller, p. 217). While bills restricting Chinese immigration were introduced in that session of Congress and again during the next session (1877–1878), none passed. In 1879 Representative Albert Willis from Kentucky offered grounds to dispute the view that the Burlingame Treaty did not permit legislation to exclude Chinese. The power to make treaties was limited by certain "objects for which the Constitution was formed," including "the general welfare, justice, domestic tranquility, and the blessings of liberty," which, Willis argued, "cannot be taken from the people by any treaty however solemnly ratified." Here and now, he said, "the presence of the Chinese endangers the peace and prosperity of our people" (Miller, 220).

Despite Willis's arguments to the contrary, existing treaty arrangements stood as a barrier to Chinese exclusion. Early in 1879 Congress passed the Fifteen Passenger Bill, constricting Chinese immigration by limiting the number of Chinese passengers permitted on board any ship making harbor in an American port. President Rutherford B. Hayes vetoed the bill, and Congress failed to override it. In his veto message, Hayes reasoned that this manner of inhibiting Chinese immigration was neither constitutionally proper nor politically sound. First, by offending the provision of the Burlingame Treaty that protected free immigration by Chinese to the United States the legislation made a new treaty;

treaty making is a presidential and not a congressional power. Second, any change in the Burlingame Treaty that amended the Treaty of Tien-tsin, meant that China no longer would be obliged to supply protections to U.S. citizens in China ensured by the latter instrument.

President Hayes's veto of the Fifteen Passenger Bill, however, did not mean that he was against restricting Chinese immigration. His veto message to Congress expressly stated that provisions of the Burlingame Treaty might require change—meaning tighter restrictions on permission for Chinese to travel to and reside in the United States.

In very short order, the Angell Treaty, negotiated by the Hayes administration in the fall of 1880, supplied the means for Congress to restrict Chinese immigration. "Whenever in the opinion of the Government of the United States, the coming of Chinese laborers to the United States, or their residence therein, affects or threatens to affect the interests of that country or of any locality within the territory thereof," reads Article I of the Angell Treaty, "the Government of China agrees that the Government of the United States may regulate, limit, or suspend such coming or residence, but may not absolutely prohibit it." On a pedestal constructed of this provision the Congress sets squarely its "Act to Execute Certain Treaty Stipulations relating to Chinese."

Tailored neatly to the Angell Treaty's precondition for limiting Chinese migration, the act's first sentence in the opening section reads: "Whereas in the opinion of the Government of the United States the coming of Chinese laborers to this country endangers the good order of certain localities within the territory thereof." The campaign to exclude Chinese began and was most vociferous on the West Coast, where the majority of Chinese laborers in the United States lived and worked. In 1876, at the request of congressmen from the West Coast states, members of a joint special congressional committee made a fact-finding visit to the West Coast. The committee's "Report on Chinese Immigration," issued in 1877, provided fodder for the government to form an opinion, five years later, on the necessity to exclude Chinese from the United States.

According to the report, in the localities where Chinese lived and worked, they endangered public health and safety. "They live in filthy dwellings, upon poor food, crowded together in narrow quarters, disregarding health and fire ordinances." Chinese laborers forced whites out of work and into economic ruin: "The Chinese have reduced wages to what would be starvation prices for white men and women, and engrossed so much of the labor in the various callings that there is a lack of employment for whites." The report also contended that the presence of the Chinese threatened free government: "An indigestible mass in the community, distinct in language, pagan in religion, inferior in mental and moral qualities, and all peculiarities, is an undesirable element in a republic, but becomes especially so if political power is placed in its hands." The solution "would seem to be that the laws should discourage the large influx of any class of population to whom the ballot cannot be safely confided" (Miller, pp. 212–213).

Time Line

1904

■ **April 27**
The Chinese Exclusion Extension Act of 1904 is signed by President Theodore Roosevelt and removes time limitations on the Chinese Exclusion Act of 1882.

1943

■ **December 17**
The Magnuson Act is signed by President Franklin D. Roosevelt and repeals the Chinese Exclusion Act and the Chinese Exclusion Extension Act, leaving Chinese immigration regulated by the quota system.

1965

■ **October 4**
The Immigration and Nationalization Act is signed by President Lyndon Baines Johnson and greatly increases the number of Chinese who may immigrate to the United States.

The opening section of the act concludes with the basic terms of such exclusion: that ninety days following passage of the act and for the next ten years, "the coming of Chinese laborers to the United States be … suspended." The ten-year suspension period permitted the legislation to clear a final hurdle. After the Angell Treaty was enacted, Congress's first exclusion bill suspended the immigration of Chinese laborers for twenty years. On April 4, President Arthur vetoed the bill. His primary objection to the legislation was that the twenty-year suspension was too long, in view of the Angell Treaty's provision permitting the United States to regulate, limit, or suspend Chinese immigration but not to prohibit it.

Following an unsuccessful vote to override the veto, Congress rewrote the legislation to suspend entry of Chinese laborers for ten years. This shorter period met with presidential approval, and on May 6, 1882, Arthur signed into law the Chinese Exclusion Act of 1882. The act made race and national origin the basis to exclude someone from entering the United States. The ten-year time frame proved no barrier to making Chinese exclusion a more permanent fixture of U.S. policy. One decade following the act's passage, Congress extended Chinese exclusion for another ten-year period when it passed the Geary Act in 1892. In 1904 Congress extended the policy again, this time with no limit.

◆ Section 2

This section makes the master of a vessel subject to criminal prosecution for bringing any Chinese laborer to land.

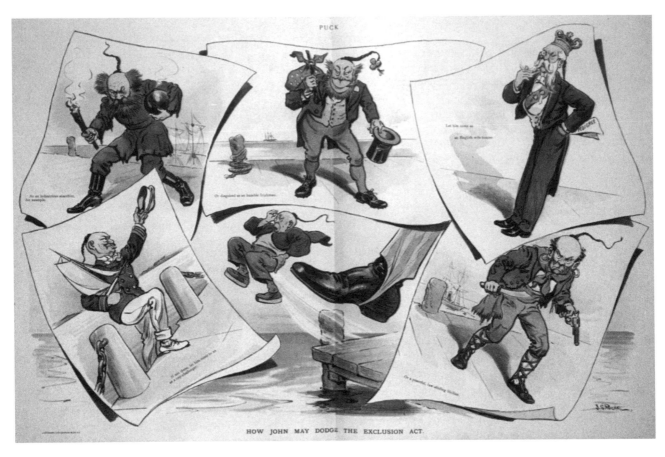

This drawing from 1905, titled "How John May Dodge the Exclusion Act," displays the hostile attitudes toward Chinese trying to immigrate to the United States. (Library of Congress)

◆ Section 3

To comply with the Burlingame Treaty (permitting Chinese subjects to travel to and reside in the United States) and the Angell Treaty (permitting the U.S. government to suspend but not prohibit Chinese laborers from coming to or residing in the United States), the Chinese Exclusion Act "shall not apply to Chinese laborers who were in the United States on the seventeenth day of November, eighteen hundred and eighty," the date the Angell Treaty was signed. Nor does the act apply to Chinese laborers "who shall have come into the same before the expiration of ninety days next after the passage of this act." Thus, Chinese laborers already in the United States were not expelled by the act.

In an important way, however, their ability to continue residence in the United States was highly regulated. The act required any Chinese laborer who leaves the country to produce, upon his return, evidence proving prior residence "to the collector of the port in the United States at which such vessel shall arrive." The collector was a U.S. customs official, and the scheme to identify laborers allowed to return was extremely complex.

◆ Sections 4 and 5

In Sections 4 and 5, Congress sets forth regulations "for the purpose of properly identifying Chinese laborers ... and

in order to furnish them with the proper evidence of their right to go from and come to the United States of their free will and accord." According to these sections, detailed information describing a laborer about to leave the country were to be recorded on a list prepared by the local collector of customs, and the laborer would receive a certificate from the collector. Upon return to the United States, the laborer would be required to produce that certificate, proving prior residence in the United States, "to the collector of customs of the district at which such Chinese laborer shall seek to re-enter."

The procedural labyrinth described in Sections 4 and 5 resulted in disorganized, underfunded, and inconsistent application of the act. The Treasury Department, which supervised customs officials, did not readily provide prescriptions for its enforcement. Because they were so detailed, the duties described in these two sections severely overburdened customs offices in West Coast ports. Customs collectors, operating without centralized planning and procedures, exercised local preference and discretion and enforced the act inconsistently. Some customs offices were accused of improperly excluding Chinese laborers. At other ports allegations arose that some Chinese fraudulently entered the country. Federal court dockets on the West Coast filled with hearings to determine the status of Chinese trying to reenter the United States who were detained under the act.

Congress responded with legislation that tightened the act's enforcement. The Exclusion Law of 1884, amending the 1882 act, established additional requirements for the evidence that customs collectors had to record when Chinese laborers left the United States and then use later to determine legal reentry. More dramatically, in the Scott Act of 1888, Congress barred Chinese laborers who left the United States from reentering at all.

◆ Section 6

Section 6 has the first reference to a "Chinese person other than a laborer who may be entitled by said treaty and this act to come within the United States." To construct the classes of Chinese persons exempt from the Chinese Exclusion Act of 1882, and thus permitted to travel to and reside in the United States, requires reading Sections 6, 13, and 15 in light of the Angell Treaty.

Section 13 of the act exempts "diplomatic and other officers of the Chinese Government traveling upon the business of that government" and their personal and household servants. Section 15 construes the term "Chinese laborers" broadly "to mean both skilled and unskilled laborers and Chinese employed in mining." This designation, though very inclusive, does not cover all Chinese who might visit the United States.

A higher class of Chinese is made exempt from the act by terms of the Angell Treaty, signed in 1880 and permitting the act's exclusion of laborers. Article II of that treaty allows "Chinese subjects, whether proceeding to the United States as teachers, students, merchants or from curiosity, together with their body and household servants" to freely travel to and from the United States. By not listing them in the act that excluded Chinese laborers, Congress kept this group of Chinese persons free of the act's reach. And by not listing merchants in the act, Congress protected profitable trade relations between the United States and China.

An individual could obtain a "Section 6 Certificate" from the Chinese government, which identified the holder as a member of an exempt class. Amid allegations that this status was being given to individuals not fitting the description, Congress included in its Exclusion Law of 1884 more specific requirements for awarding Section 6 certification.

◆ Section 7

The act recognizes the value of a "Section 6 Certificate," which exempted the holder from exclusion, by criminalizing fraudulent preparation or use of one. These were common practices.

◆ Section 8

The attempt to use ship officials to help administer the complex set of requirements the act put into place did not work well. Employees of the shipping companies were not always informed of the many regulations imposed by Congress and likely had less interest and expertise in carrying them out than did customs officials.

◆ Section 9

The act directs that upon arriving at port, but before passengers disembark, a customs official will board the ship and, using procedures previously described, identify any Chinese laborer excluded by the act. The customs official will instruct the master of the vessel to detain on board excluded laborers.

Many Chinese excluded under the act brought legal challenges, grounded in a strong and fundamental principle of U.S. law. Laborers excluded and detained on board might petition a federal court for a writ of habeas corpus, requiring the government to offer just grounds for their detainment. Federal courts took these petitions seriously. Many resulted in a court order to the collector to allow entry of the individual bringing the petition. This very active use of federal courts by Chinese to challenge their exclusion helped shape the act's enforcement, and the success of these legal efforts became an important, early chapter in the history of Asian Americans' struggle for rights in this system.

◆ Sections 10 and 11

In Sections 10 and 11, Congress outlines additional penalties for persons, including non-Chinese, violating or failing to enforce the act. The act relies heavily on a complex system of evidence, registration, and certification (see Sections 4, 5, 6, 8, and 9) to identify and keep out of the U.S. those Chinese laborers the act excluded. Alongside these attempts to accomplish the act's aim through administrative procedures, however, Congress also wrote into the act criminal sanctions to be imposed against anyone eluding or violating these procedures. To appreciate these procedures in full force, read the attempts in Sections 10 and 11 to compel adherence to the act by punishing anyone failing to do so alongside other punishments described in Sections 2, 7, and 8.

◆ Section 12

The hostility toward the Chinese that Congress expresses in the act is fully felt in this section. First, "no Chinese person shall be permitted to enter the United States by land without producing" in the proper way the required permission. A Chinese laborer wanting to come to the United States for the first time could not legally obtain permission. Returning Chinese laborers who qualified for the required permission confronted a complex and confusing system, one administrated with great inconsistency, created by the act to provide them their only legal means of reentry. Soon, even this road to reentry was closed. The Scott Act of 1888 barred reentry of Chinese laborers who had resided in the United States legally if they left the country.

Next, the act decrees that any Chinese person "found unlawfully within the United States" shall be removed. Zealous believers that Chinese laborers threatened the good order of the United States readily found empowerment in these words. Ten years later, stronger dictates were passed. The Geary Act of 1892 required any Chinese person residing in the United States who was arrested for vio-

"Whereas in the opinion of the Government of the United States the coming of Chinese laborers to this country endangers the good order of certain localities within the territory thereof."

(Opening Section)

"That from and after the expiration of ninety days next after the passage of this act, and until the expiration of ten years next after the passage of this act, the coming of Chinese laborers to the United States be, and the same is hereby, suspended; and during such suspension it shall not be lawful for any Chinese laborer to come, or having so come after the expiration of said ninety days to remain within the United States."

(Opening Section)

"That hereafter no State court or court of the United States shall admit Chinese to citizenship; and all laws in conflict with this act are hereby repealed."

(Section 14)

lating the act to prove that he or she lived lawfully in the United States. In other words, the government was not required to prove guilt; rather, the individual had to prove innocence. The Geary Act also required Chinese laborers then living in the United States, and not barred by the 1882 act from residing in the United States, to apply to the government for a certificate that proved legal residence.

◆ **Section 13**

The Treaty of Tien-tsin, signed in 1858, secured diplomatic relations with China. This section recognizes this treaty along with the practical necessity of permitting officials of the Chinese government to reside legally within the United States.

◆ **Section 14**

The act expressly denies naturalized citizenship to all Chinese, not just laborers. The sentiment ran strong in Congress and in the nation that Chinese were not fit to be citizens.

By adding the instruction that "all laws in conflict with this act are hereby repealed," Congress shows its determination to slam shut all doors on Chinese rights to naturalization. Statutes passed after the Civil War had extended naturalization rights, originally available only to whites, to per-

sons of African descent. Congress's intent here is to make it very clear that Chinese cannot become naturalized citizens.

Not addressed in the act, and a subject litigated in the years following its passage, is the question of whether a person of Chinese descent born in the United States is a citizen.

◆ **Section 15**

The broad construction expressly given in the term "Chinese laborers" demonstrates the long reach Congress intended the act to have. These laborers were the targets of hatred and hostility, and labor union leaders and white workers railed against them. Politicians and newspapers called for their exclusion. With the Chinese Exclusion Act of 1882, Congress responds to and these voices and makes them legitimate.

Audience

Early angry calls to exclude Chinese from the United States came from the West Coast, where most Chinese laborers lived and worked. The congressional committee whose fact-finding mission supported legislation to exclude the Chinese included a representative and a senator from California. A California senator introduced the bill that became the Chinese Exclusion Act of 1882. On the West Coast, white workers, labor leaders (among them, Denis Kearney, who notoriously fanned flames of hatred toward Chinese workers), newspaper editors, and politicians celebrated its passage and immediately began to lobby for changes to strengthen the act. The act, then, was written in part to please West Coast Americans who claimed it was necessary to preserve jobs and good wages for whites, to promote health and safety in cities, and to protect American society against alien influence.

The movement to exclude had support throughout the nation, however. Critics of Chinese laborers from the eastern and southern states, where far fewer Chinese lived, often cast the immigrants as a new class of slaves, undesirable in post-Civil War times. "It is servile labor," said James Blaine, Republican from Maine and in the forefront of the movement to exclude on the Senate floor during debates in 1879. "It is not free labor such as we intend to develop and encourage and build up in this country" (Miller, p. 251). Support for exclusion was far from unanimous, but it existed across the United States. Leaders from both major parties recognized in the movement to exclude a chance to attract electoral support, especially from the white working class. Thus, the Chinese Exclusion Act of 1882, which responded to highly organized protests on the West Coast, spoke to a national audience.

Impact

The Chinese Exclusion Act of 1882 curbed the influx of Chinese immigrants to the United States. It placed burdens on Chinese laborers living in the United States who wished to leave the country and then reenter. Laws passed to strengthen the 1882 act made reentry of laborers illegal and required laborers living in the United States to prove that their residence was legal. In the long run, these laws had profound, adverse effects on Chinese communities in the United States and on their relation to the larger society. The act and the exclusion laws passed after it were designed to reduce the number of Chinese in the United States and delivered on that intent. According to U.S. Census reports, the number of Chinese in the country grew from around sixty-three thousand in 1870 to between one hundred thousand and one hundred and ten thousand in 1880 and 1890. Less than ninety thousand Chinese were counted in the 1900 census, and the number fell to approximately seventy-two thousand in 1910 and to sixty-two thousand a decade later.

Because they were passed so soon after the original bill went into force, the laws to strengthen the 1882 act show that the forces pressing for exclusion inside and outside of Congress felt the original act had not effectively dealt with the so-called "Chinese question." Regardless of whether it satisfied supporters of exclusion, however, the 1882 act legitimated hostile treatment of a particular race and paved the way for more of the same. The push for subsequent legislation drew on the same racial and ethnic biases and

attacks motivating and inspiring support for the 1882 act. The laws passed to strengthen the 1882 act upped the ante in the campaign against Chinese laborers.

The act itself stayed in place, securing the exclusion of Chinese workers and limiting Chinese immigration to the United States, until World War II. The Magnuson Act, passed in 1943, repealed the Chinese Exclusion Laws passed in 1882, 1884, 1888, 1892, and 1904. Chinese immigration was then folded into the system regulating immigration from other countries, which set limits on the number permitted to enter according to national origin. The annual quota for Chinese immigration was set at 105 per year. Not until it passed the Immigration and Nationalization Act in 1965 did Congress liberalize the number of Chinese permitted to enter and reside in the United States.

Related Documents

Angell Treaty. San Francisco Chinatown.com Web site. http:// www.sanfranciscochinatown.com/history/1880proclaimation.html. Accessed on August 30, 2007. The Angell Treaty modified prior treaties to allow the U.S. government "to regulate, limit, or suspend" the coming of Chinese laborers to the United States.

"Burlingame-Seward Treaty of 1868." University of Dayton Law School Web site. http://academic.udayton.edu/race/02rights/treaty 1868.htm. Accessed on January 21, 2008. Commonly called simply the Burlingame Treaty, this treaty assured Chinese the right to travel and reside in the United States.

"Geary Act of 1892." San Francisco Chinatown.com Web site. http://www.sanfranciscochinatown.com/history/1892gearyact.html. Accessed on August 30, 2007. The Geary Act extended the Chinese Exclusion Act of 1882 for ten additional years, established a presumption of unlawful residence for any Chinese person arrested under the Exclusion Act, and required Chinese laborers living in the United States to apply for certificates of residence.

"The Scott Act of 1888." Everything2 Web site. http://everything2. com/index.pl?node_id=448155. Accessed on August 30, 2007. The Scott Act amended the Chinese Exclusion Act of 1882 by denying reentry to Chinese laborers once they left the United States.

Bibliography

■ Articles

Salyer, Lucy. "Captives of Law: Judicial Enforcement of the Chinese Exclusion Laws, 1891–1905." *Journal of American History* 76, no. 1 (1989): 91–117.

■ Books

Coolidge, Mary Roberts. *Chinese Immigration*. New York: Henry Holt and Company, 1909.

Fritz, Christian G. "Due Process, Treaty Rights, and Chinese Exclusion, 1882–1891." *Entry Denied: Exclusion and the Chinese*

Community in America, 1882–1943, ed. Sucheng Chan. Philadelphia: Temple University Press, 1991.

Gyory, Andrew. *Closing the Gate: Race, Politics, and the Chinese Exclusion Act*. Chapel Hill: University of North Carolina Press, 1998.

Lee, Erika. *At America's Gate: Chinese Exclusion during the Exclusion Era, 1882–1943*. Chapel Hill: University of North Carolina Press, 2003.

McClain, Charles J. *In Search of Equality: The Chinese Struggle against Discrimination in Nineteenth-Century America*. Berkeley: University of California Press, 1994.

Miller, Marion Mills. "Chinese Exclusion." In *Great Debates in American History: From the Debates in the British Parliament on the Colonial Stamp Act (1764–1765) to the Debates in Congress at the Close of the Taft Administration (1912–1913)*, vol. 11. New York: Current Literature Publishing Company, 1913.

Saxton, Alexander. *The Indispensable Enemy: Labor and the Anti-Chinese Movement in California*. Berkeley: University of California Press, 1971.

Wong, Marie Rose. *Sweet Cakes, Long Journey: The Chinatowns of Portland, Oregon*. Seattle: University of Washington Press, 2004.

■ **Web Sites**

"Chinese Immigration: Origins and Opinions." American University Web site.
> http://www.american.edu/bgriff/dighistprojects/boyle/index.htm. Accessed on August 30, 2007.

"Chinese Immigration to the United States, 1851–1900." The Library of Congress "Learning Page" Web site.
> http://memory.loc.gov/learn/features/timeline/riseind/chinimms/chinimms.html. Accessed on August 30, 2007.

Lyman, Stanford M. "Engels Was Right! Organized Labor's Opposition to Chinese in the U.S.: Stanford M. Lyman Responds." William Patterson University Web site.
> http://www.wpunj.edu/newpol/issue29/lyman29.htm. Accessed on August 30, 2007.

—By Randy Wagner

1. Compare and contrast the movement to exclude Chinese laborers, which resulted in the 1882 Act, and the current movement to stop illegal Mexican immigrants from entering and residing in the United States. Which factors driving today's campaign against illegal Mexican immigrants are similar to those motivating the push to exclude Chinese? What are the biggest differences between the two movements?

2. Consider Section 14 of the Chinese Exclusion Act of 1882, which denies U.S. citizenship to Chinese, in light of the Fifteenth Amendment to the U.S. Constitution, ratified in 1870 and prohibiting the United States from denying its citizens the right to vote based on race. What results if both dictates are followed? Can the two be consistent? Is it a representative democracy when persons excluded by law cannot vote to choose senators and representatives who will determine whether or how to change that law? Can you identify other examples in U.S. history (or in the present) where a group of persons has been (or is) kept from voting for the legislators who pass the laws governing them? Can you argue that it is justifiable?

3. The Chinese were not the only group characterized in the nineteenth century as "an indigestible mass in the community" and "an undesirable element in a republic" (Miller, p. 213). Native Americans, African Americans, and Catholic immigrants were also at times portrayed as unfit to participate fully or equally in American society. What is the purpose when political leaders and opinion makers express these negative portrayals? Do these characterizations ever go away? Have the laws of this nation tended more to challenge or to reinforce these kinds of views?

4. Far fewer Japanese than Chinese lived in the United States during the period when the movement to exclude Chinese laborers was raging. The 1890 U.S. Census reported only 2,039 Japanese and more than 100,000 Chinese among the entire U.S. population. The Gentlemen's Agreement of 1907 between the United States and Japan ended immigration of Japanese persons to the United States. That document resulted from quiet negotiations between the two governments, a process not at all like the complicated set of diplomatic and legislative steps leading to the Chinese Exclusion Act of 1882. Read about the Gentlemen's Agreement of 1907 and then compare and contrast its development and its content with the Chinese Exclusion Act of 1882.

Glossary

abet	to encourage and assist someone in committing a crime
collector of customs	a local official in the Customs Service responsible for monitoring the movement of people and goods
master of any vessel	commander or captain of a ship
prima-facie evidence	evidence to establish a fact unless contradictory evidence is produced
treaty stipulations	conditions or requirements in an agreement between nations

CHINESE EXCLUSION ACT

An Act to execute certain treaty stipulations relating to Chinese.

Whereas in the opinion of the Government of the United States the coming of Chinese laborers to this country endangers the good order of certain localities within the territory thereof: Therefore,

Be it enacted by the Senate and House of Representatives of the United States of America in Congress assembled, That from and after the expiration of ninety days next after the passage of this act, and until the expiration of ten years next after the passage of this act, the coming of Chinese laborers to the United States be, and the same is hereby, suspended; and during such suspension it shall not be lawful for any Chinese laborer to come, or having so come after the expiration of said ninety days to remain within the United States.

SEC. 2. That the master of any vessel who shall knowingly bring within the United States on such vessel, and land or permit to be landed, any Chinese laborer, from any foreign port or place, shall be deemed guilty of a misdemeanor, and on conviction thereof shall be punished by a fine of not more than five hundred dollars for each and every such Chinese laborer so brought, and maybe also imprisoned for a term not exceeding one year.

SEC. 3. That the two foregoing sections shall not apply to Chinese laborers who were in the United States on the seventeenth day of November, eighteen hundred and eighty, or who shall have come into the same before the expiration of ninety days next after the passage of this act, and who shall produce to such master before going on board such vessel, and shall produce to the collector of the port in the United States at which such vessel shall arrive, the evidence hereinafter in this act required of his being one of the laborers in this section mentioned; nor shall the two foregoing sections apply to the case of any master whose vessel, being bound to a port not within the United States, shall come within the juris-

diction of the United States by reason of being in distress or in stress of weather, or touching at any port of the United States on its voyage to any foreign port or place: Provided, That all Chinese laborers brought on such vessel shall depart with the vessel on leaving port.

SEC. 4. That for the purpose of properly identifying Chinese laborers who were in the United States on the seventeenth day of November eighteen hundred and eighty, or who shall have come into the same before the expiration of ninety days next after the passage of this act, and in order to furnish them with the proper evidence of their right to go from and come to the United States of their free will and accord, as provided by the treaty between the United States and China dated November seventeenth, eighteen hundred and eighty, the collector of customs of the district from which any such Chinese laborer shall depart from the United States shall, in person or by deputy, go on board each vessel having on board any such Chinese laborers and cleared or about to sail from his district for a foreign port, and on such vessel make a list of all such Chinese laborers, which shall be entered in registry-books to be kept for that purpose, in which shall be stated the name, age, occupation, last place of residence, physical marks of peculiarities, and all facts necessary for the identification of each of such Chinese laborers, which books shall be safely kept in the custom-house; and every such Chinese laborer so departing from the United States shall be entitled to, and shall receive, free of any charge or cost upon application therefor, from the collector or his deputy, at the time such list is taken, a certificate, signed by the collector or his deputy and attested by his seal of office, in such form as the Secretary of the Treasury shall prescribe, which certificate shall contain a statement of the name, age, occupation, last place of residence, persona description, and facts of identification of the Chinese laborer to whom the certificate is issued, corresponding with the said list and registry in all particulars. In case any Chinese laborer after having received such certificate shall leave such vessel before her departure he shall deliver his certificate to the master of the vessel, and if such Chinese laborer shall fail to return to such vessel before her departure from port the certificate shall be delivered by the master to the collector of customs for cancellation. The certificate herein provided for shall entitle the Chinese laborer to whom the same is issued to return to and re-enter the United States upon producing and delivering the same to the collector of customs of the district at which such Chinese laborer shall seek to re-enter; and upon delivery of such certificate by such Chinese laborer to the collector of customs at the time of re-entry in the United States said collector shall cause the same to be filed in the custom-house anti duly canceled.

SEC. 5. That any Chinese laborer mentioned in section four of this act being in the United States, and desiring to depart from the United States by land, shall have the right to demand and receive, free of charge or cost, a certificate of identification similar to that provided for in section four of this act to be issued to such Chinese laborers as may desire to leave the United States by water; and it is hereby made the duty of the collector of customs of the district next adjoining the foreign country to which said Chinese laborer desires to go to issue such certificate, free of charge or cost, upon application by such Chinese laborer, and to enter the same upon registry-books to be kept by him for the purpose, as provided for in section four of this act.

SEC. 6. That in order to the faithful execution of articles one and two of the treaty in this act before mentioned, every Chinese person other than a laborer who may be entitled by said treaty and this act to come within the United States, and who shall be about to come to the United States, shall be identified as so entitled by the Chinese Government in each case, such identity to be evidenced by a certificate issued under the authority of said government, which certificate shall be in the English language or (if not in the English language) accompanied by a translation into English, stating such right to come, and which certificate shall state the name, title or official rank, if any, the age, height, and all physical peculiarities, former and present occupation or profession, and place of residence in China of the person to whom the certificate is issued and that such person is entitled, conformably to the treaty in this act mentioned to come within the United States.

Such certificate shall be prima-facie evidence of the fact set forth therein, and shall be produced to the collector of customs, or his deputy, of the port in the district in the United States at which the person named therein shall arrive.

SEC. 7. That any person who shall knowingly and falsely alter or substitute any name for the name written in such certificate or forge any such certificate, or knowingly utter any forged or fraudulent certificate, or falsely personate any person named in any such certificate, shall be deemed guilty of a misdemeanor; and upon conviction thereof shall be fined in a sum not exceeding one thousand dollars, and imprisoned in a penitentiary for a term of not more than five years.

SEC. 8. That the master of any vessel arriving in the United States from any foreign port or place shall, at the same time he delivers a manifest of the cargo, and if there be no cargo, then at the time of making a report of the entry of the vessel pursuant to law, in addition to the other matter required to be reported, and before landing, or permitting to land, any Chinese passengers, deliver and report to the collector of customs of the district in which such vessels shall have arrived a separate list of all Chinese passengers taken on board his vessel at any foreign port or place, and all such passengers on board the vessel at that time. Such list shall show the names of such passengers (and if accredited officers of the Chinese Government traveling on the business of that government, or their servants, with a note of such facts), and the names and other particulars, as shown by their respective certificates; and such list shall be sworn to by the master in the manner required by law in relation to the manifest of the cargo. Any willful refusal or neglect of any such master to comply with the provisions of this section shall incur the same penalties and forfeiture as are provided for a refusal or neglect to report and deliver a manifest of the cargo.

SEC. 9. That before any Chinese passengers are landed from any such line vessel, the collector, or his deputy, shall proceed to examine such passenger, comparing the certificate with the list and with the passengers; and no passenger shall be allowed to land in the United States from such vessel in violation of law.

SEC. 10. That every vessel whose master shall knowingly violate any of the provisions of this act shall be deemed forfeited to the United States, and shall be liable to seizure and condemnation in any district of the United States into which such vessel may enter or in which she may be found.

SEC. 11. That any person who shall knowingly bring into or cause to be brought into the United States by land, or who shall knowingly aid or abet the same, or aid or abet the landing in the United States from any vessel of any Chinese person not lawfully entitled to enter the United States, shall be deemed guilty of a misdemeanor, and shall, on conviction thereof, be fined in a sum not exceeding one thousand dollars, and imprisoned for a term not exceeding one year.

SEC. 12. That no Chinese person shall be permitted to enter the United States by land without producing to the proper officer of customs the certificate in this act required of Chinese persons seeking to land from a vessel. And any Chinese person found unlawfully within the United States shall be caused to be removed therefrom to the country from whence he came, by direction of the President of the United States, and at the cost of the United States, after being brought before some justice, judge, or commissioner of a court of the United States and found to be one not lawfully entitled to be or remain in the United States.

SEC. 13. That this act shall not apply to diplomatic and other officers of the Chinese Government traveling upon the business of that government, whose credentials shall be taken as equivalent to the certificate in this act mentioned, and shall exempt them and their body and house-hold servants from the provisions of this act as to other Chinese persons.

SEC. 14. That hereafter no State court or court of the United States shall admit Chinese to citizenship; and all laws in conflict with this act are hereby repealed.

SEC. 15. That the words "Chinese laborers", wherever used in this act shall be construed to mean both skilled and unskilled laborers and Chinese employed in mining.

Approved, May 6, 1882.

Forty-Seventh Congress of the United States of America;

At the Second Session,

Begun and held at the City of Washington on Monday, the fourth day of December, one thousand eight hundred and eighty-two

AN ACT

To regulate and improve the civil service of the United States.

Be it enacted by the Senate and House of Representatives of the United States of America in Congress assembled, That the President is authorized to appoint, by and with the advice and consent of the Senate, three persons, not more than two of whom shall be adherents of the same party, as Civil Service Commissioners, and said three commissioners shall constitute the United States Civil Service Commission. Said commissioners shall hold no other official place under the United States.

The President may remove any commissioner; and any vacancy in the position of commissioner shall be so filled by the President, by and with the advice and consent of the Senate, as to conform to said conditions for the first selection of commissioners.

The commissioners shall each receive a salary of three thousand five hundred dollars a year. And each of said commissioners shall be paid his necessary traveling expenses incurred in the discharge of his duty as a commissioner.

Sec. 2. That it shall be the duty of said commissioners:

First. To aid the President, as he may request, in preparing suitable rules for carrying this act into effect, and when said rules shall have been promulgated it shall be the duty of all officers of the United States in the departments and offices to which any such rules may relate to aid, in all proper ways, in carrying said rules, and any modifications thereof, into effect.

Second. And, among other things, said rules shall provide and declare, as nearly as the conditions of good administration will warrant, as follows:

First, for open, competitive examinations for testing the fitness of applicants for the public service now classified or to be classified hereunder. Such examinations shall be practical in their character, and so far as may be shall relate to those matters which will fairly test the relative capacity and fitness

The Pendleton Civil Service Act (National Archives and Records Administration)

"No person in the public service is ... under any obligations to contribute to any political fund, or to render any political service."

Overview

Named after Senator George Hunt Pendleton of Ohio, the Pendleton Civil Service Act was written by the civil service reformer Dorman B. Eaton and was signed into law on January 16, 1883. Traditionally, federal government jobs had been gained by those who contributed to political campaigns, a process known as the "spoils system" in reference to the idea that "to the victor belong the spoils." The Pendleton Act instituted examinations to appoint people based on merit rather than patronage. The Pendleton Act essentially created "classified" positions that would be filled from a list of eligible applicants based on the results of their examinations. The act also established the United States Civil Service Commission to administer federal government employment. Initially, the act covered only approximately ten thousand federal positions. Presidents, however, were authorized to add to these positions. By 1932 more than 80 percent of federal jobs had been brought under the umbrella of the civil service system.

Context

Beginning with President Andrew Jackson, whose philosophy of granting spoils to the victor dictated the process of appointing people to jobs in the federal civil service, the spoils system was firmly entrenched by the time the Pendleton Act was written. While there were fewer than one thousand civil service employees in 1800, there were more than one hundred thousand by 1883. Until the end of the Civil War, friends, family members, and financial supporters could virtually count on obtaining a job with the civil service. During elections, office seekers continually sought jobs, contributing money to political campaigns and even going so far as to place advertisements in the newspapers. As each new administration took office, however, it appointed new people to posts, so there was no job security. People feared losing their jobs as soon as new administrators were elected or their political patrons lost power. Consequently, before the passage of the Pendleton Act, loyalty and morale in the civil service were low, since employees had little hope for promotion and were often treated unprofessionally.

In his book *Since the Civil War*, the historian Charles R. Lingley summarizes the sentiment best when he says, "It is the duty of the citizen, therefore, to support the party that stands for right policies and to adhere closely to its official organization. Loyalty should be rewarded by appointment to positions within the gift of the party; and disloyalty should be looked upon as political treason" (Lingley, p. 118). Patricia Ingraham writes that the spoils system was especially out of control between 1845 and 1865. At President Zachary Taylor's inauguration, Senator William Seward jokingly remarked that "the world seems almost divided into two classes: those who are going to California in search of gold, and those going to Washington in quest of office" (Ingraham, p. 21). Of the hordes of hungry office seekers on the White House lawn, President Abraham Lincoln even commented, "There you see something which will, in the course of time, become a greater danger to the public than the rebellion itself" (Ingraham, p. 22).

Over the years, several politicians, including Henry Clay and Daniel Webster, sought to reform the current civil service management. Although it was unsuccessful, Senator Charles Sumner of Massachusetts in 1864 introduced a reform bill based on the British model of civil service. Four years later, Representative Thomas Allen Jenckes of Rhode Island submitted a bill to reform the civil service. The following year, Congress established the Select Committee on the Reorganization of the Civil Service of the Government and appointed Jenckes head of the committee. Passed on March 3, 1871, Jenckes's bill empowered the president to make regulations for hiring civil service employees and to appoint a body to oversee the hiring. President Grant established the Civil Service Advisory Board with a fifteen-thousand-dollar appropriation from Congress. Grant chose the reformer George William Curtis to head the board. After a few years, however, Congress refused to appropriate any more funds to the Civil Service Advisory Board.

While Congress may have abandoned the idea of civil service reform, individual reformers refused to give up and formed the New York Civil Service Reform League in 1877 under the leadership of Dorman B. Eaton. In 1881 the National Civil Service Reform League was formed in

1829

■ **March 4**
President Andrew Jackson
develops the "spoils system."

1864

■ Senator Charles Sumner
introduces a bill to provide for
competitive examinations in
the civil service.

1865

■ **December 20**
Representative Thomas Allen
Jenckes introduces a bill to
provide civil service jobs
based on merit.

1871

■ **March 3**
Jenckes's Civil Service Bill is
established to ensure the
adoption of the merit system;
President Ulysses S. Grant
creates the Civil Service
Advisory Board and places
George William Curtis in
charge.

1876

■ President Rutherford B.
Hayes appoints Dorman B.
Eaton to conduct a study of
the British Civil Service.

1877

■ **May**
Civil service reform movement
begins in New York with the
development of the New York
Civil Service Reform League.

1881

■ **July 2**
President James A. Garfield is
shot by a disappointed office
seeker Charles Guiteau.
Garfield later dies on
September 19, 1881.

■ **January 10**
Pendleton introduces the New
York Civil Service Reform
Association's bill to regulate
the civil service.

■ **August 11**
National Civil Service Reform
League is organized in Rhode
Island.

1883

■ Roughly 11 percent of
those employed with the civil
service are classified.

Rhode Island, and George William Curtis was elected as the organization's first president. By January 1883 there were more than fifty local associations across the country.

Although President Rutherford B. Hayes advocated for civil service reform, the matter was not discussed again in Congress until President James A. Garfield was assassinated by Charles Guiteau, an upset office seeker hoping to be appointed the U.S. consul in Paris in 1881. After Garfield's death, the public and reformers alike sensationalized the evils of the spoils system. A special committee of the New York Civil Service Reform League distributed a pamphlet containing some of Garfield's best quotes on reform and posted signs in all post offices. Congress could no longer ignore the public clamor for reform in the civil service. Something had to be done.

About the Author

Born in Hardwick, Vermont, in 1823 to a Unitarian minister, Dorman Bridgeman Eaton was a longtime advocate of civil service reform. He attended Harvard Law School and became a lawyer in New York City. While he was there he joined the Citizens Association, a group dedicated to social and political reform. As chairman of the group's legislative committee, Eaton drafted a bill to establish the Metropolitan Fire Commission to replace volunteer firefighters with professionals. Buoyed by success, Eaton and the association next tackled the city's health care problems and political issues. Eaton firmly believed that New York City's elected and appointed officials were unable to do their jobs because they feared that they could be ousted soon or that they might estrange the people who had voted for them. Writing exhaustively on the subject in publications such as the *New York Times* and *Atlantic Monthly*, he felt that public occupations should be filled with experts who had passed a competitive exam.

In 1873 President Ulysses S. Grant appointed Eaton head of the newly created Civil Service Commission. Eaton worked to make progress in civil service reform, but just two years later the commission was dismantled by Grant after Congress refused to appropriate funds. Eaton, however, was not deterred in his quest for reform. In 1877 he organized the first civil service reform association in the country, the New York Civil Service Reform Association. Though the commission was inactive, Eaton continued in his role as commissioner, serving without compensation for presidents Rutherford B. Hayes, James A. Garfield, and Chester A. Arthur. In 1880 Eaton traveled to England to study the British Civil Service system. His book on the subject, *Civil Service in Great Britain*, became an instant success. During this time, he also assessed New York City's post office as well as the New York Custom House.

In early 1882, Senator George Hunt Pendleton of Ohio drafted a bill to reform the federal civil service. Composing a similar document for the New York Civil Service Reform Association, Eaton persuaded Senator Pendleton to use the association's proposal rather than his own. When Congress passed the bill in January 1883, President Arthur appointed Eaton to administer it. Eaton oversaw the enforcement of the Pendleton Act until he resigned in 1886 to go back home to New York City. In 1899 he published *The Government of Municipalities*, which summarized his activities as a reformer. He remained a staunch supporter of reform movements until his death later that year.

Explanation and Analysis of the Document

◆ Section 1.

In the introduction to the Pendleton Act, the authors, Eaton and Pendleton, establish that the president of the United States, with the advice and consent of the Senate, has the authority to appoint three people to form the Civil Service Commission. Only two of the three commissioners could belong to the same political party. The introduction specifies that the commissioners can hold no other official office. The Pendleton Act provides that each of the three commissioners receive an annual salary of $3,500.

◆ Section 2.

Section 2 pertains to the five duties of the commissioners. Their first duty is to assist the president in determining appropriate regulations to enforce the Pendleton Act. The second responsibility is to "provide and declare, as nearly as the conditions of good administration will warrant" open and competitive examinations to determine whether applicants are suitable for classified positions. The commissioners are instructed to select those candidates who score highest on the examinations. Civil service positions are to be filled proportionately to the population of each state or territory. Applicants are required to pledge an oath affirming that they actually live where they say they live. In addition, there is a prescribed period of probation during which no appointments will be made. The second duty also specifies that civil service employees cannot be required to contribute any money to a political campaign and that the employees will not be removed from their positions if they refuse to contribute. Civil service employees are prohibited from using their positions to influence or coerce anyone into political action. If no one applies for the competitive examinations, the positions will be opened to allow for noncompetitive examinations. Records of all appointments, including any transfers, resignations, or removals, are to be kept by the commission.

The third duty is to make regulations for, supervise, and preserve the records of all examinations. The commission is also instructed to keep records of all its proceedings. The fourth duty allows the commissioners to investigate the enforcement of the commission's rules and regulations, including the actions of any examiners and anyone in the public service. The fifth duty provides that the commissioners make an annual report to the president, discussing the commission's "action[s], the rules and regulations and the exceptions thereto in force, the practical effects there-

Time Line

1883

■ January 16
Pendleton Act is passed by Congress and signed into law by President Chester A. Arthur; Civil Service Commission is established.

1889

■ The combined salaries of classified officers equals that of all unclassified employees.

■ President Benjamin Harrison appoints Theodore Roosevelt to head the Civil Service Commission.

1900

■ More than 46 percent of civil service employees are under the merit system.

of, and any suggestions it may approve for the more effectual accomplishment of the purposes of this act."

◆ Section 3.

Section 3 authorizes the commission to hire a chief examiner to act as liaison to the examining boards in Washington to "secure accuracy, uniformity, and justice in all their proceedings." The chief examiner's salary was set at $3,000 per year in addition to traveling expenses. Section 3 also specifies that the commission could have a secretary appointed by the president at an annual salary of $600. Along those lines, the commission is also instructed to hire a stenographer and a messenger if necessary.

The commission is instructed in Section 3 to appoint at least three persons to serve on the board of examiners wherever examinations would take place. The act prescribes that examinations must take place at least twice per year, given that there are applicants to be examined. Public officials, including collectors and postmasters, are directed to allow the "reasonable use" of the public buildings for the examinations.

◆ Section 4.

Section 4 instructs the secretary of the interior to provide "suitable and convenient rooms and accommodations ... to be furnished, heated, and lighted" in Washington, D.C., for the commission and for any examinations. The secretary of the interior is also responsible for providing stationary and supplies and printing for the commission.

◆ Section 5.

Section 5 states that a commissioner, examiner, or anyone involved in the civil service "who shall willfully and corruptly ... defeat, deceive, or obstruct any person in respect of his or her right of examination" will be judged guilty of a misdemeanor. This also applies to anyone false-

George Hunt Pendleton (Library of Congress)

ly grading an examination and to those who supply secret information to candidates "either improving or injuring the prospects or chances of any person so examined, or to be examined, being appointed, employed, or promoted." If one is convicted of this misdemeanor, the fine is set at between $100 and $1,000. The convicted also faces possible imprisonment, between ten days and one year, instead of or in addition to the monetary fine.

◆ Section 6.

This section deals with the duties of various other officials. The secretary of the treasury is instructed, within sixty days of the passage of the Pendleton Act, to arrange the clerks and employees of the collector, naval officer, surveyor, and appraisers in classes in each customs district. Each customs district can have as many as fifty people in a classified group. All arrangements and classifications must be reported to the president. Likewise, the postmaster general is also responsible for arranging the clerks and other people employed at each post office. Both the secretary of the treasury and the postmaster general can, at any time, be authorized by the president to make other classifications. In addition, the secretary of the treasury, postmaster

general, and other heads of departments or offices are instructed to enforce the Pendleton Act and to revise "any then existing classification or arrangement of those in their respective departments."

◆ Section 7.

This section stipulates that once six months has passed from the passage of the Pendleton Act, no one should be appointed, employed, or promoted until he or she has passed an examination or it is proved that he or she is exempted from taking an examination. Section 7 specifically mentions that the Pendleton Act does not intend to deprive those discharged from the military or navy of the benefits given by the 1754 section of the Revised Statutes. In addition, Section 7 indicates that laborers, workmen, and officers of any other branch of the government except the executive branch will not be required to take the classified examinations. Those appointed by the Senate also do not have to take the examinations unless required by the Senate.

◆ Section 8.

Section 8 specifies that anyone who regularly abuses "intoxicating beverages to excess" will not be employed in the civil service.

◆ Section 9.

According to Section 9, if there are already two or more members of the same family employed in public service, no other member of the family will be eligible.

◆ Section 10.

Section 10 requires that senators and representatives not give applicants recommendations "except as to the character or residence of the applicant."

◆ Section 11.

As hinted at in Section 2 regarding campaign contributions, Section 11 specifies that elected officials, employees of the Senate or House of Representatives, military officers, or other employees may not, "directly or indirectly, solicit or receive" any financial contributions for political purposes from officers, clerks, and employees of the United States or anyone "receiving any salary or compensation from moneys derived from the Treasury of the United States."

◆ Section 12.

Similarly to Section 11, this section mandates that no one is allowed to receive any financial contribution or anything of value while in any naval yard, fort, or arsenal or in any room or building being used for official duties of the United States.

◆ Section 13.

Section 13 also deals with financial contributions. It specifies that no officer or employee mentioned in the Pendleton Act may fire, promote, or "change the official rank or compensation of any other officer or employee, or

"*That no person in the public service is for that reason under any obligations to contribute to any political fund, or to render any political service, and that he will not be removed or otherwise prejudiced for refusing to do so.*"

(Section 2, fifth component of the second part)

"*That all the offices, places, and employments so arranged or to be arranged in classes shall be filled by selections according to grade from among those graded highest as the results of such competitive examinations.*"

(Section 2, second component of the second part)

"*That no person habitually using intoxicating beverages to excess shall be appointed to, or retained in, any office, appointment, or employment to which the provisions of this act are applicable.*"

(Section 8)

promise or threaten so to do" for either contributing or refusing to contribute money or items of value for a political campaign.

◆ **Section 14.**

Section 14 also pertains to contributions to political campaigns. According to Section 14, "no officer, clerk, or other employee of the United States shall, directly or indirectly," give any one money or valuables for political purposes.

◆ **Section 15.**

Section 15 states that anyone found guilty of the conditions in Sections 11 through 14 will be found guilty and convicted of a misdemeanor. The penalty for such misdemeanor is set at no less than $5,000, imprisonment for no more than three years, or both.

Audience

The Pendleton Act was written for both American politicians and the American populace. When Senator George Pendleton introduced his bill to the Senate in December 1880, the proposal received little attention. Eaton soon approached Pendleton in the hope of persuading him to submit the document drafted by the New York Civil Service Reform Association. Pendleton agreed and introduced the bill, yet no action was taken. After President Garfield's assas-

sination, the American people demanded that the civil service be reformed. Many politicians failed to realize how strongly the people felt on the matter, refusing to make any changes. This attitude, however, cost them votes in the 1882 mid-year election. When Pendleton's bill went before the Senate again in December 1882, it was immediately passed.

The Pendleton Act was written primarily for the American people, and so is its language. It is written in language that the layperson can understand and is not filled with technical wording. However, the act does cite very specific actions that the president and his appointed commissioners must take.

Impact

The Pendleton Act provided a way to "reduce the costs of patronage by improving the quality of federal workers and to constrain competition among politicians over the control of federal positions" (Johnson and Libecap, p. 14). The passage of the Pendleton Act had an immediate impact on American politics. Civil service reform stayed on the minds of the American public. In future presidential elections, voters tended to elect the candidate who had not risen up through the spoils system, opting instead to vote for the candidate who advocated for civil service reform and the merit system. Congressmen themselves even acted in opposition to the Civil Service Commission, introducing no fewer than seven bills to repeal the Pendleton Act during President Grover Cleveland's first term in office. The bills never passed, however, and by 1904, just twenty-one years after the Pendleton Act went into effect, more than 50 percent of civil service jobs were based on merit examinations.

In 1883 the Pendleton Act placed just over thirteen thousand positions, and only 11 percent were categorized as classified. Hoogenboom writes that "from its start, the new system included places close to policymaking positions, perhaps even encroached upon them, and subsequently moved downward to include progressively minor positions" (1961, p. 304). While the Pendleton Act also protected employees from being removed from their positions based on political or religious beliefs, many politicians found ways around the commission's rules, transferring an employee from one job to another and creating temporary positions. As Hoogenboom notes, "the smaller the office and the more remote it was from Washington, the greater were the chances for evasion of the rules" (1961, p. 309). In 1888 President Cleveland even altered the rules of the Pendleton Act, waiving the requirement that incumbent employees must take the merit exams. Along those lines, presidents also had the authority to assist patronage employees by reclassifying the positions. By the 1890s, however, the Pendleton Act was generally followed, and in 1900 more than 40 percent of the civil service was classified.

One of the major impacts of the Pendleton Act was that it forbade giving campaign contributions in return for a job. Before the Pendleton Act, these types of campaign contributions, called political assessments, made up 75 percent of all campaign contributions. Sean Theriault points out that before the Pendleton Act, between the beginning of the Civil War and 1881, the number of political appointees rose by 173 percent. Following the passage of the Pendleton Act, ten states and more than four hundred cities, as well as the Philippines and Puerto Rico, adhered to the merit system. Presidents William McKinley, Grover Cleveland, and Theodore Roosevelt worked to expand the Pendleton Act, requiring political neutrality from all government employees and establishing job tenure and appeals processes. In 1923 Congress passed the Classification Act, establishing the standard of equal pay for equal work.

Related Documents

Berens, Ruth McMurry. "Blueprint for Reform: Curtis, Eaton, and Schurz." M.A. thesis, University of Chicago, 1943. Beren's work examines the works of civil service reformers George William Curtis, Dorman B. Eaton, and Carl Schurz.

Dorman B. Eaton. 1823–1899. New York: 1900. Biographical sketch of Eaton's life and works in addition to memorials written after his death.

Eaton, Dorman B. *Civil Service in Great Britain: A History of Abuses and Reforms, and Their Bearing upon American Politics.* 1880.

Reprint. Eastbourne, U.K.: Gardners Books, 2007. Eaton's study of the British Civil Service system at the request of President Rutherford B. Hayes is presented in this book.

———. *The "Spoils" System and Civil-Service Reform in the Custom-House and Post Office at New York.* New York: G. P. Putnam's Sons, 1882. In this book, Eaton's gives his views of the spoils system and the first attempts at civil service reform in the New York Custom House and Post Office.

Kellogg, S.W. "The Beginnings of Civil Service Reform." *Yale Law Journal* 8, no. 3 (December 1898): 134–146. Kellogg, a member of Congress during the time the Pendleton Act was passed, recalls the evolution of civil service reform in America in this article.

Smith, Stephen. *The City That Was.* New York: F. Allaben, 1911. Smith's book examines the sanitary conditions in New York City and Britain as well as the works of Dorman B. Eaton.

Bibliography

■ Articles

Fleming, Thomas. "The Long, Stormy Marriage of Money and Politics." *American Heritage* 49, no. 7 (November 1998): 45–53.

Ford, Henry Jones. "Political Evolution and Civil Service Reform." *Annals of the American Academy of Political and Social Science* 15 (March 1900): 1–15.

Hoogenboom, Ari. "The Pendleton Act and the Civil Service." *American Historical Review* 64, no. 2 (January 1959): 301–318.

———. "Thomas A. Jenckes and Civil Service Reform." *Mississippi Valley Historical Review* 47, no. 2 (March 1961): 636–658.

Kaplan, H. Eliot. "Accomplishments of the Civil Service Reform Movement." *Annals of the American Academy of Political and Social Science* 189 (January 1937): 142–147.

McFarland, Gerald W. "Partisan of Nonpartisanship: Dorman B. Eaton and the Genteel Reform Tradition." *Journal of American History* 54, no. 4 (March 1968): 806–822.

Montgomery, W. W., Jr. "Problems and Progress of the Merit System." *Annals of the American Academy of Political and Social Science* 189 (January 1937): 192–198.

Reeves, Thomas C. "Chester A. Arthur and the Campaign of 1880." *Political Science Quarterly* 84, no. 4 (December 1969): 628–637.

Richardson, Lyon N., and Curtis W. Garrison. "George William Curtis, Rutherford B. Hayes, and Civil Service Reform." *Mississippi Valley Historical Review* 32, no. 2 (September 1945): 235–250.

Theriault, Sean M. "Patronage, the Pendleton Act, and the Power of the People." *Journal of Politics* 65, no. 1 (February 2003): 50–68.

Wheeler, Everett P. "The Rise and Progress of the Merit System." *Political Science Quarterly* 34, no. 3 (September 1919): 486–492.

■ Books

Halloran, Matthew F. *The Romance of the Merit System: Forty-Five Years' Reminiscences of the Civil Service.* Washington, D.C.: Juddy & Detweiler, 1929.

Harvey, Donald R. *The Civil Service Commission.* New York: Praeger Publishers, 1970.

Hollander, Herbert S. *Spoils!* Washington, D.C.: William Ullman, 1936.

Hoogenboom, Ari. *Outlawing the Spoils: A History of the Civil Service Reform Movement, 1865–1883.* Urbana: University of Illinois Press, 1961.

Hoogenboom, Ari, ed. *Spoilsmen and Reformers.* Chicago: Rand McNally, 1964.

Huddleston, Mark W., and William W. Boyer. *The Higher Civil Service in the United States: Quest for Reform.* Pittsburgh: University of Pittsburgh Press, 1996.

Ingraham, Patricia Wallace. *The Foundation of Merit: Public Service in American Democracy.* Baltimore, Md.: Johns Hopkins University Press, 1995.

Johnson, Ronald N., and Gary D. Libecap. *The Federal Civil Service System and the Problem of Bureaucracy: The Economics and Politics of Institutional Change.* Chicago: University of Chicago Press, 1994.

Lingley, Charles Ramsdell. *Since the Civil War.* Revised edition. New York: Century Company, 1926.

Prince, Carl E. *The Federalists and the Origins of the U.S. Civil Service.* New York: New York University Press, 1977.

Rosenbloom, David H., ed. *Centenary Issues of the Pendleton Act of 1883: The Problematic Legacy of Civil Service Reform.* New York: Marcel Dekker, 1982.

Sageser, Adelbert Bower. *The First Two Decades of the Pendleton Act: A Study of Civil Service Reform.* Lincoln: University of Nebraska, 1935.

Stewart, Frank Mann. *The National Civil Service Reform League: History, Activities, and Problems.* Austin: University of Texas, 1929.

Titlow, Richard E. *Americans Import Merit: Origins of the United States Civil Service and the Influence of the British Model.* Washington, D.C.: University Press of America, 1979.

United States Civil Service Commission. *History of the Federal Civil Service, 1789 to the Present.* Washington, D.C.: U.S. Government Printing Office, 1941.

Van Riper, Paul P. *History of the United States Civil Service.* Westport, Conn.: Greenwood Press, 1976.

■ Web Sites

United States Civil Service Commission Web site. http://www.csc.gov.ph/. Accessed on September 12, 2007.

—By Nicole Mitchell

1. Compare and contrast the modern civil service system with that enacted by the passage of the Pendleton Act in 1883. What are some similarities? What are some differences?

2. Compare and contrast the American civil service system with the model British civil service system. How are the two systems modeled on civil service systems in other countries? Focus on the documents' intended audience, overall impact, and so on.

3. Given the history of the spoils system, the civil service, and the political climate before 1883, was the Pendleton Act necessary for reforming the civil service? Why or why not? Why did the Pendleton Act succeed when so many other bills failed? Where would America be today if the Pendleton Act had not been enacted?

4. With no funding and little commitment from Congress, the first Civil Service Commission failed in just two years. Was the first Civil Service Commission destined to fail? Why or why not?

5. One of the Civil Service Commission's most famous commissioners was the future president Theodore Roosevelt. Roosevelt took strides to strengthen the authority of the commission and to classify more positions. Why do you think he did this? Is his work as commissioner indicative of his future presidential goals?

6. Before the passage of the Pendleton Act, most government jobs were obtained through patronage. Today, virtually all federal government jobs are under the purview of the Civil Service Commission. Compare and contrast the two systems. What are the advantages and disadvantages of each system?

Glossary

classified	positions that have been determined as professional and require professional skills and training
grade	a degree or rank in terms of advancement or promotion

PENDLETON CIVIL SERVICE ACT

An act to regulate and improve the civil service of the United States

Be it enacted by the Senate and House of Representatives of the United States of America in Congress assembled, That the President is authorized to appoint, by and with the advice and consent of the Senate, three persons, not more than two of whom shall be adherents of the same party, as Civil Service Commissioners, and said three commissioners shall constitute the United States Civil Service Commission. Said commissioners shall hold no other official place under the United States.

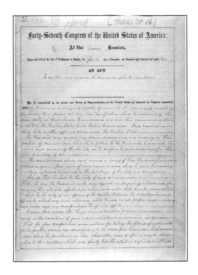

The President may remove any commissioner; and any vacancy in the position of commissioner shall be so filled by the President, by and with the advice and consent of the Senate, as to conform to said conditions for the first selection of commissioners.

The commissioners shall each receive a salary of three thousand five hundred dollars a year. And each of said commissioners shall be paid his necessary traveling expenses incurred in the discharge of his duty as a commissioner.

SEC. 2. That it shall be the duty of said commissioners:

FIRST. To aid the President, as he may request, in preparing suitable rules for carrying this act into effect, and when said rules shall have been promulgated it shall be the duty of all officers of the United States in the departments and offices to which any such rules may relate to aid, in all proper ways, in carrying said rules, and any modifications thereof; into effect.

SECOND. And, among other things, said rules shall provide and declare, as nearly as the conditions of good administration will warrant, as follows:

First, for open, competitive examinations for testing the fitness of applicants for the public service now classified or to be classified here-under. Such examinations shall be practical in their character, and so far as may be shall relate to those matters which will fairly test the relative capacity and fitness of the persons examined to discharge the duties of the service into which they seek to be appointed.

Second, that all the offices, places, and employments so arranged or to be arranged in classes shall be filled by selections according to grade from among those graded highest as the results of such competitive examinations.

Third, appointments to the public service aforesaid in the departments at Washington shall be apportioned among the several States and Territories and the District of Columbia upon the basis of population as ascertained at the last preceding census. Every application for an examination shall contain, among other things, a statement, under oath, setting forth his or her actual bona fide residence at the time of making the application, as well as how long he or she has been a resident of such place.

Fourth, that there shall be a period of probation before any absolute appointment or employment aforesaid.

Fifth, that no person in the public service is for that reason under any obligations to contribute to any political fund, or to render any political service, and that he will not be removed or otherwise prejudiced for refusing to do so.

Sixth, that no person in said service has any right to use his official authority or influence to coerce the political action of any person or body.

Seventh, there shall be non-competitive examinations in all proper cases before the commission, when competent persons do not compete, after notice has been given of the existence of the vacancy, under such rules as may be prescribed by the commissioners as to the manner of giving notice.

Eighth, that notice shall be given in writing by the appointing power to said commission of the persons selected for appointment or employment from among those who have been examined, of the place of residence of such persons, of the rejection of any such persons after probation, of transfers, resignations, and removals and of the date thereof, and a record of the same shall be kept. by said commission. And any necessary exceptions from said eight fundamental provisions of the rules shall be set forth in connection with such rules, and the reasons there-for shall be stated in the annual reports of the commission.

THIRD. Said commission shall, subject to the rules that may be made by the President, make regulations for, and have control of, such examinations, and, through its members or the examiners, it shall supervise and preserve the records of the same; and said commission shall keep minutes of its own proceedings.

FOURTH. Said commission may make investigations concerning the facts, and may report upon all matters touching the enforcement and effects of said rules and regulations, and concerning the action of any examiner or board of examiners hereinafter provided for, and its own subordinates, and those in the public service, in respect to the execution of this act.

FIFTH. Said commission shall make an annual report to the President for transmission to Congress, showing its own action, the rules and regulations and the exceptions thereto in force, the practical effects thereof, and any suggestions it may approve for the more effectual accomplishment of the purposes of this act.

SEC.3. That said commission is authorized to employ a chief examiner, a part of whose duty it shall be, under its direction, to act with the examining boards, so far as practicable, whether at Washington or elsewhere, and to secure accuracy, uniformity, and justice in all their proceedings, which shall be at all times open to him. The chief examiner shall be entitled to receive a salary at the rate of three thousand dollars a year, and he shall be paid his necessary traveling expenses incurred in the discharge of his duty The commission shall have a secretary, to be appointed by the President, who shall receive a salary of one thousand six hundred dollars per annum. It may, when necessary, employ a stenographer, and a messenger, who shall be paid, when employed, the former at the rate of one thousand six hundred dollars a year, and the latter at the rate of six hundred dollars a year. The commission shall, at Washington, and in one or more places in each State and Territory where examinations arc to take place, designate and select a suitable number of persons, not less than three, in the official service of the United States, residing in said State or Territory, after consulting the head of the department or office in which such persons serve, to be members of boards of examiners, and may at any time substitute any other person in said service living in such State or Territory in the place of anyone so selected. Such boards of examiners shall be so located as to make it reasonably convenient and inexpensive for applicants to attend before them; and where there are persons to be examined in any State or Territory, examinations shall be held therein at least twice in each year. It shall be the duty of the collector, postmaster, and other officers of the United States at any place outside of the District of Columbia where examinations are directed by the President or by said board to be held, to allow the reasonable use of the public buildings for holding such examinations, and in all proper ways to facilitate the same.

SEC. 4. That it shall be the duty of the Secretary of the Interior to cause suitable and convenient rooms and accommodations to be assigned or provided, and to be furnished, heated, and lighted, at the city of Washington, for carrying on the work of said commission and said examinations, and to cause the necessary stationery and other articles to be supplied, and the necessary printing to be done for said commission.

SEC. 5. That any said commissioner, examiner, copyist, or messenger, or any person in the public service who shall willfully and corruptly, by himself or in co-operation with one or more other persons, defeat, deceive, or obstruct any person in respect of his or her right of examination according to any such rules or regulations, or who shall willfully, corruptly, and falsely mark, grade, estimate, or report upon the examination or proper standing of any person examined hereunder, or aid in so doing, or who shall willfully and corruptly make any false representations concerning the same or concerning the person examined, or who shall willfully and corruptly furnish to any person any special or secret information for the purpose of either improving or injuring the prospects or chances of any person so examined, or to be examined, being appointed, employed, or promoted, shall for each such offense be deemed guilty of a misdemeanor, and upon conviction thereof, shall be punished by a fine of not less than one hundred dollars, nor more than one thousand dollars, or by imprisonment not less than ten days, nor more than one year, or by both such fine and imprisonment.

SEC. 6. That within sixty days after the passage of this act it shall be the duty of the Secretary of the Treasury, in as near conformity as may be to the classification of certain clerks now existing under the one hundred and sixty-third section of the Revised Statutes to arrange in classes the several clerks and persons employed by the collector, naval officer, surveyor, and appraisers, or either of them, or being in the public service, at their respective offices in each customs district where the whole number of said clerks and persons shall be all together as many as fifty. And thereafter, from time to time, on the direction of the President, said Secretary shall make the like classification or arrangement of clerks and persons so employed, in connection with any said office or offices, in any other customs district. And, upon like request, and for the purposes of this act, said Secretary shall arrange in one or more of said classes, or of existing classes, any other clerks, agents, or persons employed under his department in any said district not now classified; and every such arrangement and classification upon being made shall be reported to the President.

Second. Within said sixty days it shall be the duty of the Postmaster-General, in general conformity to said one hundred and sixty-third section, to separately arrange in classes the several clerks and persons employed, or in the public service at each post-office, or under any post-master of the United States, where the whole number of said clerks and persons shall together amount to as many as fifty. And thereafter, from time to time, on the direction of the President, it shall be the duty of the Postmaster-General to arrange in like classes the clerks and persons so employed in the postal service in connection with any other post-office; and every such arrangement and classification upon being made shall be reported to the President.

Third. That from time to time said Secretary, the Postmaster-General, and each of the heads of departments mentioned in the one hundred and fifty-eighth section of the Revised Statutes, and each head of an office, shall, on the direction of the President, and for facilitating the execution of this act, respectively revise any then existing classification or arrangement of those in their respective departments and offices, and shall, for the purposes of the examination herein provided for, include in one or more of such classes, so far as practicable, subordinate places, clerks, and officers in the public service pertaining to their respective departments not before classified for examination.

SEC. 7. That after the expiration of six months from the passage of this act no officer or clerk shall be appointed, and no person shall be employed to enter or be promoted in either of the said classes now existing, or that may be arranged hereunder pursuant to said rules, until he has passed an examination, or is shown to be specially exempted from such examination in conformity herewith. But nothing herein contained shall be construed to take from those honorably discharged from the military or naval service any preference conferred by the seventeen hundred and fifty-fourth section of the Revised Statutes, nor to take from the President any authority not inconsistent with this act conferred by the seventeen hundred and fifty-third section of said statutes; nor shall any officer not in the executive branch of the government, or any person merely employed as a laborer or workman, be required to be classified hereunder; nor, unless by direction of the Senate, shall any person who has been nominated for confirmation by the Senate be required to be classified or to pass an examination.

SEC. 8. That no person habitually using intoxicating beverages to excess shall be appointed to, or retained in, any office, appointment, or employment to which the provisions of this act are applicable.

SEC. 9. That whenever there are already two or more members of a family in the public service in the grades covered by this act, no other member of such family shall be eligible to appointment to any of said grades.

SEC. 10. That no recommendation of any person who shall apply for office or place under the provisions of this act which may be given by any Senator or member of the House of Representatives, except as to the character or residence of the applicant, shall be received or considered by any person concerned in making any examination or appointment under this act.

SEC. 11. That no Senator, or Representative, or Territorial Delegate of the Congress, or Senator, Representative, or Delegate elect, or any officer or employee of either of said houses, and no executive, judicial, military, or naval officer of the United States, and no clerk or employee of any department, branch or bureau of the executive, judicial, or military or naval service of the United States, shall, directly or indirectly, solicit or receive., or be in any manner concerned ill soliciting or receiving, any assessment, subscription, or contribution for any political purpose whatever, from any officer, clerk, or employee of the United States, or any department, branch, or bureau thereof, or from any person receiving any salary or compensation from moneys derived from the Treasury of the United States.

SEC. 12. That no person shall, in any room or building occupied in the discharge of official duties by any officer or employee of the United States mentioned in this act, or in any navy-yard, fort, or arsenal, solicit in any manner whatever, or receive any contribution of money or any other thing of value for any political purpose whatever.

SEC. 13. No officer or employee of the United States mentioned m this act shall discharge, or promote, or degrade, or in manner change the official rank or compensation of any other officer or employee, or promise or threaten so to do, for giving or withholding or neglecting to make any contribution of money or other valuable thing for any political purpose.

SEC. 14. That no officer, clerk, or other person in the service of the United States shall, directly or indirectly, give or hand over to any other officer, clerk, or person in the service of the United States, or to any Senator or Member of the House of Representatives, or Territorial Delegate, any money or other valuable thing on account of or to be applied to the promotion of any political object whatever.

SEC. 15. That any person who shall be guilty of violating any provision of the four foregoing sections shall be deemed guilty of a misdemeanor, and shall, on conviction thereof, be punished by a fine not exceeding five thousand dollars, or by imprisonment for a term not exceeding three years, or by such fine and imprisonment both, in the discretion of the court.

Approved, January sixteenth, 1883.

Forty-Ninth Congress of the United States of America;

At the Second Session,

Begun and held at the City of Washington on Monday, the sixth day of December, one thousand eight hundred and eighty-six

AN ACT

To regulate Commerce.

Be it enacted by the Senate and House of Representatives of the United States of America in Congress assembled, That the provisions of this act shall apply to any common carrier or carriers engaged in the transportation of passengers or property wholly by railroad, or partly by railroad and partly by water when both are used, under a common control, management, or arrangement, for a continuous carriage or shipment, from one State or Territory of the United States or the District of Columbia, to any other State or Territory of the United States, or the District of Columbia, or from any place in the United States to an adjacent foreign country, or from any place in the United States through a foreign country to any other place in the United States, and also to the transportation in like manner of property shipped from any place in the United States to a foreign country and carried from such place to a port of transshipment, or shipped from a foreign country to any place in the United States and carried to such place from a port of entry either in the United States or an adjacent foreign country: Provided, however, That the provisions of this act shall not apply to the transportation of passengers or property, or to the receiving, delivering, storage, or handling of property, wholly within one State, and not shipped to or from a foreign country from or to any State or Territory as aforesaid.

The term "railroad" as used in this act shall include all bridges and ferries used or operated in connection with any railroad, and also all the road in use by any corporation operating a railroad, whether owned or operated under a contract, agreement, or lease; and the term "transportation" shall include all instrumentalities of shipment or carriage.

All charges made for any service rendered or to be rendered in the transportation of passengers or property as aforesaid, or in connection there

The Interstate Commerce Act (National Archives and Records Administration)

"Every common carrier ... shall print and keep for public inspection schedules showing the rates and fares and charges for the transportation of passengers and property."

Overview

The Interstate Commerce Act of 1887, also known as an Act to Regulate Commerce, was signed by President Grover Cleveland on February 4, 1887. With the enactment of the Interstate Commerce Act, the railroads became the first federally regulated industry in the United States. The passage of this act was a challenge to the nineteenth-century notion of laissez-faire. Laissez-faire is the idea that economic and business industries would thrive better with little government interference or regulation, other than that which is necessary to protect individual and property rights. This act also created the Interstate Commerce Commission, a five-member committee that would oversee the investigation of railroad abuses and the enforcement of the act. While the Interstate Commerce Commission was unique in its time, it became the model for future government regulatory agencies. Its initial purpose was to address the issues of railroad abuses and discrimination, in which large markets received greater pricing benefits and preferential treatment than did their smaller counterparts.

During the second half of the nineteenth century the railroad industry was rapidly growing and expanding. At that time, the railroads were privately owned and were not government regulated, resulting in cutthroat competition and rate wars among competitors. Abuses were widespread and rampant. This in turn caused a great deal of antirailroad sentiment, particularly among merchants and farmers. The Interstate Commerce Act of 1887 was a federal attempt to address the issue of the growing power of the railroads and their monopolistic tendencies. Directly aiming at commerce that crossed state lines on the railroad, the act shifted the responsibility of regulation from the individual states to the federal government. It would have a significant influence on interstate transportation issues as well as on future legislation of public utilities.

Context

By the end of the Civil War in 1865, the railroad was growing in track mileage and in importance to the American economy. At that time, the railroads were independently owned and unregulated, and the industry was highly competitive. Farmers and merchants, from the East Coast to the West Coast, dependent upon the railroad for survival, were affected by what was perceived to be the growing power of the railroad monopolies. Rate wars, cutthroat competition, and stock manipulation were widespread throughout the industry. The atmosphere was ripe for change.

By the 1870s Americans had begun to raise objections to the discriminatory practices of the railroads, particularly those involved in interstate commerce. Many called for regulatory measures. Numerous bills were proposed to regulate rates, investigate abuses and complaints, and curtail the railroad's use of pooling, rebating, and drawbacks, which many saw as discriminatory and unfair practices. For the railroad industry, pooling was the practice of railroads uniting to combine their resources. The practice of pooling also included the sharing of cargo and the sharing of profits and losses of freight shipments. In rebating, the railroads offered certain large customers money back or credit to their accounts, giving them an unfair pricing advantage over smaller companies. In a drawback, which is similar to a rebate, the railroads offered to certain customers the return of a portion of money already paid.

On the state level, the so-called Granger laws were passed in an effort to regulate the railroads within the individual states. During the 1870s, voluntary railroad associations were established, with the hope that the railroad industry might be able to fix the problems from within and regulate itself. In 1877 the U.S. Supreme Court upheld these state laws in *Munn v. Illinois*, which said the laws were just because they protected the public interest. This decision was reversed in *Wabash, St. Louis, & Pacific Railroad Co. v. Illinois* (1886), in which the Supreme Court ruled that the state regulations were unconstitutional because they interfered with interstate commerce. According to the Supreme Court, jurisdiction and regulation of interstate commerce were exclusively under the authority of the U.S. Congress.

In 1877, John H. Reagan introduced a bill into Congress known as the Reagan Bill, which was intended to reg-

1877

- Supreme Court decision in *Munn v. Illinois* upholds the state control of intrastate businesses, including railroads, through the so-called Granger laws.

1884

- The Reagan Bill is passed by the U.S. House of Representatives in an attempt to impose national regulation on the railroad industry.

1885

- The Cullom Bill is passed in the U.S. Senate, seeking to federally regulate interstate commerce and the railroad and calling for the establishment of an Interstate Commerce Commission.

1886

- In *Wabash, St. Louis, & Pacific Railroad Co. v. Illinois* the U.S. Supreme Court rules that state laws regulating interstate railroads are unconstitutional because they violate the commerce clause of the U.S. Constitution.

1887

- **February 4**
President Grover Cleveland signs the Interstate Commerce Act.

- **April 5**
The first session of the Interstate Commerce Commission convenes.

1879

- The congressional Hepburn Committee investigates alleged railroad abuses.

1889

- The National Association of Railroad Commissioners, a voluntary association, is established.

1890

- **July 2**
The Sherman Anti-Trust Act outlawing trusts and monopolies is signed by President Benjamin Harrison.

ulate the railroad industry by outlawing rebates and discrimination, regulate short- and long-haul commerce, and outlaw railroad pooling. Not longer after, Senator Shelby M. Cullom introduced the Cullom Bill into the Senate, where it was first passed in 1885. That same year Cullom chaired the Select Committee to Investigate Interstate Commerce, created to hear and investigate complaints regarding railroad abuses. Dozens of railroad men were called to the Senate to testify before the committee. Some of the key issues included rate discrepancies and discrimination between similarly situated customers and communities, accusations that the railroads were unduly influencing local and state governments, and free transportation to certain elected officials.

The Interstate Commerce Act of 1887 attempted to grant to the federal government some regulatory control over the railroad industry, particularly in regard to interstate commerce and transportation. It created the Interstate Commerce Commission as a vehicle to investigate complaints and abuses as well as to enforce the provisions of the act. This act shifted the responsibility of the regulation of interstate commerce from the states to the federal government. The act banned discriminatory practices, gave the commission the power to determine "reasonable and just" rates, and required that the railroads publicly disclose and publish their rates.

About the Author

The Interstate Commerce Act of 1887 was an act of Congress and, as such, does not have a specific author. Two men, however, played a major role in its creation: John H. Reagan and Shelby M. Cullom.

Born on October 8, 1818, in Sevierville, Tennessee, John Henninger Reagan moved to Texas in 1839. Trained as a surveyor, he later began to practice law. He was a member of the state house of representatives from 1847 to 1849. In 1852 he became a district judge of Navarro County. Involved in Democratic Party politics in Texas throughout the 1850s, he was elected to the U.S. House of Representatives from the Eastern District of Texas in 1857. On January 15, 1861, Reagan resigned from his seat in Congress. When the Civil War broke out, he served as the Confederate postmaster general. He was captured on May 9, 1865, and sent to Fort Warren in Boston harbor.

After the war, Reagan was a member of the Texas state constitutional convention in 1875. Reagan served as a U.S. congressman from March 4, 1875, to March 4, 1887, when he became a U.S. senator until his resignation on June 10, 1891. As a congressman, he introduced the Reagan Bill, legislation that attempted to regulate the railroad industry by outlawing rebates and discrimination, to regulate short- and long-haul commerce, and to outlaw railroad pooling. Some of the proposals in the bill were incorporated into the Interstate Commerce Act of 1887. In 1887, Reagan was chairman of the Committee' on Commerce, and after his resignation from the Senate he was appointed as a member of the railroad commission in Texas. He died in Palestine, Texas, on March 6, 1905.

Shelby Moore Cullom was born in Wayne County, Kentucky, on November 22, 1829. In 1837 he moved to Tazewell County, Illinois, and later made his home in Springfield. He was admitted to the bar in 1855 and was elected city attorney in Springfield that year. He served as a member of the Illinois House of Representatives in 1856 and again from 1860 to 1861. He was elected as a Republican to the U.S. Congress and served from March 4, 1865, to March 3, 1871. He was again elected as a member of the state house of representatives from 1873 to 1874. He served as governor of Illinois from 1877 to 1883. He resigned his post as governor to be a U.S. senator from March 4, 1883, to March 3, 1913. In the Senate he wrote and sponsored the Cullom Bill, first passed in 1885, which attempted to regulate interstate commerce and the railroad. Cullom chaired the Select Committee to Investigate Interstate Commerce, also known as the Cullom Committee, which was established on March 17, 1885, to investigate complaints against and abuses by the railroad and water routes traveling across state lines. One of the provisions in the Cullom Bill called for the establishment of an Interstate Commerce Commission. Several of his proposals from this bill were incorporated into the Interstate Commerce Act of 1887. While in the Senate, he also served on the Committee on Expenditures of Public Money, the Committee on Interstate Commerce, and the Committee on Foreign Relations; he was the Republican Conference chairman and regent of the Smithsonian Institution. Cullom also served as chairman of the Lincoln Memorial Commission. He died on January 28, 1914.

Explanation and Analysis of the Document

◆ Section 1

The opening section of the Interstate Commerce Act of 1887 acknowledges that the act was approved by both the Senate and the House of Representatives of the United States of America. It explains that the act applies to any carrier that transports either passengers or goods, by railroad or by water or a combination of both, across state lines, from one U.S. territory to another, or through the District of Columbia. It also covers transportation of passengers or goods to and from any country adjacent to the United States, such as Canada or Mexico, as well as other foreign countries. The act does not apply, however, to intrastate transportation of passengers or property or to receiving, delivering, storage, or handling of property within one state and not shipped to or from a foreign country from or to any state or territory. For the purpose of this act, the term *railroad* also applies to the bridges, ferries, and roads used in connection with railroad transportation. The term *transportation* as used in the act

Time Line	
1893	■ A depression causes severe problems to the railroad industry, already in economic trouble as a result of overextended trackage and rate wars.
1897	■ In the *Interstate Commerce Commission v. Alabama Midland Railway Company* case, the Supreme Court rules that competition from another railroad was sufficient to make circumstances different enough to justify exceptions to Section 4 of the Interstate Commerce Act of 1887.
1903	■ Congress passes the Elkins Act, the first of a series of significant amendments to the Interstate Commerce Act of 1887. This act is also known as the Elkins Anti-rebating Act. It was intended to end rebating in the railroad industry.
1906	■ Congress passes the Hepburn Act, the second significant amendment to the Interstate Commerce Act of 1887, extending the powers and jurisdiction of the Interstate Commerce Commission.
1910	■ The Mann-Elkins Act is passed by Congress, the third significant amendment to the Interstate Commerce Act of 1887. This act revitalized the long- and short-haul clause that had been weakened in the *Interstate Commerce Commission v. Alabama Midland Railway Company* case.

refers to any means of shipment or carriage. The act decrees that all charges in transportation services be "reasonable and just" but does not give further definition of those terms. All unjust and unreasonable charges are prohibited.

◆ Section 2

Rebates and personal discrimination of any kind are prohibited by this act. Any preferential treatment is declared "unjust discrimination."

◆ Section 3

Local discrimination and preferential treatment for passengers and property are forbidden; equal facilities for the interchange of traffic with connecting lines are ordered so as to not discriminate in carriers' rates and charges between those connecting lines. This section prohibits undue preference or prejudice in interstate commerce.

◆ Section 4

The so-called long- and short-haul clause prohibited charging higher rates for a shorter haul than for a longer haul under substantially similar circumstances and conditions. This section, however, does stipulate that a carrier may apply to the commission, under special conditions, to authorize an exception to charge less for a longer haul than for a shorter one and that the commission is authorized to do so.

◆ Section 5

All agreements to pool traffic or earnings are prohibited.

◆ Section 6

All rates are to be clearly published, conveniently posted, and adhered to. Published rates cannot be raised without ten days' public notice of the proposed changes. All rate changes must then be published and adhered to. Reductions of published rates may be made without previous public notice, but these reductions must then be published to the public. All carriers must provide copies of the schedule of rates to the commission, as well as copies of any agreements made between and among carriers. The commission has the right to determine the amount and place of publication of rates. Violations would be punishable.

◆ Section 7

It is forbidden to intentionally prevent the "continuous" carriage of freight in order to bypass the provisions of the act.

◆ Section 8

Common carriers who fail to obey the act will be liable to the person or persons injured by their actions, including payment of attorneys' fees.

◆ Section 9

Any person filing a complaint for damages may make the complaint directly to the commission or through a district or circuit court, but not both. This section also compels testimony of the defendant and the production of papers.

◆ Section 10

Each violation of the act would be subject to a fine not to exceed $5,000.

◆ Section 11

The Interstate Commerce Commission would be composed of five members, to be appointed by the president. The customary term of office for commissioners would be six years. No more than three members may be from the same political party. Commissioners may not be shareholders or financially connected with any common carriers.

◆ Section 12

The powers of the commission include investigation into the management of the common carriers as determined by this act, the right to obtain information from the carriers to enforce the act, and the power to require the attendance and testimony of witnesses and the production of books, papers, contracts and other material evidence relating to an investigation of a complaint. The commission has the right to invoke the aid of the U.S. courts to compel the appearance of witnesses and the production of papers in evidence.

◆ Section 13

This section discusses the procedures to make a complaint against a carrier. Complaints against the common carriers are to be submitted to the commission in the form of a petition; the commission in turn would forward the charges to the common carriers, who must then answer the complaint within a reasonable time. If reparations are made to the injured party, the common carrier is no longer liable for that complaint. Otherwise, the commission has the right and power to investigate the complaint.

◆ Section 14

When the commission carries out an investigation, it must make a written report of the facts that led to the conclusion of the investigation. At that time, the commission will recommend compensation. A copy of the commission's report must be kept for the record as well as sent to the person who filed the complaint and the common carrier involved in the case. The commission's decision may be used in future court appeal cases.

◆ Section 15

If, as a result of an investigation, the commission finds that the common carrier has violated a part of this act, the commission must notify the violators to "cease and desist" in violating the act, or to make reparation to the injured party.

◆ Section 16

If the violator of this act ignores the order of the commission, the commission may apply to the federal courts for assistance. The commission's report may be used as evidence in such cases. The court may then issue a written notice to the violator to stop the practice or to obey the order of the commission. The court may fine the violator up to $5,000 per day for each day that the violation continues or the commission's order remains unheeded. The court-ordered fines may be appealed to the U.S. Supreme Court by any of the parties involved.

◆ Section 17

The commission may operate in whatever way it can to conduct its business and to bring about justice. A majority vote of the commissioners is necessary, and the commis-

A STAY OF PROCEEDINGS.
The Foot of Monopoly — and the Hand of Cleveland.

This 1887 cartoon, titled "A Stay of Proceedings: The Foot of Monopoly and the Hand of Cleveland," illustrates the effect of the Interstate Commerce Act, in which Congress gave itself the power to regulate railroad monopolies.
(Library of Congress)

sion may make changes in its procedures as long as they are in keeping with the practices of the U.S. court system. All votes and officials acts of the commission must be kept in writing and be made available to the public upon request.

◆ Section 18

The annual salary for commissioners will be $7,500. The commission must appoint a secretary, who will be paid $3,500 per year. The commission may hire other employees, who will be paid as the commission decides, upon approval by the secretary of the interior. The secretary if the interior will furnish offices and supplies for the commission. After providing vouchers, the commission's business expenses will be paid by the secretary of the interior.

◆ Section 19

The main office of the commission will be in Washington, D.C., where its general meetings will be held. If necessary, the commissioners may hold meetings any-

where in the United States to address complaints or to carry out its duties.

◆ Section 20

The commission is authorized to require annual reports from all common carriers. These reports must include details about finance, profits, losses, operations, rates, regulations, and any agreements or contracts with other common carriers. The commission may also fix a period of time when all common carriers must follow a uniform system of accounts.

◆ Section 21

By December 1 of every year, the commission must provide a report to the secretary of the interior, which will be forwarded to Congress. The report should contain information and data relating to questions regarding the regulation of commerce. The commission may also include in this report any recommendations for future legislation.

"*All charges made for any service rendered or to be rendered in the transportation of passengers or property as aforesaid, or in connection therewith, or for the receiving, delivering, storage, or handling of such property, shall be reasonable and just.*"

(Section 1)

"*Unjust discrimination … is hereby prohibited and declared to be unlawful.*"

(Section 2)

"*Every common carrier subject to the provisions of this act shall according to their respective powers, afford all reasonable, proper and equal facilities for the interchange of traffic between their respective lines.*"

(Section 3)

"*That it shall be unlawful for any common carrier subject to the provisions of this act to charge or receive any greater compensation in the aggregate for the transportation of passengers or of like kind of property.*"

(Section 4)

"*That it shall be unlawful for any common carrier subject to the provisions of this act to enter into any contract, agreement, or combination with any other common carrier or carries for the pooling of freights of different and competing railroads.*"

(Section 5)

"*That every common carrier subject to the provisions of this act shall print and keep for public inspection schedules showing the rates and fares and charges for the transportation of passengers and property.*"

(Section 6)

"*That any person or persons claiming to be damaged by common carrier subject to the provisions of this act may either make complaint to the Commission as hereinafter provided for, or may bring suit in his or their own behalf for the recovery of the damages.*"

(Section 9)

Section 22

This act does not apply to the movement, storage, or handling of property belonging to federal, state, or local governments; charities; religious organizations or clergy; or employees of any railroad company. This act does not abridge or change laws already in practice but rather are in addition to them.

Section 23

The commission is appropriated the sum of $100,000 for the fiscal year ending June 30, 1888.

Section 24

Sections 11 and 18 of this act shall take effect immediately, and the rest shall take effect sixty days after its passage.

Audience

The Interstate Commerce Act of 1887 was written in an attempt to regulate and control the growing power and what seemed to be the corruption and unfair practices of the railroad industry. While the provisions of the act were directed mainly at the railroad carriers whose tracks crossed state lines in the transport of people and goods (that is, freight), it was also written as a means of protecting the customers of those railway lines. The act provided regulations and provisions that were required of all interstate commerce carriers, including the prohibition of unjust discrimination, rebates, pooling, and higher rate charges for short hauls on a long-haul line. It also, however, provided a mechanism, through the creation of the Interstate Commerce Commission, to enforce the act. In addition, the establishment of the commission became a medium for addressing complaints of abuses and infringements of the act. The commission also became the vehicle for investigating the railroads. It was through the Interstate Commerce Act that federal regulation of industry began.

Impact

The Interstate Commerce Act of 1887 was the first successful attempt to federally regulate industry in America. It specifically targeted the railroad industry and its interstate commerce practices by attempting to federally control and standardize that industry's traffic across state lines. It served as a model for future regulatory legislation, as the Interstate Commerce Commission likewise served as a model for governmental regulatory agencies. It was not long before the concept of "interstate commerce" was expanded to include much more than the transportation of goods and people across state lines. By the early twentieth century that definition grew to include motor vehicle regulations; water transportation; trucking and other interstate carriers; issues concerning railroad labor; child labor; means of communication, such as the telegraph, telephone, and cable lines; oil pipelines; aviation;

and racial discrimination on and in transportation lines or terminals. While it was not the original intention of the act, the commissioners addressed issues of civil rights complaints when they were filed. The commission's handling of these complaints often led to landmark U.S. Supreme Court cases, such as *Mitchell v. United States* (1941) and *Henderson v. United States* (1950). Both cases involved racial discrimination on railroad carriers that crossed state lines.

In 1914, under President Woodrow Wilson, the Federal Trade Commission Act, along with the Federal Trade Commission, was established to promote consumer protection and to curtail anticompetitive business practices. Other federal agencies patterned after the Interstate Commerce Commission included the Federal Communications Commission (1934), the U.S. Securities and Exchange Commission (1934), the National Labor Board (1935), the Civil Aeronautics Board (1940), and the Consumer Product Safety Commission (1972).

The Interstate Commerce Act was amended over time. As weaknesses in the act came to light, new legislation was passed to fix the inadequacies and to extend the jurisdiction of the commission: the Elkins Act (1903), the Hepburn Act (1906), the Mann-Elkins Act (1910) and the Transportation Act (1920). Further revisions were made to the Interstate Commerce Act in 1978, 1983, and 1994. When the Interstate Commerce Commission was finally disbanded in 1995, its remaining functions were transferred to the Department of Transportation.

Related Documents

Elkins Act, U.S. Statutes at Large 32 (1903): 847. The Elkins Act was intended to amend or fix the Interstate Commerce Act's inadequacy in preventing rebating in the railroad industry—that is, giving rebates to larger corporations—and it made the published rates the legal rates. This act allowed for the prosecution of the railroad companies that continued discriminatory practices, favorable rebating, and nonadherence to published rates.

Hepburn Act, U.S. Statutes at Large 584 (1906): 34. The purpose of the Hepburn Act was to amend or fix problems with the Interstate Commerce Act. The Hepburn Act extended the powers of the Interstate Commerce Commission, and thus the federal government, to include jurisdiction over railroad switches, spurs, yards, depots, terminals, express companies, companies operating pipelines transporting petroleum products, and companies operating sleeping cars on the railroads. It also gave the commission the right to replace existing rates with what it considered just and reasonable ones.

Mann-Elkins Act, U.S. Statutes at Large 36 (1910): 539. The Mann-Elkins Act was a further attempt to amend or fix the inadequacies of the Interstate Commerce Act. It revitalized the long- and short-haul clause of the Interstate Commerce Act, which had been weakened in the *Interstate Commerce Commission v. Alabama Midland Railway Company* Supreme Court case. The act allowed for the Interstate Commerce Commission to suspend changes in railroad rates until they were deemed reasonable by the commission. The Mann-Elkins Act also established the Commerce Court, which would review the commission's orders. The powers of the commission were further extended to include jurisdiction over telegraph, telephone, and cable lines.

Sherman Anti-Trust Act, U.S. Statutes at Large 26 (1890): 209. The Sherman Anti-Trust Act was the first federal law enacted by the U.S. Congress to outlaw trusts in an attempt to eliminate business monopolies. It was signed by President Benjamin Harrison on July 2, 1890.

Transportation Act, U.S. Statutes at Large 41 (1920): 476. The Transportation Act granted the Interstate Commerce Commission the right to approve pooling arrangements. The commission would also oversee the consolidation of the railroad systems. It further allowed the commission to fix minimum rates.

Bibliography

■ Articles

"Evolution of Federal Consumer Legislation." *Congressional Digest* (November 1992): 262–263.

Childs, William R. "State Regulators and Pragmatic Federalism in the United States, 1889–1945." *Business History Review* 75, no. 4 (2001): 701–738.

Doezema, William R. "Railroad Management and the Interplay of Federal and State Regulation, 1885–1916." *Business History Review* 50, no. 2 (1976): 153–178.

Freyer, Tony A. "The Federal Courts, Localism, and the National Economy, 1865–1900." *Business History Review* 53, no. 3 (1979): 343–363.

Gilligan, Thomas W., William J. Marshall, and Barry R. Weingast. "The Economic Incidence of the Interstate Commerce Act of 1887: A Theoretical and Empirical Analysis of the Short-Haul Pricing Constraint." *RAND Journal of Economics* 21, no. 2 (1990): 189–210.

Harbeson, Robert W. "Railroads and Regulation, 1877–1916: Conspiracy or Public Interest?" *Journal of Economic History* 27, no. 2. (1967): 230–242.

Hilton, George W. "The Consistency of the Interstate Commerce Act." *Journal of Law and Economics* 9 (October 1966): 87–113.

Kutler, Stanley I. "Chief Justice Taft, National Regulation, and the Commerce Power." *Journal of American History* 51, no. 4 (1965): 651–668.

Martin, Albro. "The Troubled Subject of Railroad Regulations in the Gilded Age—A Reappraisal." *Journal of American History* 61, no. 2 (1974): 339–371.

Nash, Gerald. "The Reformer Reformed: John H. Reagan and Railroad Regulation." *Business History Review* 29, no. 2. (1955), 189–196.

Peltzman, Sam. "Regulation and the Natural Progress of Opulence." Lecture presented at the AEI-Brooking Joint Center for Regulatory Studies, Washington, D.C., September 8, 2004.

Prager, Robin A. "Using Stock Price Data to Measure the Effects of Regulation: The Interstate Commerce Act and the Railroad Industry." *RAND Journal of Economics* 20, no. 2 (1989): 280–290.

Revell, Keith D. "Cooperation, Capture, and Autonomy: The Interstate Commerce Commission and the Port Authority in the 1920s." *Journal of Policy History* 12, no. 2 (2000): 177–214.

Ulen, Thomas S. "Cartels and Regulation: Late Nineteenth-Century Railroad Collusion and the Creation of the Interstate Commerce Commission." *Journal of Economic History* 40, no. 1 (March 1980): 179–181.

■ Books

Chandler, Alfred D., Jr., ed. *The Railroads: The Nation's First Big Business*. New York: Harcourt, Brace & World, 1965.

Cochran, Thomas C. *Railroad Leaders, 1845–1890: The Business Mind in Action*. New York: Russell & Russell, 1965.

Hoogenboom, Ari, and Olive Hoogenboom. *A History of the ICC: From Panacea to Palliative*. New York: W. W. Norton, 1976.

Kolko, Gariel. *Railroads and Regulation, 1877–1916*. Princeton, N.J.: Princeton University Press: 1965.

MacAvoy, Paul W., and John W. Snow, eds. *Railroad Revitalization and Regulatory Reform*. Washington, D.C.: American Enterprise Institute for Public Policy Research, 1977.

Ripley, William Z. *Railroads: Rates and Regulation*. 1912. Reprint. New York: Arno Press, 1973.

Scott, James C. *Presidents, Parties, and the State: A Party System Perspective on Democratic Regulatory Choice, 1884–1936*. New York: Cambridge University Press, 2000.

Stone, Richard D. *The Interstate Commerce Commission and the Railroad Industry: A History of Regulatory Policy*. New York: Praeger: 1991.

■ Web Sites

"Cullom, Shelby Moore, (1829–1914)." Biographical Directory of the United States Congress Web site.
   http://bioguide.congress.gov/scripts/biodisplay.pl?index=C0009 73. Accessed on December 21, 2007.

"Interstate Commerce Act." Ohio History Central, an Online Encyclopedia of Ohio History Web site.
   http://www.ohiohistorycentral.org/entry.php?rec=1477. Accessed on December 21, 2007.

"People and Events: Interstate Commerce Commission." American Experience Web site.
  http://www.pbs.org/wgbh/amex/streamliners/peopleevents/e_ica.html. Accessed on December 21, 2007.

"Reagan, John Henninger, (1818–1905)." Biographical Directory of the United States Congress Web site.
  http://bioguide.congress.gov/scripts/biodisplay.pl?index=R000098. Accessed on December 21, 2007.

van Ophem, Marieke. "Railroads and Regulation: The Interstate Commerce Act." In *The Iron Horse: The Impact of the Railroads on 19th Century American Society.* From Revolution to Reconstruction Web site.
  http://www.let.rug.nl/usa/E/ironhorse/ironhorse28.htm. Accessed on December 21, 2007.

—By Caroline Fuchs

Questions for Further Study

1. The Interstate Commerce Act of 1887 was the first legislative attempt to federally regulate industry in the United States. In recent years, what federal legislation has attempted to regulate U.S. business or industry? What event or events prompted the legislation? Who was responsible for its promotion? Would you consider this recent legislation a success or failure? Explain.

2. Often the Interstate Commerce Act of 1887 is cited as an example of Progressive Era legislation. What is meant by that statement? Who were "the Progressives"? Identify and explain three other examples of Progressive Era legislation. What did they all have in common? Identify another group that has a similar outlook today. Discuss these similarities.

3. Some early proponents of the Interstate Commerce Act argued that the federal government should not have the power to regulate or override state laws or states' rights. Can you think of a similar argument used today? Explain.

4. By the end of the eighteenth century the railroad industry was one of the fastest-growing and most powerful industries in the United States, and it was much criticized for its monopolistic policies and corruption. What growing American industry today is under similar attack? What legislation might be needed to curb its power? Imagine you are a U.S. senator. Draft a bill, with at least four parts, that would attempt to regulate the industry you have identified.

5. Lobbyists advocate for or against proposed congressional legislation. Identify at least two groups in America today that have strong lobbying power. What motivates them? What types off legislation do they favor? Why? What legislation do they oppose? Why?

Glossary

aggregate	combined total
abet	assist
carriage	means of transporting people or goods
cease and desist	stop; discontinue
common carrier	an individual or a company that transports people or goods from one place to another for a fee; a transportation company
complainant	an accuser; someone who makes a complaint
contravention	an act against or in breach of
drawback	a rebate on taxes or fees paid
lessee	leaseholder
litigation	lawsuit; legal action
pecuniarily	financially
penal	subject to punishment; legally punishable
pooling	an agreement to unite; a combining of resources; the sharing of cargo or the profit or loss from freight transport
prescribe	to recommend or order
prima facie evidence	evidence that is acceptable as proof until other evidence proves differently
quorum	the minimum number of persons who must agree for an order or decision to be binding
reparation	compensation; payment for damages
supersede	to replace; to override
writs of attachment	written court orders to seize a debtor's property in order to pay a creditor
writ of execution	a written order to enforce a court judgment; a written court order authorizing the seizure or taking of property or assets
writ of injunction	a written court order or demand for someone to cease a course of action or be prevented from following a course of action

INTERSTATE COMMERCE ACT

An act to regulate Commerce

Be it enacted by the Senate and House of Representatives of the United States of America in Congress assembled, That the provisions of this act shall apply to any common carrier or carriers engaged in the transportation of passengers or property wholly by railroad, or partly by railroad and partly by water when both are used, under a common control, management, or arrangement, for a continuous carriage or shipment, from one State or Territory of the United States, or the District of Columbia, to any other State or Territory of the United States, or the District of Columbia, or from any place in the United States to an adjacent foreign country, or from any place in the United States through a foreign country to any other place in the United States, and also to the transportation in like manner of property shipped from any place in the United States to a foreign country and carried from such place to a port of trans-shipment, or shipped from a foreign country to any place in the United States and carried to such place from a port of entry either in the United States or an adjacent foreign country: *Provided, however,* That the provisions of this act shall not apply to the transportation of passengers or property, or to the receiving, delivering, storage, or handling of property, wholly within one State, and not shipped to or from a foreign country from or to any State or Territory as aforesaid.

The term "railroad" as used in this act shall include all bridges and ferries used or operated in connection with any railroad, and also all the road in use by any corporation operating a railroad, whether owned or operated under a contract, agreement, or lease; and the term "transportation" shall include all instrumentalities of shipment or carriage.

All charges made for any service rendered or to be rendered in the transportation of passengers or property as aforesaid, or in connection therewith, or for the receiving, delivering, storage, or handling of such

property, shall be reasonable and just; and every unjust and unreasonable charge for such service is prohibited and declared to be unlawful.

Sec. 2. That if any common carrier subject to the provisions of this act shall, directly or indirectly, by any special rate, rebate, drawback, or other device, charge, demand, collect, or receive from any person or persons a greater or less compensation for any service rendered, or to be rendered, in the transportation of passengers or property, subject to the provisions of this act, than it charges, demands, collects, or receives from any other person or persons for doing for him or them a like and contemporaneous service in the transportation of a like kind of traffic under substantially similar circumstances and conditions, such common carrier shall be deemed guilty of unjust discrimination, which is hereby prohibited and declared to be unlawful.

Sec. 3. That it shall be unlawful for any common carrier subject to the provisions of this act to make or give any undue or unreasonable preference or advantage to any particular person, company, firm, corporation, or locality, or any particular description of traffic, in any respect whatsoever, or to subject any particular person, company, firm, corporation, or locality, or any particular description of traffic, to any undue or unreasonable prejudice or disadvantage in any respect whatsoever.

Every common carrier subject to the provisions of this act shall according to their respective powers, afford all reasonable, proper, and equal facilities for the interchange of traffic between their respective lines, and for the receiving, forwarding, and delivering of passengers and property to and from their several lines and those connection therewith, and shall not discriminate in their rates and charges between such connecting lines; but this shall not be construed as requiring any such common carrier to give the use of its tracks or terminal facilities to another carrier engaged in like business.

Sec. 4. That it shall be unlawful for any common carrier subject to the provisions of this act to charge or receive any greater compensation in the aggregate for the transportation of passengers or of like kind of property, under substantially similar circumstances and conditions, for a shorter than for a longer distance over the same line, in the same direction, the shorter being included within the longer distance; but this shall not be construed as authorizing any common carrier within the terms of this act to charge and receive as great compensation for a shorter as for a longer distance: *Provided, however*, That upon application to the Commission appointed under the provisions of this act, such common carrier may, in special cases, after investigation by the Commission, be authorized to charge less for longer than for shorter distances for the transportation of passengers or property; and the Commission may from time to time prescribe the extent to which such designated common carrier may be relieved from the operation of this section of this act.

Sec. 5. That it shall be unlawful for any common carrier subject to the provisions of this act to enter into any contract, agreement, or combination with any other common carrier or carriers for the pooling of freights of different and competing railroads, or to divide between them the aggregate or net proceeds of the earnings of such railroads, or any portion thereof; and in any case of an agreement for the pooling of freights as aforesaid, each day of its continuance shall be deemed a separate offense.

Sec. 6. That every common carrier subject to the provisions of this act shall print and keep for public inspection schedules showing the rates and fares and charges for the transportation of passengers and property which any such common carrier has established and which are in force at the time upon its railroad, as defined by the first section of this act. The schedules printed as aforesaid by any such common carrier shall plainly state the places upon its railroad between which property and passengers will be carried, and shall contain the classification of freight in force upon such railroad, and shall also state separately the terminal charges and any rules or regulations which in any wise change, affect, or determine any part or the aggregate of such aforesaid rates and fares and charges. Such schedules shall be plainly printed in large type, of at least the size of ordinary pica, and copies for the use of the public shall be kept in every depot or station upon any such railroad, in such places and in such form that they can be conveniently inspected.

Any common carrier subject to the provisions of this act receiving freight in the United States to be carried through a foreign country to any place in the United States shall also in like manner print and keep for public inspection, at every depot where such freight is received for shipment, schedules showing the through rates established and charged by such common carrier to all points in the United States beyond the foreign country to which it accepts freight for shipment; and any freight shipped from the United States through a foreign country into the United States, the through rate on which shall not have been made public as required by this act, shall, before it is admitted into the United States from said foreign country, be subject to customs duties as if said freight were of foreign production; and any law in conflict with this section is hereby repealed.

No advance shall be made in the rates, fares, and charges which have been established and published as aforesaid by any common carrier in compliance with the requirements of this section, except after ten days' public notice, which shall plainly state the changes proposed to be made in the schedule then in force, and the time when the increased rates, fares, or charges will go into effect; and the proposed changes shall be shown by printing new schedules, or shall be plainly indicated upon the schedules in force at the time and kept for public inspection. Reductions in such published rates, fares, or charges may be made without previous public notice; but whenever any such reduction is made, notice of the same shall immediately be publicly posted and the changes made shall immediately be made public by printing new schedules, or shall immediately be plainly indicated upon the schedules at the time in force and kept for public inspection.

And when any such common carrier shall have established and published its rates, fares, and charges in compliance with the provisions of this section, it shall be unlawful for such common carrier to charge, demand, collect, or receive from any person or persons a greater or less compensation for the transportation of passengers or property, or for any services in connection therewith, than is specified in such published schedule of rates, fares, and charges as may at the time be in force.

Every common carrier subject to the provisions of this act shall file with the Commission hereinafter provided for copies of its schedules of rates, fares, and charges which have been established and published in compliance with the requirements of this section, and shall promptly notify said Commission of all changes made in the same. Every such common carrier shall also file with said Commission copies of all contracts, agreements, or arrangements with other common carriers in relation to any traffic affected by the provisions of this act to which it may be a party. And in cases where passengers and freight pass over continuous lines or routes operated by more than one common carrier, and the several common carriers operating such lines or routes establish joint tariffs of rates or fares or charges for such continuous lines or routes, copies of such joint tariffs shall also, in like manner, be filed with said Commission. Such joint rates, fares, and charges on such continuous lines so filed as aforesaid shall be made public by such common carriers when directed by said Commission, in so far as may, in the judgment of the Commission, be deemed practicable; and said Commission shall from time to time prescribe the measure of publicity which shall be given to such rates, fares, and charges, or to such part of them as it may deem it practicable for such common carriers to publish, and the places in which they shall be published; but no common carrier party to any such joint tariff shall be liable for the failure of any other common carrier party thereto to observe and adhere to the rates, fares, or charges thus made and published.

If any such common carrier shall neglect or refuse to file or publish its schedules or tariffs of rates, fares, and charges as provided in this section, or any part of the same, such common carrier shall, in addition to other penalties herein prescribed, be subject to a writ of mandamus, to be issued by any circuit court of the United States in the judicial district wherein the principal office of said common carrier is situated or wherein such offense may be committed, and if such common carrier be a foreign corporation, in the judicial circuit wherein such common carrier accepts traffic and has an agent to perform such service, to compel compliance with the aforesaid provisions of this section; and such writ shall issue in the name of the people of the United States, at the relation of the Commissioners appointed under the provisions of this act; and failure to comply with its requirements shall be punishable as and for a contempt; and the said Commissioners, as complainants, may also apply, in any such circuit of the United States, for a writ of injunction against such common carrier, to restrain such common carrier from receiving or transporting property among the several States and Territories of the United States, or between the United States and adjacent foreign countries, or between ports of transshipment

and of entry and the several States and Territories of the United States, as mentioned in the first section of this act, until such common carrier shall have complied with the aforesaid provisions of this section of this act.

Sec. 7. That it shall be unlawful for any common carrier subject to the provisions of this act to enter into any combination, contract, or agreement, expressed or implied, to prevent, by change of time schedule, carriage in different cars, or by other means or devices, the carriage of freights from being continuous from the place of shipment to the place of destination; and no break of bulk, stoppage, or interruption made by such common carrier shall prevent the carriage of freights from being and being treated as one continuous carriage from the place of shipment to the place of destination, unless such break, stoppage, or interruption was made in good faith for some necessary purpose, and without any intent to avoid or unnecessarily interrupt such continuous carriage or to evade any of the provisions of this act.

Sec. 8. That in case any common carrier subject to the provisions of this act shall do, cause to be done, or permit to be done any act, matter, or thing in this act prohibited or declared to be unlawful, or shall omit to do any act, matter, or thing in this act required to be done, such common carrier shall be liable to the person or persons injured thereby for the full amount of damages sustained in consequence of any such violation of the provisions of this act, together with a reasonable counsel or attorney's fee, to be fixed by the court in every case of recovery, which attorney's fee shall be taxed and collected as part of the costs in the case.

Sec. 9. That any person or persons claiming to be damaged by any common carrier subject to the provisions of this act may either make complaint to the Commission as hereinafter provided for, or may bring suit in his or their own behalf for the recovery of the damages for which such common carrier may be liable under the provisions of this act, in any district or circuit court of the United States of competent jurisdiction; but such person or persons shall not have the right to pursue both of said remedies, and must in each case elect which one of the two methods of procedure herein provided for he or they will adopt. In any such action brought for the recovery of damages the court before which the same shall be pending may compel any director, officer, receiver, trustee, or agent of the corporation or company defendant in such suit to attend, appear, and testify in such case, and may compel the production of the books and papers of such corporation or company party to any such suit; the claim that any such testimony or evidence may tend to criminate the person giving such evidence shall not excuse such witness from testifying, but such evidence or testimony shall not be used against such person on the trial of any criminal proceeding.

Sec. 10. That any common carrier subject to the provisions of this act, or, whenever such common carrier is a corporation, any director or officer thereof, or any receiver, trustee, lessee, agent, or person acting for or employed by such corporation, who, alone or with any other corporation, company, person, or party, shall willfully do or cause to be done, or shall willingly suffer or permit to be done, any act, matter, or thing in this act prohibited or declared to be unlawful, or who shall aid or abet therein, or shall willfully omit or fail to do any act, matter, or thing in this act required to be done, or shall cause or willingly suffer or permit any act, matter, or thing so directed or required by this act to be done not to be so done, or shall aid or abet any such omission or failure, or shall be guilty of any infraction of this act, or shall aid or abet therein, shall be deemed guilty of a misdemeanor, and shall, upon conviction thereof in any district court of the United States within the jurisdiction of which such offense was committed, be subject to a fine of not to exceed five thousand dollars for each offense.

Sec. 11. That a Commission is hereby created and established to be known as the Inter-State Commerce Commission, which shall be composed of five Commissioners, who shall be appointed by the President, by and with the advice and consent of the Senate. The Commissioners first appointed under this act shall continue in office for the term of two, three, four, five, and six years, respectively, from the first day of January, anno Domini eighteen hundred and eighty-seven, the term of each to be designated by the President; but their successors shall be appointed for terms of six years, except that any person chosen to fill a vacancy shall be appointed only for the unexpired term of the Commissioner whom he shall succeed. Any Commissioner may be removed by the President for inefficiency, neglect of duty, or malfeasance in office. Not more than three of the Commissioners shall be appointed from the same political party. No person in the employ of or holding any official relation to any common carrier subject to the provisions of this act, or owning stock or bonds thereof, or who is in any manner pecuniarily interested therein, shall enter upon the duties of or hold

such office. Said Commissioners shall not engage in any other business, vocation, or employment. No vacancy in the Commission shall impair the right of the remaining Commissioners to exercise all the powers of the Commission.

Sec. 12. That the Commission hereby created shall have authority to inquire into the management of the business of all common carriers subject to the provisions of this act, and shall keep itself informed as to the manner and method in which the same is conducted, and shall have the right to obtain from such common carriers full and complete information necessary to enable the Commission to perform the duties and carry out the objects for which it was created; and for the purposes of this act the Commission shall have power to require the attendance and testimony of witnesses and the production of all books, papers, tariffs, contracts, agreements, and documents relating to any matter under investigation, and to that end may invoke the aid of any court of the United States in requiring the attendance and testimony of witnesses and the production of books, papers, and documents under the provisions of this section.

And any of the circuit courts of the United States within the jurisdiction of which such inquiry is carried on may, in case of contumacy or refusal to obey a subpoena issued to any common carrier subject to the provisions of this act, or other person, issue an order requiring such common carrier or other person to appear before said Commission (and produce books and papers if so ordered) and give evidence touching the matter in question; and any failure to obey such order of the court may be punished by such court as a contempt thereof. The claim that any such testimony or evidence may tend to criminate the person giving such evidence shall not excuse such witness from testifying; but such evidence or testimony shall not be used against such person on the trial of any criminal proceeding.

Sec. 13. That any person, firm, corporation, or association, or any mercantile, agricultural, or manufacturing society, or any body politic or municipal organization complaining of anything done or omitted to be done by any common carrier subject to the provisions of this act in contravention of the provisions thereof, may apply to said Commission by petition, which shall briefly state the facts; whereupon a statement of the charges thus made shall be forwarded by the Commission to such common carrier, who shall be called upon to satisfy the complaint or to answer the same in writing within a reasonable time, to be specified by the Commission. If such common carrier, within the time specified, shall make reparation for the injury alleged to have been done, said carrier shall be relieved of liability to the complainant only for the particular violation of law thus complained of. If such carrier shall not satisfy the complaint within the time specified, or there shall appear to be any reasonable ground for investigating said complaint, it shall be the duty of the Commission to investigate the matters complained of in such manner and by such means as it shall deem proper.

Said Commission shall in like manner investigate any complaint forwarded by the railroad commissioner or railroad commission of any State or Territory, at the request of such commissioner or commission, and may institute any inquiry on its own motion in the same manner and to the same effect as though complaint had been made.

No complaint shall at any time be dismissed because of the absence of direct damage to the complainant.

Sec. 14. That whenever an investigation shall be made by said Commission, it shall be its duty to make a report in writing in respect thereto, which shall include the findings of fact upon which the conclusions of the Commission are based, together with its recommendation as to what reparation, if any, should be made by the common carrier to any party or parties who may be found to have been injured; and such findings so made shall thereafter, in all judicial proceedings, be deemed prima facie evidence as to each and every fact found.

All reports of investigations made by the Commission shall be entered of record, and a copy thereof shall be furnished to the party who may have complained, and to any common carrier that may have been complained of.

Sec. 15. That if in any case in which an investigation shall be made by said Commission it shall be made to appear to the satisfaction of the Commission, either by the testimony of witnesses or other evidence, that anything has been done or omitted to be done in violation of the provisions of this act, or of any law cognizable by said Commission, by any common carrier, or that any injury or damage has been sustained by the party or parties complaining, or by other parties aggrieved in consequence of any such violation, it shall be the duty of the Commission to forth with cause a copy of its report in respect thereto to be delivered to such common carrier, together with a notice to said common carrier to cease and desist from such violation, or to make reparation for the injury so found to have been done,

or both, within a reasonable time, to be specified by the Commission; and if, within the time specified, it shall be made to appear to the Commission that such common carrier has ceased from such violation of law, and has made reparation for the injury found to have been done, in compliance with the report and notice of the Commission, or to the satisfaction of the party complaining, a statement to that effect shall be entered of record by the Commission, and the said common carrier shall thereupon be relieved from further liability or penalty for such particular violation of law.

Sec. 16. That whenever any common carrier, as defined in and subject to the provisions of this act, shall violate or refuse or neglect to obey any lawful order or requirement of the Commission in this act named, it shall be the duty of the Commission, and lawful for any company or person interested in such order or requirement, to apply, in a summary way, by petition, to the circuit court of the United States sitting in equity in the judicial district in which the common carrier complained of has its principal office, or in which the violation or disobedience of such order or requirement shall happen, alleging such violation or disobedience, as the case may be; and the said court shall have power to hear and determine the matter, on such short notice to the common carrier complained of as the court shall deem reasonable; and such notice may be served on such common carrier, his or its officers, agents, or servants, in such manner as the court shall direct; and said court shall proceed to hear and determine the matter speedily as a court of equity, and without the formal pleadings and proceedings applicable to ordinary suits in equity, but in such manner as to do justice in the premises; and to this end such court shall have power, if it think fit, to direct and prosecute, in such mode and by such persons as it may appoint, all such inquiries as the court may think needful to enable it to form a just judgment in the matter of such petition; and on such hearing the report of said Commission shall be prima facie evidence of the matters therein stated; and if it be made to appear to such court, on such hearing or on report of any such person or persons, that the lawful order or requirement of said Commission drawn in question has been violated or disobeyed, it shall be lawful for such court to issue a writ of injunction or other proper process, mandatory or otherwise, to restrain such common carrier from further continuing such violation or disobedience of such order or requirement of said Commission, and enjoining obedience to the same; and in case of any disobedience of any such writ of injunction or other proper process, mandatory or otherwise, it shall be lawful for such court to issue writs of attachment, or any other process of said court incident or applicable to writs of injunction or other proper process, mandatory or otherwise, against such common carrier, and if a corporation, against one or more of the directors, officers, or agents of the same, or against any owner, lessee, trustee, receiver, or other person failing to obey such writ of injunction or other proper process, mandatory or otherwise; and said court may, if it shall think fit, make an order directing such common carrier or other person so disobeying such writ of injunction or other proper process, mandatory or otherwise, to pay such sum of money not exceeding for each carrier or person in default the sum of five hundred dollars for every day after a day to be named in the order that such carrier or other person shall fail to obey such injunction or other proper process, mandatory or otherwise; and such moneys shall be payable as the court shall direct, either to the party complaining, or into court to abide the ultimate decision of the court, or into the Treasury; and payment thereof may, without prejudice to any other mode of recovering the same, be enforced by attachment or order in the nature of a writ of execution, in like manner as if the same had been recovered by a final decree in person in such court. When the subject in dispute shall be of the value of two thousand dollars or more, either party to such proceeding before said court may appeal to the Supreme Court of the United States, under the same regulations now provided by law in respect of security for such appeal; but such appeal shall not operate to stay or supersede the order of the court or the execution of any writ or process thereon; and such court may, in every such matter, order the payment of such costs and counsel fees as shall be deemed reasonable. Whenever any such petition shall be filed or presented by the Commission it shall be the duty of the district attorney, under the direction of the Attorney-General of the United States, to prosecute the same; and the costs and expenses of such prosecution shall be paid out of the appropriation for the expenses of the courts of the United States. For the purposes of this act, excepting its penal provisions, the circuit courts of the United States shall be deemed to be always in session.

Sec. 17. That the Commission may conduct its proceedings in such manner as will best conduce to the proper dispatch of business and to the ends of justice. A majority of the Commission shall constitute a quorum for the transaction of business, but no Commissioner shall participate in any hearing or proceeding in which he has any pecuniary interest. Said Commission may, from time to time, make or amend such general rules or orders as may be requisite for the order and regulation of proceedings before it, including forms of notices and the service thereof, which shall conform, as nearly as may be, to those in use in the courts of the United States. Any party may appear before said Commission and be heard, in person or by attorney. Every vote and official act of the Commission shall be entered of record, and its proceedings shall be public upon the request of either party interested. Said Commission shall have an official seal, which shall be judicially noticed. Either of the members of the Commission may administer oaths and affirmations.

Sec. 18. That each Commissioner shall receive an annual salary of seven thousand five hundred dollars, payable in the same manner as the salaries of judges of the courts of the United States. The Commission shall appoint a secretary, who shall receive an annual salary of three thousand five hundred dollars, payable in like manner. The Commission shall have authority to employ and fix the compensation of such other employees as it may find necessary to the proper performance of its duties, subject to the approval of the Secretary of the Interior.

The Commission shall be furnished by the Secretary of the Interior with suitable offices and all necessary office supplies. Witnesses summoned before the Commission shall be paid the same fees and mileage that are paid witnesses in the courts of the United States.

All of the expenses of the Commission, including all necessary expenses for transportation incurred by the Commissioners, or by their employees under their orders, in making any investigation in any other places than in the city of Washington, shall be allowed and paid, on the presentation of itemized vouchers therefor approved by the chairman of the Commission and the Secretary of the Interior.

Sec. 19. That the principal office of the Commission shall be in the city of Washington, where its general sessions shall be held; but whenever the convenience of the public or of the parties may be promoted or delay or expense prevented thereby, the Commission may hold special sessions in any part of the United States. It may, by one or more of the Commissioners, prosecute any inquiry necessary to its duties, in any part of the United States, into any matter or question of fact pertaining to the business of any common carrier subject to the provisions of this act.

Sec. 20. That the Commission is hereby authorized to require annual reports from all common carriers subject to the provisions of this act, to fix the time and prescribe the manner in which such reports shall be made, and to require from such carriers specific answers to all questions upon which the Commission may need information. Such annual reports shall show in detail the amount of capital stock issued, the amounts paid therefor, and the manner of payment for the same; the dividends paid, the surplus fund, if any, and the number of stockholders; the funded and floating debts and the interest paid thereon; the cost and value of the carrier's property, franchises, and equipment; the number of employees and the salaries paid each class; the amounts expended for improvements each year, how expended, and the character of such improvements; the earnings and receipts from each branch of business and from all sources; the operating and other expenses; the balances of profit and loss; and a complete exhibit of the financial operations of the carrier each year, including an annual balance sheet. Such reports shall also contain such information in relation to rates or regulations concerning fares or freights, or agreements, arrangements, or contracts with other common carriers, as the Commission may require; and the said Commission may, within its discretion, for the purpose of enabling it the better to carry out the purposes of this act, prescribe (if in the opinion of the Commission it is practicable to prescribe such uniformity and methods of keeping accounts) a period of time within which all common carriers subject to the provisions of this act shall have, as near as may be, a uniform system of accounts, and the manner in which such accounts shall be kept.

Sec. 21. That the Commission shall, on or before the first day of December in each year, make a report to the Secretary of the Interior, which shall be by him transmitted to Congress, and copies of which shall be distributed as are the other reports issued from the Interior Department. This report shall contain such information and data collected by the Commission as may be considered of value in the determination of questions connected with the regulation of commerce, together with such recommendations as to additional legislation relating thereto as the Commission may deem necessary.

Sec. 22. That nothing in this act shall apply to the carriage, storage, or handling of property free or at reduced rates for the United States, State, or municipal governments, or for charitable purposes, or to or from fairs and expositions for exhibition thereat, or the issuance of mileage, excursion, or commutation passenger tickets; nothing in this act shall be construed to prohibit any common carrier from giving reduced rates to ministers of religion; nothing in this act shall be construed to prevent railroads from giving free carriage to their own officers and employees, or to prevent the principal officers of any railroad company or companies from exchanging passes or tickets with other railroad companies for their officers and employees; and nothing in this act contained shall in any way abridge or alter the remedies now existing at common law or by statute, but the provisions of this act are in addition to such remedies: *Provided*, That no pending litigation shall in any way be affected by this act.

Sec. 23. That the sum of one hundred thousand dollars is hereby appropriated for the use and purposes of this act for the fiscal year ending June thirtieth, anno Domini eighteen hundred and eighty-eight, and the intervening time anterior thereto.

Sec. 24. That the provisions of sections eleven and eighteen of this act, relating to the appointment and organization of the Commission herein provided for, shall take effect immediately, and the remaining provisions of this act shall take effect sixty days after its passage.

Approved, February 4, 1887.

Forty-Ninth Congress of the United States of America;

At the Second Session,

Begun and held at the City of Washington on Monday, the sixth day of December, one thousand eight hundred and eighty-six.

AN ACT

To provide for the allotment of lands in severalty to Indians on the various reservations, and to extend the protection of the laws of the United States and the Territories over the Indians, and for other purposes.

Be it enacted by the Senate and House of Representatives of the United States of America in Congress assembled, **That** in all cases where any tribe or band of Indians has been, or shall hereafter be, located upon any reservation created for their use, either by treaty stipulation or by virtue of an act of Congress or executive order setting apart the same for their use, the President of the United States be, and he hereby is, authorized, whenever in his opinion any reservation or any part thereof of such Indians is advantageous for agricultural and grazing purposes, to cause said reservation, or any part thereof, to be surveyed, or resurveyed if necessary, and to allot the lands in said reservation in severalty to any Indian located thereon in quantities as follows:

To each head of a family, one-quarter of a section;

To each single person over eighteen years of age, one-eighth of a section;

To each orphan child under eighteen years of age, one-eighth of a section; and

To each other single person under eighteen years now living, or who may be born prior to the date of the order of the President directing an allotment of the lands embraced in any reservation, one-sixteenth of a section: Provided, That in case there is not sufficient land in any of said reservations to allot lands to each individual of the classes above named in quantities as above provided, the lands embraced in such reservation or reservations shall be allotted to each individual of each of said classes pro rata in accordance with the provisions of this act: And provided further, That where the treaty or act of Congress setting apart such reservation provides for the allotment of lands in severalty in quantities in excess of those herein provided, the President, in making allotments upon such reservation, shall allot the lands to each individual Indian belonging thereon in quantity as specified in such treaty or act: And provided further, That when the lands allotted are only valuable for grazing

---

The Dawes Severalty Act (National Archives and Records Administration)

DAWES SEVERALTY ACT

1887

"Every Indian born within the territorial limits of the United States to whom allotments shall have been made ... is hereby declared to be a citizen of the United States."

Overview

In the second half of the nineteenth century the federal government initiated an aggressive set of policies designed to free up western land for white settlers and to acculturate American Indians to American values and practices. Decades of work toward this end culminated in the Dawes Severalty Act of 1887. Named after the Massachusetts senator Henry L. Dawes, who headed the Senate's Committee on Indian Affairs, the act broke the land of most remaining reservations into parcels to be farmed by individual American Indians or nuclear American Indian families. Partitioning Indian land in this manner, Congress hoped, would force native peoples to give up communal living and to adopt American farming practices. Eventually, policy makers reasoned, American Indians would embrace all American cultural norms and become integrated into U.S. society.

When the Dawes Act passed in 1887, Americans' views of native peoples varied considerably. Some groups, particularly evangelicals, dedicated themselves to both the religious and the cultural conversion of American Indians. Viewing themselves as benevolent teachers, they believed that they had a duty to acculturate American Indians. Others thought that American Indians were inassimilable, racially inferior savages who were destined for extinction. Few felt that Indian tribes deserved to be treated as sovereign nations as they had been in the past. While the crafters of the Dawes Act believed themselves to have the best interests of American Indians at heart, the act ultimately hurt native peoples, dispossessing them of their lands and further marginalizing them. People unsympathetic to American Indians manipulated the Dawes Act for their own financial gain, resulting in the massive displacement of native peoples. As a consequence, by 1900 the American Indian population had fallen to its lowest point in U.S. history.

Context

Following the Civil War, Americans had a reinvigorated interest in western migration. Transnational railroads made western migration safer and faster than it had been in the past. At the same time, rapid population growth resulting largely from immigration contributed to overcrowding of urban areas and competition for jobs. Many saw the Jeffersonian hope for a nation of independent homesteaders as less and less realistic. Nevertheless, many Americans resisted "wage slavery," determined to pursue the dream of homesteading. The federal government aided potential homesteaders by passing the Homestead Act in 1862, providing land grants to hundreds of thousands of Americans.

White American migration into the West did not occur without opposition, however. The trans-Mississippi West was home to both American Indians native to that region and tribes that had been forcibly migrated from the eastern United States in the eighteenth and early nineteenth centuries. These groups did not passively accept homesteaders' claims to their land. Those who posed the greatest obstacle to American homesteaders were the Plains Indians. Primarily semisedentary people, the Plains Indians, including the Cheyenne, the Comanche, the Crow, the Kiowa, and the Sioux, subsisted mainly by hunting buffalo. Homesteaders impeded their ability to survive by breaking land into parcels protected as private property, preventing both the buffalo and the Plains Indians from roaming freely. In many cases Native Americans responded violently in an effort to deter settlers. Homesteaders in turn complained that the government should protect them from Indian attacks. The situation in the West was exacerbated because businessmen, homesteaders, and railroad companies also wanted to remove the American Indians living on reservations in the West. Although the federal government had initially set up reservations in areas considered undesirable for white settlement, as land grew scarcer, the appeal of reservation land increased. In addition, in some cases, such as in the Dakota Territory, valuable natural resources like gold were discovered on Indian lands.

Throughout the second half of the nineteenth century, Native Americans responded to white settlers in a number of ways. Many tribal leaders appealed to U.S. politicians to recognize their equality as men and to appreciate tribal sovereignty. Those who made treaties with the federal government or received promises of land rights lacked recourse when the agreements were ignored or forgotten. Conse-

Time Line

1862

■ **May 6**
Congress passes the Homestead Act, which encourages western settlement by independent homesteaders.

1864

■ **November 29**
A Colorado militia attacks and murders sleeping Cheyenne and Arapaho Indians who had been relocated to Colorado.

1865–1867

■ The Great Sioux War occurs when the Sioux attempt to defend their territory against invading gold miners in Montana.

1867

■ Congress adopts a policy of "small reservations," relegating Plains Indians to reservations in the Dakota Territory or the land that would become Oklahoma.

1876

■ **June 25–26**
The battle of the Little Bighorn occurs in the Dakota Territory. General George Armstrong Custer and his small band of troops are ambushed and massacred by Sioux and Cheyenne warriors. The incident is often referred to as Custer's Last Stand.

1879

■ **January 14**
The Nez Perce Indian chief Joseph delivers a speech to President Rutherford B. Hayes and others in Washington, D.C., deploring the U.S. government's forceful resettlement of his people to a reservation and demanding equality for Native Americans.

1887

■ **February 8**
Congress passes the Dawes Severalty Act.

1890

■ **December 29**
The battle of Wounded Knee Creek occurs; American soldiers massacre between 150 and 200 Indians, mostly women and children, who had taken part in the Ghost Dance movement.

quently, many Native Americans escalated attacks on American settlers and troops in an effort to protect their way of life. However, even protracted Indian wars, such as that waged by the Apache in the Southwest, eventually resulted in Indian surrender. Indian victories, such as the Sioux and Cheyenne defeat of General George Armstrong Custer and his troops at Little Bighorn, resulted in harsher retribution by American settlers and troops. By the 1880s many Native Americans saw acquiescence to U.S. policies as their best chance for survival.

About the Author

Crafted by the U.S. Congress, the Dawes Act was based on the contribution of many individuals, although it is primarily credited to Senator Henry L. Dawes of Massachusetts, who chaired the Senate's Indian Affairs Committee. Dawes was initially skeptical about attempts to acculturate American Indians through land allotment but was persuaded by advocates to promote the act. Dawes made an exceptional candidate because he both chaired the Indian Affairs Committee and represented the state with the largest contingent of participants in the Indian reform movement.

Henry Laurens Dawes was born in Cummington, Massachusetts, on October 30, 1816. Trained as a lawyer, Dawes entered politics at a young age. As the Republican candidate, he was elected to the Massachusetts House of Representatives at age thirty-two and continued his political career in the Massachusetts state senate followed by the U.S. House of Representatives and the U.S. Senate. During the 1850s, 1860s, and 1870s Dawes adamantly supported antislavery and Reconstruction policies. During the 1880s he became an advocate for Indian reform groups in the Senate. The meetings held by groups sympathetic to the plight of American Indians at Lake Mohonk, New York, particularly influenced Dawes. Dawes increasingly advocated allotment of reservation lands to acculturate American Indians and to integrate them into American society. He remained an active advocate for Indian rights until his death on February 5, 1903.

Explanation and Analysis of the Document

◆ Section 1

Section 1 of the Dawes Act states the main purpose of the act. The act provides the president of the United States with the right to survey and divide reservation lands among individual American Indians and American Indian families. It also stipulates the manner in which the land will be divided, providing every head of household with one-quarter section of land, every single person over age eighteen or orphan under age eighteen with one-eighth section of land, and all other unmarried people under the age of eighteen with one-sixteenth section of land. Section 1 does not specify the actual size of a section but suggests that sections will be determined based on government survey of reservations and the size of the Indian population living on each.

If an American Indian receives an allotment suitable only for ranching and not for agriculture, the act guarantees that he will get an additional allotment.

◆ Section 2

Section 2 guarantees the right of each American Indian to choose the area of land that will become his allotment. Heads of household are charged with choosing plots in the name of their minor children, and Bureau of Land Management agents are responsible for choosing land on behalf of orphaned children. If two people entitled to allotments want the same tract of land, the parcel will be divided between them, and they will receive from another area the remainder of land due to them. After Indians make their selections, agents are responsible for drawing preliminary boundaries, which they are to revise after resurveying the land and adding or subtracting from the various plots to standardize their size.

Section 2 also anticipates potential problems arising from the act. It insists that the agents responsible for choosing land on behalf of orphaned children choose land based on the best interests of those children. Suspecting some resistance to land division and allotment, Section 2 states that if an American Indian entitled to a portion of the newly divided reservations does not stake his claim to a partition of land within four years, the secretary of the interior should have a land agent choose a parcel on behalf of that Indian and issue a patent to the Indian in question for the plot of land in his name.

◆ Section 3

The purpose of Section 3 is to establish the manner in which allotments will be made, who will make them, who will appoint the officers who grant allotments, and how allotments will be documented. It states that the president will assign agents responsible for overseeing the allotment process. Records of allotment will be stored in both the Indian Office and the General Land Office.

◆ Section 4

Section 4 explains how the system of allotment will apply to American Indians who do not live on reservations. It states that an Indian residing off a reservation has the right to an allotment parcel equal to that of a native living on a reservation and that he can choose a parcel from any area of unsettled land. Although American Indians can choose their allotment from areas of unsurveyed land, the allotments will be adjusted once the land is surveyed. Section 4 also explains that the U.S. Treasury will compensate local land offices for the land settled by Indians.

◆ Section 5

Section 5 specifies the requirements for American Indians to gain ownership of their allotments. It states that once American Indians choose their plots of lands, those plots will be patented to them but held in trust by the U.S. government for twenty-five years. During those twenty-five years American Indians cannot sell the land. Furthermore,

Time Line

1893 ■ The western historian Fredrick Jackson Turner delivers his "frontier thesis," arguing that the existence of a frontier influenced the American character and was key to maintaining such qualities as freedom and independence.

1890 ■ The federal government declares the frontier officially closed.

1900 ■ The American Indian population is estimated at 250,000, the lowest in U.S. history up to that time.

Section 5 nullifies any sale of allotted land prior to the end of the twenty-five-year period. If an allottee dies during the period in which the government holds his land in trust, his heirs will inherit the right to the land.

Additionally, Section 5 discusses options for reservation land not allotted to individuals under the provision of the act. It states that the federal government can negotiate with tribes to purchase unallotted reservation land but that land purchased from tribes can be used only to encourage actual settlers. Settlers will be restricted to land grants no larger than 160 acres per person. Religious organizations engaged in converting or educating native people are also entitled to tracts of land of no more than 160 acres. Like American Indians living on allotments, non-native settlers will have their land held in trust by the federal government, but only for five years.

The fees paid by homesteaders for tracts of former Indian land are relegated to the American Indians who had previously held the rights to the land in question. The money can be used by Congress for educating or otherwise "civilizing" the American Indians from the reservation in question. Section 5 concludes by stating that American Indians who have taken advantage of the allotment policy as well as those who have become U.S. citizens will have preference in the hiring of public employees working in American Indian communities.

◆ Section 6

Section 6 deals with the legal and citizenship status of American Indians who participate in the allotment program. All American Indians who receive allotments, it states, will become American citizens and have all of the rights of American citizens. It stipulates that no local or state government can pass laws denying equal protection by law to American Indians who have taken part in the allotment program. In addition, Section 6 specifies that all American Indians who take part in the allotment process

Senator Henry Dawes of Massachusetts (Library of Congress)

will become subject to the laws of the state or territory in which they reside.

◆ Section 7

Section 7 endows the secretary of the interior with the authority to regulate water resources, if they are needed to make reservation land fertile for agricultural use. The secretary is charged with equitably distributing water among the American Indians living on a reservation. Section 7 also forbids giving water rights to one individual if doing so would hurt another.

◆ Section 8

Section 8 excludes certain tribes (Cherokee, Creek, Choctaw, Chickasaw, Fox, Osage, Miami, Peoria, Sac, and Seminole) and certain regions (Seneca Nation of New York reservations and Sioux Nation territory in Nebraska) from the provisions of the act.

◆ Section 9

Section 9 states that the cost of surveying lands authorized by the act will be paid out of a $100,000 account in the Treasury. The $100,000 will be repaid to the Treasury from the sale of land acquired from American Indians based on the standards set forth by the act.

◆ Section 10

Section 10 protects the federal government's right to exercise eminent domain over land allotted to American Indians.

◆ Section 11

Section 11 certifies that the act cannot be used to halt the relocation of the Southern Ute Indians from their current reservation in southwestern Colorado to a new reservation.

Audience

The Dawes Act was written by politicians for politicians and bureaucrats. The language is technical and verbose, but also pointedly specific. The drafters of the act, who saw themselves as friends of the American Indian, attempted to draft an act so specific that those wishing to use the new policy to displace American Indians would not be able to do so. Notably, the initial act was drafted so seamlessly that speculators had difficulty obtaining legal rights to Native allotments until after the Dawes Act was amended in 1891.

The Dawes Act was written with the understanding that employees of the General Land Office and the Bureau of Indian Affairs would frequently refer to it. For that reason these employees are specifically addressed throughout the act, and their actions are strictly proscribed. The act frequently warns agents against attempting to use their position for personal gain, stating, for example, that agents choosing plots of land for orphaned children must consider the best interests of the children and that tribes agreeing to sell reservation land to the government must be fairly compensated. Because of the extreme technicality of the language used in the Dawes Act, it was clearly not intended for an American Indian audience. Most American Indians could not read English, and even those who could read would have had difficulty interpreting the act.

Impact

Few American Indians converted to American styles of farming or adopted American cultural norms as a result of the Dawes Act. The act assigned plots of land to individual Indians but did not include a provision to train them in farming practices. Few American Indians had experience farming. They did not have the required equipment and goods to begin farming, and most encountered difficulty if they tried to buy things on credit. Although in the 1880s and 1890s Congress approved small grants for American Indians to purchase seeds and farming equipment, the grants were far too small and inconsistent to aid American Indians significantly in converting to sedentary living and farming. Those American Indians who tried to mimic American homesteaders therefore usually reaped small, unprofitable harvests and quickly abandoned their efforts.

American Indians did not immediately feel the effects of the Dawes Act. Although speculators began making agreements for the trade or sale of Indian lands almost as soon as the act passed, they rarely began settling or developing the land for fear of expropriation. Ironically, although the Dawes Act intended to Americanize Indians, because the

"*An Act to provide for the allotment of lands in severalty to Indians on the various reservations, and to extend the protection of the laws of the United States and the Territories over the Indians, and for other purposes.*"

(Section 1)

"*That upon the approval of the allotments provided for in this act by the Secretary of the Interior, he shall cause patents to issue therefor in the name of allottees ... and declare that the United States does and will hold the land thus allotted, for the period of twenty-five years, in trust for the sole use and benefit of the Indian to whom such allotment shall have been made, or, in case of his decease, of his heirs.*"

(Section 5)

"*And provided further, That at any time after lands have been allotted to all the Indians of any tribe ... it shall be lawful for the Secretary of the Interior to negotiate ... for the purchase and release ... of such portions of its reservation not allotted as such tribe shall ... consent to sell, on such terms and conditions as shall be considered just and equitable between the United States and said tribe of Indians.*"

(Section 5)

"*And every Indian born within the territorial limits of the United States to whom allotments shall have been made under the provisions of this act ... and every Indian ... who has voluntarily taken up ... his residence separate and apart from any tribe of Indians therein ... is hereby declared to be a citizen of the United States, and is entitled to all the rights, privileges, and immunities of such citizens.*"

(Section 6)

federal government held the allotments in trust for twenty-five years, American Indians were able to maintain their traditional ways of life in the years immediately following the passage of the Dawes Act. While many made agreements regarding their allotments that would ultimately lead to their displacement, during the years in which the land remained in trust, American Indians were able to continue to hunt game and to use resources throughout their reservations. Few American Indians accepted the notion of private property, and on most reservations they continued to live as though they held their lands communally.

Within the first decade of the Dawes Act's inception, state and local governments found loopholes allowing outsiders to purchase American Indian allotments. Once speculators and businesses gained ownership of Indian lands, American Indians felt the effects of the Dawes Act swiftly. Fences went up, restricting the movement of Indians as well as the game they hunted. Key resources, such as rivers and forests, were relegated to private, non-Indian owners, often eliminating the subsistence ability of American Indians.

In addition, the funds made from the sale of reservation land that the Dawes Act had earmarked for programs to improve American Indians' lives were grossly mismanaged. Compensation for land sales often did not make its way to Indian accounts for decades. Even when payments for reservation land made it to the federally held Indian accounts, they were used for ends that few Native Americans viewed as beneficial. In her study of the effects of the Dawes Act on the American Indians of Minnesota, the historian Melissa L. Meyer writes, "Facile generalizations about Anishinaabe dependence on welfare gratuities mask the fact that they essentially financed their own 'assimilation'" (p. 388). Money from the sale of Indian lands usually funded schools and social welfare programs aimed at Americanizing Indians. In 1934, when the Dawes Act was reversed through the Indian Reorganization Act, American Indians owned less than half the land that they had owned in 1887.

Related Documents

Burke Act. California State University, San Marcos, Web site. http://www.csusm.edu/nadp/a1906.htm. Accessed on January 18, 2008. In 1906 the U.S. Congress amended the Dawes Act with the Burke Act, which did away with many of the protective specifications of the initial act, most notably allowing Native Americans to sell their allotted land immediately rather than waiting twenty-five years.

Chief Joseph. "An Indian's View on Indian Affairs." *North American Review* no. 128 (April 1879). In this speech, delivered in 1879 to President Rutherford B. Hayes and other dignitaries in Washington, D.C., Chief Joseph invokes the American ideals of freedom and equality in an effort to prevent the further marginalization of his people.

Kappler, Charles J., ed. *Indian Affairs: Laws and Treaties.* 7 vols. Washington, D.C.: Government Printing Office, 1904–1941. Oklahoma State University Web site. http://digital.library.okstate.edu/kappler/. Accessed on January 6, 2008. With a variety of sources pertaining to federal Indian policy, particularly relating to the use of land, these volumes contain treaties, congressional minutes, and other primary sources relating to a variety of Indian tribes.

Pratt, Richard. "Kill the Indian ... and Save the Man." In *Reading the American Past: Selected Historical Documents*, ed. Michael P. Johnson. 4th ed. New York: Bedford/St. Martin's, 2007. Pratt, a supporter of the federal government's attempt to acculturate and "civilize" American Indians, argues for the necessity of American education for Indians who had taken part in the allotment process made possible by the Dawes Act.

Bibliography

■ Articles

Carlson, Leonard A. "The Dawes Act and Indian Farming." *Journal of Economic History* 38, no. 1 (March 1978): 274–276.

Cotroneo, Ross R., and Jack Dozier. "A Time of Disintegration: The Coeur d'Alene and the Dawes Act." *Western Historical Quarterly* 5, no. 4 (October 1974): 405–419.

Leibhardt, Barbara. "Allotment Policy in an Incongruous Legal System: The Yakima Indian Nation as a Case Study, 1887–1934." *Agricultural History* 65, no. 4 (Autumn 1991): 78–103

Meyer, Melissa L. "'We Can Not Get a Living as We Used To': Dispossession and the White Earth Anishinaabeg, 1889–1920." *American Historical Review* 96, no. 2 (April 1991): 368–394.

■ Books

Adelman, Gerard. *Major Objections to the Dawes Act of 1887: Their Content and Results.* Columbus: Ohio State University, 1970.

Carlson, Leonard A. *Indians, Bureaucrats, and Land: The Dawes Act and the Decline of Indian Farming.* Westport, Conn.: Greenwood Press, 1981.

Fritz, Henry E. *The Movement for Indian Assimilation, 1860–1980.* Philadelphia: University of Pennsylvania Press, 1963.

Greenwald, Emily. *Reconfiguring the Reservation: The Nez Perces, Jicarilla Apaches, and the Dawes Act.* Albuquerque: University of New Mexico Press, 2002.

Hauptman, Laurence M., and L. Gordon McLester, III. *The Oneida Indians in the Age of Allotment, 1860–1920.* Norman: University of Oklahoma Press, 2006.

Johnston, Robert D., and Catherine McNicol Stock, eds. *The Countryside in the Age of the Modern State: Political Histories of Rural America.* Ithaca, N.Y.: Cornell University Press, 2001.

McDonnell, Janet A. *The Dispossession of the American Indian, 1887–1934.* Bloomington: Indiana University Press, 1991.

Otis, D. S. *The Dawes Act and the Allotment of Indian Lands,* ed. Francis Paul Prucha. Norman: University of Oklahoma Press, 1973.

Prucha, Francis Paul, comp. *The Indian in American History.* New York: Holt, Rinehart, and Winston, 1971.

———, ed. *Americanizing the American Indians; Writings by the "Friends of the Indian," 1880–1900.* Cambridge, Mass.: Harvard University Press, 1973.

———. *Indian Policy in the United States: Historical Essays.* Lincoln: University of Nebraska Press, 1981.

Stubben, Jerry D. *Native Americans and Political Participation: A Reference Handbook.* Santa Barbara, Calif.: ABC-CLIO, 2006.

■ Web Sites

Autry National Center Web site. http://www.autrynationalcenter.org/. Accessed on October 20, 2007.

National Museum of the American Indian Web site.
http://www.nmai.si.edu/. Accessed on October 20, 2007.

"Native American Documents Project." California State University, San Marcos, Web site.
http://www.csusm.edu/projects/nadp/nadp.htm. Accessed on October 20, 2007.

—By G. Mehera Gerardo

Questions for Further Study

1. The Dawes Act was part of an assimilationist trend in American Indian policy that emerged after the American Civil War. It departed considerably from earlier policies that dealt with American Indians. Compare the Dawes Act to President Andrew Jackson's message to Congress on Indian Removal (1830). How do Jackson's attitudes compare with those reflected in the Dawes Act? How would you characterize Jacksonian Indian policy? How do you think assimilationists viewed Jackson's ideas?

2. One stated purpose of the Dawes Act was to "civilize" the American Indian. The act is also sometimes referred to as "An Act for the Salvation of the American Indian." What problems might arise from a bill based on a belief in the superiority of white American society and the inferiority of American Indian society?

3. Compare and contrast the Dawes Act to the Chinese Exclusion Act (1882). How do the two acts deal with ethnic groups considered to be "problems" in the late nineteenth century? Is one group treated with greater respect than the other? If so, how? Do you think the two acts were inspired by a shared ideology? Why or why not?

4. How might American Indians have responded to the Dawes Act? Do you think they understood what the federal government hoped to accomplish through it? Do you think they would have resisted efforts to acculturate them to American norms? Would they have viewed people like Dawes as "friends of the Indian"? Why or why not?

5. Scholars often describe the Dawes Act as the last of a series of policies that destroyed American Indians' traditional way of life. What elements of the Dawes Act would have changed American Indians' lifestyles? Could American Indians have maintained any of their traditional practices under the Dawes Act? If so, how?

6. A central precept of the Dawes Act was that encouraging American Indians to adopt American styles of farming and give up communal living was the crucial first step to Americanizing them. Why did policy makers consider farming so important? Does the Dawes Act fit into the Jeffersonian ideal of the United States being an agrarian republic? If so, how?

Glossary

aforesaid	previously mentioned; already referred to
allot	to allocate a portion
allottee	the receiver of an allotment
appropriation	something set aside for a specific purpose
deem	to regard as
disposition	bestowal
embrace	to contain
patent	a document granting an exclusive right
pro rata	in proportion
riparian	relating to a body of water
severalty	the quality of being distinct or autonomous
stipulation	an agreed-to condition in a contract

DAWES SEVERALTY ACT

An Act to provide for the allotment of lands in severalty to Indians on the various reservations, and to extend the protection of the laws of the United States and the Territories over the Indians, and for other purposes

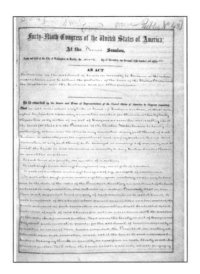

Be it enacted by the Senate and House of Representatives of the United States of America in Congress assembled, That in all cases where any tribe or band of Indians has been, or shall hereafter be, located upon any reservation created for their use, either by treaty stipulation or by virtue of an act of Congress or executive order setting apart the same for their use, the President of the United States be, and he hereby is, authorized, whenever in his opinion any reservation or any part thereof of such Indians is advantageous for agricultural and grazing purposes, to cause said reservation, or any part thereof, to be surveyed, or resurveyed if necessary, and to allot the lands in said reservation in severalty to any Indian located thereon in quantities as follows:

To each head of a family, one-quarter of a section;

To each single person over eighteen years of age, one-eighth of a section;

To each orphan child under eighteen years of age, one-eighth of a section; and

To each other single person under eighteen years now living, or who may be born prior to the date of the order of the President directing an allotment of the lands embraced in any reservation, one-sixteenth of a section:

Provided, That in case there is not sufficient land in any of said reservations to allot lands to each individual of the classes above named in quantities as above provided, the lands embraced in such reservation or reservations shall be allotted to each individual of each of said classes pro rata in accordance with the provisions of this act: And provided further, That where the treaty or act of Congress setting apart such reservation provides the allotment of lands in severalty in quantities in excess of those herein provided, the President, in making allotments upon such reservation, shall allot the lands to each individual Indian belonging thereon in quantity as specified in such treaty or act: And provided further, That when the lands allotted are only valuable for grazing purposes, an additional allotment of such grazing lands, in quantities as above provided, shall be made to each individual.

Sec. 2. That all allotments set apart under the provisions of this act shall be selected by the Indians, heads of families selecting for their minor children, and the agents shall select for each orphan child, and in such manner as to embrace the improvements of the Indians making the selection. where the improvements of two or more Indians have been made on the same legal subdivision of land, unless they shall otherwise agree, a provisional line may be run dividing said lands between them, and the amount to which each is entitled shall be equalized in the assignment of the remainder of the land to which they are entitled under his act: Provided, That if any one entitled to an allotment shall fail to make a selection within four years after the President shall direct that allotments may be made on a particular reservation, the Secretary of the Interior may direct the agent of such tribe or band, if such there be, and if there be no agent, then a special agent appointed for that purpose, to make a selection for such Indian, which selection shall be allotted as in cases where selections are made by the Indians, and patents shall issue in like manner.

Sec. 3. That the allotments provided for in this act shall be made by special agents appointed by the President for such purpose, and the agents in charge of the respective reservations on which the allotments are directed to be made, under such rules and regulations as the Secretary of the Interior may from time to time prescribe, and shall be certified by such agents to the Commissioner of Indian Affairs, in duplicate, one copy to be retained in the Indian Office and the other to be transmitted to the Secretary of the Interior for his action, and to be deposited in the General Land Office.

Sec. 4. That where any Indian not residing upon a reservation, or for whose tribe no reservation has been provided by treaty, act of Congress, or executive order, shall make settlement upon any surveyed or unsurveyed lands of the United States not otherwise appropriated, he or she shall be entitled, upon application to the local land-office for the district in which the lands arc located, to have the same allotted to him or her, and to his or her children, in quantities and manner as provided in this act for Indians residing upon reservations; and when such settlement is made upon unsurveyed lands, the grant to such Indians shall be adjusted upon the survey of the lands so as to conform thereto; and patents shall be issued to them for such lands in the manner and with the restrictions as herein provided. And the fees to which the officers of such local land-office would have been entitled had such lands been entered under the general laws for the disposition of the public lands shall be paid to them, from any moneys in the Treasury of the United States not otherwise appropriated, upon a statement of an account in their behalf for such fees by the Commissioner of the General Land Office, and a certification of such account to the Secretary of the Treasury by the Secretary of the Interior.

Sec. 5. That upon the approval of the allotments provided for in this act by the Secretary of the Interior, he shall cause patents to issue therefor in the name of the allottees, which patents shall be of the legal effect, and declare that the United States does and will hold the land thus allotted, for the period of twenty-five years, in trust for the sole use and benefit of the Indian to whom such allotment shall have been made, or, in case of his decease, of his heirs according to the laws of the State or Territory where such land is located, and that at the expiration of said period the United States will convey the same by patent to said Indian, or his heirs as aforesaid, in fee, discharged of said trust and free of all charge or incumbrance whatsoever: Provided, That the President of the United States may in any case in his discretion extend the period. And if any conveyance shall be made of the lands set apart and allotted as herein provided, or any contract made touching the same, before the expiration of the time above mentioned, such conveyance or contract shall be absolutely null and void: Provided, That the law of

descent and partition in force in the State or Territory where such lands are situate shall apply thereto after patents therefor have been executed and delivered, except as herein otherwise provided; and the laws of the State of Kansas regulating the descent and partition of real estate shall, so far as practicable, apply to all lands in the Indian Territory which may be allotted in severalty under the provisions of this act: And provided further, That at any time after lands have been allotted to all the Indians of any tribe as herein provided, or sooner if in the opinion of the President it shall be for the best interests of said tribe, it shall be lawful for the Secretary of the Interior to negotiate with such Indian tribe for the purchase and release by said tribe, in conformity with the treaty or statute under which such reservation is held, of such portions of its reservation not allotted as such tribe shall, from time to time, consent to sell, on such terms and conditions as shall be considered just and equitable between the United States and said tribe of Indians, which purchase shall not be complete until ratified by Congress, and the form and manner of executing such release prescribed by Congress: Provided however, That all lands adapted to agriculture, with or without irrigation so sold or released to the United States by any Indian tribe shall be held by the United States for the sale purpose of securing homes to actual settlers and shall be disposed of by the United States to actual and bona fide settlers only tracts not exceeding one hundred and sixty acres to any one person, on such terms as Congress shall prescribe, subject to grants which Congress may make in aid of education: And provided further, That no patents shall issue therefor except to the person so taking the same as and homestead, or his heirs, and after the expiration of five years occupancy therof as such homestead; and any conveyance of said lands taken as a homestead, or any contract touching the same, or lieu thereon, created prior to the date of such patent, shall be null and void. And the sums agreed to be paid by the United States as purchase money for any portion of any such reservation shall be held in the Treasury of the United States for the sole use of the tribe or tribes Indians; to whom such reservations belonged; and the same, with interest thereon at three per cent per annum, shall be at all times subject to appropriation by Congress for the education and civilization of such tribe or tribes of Indians or the members thereof. The patents aforesaid shall be recorded in the General Land Office, and afterward delivered, free of charge, to the allottee entitled thereto. And if any religious society or other organization is now occupying any of the public lands to which this act is applicable, for religious or educational work among the Indians, the Secretary of the Interior is hereby authorized to confirm such occupation to such society or organization, in quantity not exceeding one hundred and sixty acres in any one tract, so long as the same shall be so occupied, on such terms as he shall deem just; but nothing herein contained shall change or alter any claim of such society for religious or educational purposes heretofore granted by law. And hereafter in the employment of Indian police, or any other employees in the public service among any of the Indian tribes or bands affected by this act, and where Indians can perform the duties required, those Indians who have availed themselves of the provisions of this act and become citizens of the United States shall be preferred.

Sec. 6. That upon the completion of said allotments and the patenting of the lands to said allottees, each and every member of the respective bands or tribes of Indians to whom allotments have been made shall have the benefit of and be subject to the laws, both civil and criminal, of the State or Territory in which they may reside; and no Territory shall pass or enforce any law denying any such Indian within its jurisdiction the equal protection of the law. And every Indian born within the territorial limits of the United States to whom allotments shall have been made under the provisions of this act, or under any law or treaty, and every Indian born within the territorial limits of the United States who has voluntarily taken up, within said limits, his residence separate and apart from any tribe of Indians therein, and has adopted the habits of civilized life, is hereby declared to be a citizen of the United States, and is entitled to all the rights, privileges, and immunities of such citizens, whether said Indian has been or not, by birth or otherwise, a member of any tribe of Indians within the territorial limits of the United States without in any manner affecting the right of any such Indian to tribal or other property.

Sec. 7. That in cases where the use of water for irrigation is necessary to render the lands within any Indian reservation available for agricultural purposes, the Secretary of the Interior be, and he is hereby, authorized to prescribe such rules and regulations as he may deem necessary to secure a just and equal distribution thereof among the Indians residing upon any such reservation; and no other appropriation or grant of water by any riparian proprietor shall permitted to the damage of any other riparian proprietor.

Sec. 8. That the provisions of this act shall not extend to the territory occupied by the Cherokees, Creeks, Choctaws, Chickasaws, Seminoles, and Osage, Miamies and Peorias, and Sacs and Foxes, in the Indian Territory, nor to any of the reservations of the Seneca Nation of New York Indians in the State of New York, nor to that strip of territory in the State of Nebraska adjoining the Sioux Nation on the south added by executive order.

Sec. 9. That for the purpose of making the surveys and resurveys mentioned in section two of this act, there be, and hereby is, appropriated, out of any moneys in the Treasury not otherwise appropriated, the sum of one hundred thousand dollars, to be repaid proportionately out of the proceeds of the sales of such land as may be acquired from the Indians under the provisions of this act.

Sec. 10. That nothing in this act contained shall be so construed to affect the right and power of Congress to grant the right of way through any lands granted to an Indian, or a tribe of Indians, for railroads or other highways, or telegraph lines, for the public use, or condemn such lands to public uses, upon making just compensation.

Sec. 11. That nothing in this act shall be so construed as to prevent the removal of the Southern Ute Indians from their present reservation in Southwestern Colorado to a new reservation by and with consent of a majority of the adult male members of said tribe.

Approved, February, 8, 1887.